T0140055

Lecture Notes in Computer Science 13380

More information about this series at https://link.springer.com/bookseries/558

Osvaldo Gervasi · Beniamino Murgante ·
Sanjay Misra · Ana Maria A. C. Rocha ·
Chiara Garau (Eds.)

Computational Science and Its Applications – ICCSA 2022 Workshops

Malaga, Spain, July 4–7, 2022
Proceedings, Part IV

 Springer

Editors
Osvaldo Gervasi 🆔
University of Perugia
Perugia, Italy

Beniamino Murgante 🆔
University of Basilicata
Potenza, Potenza, Italy

Sanjay Misra 🆔
Østfold University College
Halden, Norway

Ana Maria A. C. Rocha 🆔
University of Minho
Braga, Portugal

Chiara Garau 🆔
University of Cagliari
Cagliari, Italy

ISSN 0302-9743   ISSN 1611-3349   (electronic)
Lecture Notes in Computer Science
ISBN 978-3-031-10541-8   ISBN 978-3-031-10542-5   (eBook)
https://doi.org/10.1007/978-3-031-10542-5

This Springer imprint is published by the registered company Springer Nature Switzerland AG
The registered company address is: Gewerbestrasse 11, 6330 Cham, Switzerland

Preface

These six volumes (LNCS 13377–13382) consist of the peer-reviewed papers from the workshops at the 22nd International Conference on Computational Science and Its Applications (ICCSA 2022), which took place during July 4–7, 2022. The peer-reviewed papers of the main conference tracks are published in a separate set consisting of two volumes (LNCS 13375–13376).

This year, we again decided to organize a hybrid conference, with some of the delegates attending in person and others taking part online. Despite the enormous benefits achieved by the intensive vaccination campaigns in many countries, at the crucial moment of organizing the event, there was no certainty about the evolution of COVID-19. Fortunately, more and more researchers were able to attend the event in person, foreshadowing a slow but gradual exit from the pandemic and the limitations that have weighed so heavily on the lives of all citizens over the past three years.

ICCSA 2022 was another successful event in the International Conference on Computational Science and Its Applications (ICCSA) series. Last year, the conference was held as a hybrid event in Cagliari, Italy, and in 2020 it was organized as virtual event, whilst earlier editions took place in Saint Petersburg, Russia (2019), Melbourne, Australia (2018), Trieste, Italy (2017), Beijing, China (2016), Banff, Canada (2015), Guimaraes, Portugal (2014), Ho Chi Minh City, Vietnam (2013), Salvador, Brazil (2012), Santander, Spain (2011), Fukuoka, Japan (2010), Suwon, South Korea (2009), Perugia, Italy (2008), Kuala Lumpur, Malaysia (2007), Glasgow, UK (2006), Singapore (2005), Assisi, Italy (2004), Montreal, Canada (2003), and (as ICCS) Amsterdam, The Netherlands (2002) and San Francisco, USA (2001).

Computational science is the main pillar of most of the present research, and industrial and commercial applications, and plays a unique role in exploiting ICT innovative technologies. The ICCSA conference series provides a venue to researchers and industry practitioners to discuss new ideas, to share complex problems and their solutions, and to shape new trends in computational science.

Apart from the 52 workshops, ICCSA 2022 also included six main tracks on topics ranging from computational science technologies and application in many fields to specific areas of computational sciences, such as software engineering, security, machine learning and artificial intelligence, and blockchain technologies. For the 52 workshops we have accepted 285 papers. For the main conference tracks we accepted 57 papers and 24 short papers out of 279 submissions (an acceptance rate of 29%). We would like to express our appreciation to the Workshops chairs and co-chairs for their hard work and dedication.

The success of the ICCSA conference series in general, and of ICCSA 2022 in particular, vitally depends on the support of many people: authors, presenters, participants, keynote speakers, workshop chairs, session chairs, organizing committee members, student volunteers, Program Committee members, advisory committee members, international liaison chairs, reviewers, and others in various roles. We take this opportunity to wholehartedly thank them all.

We also wish to thank our publisher, Springer, for their acceptance to publish the proceedings, for sponsoring some of the best papers awards, and for their kind assistance and cooperation during the editing process.

We cordially invite you to visit the ICCSA website https://iccsa.org where you can find all the relevant information about this interesting and exciting event.

July 2022

Osvaldo Gervasi
Beniamino Murgante
Sanjay Misra

Welcome Message from Organizers

The ICCSA 2021 conference in the Mediterranean city of Cagliari provided us with inspiration to offer the ICCSA 2022 conference in the Mediterranean city of Málaga, Spain. The additional considerations due to the COVID-19 pandemic, which necessitated a hybrid conference, also stimulated the idea to use the School of Informatics of the University of Málaga. It has an open structure where we could take lunch and coffee outdoors and the lecture halls have open windows on two sides providing optimal conditions for meeting more safely.

The school is connected to the center of the old town via a metro system, for which we offered cards to the participants. This provided the opportunity to stay in lodgings in the old town close to the beach because, at the end of the day, that is the place to be to exchange ideas with your fellow scientists. The social program allowed us to enjoy the history of Malaga from its founding by the Phoenicians...

In order to provoke as much scientific interaction as possible we organized online sessions that could easily be followed by all participants from their own devices. We tried to ensure that participants from Asia could participate in morning sessions and those from the Americas in evening sessions. On-site sessions could be followed and debated on-site and discussed online using a chat system. To realize this, we relied on the developed technological infrastructure based on open source software, with the addition of streaming channels on YouTube. The implementation of the software infrastructure and the technical coordination of the volunteers were carried out by Damiano Perri and Marco Simonetti. Nine student volunteers from the universities of Málaga, Minho, Almeria, and Helsinki provided technical support and ensured smooth interaction during the conference.

A big thank you goes to all of the participants willing to exchange their ideas during their daytime. Participants of ICCSA 2022 came from 58 countries scattered over many time zones of the globe. Very interesting keynote talks were provided by well-known international scientists who provided us with more ideas to reflect upon, and we are grateful for their insights.

Eligius M. T. Hendrix

Organization

ICCSA 2022 was organized by the University of Malaga (Spain), the University of Perugia (Italy), the University of Cagliari (Italy), the University of Basilicata (Italy), Monash University (Australia), Kyushu Sangyo University (Japan), and the University of Minho, (Portugal).

Honorary General Chairs

Norio Shiratori	Chuo University, Japan
Kenneth C. J. Tan	Sardina Systems, UK

General Chairs

Osvaldo Gervasi	University of Perugia, Italy
Eligius Hendrix	University of Malaga, Italy
Bernady O. Apduhan	Kyushu Sangyo University, Japan

Program Committee Chairs

Beniamino Murgante	University of Basilicata, Italy
Inmaculada Garcia Fernandez	University of Malaga, Spain
Ana Maria A. C. Rocha	University of Minho, Portugal
David Taniar	Monash University, Australia

International Advisory Committee

Jemal Abawajy	Deakin University, Australia
Dharma P. Agarwal	University of Cincinnati, USA
Rajkumar Buyya	Melbourne University, Australia
Claudia Bauzer Medeiros	University of Campinas, Brazil
Manfred M. Fisher	Vienna University of Economics and Business, Austria
Marina L. Gavrilova	University of Calgary, Canada
Sumi Helal	University of Florida, USA, and University of Lancaster, UK
Yee Leung	Chinese University of Hong Kong, China

International Liaison Chairs

Ivan Blečić	University of Cagliari, Italy
Giuseppe Borruso	University of Trieste, Italy

Elise De Donker	Western Michigan University, USA
Maria Irene Falcão	University of Minho, Portugal
Robert C. H. Hsu	Chung Hua University, Taiwan
Tai-Hoon Kim	Beijing Jiaotong University, China
Vladimir Korkhov	St Petersburg University, Russia
Sanjay Misra	Østfold University College, Norway
Takashi Naka	Kyushu Sangyo University, Japan
Rafael D. C. Santos	National Institute for Space Research, Brazil
Maribel Yasmina Santos	University of Minho, Portugal
Elena Stankova	St Petersburg University, Russia

Workshop and Session Organizing Chairs

Beniamino Murgante	University of Basilicata, Italy
Chiara Garau	University of Cagliari, Italy
Sanjay Misra	Ostfold University College, Norway

Award Chair

| Wenny Rahayu | La Trobe University, Australia |

Publicity Committee Chairs

Elmer Dadios	De La Salle University, Philippines
Nataliia Kulabukhova	St Petersburg University, Russia
Daisuke Takahashi	Tsukuba University, Japan
Shangwang Wang	Beijing University of Posts and Telecommunications, China

Local Arrangement Chairs

Eligius Hendrix	University of Malaga, Spain
Inmaculada Garcia Fernandez	University of Malaga, Spain
Salvador Merino Cordoba	University of Malaga, Spain
Pablo Guerrero-García	University of Malaga, Spain

Technology Chairs

| Damiano Perri | University of Florence, Italy |
| Marco Simonetti | University of Florence, Italy |

Program Committee

| Vera Afreixo | University of Aveiro, Portugal |
| Filipe Alvelos | University of Minho, Portugal |

Hartmut Asche	Hasso-Plattner-Institut für Digital Engineering gGmbH, Germany
Ginevra Balletto	University of Cagliari, Italy
Michela Bertolotto	University College Dublin, Ireland
Sandro Bimonte	TSCF, INRAE, France
Rod Blais	University of Calgary, Canada
Ivan Blečić	University of Sassari, Italy
Giuseppe Borruso	University of Trieste, Italy
Ana Cristina Braga	University of Minho, Portugal
Massimo Cafaro	University of Salento, Italy
Yves Caniou	ENS Lyon, France
Ermanno Cardelli	University of Perugia, Italy
José A. Cardoso e Cunha	Universidade Nova de Lisboa, Portugal
Rui Cardoso	University of Beira Interior, Portugal
Leocadio G. Casado	University of Almeria, Spain
Carlo Cattani	University of Salerno, Italy
Mete Celik	Erciyes University, Turkey
Maria Cerreta	University of Naples Federico II, Italy
Hyunseung Choo	Sungkyunkwan University, South Korea
Rachel Chieng-Sing Lee	Sunway University, Malaysia
Min Young Chung	Sungkyunkwan University, South Korea
Florbela Maria da Cruz Domingues Correia	Polytechnic Institute of Viana do Castelo, Portugal
Gilberto Corso Pereira	Federal University of Bahia, Brazil
Alessandro Costantini	INFN, Italy
Carla Dal Sasso Freitas	Universidade Federal do Rio Grande do Sul, Brazil
Pradesh Debba	Council for Scientific and Industrial Research (CSIR), South Africa
Hendrik Decker	Instituto Tecnológico de Informática, Spain
Robertas Damaševičius	Kaunas University of Technology, Lithuania
Frank Devai	London South Bank University, UK
Rodolphe Devillers	Memorial University of Newfoundland, Canada
Joana Matos Dias	University of Coimbra, Portugal
Paolino Di Felice	University of L'Aquila, Italy
Prabu Dorairaj	NetApp, India/USA
M. Noelia Faginas Lago	University of Perugia, Italy
M. Irene Falcao	University of Minho, Portugal
Florbela P. Fernandes	Polytechnic Institute of Bragança, Portugal
Jose-Jesus Fernandez	National Centre for Biotechnology, Spain
Paula Odete Fernandes	Polytechnic Institute of Bragança, Portugal
Adelaide de Fátima Baptista Valente Freitas	University of Aveiro, Portugal
Manuel Carlos Figueiredo	University of Minho, Portugal
Maria Celia Furtado Rocha	Federal University of Bahia, Brazil
Chiara Garau	University of Cagliari, Italy
Paulino Jose Garcia Nieto	University of Oviedo, Spain

Raffaele Garrisi	Polizia di Stato, Italy
Jerome Gensel	LSR-IMAG, France
Maria Giaoutzi	National Technical University of Athens, Greece
Arminda Manuela Andrade Pereira Gonçalves	University of Minho, Portugal
Andrzej M. Goscinski	Deakin University, Australia
Sevin Gümgüm	Izmir University of Economics, Turkey
Alex Hagen-Zanker	University of Cambridge, UK
Shanmugasundaram Hariharan	B.S. Abdur Rahman Crescent Institute of Science and Technology, India
Eligius M. T. Hendrix	University of Malaga, Spain and Wageningen University, The Netherlands
Hisamoto Hiyoshi	Gunma University, Japan
Mustafa Inceoglu	Ege University, Turkey
Peter Jimack	University of Leeds, UK
Qun Jin	Waseda University, Japan
Yeliz Karaca	UMass Chan Medical School, USA
Farid Karimipour	Vienna University of Technology, Austria
Baris Kazar	Oracle Corp., USA
Maulana Adhinugraha Kiki	Telkom University, Indonesia
DongSeong Kim	University of Canterbury, New Zealand
Taihoon Kim	Hannam University, South Korea
Ivana Kolingerova	University of West Bohemia, Czech Republic
Nataliia Kulabukhova	St. Petersburg University, Russia
Vladimir Korkhov	St. Petersburg University, Russia
Rosa Lasaponara	National Research Council, Italy
Maurizio Lazzari	National Research Council, Italy
Cheng Siong Lee	Monash University, Australia
Sangyoun Lee	Yonsei University, South Korea
Jongchan Lee	Kunsan National University, South Korea
Chendong Li	University of Connecticut, USA
Gang Li	Deakin University, Australia
Fang (Cherry) Liu	Ames Laboratory, USA
Xin Liu	University of Calgary, Canada
Andrea Lombardi	University of Perugia, Italy
Savino Longo	University of Bari, Italy
Tinghuai Ma	Nanjing University of Information Science and Technology, China
Ernesto Marcheggiani	Katholieke Universiteit Leuven, Belgium
Antonino Marvuglia	Public Research Centre Henri Tudor, Luxembourg
Nicola Masini	National Research Council, Italy
Ilaria Matteucci	National Research Council, Italy
Nirvana Meratnia	University of Twente, The Netherlands
Fernando Miranda	University of Minho, Portugal
Giuseppe Modica	University of Reggio Calabria, Italy
Josè Luis Montaña	University of Cantabria, Spain

Zequn Wang	Intelligent Automation Inc, USA
Robert Weibel	University of Zurich, Switzerland
Frank Westad	Norwegian University of Science and Technology, Norway
Roland Wismüller	Universität Siegen, Germany
Mudasser Wyne	National University, USA
Chung-Huang Yang	National Kaohsiung Normal University, Taiwan
Xin-She Yang	National Physical Laboratory, UK
Salim Zabir	France Telecom Japan Co., Japan
Haifeng Zhao	University of California, Davis, USA
Fabiana Zollo	Ca' Foscari University of Venice, Italy
Albert Y. Zomaya	University of Sydney, Australia

Workshop Organizers

International Workshop on Advances in Artificial Intelligence Learning Technologies: Blended Learning, STEM, Computational Thinking and Coding (AAILT 2022)

Alfredo Milani	University of Perugia, Italy
Valentina Franzoni	University of Perugia, Italy
Osvaldo Gervasi	University of Perugia, Italy

International Workshop on Advancements in Applied Machine-Learning and Data Analytics (AAMDA 2022)

Alessandro Costantini	INFN, Italy
Davide Salomoni	INFN, Italy
Doina Cristina Duma	INFN, Italy
Daniele Cesini	INFN, Italy

International Workshop on Advances in Information Systems and Technologies for Emergency Management, Risk Assessment and Mitigation Based on the Resilience (ASTER 2022)

Maurizio Pollino	ENEA, Italy
Marco Vona	University of Basilicata, Italy
Sonia Giovinazzi	ENEA, Italy
Benedetto Manganelli	University of Basilicata, Italy
Beniamino Murgante	University of Basilicata, Italy

International Workshop on Advances in Web Based Learning (AWBL 2022)

Birol Ciloglugil	Ege University, Turkey
Mustafa Inceoglu	Ege University, Turkey

International Workshop on Blockchain and Distributed Ledgers: Technologies and Applications (BDLTA 2022)

Vladimir Korkhov	St Petersburg State University, Russia
Elena Stankova	St Petersburg State University, Russia
Nataliia Kulabukhova	St Petersburg State University, Russia

International Workshop on Bio and Neuro Inspired Computing and Applications (BIONCA 2022)

Nadia Nedjah	State University of Rio De Janeiro, Brazil
Luiza De Macedo Mourelle	State University of Rio De Janeiro, Brazil

International Workshop on Configurational Analysis For Cities (CA CITIES 2022)

Claudia Yamu	Oslo Metropolitan University, Norway
Valerio Cutini	Università di Pisa, Italy
Beniamino Murgante	University of Basilicata, Italy
Chiara Garau	Dicaar, University of Cagliari, Italy

International Workshop on Computational and Applied Mathematics (CAM 2022)

Maria Irene Falcão	University of Minho, Portugal
Fernando Miranda	University of Minho, Portugal

International Workshop on Computational and Applied Statistics (CAS 2022)

Ana Cristina Braga	University of Minho, Portugal

International Workshop on Computational Mathematics, Statistics and Information Management (CMSIM 2022)

Maria Filomena Teodoro	University of Lisbon and Portuguese Naval Academy, Portugal

International Workshop on Computational Optimization and Applications (COA 2022)

Ana Maria A. C. Rocha   University of Minho, Portugal
Humberto Rocha   University of Coimbra, Portugal

International Workshop on Computational Astrochemistry (CompAstro 2022)

Marzio Rosi   University of Perugia, Italy
Nadia Balucani   University of Perugia, Italy
Cecilia Ceccarelli   Université Grenoble Alpes, France
Stefano Falcinelli   University of Perugia, Italy

International Workshop on Computational Methods for Porous Geomaterials (CompPor 2022)

Vadim Lisitsa   Sobolev Institute of Mathematics, Russia
Evgeniy Romenski   Sobolev Institute of Mathematics, Russia

International Workshop on Computational Approaches for Smart, Conscious Cities (CASCC 2022)

Andreas Fricke   University of Potsdam, Germany
Juergen Doellner   University of Potsdam, Germany
Salvador Merino   University of Malaga, Spain
Jürgen Bund   Graphics Vision AI Association, Germany/Portugal
Markus Jobst   Federal Office of Metrology and Surveying, Austria
Francisco Guzman   University of Malaga, Spain

International Workshop on Computational Science and HPC (CSHPC 2022)

Elise De Doncker   Western Michigan University, USA
Fukuko Yuasa   High Energy Accelerator Research Organization (KEK), Japan
Hideo Matsufuru   High Energy Accelerator Research Organization (KEK), Japan

International Workshop on Cities, Technologies and Planning (CTP 2022)

Giuseppe Borruso   University of Trieste, Italy
Malgorzata Hanzl   Lodz University of Technology, Poland
Beniamino Murgante   University of Basilicata, Italy

Anastasia Stratigea   National Technical University of Athens, Grece
Ginevra Balletto   University of Cagliari, Italy
Ljiljana Zivkovic   Republic Geodetic Authority, Serbia

International Workshop on Digital Sustainability and Circular Economy (DiSCE 2022)

Giuseppe Borruso   University of Trieste, Italy
Stefano Epifani   Digital Sustainability Institute, Italy
Ginevra Balletto   University of Cagliari, Italy
Luigi Mundula   University of Cagliari, Italy
Alessandra Milesi   University of Cagliari, Italy
Mara Ladu   University of Cagliari, Italy
Stefano De Nicolai   University of Pavia, Italy
Tu Anh Trinh   University of Economics Ho Chi Minh City, Vietnam

International Workshop on Econometrics and Multidimensional Evaluation in Urban Environment (EMEUE 2022)

Carmelo Maria Torre   Polytechnic University of Bari, Italy
Maria Cerreta   University of Naples Federico II, Italy
Pierluigi Morano   Polytechnic University of Bari, Italy
Giuliano Poli   University of Naples Federico II, Italy
Marco Locurcio   Polytechnic University of Bari, Italy
Francesco Tajani   Sapienza University of Rome, Italy

International Workshop on Ethical AI Applications for a Human-Centered Cyber Society (EthicAI 2022)

Valentina Franzoni   University of Perugia, Italy
Alfredo Milani   University of Perugia, Italy

International Workshop on Future Computing System Technologies and Applications (FiSTA 2022)

Bernady Apduhan   Kyushu Sangyo University, Japan
Rafael Santos   INPE, Brazil

International Workshop on Geodesign in Decision Making: Meta Planning and Collaborative Design for Sustainable and Inclusive Development (GDM 2022)

Francesco Scorza   University of Basilicata, Italy
Michele Campagna   University of Cagliari, Italy
Ana Clara Mourão Moura   Federal University of Minas Gerais, Brazil

International Workshop on Geomatics in Agriculture and Forestry: New Advances and Perspectives (GeoForAgr 2022)

Maurizio Pollino	ENEA, Italy
Giuseppe Modica	University of Reggio Calabria, Italy
Marco Vizzari	University of Perugia, Italy

International Workshop on Geographical Analysis, Urban Modeling, Spatial Statistics (Geog-An-Mod 2022)

Giuseppe Borruso	University of Trieste, Italy
Beniamino Murgante	University of Basilicata, Italy
Harmut Asche	Hasso-Plattner-Institut für Digital Engineering gGmbH, Germany

International Workshop on Geomatics for Resource Monitoring and Management (GRMM 2022)

Alessandra Capolupo	Polytechnic of Bari, Italy
Eufemia Tarantino	Polytechnic of Bari, Italy
Enrico Borgogno Mondino	University of Turin, Italy

International Workshop on Information and Knowledge in the Internet of Things (IKIT 2022)

Teresa Guarda	State University of Santa Elena Peninsula, Ecuador
Filipe Portela	University of Minho, Portugal
Maria Fernanda Augusto	Bitrum Research Center, Spain

13th International Symposium on Software Quality (ISSQ 2022)

Sanjay Misra	Østfold University College, Norway

International Workshop on Machine Learning for Space and Earth Observation Data (MALSEOD 2022)

Rafael Santos	INPE, Brazil
Karine Reis Ferreira Gomes	INPE, Brazil

International Workshop on Building Multi-dimensional Models for Assessing Complex Environmental Systems (MES 2022)

Vanessa Assumma	Politecnico di Torino, Italy
Caterina Caprioli	Politecnico di Torino, Italy
Giulia Datola	Politecnico di Torino, Italy

Federico Dell'Anna   Politecnico di Torino, Italy
Marta Dell'Ovo   Politecnico di Milano, Italy

International Workshop on Models and Indicators for Assessing and Measuring the Urban Settlement Development in the View of ZERO Net Land Take by 2050 (MOVEto0 2022)

Lucia Saganeiti   University of L'Aquila, Italy
Lorena Fiorini   University of L'aquila, Italy
Angela Pilogallo   University of Basilicata, Italy
Alessandro Marucci   University of L'Aquila, Italy
Francesco Zullo   University of L'Aquila, Italy

International Workshop on Modelling Post-Covid Cities (MPCC 2022)

Beniamino Murgante   University of Basilicata, Italy
Ginevra Balletto   University of Cagliari, Italy
Giuseppe Borruso   University of Trieste, Italy
Marco Dettori   Università degli Studi di Sassari, Italy
Lucia Saganeiti   University of L'Aquila, Italy

International Workshop on Ecosystem Services: Nature's Contribution to People in Practice. Assessment Frameworks, Models, Mapping, and Implications (NC2P 2022)

Francesco Scorza   University of Basilicata, Italy
Sabrina Lai   University of Cagliari, Italy
Silvia Ronchi   University of Cagliari, Italy
Dani Broitman   Israel Institute of Technology, Israel
Ana Clara Mourão Moura   Federal University of Minas Gerais, Brazil
Corrado Zoppi   University of Cagliari, Italy

International Workshop on New Mobility Choices for Sustainable and Alternative Scenarios (NEWMOB 2022)

Tiziana Campisi   University of Enna Kore, Italy
Socrates Basbas   Aristotle University of Thessaloniki, Greece
Aleksandra Deluka T.   University of Rijeka, Croatia
Alexandros Nikitas   University of Huddersfield, UK
Ioannis Politis   Aristotle University of Thessaloniki, Greece
Georgios Georgiadis   Aristotle University of Thessaloniki, Greece
Irena Ištoka Otković   University of Osijek, Croatia
Sanja Surdonja   University of Rijeka, Croatia

International Workshop on Privacy in the Cloud/Edge/IoT World (PCEIoT 2022)

Michele Mastroianni	University of Campania Luigi Vanvitelli, Italy
Lelio Campanile	University of Campania Luigi Vanvitelli, Italy
Mauro Iacono	University of Campania Luigi Vanvitelli, Italy

International Workshop on Psycho-Social Analysis of Sustainable Mobility in the Pre- and Post-Pandemic Phase (PSYCHE 2022)

Tiziana Campisi	University of Enna Kore, Italy
Socrates Basbas	Aristotle University of Thessaloniki, Greece
Dilum Dissanayake	Newcastle University, UK
Nurten Akgün Tanbay	Bursa Technical University, Turkey
Elena Cocuzza	University of Catania, Italy
Nazam Ali	University of Management and Technology, Pakistan
Vincenza Torrisi	University of Catania, Italy

International Workshop on Processes, Methods and Tools Towards Resilient Cities and Cultural Heritage Prone to SOD and ROD Disasters (RES 2022)

Elena Cantatore	Polytechnic University of Bari, Italy
Alberico Sonnessa	Polytechnic University of Bari, Italy
Dario Esposito	Polytechnic University of Bari, Italy

International Workshop on Scientific Computing Infrastructure (SCI 2022)

Elena Stankova	St Petersburg University, Russia
Vladimir Korkhov	St Petersburg University, Russia

International Workshop on Socio-Economic and Environmental Models for Land Use Management (SEMLUM 2022)

Debora Anelli	Polytechnic University of Bari, Italy
Pierluigi Morano	Polytechnic University of Bari, Italy
Francesco Tajani	Sapienza University of Rome, Italy
Marco Locurcio	Polytechnic University of Bari, Italy
Paola Amoruso	LUM University, Italy

14th International Symposium on Software Engineering Processes and Applications (SEPA 2022)

Sanjay Misra	Østfold University College, Norway

International Workshop on Ports of the Future – Smartness and Sustainability (SmartPorts 2022)

Giuseppe Borruso	University of Trieste, Italy
Gianfranco Fancello	University of Cagliari, Italy
Ginevra Balletto	University of Cagliari, Italy
Patrizia Serra	University of Cagliari, Italy
Maria del Mar Munoz Leonisio	University of Cadiz, Spain
Marco Mazzarino	University of Venice, Italy
Marcello Tadini	Università del Piemonte Orientale, Italy

International Workshop on Smart Tourism (SmartTourism 2022)

Giuseppe Borruso	University of Trieste, Italy
Silvia Battino	University of Sassari, Italy
Ainhoa Amaro Garcia	Universidad de Alcalà and Universidad de Las Palmas, Spain
Maria del Mar Munoz Leonisio	University of Cadiz, Spain
Carlo Donato	University of Sassari, Italy
Francesca Krasna	University of Trieste, Italy
Ginevra Balletto	University of Cagliari, Italy

International Workshop on Sustainability Performance Assessment: Models, Approaches and Applications Toward Interdisciplinary and Integrated Solutions (SPA 2022)

Francesco Scorza	University of Basilicata, Italy
Sabrina Lai	University of Cagliari, Italy
Jolanta Dvarioniene	Kaunas University of Technology, Lithuania
Iole Cerminara	University of Basilicata, Italy
Georgia Pozoukidou	Aristotle University of Thessaloniki, Greece
Valentin Grecu	Lucian Blaga University of Sibiu, Romania
Corrado Zoppi	University of Cagliari, Italy

International Workshop on Specifics of Smart Cities Development in Europe (SPEED 2022)

Chiara Garau	University of Cagliari, Italy
Katarína Vitálišová	Matej Bel University, Slovakia
Paolo Nesi	University of Florence, Italy
Anna Vanova	Matej Bel University, Slovakia
Kamila Borsekova	Matej Bel University, Slovakia
Paola Zamperlin	University of Pisa, Italy

Federico Cugurullo   Trinity College Dublin, Ireland
Gerardo Carpentieri   University of Naples Federico II, Italy

International Workshop on Smart and Sustainable Island Communities (SSIC 2022)

Chiara Garau   University of Cagliari, Italy
Anastasia Stratigea   National Technical University of Athens, Greece
Paola Zamperlin   University of Pisa, Italy
Francesco Scorza   University of Basilicata, Italy

International Workshop on Theoretical and Computational Chemistry and Its Applications (TCCMA 2022)

Noelia Faginas-Lago   University of Perugia, Italy
Andrea Lombardi   University of Perugia, Italy

International Workshop on Transport Infrastructures for Smart Cities (TISC 2022)

Francesca Maltinti   University of Cagliari, Italy
Mauro Coni   University of Cagliari, Italy
Francesco Pinna   University of Cagliari, Italy
Chiara Garau   University of Cagliari, Italy
Nicoletta Rassu   Univesity of Cagliari, Italy
James Rombi   University of Cagliari, Italy
Benedetto Barabino   University of Brescia, Italy

14th International Workshop on Tools and Techniques in Software Development Process (TTSDP 2022)

Sanjay Misra   Østfold University College, Norway

International Workshop on Urban Form Studies (UForm 2022)

Malgorzata Hanzl   Lodz University of Technology, Poland
Beniamino Murgante   University of Basilicata, Italy
Alessandro Camiz   Özyeğin University, Turkey
Tomasz Bradecki   Silesian University of Technology, Poland

International Workshop on Urban Regeneration: Innovative Tools and Evaluation Model (URITEM 2022)

Fabrizio Battisti   University of Florence, Italy
Laura Ricci   Sapienza University of Rome, Italy
Orazio Campo   Sapienza University of Rome, Italy

International Workshop on Urban Space Accessibility and Mobilities (USAM 2022)

Chiara Garau	University of Cagliari, Italy
Matteo Ignaccolo	University of Catania, Italy
Enrica Papa	University of Westminster, UK
Francesco Pinna	University of Cagliari, Italy
Silvia Rossetti	University of Parma, Italy
Wendy Tan	Wageningen University and Research, The Netherlands
Michela Tiboni	University of Brescia, Italy
Vincenza Torrisi	University of Catania, Italy

International Workshop on Virtual Reality and Augmented Reality and Applications (VRA 2022)

Osvaldo Gervasi	University of Perugia, Italy
Damiano Perri	University of Florence, Italy
Marco Simonetti	University of Florence, Italy
Sergio Tasso	University of Perugia, Italy

International Workshop on Advanced and Computational Methods for Earth Science Applications (WACM4ES 2022)

Luca Piroddi	University of Cagliari, Italy
Sebastiano Damico	University of Malta, Malta

International Workshop on Advanced Mathematics and Computing Methods in Complex Computational Systems (WAMCM 2022)

Yeliz Karaca	UMass Chan Medical School, USA
Dumitru Baleanu	Cankaya University, Turkey
Osvaldo Gervasi	University of Perugia, Italy
Yudong Zhang	University of Leicester, UK
Majaz Moonis	UMass Chan Medical School, USA

Additional Reviewers

Akshat Agrawal	Amity University, Haryana, India
Waseem Ahmad	National Institute of Technology Karnataka, India
Vladimir Alarcon	Universidad Diego Portales, Chile
Oylum Alatlı	Ege University, Turkey
Raffaele Albano	University of Basilicata, Italy
Abraham Alfa	FUT Minna, Nigeria
Diego Altafini	Università di Pisa, Italy
Filipe Alvelos	Universidade do Minho, Portugal

Marina Alexandra Pedro Andrade	ISCTE-IUL, Portugal
Debora Anelli	Polytechnic University of Bari, Italy
Gennaro Angiello	AlmavivA de Belgique, Belgium
Alfonso Annunziata	Università di Cagliari, Italy
Bernady Apduhan	Kyushu Sangyo University, Japan
Daniela Ascenzi	Università degli Studi di Trento, Italy
Burak Galip Aslan	Izmir Insitute of Technology, Turkey
Vanessa Assumma	Politecnico di Torino, Italy
Daniel Atzberger	Hasso-Plattner-Institute für Digital Engineering gGmbH, Germany
Dominique Aury	École Polytechnique Fédérale de Lausanne, Switzerland
Joseph Awotumde	University of Alcala, Spain
Birim Balci	Celal Bayar University, Turkey
Juliana Balera	INPE, Brazil
Ginevra Balletto	University of Cagliari, Italy
Benedetto Barabino	University of Brescia, Italy
Kaushik Barik	University of Alcala, Spain
Carlo Barletta	Politecnico di Bari, Italy
Socrates Basbas	Aristotle University of Thessaloniki, Greece
Rosaria Battarra	ISMed-CNR, Italy
Silvia Battino	University of Sassari, Italy
Chiara Bedan	University of Trieste, Italy
Ranjan Kumar Behera	National Institute of Technology Rourkela, India
Gulmira Bekmanova	L.N. Gumilyov Eurasian National University, Kazakhstan
Mario Bentivenga	University of Basilicata, Italy
Asrat Mulatu Beyene	Addis Ababa Science and Technology University, Ethiopia
Tiziana Binda	Politecnico di Torino, Italy
Giulio Biondi	University of Firenze, Italy
Alexander Bogdanov	St Petersburg University, Russia
Costanza Borghesi	University of Perugia, Italy
Giuseppe Borruso	University of Trieste, Italy
Marilisa Botte	University of Naples Federico II, Italy
Tomasz Bradecki	Silesian University of Technology, Poland
Ana Cristina Braga	University of Minho, Portugal
Luca Braidotti	University of Trieste, Italy
Bazon Brock	University of Wuppertal, Germany
Dani Broitman	Israel Institute of Technology, Israel
Maria Antonia Brovelli	Politecnico di Milano, Italy
Jorge Buele	Universidad Tecnológica Indoamérica, Ecuador
Isabel Cacao	University of Aveiro, Portugal
Federica Cadamuro Morgante	Politecnico di Milano, Italy

Rogerio Calazan	IEAPM, Brazil
Michele Campagna	University of Cagliari, Italy
Lelio Campanile	Università degli Studi della Campania Luigi Vanvitelli, Italy
Tiziana Campisi	University of Enna Kore, Italy
Antonino Canale	University of Enna Kore, Italy
Elena Cantatore	Polytechnic University of Bari, Italy
Patrizia Capizzi	Univerity of Palermo, Italy
Alessandra Capolupo	Polytechnic University of Bari, Italy
Giacomo Caporusso	Politecnico di Bari, Italy
Caterina Caprioli	Politecnico di Torino, Italy
Gerardo Carpentieri	University of Naples Federico II, Italy
Martina Carra	University of Brescia, Italy
Pedro Carrasqueira	INESC Coimbra, Portugal
Barbara Caselli	Università degli Studi di Parma, Italy
Cecilia Castro	University of Minho, Portugal
Giulio Cavana	Politecnico di Torino, Italy
Iole Cerminara	University of Basilicata, Italy
Maria Cerreta	University of Naples Federico II, Italy
Daniele Cesini	INFN, Italy
Jabed Chowdhury	La Trobe University, Australia
Birol Ciloglugil	Ege University, Turkey
Elena Cocuzza	Univesity of Catania, Italy
Emanuele Colica	University of Malta, Malta
Mauro Coni	University of Cagliari, Italy
Elisete Correia	Universidade de Trás-os-Montes e Alto Douro, Portugal
Florbela Correia	Polytechnic Institute of Viana do Castelo, Portugal
Paulo Cortez	University of Minho, Portugal
Lino Costa	Universidade do Minho, Portugal
Alessandro Costantini	INFN, Italy
Marilena Cozzolino	Università del Molise, Italy
Alfredo Cuzzocrea	University of Calabria, Italy
Sebastiano D'amico	University of Malta, Malta
Gianni D'Angelo	University of Salerno, Italy
Tijana Dabovic	University of Belgrade, Serbia
Hiroshi Daisaka	Hitotsubashi University, Japan
Giulia Datola	Politecnico di Torino, Italy
Regina De Almeida	University of Trás-os-Montes and Alto Douro, Portugal
Maria Stella De Biase	Università della Campania Luigi Vanvitelli, Italy
Elise De Doncker	Western Michigan University, USA
Itamir De Morais Barroca Filho	Federal University of Rio Grande do Norte, Brazil
Samuele De Petris	University of Turin, Italy
Alan De Sá	Marinha do Brasil, Brazil
Alexander Degtyarev	St Petersburg University, Russia

Federico Dell'Anna	Politecnico di Torino, Italy
Marta Dell'Ovo	Politecnico di Milano, Italy
Ahu Dereli Dursun	Istanbul Commerce University, Turkey
Giulia Desogus	University of Cagliari, Italy
Piero Di Bonito	Università degli Studi della Campania, Italia
Paolino Di Felice	University of L'Aquila, Italy
Felicia Di Liddo	Polytechnic University of Bari, Italy
Isabel Dimas	University of Coimbra, Portugal
Doina Cristina Duma	INFN, Italy
Aziz Dursun	Virginia Tech University, USA
Jaroslav Dvořak	Klaipėda University, Lithuania
Dario Esposito	Polytechnic University of Bari, Italy
M. Noelia Faginas-Lago	University of Perugia, Italy
Stefano Falcinelli	University of Perugia, Italy
Falcone Giacomo	University of Reggio Calabria, Italy
Maria Irene Falcão	University of Minho, Portugal
Stefano Federico	CNR-ISAC, Italy
Marcin Feltynowski	University of Lodz, Poland
António Fernandes	Instituto Politécnico de Bragança, Portugal
Florbela Fernandes	Instituto Politecnico de Braganca, Portugal
Paula Odete Fernandes	Instituto Politécnico de Bragança, Portugal
Luis Fernandez-Sanz	University of Alcala, Spain
Luís Ferrás	University of Minho, Portugal
Ângela Ferreira	Instituto Politécnico de Bragança, Portugal
Lorena Fiorini	University of L'Aquila, Italy
Hector Florez	Universidad Distrital Francisco Jose de Caldas, Colombia
Stefano Franco	LUISS Guido Carli, Italy
Valentina Franzoni	Perugia University, Italy
Adelaide Freitas	University of Aveiro, Portugal
Andreas Fricke	Hasso Plattner Institute, Germany
Junpei Fujimoto	KEK, Japan
Federica Gaglione	Università del Sannio, Italy
Andrea Gallo	Università degli Studi di Trieste, Italy
Luciano Galone	University of Malta, Malta
Adam Galuszka	Silesian University of Technology, Poland
Chiara Garau	University of Cagliari, Italy
Ernesto Garcia Para	Universidad del País Vasco, Spain
Aniket A. Gaurav	Østfold University College, Norway
Marina Gavrilova	University of Calgary, Canada
Osvaldo Gervasi	University of Perugia, Italy
Andrea Ghirardi	Università di Brescia, Italy
Andrea Gioia	Politecnico di Bari, Italy
Giacomo Giorgi	Università degli Studi di Perugia, Italy
Stanislav Glubokovskikh	Lawrence Berkeley National Laboratory, USA
A. Manuela Gonçalves	University of Minho, Portugal

Leocadio González Casado	University of Almería, Spain
Angela Gorgoglione	Universidad de la República Uruguay, Uruguay
Yusuke Gotoh	Okayama University, Japan
Daniele Granata	Università degli Studi della Campania, Italy
Christian Grévisse	University of Luxembourg, Luxembourg
Silvana Grillo	University of Cagliari, Italy
Teresa Guarda	State University of Santa Elena Peninsula, Ecuador
Carmen Guida	Università degli Studi di Napoli Federico II, Italy
Kemal Güven Gülen	Namık Kemal University, Turkey
Ipek Guler	Leuven Biostatistics and Statistical Bioinformatics Centre, Belgium
Sevin Gumgum	Izmir University of Economics, Turkey
Martina Halásková	VSB Technical University in Ostrava, Czech Republic
Peter Hegedus	University of Szeged, Hungary
Eligius M. T. Hendrix	Universidad de Málaga, Spain
Mauro Iacono	Università degli Studi della Campania, Italy
Oleg Iakushkin	St Petersburg University, Russia
Matteo Ignaccolo	University of Catania, Italy
Mustafa Inceoglu	Ege University, Turkey
Markus Jobst	Federal Office of Metrology and Surveying, Austria
Issaku Kanamori	RIKEN Center for Computational Science, Japan
Yeliz Karaca	UMass Chan Medical School, USA
Aarti Karande	Sardar Patel Institute of Technology, India
András Kicsi	University of Szeged, Hungary
Vladimir Korkhov	St Petersburg University, Russia
Nataliia Kulabukhova	St Petersburg University, Russia
Claudio Ladisa	Politecnico di Bari, Italy
Mara Ladu	University of Cagliari, Italy
Sabrina Lai	University of Cagliari, Italy
Mark Lajko	University of Szeged, Hungary
Giuseppe Francesco Cesare Lama	University of Napoli Federico II, Italy
Vincenzo Laporta	CNR, Italy
Margherita Lasorella	Politecnico di Bari, Italy
Francesca Leccis	Università di Cagliari, Italy
Federica Leone	University of Cagliari, Italy
Chien-sing Lee	Sunway University, Malaysia
Marco Locurcio	Polytechnic University of Bari, Italy
Francesco Loddo	Henge S.r.l., Italy
Andrea Lombardi	Università di Perugia, Italy
Isabel Lopes	Instituto Politécnico de Bragança, Portugal
Fernando Lopez Gayarre	University of Oviedo, Spain
Vanda Lourenço	Universidade Nova de Lisboa, Portugal
Jing Ma	Luleå University of Technology, Sweden
Helmuth Malonek	University of Aveiro, Portugal
Francesca Maltinti	University of Cagliari, Italy

Benedetto Manganelli	Università degli Studi della Basilicata, Italy
Krassimir Markov	Institute of Electric Engineering and Informatics, Bulgaria
Alessandro Marucci	University of L'Aquila, Italy
Alessandra Mascitelli	Italian Civil Protection Department and ISAC-CNR, Italy
Michele Mastroianni	University of Campania Luigi Vanvitelli, Italy
Hideo Matsufuru	High Energy Accelerator Research Organization (KEK), Japan
Chiara Mazzarella	University of Naples Federico II, Italy
Marco Mazzarino	University of Venice, Italy
Paolo Mengoni	University of Florence, Italy
Alfredo Milani	University of Perugia, Italy
Fernando Miranda	Universidade do Minho, Portugal
Augusto Montisci	Università degli Studi di Cagliari, Italy
Ricardo Moura	New University of Lisbon, Portugal
Ana Clara Mourao Moura	Federal University of Minas Gerais, Brazil
Maria Mourao	Polytechnic Institute of Viana do Castelo, Portugal
Eugenio Muccio	University of Naples Federico II, Italy
Beniamino Murgante	University of Basilicata, Italy
Giuseppe Musolino	University of Reggio Calabria, Italy
Stefano Naitza	Università di Cagliari, Italy
Naohito Nakasato	University of Aizu, Japan
Roberto Nardone	University of Reggio Calabria, Italy
Nadia Nedjah	State University of Rio de Janeiro, Brazil
Juraj Nemec	Masaryk University in Brno, Czech Republic
Keigo Nitadori	RIKEN R-CCS, Japan
Roseline Ogundokun	Kaunas University of Technology, Lithuania
Francisco Henrique De Oliveira	Santa Catarina State University, Brazil
Irene Oliveira	Univesidade Trás-os-Montes e Alto Douro, Portugal
Samson Oruma	Østfold University College, Norway
Antonio Pala	University of Cagliari, Italy
Simona Panaro	University of Porstmouth, UK
Dimos Pantazis	University of West Attica, Greece
Giovanni Paragliola	ICAR-CNR, Italy
Eric Pardede	La Trobe University, Australia
Marco Parriani	University of Perugia, Italy
Paola Perchinunno	Uniersity of Bari, Italy
Ana Pereira	Polytechnic Institute of Bragança, Portugal
Damiano Perri	University of Perugia, Italy
Marco Petrelli	Roma Tre University, Italy
Camilla Pezzica	University of Pisa, Italy
Angela Pilogallo	University of Basilicata, Italy
Francesco Pinna	University of Cagliari, Italy
Telmo Pinto	University of Coimbra, Portugal

Fernando Pirani	University of Perugia, Italy
Luca Piroddi	University of Cagliari, Italy
Bojana Pjanović	University of Belgrade, Serbia
Giuliano Poli	University of Naples Federico II, Italy
Maurizio Pollino	ENEA, Italy
Salvatore Praticò	University of Reggio Calabria, Italy
Zbigniew Przygodzki	University of Lodz, Poland
Carlotta Quagliolo	Politecnico di Torino, Italy
Raffaele Garrisi	Polizia Postale e delle Comunicazioni, Italy
Mariapia Raimondo	Università della Campania Luigi Vanvitelli, Italy
Deep Raj	IIIT Naya Raipur, India
Buna Ramos	Universidade Lusíada Norte, Portugal
Nicoletta Rassu	Univesity of Cagliari, Italy
Michela Ravanelli	Sapienza Università di Roma, Italy
Roberta Ravanelli	Sapienza Università di Roma, Italy
Pier Francesco Recchi	University of Naples Federico II, Italy
Stefania Regalbuto	University of Naples Federico II, Italy
Marco Reis	University of Coimbra, Portugal
Maria Reitano	University of Naples Federico II, Italy
Anatoly Resnyansky	Defence Science and Technology Group, Australia
Jerzy Respondek	Silesian University of Technology, Poland
Isabel Ribeiro	Instituto Politécnico Bragança, Portugal
Albert Rimola	Universitat Autònoma de Barcelona, Spain
Corrado Rindone	University of Reggio Calabria, Italy
Ana Maria A. C. Rocha	University of Minho, Portugal
Humberto Rocha	University of Coimbra, Portugal
Maria Clara Rocha	Instituto Politécnico de Coimbra, Portugal
James Rombi	University of Cagliari, Italy
Elisabetta Ronchieri	INFN, Italy
Marzio Rosi	University of Perugia, Italy
Silvia Rossetti	Università degli Studi di Parma, Italy
Marco Rossitti	Politecnico di Milano, Italy
Mária Rostašová	Universtiy of Žilina, Slovakia
Lucia Saganeiti	University of L'Aquila, Italy
Giovanni Salzillo	Università degli Studi della Campania, Italy
Valentina Santarsiero	University of Basilicata, Italy
Luigi Santopietro	University of Basilicata, Italy
Stefania Santoro	Politecnico di Bari, Italy
Rafael Santos	INPE, Brazil
Valentino Santucci	Università per Stranieri di Perugia, Italy
Mirko Saponaro	Polytechnic University of Bari, Italy
Filippo Sarvia	University of Turin, Italy
Andrea Scianna	ICAR-CNR, Italy
Francesco Scorza	University of Basilicata, Italy
Ester Scotto Di Perta	University of Naples Federico II, Italy
Ricardo Severino	University of Minho, Portugal

Jie Shen	University of Michigan, USA
Luneque Silva Junior	Universidade Federal do ABC, Brazil
Carina Silva	Instituto Politécnico de Lisboa, Portugal
Joao Carlos Silva	Polytechnic Institute of Cavado and Ave, Portugal
Ilya Silvestrov	Saudi Aramco, Saudi Arabia
Marco Simonetti	University of Florence, Italy
Maria Joana Soares	University of Minho, Portugal
Michel Soares	Federal University of Sergipe, Brazil
Alberico Sonnessa	Politecnico di Bari, Italy
Lisete Sousa	University of Lisbon, Portugal
Elena Stankova	St Petersburg University, Russia
Jan Stejskal	University of Pardubice, Czech Republic
Silvia Stranieri	University of Naples Federico II, Italy
Anastasia Stratigea	National Technical University of Athens, Greece
Yue Sun	European XFEL GmbH, Germany
Anthony Suppa	Politecnico di Torino, Italy
Kirill Sviatov	Ulyanovsk State Technical University, Russia
David Taniar	Monash University, Australia
Rodrigo Tapia-McClung	Centro de Investigación en Ciencias de Información Geoespacial, Mexico
Eufemia Tarantino	Politecnico di Bari, Italy
Sergio Tasso	University of Perugia, Italy
Vladimir Tcheverda	Institute of Petroleum Geology and Geophysics, SB RAS, Russia
Ana Paula Teixeira	Universidade de Trás-os-Montes e Alto Douro, Portugal
Tengku Adil Tengku Izhar	Universiti Teknologi MARA, Malaysia
Maria Filomena Teodoro	University of Lisbon and Portuguese Naval Academy, Portugal
Yiota Theodora	National Technical University of Athens, Greece
Graça Tomaz	Instituto Politécnico da Guarda, Portugal
Gokchan Tonbul	Atilim University, Turkey
Rosa Claudia Torcasio	CNR-ISAC, Italy
Carmelo Maria Torre	Polytechnic University of Bari, Italy
Vincenza Torrisi	University of Catania, Italy
Vincenzo Totaro	Politecnico di Bari, Italy
Pham Trung	HCMUT, Vietnam
Po-yu Tsai	National Chung Hsing University, Taiwan
Dimitrios Tsoukalas	Centre of Research and Technology Hellas, Greece
Toshihiro Uchibayashi	Kyushu University, Japan
Takahiro Ueda	Seikei University, Japan
Piero Ugliengo	Università degli Studi di Torino, Italy
Gianmarco Vanuzzo	University of Perugia, Italy
Clara Vaz	Instituto Politécnico de Bragança, Portugal
Laura Verde	University of Campania Luigi Vanvitelli, Italy
Katarína Vitálišová	Matej Bel University, Slovakia

Daniel Mark Vitiello	University of Cagliari, Italy
Marco Vizzari	University of Perugia, Italy
Alexander Vodyaho	St. Petersburg State Electrotechnical University "LETI", Russia
Agustinus Borgy Waluyo	Monash University, Australia
Chao Wang	USTC, China
Marcin Wozniak	Silesian University of Technology, Poland
Jitao Yang	Beijing Language and Culture University, China
Fenghui Yao	Tennessee State University, USA
Fukuko Yuasa	KEK, Japan
Paola Zamperlin	University of Pisa, Italy
Michal Žemlička	Charles University, Czech Republic
Nataly Zhukova	ITMO University, Russia
Alcinia Zita Sampaio	University of Lisbon, Portugal
Ljiljana Zivkovic	Republic Geodetic Authority, Serbia
Floriana Zucaro	University of Naples Federico II, Italy
Marco Zucca	Politecnico di Milano, Italy
Camila Zyngier	Ibmec, Belo Horizonte, Brazil

Sponsoring Organizations

ICCSA 2022 would not have been possible without tremendous support of many organizations and institutions, for which all organizers and participants of ICCSA 2022 express their sincere gratitude:

 Springer International Publishing AG, Germany (https://www.springer.com)

 Computers Open Access Journal (https://www.mdpi.com/journal/computers)

 Computation Open Access Journal (https://www.mdpi.com/journal/computation)

 University of Malaga, Spain (https://www.uma.es/)

University of Perugia, Italy
(https://www.unipg.it)

University of Basilicata, Italy
(http://www.unibas.it)

Monash University, Australia
(https://www.monash.edu/)

Kyushu Sangyo University, Japan
(https://www.kyusan-u.ac.jp/)

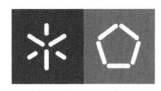

University of Minho, Portugal
(https://www.uminho.pt/)

Universidade do Minho
Escola de Engenharia

Contents – Part IV

**International Workshop on Building Multi-dimensional Models
for Assessing Complex Environmental Systems (MES 2022)**

**International Workshop on Models and Indicators for Assessing
and Measuring the Urban Settlement Development in the View
of ZERO Net Land Take by 2050 (MOVEto0 2022)**

International Workshop on Modelling Post-Covid Cities (MPCC 2022)

International Workshop on Ecosystem Services: Nature's Contribution to People in Practice. Assessment Frameworks, Models, Mapping, and Implications (NC2P 2022)

International Workshop on New Mobility Choices For Sustainable and Alternative Scenarios (NEWMOB 2022)

**International Workshop on Processes, Methods and Tools Towards
Resilient Cities and Cultural Heritage Prone to SOD and ROD
Disasters (RES 2022)**

**International Workshop on Scientic Computing Infrastructure
(SCI 2022)**

International Workshop on Information and Knowledge in the Internet of Things (IKIT 2022)

The Impact of Quantum Computing on Businesses

Teresa Guarda[1,2,3](✉) ⓘ, Washington Torres[1,2] ⓘ, and Maria Fernanda Augusto[1,2,4] ⓘ

[1] Universidad Estatal Penisula de Santa Elena, La Libertad, Ecuador
tguarda@gmail.com
[2] CIST – Centro de Investigación en Sistemas y Telecomunicaciones, La Libertad, Ecuador
[3] Algoritmi Centre, Minho University, Guimarães, Portugal
[4] BITrum-Research Group, C/San Lorenzo 2, 24007 León, Spain

Abstract. Despite the fact that data science continues in a constant evolution, there are still many problems that are still impossible to solve due to processing issues, either due to the exorbitant amount of data collected, or related to the different types of data to be processed. Quantum computing in the last decade has experienced a significant boom which has allowed researchers to pose problems that until now were impossible to solve in the classical paradigm. Quantum computing promises gains by solving how we solve these challenging computational problems. Currently, creating added value and achieving new experiences for the consumer, enhanced with it combination with artificial intelligence and machine learning, being a determining factor to promote business competitive advantage. This article aims to assess the impact of quantum computing on businesses competitive advantage, through a qualitative bibliographic analysis. In this context, an extensive research was carried out in this area on Web of Science and Scopus for the period 2016–2021. The survey covers 162 papers selected for this study, 92 from Scopus and 70 from Web of Science.

Keywords: Quantum artificial intelligence applications · Quantum machine learning · Quantum computing · Business competitive advantage

1 Introduction

With the acceleration of the digital transformation caused by the pandemic, technology has had a major impact on the world economy through the new opportunities that have arisen for companies in terms of implementing various digital solutions that have allowed them to improve, expand and facilitate their processes.

Quantum computing (QC) in the last decade has experienced a significant boom which has allowed researchers to pose problems that until today were impossible to solve in the classical paradigm [1].

Computers automating virtually all processes and systems that facilitate decision-making in any company are no longer as far away as they seemed. Quantum computing is leaving the laboratories of large technology companies to enter the daily lives of companies of all sizes and in any market segment.

O. Gervasi et al. (Eds.): ICCSA 2022 Workshops, LNCS 13380, pp. 3–14, 2022.
https://doi.org/10.1007/978-3-031-10542-5_1

There are several works that today focus on studying the potential applications of QC, in different sectors. In organizations, there are many challenging issues, and QC promises gains by solving how we solve these challenging computational problems.

Currently, creating added value and achieving new experiences for the consumer, enhanced with artificial intelligence, has become a determining factor that can promote business competitive advantage [2].

This research was supported by a bibliographical review and analysis in the areas of QC, artificial intelligence (AI), and machine learning (ML), with the aim of evaluating the impact of QC on business. In addition to understanding the impact at business competitive advantage by providing support regarding decision making.

For the survey, the chosen international databases responsible for scientific publications of an interdisciplinary nature, was Web of Science (WoS) and the Scopus. The terms used for the search was "Quantum Computing". Having presented a total of 33,368 documents, distributed between 2016 and 2021 (Fig. 1), being 34% Scopus and 66% Web of Science.

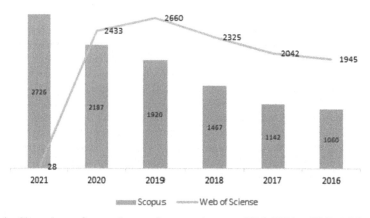

Fig. 1. Chronology of research terms between the years 2016–2021 at WoS and Scopus.

The research area with the most publications, in the case of WoS is Physics and Astronomy Astrophysics, totaling 63%, followed by Chemistry with 21%. In the case of Scopus is Computer Science with 22% of publications, followed by Physics and Astronomy Astrophysics, with 21%. Although there is some balance between the areas with more publications between the two indexing platforms, it is possible verify at Fig. 2, that 3 these research areas stand out due to their asymmetry: Physics and Astronomy Astrophysics; Chemistry; and Mathematics.

Although Scopus and WoS publications have the same countries in the top 9, in terms of number of publications they only present the two countries with the highest number of publications in the same order, United States and China (Fig. 3), in the case of WoS the 3rd was changed with India.

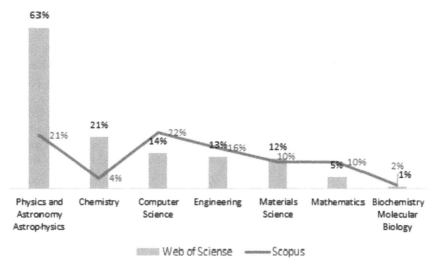

Fig. 2. Distribution by research areas between the years 2016–2021 at WoS and Scopus.

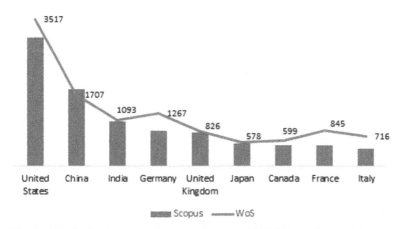

Fig. 3. Distribution by country between the years 2016–2021 at WoS and Scopus.

2 Quantum Computing

In the 1980s, two important fields of research focused on the domain of quantum mechanics emerged: quantum information and quantum computing. Both with the aim of applying the quantum systems in a computational apparatus, for the manipulation of information [3].

The quantum computer is a programmable device capable of performing calculations and algorithms by manipulating and reading information stored in quantum systems, such as atoms, molecules, protons, electrons and photons. In this type of computer, quantum bits are used, which, due to their nature, make this type of computer capable of performing tasks that would take thousands, or even millions of years to be done by electronic computers [4].

A quantum computer is a collection of n qubits on which it is possible to prepare in a state known as | 0 > which can be measured in the basis (|0 >, |1 >). This foundation of computing is based on the principles of superposition of matter and quantum entanglement to develop a different computation [5].

Traditional computers work on binary numbers and allow us to input information to obtain results. Which means, when performing calculations, we need to establish a series of rules that determine exactly what kinds of answers we are able to get. The whole process involves adding, subtracting, multiplying and dividing data to obtain valid variables.

The difference between electronic and quantum computers is that, due to the probabilistic nature of quantum physics, before be read the quantum bit, its state can be not only 0 or 1, but also the intersection between these states. It is as if quantum computers accepted answers like yes, no and both simultaneously. If you want to better understand the probabilities of the quantum world [1, 6].

The quantum computers being developed today use light particles, trapped ions, superconducting qubits and observing nitrogen in imperfect diamonds [7].

QC will have the ability to address and help solve a varied range of problems, from process optimization to simulation and machine learning [8, 9]. Therefore, some potential applications can already be seen on the horizon of quantum computing in the industry. Being related to the resolution of mathematical problems; the use of quantum artificial intelligence; training deep learning and cybersecurity models; the development of batteries with greater capacity and charging speed.

The potential of QC is so great, and technology advances so fast, that companies need to have a basic understanding of how the technology works, what kinds of problems it can solve, and how they can take advantage of it. There are several sectors already involved: logistics, financial, chemical, energy, pharmaceutical, cybersecurity, and industrial; where quantum computing has great potential [10–15].

The high processing capacity of these computers will be able to trace complex paths and make projections of each possible decision to be taken by companies, such as investment management, risk measurement in different scenarios and research, leaving companies even more capable and planned for any event.

Developing applications with this new technology can make cloud computing services much more agile and powerful. In addition, quantum computing research talks about hardware that could be offered in the future as a cloud service [16].

Given this, giant technology companies are investing heavily in technology to get ahead and have computers capable of solving unimaginable problems. Everything is still recent and companies are not sure how this quantum future will work, but that hasn't stopped them all from starting some wild project.

Organizations with precarious computing resources in the area of optimization or data security must begin to understand how this technology could solve their problems, since through quantum formulations it will be possible to retain any and all knowledge in an optimized way and still receive suggestions with statistical data calculated according to the organizations objective.

There are three main types of quantum computing: Quantum Annealing (QA); Quantum Simulation (QS); and Universal Quantum (UQ). Each has different processing power and time, as well as the time it takes to be commercially viable [17, 18].

QA it's the least powerful (like traditional computers) and most restrictive type; it's easy to build; and a good option to optimizing problems.

In the case of QS, it is capable of simulating complex quantum interactions that are intractable for any known conventional machine; with an average difficulty in build-up; containing between 50 and 100 qubits. It can be apply at quantum chemistry; material science; optimization problems; and sampling quantum dynamics.

The third type, UQ, it's the most powerful, but posing a series of difficult technical challenges; it's the hardest to build; and compromise more than 1000,000 physical qubits [19]. This type has a wide application areas: machine learning; secure computing; cryptography; quantum chemistry; material science; optimization problems; and sampling quantum dynamics.

3 Quantum Machine Learning

The goal of Machine Learning (ML) is to teach the machine how to perform a specific task, without providing explicit instructions. It is divided into three main families: supervised learning; unsupervised learning; and reinforced learning.

Supervised learning is without doubt the most famous and developed aspect of automatic learning, both in academic and industrial research. It is also the case of quantum automatic learning, and many works have attempted to adapt classical supervised algorithms to the quantum configuration [20, 21].

The neural networks are one of the most commonly used supervised algorithms, due to their ability to classify and make accurate predictions. In the literature, several models of quantum and quantum neural networks have been proposed, with different ways of encoding the data [22].

QC was also introduced to various unsupervised learning algorithms, providing new quantum-enhanced machine learning algorithms.

Quantum principal component analysis (QPCA), was proposed by Llyod et al. [23], and exploits the spectral decomposition of the Variational Quantum Eigensolver. Many works have been derived from it, providing improvements in the performance or precision of QPCA [24].

Recently, QPCA was used in finance to simulate the Heath-Jarrow-Morton model for the pricing of interest rate financial derivatives [25].

Reinforced learning has received less interest than the other two machine learning approaches, but interesting proposals were made nonetheless. Many jobs were derived from it, providing improvements in performance with the precision of QPCA. Recently, QPCA has been used in finance to simulate the Heath-Jarrow-Morton model for fixing the prices of financial derivatives of interest types [23–25].

Most of the works are based on the agent model, where an agent interacts with its environment and selects the best actions to maximize a reward function [26]. In others works experimental experiments have been proposed, using superconducting circuits [27], quantum optical neural networks [28], and others.

In the last few years, with the development of Machine Learning techniques, many problems have been addressed using these algorithms with the help of a large amount of compiled data. However, considering the most difficult problems that our society faces, the algorithms and real machine learning approaches show some limitations in terms of size and the amount of data that can be processed, but also from the point of view of efficiency and the income.

Quantum Machine Learning (QML), have three different approaches. The first is to apply classical machine learning to solve problems in quantum physics or quantum information. The second is to use quantum computations to speed up classical machine learning techniques, sometimes leading to hybrid algorithms. This is also known as quantum enhanced machine learning. The last one is to use pure quantum models or adaptations of learning algorithms to exploit the full potential of quantum mechanics and quantum information processing [21, 29].

QML has the potential, to exploit the advantages of the quantum computing and the quantum information process, to help the machines to learn faster and to tackle the most difficult tasks.

4   Quantum Artificial Intelligence Applications

The quantum artificial intelligence makes reference to the use of quantum computers for the processes of machine learning algorithms. The objective is to take advantage of the superiority of the processing of the quantum computing to obtain unattainable results with classic computer technologies. There are several possible applications like: data sets integration; process large data series; agile resolution of complex problems; and increased business insight and improved business models.

To handle and integrate multiple data sets from different sources, quantum computers also offer great help, speeding up processes and facilitating analysis.

The ability to handle volumes of such complex information makes quantum computing the ideal choice for solving business problems in a wide range of fields.

We produce 2.5 exabytes of data every day. An amount equivalent tof 5 million laptops. Every minute of every day, the 3.2 billion Internet users in the world continue to feed the databases adding 9,722 pins on Pinterest, 347,222 tweets, 4.2 million "likes" on Facebook, in addition to an infinity of other data in other formats, such as photos, videos, documents, information to create accounts, and others [30].

Quantum computers are designed to handle large volumes of data, as well as discover patterns and detect anomalies extremely quickly. Successive iterations of quantum computer designs and improvements in quantum error-correcting code are allowing developers to harness more and more of the potential of quantum bits. At the same time, they make it possible to optimize said potential to solve all kinds of problems that companies face when making decisions.

Quantum computers are capable of solving calculations in a matter of seconds that a current computer would take years. With quantum computing, developers can simultaneously perform multiple calculations on multiple input data. Quantum computers are essential for processing the endless stream of data that companies generate on a daily basis. In terms of calculation speed, these computers are capable of quickly solving extremely complex problems [31]. This ability is what is known as quantum supremacy. Thus, a quantum computer can carry out calculations in 200 s that would take a traditional computer 10,000 years. The key is to translate the real-world problems that companies face into quantum language [32].

With the increasing amount of data generated in industries such as pharmaceuticals, financials and life sciences, companies are losing their ties to classical computing rope. In order to have a better data framework, these companies now need complex models with enough processing power to model the most complex situations. And that is where quantum computers are called to play a very important role. The creation of better models with quantum technology will speed up many processes. Thus, in the health sector, it will make it possible to greatly shorten the development cycles of disease treatments, as in the case of COVID-19, shortening the cycle of research, testing, monitoring and treatment of the virus. On the other hand, in the banking sector, it will help reduce cases of financial implosion, or improve the logistics chain of the manufacturing sector.

5 Impact of QC on Businesses

Quantum computers will be disruptive for all industries, this dysfunction could influence / benefit companies at various levels.

One of the main differentiators that can be expected with quantum computing is an increase in online security, whose only negative point is the obsolescence of the encryption systems we use today [33]. QC will allow for a more organized distribution of information and the creation of extremely secure communication methods.

Although the impact of AI already makes a difference in the daily lives of companies, with quantum computing this impact will be much greater, since these systems are able to absorb and analyze more information simultaneously, and will be better to provide AI with the information and feedback they need to perform optimally [34]. This will reduce the systems learning curve, and they will be able to correct their errors quickly and self-sufficiently. The result is a technology that is more intuitive and advances faster.

The market value of quantum computing is expected to be around $2.2 billion in 2026. By then, it is estimated that there will be a total of around 180 installed quantum computers (45 of them produced in the same year). These figures include both equipment installed in the quantum computing companies themselves that offer quantum services, as well as local machines in customer premises [35].

For businesses to survive and acquire or maintain a competitive advantage, they need to be able to determine a number of likely outcomes from existing information (internal and external), that is, predictability, which increases with quantum superposition.

As quantum computers are able to analyze multiple data matrices at the same time and without losing efficiency, they will allow for much greater predictability, improving results.

Currently, there is still no passive production or sale of viable quantum computers. However, this is a technology that will be part of our future and that organizations should be aware of, as it represents a series of possibilities that will help deliver a better level of service and more efficiency to their consumers.

Microsoft developed Microsoft Quantun, an open Cloud Quantum Computing and Optimization ecosystem that features partner solutions, learning resources for developers, researchers, and students. It is from this ecosystem that Microsoft believes it is possible to accelerate the development and growth of Quantum Computing, since it has pre-built solutions that guarantee rapid development. The solutions are customized and prepared for both integration and data submission. Thus, the optimized development process with Azure Quantum guarantees cost savings in the medium and long term [36, 37].

As a complement, Microsoft launched a Quantum Development Kit, which allows developers to build algorithms using the Quantum language Q#, created by the company. With applications being able to be tested in local simulators, such as notebooks or desktops, with up to 30 logical qubits of power for quantum circuits, or even via Microsoft Azure, with a power close to 40 qubits [38].

Quantum computing is reaching a commercialization phase that could change our world. Early adopters of quantum's unique ability to solve certain types of problems can make breakthroughs that enable new business models.

Visionary organizations are already lining up with the emerging quantum computing ecosystem to become "quantum-ready" [39]. These pioneering companies are exploring use cases and associated algorithms that address complex business problems. This report discusses the paradigm shift that quantum computing represents for business, explains why your company may need to act now, and provides five recommendations for leveraging your organization through the business advantage that quantum provides. Quantum computing is reaching a commercialization phase that could change our world. Early adopters of quantum's unique ability to solve certain types of problems can make breakthroughs that enable new business models [40].

Quantum systems can trigger the discovery of new materials and new drugs, and allows that logistics and supply chains to be extremely efficient, as well as helping to find new ways to model financial data and isolate key risk factors to make better investments. Quantum computing can contribute to more dynamic artificial intelligences capable of dealing with a greater number of problems [8, 11, 13, 18, 29].

The encryption, one of the main data security mechanisms, will need to be revised, as the speed of calculations of a quantum computer will be able to unravel current codes in seconds. But on the other hand, quantum cryptography would be totally secure and virtually unbreakable.

Digital transformation in companies grows at exponential speed and the arrival of this technology will change the shape of many business models, opening doors for innovation. Company's IT area needs to be up to date and prepared for all the changes that are to come.

It is evident that we have to wait, but we have one certainty: quantum computing brings a vast world of possibilities to the corporate universe. Current industry trends related to quantum computing are (Fig. 4): chemicals & pharma; computer science; cybersecurity; energy & utilities; financial services; logistics & transport; media & marketing; military; and telecommunications.

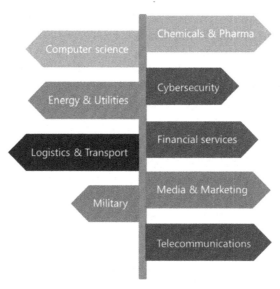

Fig. 4. Quantum computing current industry trends.

6   Conclusions

Quantum computing it's a real technology that will transform our future and that of virtually every industry. It is a disruptive technology that will solve several problems in today's business ecosystem.

Quantum computers are very different from the computers we use on a daily basis because the information processing is done following the rules of Quantum Physics. In a traditional computer, information is processed in 0 and 1 (bits), while in a quantum computer, information can be 0 and 1 at the same time (quantum bits or qubits), which exponentially increases the information processing capacity.

Quantum computers solve problems that classical computers are no longer able to answer. It is this additional information processing power that will dictate new opportunities in the business world.

There is a lot of promise around quantum computing, although there is still no transformative solution based on it. However, today, a lot is already known, due to the various tests and developments carried out with the technology in recent years.

The potential is so great, and technology advances so fast, that every leader needs to have a basic understanding of how technology works, the types of problems it can solve, and how to prepare to harness its potential.

In the near future, quantum computing will transform almost every aspect of technology, taking a broad approach to a range of problems, from process optimization to simulation and machine learning.

Access to cloud-hosted quantum services (Quantum Computing as a Service (QCaaS)) will be the main source of revenue for quantum computing companies, accounting for 75 percent of all quantum computing revenue by 2026. In the long term the acquisition of quantum equipment becomes a more frequent option, at present, the interest of potential end users is focused more on access to quantum computing capabilities through the cloud, avoiding making technologically risky and expensive investments in quantum computing equipment [41].

Quantum computing is a bet for the future of business and should have an impact on our routine in the next 5 to 10 years. To take the technology from the labs to the day to day of companies, big corporations, such as IBM, Google and Microsoft, and startups are investing their efforts in improving this solution.

In the next 5 years we will see a boom in the number of quantum software applications, quantum development tools, and quantum engineers and experts, as infrastructures expand, and this will allow more organizations to harness the power of two transformational technologies of quantum computing and AI, so many universities will begin to incorporate quantum computing subjects as core subjects in their curricula.

References

1. Kaye, P., Laflamme, R., Mosca, M.: An Introduction to Quantum Computing. TEAM LinG, Oxford (2006)
2. Mosteanu, N., Faccia, A.: Fintech frontiers in quantum computing, fractals, and blockchain distributed ledger: paradigm shifts and open innovation. J. Open Innovation: Technol., Market an Complexity 7(19), 1 (2021)
3. Ladd, T.D., Jelezko, F., Laflamme, R., Nakamura, Y., Monroe, C., O'Brien, J.L.: Quantum computers. Nature 464(7285), 45–53 (2010)
4. Lloyd, S.: The Universe as Quantum Computer. A Computable Universe: Understanding and Exploring Nature as Computation, 567–581 (2013)
5. Egger, D.J., et al.: Quantum computing for finance: State-of-the-art and future prospects. IEEE Trans. Quantum Eng. 1, 1–24 (2000)
6. McMahon, D.: Quantum Computing Explained, John Wiley & Sons (2007)
7. Vignesh, R., Poonacha, P.G.: Quantum computer architectures: an idea whose time is not far away. In: International Conference on Computers, Communications, and Systems (ICCCS) (2015)
8. Ajagekar, A., You, F.: Quantum computing based hybrid deep learning for fault diagnosis in electrical power systems. Appl. Energy 303, 117628 (2021)
9. Altman, E.B.K.R., Carleo, G., Carr, L.D., Demler, E., Chin, C., Zwierlein, M.: Quantum simulators: Architectures and opportunities. PRX Quantum 2(1), 017003 (2021)
10. Cheung, K.F., Bell, M.G., Bhattacharjya, J.: Cybersecurity in logistics and supply chain management: an overview and future research directions. Transportation Res. Part E: Logistics Transportation Review 146, 102217 (2021)
11. Orus, R., Mugel, S., Lizaso, E.: Quantum computing for finance: Overview and prospects. Reviews in Physics 4, 100028 (2019)
12. Ajagekar, A., You, A.: New frontiers of quantum computing in chemical engineering. Korean Journal of Chemical Eng. pp. 1–10 (2022)
13. Ajagekar, A., You, F.: Quantum computing for energy systems optimization: challenges and opportunities. Energy 179, 76–89 (2019)
14. Fernandez-Carames, T.M., Fraga-Lamas, P.: Towards post-quantum blockchain: a review on blockchain cryptography resistant to quantum computing attacks. IEEE access 8, 21091–21116 (2020)
15. Luckow, A., Klepsch, J., Pichlmeier, J.: Quantum computing: towards industry reference problems. Digitale Welt 5(2), 38–45 (2021)

16. Kumar, R.A., Kambalapally, V.: A contingent review on cloud computing trends predicting viable possibilities for future of computing. **1042**(1), 1–8 (2021)
17. Hauke, P., Katzgraber, H.G., Lechner, W., Nishimori, H., Oliver, W.D.: Perspectives of quantum annealing: Methods and implementations. Rep. Prog. Phys. **83**(5), 1–21 (2020)
18. National Academies of Sciences: Engineering, and Medicine, Quantum computing: progress and prospects, Washington. National Academies Press, DC (2019)
19. Amoroso, R.L.: Universal Quantum Computing: Supervening Decoherence-Surmounting Uncertainty. World Scientific (2017)
20. Kulkarni, V., Kulkarni, M., Pant, A.: Quantum computing methods for supervised learning. Quantum Machine Intelligence **3**(2), 1–14 (2021). https://doi.org/10.1007/s42484-021-000 50-0
21. Nivelkar, M., Bhirud, S.G.: Modeling of supervised machine learning using mechanism of quantum computing. J. Phys: Conf. Ser. **161**(1), 1–10 (2022)
22. Jiang, W., Xiong, J., Shi, Y.: When machine learning meets quantum computers: a case study. In: 26th Asia and South Pacific Design Automation Conference (2021)
23. Lloyd, S., Mohseni, M., Rebentrost, P.: Quantum principal component analysis. Nat. Phys. **10**(9), 631–633 (2014)
24. Li, Z., et al.: Resonant quantum principal component analysis. Science Advances, **7**(34), eabg2589 (2021)
25. Martin, A., et al.: Toward pricing financial derivatives with an ibm quantum computer. Physical Review Res. **3**(1), 013167 (2021)
26. Paparo, G.D., Dunjko, V., Martin-Delgado, M.A.M.A., Briegel, H.J.: Quantum speedup for active learning agents. Phys. Rev. X **4**(3), 1–14 (2014)
27. Lamata, L., Parra-Rodriguez, A., Sanz, M., Solano, E.: Digital-analog quantum simulations with superconducting circuits. Advances in Physics: X, **3**(1), 1457981 (2018)
28. Steinbrecher, G.R., Olson, J.P., Englund, D., Carolan, J.: Quantum optical neural networks. npj Quantum Information **5**(1), 1-9 (2019)
29. Biamonte, J., Wittek, P., Pancotti, N., Rebentrost, P., Wiebe, N., Lloyd, S.: Quantum machine learning. Nature **549**, 195–202 (2017)
30. Khan, T.M., Robles-Kelly, A.: Machine learning: quantum vs classical. IEEE Access **8**, 219275–219294 (2020)
31. Denning, P.J., Tedre, M.: Computational Thinking, Mit Press (2019)
32. Arute, F., et al.: Quantum supremacy using a programmable superconducting processor. Nature **574**(1–67), 505–510 (2019)
33. Easttom, W.:Quantum computing and cryptography. In: Modern Cryptography, Springer, Cham, pp. 385-390 (2021)
34. Rawat, B., Mehra, N., Bist, A.S., Yusup, M., Sanjaya, Y.P.A.: Quantum computing and AI: impacts & possibilities. ADI J. Recent Innovation **3**(2), 202–207 (2022)
35. Srivastava, S.: Artificial intelligences last news quantum computing. Analytics Insight, (2020). https://www.analyticsinsight.net/ai-quantum-computing-can-enable-much-anticipated-advancements/
36. Marx, V.: Biology begins to tangle with quantum computing. Nat. Methods **18**(7), 715–719 (2021)
37. Azure: Azure Quantum. Azure, (2022). https://azure.microsoft.com/en-us/solutions/qua ntum-computing/
38. Hooyberghs, J.: "What's Next?," in Introducing Microsoft Quantum Computing for Developers, pp. 341–353. Apress, Berkeley (2022)
39. Nallamothula, L.: Quantum ecosystem development using advanced cloud services. In: Elbiaze, H., Sabir, E., Falcone, F., Sadik, M., Lasaulce, S., Ben Othman, J. (eds.) UNet 2021. LNCS, vol. 12845, pp. 163–171. Springer, Cham (2021). https://doi.org/10.1007/978-3-030-86356-2_14

40. Gil, D., Mantas, J., Sutor, R., Kesterson-Townes, L., Flöther, F., Schnabel, C.: Coming soon to your business- quantum computing. IBM Institute for business value (2018)
41. Inside Quantum Technology: Quantum Computing: A Seven-year Market Forecast. Report IQT-QCM-1020 (2020)

Educational Resource Recommender Systems Using Python and Moodle

Alicia Andrade Vera$^{(\boxtimes)}$ (ID) and Carlos Mendoza González

Universidad Estatal Península de Santa Elena, La Libertad, Ecuador
`aandrade@upse.edu.ec`

Abstract. This paper presents the implementation in Phyton of an algorithm for recommending educational resources based on the user's needs, where these resources will be obtained through the use of the YouTube API that suggests videos of educational materials focused on the student's level of knowledge to customize the recommendations, taking into consideration data obtained from a knowledge survey and the academic grades obtained from different resources made from the Moodle learning platform. The emphasis is on building an RS with the capacity to assist in educational settings. The RSs applied in education allow students to find materials that fit their needs and preferences, and the recommended materials are adapted to the pedagogical objectives of the teachers. It should be noted that the implementation of the project was carried out in a controlled environment, with the interaction of a group of students of a particular subject and semester.

Keywords: Recommendation system · Collaborative filtering · Moodle · Python

1 Introduction

The use of recommender systems as information retrieval techniques and strategies aims to solve the problem of data overload. They help filter the information available on the web and find the information that is most interesting and valuable to users, allowing them to discover new content more quickly and efficiently.

Recommender systems are used in various applications, such as recommending books, music, movies or news. The task of RS is to automatically select the most appropriate items based on each user's personal interests and preferences. Typically, RS focuses on a specific type of item to recommend, such as in travel e-commerce or an educational repository, and generates personalized recommendations that provide useful and effective recommendations [1].

Nowadays, the adoption of personalized learning approaches, especially RS, is justified due to the high demand for interpretation of data stored in educational institutions and in various virtual environments or services. Almost all student behaviors and actions are stored on the servers of educational institutions [2].

In addition, learning activities take place in a virtual environment that includes a variety of tools and systems. For example, virtual teaching and learning environments (VLEEs) provide access to learning resources, but do not guarantee that a teacher or learner will use them in the course. Students often use additional tools to collaborate or find resources, as if the educational materials presented in a virtual environment are insufficient. Learning situations are also becoming increasingly complex due to the different pedagogical approaches between formal and informal learning, which have different requirements for the learning environment and, as such, for reinforcement in learning [3].

In terms of the recommendation techniques used, RSs are generally based on collaborative filtering, content-based filtering, knowledge-based filtering or link recommendation algorithms. These algorithms use the user's information and resources to generate recommendations.

In general, recommender systems are evaluated using three types of tests driven by protocol evaluation in areas such as information retrieval and machine learning [4].

The aim of this work is to search for resources with the help of the YouTube API, and suggest those that best suit not only the search, but also the educational needs of the student, so the first part of this work focuses on the recommendation of videos based on a survey of knowledge that the student has previously assessed. In addition, we work with the results obtained from the lessons, workshops and practices carried out on the MOODLE platform.

2 Theoretical Background

This section presents the theoretical and technological bases on which the proposed recommender system is based. First, the concept of the Moodle learning platform, the environment on which this work is focused, is described. Secondly, the types of recommender systems are presented.

2.1 E-Learning Platforms

The e-learning platform is an online learning management system (LMS) that allows you to manage, deliver, monitor, evaluate and support various pre-planned and designed activities in the process of fully virtual training (e-learning) [5].

The use of LMS platforms offers many advantages to support direct instruction, leading to better results than through traditional teaching methods.

The correct use of the LMS allows access to information and communication, expands learning strategies and offers the possibility of improving certain cognitive skills that depend directly on the specific stimuli of each person and the creative techniques used in learning. In the publication and creation of content.

Of all the information platforms that exist in the market, this paper focuses on Moodle because it is the one used in this work.

The Moodle distance learning platform is an LMS, it allows you to keep track of the content and the different users that interact within it. In this case, Moodle has most of the tools to communicate and monitor the activities of the participants [6].

Moodle facilitates the teaching and learning process, teamwork activities and collaboration in projects, and because of the interaction it provides it promotes the existence of three models: (teaching model in transmitting knowledge, teaching model in acquiring, compiling and accumulating knowledge and the teaching model for developing, inventing and creating knowledge), and the five different types of content management systems with educational value (pure CMS system, weblog content management systems, CMS systems oriented to collaboration, community and collaborative content management systems, and wiki systems) [7].

2.2 Recommender Systems

A recommender system is defined as a tool, platform or software module for the purpose of providing recommendations that are useful to users [8].

Most experts are thinking of four architectures of recommender systems: content-based systems, knowledge-based systems, collaborative filtering systems, and hybrid systems. All four architectures are often used, and the data mappings refer to user choices for specific factors. Each quantity within the matrix shows a pair of user agents, which serves this information on multiple supports to create recommendations [9].

Of all the recommender system architectures, this paper will focus on collaborative filtering because it is the one used in this work.

Collaborative filtering (CF) systems their make their recommendations based on the relationships between users and objects. RS recommends an active user, and items that it wants other users to have the same options. The similarity between users is calculated, taking into account the similarity between their levels [10]. Within CF, nearest neighbor methods have high popularity, efficiency and capabilities to create accurate and personal recommendations. In this approach: (1) the utility matrix is completed for different users and (2) the similarity between users is determined between users from the Jaccard index or the degree of cosine [11].

Memory-based collaborative filtering algorithms, or nearest-neighbor algorithms they use a comprehensive database of items and users to create forecasts [12]. First, they used statistical techniques to find neighbors, using items with similar rating histories to existing users [13]. Once a list of neighbors is created, their choices are combined to create a list containing the N most recommended items for the current user. Among its limitations is the need to have a minimum number of users with a minimum number of predictions for each person, including which users the recommendation is targeted [14].

In addition to the above systems, other authors consider other recommender systems, such as those based on demographics or utility, to be particularly relevant. These systems are actually subcategories of the aforementioned recommender system architecture [15].

3 Python Recommender System

This section describes the Phyton implementation of a user-based collaborative filtering recommendation system that connects to the YouTube API, whose main objective is to suggest educational resources to users based on the score that will be a discrete numerical value between a maximum and minimum that each student placed in a survey generated at the end of the academic cycle on the knowledge they consider to have in the different topics covered during the academic period, using the nearest neighbor algorithm. In addition, based on the lowest overall average grades of the lessons, practices and workshops carried out within the Moodle platform, videos will be suggested.

Because the proposed RS focuses on fostering learning, it must have access to: (1) student information, (2) lesson information, (3) workshop and practice information, and (4) knowledge survey information.

3.1 Development Environment

Open-source development tools were used for this work. First, the Visual Studio Code source code editor was installed, where the repository containing the Python files with the algorithm was created. Secondly, the Python programming language was installed, which was used due to the number of libraries that the developer community has created, among them: NumPy, which was used to work with the data in a multidimensional way; Pandas was used to read and manage the dataset, creating the DataFrame with integrated indexing; Strealim, which allowed converting the data scripts into web applications and due to the great flexibility of this language to integrate with the YouTube API. In addition, a Python-mysql-connector module was installed, used in the Windows operating system; in order to install the module, it is necessary to have Python and PIP pre-installed in the system.

3.2 API YouTube

The YouTube website plays a relevant role, since the information of the educational elements is obtained through its API. To make the recommendation, the collaborative filtering technique is used, implementing an algorithm that recommends "elements" to the user based on the grades obtained according to the knowledge survey executed. Additionally, using the most popular recommendation technique, the student will be able to have recommendations based on the grades obtained in lessons, workshops and practices.

To make use of the resources of the YouTube platform using other software such as Python, it is necessary to make use of the YouTube resources Data API which will allow us to access the resources and related information of the entire platform such as channels, playlists, comments, subscriptions, thumbnails, categories and videos.

An API key is required to make use of the Data API, so it is necessary to have a Google account to access the Google API Console where the API key is requested, and the application that will make use of the resources is registered through requests.

The main resources of the YouTube API are: activity, channel, channeBanner, guide-Category, playlist, playlistItem, search result, subscription, thumbnail, video and video-Category. Of these the RS shows only videos of the topics that the algorithm determines that the student should reinforce, through the following request: GET https://www.goo gleapis.com/youtube/v3/search, this request requires a parameter "q" of type string that specifies the query term to be searched, the same that will be determined by the RS.

3.3 Moodle Virtual Platform

This system is based on the results obtained in a knowledge survey, considering student preferences, the recommendations in this case are made taking into account the three most similar profiles based on student responses and thus recommending different topics seen throughout the academic period [16]. Additionally, recommendations are also made considering the subjects with the lowest overall average and lowest individual grades.

This system is mainly aimed at students, obtains automatic feedback information and can be applied to any domain, as it is web-based and recommends resources. The Moodle recommendation system was implemented in a sixteen-week course.

The knowledge survey is elaborated with twenty-five (25) questions in relation to the topics contained in the syllabus of the Fundamentals of Redes course and the following Likert scale was used to rate: (5) Very well, (4) well, (3) Fair, (2) Little, (1) Not at all.

The Moodle gradebook configuration is composed of two parent categories: cycle I and cycle II that contain the subcategories assessment strategies and final exam. The evaluative strategies subcategory is composed of the components teaching, practice and experimentation and autonomous work as shown in Table 1.

Table 1. Moodle grade chart.

Assessment strategies	Teaching component	Lesson 1
		Lesson 2
		Lesson n
	Total teaching component	
	Practice and experimentation component	Practice 1
		Practice 2
		Practice n
	Total practice and experimentation component	
	Autonomous work component	Task 1
		Task 2
		Task n
	Total autonomous work component	
Total assessment strategies		
Final exam		
Total course = Assessment strategies + Final exam		

3.4 Connecting to the Moodle Database

To connect the MySQL database with Python is done in two ways:

1. The MySQL Connector Python module is used to execute the queries and the following steps were performed.

   a. Using the pip command to install the MySQL Python connector.
      ```
      pip install mysql-connector-python
      ```
   b. Import using a statement so that you can use the methods of this module to communicate with the MySQL database.
      ```
      import mysql.connector
      ```

c. Use the connect () method with the necessary arguments to connect to MySQL.

```
db = mysql.connect(
host="localhost",
user="root",
passwd="",
database="Moodle
)
```

2. To convert a table in MySQL to Pandas DataFrame the connection is as follows.
a. Connection to the database.

```
db_connection_str = "mysql+pymysql://"+UserName+ ":"
+Password +"@localhost/"+ DatabaseName
```

3.5 Algorithm Creation and Implementation of the Recommender System

The recommendation system will show information to students and teachers of a particular course regarding general topics such as: (1) the most failed questions in each of the tests (lessons and exams), (2) the in-class workshop with the lowest overall average, (3) the practice performed with the lowest overall average, and specifically (4) information on a knowledge survey of topics covered throughout the semester and the scale of difficulty it represented for each student [17].

For the first three cases the mechanism of the most popular without using collaborative filtering will be used, this is a basic way without using machine learning to offer recommendations in more general and not personalized aspects being the same for all users, which is accurate for these cases where it is expected that both the teacher and students are shown this general information about the course activities, despite this for the first case on the questions that most students failed in the tests; students will be shown information only of the tests they took, and as for the teacher if you can see all existing tests.

The last recommendation topic on the knowledge evaluation survey, being of a personalized nature, will make use of the user-based collaborative filtering technique with the nearest neighbor algorithm, so this section will cover the detail of the implementation of this resource to be recommended [18].

The nearest neighbor method essentially consists of determining similar users within a set through a quantifiable element that relates them on a topic or preference. In this case there is a set of students where the preferences of other similar students will be taken into account, i.e., the "neighbor" that most resembles him/her with respect to a preference, in this case the scale of values of the questions of the knowledge survey [19].

This process is defined by the following Eq. (1).

$$r_{ij} = \frac{\sum_k Similaries(u_i, u_k)r_{kj}}{numberofratings} \tag{1}$$

There are two ways to calculate preferences: (1) user-based collaborative filtering and (2) item-based collaborative filtering.

[20]The recommendation is to show a student the topics that are most difficult for the general population to understand considering the weaknesses of users whose scores are similar to the first student. Considering these aspects, the following resources will be available:

- Matrix of Survey Items (Items Feedback): Preferences.
- Matrix of ratings by user and topic (Values Item Feedback): Set of elements that represent the preferences of users regarding topics.

From these resources the goal is to calculate a student's preferences through the preferences of similar students or "near neighbors" on the topics he or she may be interested in reinforcing. This process will be detailed as a series of steps for better explanation:

1. Creation of the resource sets (Matrixes of survey topics and ratings by user and topic).
2. Find similarity among students.
3. Develop a recommendation mechanism.

Creation of Resource Sets. The necessary matrixes are created by querying the Moodle database hosted in MYSQL through sqlalchemy to be converted into a DataFrame for better handling, as follows:

```
db_connection = create_engine(db_connection_str)
```

Survey topic matrix.

```
df_items_feedback = pd.read_sql(listFeedbackItems(),
con=db_connection_str)
```

Matrix of ratings by user and topic.

```
df_values_items_feedback = pd.read_sql(listItemsVal-
uesByUser(), con=db_connection_str)
```

This process must be carried out with due analysis since the information provided to the recommender system is essential if reliable information is to be obtained. That is why at this point it is necessary to limit the margin of error of the records, i.e., redundant or unnecessary data. In this case the data shown are filtered through the queries directly and not at the DataFrame level with the panda library.

The data obtained in the subject matrix of the survey show a total of 25 subjects and about the grades per user and subject there are a total of 975 records regarding 39 students with 25 grades each.

Find Similarities Among Students. For this purpose, a function for calculating nearest neighbors must be created. Similarity can be calculated in two ways: Pearson correlation and cosine similarity [21]. In this case, the second option has been used to find three students with similar grades.

Cosine similarity Eq. (2).

$$\cos(x_1, x_2) = \frac{\vec{x}_1 . \vec{x}_2}{[[\vec{x}_1 \, \Delta \, \vec{x}_2]]} \tag{2}$$

The function will receive three parameters the student's unique user identifier (user_id), the pivot matrix of grades per user and subject, and the number of similar users required. The first parameter `user_id` will be entered through the web interface after typing the user's name and retrieved by a database query. The second parameter matrix will be obtained from the matrix ratings per user and topic using the `pivot_table` statement in Python. Finally, the third parameter is an integer previously defined in the programming of the interface, which will represent a parameter "k" that will vary depending on what is required.

Function for generation of similar users:

```
def generateSimilarUsers(user_id, matrix, k=3):
    user = matrix[matrix.index == user_id]
    other_users = matrix[matrix.index != user_id]
    similarities = co-
sine_similarity(user,other_users)[0].tolist()
    indices = other_users.index.tolist()
    index_similarity = dict(zip(indices, similarities))
    index_similarity_sorted = sort-
ed(index_similarity.items(), key=operator.itemgetter(1))
    index_similarity_sorted.reverse()
    top_users_similarities = index_similarity_sorted[:k]
    users = [u[0] for u in top_users_similarities]
    return users
```

Second function parameter:

```
grade_matrix = df_values_items_feedback.pivot_table(in-
dex='user_id', columns='item_feedback_id', val-
ues='grade')
```

The function will first create a DataFrame with the current user that has been provided, and then another one with the remaining users. Using the "cosine_similarity" function imported from the sklearn module, the similarity between students is calculated, and then a list is created with the indexes of these students, then key/value pairs are created for each user index and its similarity, where they are ordered to finally show the number of similar neighbors according to the number that has been defined.

Import sklearn module.

```
from sklearn.metrics.pairwise import cosine_similarity
```

The Python sklearn module that integrates classical machine learning algorithms into the tightly coupled world of Python science packages. Its goal is to provide simple and efficient solutions to learning problems that are accessible to all and reusable in various contexts: machine learning as a versatile tool for science and engineering.

Develop Recommendation Mechanism. The recommendations listed will also be provided by a function that receives 4 parameters: the unique identifier of the student's user (user_id), the matrix of similar users obtained previously, again the pivot matrix of the grades per user and subject, and the number of recommendations to display. The first parameter User_id is obtained in the same way as the previous function. The second parameter matrix of similar users will be obtained by the function GenerateSimilarUsers and, finally, the fourth parameter is an integer previously defined in a global variable.

Function to generate personalized recommendations:

```
def recommend_item(user_index, similar_user_indices, ma-
trix, items=max_item_recomended):
    similar_users = matrix[matrix.index.isin(simi-
lar_user_indices)]
    similar_users = similar_users.mean(axis=0)
    similar_users_df = pd.DataFrame(similar_users, col-
umns=['mean'])
    similar_users_df.head()
    user_df = matrix[matrix.index == user_index]
    user_df_transposed = user_df.transpose()
    user_df_transposed.columns = ['grade']
    user_df_transposed = user_df_trans-
posed[user_df_transposed['grade']==0]
    animes_unseen = user_df_transposed.index.tolist()
    similar_users_df_filtered = similar_users_df[simi-
lar_users_df.index.isin(animes_unseen)]
    similar_users_df_ordered = similar_users_df.sort_val-
ues(by=['mean'], ascending=True)
    top_n_item_feedback = similar_users_df_or-
dered.head(items)
    top_n_items_feedback_indices = top_n_item_feed-
back.index.tolist()
    items_feedback_information = df_items_feed-
back[df_items_feedback['item_feed-
back_id'].isin(top_n_items_feedback_indices)]
    return items_feedback_information
```

The function will initially create a matrix of the grades per topic only considering the list of similar users, then it calculates the average grade of all the questions on the matrix, which is converted into a DataFrame for better use, it creates a vector with the matrix of grades only with the current user entered, it reduces redundant data if any. After that, a list of the topics that are difficult for the current student is created, and the average grades of similar users are filtered, the DataFrame is sorted to list the items with lower scores that represent the recommendations.

After obtaining the personalized recommendations, the suggestions are supplemented by displaying a number of YouTube videos. This process is best shown in the graphical interface to be used by students and teachers, which is described below.

4 Results

The generated recommendations are displayed in a graphical interface through a web application. There are several ways to interpret the native Pyhton code in the browser, in this particular case the use of Streamlit has been chosen, which is an extremely pow-erful tool that provides the user with an extensive set of text components, data visualization, and data visualization, graphics, multimedia and many others, thus facilitating the creation and dynamism of web applications. In this particular case the following was used:

Streamlit library import:

```
import streamlit as st
```

— st.title: title creation; st.image: image display.;st.text_input: data input; st.header y st.subheader: for texts in header and subheader formats; st.table: Display a static table; st.write: display any text string; st.checkbox: checkbox usage; st.error: display error messages; st.warning: display warning messages; st.success: display a success message.

In terms of interface construction, this is done in a very similar way to traditional web applications, only that instead of using hmtl elements in a file of the same extension, the view is coded directly in the Python file with.py extension making use of the Streamlit library, and using the elements that it provides and are previously detailed. The structure of the extension then results in a combination of graphical elements of Streamlit calling functions implemented through Python code such as the nearest neighbor algorithm and many others, and which in turn makes use of the necessary information extracted from the database queries. These resources and their interaction will result in a list of recommendations suggesting content from the YouTube platform. The structure of the application can best be described by the following graph presented in Fig. 1.

4.1 Display of Recommendations

In general terms, the recommendation system will show the information in a web application, which can be accessed from a link published in the Moodle virtual environment. The application will ask for the user's name as a parameter as a validation mechanism. Once the user is verified, four types of recommendations will be displayed; three general

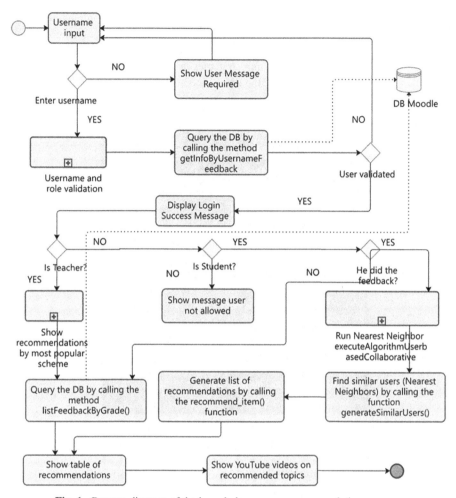

Fig. 1. Process diagram of the knowledge survey recommendation process.

ones for any user using the most popular scheme without collaborative filtering and one specific recommendation using the nearest neighbor algorithm previously developed and explained.

The information that will be displayed to the student and teacher user of a course is: (1) the most failed questions in each of the tests (lessons and exams), (2) the workshop in class with the lowest overall average, (3) the practice performed with the lowest overall average, (4) recommendations on topics covered throughout the semester through a knowledge survey, to evaluate the difficulty that represented for each student a particular topic.

The results obtained from all types of recommendations will be complemented by showing a certain number of YouTube videos regarding the suggestions obtained so that students have support material to reinforce knowledge in those topics, and in the case of the teacher to implement new teaching strategies in those areas where students have difficulties. The web application once the link is accessed from the virtual classroom is dis-played as shown in Fig. 2.

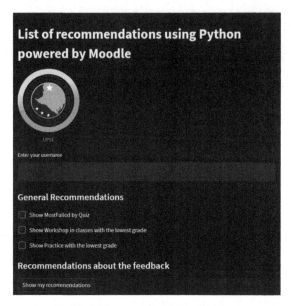

Fig. 2. Main recommendation interface.

To access the first three recommendations, it will be necessary to enter the user's name and select the desired item to display the respective recommendations, these are general, but despite this only the information related to the student will be displayed. For example, in the first case of the most failed items, only the information of the evaluations that the student has taken will be shown, as shown in Fig. 3.

Figure 4 show the recommendations according to the three workshops and three practices with the lowest overall average, since the same content is shown to all students when determined by the lowest average score.

Regarding the last recommendation on the knowledge survey, this will be personalized and will make use of the nearest neighbor algorithm, and in the same way as the previous cases will require the entry of the user's name.

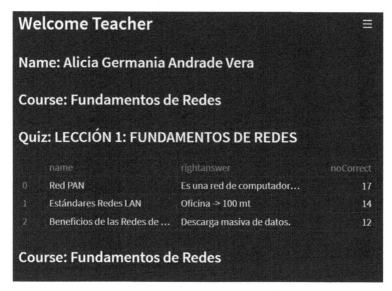

Fig. 3. Items most failed by quizzes.

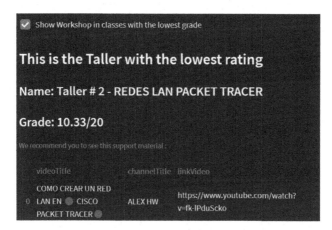

Fig. 4. Workshop in classes with the lowest grade.

Figure 5 shows the results when the student takes the survey, but what happens when the student using the recommendation system did not take the survey based on the theory, the collaborative filtering technique is based on the user's interactions with respect to a preference, and when the user does not have interactions, it is simply not possible to make use of this method.

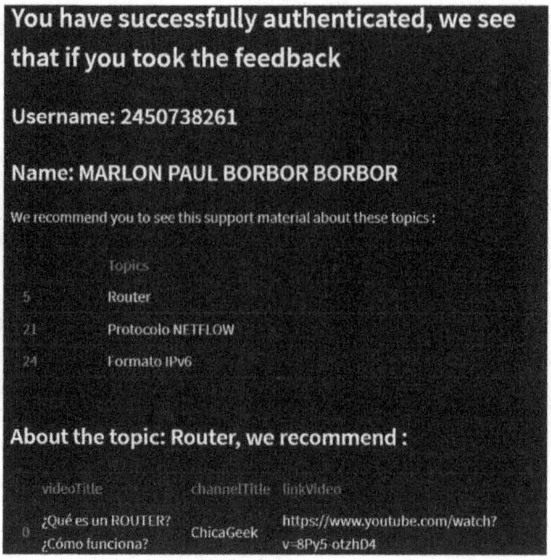

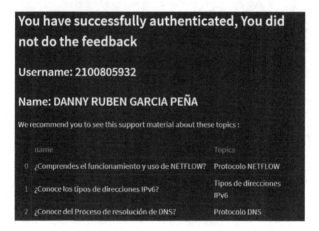

Fig. 5. Rendered the survey.

The solution to this situation is to make random recommendations to the user, but in this case the most popular mechanism will be used to show the most difficult topics for the general student population as shown in Fig. 6.

Fig. 6. Did not submit the survey.

5 Conclusions

The application of RS in education can benefit both educators and students. On the one hand, they reduce the need for teachers to search for and select educational materials; on the other hand, they improve students' decision-making process because they have access to high-quality materials and accurate, personalized information.

The application of this type of systems is extremely useful and practical by globally providing all users of a course with recommendations on specific topics by providing multimedia support material from platforms such as YouTube. In addition to this fact, all the tools used in the development of the system were open source, so it does not represent economic costs but only time investment in the development process.

Finally, it should be noted that the implementation of the project was carried out in a controlled environment, with the interaction of a group of students of a particular subject and semester. From the results obtained in the present work, it was possible to show how the Collaborative Filtering approaches offer good results. However, it is important to keep in mind that the results presented serve only as a first step towards understanding and appropriate specialization for recommendations.

This work should be complemented with experiments in a production environment, in cloud servers maximizing the scope of the work by employing it in the subjects of a semester or in all subjects of an institution, considering the independent characteristics, needs, level of knowledge, and expectations of each student who is part of the RS users, as well as their information search tasks and how to use the recommended resources in their learning activities, by using new rule patterns and extending the recommendation criteria designed to increase the type and number of recommendations.

References

1. Ricci, F., Rokach, L., Shapira, B.: Recommender systems: introduction and challenges. In: Recommender systems handbook. Springer, pp. 1–34 (2015). https://doi.org/10.1007/978-1-4899-7637-6_1
2. Durovic, G., Holenko Dlab, M., Hoic-Bozic, N.: Educational recommender systems: An overview and guidelines for further research and development. Sveucilista u Zagrebu, **20** (2018)
3. El Guabass, I., Al Achhab, M., Jellouli, I., Mohajir, B.: Context-aware recommender systems for learning. Int. J. Inf. Sci. **1**(1), 17–25 (2018)
4. Guy Shani, Asela Gunawardana,: Evaluating recommendation systems. In: Francesco Ricci, Lior Rokach, Bracha Shapira, Paul B Kantor, (ed.) Recommender systems handbook, pp. 257–297. Springer, Boston, MA (2011). https://doi.org/10.1007/978-0-387-85820-3_8
5. Simanullang, N.H.S., Rajagukguk, J.: Learning Management System (LMS) Based On Moodle To Improve Students Learning Activity. J. Physics: Conference Series **1462**(1), 012067 (2020)
6. Harrathi, M., Touzani, N., Braham, R.: Toward a personalized recommender system for learning activities in the context of MOOCs. In: De Pietro, G., Gallo, L., Howlett, R.J., Jain, L.C. (eds.) KES-IIMSS 2017. SIST, vol. 76, pp. 575–583. Springer, Cham (2018). https://doi.org/10.1007/978-3-319-59480-4_57
7. Gamage, S.H.P.W., Ayres, J.R., Behrend, M.B.: A systematic review on trends in using Moodle for teaching and learning. Int. J. STEM Educ. **9**(1), 1-24 (2022)
8. Rickard, P., Stiles, R.: Comprehensive adult student assessment system (casas) design for effective assessment in correctional educational programs, Journal of Correctional, **32**, 51–53 (1985)
9. Ullman, J., Leskovec, J., Rajaraman, A.: Mining of Massive Datasets (2011). http://www.mmds.org/
10. Yago Corral, H.: Dialnet (2019). https://dialnet.unirioja.es/servlet/tesis?codigo=251131. [Último acceso: 22 octubre 2021]

11. Sapountzi, A., Psannis, K.E.: Social networking data analysis tools & challenges. ScienceDirect, **86**, 893–913 (2018)
12. Cunha, T., Soares, C., De Carvalho, A.C.: Metalearning and Recommender Systems: A literature review and empirical study on the algorithm selection problem for Collaborative Filtering. ScienceDirect **423**, 128–144 (2018)
13. Tarus, J., Niu, Z., Mustafa, G.: Knowledge-based recommendation: a review of ontology-based recommender systems for e-learning. Artif Intell Rev **50**, 21–48 (2018)
14. Galán Nieto, S.M.: UC3M Research Portal. (2007). https://www.it.uc3m.es/jvillena/irc/practicas/06-07/31.pdf. [Último acceso: 23 noviembre 2021]
15. Li, H., Shi, J., Zhang, S., Yun, H.: Implementation of intelligent recommendation system for learning resources. In: 12th International Conference on Computer Science and Education (ICCSE), pp. 139–144 (2017)
16. Kulkarn, P.V., Rohini Kale, S.R.: Recommender System in eLearning: A Survey. In: Proceeding of International Conference on Computational Science and Applications , pp. 119–126 (2020)
17. Bansal, S., Baliyan, N.: A Study of Recent Recommender System Techniques. International Journal of Knowledge and Systems Science, **10**(2), 13–41 (2019)
18. Liang, D., Krishnan, R.G., Hoffman, M.D., Jebara, T.: Variational Autoencoders for Collaborative Filtering. Advancing Computing as a Science & Profession, 689–698 (2018)
19. Zhang, S., Yao, L., Sun, A., Tay, Y.: Deep Learning Based Recommender System: A Survey and New Perspectives. ACM Comput Surv, **52** (2019)
20. Kharita, M.K., Kumar, A., Singh, P.: Item-Based Collaborative Filtering in Movie Recommendation in Real time. In: 2018 First International Conference on Secure Cyber Computing and Communication (ICSCCC). pp. 340–342. IEEE (2018)
21. Shu, J., Shen, X., Liu, H., Yi, B., Zhang, Z.: A content-based recommendation algorithm for learning resources. Multimedia Syst. **24**(2), 163–173 (2017). https://doi.org/10.1007/s00530-017-0539-8

Systematic Literature Review on Data Provenance in Internet of Things

Emrullah Gultekin[1,2(✉)] and Mehmet S. Aktas[1]

[1] Computer Engineering Department, Yildiz Technical University, Istanbul, Turkey
aktas@yildiz.edu.tr
[2] Ziraat Teknoloji, Istanbul, Turkey
egultekin@ziraatteknoloji.com

Abstract. Internet of Things(IoT) is a concept that develops day by day and is now an indispensable part of our lives. Although it has been developed a lot, it still has many problematic areas and has many aspects that need improvement. On the other hand, data provenance is a concept that covers the origin of the data, the changes made, and the processes it has gone through. Data provenance is an essential option for improvements in the IoT field. Although there are many research studies in the literature related to the use of data provenance in the IoT, we could not identify a comprehensive systematic literature review that focuses explicitly on this topic. The study aims to examine the current data provenance on the Internet of Things studies, identify potential shortcomings or improvements, determine the working areas that can be done to make the processes more efficient and solve the IoT and data provenance problems. We also aim to serve this study as a knowledge base for researchers for conducting further research and development in this area. The review is done by following a systematic literature review process. We presented an SLR-based method on data provenance in IoT. We investigated the challenges encountered in IoT applications and worked on using data provenance as a solution. We conducted a literature search covering the years 2012–2022. We found 140 published papers. After applying exclusion criteria for these papers, we have focused on the final 16 papers. In the IoT area, some challenges require work, such as constrained resources, heterogeneity, scalability, mobility, security and privacy. Our study shows that data provenance is primarily used in security, privacy, reliability, and trust. We can say that the studies in these fields have increased gradually over the last years. Blockchain is frequently used to provide data provenance.

Keywords: Data provenance · Internet of Things · IoT · Systematic literature review

1 Introduction

The Internet of Things (IoT) refers to a rapidly growing technological concept in which devices can be connected and can communicate even if they are in different

O. Gervasi et al. (Eds.): ICCSA 2022 Workshops, LNCS 13380, pp. 31–46, 2022.
https://doi.org/10.1007/978-3-031-10542-5_3

structures and platforms. Depending on the advancement of technology, new sensors and devices have emerged, and sometimes changes have been made to existing devices, and new features have been added. Although such sensors and devices have already existed, a completely new approach has emerged with the development of the internet and the connection of these devices to the internet. This approach implies that any object can be accessed by anyone by any device in any place and condition. The Internet of Things has now entered every aspect of our lives, from our homes to our cars, outside to inside, and even our bodies. It is estimated that by 2030, organizations can generate value using data generated by 8 billion people and 25 billion connected devices [13]. This shows the importance and impact of IoT in our current lives and future. Its rapid growth causes some problems.

Provenance can find answers to what, where, when, how, and what for a data object. It enables us to obtain information about the state of an object and the processes that are made for it to come to this state, the stages it passes through, when and how these processes and stages occur [1]. In general, pure data is insufficient to understand, evaluate and reuse data. In addition to the data, meta data information such as the method in which the data is provided, the purpose of receiving the data, and the processes applied to the data are also required. IoT devices have resource limitations. These limitations may result in a device failure or service failure. Provenance capacities for all system elements can help resolve these issues [2]. Provenance makes many contributions, such as data clarity, reliability, and data reuse [12].

Using provenance data provides many benefits but can also cause some disadvantages. For example, a particular increase in network traffic is expected by adding provenance data to existing data. In addition, with this new data, the IoT, which already has limited resources, will result in memory, processor, and energy consumption in the devices. It is crucial to study how much these consumptions will be and whether they will create disadvantageous situations, and possible solutions that can be applied to eliminate or minimize disadvantageous situations.

Both the Internet of Things and the use of provenance are among the popular topics studied recently. This study investigated academic studies on data provenance in the Internet of Things.

2 Review Approach

2.1 Research Questions

Although there are studies on data provenance on the Internet of Things, there is a lack of detailed studies. There are review studies related to data provenance and IoT; for example, Bai et al. [24] conducted a systematic literature review, but they focused on security and the Internet of Health Things (IoHT), an extension of the IoT. We could not identify a comprehensive systematic literature review that focuses explicitly on the use of data provenance on the Internet of Things. This literature review aims to fill this gap to some extent, as there is no comprehensive review of the use of data provenance in the field of the Internet of Things. For this purpose, the main difficulties encountered in the current Internet of Things applications and data provenance to solve these problems have been studied and it has been tried to find answers to the following research questions.

RQ1: How much research activity has there been in IoT and Data provenance since 2012? How often and in which journals are articles published? The frequency of publication will show a trend analysis on the usage of provenance in the Internet of Things issues.

RQ2: What research topics are being addressed? What are the main categories to which the issues are related? What are the main subjects, and what keywords do they use? The keywords used will show their relationship with other topics.

RQ3: What are the main problems being tried to find a solution for the Internet of Things using data provenance?

RQ4: What are the open issues and the future research directions of data provenance and the Internet of Things?

2.2   Identification of Relevant Articles

The study begins with searching in known digital libraries to find articles. For searches, popular digital libraries such as IEEE Xplore (https://ieeexplore.ieee.org/Xplore/home.jsp), ScienceDirect (https://www.sciencedirect.com), ACM (https://dl.acm.org/dl.cfm) and Scopus (https://www.scopus.com) were scanned. These libraries were searched with "(data provenance OR provenance) AND (Internet of Things OR IoT)" search criteria. The abstract section of the results was read by eliminating those not relevant. The articles related to data provenance in the Internet of Things were identified, and those that were more distant from the subject or those that were not suitable for the study were eliminated. The articles that conveyed the subject most efficiently were included in the study.

2.3   Inclusion and Exclusion Criteria

The criteria for the inclusion of articles in the research are as follows: Within the scope of the article, we tried to identify the articles directly related to the internet of things and data provenance. "Internet of Things AND Data Provenance", "Internet of Things AND Provenance", "IoT AND Data Provenance" and "IoT AND Provenance" search criteria were searched. In order to narrow the search results, the articles with document title or abstract or index terms containing these search criteria and published in the last 10 years (2012–2022) were selected.

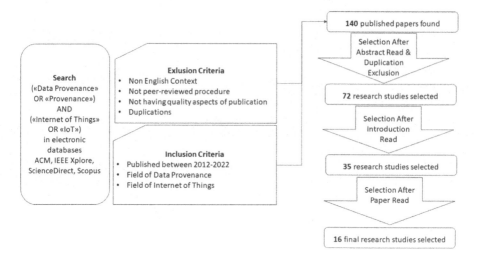

Fig. 1. Search progress

There are 27 articles searched by these search criteria from the IEEE Xplore database, 13 articles from the ScienceDirect database, 82 articles from the Scopus database, and 18 from the ACM database. 140 articles were found in total.

- 14 articles were filtered due to duplication.
- 54 articles were excluded after abstract reading because they were irrelevant.
- In total, 68 articles were filtered after abstract reading due to irrelevant to the data provenance in Internet of Things.
- 72 articles were selected to be read.
- 37 of 72 articles were eliminated after abstract and introduction reading because they were irrelevant.
- 35 articles were downloaded.
- After reading these 35 articles, 16 articles were selected to be studied.
- Only the manuscripts in English were included in the study.

2.4   Quality Assessment of Studies

When selecting the articles, it was put as a quality criterion that they were published in a well-known prestigious digital library and published after a particular examination. It was considered sufficient to be a primary research article evaluated and accepted by the referees and published in the last 10 years. No other criteria have been searched for.

2.5   Extraction and Synthesis of Data

The following data were extracted from studies that met the inclusion criteria, and the results were synthesized.

- Title
- Author
- Year of publication
- Publication database
- Data provenance and Internet of Things approaches discussed.
- Category of study
- Evaluation methods
- Implementation and simulation status
- Keywords used

3   Conducting the Review

3.1   Initial Search

Table 1 summarizes the search texts used in each digital library database. Inquiries were not made in the full text but on metadata fields such as article title, abstract and keywords (index terms).

Table 1. Search Strings

Search String ID	Search String
SS1	Internet of things and data provenance
SS2	Internet of things and provenance
SS3	IoT and data provenance
SS4	IoT and provenance

The database search took place on October 17th, 2021. The search was done for the last 10 years. The total number of papers from all databases was too much for a study. Then a preliminary screening of the search results was performed.

The keywords in the query texts return a large number of results. However, repetitive or irrelevant studies were eliminated from the query results. At the end of this phase, a total of 140 works remain. Figure-1 shows the search progress of the study.

4   Summary of Primary Studies

4.1   List of Primary Studies

Table 2. Selected papers

Paper name	Paper Id
Using Provenance and CoAP to track Requests/Responses in IoT	P1
Secure data provenance in Internet of Things based networks by outsourcing attribute based signatures and using Bloom filters	P2
Data provenance to audit compliance with privacy policy in the Internet of Things	P3
Secure data provenance in home energy monitoring networks	P4
Light-Weight Security and Data Provenance for Multi-Hop Internet of Things	P5
Towards a provenance collection framework for Internet of Things devices	P6
Enhancing privacy in wearable IoT through a provenance architecture	P7
Blockchain-based Data Provenance for the Internet of Things	P8
Secure and efficient distributed network provenance for IoT: A blockchain- based approach	P9
An index-based provenance compression scheme for identifying malicious nodes in multihop IoT network	P10
BlockTrack-L: A lightweight blockchain-based provenance message tracking in IoT	P11
Provenance-enabled packet path tracing in the RPL-based internet of things	P12
A lightweight protocol for secure data provenance in the internet of things using wireless fingerprints	P13
IoT big data provenance scheme using blockchain on hadoop ecosystem	P14
Secure data provenance in internet of things using hybrid attribute based crypt technique	P15
Provenance-based data flow control mechanism for internet of things	P16

The IoT vision, which benefits from the consistent advances in microelectronics, communications, and information technology, seems achievable. IoT-related applications and services are making more and more contributions to facilitating human life day by day. Therefore, this creates a diverse and large number of entities and services that require interaction with each other in various conditions and environments. The Internet of Things is expected to enable a world of intelligence and automation powered by seamless interactions between humans and their intelligent environments. The IoT offers many exciting solutions to problems encountered in various application areas. The potentially large number of things, their diversity, their constraints, and the heterogeneous nature of communications encountered in the IoT create many significant challenges in terms of management, security, privacy, and interoperability, amongst many others [4]. Data provenance can be used for diverse purposes, such as evaluating the quality and reliability of data, trustworthiness, reproducibility of experiments, audit processes, data versioning, establishing property data, and discovering new data. However, scientists need to save provenance metadata during the data lifecycle stages to obtain the benefits of data provenance [11]. Provenance is not limited to data only. It is a crucial concept that provides features such as integrity, authenticity, and repeatability when it comes to digital information. These features help in detecting errors, analyzing errors, preventing unwanted behaviors and failures, and understanding the process of converting inputs into outputs, thus understanding the system [5].

This section summarizes studies on the use of data provenance in IoT applications. The studies are given by grouping according to their main categories. Sometimes a study may be close to more than one category. In this case, the closest category is selected. What we mean by the category is not the subject to be solved, but the main subject that the study focuses on. For example, in a study conducted in the field of security using blockchain for data provenance, security is the area where the solution is tried to be found, while blockchain is the method used. In this case, work can sometimes be categorized as blockchain and sometimes as security. The main focus of the study was chosen as the category.

Blockchain: Sigwart et al. [15] proposed a generic blockchain-based data provenance framework for the Internet of Things which can be applied to various use cases. They evaluated the framework concerning the defined requirements using an implementation with Ethereum smart contracts. An example of using provenance data in vaccine procurement is discussed. This example aims to determine whether the values, such as the temperature of the vaccine, go out of the desired value and thus whether the vaccine is spoiled or not with the provenance data. In another usage scenario, an example of provenance is given in a system where patient values are monitored, and assistants or health personnel are warned in case of an emergency. They proposed a generic data provenance architecture.

Siddiqui et al. [16] have proposed a permissioned blockchain solution for maintaining secure data provenance, utilizing outsourced attribute-based encryption. They use partial signatures to reduce the overhead of authentication and blockchain mechanisms from the IoT node to the Edge node.

Porkodi et al. [23] proposed a framework for securing data provenance in IoT systems, privacy and access control policies, and cryptographic techniques in the blockchain. They used Hybrid Attribute-Based Encryption (HABE) as a blockchain cryptographic technique. The proposed hybrid attribute-based encryption assures data security.

Liu et al. [21] inspected security challenges for operating distributed network provenance for the Internet of Things. They utilized the blockchain as the essential architecture for storing and querying cross-domain provenance data. They also presented a unified model for efficiently instantiating provenance query modules in the verifiable computation framework.

Pacooh et al. [22] proposed a secure framework that is blockchain-enabled. The framework is for large-scale IoT data storage. They considered Edge computing to be merged to facilitate the management of the authentications of the small IoT devices and perform data storage. They also deployed a lightweight mutual authentication scheme that enables performing authorization and authentication of IoT devices. They presented the implementation of the proposed security scheme for IoT data to ensure data provenance, verifiability, integrity, and traceability.

Security: Liu et al. [18] proposed an index-based provenance compression algorithm. It adopts the idea of typical substring matching, combined with path identifier and path index to represent the path information in the data provenance, thereby reducing the size of data provenance. Similarly, they amplify the data provenance scheme to attack detection and propose a based malicious node identification.

Aman et al. [14] used an analytical model to develop a mechanism to establish data provenance in IoT systems. They also proposed a lightweight security protocol for data provenance. They use physical unclonable functions (PUFs) and fingerprints extracted from the wireless channel, mutual authentication, and anonymity to achieve data provenance.

Kaku et al. [6] presented studies on provenance in the IoT field, it is emphasized that most of the studies aim to provide authenticity, trust, and quality of data by following the source of the data. Furthermore, it is stated that provenance is still an important issue when IoT considers it. It is necessary to look for answers such as who, timestamps, periods of processes, and why, where, and when from the data provenance IoT framework. In the IoT CoAP area, they discussed the use of provenance for request/response calls from a machine perspective. In addition, they presented the results by performing response time and throughput values and performance values.

In the study conducted by Chia et al. [3], A method for home energy monitoring networks that provides cross-check validation to prevent fraud in energy consumption is presented. With this method, it is aimed to prevent the manipulation of smart meters and to ensure that the correct measurement is transmitted. The proposed solution tried to validate the data sent via an independent sensor placed with a smart plug. Thus, it has been tried to provide secure data provenance. Their work investigated provenance models to reduce data integrity attacks in IoT systems. To identify the origin of the data, they used PUFs and wireless link fingerprints. They ensure the integrity of an information's origin since PUFs are difficult to clone. No provenance model and framework were used in the study.

Nwafor et al. [8] emphasize the need for integrating provenance into the Internet of Things system. They propose a provenance collection framework that provides provenance collection capabilities for devices in an Internet of

Things system. They record IoT devices' I/O data transformations and generate provenance data. In the confidential procurement of origin data, they presented a framework for collecting provenances traced data can be converted into provenance logs. With a sensor track with different configurations, their built-in solution achieves data lineage for IoT devices. The integrity of lineage logs is neglected.

Kamal and Tariq [7] introduced a lightweight solution for security and data provenance in a multi-hop IoT environment. They created link fingerprints using the Received Signal Strength Indicator (RSSI) value of the IoT devices. They used the correlated coefficient based on matching the link fingerprints to identify the path to the source node. To ensure security without an authorization mechanism, they relied on the physical parameters of RSSI. In this case, RSSI values can be easily manipulated. The system is vulnerable to external attacks.

In the study of Siddiqui et al. [10], It is stated that the use of data provenance is necessary for IoT devices. However, it is emphasized that these data can be manipulated from outside, and therefore it is crucial to use secure data provenance mechanisms. Since IoT devices have resource constraints, they focus on the appropriate solution. A secure data provenance mechanism based on attribute-based encryption has been proposed. In this mechanism, ciphertext policy attribute-based encryption (CP-ABE) is used instead of public-key encryption. A bloom filter stores provenance information to reduce storage costs due to resource constraints on IoT devices. In order to reduce the computation load of IoT devices, operations that require more computation were performed on edge nodes. The system was tested in a simulation environment, and the results were evaluated.

Data Flow: Rong-na et al. [19] proposed a provenance-based data flow control mechanism that uses provenance data to implement direct and indirect data flow control. Thus, they aimed to reduce the risk of indirect leakage. Provenance data is becoming more and more prominent as there is data flow between different devices; therefore, indirect control on the provenance data takes an increasing amount of time, critically affecting control performance. They simplified provenance data according to the type of operation generating the data and the association degree of data, and their provenance data; thus, they wanted to increase the control efficiency of the data flow. In order to reduce the storage space and improve the efficiency of querying the provenance data, they also proposed a provenance tree that records the relationship between data and their provenance data. They demonstrated the implementation and optimization method of provenance-based data flow control.

Data Trustworthiness: To ensure data trustworthiness during packet traversal, Suhail et al. [20] proposed a Provenance-enabled Packet Path Tracing scheme for RPL-connected IoT devices. They introduced a node-level provenance by embedding sequence numbers against the routing entry at the routing table of the respective forwarding node. They also added a system-level provenance.

This provenance type included destination and source node IDs and was used for capturing the complete packet trace. They aimed to verify the provenance with node-level and system-level sources.

Privacy: Lomotey et al. [17] proposed a broadcast-subscriber IoT model where users' data only is shared with healthcare facilities or user-authorized devices and nodes. For this purpose, they proposed two main approaches. In the first approach, uniquely identifiable components in communication devices encrypted with meta-data level encryption techniques and keys are known only to devices in the subscription pool. This hardware and software level encryption technique means that privacy breaches are minimal, as demonstrated in various experiments. It is tested with various encryption-decryption algorithms, including AES, DES, 3DES, MD5, and SHA. The second approach proposes the provenance technique in broadcast subscriber IoT architecture. In this way, transparency and a full digital audit trail are targeted. Provenance information from the data source to its current state facilitates the audit of the IoT data. The interconnectedness of Wearable IoT Devices is also investigated to determine who receives what data in the IoT architecture. The proposed system was tested with several evaluations, and its contributions were presented.

Pasquier et al. [9] examine provenance to provide privacy policy and control mechanisms in the IoT area. They explain the idea of the study as follows: Provenance can be analyzed to determine whether the implementation mechanisms and the objectives of the regulations are met. Expected behaviors and

Table 3. Category of Papers

Paper Id	Category	Implementation	Simulation
P1	Network	✓	✓
P2	Security	✓	✓
P3	Privacy Policy	✗	✗
P4	Security, Privacy	✓	✓
P5	Security	✓	✓
P6	Data collection	✓	✗
P7	Privacy	✓	✓
P8	Blockchain	✓	✗
P9	Trust, Blockchain	✓	✓
P10	Security	✓	✓
P11	Blockchain, Security	✓	✓
P12	Data trustworthiness, Routing	✓	✓
P13	Authentication	✓	✓
P14	Big data, Blockchain	✓	✓
P15	Security, Blockchain	✓	✓
P16	Data flow	✓	✓

actual behaviors can be reported to improve the implementation mechanism. The difficulties encountered in obtaining provenance data were also discussed.

5   Results and Discussion

In this section, the study results are presented and discussed regarding the aim. Answers to the research questions determined for the study were presented.

RQ1: How much research activity has there been in IoT and Data provenance since 2012? How often and in which journals are articles published? The frequency of publication will show a trend analysis on the usage of provenance in the Internet of Things issues.

When the frequency of studies and the databases from which the studies are located are analyzed, it can be seen that data provenance and IoT issues have been studied more in recent years.

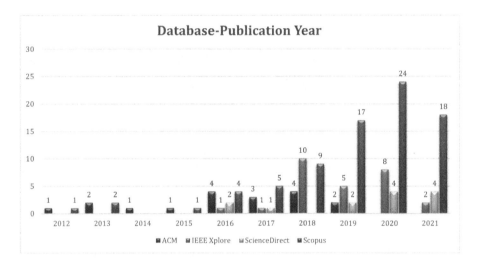

Fig. 2. Publication years of the papers

Figure-2 shows a graph of working years and journals. In 2012, there were 1 IEEE Xplore and 1 ACM work in total 2, 3 in 2013, 2 in 2015,11 in 2016, 10 in 2017, 23 in 2018, 26 in 2019, 36 in 2020 and 24 in 2021 140 articles in total. When evaluating these data, it should be considered that 2021 has not yet been completed. Therefore, there may be articles in progress and are in the process of publication. These data show an increasing trend, especially in the number of studies in recent years. There is a steady increase here until 2021. It should not be overlooked that the rates here are the rates of the papers we work with. Considering the studies that we did not include, different rates may occur. However, in general, it is possible to observe that data provenance studies in the field of IoT have increased recently.

A total of 140 articles were found from the 4 researched databases. 27 of 140 articles were found in IEEE Xplore, 13 in ScienceDirect, 82 in Scopus, and 18 in ACM. Some of these articles (14) were found in more than one database. Detailed information was described in the Search Strategy section.

As a result, there is an increasing trend in the field of data provenance in IoT with the increasing popularity of these fields.

RQ2: What research topics are being addressed? What are the main categories to which the issues are related? What are the main subjects, and what keywords do they use? The keywords used will show their relationship with other topics.

Table-3 shows the category of selected 16 articles and the work done. The article states whether there is Implementation and whether the results are evaluated by simulation.

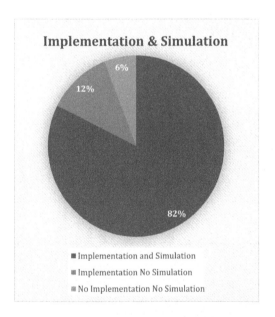

Fig. 3. Implementation/Simulation

Figure-3 shows the implementation and simulation status of selected papers. Studies have been conducted in security, privacy, network, request/response, verification, data trustworthiness, privacy policy, blockchain, trust, data collection, and authentication. These are related studies. Data provenance and IoT are the main fields of study. IoT and data provenance issues such as security, privacy, reliability, confidentiality, and trust have been frequently addressed.

The keywords used will show their relationship with other topics. The keywords used in conjunction with data provenance and IoT can give information about the areas in which these studies are carried out. Figure-4 shows the distribution of most keywords used in the articles studied. From the perspective of keywords, we can see that Internet of Things (IoT) and Data Provenance (Provenance) keywords are mostly used. This is natural because these keywords are our search criteria. By looking at other commonly used keywords, we can understand the topics covered in this field. Blockchain, Security and Cloud Computing are used frequently. We can say that the studies in these areas are more intense. The Other keywords used are:Smart Contract, Authentication, Link Quality Indicator, Wireless Channel Characteristics, Physical Unclonable Functions, Attack Detection, Compression, Cloud-based IoT, Privacy, Bloom Filter, Sensors, Lightweight Authentication, Light-weight Signature Generation, Mobile Devices, Middleware, Wearables, Hyperledger Fabric, Attribute Based Encryption, Hadoop, Big Data, Traceability, Link-fingerprints, Light-weight, Multihop, Data Trustworthiness, Access Control, LLN, URI, REST, RPL, Cryptography, Sensor Networks, 6LowPAN, Home Area Networks, Location Authenticity, Smart Grid, IPv6, Distributed Network Provenance, Trust, Ciphertext Policy Attribute Based Encryption, Hybrid attribute based crypt technique, History, Lossless provenance, Data Models, Temperature sensors, Computational Modeling, Meta Data, COAP

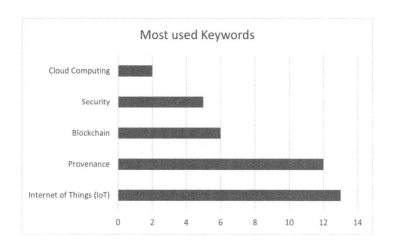

Fig. 4. Keywords most used

RQ3: What are the main problems being tried to find a solution for the Internet of Things using data provenance?

Data provenance is primarily used to solve security, privacy, reliability, and trust-related problems. We can say that the studies in these fields have increased gradually towards the last years. Blockchain is frequently used to provide data provenance.

RQ4: What are the open issues and the future research directions of data provenance and the Internet of Things?

In the IoT and data provenance studies, security and privacy are often the natural subjects of the study, even if it is not the main topic of the study. IoT devices have some security difficulties due to resource constraints. Therefore, it may be necessary to take additional precautions to ensure security in IoT devices. Privacy is an essential issue in IoT applications because it often senses information in these environments. Data provenance can provide security, reliability, and trust in IoT devices from a data provenance perspective. However, data provenance can provide these plus features while at the same time creating a disadvantageous situation because data provenance provides features such as security, reliability, trust, not only the current state of the data but also the origin, the stages, and processes it undergoes, the information such as when and by whom these processes are performed. Therefore, this information may also create privacy issues. Security mechanisms such as encryption and authentication are required to restore privacy. The issues of security, reliability, trust, and privacy in IoT devices and data provenance are open issues that will continue to be worked on in the future.

6   Conclusions and Future Work

This review presented an SLR-based method on data provenance in IoT. We investigated the challenges encountered in IoT applications and worked on the use of data provenance as a solution. We conducted a literature search covering the years 2012–2022. We found 140 published papers between these years. After applying exclusion criteria for these papers, we have focused on the final 16 papers. In the IoT area, some challenges require work such as constrained resources, heterogeneity, scalability, identity, mobility, searching and discovering, security and privacy. In our studies, we have seen that data provenance is mainly used in security, privacy, transparency, reliability, confidentiality, and verification. We can say that the studies in these fields have increased gradually towards the last years. Security, reliability, trust, and privacy are currently being studied and needed in the future. Regarding the SLR-based method, we may not have analyzed all available studies. Non-English, non-peers were reviewed, and editorial articles, book chapters, and survey articles were excluded. In this review, we conducted a comprehensive survey of approaches to using data provenance in IoT through the findings of more than 100 authors and different studies. However, given the increasing number of studies in this area, it is impossible to ensure that all studies are considered. Our research ended in March 2022.

Acknowledgement. The authors would like to express to thank to Ziraat Teknoloji for their support. This study was produced from the first author's doctoral thesis, prepared under the supervision of the second author.

References

1. Aktas, M.S., Astekin, M.: Provenance aware run-time verification of things for self-healing Internet of Things applications. Concurrency Computat. Pract. Exper. **31**, e4263 (2019). https://doi.org/10.1002/cpe.4263

2. Dundar, B., Astekin, M., Aktas, M.S.: A big data processing framework for self-healing internet of things applications. In: 2016 12th International Conference on Semantics, Knowledge and Grids (SKG), pp. 62–68 (2016). https://doi.org/10.1109/SKG.2016.017

3. Ming H.C., Sye L.K., Tang, Z.: Secure Data Provenance in Home Energy Monitoring Networks. In: Proceedings of the 3rd Annual Industrial Control System Security Workshop (ICSS 2017), pp. 7–14. ACM, New York (2017). https://doi.org/10.1145/3174776.3174778

4. Elkhodr, M., Alsinglawi, B., Alshehri, M.: Data provenance in the internet of things. In: 2018 32nd International Conference on Advanced Information Networking and Applications Workshops (WAINA), Krakow, pp. 727–731 (2018). https://doi.org/10.1109/WAINA.2018.00175

5. Kaku, E., Orji, R., Pry, J., Sofranko, K., Lomotey, R., Deters, R.: Privacy Improvement Architecture for IoT. In: 2018 IEEE International Congress on Internet of Things (ICIOT), San Francisco, CA, pp. 148–155 (2018). https://doi.org/10.1109/ICIOT.2018.00028

6. Kaku, E., Lomotey, R.K., Deters, R.: Using Provenance and CoAP to track Requests/Responses in IoT. Proc. Comput. Sci. **94**, 144–151 (2016). https://doi.org/10.1016/j.procs.2016.08.023, ISSN 1877–0509

7. Kamal, M., Tariq, S .: Light-Weight Security and Data Provenance for Multi-Hop Internet of Things. IEEE Access **6**, 34439–34448 (2018). https://doi.org/10.1109/ACCESS.2018.2850821

8. Nwafor, E., Campbell, A., Hill, D., Bloom, G.: Towards a provenance collection framework for Internet of Things devices. In: 2017 IEEE SmartWorld, Ubiquitous Intelligence & Computing, Advanced & Trusted Computed, Scalable Computing & Communications, Cloud & Big Data Computing, Internet of People and Smart City Innovation (SmartWorld/SCALCOM/UIC/ATC/CBDCom/IOP/SCI), San Francisco, CA, pp. 1–6 (2017). https://doi.org/10.1109/UIC-ATC.2017.8397531

9. Pasquier, T., Singh, J., Powles, J., Eyers, D., Seltzer, M., Bacon, J.: Data provenance to audit compliance with privacy policy in the Internet of Things. Pers. Ubiquit. Comput. **22**(2), 333–344 (2017). https://doi.org/10.1007/s00779-017-1067-4

10. Siddiqui, M.S., Rahman, A., Nadeem, A., Alzahrani, A.M.: Secure data provenance in internet of things based networks by outsourcing attribute based signatures and using bloom filters. Int. J. Adv. Comput. Sci. Appli. (IJACSA) **10**(5), 221–226 (2019). http://dx.doi.org/10.14569/IJACSA.2019.0100529

11. de Silva, D.L. Batista, A., Corrêa, P.L.P.: Data Provenance in Environmental Monitoring. In: 2016 IEEE 13th International Conference on Mobile Ad Hoc and Sensor Systems (MASS), Brasilia, pp. 337–342 (2016). https://doi.org/10.1109/MASS.2016.050

12. Jensen, S., Plale, B., Aktas, M.S., Luo, Y., Chen, P., Conover, H.: Provenance capture and use in a satellite data processing pipeline. IEEE Trans. Geosci. Remote Sens. **51**(11), 5090–5097 (2013). https://doi.org/10.1109/TGRS.2013.2266929

13. Nitschke, P., Williams, S.P.: Conceptualizing the internet of things data supply. Proc. Comput. Sci. **181**, 642–649 (2021). https://doi.org/10.1016/j.procs.2021.01.213, ISSN 1877–0509

14. Aman, M.N., Basheer, M.H., Sikdar, B.: A lightweight protocol for secure data provenance in the internet of things using wireless fingerprints. IEEE Syst. J. **15**(2), 2948–2958 (2021). https://doi.org/10.1109/JSYST.2020.3000269

15. Sigwart, M., Borkowski, M., Peise, M., Schulte, S., Tai, S.: Blockchain-based Data Provenance for the Internet of Things. In: 9th International Conference on the

Internet of Things (IoT 2019), Bilbao, Spain, October 22–25, 8 pages. ACM, New York (2019). htttps://doi.org/10.1145/3365871.3365886

16. Siddiqui, M.S., Syed, T.A., Nadeem, A., Nawaz, W., Albouq, S.S.: BlockTrack-L: a lightweight blockchain-based provenance message tracking in IoT. Int. J. Adv. Comput. Sci. Appli. (IJACSA) **11**(4) (2020). https://doi.org/10.14569/IJACSA. 2020.0110462

17. Lomotey, R.K., Sofranko, K., Orji, R.: Enhancing privacy in wearable iot through a provenance architecture. Multimodal Technol. Interact. **2**, 18 (2018). https://doi.org/10.3390/mti2020018

18. Liu, Z., Wu, Y.: An index-based provenance compression scheme for identifying malicious nodes in multihop IoT network. IEEE Internet Things J. **7**(5), 4061–4071 (2020). https://doi.org/10.1109/JIOT.2019.2961431

19. Rong-na, X., Hui, L., Guo-zhen, S., Yun-chuan, G., Ben, N., Mang, S.: Provenance-based data flow control mechanism for Internet of things. Trans. Emerging Tel. Tech. **32**, e3934 (2021). https://doi.org/10.1002/ett.3934

20. Suhail, S., Hussain, R., Abdellatif, M., Pandey, S.R., Khan, A., Hong, C.S.: Provenance-enabled packet path tracing in the RPL-based internet of things. Comput. Netw. **173**, 107189 (2020). https://doi.org/10.1016/j.comnet.2020.107189, ISSN 1389-1286

21. Liu, D., Ni, J., Huang, C., Lin, X., Shen, X.S.: Secure and efficient distributed network provenance for IoT: a blockchain-based approach. IEEE Internet Things J. **7**(8), 7564–7574 (2020). https://doi.org/10.1109/JIOT.2020.2988481

22. Honar Pajooh, H., Rashid, M.A., Alam, F., Demidenko, S.: IoT Big Data provenance scheme using blockchain on Hadoop ecosystem. J. f Big Data **8**(1), 1–26 (2021). https://doi.org/10.1186/s40537-021-00505-y

23. Porkodi, S., Kesavaraja, D.: Secure data provenance in Internet of Things using hybrid attribute based crypt technique. Wireless Pers. Commun. **118**(4), 2821–2842 (2021). https://doi.org/10.1007/s11277-021-08157-0

24. Baogang, B., Shah, N., Yuhe, B., Amir, A.: Security and provenance for Internet of Health Things: a systematic literature review. J. Soft. Evolution Process **33**, e2335 (2021). https://doi.org/10.1002/smr.2335

13th International Symposium on Software Quality (ISSQ 2022)

A Feature Selection-Based K-NN Model for Fast Software Defect Prediction

Joseph Bamidele Awotunde[1][(✉)] , Sanjay Misra[2] ,
Abidemi Emmanuel Adeniyi[2] , Moses Kazeem Abiodun[1,3] , Manju Kaushik[4],
and Morolake Oladayo Lawrence[5]

[1] Department of Computer Science, University of Ilorin, Ilorin, Nigeria
`awotunde.jb@unilorin.edu.ng`
[2] Department of Computer Science and Communication, Ostfold University College,
Halden, Norway
`Sanjay.misra@hiof.no, adeniyi.emmanuel@lmu.edu.ng`
[3] Department of Computer Science, Landmark University, Omu-Aran, Nigeria
`moses.abiodun@lmu.edu.ng`
[4] Amity Institute of Information Technology, Amity University, Jaipur, Rajasthan, India
`mkaushik@jpr.amiy.edu`
[5] Department of Computer Science, Baze University, Abuja, Nigeria
`morolake.lawrence@bazeuniversity.edu.ng`

Abstract. Software Defect Prediction (SDP) is an advanced technological method of predicting software defects in the software development life cycle. Various research works have been previously being done on SDP but the performance of these methods varied from several datasets, hence, making them inconsistent for SDP in the unknown software project. But the hybrid technique using feature selection enabled with machine learning for SDP can be very efficient as it takes the advantage of various methods to come up with better prediction accuracy for a given dataset when compared with an individual classifier. The major issues with individual ML-based models for SDP are the long detection time, vulnerability of the software project, and high dimensionality of the feature parameters. Therefore, this study proposes a hybrid model using a feature selection enabled Extreme Gradient Boost (XGB) classifier to address these mentioned challenges. The cleaned NASA MDP datasets were used for the implementation of the proposed model, and various performance metrics like F-score, accuracy, and MCC were used to reveal the performance of the model. The results of the proposed model when compared with state-of-the-art methods without feature selection perform better in terms of the metrics used. The results reveal that the proposed model outperformed all other prediction techniques.

Keywords: Software defect prediction · Machine learning · Extreme gradient boost · Feature selection · Prediction · Software development life cycle

A. E. Adeniyi and M. K. Abiodun—Landmark University SDG 4 (Quality Education)

M. K. Abiodun—Landmark University SDG 16 (Peace and Justice, Strong Institution)

A. E. Adeniyi—Landmark University SDG 11 (Sustainable Cities and Communities)

O. Gervasi et al. (Eds.): ICCSA 2022 Workshops, LNCS 13380, pp. 49–61, 2022.
https://doi.org/10.1007/978-3-031-10542-5_4

1 Introduction

In recent time, the software has been the heart of the technological era where factually all organizations are in needs of one software or others [1]. But if there are frequent software defects the main aim of creating them is defeated, and reduce its credibility and reliability [2]. ally Software is the heart of this technological era. If there are frequent defects in software, it reduces reliability and credibility [3, 4]. This resulted into software dissatisfied the customers and thereby worsening the software company's images [4, 5]. If flaws are discovered beginning of the software development process, resources can be allocated to only the software components that are required. Hence, software defect prediction (SDP) is one of the key features with the continual increases in software industry for manufacturing quality software. The discovery of defects in software in time will help the industries in saving effort, money and resources.

Machine learning (ML) models have been gaining greater attention in recent time in the prediction of software defection [6]. This was done in other to give timely delivery of software products with optimal deployment of the available resources [7]. But the problems of imbalanced and high dimensionality of software datasets have hindered the performance of the ML-based models [8]. Accuracy has been identified as a good evaluation metric for comparison when consider the binary problems [9], but in a situation where the number of instances of one class is huge that another, the accuracy of such model will not be efficient. For instance, if there are 10 defects out of 100 instances and 90 instances are free of defect, the result of the validation results will be affected when ML-based model is trained on such imbalanced data. The results will of sequence be biased towards the mainstream class. The problem of imbalance is common among real-world problems [10, 11].

The feature selection can be used to handle large dataset with huge amount of features that the classifiers need to select from before the prediction or classification of such dataset [12]. This is used to identify the most relevant parameters that can greatly contributed to high efficient software defect prediction using various ML-based models. The redundant within datasets can remove using feature selection techniques, the classifiers will remove non-independent features from the dataset [13]. The feature selection method will enhance the efficient handling of irrelevant and redundant parameters in the datasets used for software defect prediction [14]. Feature selection is very important in software defect prediction. The application of this classifier has a great influence on the prediction accuracy, thus become necessary to use proper feature selection classifier for dimensionality reduction.

Therefore, this paper proposes a hybrid feature selection enabled Extreme Gradient Boost model for software defect prediction. The feature selection was used to reduce the dimensionality of the dataset before applying XGBoost classifier on the software defect dataset. The case of imbalance and feature redundancy dataset was handle using data normalization mothed. The XGBoost ensemble algorithm was used because of stronger robustness to irrelevant and redundant features. The major contributions of the study are:

(i) the application of feature selection to reduce the high dimensionality of the software defect dataset.

(ii)   resampling method was applied to handle the imbalanced instances within the dataset.

(iii) the prediction of the software defection dataset was perform using XGBoost algorithm to successfully classifier irrelevant and redundant data after the application of feature selection and data normalization methods.

2   Related Work

ML-based models have been applied by various researchers to solve twofold (binary) classification in various fields like in rainfall prediction [15, 16], sentiment analysis [17–19], network intrusion detection [11, 20–22], and software defect prediction [1, 2, 4, 23–25]. Some of the SDP related works are discussed in this study.

The authors in [26] reviewed the analysis of ML-based models on SDP using twelve cleaned NASA datasets for the performance of their classifiers. The algorithms employed are Support Vector Machine (SVN), K-Nearest Neighbor (K-NN), Naïve Bayes (NB), Radial Basis Function (RBF), Decision Tree (DT), Multi-Layer Perceptron (MLP), and Random Forest (RF). The performance metrics used on the analyzed models are recall, accuracy, ROC, MCC, and F1-score. The results of the experiment shown that RF performed better when compared with other classifiers followed by the SVM model. In another similar work, the authors in [27] used ensemble classification model after using feature selection to reduce the irrelevant features from the dataset used for testing the model. The proposed model was implemented in a binary dimension, using feature selection with the classifier and secondly applied the model without feature selection method. The NASA datasets was used with various performance metrics to evaluated the performance of the proposed models. The results of the model are compared with other state-of-the-art used prediction methods. The results shown great improvement on some datasets but the model was unable to perform well in class imbalanced dataset because the issue was not well resolved by the proposed model.

The authors in [28], proposed six classifiers for SDP techniques using Principal Component Analysis (PCA) for feature reduction, the algorithms used are Holographic Networks, Layered Neural network, LR, and Discriminant Analysis. The performance metrics are Misclassification Rate, Verification Cost, Predictive Validity, and Achieved Quality. The results of the proposed models revealed 100% accuracy especially the one with the application of PCA for dimensionality reduction without error. In [4], the authors provided experimental appraisal of SDP models using several boosting enabled ensemble techniques on three open source JAVA projects. Stable performance metrics like AUC, Balance, and G-Mean are used to evaluated the models. The resampling methods with four ensemble classifiers were used within the JAVA projects. The resampling methods enabled classifiers performed better when compared with classifiers without resampling techniques. This shown that the resampling has great impact on the ensemble classifiers, and has significantly improved the SDP models when compared with classic boosting classifiers. Among the resampling techniques used, RUSBoost performed greatly followed by MSMOTEBoost, and the poorest among them is the SMOTEBoost.

In another study by [1], presented a model using several ensemble learning for prediction of faults within software modules. The proposed system combined both linear and non-linear combination rule for the ensemble models. Several software fault datasets that are publicly available was used for the design and conduct of the experiments. The proposed system was able to predict software faults with high accuracy, and the results was reliable throughout the datasets used for performance evaluation. The prediction at level l (Pred(l)) was further used on the ensemble classifiers to measures the completeness of the results. The result shows that average relative error of the number of modules in a dataset is less than or equal to a threshold value of l. this analysis and evaluation using the metric confirmed the effectiveness of the proposed system for the prediction of software faults. The ensemble techniques performance improved when compared with single fault prediction method for software faults prediction. The main contribution of the model is the quick identification of the faults in the software products with the utilization of testing resources.

In [23], the authors presented a model for SDP contains four stages: (i) feature selection, (ii) Pre-processing (iii) classification, and (iv) Reflection of results. The feature selection model was use to remove irrelevant features from the dataset before applying ensemble learning classifiers. The cleaned NASA MDP datasets was used for the implementation of the proposed model by the authors. Various performance metrics like accuracy, F1-score, MCC, and ROC for the evaluation of the model. The model was tested on each of the dataset to compare them to know the highest scores among the six datasets. Ten well-known supervised classifiers models were used to compared with the proposed model, the search methods and the results of the proposed system revealed that the model outperformed all the other classifiers methods. In a study by [29], the authors proposed SVM for the prediction of software faults using NASA datasets for the implementation of the model. The proposed framework was compared with other models like LR, K-NN, RF, NB, RBF, and MLP. The results show that the proposed method outperformed some of the classification methods used to test the performance.

The authors in [30] shown the importance of feature selection for SDP systems by show that some parameters or features are more relevant than others. The ANN enabled with feature selection for the implementation of the framework. The selected features are used to predict the SDP using ANN classifiers. The Gaussian Kernel SVM and JM1 NASA dataset was used to tested the performance of the proposed method for experiment. From the results by the proposed model, SVM outperformed the model in the twofold defect classification. In [31], the authors used hybrid Genetic Algorithm (GA) with Deep Neural Network (DNN) SDP using several datasets from PROMISE repository. The Hybrid GA is used for feature selection in other to select the optimal features for the model, and DNN was used to performed the prediction of the system. The results of the proposed model outperformed other techniques used to test the performance of the model.

From the existing research, it was discovered that the imbalanced nature of software data can hinder the performance of models leading to incorrect interpretations of results, and high dimensionality of features in any dataset will reduce the performance of any ensemble algorithms. Therefore, this study proposed a hybrid model can consist of feature selection, data normalization, and XGBoost for the classification of software products to predict whether a software has defects or not.

3 Materials and Methods

3.1 Proposed Hybrid Software Defect Prediction Model

The proposed system aims at enhancing the performance of SDP for software development faults prediction using feature selection and XGBoost techniques on the NASA datasets. In recent years' various techniques like ML-based models and data mining techniques have been used to resolve various problems involved software defects prediction system performance. To improve the performance of SDP for software products, the proposed model reduced the number of features using for the prediction of software defects in software development. Figure 1 presents the framework for the proposed model. The model consists of the followings processes: (i) pre-processing, (ii) imbalance using resampling method, (iii) feature selection, and (iv) prediction. The stages are discussing in details in the following subsection.

3.2 The Pre-processing Stage

To provide an appropriate data for the SDP proposed framework, various pre-processing steps were performing on the NASA dataset. The following are the steps follows to reform the dataset used for the purpose of this study:

(i)   Removing duplicated instances: software modules with same class labels and software metric values is referred to has duplicated instances for instance defective labels. In a real-world problem, this situation is very thinkable. Regrettably, the machine learners are going to be affect negatively if there is duplicated instances, thus cause overoptimistic if they are categorized fittingly as a part of test data. This will result to over-pessimistic presentations if they are misclassified as a part of test data. Furthermore, this can create time-consuming during training process, and reduce the improvement in the performance of the models and classifiers. Hence, it become very necessary to remove duplicated instances in the datasets;

(ii) Replacement of Misplaced labels: There many instance values with multiple software metrics generally. Due to some reasons, there can be more than one values of an instance that can be missing especially when data were collected carelessly. It became very often that the instance cannot satisfy input requirement of the proposed model since this missing values has to be processed. For any missing value in this study, we replace it with then average of the equivalent metric. For instance, suppose both mt_{99} and mt_{100} are missed i.e. NaN, a metric mt and it clarifications $\{mt_1, \ldots\ldots, mt_{100}\}$. the two missing values can be replaced using Eq. (1):

$$mt_{99} = mt_{100} = \frac{1}{98}\sum\nolimits_{i=1}^{98} mt, \qquad (1)$$

(iii) Data Standardization: the values of various software metrics are of several order of magnitude, thus we need to perform data normalization on these metrics. The min-max-normalization the most commonly used method was used in this study to transform in the interval [0, 1] of all the values, and normalize the data [32, 33].

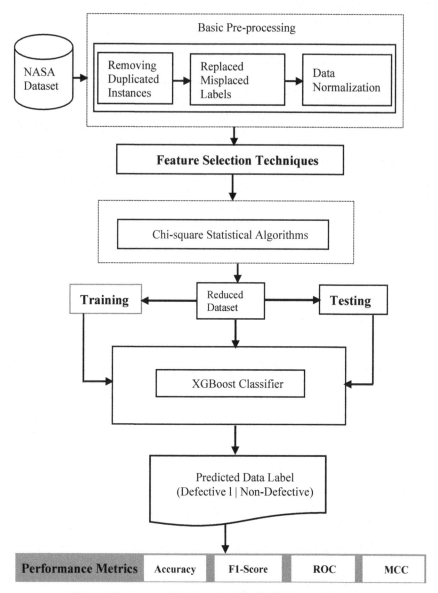

Fig. 1. The proposed Software Defects Prediction Architecture

the minimum and maximum values of a given metric x are $max(x)$ *and* $min(x)$, one-to-one. The value $\widetilde{x}_i$ for each value of x_i of metric x, can be computed as

$$\widetilde{x}_i = \frac{x_i - min(x)}{max(x) - min(x)}, \tag{2}$$

3.3 The Chi-Square Statistical Model for Feature Selection

The Chi-square statistical model was use for feature selection in this study. There are always two variables in feature selection that normally refer to incidence frequency of feature t and the category C is the likelihood of incidence respectively. In software defects prediction, in the proposed model it is consider whether features t and C are autonomous. It means if features t and C are independent, then feature t cannot be used to decide whether a label fit in to category C. In training, to find out the extent of t and C whether they are correlated is very difficult especially when not independent. Hence, Chi-square test can be used to define their significance. The relationship between feature t and category C is measures using the Chi-square statistical techniques. The label feature t and a category C was represented using bidirectional queue.

If feature t and the category C assume, and accords with the chi-square distribution with first-order degree of freedom. The more category label the feature carries is the higher chi-square score for the category c, then there is great relevance between t *and* C_j. Then the chi-square score of feature t for category C can be define as follows:

$$X^2 = (t, c)\frac{N(AD - BC)^2}{(A + C)(A + B)(B + BD)(C + D)} \tag{3}$$

The result in Eq. 3 shown the relevance between feature t and category C_j. The relevant of feature t will be the lager the class category C_j are autonomous, when $CHI(t, C_i)$, then the feature t and label class C_j is independent. Equation 3 can be used to calculated the value for a single class denoted by $X^2(t, c)$, but by combining all the value of $X^2(t, c)$ for feature label t for all classes, then we first calculate the $X^2(t, c)$ for all the feature of instance t for all classes. Then testing feature t for all the distinct $X^2(t, c)$ score, the number of the classes is then be m:

$$XAVG^2(t) = \sum_{i-1}^{m} p(c)X^2(t, c) \tag{4}$$

The average of $X^2(t, c)$ score of the feature label t for all classes is been calculated by Eq. 4.

$$\aleph MAX^2(t) = \max_{1 \leq i \leq m} \left\{ X^2(t, c) \right\} \tag{5}$$

Equation (5) is used to calculates the maximum $X^2(t, c)$ of feature label t for all classes. The feature label is finally sorted by the X scores, and a suitable quantity of feature label are designated permitting to the given threshold value.

3.4   The Extreme Gradient Boost

This is a family of GB ensemble that uses second-order products of the forfeiture function to find the finest base classifier more perfectly and proficiently. The XGB utilizes the second-order gradients, but the GB uses gradients to fit a new base classifier. Gradient Boosting algorithm is a supervised machine learning technique which tries to predict the output by combining the predictions of multiple weaker or low performing models. This ML-based method uses ensemble of DT with GB framework [34]. The error generated from the previous models is been used by the ML-based methods using boosting to minimized the errors and influence the performance of the model for enhancement. The GB minimize the errors of the ensemble efficiently when compare with Boosting. The Gradient Descent model is used by the GB to reduce errors in successive algorithms. The XGBoost is used for additional improvement to the tree-based models uses the benefits of GB model remove overfitting and offer ability to escape bias circumstances. tree-based algorithms are added by the use of XGBoost which uses the benefits of Gradient Boosting algorithm to provide facility to avoid bias or overfitting conditions, tree thinning and matching learning.

3.5   The NASA Datasets

Four widely used datasets from NASA MDP repository was used in this study, the datasets were used because selection an appropriate dataset is the most important aspect of classification and prediction of SDP for the proposed model. The NASA MDP datasets used were: PC4, PC5, JM1, and KC1 and this was presented in Table 1. Each dataset is in the form of an attribute set called module with various records where each record represents a module. Each attribute is generated during the dataset capturing and development called the software metrics (Table 2).

Table 1. D" NASA cleaned datasets

Dataset	Features	Elements	Defects	Non-Defects	Defects (%)
PC4	37	1270	176	1094	13.8
PC5	39	1694	458	1236	27.0
JM1	22	7720	1612	6108	20.8
KC1	22	1162	294	868	25.3

Table 2. Confusion matrix.

		Predicted	
		Class a	Class b
Real	Class a	TP	FN
	Class b	FP	TN

3.6 Performance Evaluation Metrics

Accuracy is the percentage of correctly classified instances as presented by Eq. (6)

$$Accuracy = \frac{tp + tn}{tp + tn + fp + fn} \tag{6}$$

The F1-Score is the harmonic mean between the recall and precision as illustrated by Eq. (7)

$$F1_{Score} = \frac{2 \times Precision \times Recall}{Precision + Recall} \tag{7}$$

The ratio of predicted and the observed classifications is used to computed the MCC as shown by Eq. (8)

$$MCC = \frac{TN * TP - FN * FP}{\sqrt{(FP + TP)(FN + TP)(TN + FP)(TN + FN)}} \tag{8}$$

4 Results and Discussion

The experiment of the study was done using Core™ i5-4200U CPU @ 1.60 GHz 2.30 Intel® GHz 8.0 GB RAM laptop running on Windows 10.1 (64bit). And WEKA programing. The proposed system used the benchmark datasets with experiment setup respectively. the experiment was perform using various performance metrics for the proposed system evaluation.

The proposed model used four NASA software that is publicly available software defects datasets. As say earlier from this study, the study uses feature selection to remove irrelevant features to enable the model to performance efficiently. This was done due to the missing values, duplicate instances, and conflicting features that the NASA datasets suffer from. Table 3 shows the original features and the selected features using Chi-square statistical model on the four NASA datasets.

Table 3. The number of features before and after features selection algorithm

	Dataset	PC4	PC5	JM1	KC1
No of Features	Before	37	39	21	21
	After	17	19	8	10
	Retention ratio (%)	45.95	48.72	38.10	47.62

Table 4 displayed the performance evaluation of the XGBoost model in terms of accuracy, F1-score, and MCC scores over the 4 software defects datasets. This show the results when the feature selection algorithm was not used on the datasets. The XGBoost model noticeable performance with PC4 dataset, and follow by the PC5 and the KC1 was the worst of all the dataset.

Table 4. The performance of the XGBoost model without feature selection

Dataset	Accuracy	F1-score	MCC
PC4	95.324	0.597	0.517
PC5	93.021	0.473	0.421
JM1	89.457	0.376	0.345
KC1	87.872	0.321	0.296

Table 5 displayed the performance evaluation of the proposed model in terms of accuracy, F1-score, and MCC scores over the 4 software defects datasets. This show the results XGBoost when the feature selection algorithm was not used on the datasets. The model noticeable performance with PC4 dataset, and follow by the PC5 and the KC1 was the worst of all the dataset. The feature selection really improved the prediction model on the datasets with an average of 4.197%.

Table 5. The performance of the XGBoost model with feature selection

Dataset	Accuracy	F1-score	MCC
PC4	99.521	0.743	0.765
PC5	96.386	0.532	0.553
JM1	91.035	0.412	0.394
KC1	88.278	0.395	0.353

5   Conclusion

The study proposed a model for the prediction of software defects prone to software modules. Early detection of defect in software modules can really reduce the cost of software development life cycle process. The proposed system used Chi-square statistical algorithm for feature selection in order to eliminate features that are irrelevant in the classification process of the model. Data normalization was used to reduce the high dimensionality of the datasets used to the performance of the proposed model. XGBoost was use for the prediction of the software metrics module on the four NASA datasets. Consider the performance of the model on the four datasets, the XGBoost with feature selection performed better on the PC4 dataset, and the worst of all the dataset is KC1. The results of the proposed framework show that the feature selection enabled model greatly increase the performance of the prediction model when compare with the model without the feature selection. Nevertheless, future research still need to optimize various classifiers with extensive set of features for more variants to be selected for ML-based models. And the applications of Deep learning models with feature selection will surely improve the classification of software modules for defects.

References

1. Rathore, S.S., Kumar, S.: Towards an ensemble based system for predicting the number of software faults. Expert Syst. Appl. **82**, 357–382 (2017)
2. Laradji, I.H., Alshayeb, M., Ghouti, L.: Software defect prediction using ensemble learning on selected features. Inf. Softw. Technol. **58**, 388–402 (2015)
3. Abisoye, O.A., Akanji, O.S., Abisoye, B.O., Awotunde, J.: Slow hypertext transfer protocol mitigation model in software defined networks. In: 2020 International Conference on Data Analytics for Business and Industry: Way Towards a Sustainable Economy, ICDABI 2020, 9325601 (2020)
4. Malhotra, R., Jain, J.: Handling imbalanced data using ensemble learning in software defect prediction. In: 2020 10th International Conference on Cloud Computing, Data Science & Engineering (Confluence), pp. 300–304. IEEE (2020)
5. Awotunde, J.B., Ayo, F.E., Ogundokun, R.O., Matiluko, O.E., Adeniyi, E.A.: Investigating the roles of effective communication among stakeholders in collaborative software development projects. Lecture Notes in Computer Science (including subseries Lecture Notes in Artificial Intelligence and Lecture Notes in Bioinformatics), 2020, 12254 LNCS, pp. 311–319 (2020)
6. Awotunde, J.B., Folorunso, S.O., Bhoi, A.K., Adebayo, P.O., Ijaz, M.F.: Disease diagnosis system for IoT-based wearable body sensors with machine learning algorithm. Intelligent Systems Reference Library **2021**(209), 201–222 (2021)
7. Awotunde, J.B., Misra, S.: Feature extraction and artificial intelligence-based intrusion detection model for a secure internet of things networks. Lecture Notes Data Eng. .ications Technol. **2022**(109), 21–44 (2022)
8. Behera, R.K., Shukla, S., Rath, S.K., Misra, S.: Software reliability assessment using machine learning technique. In: Gervasi, O., et al. (eds.) Computational Science and Its Applications – ICCSA 2018: 18th International Conference, Melbourne, VIC, Australia, July 2-5, 2018, Proceedings, Part V, pp. 403–411. Springer International Publishing, Cham (2018). https://doi.org/10.1007/978-3-319-95174-4_32
9. Chicco, D., Jurman, G.: The advantages of the Matthews correlation coefficient (MCC) over F1 score and accuracy in binary classification evaluation. BMC Genomics **21**(1), 1–13 (2020)
10. Shukla, S., Behera, R.K., Misra, S., Rath, S.K.: Software reliability assessment using deep learning technique. In: Chakraverty, S., Goel, A., Misra, S. (eds.) Towards Extensible and Adaptable Methods in Computing, pp. 57–68. Springer, Singapore (2018). https://doi.org/10.1007/978-981-13-2348-5_5
11. Awotunde, J.B., Chakraborty, C., Adeniyi, A.E.: Intrusion detection in industrial internet of things network-based on deep learning model with rule-based feature selection. Wirel. Commun. Mob. Comput. **2021**(2021), 7154587 (2021)
12. Ogundokun, R.O., Awotunde, J.B., Sadiku, P., Adeniyi, E.A., Abiodun, M., Dauda, O.I.: An enhanced intrusion detection system using particle swarm optimization feature extraction technique. Procedia Computer Science **193**, 504–512 (2021)

13. Jagdhuber, R., Lang, M., Stenzl, A., Neuhaus, J., Rahnenführer, J.: Cost-Constrained feature selection in binary classification: adaptations for greedy forward selection and genetic algorithms. BMC Bioinformatics **21**(1), 1–21 (2020)

14. Kumari, A., Behera, R.K., Sahoo, B., Sahoo, S.P.: Prediction of link evolution using community detection in social network. Computing, 1–22 (2022)

15. Mishra, N., Soni, H.K., Sharma, S., Upadhyay, A.K.: Development and analysis of artificial neural network models for rainfall prediction by using time-series data. International Journal of Intelligent Systems Applications, **10**(1) (2018)

16. Zhang, X., Mohanty, S.N., Parida, A.K., Pani, S.K., Dong, B., Cheng, X.: Annual and non-monsoon rainfall prediction modelling using SVR-MLP: an empirical study from Odisha. IEEE Access **8**, 30223–30233 (2020)

17. Jagdale, R.S., Shirsat, V.S., Deshmukh, S.N.: Sentiment analysis on product reviews using machine learning techniques. In: Mallick, P.K., Balas, V.E., Bhoi, A.K., Zobaa, A.F. (eds.) Cognitive Informatics and Soft Computing. AISC, vol. 768, pp. 639–647. Springer, Singapore (2019). https://doi.org/10.1007/978-981-13-0617-4_61

18. Hassonah, M.A., Al-Sayyed, R., Rodan, A., Ala'M, A.Z., Aljarah, I., Faris, H.: An efficient hybrid filter and evolutionary wrapper approach for sentiment analysis of various topics on Twitter. Knowledge-Based Syst.**192**, 105353 (2020)

19. Rehman, A.U., Malik, A.K., Raza, B., Ali, W.: A hybrid CNN-LSTM model for improving accuracy of movie reviews sentiment analysis. Multimedia Tools and Applications **78**(18), 26597–26613 (2019)

20. Awotunde, J.B., Abiodun, K.M., Adeniyi, E.A., Folorunso, S.O., Jimoh, R.G.: A deep learning-based intrusion detection technique for a secured IoMT system. Communications in Computer and Information Science, 2022, 1547 CCIS, pp. 50–62 (2021)

21. Verma, A., Ranga, V.: Machine learning based intrusion detection systems for IoT applications. Wireless Pers. Commun. **111**(4), 2287–2310 (2020)

22. Amouri, A., Alaparthy, V.T., Morgera, S.D.: A machine learning based intrusion detection system for mobile Internet of Things. Sensors **20**(2), 461 (2020)

23. Matloob, F., Aftab, S., Iqbal, A.: A framework for software defect prediction using feature selection and ensemble learning techniques. International Journal of Modern Education Computer Sci. **11**(12) (2019)

24. Yalçıner, B., Özdeş, M.: Software defect estimation using machine learning algorithms. In: 2019 4th International Conference on Computer Science and Engineering (UBMK), pp. 487–491. IEEE (2019)

25. Arar, Ö.F., Ayan, K.: Software defect prediction using cost-sensitive neural network. Appl. Soft Comput. **33**, 263–277 (2015)

26. Iqbal, A., et al.: Performance analysis of machine learning techniques on software defect prediction using NASA datasets. Int. J. Adv. Comput. Sci. Appl **10**(5), 300–308 (2019)

27. Iqbal, A., Aftab, S., Ullah, I., Bashir, M.S., Saeed, M.A.: A feature selection based ensemble classification framework for software defect prediction. Int. J. Modern Education Comput. Sci. **11**(9), 54 (2019)

28. Lanubile, F., Lonigro, A., Vissagio, G.: Comparing models for identifying fault-prone software components. In: SEKE, pp. 312–319 (1995)

29. Elish, K.O., Elish, M.O.: Predicting defect-prone software modules using support vector machines. J. Syst. Softw. **81**(5), 649–660 (2008)

30. Gondra, I.: Applying machine learning to software fault-proneness prediction. J. Syst. Softw. **81**(2), 186–195 (2008)

31. Manjula, C., Florence, L.: Deep neural network based hybrid approach for software defect prediction using software metrics. Clust. Comput. **22**(4), 9847–9863 (2018). https://doi.org/10.1007/s10586-018-1696-z

32. Witten, I.H., Frank, E.: Data mining: practical machine learning tools and techniques with Java implementations. ACM SIGMOD Rec. **31**(1), 76–77 (2002)
33. Dai, H., Hwang, H.G., Tseng, V.S.: Convolutional neural network based automatic screening tool for cardiovascular diseases using different intervals of ECG signals. Comput. Methods Programs Biomed. **203**, 106035 (2021)
34. Awotunde, J.B., et al.: An improved machine learnings diagnosis technique for COVID-19 pandemic using chest X-ray images. Communications in Computer and Information Science, 2021, 1455 CCIS, pp. 319–330 (2021)

Comparing Univariate and Multivariate Time Series Models for Technical Debt Forecasting

Maria Mathioudaki, Dimitrios Tsoukalas$^{(\boxtimes)}$, Miltiadis Siavvas, and Dionysios Kehagias

Centre for Research and Technology Hellas, Thessaloniki, Greece
{mariamathi,tsoukj,siavvasm,diok}@iti.gr

Abstract. Technical debt (TD) is a successful and widely used metaphor that expresses the quality compromises that can yield short-term benefits but may negatively affect the overall quality of a software product in the long run. There is a vast variety of techniques and methodologies that have been proposed over the past years to enable the identification and estimation of TD during the software development cycle. However, it is only until recently that researchers have turned towards the investigation of methods that focus on forecasting its future evolution. Getting insights on the future evolution of TD can enable on-time decision-making and allow stakeholders to plan preventive strategies regarding TD repayment. In our previous studies, we have investigated time series analysis and Machine Learning techniques in order to produce reliable TD forecasts. In our current attempt, we aim to explore the capabilities of a statistical ARIMA model both in a univariate and a multivariate fashion. More specifically, the present paper investigates whether the adoption of an ARIMA model that takes into account, in addition to the TD value itself, various TD-related indicators may lead to more accurate TD predictions than its univariate alternative. For this purpose, dedicated models are constructed, evaluated, and compared on a dataset of five long-lived, open-source software applications.

Keywords: Software quality · Technical debt · Forecasting · Time series

1 Introduction

In 1992, Ward Cunningham coined the term Technical Debt (TD) [1], to characterize technical issues of a software application that are not immediately obvious to managers and end-users, but impede developers' productivity by requiring extra maintenance effort. Poor design and implementation decisions, as well as technical shortcuts to reduce time-to-market, are common causes of TD. TD, like financial debt, must be reduced early in the software development life cycle (SDLC) by applying code refactorings. If not done so, then it can accumulate

O. Gervasi et al. (Eds.): ICCSA 2022 Workshops, LNCS 13380, pp. 62–78, 2022.
https://doi.org/10.1007/978-3-031-10542-5_5

interest in the form of future software changes or improvements that will be more expensive or even impossible to implement. In that sense, it has been discovered that wasted effort due to TD can account for up to 23% of the total developers' time [2], and in extreme cases, it can lead to an unmaintainable software [3].

TD Management is a critical but difficult challenge. To this direction, researchers have examined a wide range of methodologies and tools for detecting, estimating, and repaying TD throughout the overall SDLC [4]. However, research towards the concept of *forecasting* the future evolution of a software's TD has only recently initiated [5]. In the software development market, systematic efforts towards this direction can be proven of great value, as foreseeing how TD will evolve in the future can help project managers and developers to react quickly to its accumulation and, thus, to keep software quality at a satisfactory level [5].

In previous studies [6–10], we have conducted research towards the TD identification and forecasting concept, by examining different methods ranging from simple statistical time series models to more sophisticated approaches, such as machine learning (ML) and deep learning (DL). Our findings revealed that ML and DL algorithms are suitable for making accurate TD predictions for both short- and long-term forecasting horizons. These complex models however, despite their apparent predictive capability, lack of interpretability (black box), are computationally expensive and are prone to overfitting.

To this end, in the context of this study we revisit the concept of employing time series analysis for TD forecasting. However, unlike our previous related study [7] that focused on *univariate* time series models, i.e., models that require only the past evolution of TD itself as input, this study examines whether the adoption of *multivariate* time series models, i.e., models with exogenous variables, may lead to more accurate TD predictions. In this endeavour, our multivariate models receive as input not only the TD value, but also various TD-related indicators and their combinations. Subsequently, their performances are compared with those of the univariate approach (acting as the baseline model), on a dataset of five long-lived, open-source software applications. Finally, the results are evaluated and discussed in order to reach safer conclusions.

2   Related Work

Gaining an understanding on the future evolution of a software system might be difficult, but it can also be highly beneficial for software businesses trying to deal with rising complexity and diminishing software quality in their products [11]. As a result, the concept of analyzing, gaining insights, and being able to forecast the evolution of different aspects of a software project, either directly or indirectly associated with TD, has been extensively examined by researchers in recent years (e.g. code smells [12], number of changes [13], software security [14], and defects prediction [15]). The vast majority of these efforts attempt to solve the problem by employing statistical time series or ML models on individual software attributes based on data analysis (e.g., historical data, trends, source code metrics, etc.).

One of the most widely used methodologies for understanding the evolution of software-related quality attributes and properties, is time series analysis. In a study by Yazdi et al. [13], the authors model software design evolution of numerous applications using ARMA time series and conclude that these models may accurately forecast the changes of future software updates. Similarly, Kenmei et al. [16] apply time series models to accurately estimate the evolution of future change requests using data from three large open source applications. Likewise, Goulo et al. [17] use data acquired from the Eclipse's tracking system for developing a time series model that forecasts the evolution of change requests. Moreover, they identify seasonal trends to validate that including seasonal information greatly improves the model's performance. In a different study, Raja et al. [15] apply time series techniques to forecast software defect-proneness, based on a dataset of defect reports from eight software projects. They point out that these models can facilitate budget and resource allocation planning. Finally, Antoniol et al. [18] build an ARIMA model to forecast the evolution of software metrics, such as size and complexity, based on related historical data from the Linux Kernel. Their findings suggest that forecasting the evolution of these software metrics can be utilized to improve the management of software artifacts or processes.

The significance of quality prediction in the software engineering domain is demonstrated by the numerous studies for predicting the evolution of software quality parameters, either directly or indirectly associated with TD. However, as a software system evolves, so does the amount of its accumulated TD. In a study by Tsoukalas et al. [5], the authors highlight the need for forecasting the evolution of TD and emphasize the importance of future research on this topic. The same authors contribute to the TD forecasting challenge by examining a variety of different forecasting techniques, ranging from simple statistical time series models to more complex ML and DL approaches [7–10]. Notably, in an initial endeavor to predict the TD evolution of long-lived open-source software projects, the authors present a single univariate ARIMA model [7] and conclude that it can yield reliable short-term TD forecasts for each of the five projects studied. They do observe, however, that the model's accuracy drops significantly for forecasting horizons greater than eight steps ahead. In an attempt to extend their previous work and introduce a more holistic TD forecasting methodology, the same authors conduct two follow-up studies [8,10], where they examine the ability of ML and DL methods to predict the TD evolution of 15 open-source projects. Their findings showcase that a nonlinear Random Forest regression can achieve sufficient accuracy for forecasts up to 40 horizons ahead [8], while a more complicated Multi-layer Perceptron model can produce reliable predictions for up to 150 steps ahead into the future [10].

3 Methodology and Experimental Setup

This section presents the overall methodology that was followed in the present paper. More specifically, it provides detailed information on the employed dataset, the data pre-processing, the model construction and parameter tuning, and last but not least, the strategy that was followed for the experimental execution.

3.1 Dataset and Preparation

The first step of the proposed methodology is the construction of the dataset. For the purposes of TD forecasting, the dataset needs to consist of multiple software projects along with their history of TD measurements (TD and TD indicators' values), across their commit history. This data will serve as input to train and evaluate our univariate and multivariate models.

Hence, we decided to exploit the "Technical Debt dataset"[1], i.e., a dataset that was constructed and made publicly available to facilitate TD research [19]. This dataset is based on 33 real-world open-source Java projects obtained from the Apache Software Foundation and contains TD measurements for all available commits of the aforementioned projects. TD measurements were obtained using SonarQube[2], a widely-used open-source static code analysis platform that has been used as proof of concept in multiple research studies [4]. Each one of the 33 projects is provided as a csv file, where the columns contain the software-related metrics (including TD measurements), as extracted from SonarQube, and the rows correspond to the different commits through time.

In the context of the present work, we decided to select five long-lived Apache projects, namely Ambari, Commons-codec, Commons-io, Httpcomponents-client and Mina-sshd, for constructing and evaluating our TD forecasting models. We limited the number of examined projects to 5 out of 33, as the construction of individual time series models tailored to each dataset requires extensive manual effort with respect to ARIMA modeling, parameterization, and analysis. Eventually, the selection criteria were based on the projects' commit life (at least 3 years of evolution) and commit frequency (the higher the better). The selected projects are presented in Table 1, accompanied by additional information on the total number of analyzed commits and the analysis lifetime.

Pre-processing. In order to apply any time series model for forecasting purposes, fixed time intervals between the retrieved samples (i.e., commits) need to be ensured. This part is critical for the reliability of the models. However, the datasets used in this study are obtained from real-world applications. This means that, in some cases, multiple commits may have taken place during a particular period of time, whereas in other cases, a long period of inactivity (i.e. no commits at all) may have occurred. To alleviate this issue, we applied a filtering method in order to ensure that the final datasets will include time points corresponding to one commit per week, maintaining in this way fixed time intervals between the samples. Specifically, if multiple commits have taken place during a week, we isolate and keep the last commit of the week. If a period of more than one week

---

[1] https://github.com/clowee/The-Technical-Debt-Dataset.

[2] https://www.sonarqube.org/.

has passed without commits, we assign to that week the last available commit. By applying the aforementioned approach, we maintain the initial life span of a project, but reduce the frequency of commits to one per week. More details on the final number of samples (i.e., commits) per each dataset (i.e., project) are presented in Table 1.

Table 1. Selected projects of the TD dataset

Project name	Analyzed commits	Analysis lifetime	Filtered commits
Ambari	13397	09/11 – 06/15	192
Commons-codec	1726	04/03 – 05/18	532
Commons-io	2118	01/02 – 06/18	632
Httpcomponents-client	2867	12/05 – 06/18	576
Mina-sshd	1370	12/08 – 06/18	360

Feature Selection. As already mentioned, the purpose of the present study is to compare the performance of *univariate* time series models to that of time series models that follow a *multivariate* modeling approach. The rationale behind this, is that we are interested in investigating whether models that take into account various TD-related indicators and their combinations, may be able to discover underlying patterns on the TD evolution more effectively than models that consider only the TD value itself.

That being said, to apply any form of analysis following the multivariate approach, the independent variables need to be carefully selected. There is a total of 61 software-related metrics in the dataset that could potentially act as independent variables for the current problem. However, providing a model with such an input may result to what is called the "curse of dimensionality", which is the unlikely event of a significant drop in the model's predictive performance when a large dimension of variables is provided as input. Consequently, features that are not (or are slightly) associated with the target variable, i.e., total TD, should be filtered out before any model construction attempt.

To identify the most important TD indicators that could act as strong predictors for TD forecasting, in one of our previous studies [9] (where the same dataset was used for similar purposes), we performed an extensive feature selection analysis. More specifically, different feature selection algorithms were put in practice, including filter-based, wrapper-based and embedded methods. The results led to the selected TD indicators presented in Table 2. Therefore, the same TD indicators will be used as independent variables also in this study, during the next steps of the methodology.

That being said, similarly to our previous work [8], we also specify the *total technical debt* as our target variable, i.e., the variable that we will generate forecasts for. We define *total_technical_debt* as the total remediation effort (in minutes) that is required in order to fix all reliability, maintainability and security issues detected in the source code of a software project.

Table 2. Metrics used as TD indicators

Metric	Description
Technical debt metrics	
sqale_index	Effort in minutes to fix all Code Smells
reliability_remediation_effort	Effort in minutes to fix all bug issues
security_remediation_effort	Effort in minutes to fix all vulnerability issues
total_technical_debt	Effort in minutes to fix all issues. The sum of code smell, bug and vulnerability remediation effort
Reliability metrics	
bugs	Total number of bug issues of a project
Maintainability metrics	
code_smells	Total number of code smell issues of a project
Size metrics	
comment_lines	Total number of lines that correspond to comments
ncloc	Total number of lines that are not part of a comment
Security metrics	
vulnerabilities	Total number of vulnerability issues of a project
Complexity metrics	
complexity	Total cyclomatic complexity calculated based on the number of paths through the code
Coverage metrics	
uncovered_lines	Total number of code lines that are not covered by unit tests
Duplication metrics	
Duplicated_blocks	Total number of lines that belong to duplicated blocks

3.2 Forecasting with ARIMA and ARIMAX Models

A time series is a collection of consecutive observations made at equally spaced time intervals. Prior to any time series analysis, stationarity needs to be assured, so that the statistical properties of the time series data (e.g., mean, variance, and auto-correlation) become constant over time. In this respect, Box and Jenkins introduced the Autoregressive Integrated Moving Average (ARIMA) technique for modeling non-stationary time series data [20]. These models work with both stationary and non-stationary data and can be easily adjusted in cases where the underlying patterns alter significantly. Since then, ARIMA models have been widely employed for modeling software evolution [13,15–17].

ARIMA models usually require only the historical data of the target variable, i.e., the variable that we are interested in making forecasts for (univariate approach). However, they can also be extended to take into account "exogenous" variables, i.e., independent variables that may act as predictors for the target variable. This type of models are called ARIMAX and are essentially the multivariate version of the univariate ARIMA. The methodology that follows in this part is applied for both the ARIMA and the ARIMAX modeling approach.

ARIMA (and thus ARIMAX) models are fine-tuned by specifying three integers, namely p, d and q. Parameter p is the order of the autoregressive model

(AR), representing the number of values in the past that affect the current value of the time series. Parameter d represents the integrated (I) part of the model. It stands for the number of times the time series needs to be differenced so that it becomes stationary. Lastly, parameter q is the order of the moving-average (MA) model. It basically describes that the current error depends on previous errors with some lag equal to q. There are four key steps that form the Box and Jenkins ARIMA modelling strategy:

Identification: Before parameterizing the ARIMA model, stationarity of the time series needs to be ensured. Thus, during this step, if the observed data is found to be non-stationary, the effect can be removed by differencing the time series. The number of times that a series needs to be differenced in order to become stationary corresponds to the d parameter.

Estimation: During this step, the p and q parameters can be determined by inspecting the Auto-Correlation Function (ACF) and Partial Auto-Correlation Function (PACF) plots. The ACF correlogram reveals the correlation between the residuals of the data at specific lags. However, identifying the p and q parameters via the ACF and PACF plots is not always a trivial task. In such cases, the optimal p and q parameters are specified in the next step, by comparing the *goodness of fit* of various competing models.

Diagnostic Testing: During this step, appropriate tests are performed in order to define the best ARIMA model. Specifically, the Akaike Information Criterion (AIC) and the Bayesian Information Criterion (BIC) are used and the goal is to minimize these scores through the testing of numerous ARIMA models with different p and q combinations.

Application: The final and most crucial step is to apply the selected model on unseen observations that were not used during the previous steps. Hence, to ensure the ability of the model to generalize well and, thus, to generate accurate predictions, it is of paramount importance to hold out some observations for evaluation purposes.

Performance Metrics. As in any forecasting task, predictions need to be as close to the real values as possible, while avoiding model overfitting. For evaluating the models' predictive power, similarly to our previous works [7–9] we used the *Mean Absolute Percentage Error* (MAPE). MAPE is a commonly used measure for the evaluation of forecasting models that uses absolute values to calculate the error in percentage terms.

To complement the evaluation of our results and at the same time remain inline with our previous studies [7–9], we also calculated the *Mean Absolute Error* (MAE) and the *Root Mean Squared Error* (RMSE), whose presence is usual when it comes to forecasting tasks. MAE calculates the magnitude of the errors coming from a group of forecasts by not taking under consideration their trend. RMSE represents the quantification of the quadratic mean of the differences between the observed and the predicted values.

4 Analysis, Results and Discussion

This section presents the results regarding the five different projects that comprise our dataset. Due to space limitation, we offer a detailed description of the ARIMA modelling approach for the Mina-sshd project. For the rest of the projects we provide only the final results for comparison purposes and discussion but we note that the exact same steps were followed.

4.1 Mina-sshd

Identification: As explained in Sect. 3.2, the first step of the time series analysis is to visualize the time series so that we can gain an initial insight on its nature. Figure 1 (a) illustrates the TD evolution of the Mina-sshd dataset over time.

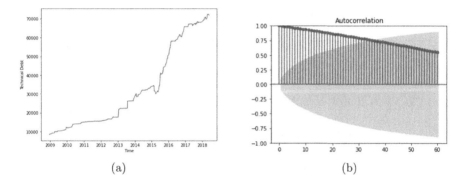

(a)   (b)

Fig. 1. TD evolution and ACF Correlogram of Mina-sshd original data

By inspecting Fig. 1 (a), it is clear that the data is non-stationary with an upward trend, i.e., the TD value of Mina-sshd increases over time. This can be further supported by the fact that the ACF chart depicted in Fig. 1 (b) is characterized by the slow linear decay in the spikes. Therefore, we need to make the time series stationary before proceeding to further analysis. A common way for making a series stationary is to transform it through *differencing*. Therefore, we took the first-order difference of the data to eliminate the overall trend from the series. If the original series is Y_t, then the differenced series is indicated by $Y_t = Y_t - Y_{t-1}$. The ACF and PACF plots of the first-order differenced time series are presented in Fig. 2.

To ensure that a first-order differencing made the time series stationary, we employed the Dickey-Fuller test [21], which tests the null hypothesis that a unit root is present in an autoregressive model. The results of the Dickey-Fuller test showed that the "Test Statistic" value is lower that the "Critical Value" (with p-value < 0.05), which means that the time series has become stationary. This is further supported by the illustrated first-order differenced data on Fig. 2 (a) which demonstrates no apparent trend. As mentioned earlier, the number of transformations that take place until the time series becomes stationary corresponds to the d parameter of the $ARIMA(p,d,q)$ model. Hence, setting the value of $d = 1$ can be safely supported by the above analysis.

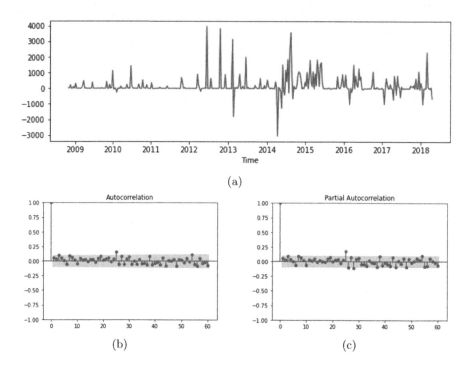

(a)

(b)   (c)

Fig. 2. Dickey-Fuller, ACF and PACF of the first-order differenced time series data

Estimation: During this step, we aim to identify the p (AR) and q (MA) parameters of the $ARIMA(p,d,q)$ model, following the practical recommendations through visual inspection of the ACF and PACF correlograms [22]. For this purpose, we analyzed Fig. 2 (b) and (c) representing the ACF and PACF correlograms of the first-order differenced time series. In general, the x-axis of the ACF plot indicates the lag at which the autocorrelation is computed, while, the y-axis indicates the value of the correlation (between -1 and 1). In our case, the two plots indicate no clear cut-off as all correlation values are found to be within the intervals of 95% confidence, except for a few exceptions which occur for rather high lag values. In this case, p and q parameters will be determined during our next step, i.e., the *Diagnostic testing*.

Diagnostic testing: As mentioned in Sect. 3.2, when no clear cut-off is indicated in the ACF and PACF correlograms, we turn towards the AIC and BIC error minimization criteria. Therefore, we conducted experiments by assigning various combinations of values (between 0 and 5) to the p and q parameters, while keeping the d parameter equal to 1. We excluded ARIMA (0,1,0) from our analysis as this is the "random walk" model and, thus, the simplest one. By inspecting the results, the models that provided the lowest AIC and BIC values were ARIMA (1,1,0), ARIMA (0,1,1) and ARIMA (1,1,1). The results of the three best performing models can be found in Table 3.

Table 3. ARIMA candidate model results for Mina-sshd

Model	AIC	BIC	Ljung-box	Prob	$Coef.$ P > $\mid z \mid$
ARIMA (0,1,1)	5639.89	5647.65	1.16	0.28	*ma* 0.001
ARIMA (1,1,0)	5638.97	5646.74	1.97	0.16	*ar* 0.000
ARIMA (1,1,1)	5616.71	5628.36	0.14	0.70	*ar* 0.000 *ma* 0.000

The coef P > $\mid z \mid$ column of Table 3 indicates the significance of each feature weight. As can be seen, all of the AR and MA parameters of the examined models have p-values lower than 0.05. This means that it is both reasonable and safe to consider any of these candidate models for our experiments. In addition, Table 3 also presents the Ljung-Box [23] statistics for residual analysis. Ljung-Box Q test is considered one of the most common goodness of fit tests. As can be seen, the Ljung-Box test of the models provides values higher than 0.05, which indicates that the residuals are independent and all three models are suitable and well-adjusted to the time series.

Since the above metrics cannot facilitate our decision on the selection of best model, we focus our efforts on the AIC and BIC indicators. AIC and BIC measure the goodness of fit of statistical models for a given set of data by estimating the quality of each model, relative to each of the other models. Models that have a better fit receive a better (lower) AIC and BIC score than models that fit worse. By inspecting Table 3, we can see that while the AIC and BIC values of the three models are similar, for ARIMA(1,1,1) the values are slightly lower (better), i.e. 5616.71 and 5628.36 respectively.

To conclude, the three models seem identical and their scores are close. However, the fact that ARIMA(1,1,1) has a slightly better AIC, BIC and Ljung-Box Q test score indicates that it is a more appropriate candidate. Therefore, we chose ARIMA(1,1,1) as the most suitable model. The next step is to evaluate the performance of the selected model on the Mina-sshd dataset.

Application: The fourth and final step of the ARIMA modelling methodology is the Application. During this step, the model is trained on a subset of the data, and then it is tested on "unseen" observations to ensure the ability of the model to generalize well. In time series analysis tasks, *Walk-forward validation* [24] is a commonly used technique to assess the models accuracy, based on the concept that models are updated when new observations are made available (i.e., by respecting the temporal order in which the samples were collected). It involves the split of the timeseries at n-1 equally distanced points. In this way, n folds are

Table 4. ARIMA(1,1,1) and ARIMAX(1,1,1) forecasting results for Mina-sshd

Model	Steps ahead	MAPE %	RMSE	MAE
ARIMA (1,1,1)	4	0.683	290.279	268.227
	8	1.197	485.614	432.432
	12	1.518	575.076	483.292
	Total average	**1.132**	**450.323**	**394.650**
ARIMAX(1,1,1)	4	0.240	122.872	102.095
	8	0.539	300.040	249.715
	12	0.538	296.198	232.803
	Total average	**0.438**	**239.703**	**194.871**

formed. Initially, the first fold is used to train a model whose accuracy is tested against the consecutive folds. Then, the first fold is merged with the second one and a new model is trained and tested against the consecutive remaining folds. The process is repeated until there is only one fold left to serve as a test set. Subsequently, *n-1* errors are obtained and the average of these errors is calculated to obtain one single value representing the overall performance of the model. In our case, taking under consideration that the filtered datasets are characterized by an average length, we chose the number of splits to be 3.

Therefore, we used the *Walk-forward validation* to conduct our experiments, by employing ARIMA(1,1,1) as the baseline model and ARIMAX(1,1,1) as the model that would prove that the inclusion of exogenous variables (i.e., TD-related indicators) in the ARIMA process may lead to more accurate TD predictions than its univariate alternative. We compared their results using MAPE, MAE and RMSE. In Table 4, we present the results for multiple (4, 8 and 12) time steps into the future. The results indicate that indeed the multivariate ARIMAX(1,1,1) model provides us with remarkably lower errors compared to its univariate alternative ARIMA(1,1,1). The average values of the errors for the different steps ahead are calculated to enable a smoother assessing of the results.

4.2   Ambari, Commons-codec, Commons-io, Httpcomponents-client

Identification: The steps that we followed during Sect. 4.1, were also repeated for the rest of the four datasets (i.e., software projects). Initially, by employing Dickey-Fuller tests for each one of the datasets we confirmed that a first-order difference is sufficient for the four time series to become stationary. Therefore, as explained in detail earlier, the d parameter of the ARIMA(p,d,q) model for all of the projects can be set to $d = 1$.

Estimation: During this phase of the analysis, we need to specify the (AR) p and (MA) q parameters for each of the datasets. We analyzed the corresponding ACF and PACF plots, but similarly to the Mina-sshd case, we were not able to draw safe conclusions as there were no clear cut-offs. Consequently, we turned again towards the minimization criteria approach by testing competitive ARIMA models, while keeping d equal to 1 according to our previous step. The three best performing models for each one of the datasets are the following:

- *Ambari*: ARIMA(1,1,0), ARIMA(0,1,1) and ARIMA(1,1,1).
- *Commons-codec*: ARIMA(1,1,1), ARIMA(2,1,1) and ARIMA(2,1,2).
- *Commons-io*: ARIMA(1,1,1), ARIMA(2,1,1) and ARIMA(1,1,2).
- *Httpcomponents-client*: ARIMA(0,1,1), ARIMA(1,1,0) and ARIMA(2,1,2).

Diagnostic Testing: During this step, we compare the best performing models in terms of goodness of fit and residuals. Through this process we aim to conclude on which of the candidate ARIMA models is more suitable for each dataset. The summary of the fitted models is presented on Table 5.

Table 5. ARIMA candidate model results for the rest of the projects

Model	AIC	BIC	Ljung-box	Prob	*Coef.* P $> \mid z \mid$
Ambari					
ARIMA(0,1,1)	4418.97	4425.47	0.09	0.77	*ma* 0.927
ARIMA(1,1,0)	4418.92	4425.42	0.10	0.75	*ar* 0.917
ARIMA(1,1,1)	4418.51	4428.27	0.02	0.88	*ar* 0.000 *ma* 0.014
Commons-codec					
ARIMA(1,1,1)	7158.41	7171.23	0.76	0.38	*ar* 0.000 *ma* 0.000
ARIMA(2,1,1)	7152.83	7169.93	0.00	0.98	*ar* 0.748 *ma* 0.000
ARIMA(2,1,2)	7152.35	7173.73	0.67	0.41	*ar* 0.191 *ma* 0.931
Commons-io					
ARIMA(1,1,1)	9817.35	9830.69	0.08	0.77	*ar* 0.000 *ma* 0.000
ARIMA(2,1,1)	9819.13	9836.92	0.00	0.98	*ar* 0.921 *ma* 0.000
ARIMA(1,1,2)	9819.21	9836.99	0.00	0.97	*ar* 0.000 *ma* 0.918
Httpcomponents-client					
ARIMA(0,1,1)	9894.14	9902.85	0.06	0.80	*ma* 0.928
ARIMA(1,1,0)	9894.13	9902.84	0.06	0.81	*ar* 0.928
ARIMA(2,1,2)	9895.41	9917.19	0.19	0.66	*ar* 0.647 *ma* 0.626

After carefully inspecting the results and mainly the AIC values, we identified that for the Ambari dataset the optimal model is the ARIMA(1,1,1), for the Commons-io dataset the ARIMA(1,1,1) and for the Httpcomponents-client the ARIMA(1,1,0). In the case of the Commons-codec dataset, we observed that while the lowest AIC is obtained using the ARIMA(2,1,2) and ARIMA(2,1,1) models, their AR and MA parameters have p-values higher than 0.05 (see coef P $> \mid z \mid$ column), which raises awareness on the goodness of fit of these models. For this reason, we decided to choose the third model, namely the ARIMA(1,1,1). We note that the coef P of the AR and MA parameters are higher than 0.05 also in the case of the Httpcompoents-client dataset. However, since this applies to all candidate models, we chose the model with the lowest AIC value.

Diagnostic Testing: During final step, similarly to the case of Mina-sshd, we compared the best performing ARIMA models for each of the datasets with their corresponding multivariate (ARIMAX) alternatives. Again, predictions were generated for 4, 8 and 12 versions ahead. The obtained errors are presented on Table 6. By inspecting Table 6, it is clear that the outcome that was obtained while inspecting the results for Mina-sshd is in line with the performance results obtained also for the rest of the datasets. More specifically, in all cases, the results

Table 6. ARIMA(1,1,1) and ARIMAX(1,1,1) forecasting results for the rest of the projects

Model	Steps ahead	MAPE %	RMSE	MAE
Ambari				
ARIMA(1,1,1)	4	3.698	4023.305	3744.349
	8	5.435	9457.667	7840.039
	12	6.759	11959.119	10389.987
	Average	**5.297**	**8480.030**	**7324.791**
ARIMAX(1,1,1)	4	1.237	1411.385	1296.111
	8	2.712	2663.183	2133.263
	12	3.440	2904.759	2456.603
	Average	**2.463**	**2326.442**	**1961.991**
Commons-codec				
ARIMA(1,1,1)	4	0.545	62.362	56.972
	8	0.911	106.136	95.587
	12	1.462	200.555	157.840
	Average	**0.972**	**123.017**	**103.466**
ARIMAX(1,1,1)	4	0.051	7.479	6.827
	8	0.308	43.414	32.988
	12	0.608	95.008	69.639
	Average	**0.322**	**48.633**	**36.484**
Commons-io				
ARIMA(1,1,1)	4	0.318	108.159	56.337
	8	3.515	994.881	717.263
	12	4.804	1173.283	965.836
	Average	**2.879**	**758.774**	**579.812**
ARIMAX(1,1,1)	4	0.197	24.022	21.461
	8	0.417	51.200	43.942
	12	0.696	99.657	78.653
	Average	**0.683**	**159.083**	**127.635**
Httpcomponents-client				
ARIMA(1,1,0)	4	3.032	3694.202	1948.633
	8	7.000	5691.715	4535.235
	12	8.343	6236.742	5420.759
	Average	**6.125**	**5207.553**	**3968.209**
ARIMAX(1,1,0)	4	1.120	915.976	745.284
	8	1.427	1046.078	922.350
	12	1.543	1077.187	977.793
	Average	**1.363**	**1013.080**	**881.809**

indicate that the multivariate ARIMAX models provide significantly lower errors when compared to their univariate alternative ARIMA models. Therefore, we can safely conclude that by bringing into the equation, in addition to the TD value itself, various TD-related indicators and their combinations, time series TD forecasting models can be significantly improved.

In order to visualize the above conclusions, Fig. 3 provides an example of forecasting the TD evolution of the Mina-sshd project for 35 commits ahead, using ARIMA(1,1,1) and ARIMAX(1,1,1). As can be seen, both models generated predictions that are close to the ground truth. However, the ARIMAX(1,1,1) model has managed to catch the fluctuations of the original time series much more accurately. Hence, as far as our dataset is concerned, the ARIMAX(1,1,1) models are able to capture the underlying TD evolution patterns in a much more effective way compared to the ARIMA(1,1,1).

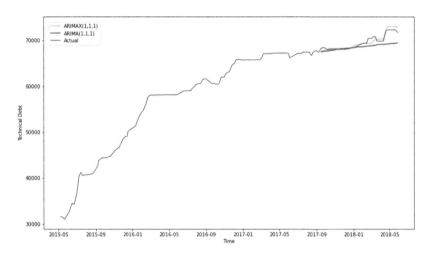

Fig. 3. Mina-sshd TD forecasting for 35 versions ahead using ARIMAX(1,1,1) and ARIMA(1,1,1)

4.3 Discussion

Across the five independent datasets, we have successfully applied the Box and Jenkins modelling strategy to identify the optimal ARIMA and ARIMAX models and compare their performances. Results showed that both models are able to fit and provide meaningful forecasts of TD evolution. However, when comparing their performance metrics, it was observed that a more complex model that relies on the historical data of both the target variable and the related independent variables outperforms a model that relies only on the target variable. Furthermore, this outcome was consistent for all forecasting horizons tested across all five projects. Relying also on our previous work, we note that time series analysis consists a useful technique for modeling the TD evolution of long-lived software projects. Through the present study we conclude that when exogenous variables are considered during the model construction, accuracy is significantly improved.

5   Conclusions

The purpose of the current work, was to extend our knowledge on the predictive performance of time series models for the purposes of TD forecasting. More specifically, we strove towards getting an understanding on whether ARIMAX models that take under consideration independent variables acting as TD predictors can provide more accurate TD forecasts than common ARIMA models. For the purpose of our study we employed 5 datasets containing the evolution history of software-metrics, computed from static code analysis for 5 long-lived projects. Based on this data, we generated forecasts for different horizons using ARIMA and ARIMAX models. The obtained results lead to a single concrete conclusion. Across the 5 independent datasets, the accuracy of the ARIMAX models was significantly higher than the accuracy provided by the ARIMA models. Thus, we conclude that taking under consideration exogenous variables when employing ARIMA models for TD forecasting purposes, escalates the model's accuracy.

While our previous studies revealed that ML and DL approaches provide reliable forecasts for both short- and long-term TD predictions, the fact that they lack interpretability and are computationally"hungry" limits their practicality. Therefore, in the context of the current study, we turned our focus towards statistical time series models, focusing on rather short-term forecasting horizons, as our main goal was to compare the performances of the two ARIMA approaches (i.e., univariate and multivariate). However, the promising results obtained using ARIMAX models urge for further investigation. To this end, as a future work, we plan to generalize the outcomes of this research towards broader forecasting horizons, in order to directly compare ARIMAX to the ML and DL models of our previous studies, potentially contributing to new milestones that can and should be added in the TD forecasting field.

Acknowledgements. This work is partially funded by the European Union's Horizon 2020 Research and Innovation Programme through SmartCLIDE project under Grant Agreement No. 871177.

References

1. Cunningham, W.: The WyCash portfolio management system. ACM SIGPLAN OOPS Messenger **4**(2), 29–30 (1993)
2. Besker, T., Martini, A., Bosch, J.: Software developer productivity loss due to technical debt-A replication and extension study examining developers' development work. J. Syst. Softw. **156**, 41–61 (2019)
3. Suryanarayana, G., Samarthyam, G., Sharma, T.: Refactoring for Software Design Smells: Managing Technical Debt. Morgan Kaufmann (2014)

4. Li, Z., Avgeriou, P., Liang, P.: A systematic mapping study on technical debt and its management. J. Syst. Soft. **101**, 193–220 (2015)
5. Tsoukalas, D., Siavvas, M., Jankovic, M., Kehagias, D., Chatzigeorgiou, A., Tzovaras, D.: Methods and tools for td estimation and forecasting: a state-of-the-art survey. In: International Conference on Intelligent Systems (IS 2018) (2018)
6. Tsoukalas, D., et al.: Machine learning for technical debt identification. IEEE Trans. Soft. Eng. (2021)
7. Tsoukalas, D., Jankovic, M., Siavvas, M., Kehagias, D., Chatzigeorgiou, A., Tzovaras, D.: On the applicability of time series models for technical debt forecasting. In: 15th China-Europe International Symposium on Software Engineering Education (CEISEE 2019) (2019) (in press)
8. Tsoukalas, D., Kehagias, D., Siavvas, M., Chatzigeorgiou, A.: Technical Debt Forecasting: an empirical study on open-source repositories. J. Syst. Soft. **170**, 110777 (2020)
9. Tsoukalas, D., Mathioudaki, M., Siavvas, M., Kehagias, D., Chatzigeorgiou, A.: A clustering approach towards cross-project technical debt forecasting. SN Comput. Sci. **2**(1), 1–30 (2021)
10. Mathioudaki, M., Tsoukalas, D., Siavvas, M., Kehagias, D.: Technical debt forecasting based on deep learning techniques. In: Gervasi, O., et al. (eds.) ICCSA 2021. LNCS, vol. 12955, pp. 306–322. Springer, Cham (2021). https://doi.org/10.1007/978-3-030-87007-2_22
11. Gall, H.C., Lanza, M.: Software evolution: analysis and visualization. In: 28th International Conference On Software Engineering, pp. 1055–1056. ACM (2006)
12. Arcelli Fontana, F., Mäntylä, M.V., Zanoni, M., Marino, A.: Comparing and experimenting machine learning techniques for code smell detection. Empir. Softw. Eng. **21**(3), 1143–1191 (2015). https://doi.org/10.1007/s10664-015-9378-4
13. Shariat Yazdi, H., Mirbolouki, M., Pietsch, P., Kehrer, T., Kelter, U.: Analysis and prediction of design model evolution using time series. In: Iliadis, L., Papazoglou, M., Pohl, K. (eds.) CAiSE 2014. LNBIP, vol. 178, pp. 1–15. Springer, Cham (2014). https://doi.org/10.1007/978-3-319-07869-4_1
14. Siavvas, M., Tsoukalas, D., Jankovic, M., Kehagias, D., Tzovaras, D.: Technical debt as an indicator of software security risk: a machine learning approach for software development enterprises. Enterprise Information Systems (2020)
15. Raja, U., Hale, D.P., Hale, J.E.: Modeling software evolution defects: a time series approach. J. Softw. Maint. Evol. Res. Pract. **21**(1), 49–71 (2009)
16. Kenmei, B., Antoniol, G., Di Penta, M.: Trend analysis and issue prediction in large-scale open source systems. In: 2008 12th European Conference on Software Maintenance and Reengineering, pp. 73–82. IEEE (2008)
17. Goulão, M., Fonte, N., Wermelinger, M., Abreu, F.B.: Software evolution prediction using seasonal time analysis: a comparative study. In: 2012 16th European Conference on Software Maintenance and Reengineering, pp. 213–222. IEEE (2012)
18. Antoniol, G., Di Penta, M., Gradara, S.: Predicting Software Evolution: An Approach and a Case Study
19. Lenarduzzi, V., Saarimäki, N., Taibi, D.: The technical debt dataset. In: 15th International Conference on Predictive Models and Data Analytics, pp. 2–11 (2019)
20. Box, G.E.P., Jenkins, G.M.: Time Series Analysis: Forecasting and Control, pp. 161–215. Palgrave Macmillan, UK (2013)
21. Dickey, D.A., Fuller, W.A.: Distribution of the estimators for autoregressive time series with a unit root. J. Am. Stat. Assoc. **74**(366), 427–431 (1979)
22. McCleary, R., Hay, R.: Applied Time Series Analysis For The Social Sciences. Sage Publications, Beverly Hills (1980)

23. Ljung, G.M., Box, G.E.P.: On a measure of lack of fit in time series models. Biometrika **65**(2), 297–303 (1978)
24. Stone, M.: Cross-validatory choice and assessment of statistical predictions. J. Royal Stat. Soc. Ser. B (Methodol.) **36**(2), 111–147 (1974)

Fine-Tuning GPT-2 to Patch Programs, Is It Worth It?

Márk Lajkó[1,2](✉) 🆔, Dániel Horváth[1,2] 🆔, Viktor Csuvik[1,2] 🆔,
and László Vidács[1,2] 🆔

[1] Department of Software Engineering, University of Szeged, Szeged, Hungary
{mlajko,hoda,csuvikv,lac}@inf.u-szeged.hu
[2] MTA-SZTE Research Group on Artificial Intelligence, Szeged, Hungary
https://www.sed.inf.u-szeged.hu

Abstract. The application of Artificial Intelligence (AI) in the Software Engineering (SE) field is always a bit delayed compared to state-of-the-art research results. While the Generative Pre-trained Transformer (GPT-2) model was published in 2018, only a few recent works used it for SE tasks. One of such tasks is Automated Program Repair (APR), where the applied technique should find a fix to software bugs without human intervention. One problem emerges here: the creation of proper training data is resource-intensive and requires several hours of additional work from researchers. The sole reason for it is that training a model to repair programs automatically requires both the buggy program and the fixed one on large scale and presumably in an already pre-processed form. There are currently few such databases, so teaching and fine-tuning models is not an easy task. In this work, we wanted to investigate how the GPT-2 model performs when it is not fine-tuned for the APR task, compared to when it is fine-tuned. From previous work, we already know that the GPT-2 model can automatically generate patches for buggy programs, although the literature lacks studies where no fine-tuning has taken place. For the sake of the experiment we evaluated the GPT-2 model out-of-the-box and also fine-tuned it before the evaluation on 1559 JavaSript code snippets. Based on our results we can conclude that although the fine-tuned model was able to learn how to write syntactically correct source code almost on every attempt, the non-fine-tuned model lacked some of these positive features.

Keywords: Automated Program Repair · Machine learning · JavaScript · Code refinement · GPT-2 · Fine-tune

1 Introduction

Recent researches in NLP led to the release of multiple massive-sized pre-trained text generation models like the Generative Pre-trained Transformer. There are currently three versions of it (GPT-1,2,3), from which we used GPT-2. Although OpenAI, the original creator of the GPT family, did not make the implementation of the model publicly available, thanks to the efforts of the NLP and AI

O. Gervasi et al. (Eds.): ICCSA 2022 Workshops, LNCS 13380, pp. 79–91, 2022.
https://doi.org/10.1007/978-3-031-10542-5_6

research community where there are several open-access implementations of it. These are pre-trained on a very large corpus of data in a self-supervised fashion. Since GPT-2 is trained to guess the next word in sentences, the training process does not require any special data, it can be easily obtained from scrapping web pages from the internet (it was originally trained on the text from 8 million websites). It is known that unfiltered data from the web is far from neutral, and the OpenAI team themselves pointed out that *"...GPT-2 do not distinguish fact from fiction, we don't support use-cases that require the generated text to be true..."* and *"...GPT-2 reflect the biases inherent to the systems they were trained on..."* [24]. Although this training procedure has some limitations, the outcome of it made the GPT family famous by writing stories about talking unicorns [2]. There are no fundamental algorithmic breakthroughs concerning GPT-2, the original model was essentially scaled-up, resulting in a model with 10x more parameters than the original. Although GPT-2 is not the latest GPT model we hypothesize that the results would be roughly the same with more-recent model variants as well. Although it limits our work to some degree, the training data we assembled and the experiments are reproducible with larger models as well, for any future researchers in the field.

The ease with which the GPT family can be used for a completely new unseen task is thrilling, without training for a single epoch. This combined with the availability of cheap computing capacities has led many software engineers to use these models without any special background knowledge [33]. On the other hand, fine-tuning a model requires more computational power and also competent people. While the pre-trained models are usually okay for experiments, for real production scenarios fine-tuning to the downstream task (e.g. sentiment detection, dialogue response generation, code completion, etc.) is usually recommended. This is especially true for those special cases when the downstream task is rather specific or its domain differs from the one it was trained on. Although it is true that the training data of GPT-2 contain source code as well, natural language is present in the majority. Automated Program Repair is such a downstream task where fine-tuning might worth it, since in it the input and the output of the model is source code. The goal of it is that by giving a buggy program the model should automatically create a patch for it without human intervention. This so-called patch is considered to be correct when it is syntactically identical (except for white-spaces) to the developer fix. This criterion is rather strict, by comparison tools that follow the Generate and Validate approach, validation is usually done against an oracle, which is usually the test suite. A program is marked as a possible fix, if it passes all the available test cases. This latter condition gives no assurance that the program is *correct*, since over- and underfitting [18] often occurs, resulting in inadequate patches. Although there are some approaches that tried to tackle this problem [3,5,8], the question of patch correctness is considered to be still open [9].

Encouraged by the excellent recent results of data-driven APR approaches [4, 5,15,22,31], in this work we wanted to investigate whether is it worth fine-tuning the GPT-2 model. At the time of writing this article the top three approaches are CoTexT [23], PLBART [1] and DeepDebug [5]. Although none of these approaches use the GPT-2 model, their operating principle is similar. From previous work we know that the fine-tuned GPT model is able to repair programs automatically, although it is of question what is the performance of the raw pre-trained model on the same task. We used the GPT-2 implementation of the Hugging Face [14] community. We fine-tuned the model on JavaScript [27] samples and evaluated it, and also used the pre-trained version out-of-the-box and simply evaluated the test data on it. The choice of JavaScript is arbitrary, although it is the de-facto web programming language globally and the most adopted language on GitHub [10], the study could be executed on any other languages as well.

To be able to fine-tune the GPT model, we mined 18736 bug-fixing commits from GitHub and preprocessed them before fed to the model. These samples are divided in the classic train-test-validation sets and the model was evaluated on these samples. On the other hand, the pre-trained model was not fine-tuned, simply evaluated on the test set. Based on our experiments the fine-tuned GPT-2 was able to repair 126 programs on first try, while when no fine-tuning was applied the model was able to repair only 10 programs on first try. On the other hand, when the non-fine-tuned model had more chances to generate a patch, it was able to generate fixes in 269 cases.

The paper is organized as follows. After a high-level overview of our research, the dataset and the model are described in Sect. 2. Thereafter Sect. 2.1 and Sect. 3.2 describe the preprocessing and fine-tuning steps. After that the process of patch generation is depicted in Sect. 3.3 and we present the settings with which the experiments were carried out. Evaluation and analysis are presented in Sect. 4, followed by the discussion of this experiment. Related work is discussed in Sect. 5, and we conclude the paper in the last section.

2   Approach

In Fig. 1 we depicted the high-level approach we present in this paper. First, JavaScript files are being fetched from GitHub and stored locally. Afterwards these files are preprocessed to form samples that can be fed to the GPT-2 model. These samples form a (p_{buggy}, p_{fixed}) tuple, where p_{buggy} is the state of the program before the code change, while p_{fixed} is the program after the patch has been applied. Note that we focused on bugs which affect only one line, thus p_{fixed} is always a single line, while p_{buggy} is the 900 tokens before that. From the retrieved 18736 JS files we extracted 18422 samples (18422 (p_{buggy}, p_{fixed}) pairs). These tuples are next split into two separate parts: training and test samples. The training samples are used to fine-tune the GPT-2 model, while the test samples are for evaluation. We conducted two experiments: (1) in which we did not fine-tune the GPT-2 model, just evaluated the pre-trained model on the test samples and (2) first the model is being fine-tuned and next it is being evaluated on the same test set as the non-fine-tuned version. In both cases the output is a list of the generated patches, since on multiple runs the

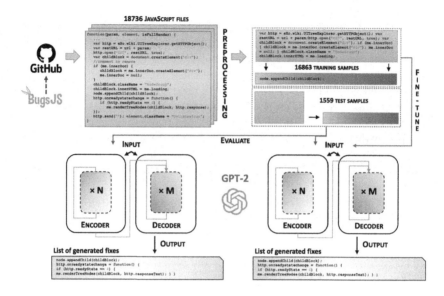

Fig. 1. The high-level approach of patch generation.

model gives back different results. Taking advantage of this, we handled the output as an ordered list and made experiments that investigate not only the first line (candidate patch) but the ones that follow as well. At the end, these ordered lists are compared against the developer fix and thus it can be easily decided whether the patch is correct or not. Finally we calculate the percentage of correctly patched programs in both cases and analyze that. A more detailed description about the approach can be found in [17].

2.1   Dataset

For the experiments we created our own dataset based on Github projects, also contained by BugsJS [12], which contains reproducible JavaScript bugs from 10 open-source projects. However we did not restricted ourselves to bugs only. In this dataset one can find changes containing bug fixes, code refinements, refactorings, etc. For the sake of simplicity, in the paper we refer to these code-refinements, as bugs. The dataset contains both single- and multi-line bugs as well. The detailed description of these code-refinements are beyond the scope of this research, but the interested reader is encouraged to take a look at the original paper or the aforementioned projects themselves, for further details. We retrieved commits using the GitPython [11] package. First we downloaded the repository, then iterated through commits one-by-one, collecting code changes for files with *.js* extension. At the end of this phase we identified 18736 files. These files served as the basis of our preprocessing step.

Preprocessing. From the mined JavaScript files every comment is being removed since they do not affect the execution. Then we split the 18736 files into 16863 training and 1559 test samples (some of the files were ignored because the code-change environment is not always adequate). Each file is preprocessed from the start until we reach the modified location and additional 10 lines. Note that for fine-tuning we picked the fixed version of the files, so the model only learns refined code and not its previous version. The evaluation samples on the other hand contain the change as well, so it can be compared to the code generated by the model. Since the model takes input sequences of fixed length, we had pad these sequences to be of equal length (2040 tokens). The input is then saved to a file where every line consists of 2040 tokens and it will be fed to the model line-by-line. Keep in mind that the preprocessing steps are different for fine-tuning and prediction depending on whether we are using the model for training or inference.

3   Experiment Setup

3.1   GPT-2

The original Generative Pre-trained Transformer, or in short GPT, model was published in 2018, a descendant and improved version of it is GPT-2 [2]. Its architecture is based on the Transformer, which is an attention model - it learns to focus attention on the previous words that are the most relevant to the task at hand: predicting the next word in the sentence. Since it was designed to generate sentences, it has fixed input and output dimensions. Since it is a statistical architecture, no linguistic information is hardcoded into it. This property allows it to generate not just natural language but source code as well. Although the pre-trained model is suitable for some experimental tasks, it is adviseable in special cases to fine-tune it for downstream tasks.

3.2   Fine-Tuning

Text sequences serve as the input of the GPT-2 model, which is usually plain English text in natural language processing. While fine-tuning the model there is no target like in classic machine learning, the model itself can learn on plain text to generate additional text (while it was trained its goal was to predict the next word in a sequence). In this paper the models input is a simple text file but instead of natural language we train on source code.

In our experiments we used HugginFace [14] implementation of the pre-trained GPT-2 model. It was used in two scenarios: generation without and with fine-runing. The fine-tuning took place on an Nvidia GeForce RTX 3090 with batch size of 7 due to the limited GPU memory. Fine-tuning took 3 h and 13 min. As tokenizer we used GPT-2 pretrained tokenizer with additional tokens: bos_token= '<—startoftext—>, eos_token= '<—endoftext—>', pad_token= '<—pad—>'. For the training we built a custom pytorch dataset and used it for our custom data loader. As optimizer we used AdamW optimizer and used linear learning rate scheduler with warmup (warmup_steps = 1e2, total_steps = len(train_dataloader)

Table 1. Results of the GPT-2 model to generate patches automatically. The upper table shows the results of the fine-tuned model and the lower table shows the results of the pre-trained model. In each generation the model created a list of patches. We considered the generations in an accumulative fashion: if we consider the first generation and the Top_1 result, only one patch is examined, in contrast in the fifth generation there are five candidate patches (one patch per generation). In this sense, the Top_1 results in the fifth generation includes 5 candidate patches. The abbreviations used are the following: EM - Exact Match, ED_N - Edit Distance within the range N (candidates with character differences less than N). For example in the upper left corner 8.08% means that the fine-tuned model was able to generate identical patches to the target in 8.08%(126/1559) in the first generation as first candidate.

| | GPT-2 fine-tuned | | | | | | | | |
| | Top_1 | | | Top_5 | | | Top_{10} | | |
Generation	# EM	# ED_5	ED_{10}	# EM	# ED_5	ED_{10}	# EM	# ED_5	ED_{10}
#1	8.08%	10.71%	11.61%	12.89%	16.23%	17.7%	13.73%	17.32%	19.24%
#2	8.98%	11.61%	12.51%	14.24%	17.77%	19.31%	15.2%	19.05%	21.17%
#3	9.69%	12.44%	13.53%	15.14%	18.92%	20.78%	16.36%	20.53%	23.16%
#4	9.81%	12.63%	13.73%	15.59%	19.5%	21.49%	16.87%	21.3%	24.12%
#5	9.94%	13.09%	14.18%	15.91%	20.4%	22.45%	17.25%	22.45%	25.53%
	GPT-2 pre-trained								
#1	0.64%	1.15%	2.5%	1.22%	1.86%	5.52%	1.48%	2.25%	7.12%
#2	0.71%	1.41%	3.08%	1.28%	2.37%	6.86%	1.54%	2.82%	8.92%
#3	0.77%	1.48%	3.78%	1.35%	2.69%	8.21%	1.67%	3.34%	10.78%
#4	0.83%	1.67%	4.17%	1.41%	2.95%	9.17%	1.73%	3.66%	11.93%
#5	0.83%	1.67%	4.17%	1.41%	2.95%	9.17%	1.73%	3.66%	11.93%

* epochs). As early stopping parameter we used patience 3. We set 100 as maximum number of epochs. Additional parameters of the GPT-2 model: top_k=50, top_p=0.8, do_sample=True, max_length=1024, num_return_sequences=1.

3.3   Patch Generation

First we expanded the GPT-2 models generate function so that the function returns a list of lines of the generated code without the input given to the model. For every bug we called this generate function 10 times which means we generated 10 patches for every input sample. The expanded generate function returns 124 tokens each time it is being called, thus the number of generated lines varies by sample and generation. In every generation we compared each generated line to our target text, which means for every bug we have 10*x candidate one-liner patches, where x corresponds to the generated 124 tokens divided by the number of line separators in our generated text. By doing so we ended up with a lot of candidates, but in an ordered manner: the first line in the first generation is treated as the "first guess of the model", so it has a privilege in some sense. As we move forward in generations and lines, the less focus is on the candidate. This patch generation process is executed for both the pre-trained and the fine-tuned model which are evaluated separately. In the next sections we compare the results in more details.

4   Results

In the previous section we described how we created candidate files for each bug. The evaluation of the results was based on these candidate text files where all candidates can be found for each bug. We compared each of these candidate patches to the target text by edit distance.

In this section we are going to compare the results of the pre-trained and the fine-tuned version of the model then analyze the results manually. The model, the preprocessing and the generation of the candidates are essentially the same, the only difference is whether we are using fine-tuning or not. Before our experiment we expected the fine-tuned model to be much more effective and we also supposed that the fine-tuned version was going to be a lot better in predicting variable names as well.

```
//2
rendererSync=require('
    ./extend').
    rendererSync.list()
//113
queryParams=util.
    parseQueryParams(
    location.search)
//115
it('should invoke the
    callback 404',
    function(done)
//180
expect(console.log.
    calledWith(sinon.
    match('Name'))).be.
    true;
//261
fs.readdirSync(
    __dirname + '/../
    controllers').
    forEach(function(
    name){
//354
for (let i = 0, len =
    args.length; i <
    len; i++) {
```

```
//2
let renderer = renderer
    .render.init()

//113
var errors = error.
    errors();

//115
it('should invoke the
    callback when
    complete', function
    (done){
//180
console.log('Called')


//261
module.exports.forEach
    = function(name,
    data) {



//354
if (args.length > 0) {
```

Listing 1: Examples of correct fixes generated by the fine-tuned GPT-2 model (left) and fixes for these samples generated by the pre-trained model (right).

For our quantitative evaluation we used edit distance. Our strictest condition was to generate identical patches, in this case we didn't accept patches that would be identical without white spaces. We evaluated the results with different edit distances so that we can see how close were our candidates to the correct patch. For both cases (pre-trained and fine-tuned model) we generated patches for one bug 5 times and considered each generated line as a candidate. The results are aggregated by generations so in each following generation there are greater or equal number of correct patches, it is also obvious that the more generations we use the less likely we are to find new additional correct patches (for example after the first generation we are more likely to find correct patches than after the 4th generation).

```
//12
if (2 == arguments.
    length) {
//213
register('data');
//214
if (browser) {
//720
else {
//914
'',
//1097
app.get('/movie',
    function(req, res){
```

```
//12
return this;
//213
''
//214
} : () => {
//720
else {
//914
{
//1097
NULL
```

Listing 2: Examples of correct patches generated by the pre-trained model (left) and fixes for these samples generated by the fine-tuned model (right)

Observing Table 1 we can clearly see that the fine-tuned model performed much better than the pre-trained one (upper table: fine-tuned, lower table pre-trained). The pre-trained model was able to generate 10 correct patches in the first generation and the first line, while the fine-tuned model was able to generate 126 correct patches in the first generation and the first line. As we mentioned earlier the results are aggregated by generation so in each generation the number of found identical patches can not be less than before. From the two observed tables we can also see that the total generated identical patches are 27 for the pre-trained model and 269 for the fine-tuned one. We can also observe that the less strict we are concerning the number of candidate lines per generation the better results we get. It is also clear that the more additional candidate lines we consider per generation better the results get. As we stated above we generate more than just the first line after the input code snippet given to our model (these are the candidate lines) despite the location of the one-liner bug is right after the input code snippet. Because gpt-2 is capable of understanding the input code snippet the first candidate line is the most likely to be a correct patch and as we check for later candidate lines the less likely the model is to generate the identical patch.

Next we analyze the generated patches manually and we are going to see that both the pre-trained and the fine-tuned model are really good at generating correct variable names and human readable error messages, although the fine-tuned model can generate more complex patches. On **Listing 1** we can see the identical candidate patches generated by the fine-tuned model compared to the fixes generated by the pre-trained model. Among these correct patches we can see that the fine-tuned version was able to generate more complex identical (to the target) patches than the pre-trained one. Both the pre-trained and the fine-tuned model can predict correct variable names, and there are also examples of the fine-tuned model generating human readable error messages. On **Listing 2** we can find the identical fixes of the pre-trained model compared to the fixes generated by the fine-tuned model. It seems like that the pre-trained model only generated easy fixes (i.e. short patches). Interestingly the fine-tuned model seems to "over learn" on these simple cases. In future research we plan to investigate it in more details. On the other hand on **Listing 3** we listed only incorrect patches generated by the pre-trained model, but as can be seen they are really close to the target. As we described earlier our evaluation was strict so we didn't consider these patches correct. Knowing the fact that the pre-trained model was not trained on any hexo (JS project) files, we can state that the reason for generating so accurate regular expressions (bug 37) is not data leakage. Note that the patches generated by the pre-trained model make sense in most of the cases, even a developer cannot decide whether it is correct or not without knowing the context.

```
//37
var rSwigVar = /\{[\s\S]*?\}\}/g;              //Pre-trained
var rSwigComment = /\\{#[\\s\\S]*?#\\}/g;      //Fine-tuned
var rSwigComment = /\{#[\s\S]*?#\}/g;          //Target
//270
Resolver.prototype.resolveTarget=function() // pre-trained
Resolver.prototype.getDependencies=function() // fine-
    tuned
Resolver.prototype.getDependencies=function() // target
//1065
app.get('/error', function(err, res){ // pre-trained
app.get('/error', function(req, res){ // fine-tuned
app.get('/error', function(req, res){ // target
//1096
var paths = require('path'); // pre-trained
var pathspec = require('pathspec'); // fine-tuned
var pathspec = require('pathspec'); // target
```

Listing 3: Patches generated by the observed models that are nearly identical to the developer change.

5   Related Work

In this work we used our own dataset to create the train-test-evaluation set of data for our model, although there are others available. Defects4J [16] is a popular dataset consisting 395 Java bugs. The ManyBugs [19] dataset contains bugs written in C - they were used to evaluate many well-known APR tools (Genprog [29], Prophet [20], etc.). Bugs.jar [26] is another well-known dataset, which is comprised of 1,158 Java bugs and their patches. Hovewer, despite their popularity, none of the aforementioned datasets contain bugs for JavaScript. The seminal work of Tufano *et al.* [28] includes the creation of a dataset for Java program repair and evaluation an NMT (Neural Machine Translation) model on it. This work is also included in the CodeXGLUE benchmark [21] which includes a collection of code intelligence tasks and a platform for model evaluation and comparison. The CodeXGLUE team also operate a leaderboard of the best-performing tools, where an approach called NSEdit [30] comes first at the time of writing this paper.

NSEdit [30] is a pre-trained, transformer based encoder-decoder model that predicts an editing sequence that can fix bugs. The encoder parts are initialized using weights from the pre-trained CodeBERT [7] model, while the decoder weights are initialized using CodeGPT [21]. They achieve an astonishing result of 24.04% fix rate on the small -, and 13.87% on the medium CodeXGLUE [21] dataset.

In this paper our aim was to use the GPT-2 [2] architecture to repair bugs automatically. While we did not achieve state-of-the-art results (although hard to compare because of the lack of publicly available datasets), to the best of our knowledge we used this model for this task first. In the previously mentioned CodeXGLUE benchmark [21] the capabilities of GPT were also utilized. They used their CodeGPT model for several tasks, including code completion. In fact, CodeGPT achieved an overall score of 71.28 in this task. Although these results are state-of-the-art performances, in the papers the GPT model was not used for Automated Program Repair.

Since the original article of GPT-2, several works have investigated the capabilities and limits of the model [32]. Thanks to its availability the internet is full of examples of the amazing generative capabilities of the model, from poetry, news or essay writing [6]. Despite the fact that the latest descendant of the GPT model family writes better than many people [25], they were used less for software engineering tasks. In a recent work the authors introduce Text2App [13], that allows users to create functional Android applications from natural language specifications.

In this paper we investigate whether it is useful to fine-tune GPT-2 for code repair task or not and we compare our results with one of our previous work which is about generating patches with the fine-tuned GPT-2 model [17].

6   Conclusions

Although it is known from the literature that GPT-2 can be used for coherent natural text generation without fine-tuning, it is little known whether its source code generation capabilities improve significantly when it is fine-tuned or not. To follow up on this issue, we evaluated both the pre-trained (non fine-tuned) and the fine-tuned GPT-2 model on a dataset that has been created from Github commits. The fine-tuned model was trained on 16863 JavaScript samples, while the pre-trained model was used out-of-the-box. The models were evaluated on the same set of test samples, and it turned out that both are able to generate syntactically and semantically correct source code. While the fine-tuned model was able to correctly refine 126 programs on first try, the pre-trained model was only be able to refine programs correctly in 10 cases. When both models had multiple chances to generate patches, the fine-tuned generated correct pathes in 269 cases, while the pre-trained in 27 cases. Although the GPT-2 model was designed for Natural Language processing and its training data mostly consists of natural language texts, based on the results, we can conclude that without fine-tuning it is still able to generate source code as well. On the other hand, it seems that fine-tuning it to this downstream task boosts its performance significantly, thus in this special case it did worth the extra computational power. We also concluded that both the pre-trained and the fine-tuned model are effective for using existing variable names, creating human readable error messages and creating reasonable complex regular expressions.

Acknowledgements. The research presented in this paper was supported in part by the ÚNKP-21-3-SZTE and ÚNKP-21-5-SZTE New National Excellence Programs, by Project no. TKP2021-NVA-09 and by the Artificial Intelligence National Laboratory Programme of the Ministry of Innovation and the National Research, Development and Innovation Office, financed under the TKP2021-NVA funding scheme. László Vidács was also funded by the János Bolyai Scholarship of the Hungarian Academy of Sciences.

References

1. Ahmad, W., Chakraborty, S., Ray, B., Chang, K.W.: Unified Pre-training for Program Understanding and Generation, pp. 2655–2668, March 2021. https://doi.org/10.18653/v1/2021.naacl-main.211
2. Radford, A., Wu, J., Child, R., Luan, D., Dario Amodei, I.S.: [GPT-2] Language Models are Unsupervised Multitask Learners. OpenAI Blog **1** 1–7 (2020)
3. Csuvik, V., Horvath, D., Horvath, F., Vidacs, L.: Utilizing source code embeddings to identify correct patches. In: 2020 IEEE 2nd International Workshop on Intelligent Bug Fixing (IBF), pp. 18–25. IEEE (2020). https://doi.org/10.1109/IBF50092.2020.9034714
4. Dinella, E., et al.: Hoppity: Learning Graph Transformations To Detect and Fix Bugs in Programs. Tech. rep. (2020)
5. Drain, D., Wu, C., Svyatkovskiy, A., Sundaresan, N.: Generating bug-fixes using pretrained transformers. In: MAPS 2021 - Proceedings of the 5th ACM SIGPLAN International Symposium on Machine Programming, co-located with PLDI 2021, pp. 1–8, June 2021. https://doi.org/10.1145/3460945.3464951

6. Elkins, K., Chun, J.: Can GPT-3 pass a writer's turing test? J. Cultural Analy. (2020). https://doi.org/10.22148/001c.17212

7. Feng, Z., et al.: Codebert: a pre-trained model for programming and natural languages (2020). https://doi.org/10.48550/ARXIV.2002.08155, https://arxiv.org/abs/2002.08155

8. Gazzola, L., Micucci, D., Mariani, L.: Automatic software repair: a survey. IEEE Trans. Software Eng. **45**(1), 34–67 (2019). https://doi.org/10.1109/TSE.2017.2755013

9. Luca, G., Micucci Daniela, M.L.: Automatic software repair: a survey. IEEE Trans. Soft. Eng. **45**(1), 34–67 (2019). https://doi.org/10.1109/TSE.2017.2755013

10. The 2020 state of the octoverse (2021). https://octoverse.github.com

11. Gitpython home (2021). https://gitpython.readthedocs.io/en/stable/

12. Gyimesi, P., et al.: BugsJS: a benchmark of javascript bugs. In: Proceedings - 2019 IEEE 12th International Conference on Software Testing, Verification and Validation, ICST 2019, pp. 90–101 (April 2019). https://doi.org/10.1109/ICST.2019.00019

13. Hasan, M., Mehrab, K.S., Ahmad, W.U., Shahriyar, R.: Text2App: A Framework for Creating Android Apps from Text Descriptions (2021)

14. Hugging face website (2022). https://huggingface.co

15. Jiang, N., Lutellier, T., Tan, L.: CURE: code-aware neural machine translation for automatic program repair, pp. 1161–1173, May 2021

16. Just, R., Jalali, D., Ernst, M.D.: Defects4J: a database of existing faults to enable controlled testing studies for Java programs. In: 2014 International Symposium on Software Testing and Analysis. ISSTA 2014 - Proceedings, pp. 437–440. Association for Computing Machinery, Inc., July 2014

17. Lajko, M., Csuvik, V., Vidacs, L.: Towards JavaScript program repair with generative Pre-rained transformer (GPT-2). In: 2022 3rd International Workshop on Automated Program Repair (APR 2022). ACM Press (2022)

18. Le, X.B.D., Thung, F., Lo, D., Goues, C.L.: Overfitting in semantics-based automated program repair. Empir. Softw. Eng. **23**(5), 3007–3033 (2018). https://doi.org/10.1007/s10664-017-9577-2

19. Le Goues, C., et al.: The ManyBugs and IntroClass Benchmarks for automated repair of C Programs. IEEE Trans. Soft. Eng. **41**(12), 1236–1256 (2015). https://doi.org/10.1109/TSE.2015.2454513

20. Long, F., Rinard, M.: Automatic patch generation by learning correct code. In: Proceedings of the 43rd Annual ACM SIGPLAN-SIGACT Symposium on Principles of Programming Languages - POPL 2016, pp. 298–312 (2016). https://doi.org/10.1145/2837614.2837617

21. Lu, S., et al.: CodeXGLUE: A Machine Learning Benchmark Dataset for Code Understanding and Generation. undefined (2021)

22. Lutellier, T., Pham, H.V., Pang, L., Li, Y., Wei, M., Tan, L.: CoCoNuT: Combining context-aware neural translation models using ensemble for program repair. In: ISSTA 2020 - Proceedings of the 29th ACM SIGSOFT International Symposium on Software Testing and Analysis, vol. 20, pp. 101–114 (2020)

23. Phan, L., et al.: CoTexT: Multi-task Learning with Code-Text Transformer, pp. 40–47, May 2021. https://doi.org/10.18653/v1/2021.nlp4prog-1.5

24. Radford, A., Narasimhan, T., Salimans, T., Sutskever, I.: [GPT-1] Improving Language Understanding by Generative Pre-Training. Preprint, pp. 1–12 (2018)

25. Radford, A., et al.: Better Language Models and Their Implications (2019)

26. Saha, R.K., Lyu, Y., Lam, W., Yoshida, H., Prasad, M.R.: Bugs.jar: a large-scale, diverse dataset of real-world Java bugs. In: Proceedings - International Conference on Software Engineering, pp. 10–13 (2018). https://doi.org/10.1145/3196398. 3196473

27. Stack overflow developer survey results (2021). https://insights.stackoverflow.com/survey/2021

28. Tufano, M., Watson, C., Bavota, G., Penta, M.D., White, M., Poshyvanyk, D.: An empirical study on learning bug-fixing patches in the wild via neural machine translation. ACM Trans. Soft. Eng. Methodol. **28**(4), 1–29 (2019). https://doi.org/10.1145/3340544

29. Weimer, W., Nguyen, T., Le Goues, C., Forrest, S.: Automatically finding patches using genetic programming. In: Proceedings of the 31st International Conference on Software Engineering, ICSE 2009, pp. 364–374. IEEE Computer Society, USA (2009). https://doi.org/10.1109/ICSE.2009.5070536

30. Yaojie, H., Xingjian, S., Qiang, Z., Lee, P.: Fix Bugs with Transformer through a Neural-Symbolic Edit Grammar

31. Yi, L., Wang, S., Nguyen, T.N.: Dlfix: context-based code transformation learning for automated program repair. In: Proceedings - International Conference on Software Engineering, pp. 602–614. IEEE Computer Society, June 2020. https://doi.org/10.1145/3377811.3380345

32. Zhao, T.Z., Wallace, E., Feng, S., Klein, D., Singh, S.: Calibrate before use: improving few-shot performance of language models (2021)

33. Zhuang, Y., Cai, M., Li, X., Luo, X., Yang, Q., Wu, F.: The next breakthroughs of artificial intelligence: the interdisciplinary nature of AI. Engineering **6**(3), 245–247 (2020)

Comparing ML-Based Predictions and Static Analyzer Tools for Vulnerability Detection

Norbert Vándor, Balázs Mosolygó, and Péter Hegelűs[✉]

Department of Software Engineering, University of Szeged, Szeged, Hungary
{vandor,mbalazs,hpeter}@inf.u-szeged.hu

Abstract. Finding and eliminating security issues early in the development process is critical as software systems are shaping many aspects of our daily lives. There are numerous approaches for automatically detecting security vulnerabilities in the source code from which static analysis and machine learning based methods are the most popular. However, we lack comprehensive benchmarking of vulnerability detection methods across these two popular categories. In one of our earlier works, we proposed an ML-based line-level vulnerability prediction method with the goal of finding vulnerabilities in JavaScript systems. In this paper, we report results on a systematic comparison of this ML-based vulnerability detection technique with three widely used static checker tools NodeJSScan (https://github.com/ajinabraham/nodejsscan), ESLint (https://eslint.org), and CodeQL (https://codeql.github.com) using the OSSF CVE Benchmark (https://github.com/ossf-cve-benchmark/ossf-cve-benchmark). We found that our method was more than capable of finding vulnerable lines, managing to find 60% of all vulnerabilities present in the examined dataset, which corresponds to the best recall of all tools. Nonetheless, our method had higher false-positive rate and running time than that of the static checkers.

Keywords: Vulnerability detection · ML models · Static analyzers · OSSF benchmark

1 Introduction

Software security is becoming more and more crucial as software systems are shaping many aspects of our daily lives. A seemingly minor programming error

This research was supported by the Ministry of Innovation and Technology of Hungary from the National Research, Development and Innovation Fund, financed under the TKP2021-NVA funding scheme and the framework of the Artificial Intelligence National Laboratory Program (MILAB). Furthermore, Péter Hegelűs was supported by the Bolyai János Scholarship of the Hungarian Academy of Sciences and the ÚNKP-21-5-SZTE-570 New National Excellence Program of the Ministry for Innovation and Technology.

O. Gervasi et al. (Eds.): ICCSA 2022 Workshops, LNCS 13380, pp. 92–105, 2022.
https://doi.org/10.1007/978-3-031-10542-5_7

might turn out to be a serious vulnerability that causes major losses in money or reputation, threatens human lives, or allows attackers to stop vital services or block infrastructure. Therefore, finding and eliminating security issues early in the development process is very important.

Since security testing is very hard and requires lots of expertise and has high costs, automated solutions are highly desirable. There are numerous approaches for detecting security vulnerabilities in the source code from which static analysis [20] and machine learning based methods [11] are the most popular. Even though tools are compared to each other within their categories (static analysis tools with other static analysis tools or ML models with other ML models), we lack comprehensive benchmarking of vulnerability detection methods across categories.

Empirical comparison of ML based vulnerability detection and static analysis tools might bring in useful insights that could help determining if one of the technologies are more beneficial than others, are there categories of security issues that can be detected more effectively with certain technique, or is combining these techniques bring anything performance-wise.

In one of our earlier works [18], we proposed an ML-based line-level vulnerability prediction method with the goal of finding vulnerabilities in JavaScript systems, while being both granular and explainable. Since our method provided favorable results, it was the next natural step to see how it fares against other static analyzers. Therefore, in this paper we report results on a systematic comparison of this ML-based vulnerability detection technique with three widely used static checker tools (NodeJSScan, ESLint, and CodeQL) for identifying vulnerabilities.

As a benchmark, we selected the OpenSSF (OSSF) CVE Benchmark[1] that consists of code and metadata for over 200 real life CVEs[2] It also contains tooling to analyze the vulnerable codebases using a variety of static analysis security testing (SAST) tools and generate reports to evaluate those tools. We extended the benchmark with the integration of our own ML-based prediction tool and evaluated the results on the data contained in the benchmark.

We found that our method was more than capable of finding vulnerable lines, managing to find 60% of all vulnerabilities present in the examined dataset. We also showed that it is capable of finding vulnerabilities that other tools would likely miss, as it has a higher likelihood of finding issues belonging to CWEs[3], which the others find significantly less of. Nonetheless, our method had higher false-positive rate and running time than that of the static checkers.

The rest of the paper is organized as follows. Section 2 describes our ML-based methods, the static analyzer tools and the benchmark we used for comparison. We provided detailed results on the 200 CVEs contained in the benchmark in Sect. 3. We present related literature in Sect. 4 and enumerate the possible threats to our work in Sect. 5. Finally, we conclude the paper in Sect. 6.

---

[1] https://github.com/ossf-cve-benchmark/ossf-cve-benchmark.

[2] Common Vulnerabilities and Exposures, https://www.cve.org.

[3] Common Weakness Enumeration, https://cwe.mitre.org.

2   Approach

Our main goal in this paper is to compare how well a JavaScript line-level ML-based vulnerability prediction method works when compared to classical static analyzer tools for vulnerability detection. Therefore, in this section, we describe the essence of an ML-based vulnerability detection method [18] we developed for identifying vulnerable JavaScript code lines and the benchmark we used for comparing it to other static analysis vulnerability checkers.

2.1   The VulnJS4Line Method

The method we have created aims to detect vulnerable lines in code bases by comparing each one to a preexisting database of known vulnerabilities. The process can be broken up into 2 major parts:

The first part is the creation of the knowledge base, and word2vec[4] model, that will be used to create vectors from the lines in question. This step needs to be executed only once, since the knowledge base can easily be extended after its creation, and the model does not need to be retrained.

The second part is the actual prediction process, during which each line of the system under investigation is tested against each line of the vulnerability database, in order to find the "most similar" vulnerable line. The probability of a line being vulnerable is calculated based on its distance from its closest pair in the database, and some static rules, such as the lines' complexity. If this probability exceeds a certain threshold, we mark it as vulnerable.

During the creation of the results presented in this paper, we used the parameters we found to be most successful during our initial testing.

2.2   OSSF CVE Benchmark

To evaluate our tool, we used the OSSF CVE Benchmark. This project consists of code and metadata for over 200 real life CVEs (belonging to 42 CWEs) from over 200 GitHub projects, while also providing the required tooling to test the performance of static analyzers. Each project contains one CVE and the patch for it; and each CVE affects one file. In total, there are 223 affected files, which translates to 222752 lines of code. For proper testing, it is invaluable to use examples from real life, rather than synthetic test code.

How It Works. The benchmark uses drivers to run the different tools on all CVEs, both pre- and post-patch, then determines two things: 1) was the tool able to detect the vulnerability, or did it produce a false negative? 2) when ran against the patched codebase, did it recognize the patch, or did it produce a false positive? After the run, all drivers generate reports, which then the benchmark parses and presents as an HTML or text file. In the report made by the benchmark, one can see certain statistics, such as the number of correctly identified

---

[4] https://radimrehurek.com/gensim/models/word2vec.html.

vulnerabilities and the number of correctly recognized patches. Besides these, there is also the file containing the vulnerabilities, with icons denoting which tool flagged which line and for what reason.

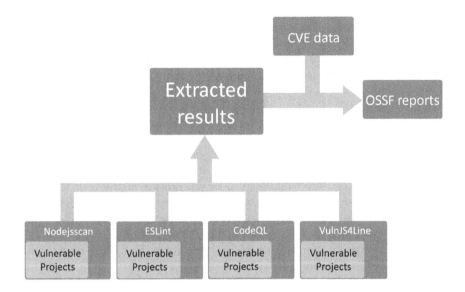

Fig. 1. A vizualization of the benchmarking process

VulnJS4Line Driver. For our own tool, we had to write a driver file in Type-Script, whose main function is to run the tool, collect the output, and produce a report compatible with the benchmark. First, the driver runs our tool on the project folder the benchmark has provided for a specific CVE. To be able to do this, we had to upgrade our tool to accept folders as input, and search for and check all JavaScript files inside them. For easier handling of outputs, we also added the option to get the results as a JSON file. To get the best results, we set the parameters to those that we outlined during our previous work. In other words, we used the SpecialValues model with 92% using the prefer_complex rule.

After this, the driver collects the results and creates an output JSON file. The files read by the benchmark must contain pairs of data: the first element is the rule the CVE violates, and the second element is a location consisting of the path to the file and the line the vulnerability is in. The rules are, in other words, the reason why a tool flags a certain line. For us, it's the lexed version of the line the CVE is the most similar to. And finally, the output file is passed to the benchmark, which stores it.

2.3   Other Tools in the Benchmark

We used three different static analyzers to which we compared our method. All of them, including the necessary drivers, were provided by the benchmark.

NodeJSScan is an open source static code scanner used to find security flaws specifically in Node.js applications. It is a user interface built upon njsscan[5], a command-line interface that uses regex-based pattern matching to find bugs and enforce code standards.

ESLint[6] is a static code analysis tool for identifying problematic patterns found in JavaScript code. It can be used for both code quality and coding style issues. It supports the current standards for ECMAScript, and is also able to analyze TypeScript code. ESLint is the most commonly used JavaScript linter.

CodeQL[7] is a semantic code analysis engine, which lets users query code as it was data. First, CodeQL has to create a relational database from each source file in the codebase by monitoring compiler activity and extracting relevant information in the case of compiled languages, or simply running the extractor directly on the source code to resolve dependencies in the case of interpreted languages. The database contains a full hierarchical representation of the code, including the abstract syntax tree, the data flow graph, and the control flow graph. Then it uses queries to find specific issues in the code. It achieves that by performing variant analysis, which is the process of identifying "seed vulnerabilities"- in other words, an already known security vulnerability - and using them to find similar problems in the code.

2.4 Statistics for the Comparison

As presented in Sect. 3, the three main statistics we were interested in were prediction quality, the time required to analyze a project and the most detected vulnerability types. To get the necessary data for these statistics, we had to extract some extra information that is not normally used in the reports the benchmark generates. While the reports contain a list of lines the tools flagged as vulnerable, to create the statistics regarding the average number of flagged lines, we also had to get the total number of lines in a file. Fortunately, this is included in the source of the benchmarking tool, along with important information regarding the CVEs.

After getting the average statistics, the next step was to create the time statistics. Unfortunately, the benchmark does not provide a conventional way to measure the time required for each tool. To remedy this, we analyzed the console logs produced by the benchmark. Before running a tool, the benchmark prints a crucial piece of information for us: the timestamp for when it will shut a running tool down. In other words, since we know that a tool will timeout after exactly 30 min, we could measure how long it ran based on the previously mentioned timestamps.

---

[5] https://github.com/ajinabraham/njsscan.

[6] https://eslint.org.

[7] https://codeql.github.com.

For the third statistic, as mentioned, we did have all information regarding CVEs, including their CWEs, which we were interested in. However, to determine whether a tool properly found a certain CWE, we also needed to check if it flagged a relevant line - this information is provided in the reports. So to create this statistic, we simply counted how many relevant flags were produced for each CVE, and from that we could check which CWE it belongs to.

3 Results

In this section, we will discuss the performance of our approach compared to three well-established and widely used static analysis tools, when it comes to detecting vulnerabilities. We have selected 3 metrics to showcase here in order to properly demonstrate the potential of our approach. These metrics are what we believe to be the most important when it comes to usability.

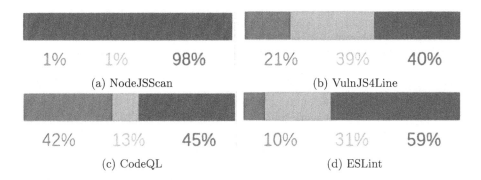

Fig. 2. Visualization of the tools' performances

3.1 Prediction Quality

When it comes to usability, the most important property of a vulnerability detection tool is its ability to produce accurate results.

As mentioned in 2 the OSSF CVE Benchmark checks whether a method flags a vulnerable lines before and after it has been patched or not. In an optimal scenario, a method would only mark actually vulnerable lines as vulnerable, however that is unfortunately not the case in most situations. In many cases the tools detect potentially faulty lines based on characteristics that do not change after the actual issue has been fixed, and as such continue to flag the lines as vulnerable, even after it has been dealt with.

The results shown in Fig. 2 demonstrate the above point. Percentage of perfect cases, where the line is only marked before a fix has been issued is represented in green, while orange represents cases where a line has been marked both before and after the related issue has been dealt with. Naturally, red represents the lines that were never marked as vulnerable.

We can see, that our method finds the most lines overall, while perfectly handling the second most lines, outperforming both NodeJSScan and ESLint by a significant margin when it comes to both metrics. CodeQL finds less vulnerable lines overall, however stops flagging most of them after they have been fixed.

We consider our results to be the second best, when it comes to this measure of predictive quality, since our method correctly handles more than twice as many vulnerabilities as ESLint does. However, the amount of "orange" or partially handled vulnerabilities is a cause for concern, since it is a sign of a higher false positive rate. Technically, in this metric, our method is outdone by NodeJSScan, since that tool fully handles half of the lines it finds, meaning that only half of the vulnerabilities will be marked after they have been fixed. We still would not consider this to be the second best result in this area, because the low probability of NodeJSScan actually finding a vulnerability would still lead to a user that solely depends on the tool missing a large majority of issues.

A similar metric, unfortunately omitted by the benchmarking tool, is the amount of lines flagged by each tool overall. The tool only measures the false positive rate of the methods in question in relation to finding vulnerabilities, but not their overarching performance, when it comes to marking lines. This means, that a method, that flags every line, would achieve a 100% "orange" rating.

As we can see in Fig. 3 on average, our method flags the most lines, followed by ESLint. The average examined file is approximately 1000 lines long, getting a bit longer post patch, meaning that while our method performs the worst, it still only flags about 10% of all lines. While this is a major issue when it comes to usability, since a large false positive rate can render a tool completely useless in a commercial setting where development time is a key asset, with manageable improvements, our tool could compete with a widespread solution such as ESLint.

3.2   Time Requirement

The effectiveness of a vulnerability detection tool can be greatly improved, if it is runnable in real time, during the process of writing code, or even in a just in time fashion, after a commit is created. The sooner a developer is notified about a potential issue, the easier it is to double check the results, and discard false positives. Even if a method is capable of producing high quality results, a massive time requirement can still hinder its large scale adoption. This metric is unfortunately omitted from the OSSF CVE Benchmark.

As we can see in Fig. 4 our method takes 6 min on average to create a set of results, while the overall best performing tool CodeQL takes a little over a minute. This is a major blow to the possibility of practical use, when it comes to our method. Improvements could still be made, since the tested version was

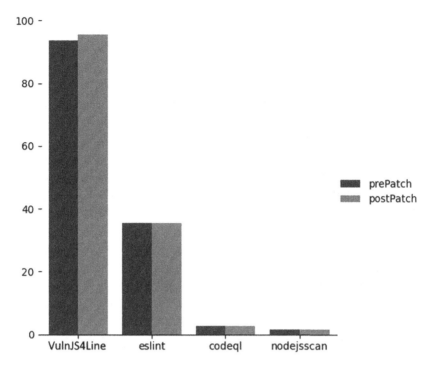

Fig. 3. Average number of lines marked per file

written in Python, a language generally known for its poor performance, when it comes to computation speed. Since the theoretical complexity of our method is low, it is possible, that with major technical improvements, it could become competitive, with its widely used counterparts.

3.3 Most Detected Vulnerability Type

Related literature [2, 10, 13, 14] agrees that static analyzers are performing better when it comes to finding SQL Injection and XSS related vulnerabilities. We investigated, whether our method showed similar preferences, when it came to finding different vulnerability types, or not.

As mentioned in Sect. 2.4 the Benchmark we used contains the CWE[8] categories of the vulnerabilities in question.

In Table 1 we showcase the CWEs that showed significant performance gaps between the tools, while having over 10 occurrences. Our main goal with presenting these results is not to show differences in the tools' capabilities, rather to point out potential areas, where one may be preferable. For this reason, we omit information about vulnerability types that rarely appear, or those where the tools' performance is similar.

---

[8] Common Weakness Enumeration.

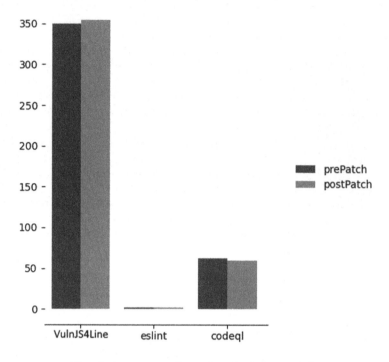

Fig. 4. Average runtime of methods in seconds

We do not showcase the results produced by NodeJSScan, since it marks too few lines, for its performance to be comparable, when it comes to finding different vulnerability types.

SQL Injection and Cross Site Scripting. Despite our notion of only showcasing CWEs with a relevant presence, we include CWE-94 even though it appears only 4 times in the dataset. CWE-89 is the id given to SQL Injection related vulnerabilities, and as such its inclusion is warranted.[9] We can see, that none of the tools manage to find a significant number of lines containing issues of this category.

Cross-site scripting or XSS related vulnerabilities, with the CWE id of 79, also do not present outstanding numbers, in this context.[10] We can see, that out of the portrayed tools, even the highest performing one, does not reach 50% detection rate.

---

[9] https://cwe.mitre.org/data/definitions/89.html.
[10] https://cwe.mitre.org/data/definitions/79.html.

Table 1. The amount of CWEs found by three of the tested tools

	CWE-78	CWE-79	CWE-88	CWE-89	CWE-94	CWE-116	CWE-400	CWE-730	CWE-915
VulnJS4Line	70%	37%	72%	25%	58%	22%	56%	55%	65%
CodeQL	40%	44%	44%	25%	35%	52%	32%	27%	35%
ESLint	55%	40%	16%	0%	78%	17%	62%	27%	95%

In view of the above mentioned results, we conclude, that in this context, the tools do not perform as previous research would indicate. As seen in Sect. 4.2 these 2 vulnerability types are the ones that are generally found with the highest success rate.

3.4 Key Differences Between the Observed Performance of the Methods

Our method performs outstandingly well, when it comes to CWE-78 (OS Command Injection), CWE-88 (Argument Injection) and CWE-730 (vulnerability related to A9 Denial of Service). It is important to point out, that while in all of these cases, our method manages to find over half of all vulnerabilities present, while the other tools struggle to get above the half way mark, except for ESLint, in the case of CWE-78. In the case of CWE-730, our method manages to find over twice as many vulnerable lines as the other two, while in the other 2 cases, it manages to gather over 70% of the lines related to the issue at hand.

When it is not the highest performing approach, it still does not fall too far behind, providing similar results, to at least one of the tools.

We can also see, that in multiple cases one tool clearly outperforms the rest, especially in the cases of CWE-915 and CWE-116. This is effect has been previously observed in different environments, and leads to th suggestion of using multiple solutions, that have clear, differing strength in tandem, to achieve an overall boosted performance.

Since out method performs distinctly better in areas, the other examined tools falter, it might have place as a specialist tool, when it comes to finding certain kinds of issues.

4   Related Work

Numerous works have been created to either compare vulnerability scanners, check the effectiveness of static analyzers, and to check the validity of benchmarks.

4.1 Effectiveness of the Static Analyzers

V. Benjamin Livshits and Monica S. Lam [15] formulated a general class of security errors in Java programs. Using these they were able to create a precise and scalable static analysis tool that was capable of finding security vulnerabilities such as XSS, SQLI, HTTP split attacks and more.

Nathaniel Ayewah et al. [6] created and evaluated FindBugs. A static software analysis tool capable of not only finding generic bugs, but security vulnerabilities such as SQL injections.

Katerina Goseva-Popstojanova and Andrei Perhinschi [12] evaluated 3 static analysis tools in the context of C/C++ and Java. They found that a significant portion of vulnerabilities was missed by all three tools, and less then half of the vulnerabilities were found by all three, in both environments.

Elisa Burato et al. [7] were able to create Julia, a static analyzer tool capable of finding 90% of security issues present in the OWASP benchmark, greatly outperforming previous scanners.

4.2   Comparing Vulnerability Scanners

S. El Idrissi et al. [13] found, during their evaluation of multiple vulnerability scanners, that the performance of each scanner differs for different vulnerability types. They found, that the scanners were more effective at finding SQLI and XSS related issues.

Jose Fonseca et al. [10] compared the performance of three commercially used scanning tools, when it came to finding SQLI and XSS related issues. They found that the tested methods produced high false positive rates and relatively low coverage.

Chanchala Joshi and Umesh Kumar Singh [14] also found, that vulnerability scanners are more successful at detecting SQLI and XSS related faults in code.

Mansour Alsaleh et al. [1] examined multiple open source web vulnerability scanners using an approach that allowed evaluation from multiple angles. They found that, while overall there were only minor differences between the performance of each scanner, there was considerable variance when it came to both the type and number of detected vulnerabilities in each tools' results.

Nataša Šuteva et al. [22] tested 6 web vulnerability scanners on the WackoPicko app. The scanners found similar amounts of vulnerabilities, all with a high false positive and false negative rates.

Balume Mburano and Weisheng Si [17] compared not only the performance of different scanners, but 2 different benchmarking tools as well. They found, that using multiple benchmarks to evaluate scanners provides a more accurate picture of their performance. They also found that no scanner can be considered as an all-rounder, since each performs differently in for different vulnerability types.

Andreq Austin and Lauries Williams [5] found that automated penetration testing found more vulnerabilities per hour than static analysis tools, however manual testing was still more effective.

Nuno Antunes and Marco Vieira [2] also investigated the differences between penetration testing and static code analysis. They found, that when it came to detecting SQL Injection related vulnerabilities static analyzers outperformed their counterparts. They also note, that even tools implementing the same approach to finding issues, might present different results.

Malaka El et al. [9] benchmarked automatic vulnerability detection tools for SCADA devices and scientific instruments. They found that not only did the tools find different vulnerability types with differing efficiency, but their scalability also varied. They propose the idea of using multiple analysis tools in tandem, in order to achieve better results.

4.3   Benchmarks

Creating powerful bechmarking tools even in itself is a challenge.

Valentin Dallmeier and Thomas Zimmermann [8] proposed a technique that allows the automatic collection of successes and failures from a projects history in order to create a large set of benchmarking data.

Reza M. Parizi et al. [16] created a set of guidelines for benchmarking projects.

Nuno Antunes and Marco Vieira [3,4] created a benchmark for web services focusing on SQL Injection related vulnerabilities.

Ivan Pashchenko et al. [19] created a benchmark that aims to reproduce real world scenarios through the use of automatically generated test cases based on prior vulnerability fixes in Open Source software repositories.

Hui-zhong Shi et al. [21] propose a generic framework of Web security evaluation.

5   Threats to Validity

Our evaluation depends on the quality of the data contained in the OSSF benchmark. However, it is manually collected and adopted by other researchers as well, therefore, it poses minor threats to the validity of our conclusions.

We compare a single ML-based method with three different static analysis tools. Therefore, our conclusions might not generalize to other ML-based techniques. Nonetheless, it already gives a first insight into how these different techniques compare to each other for vulnerability detection. However, further studies in this area is needed.

The only evaluation metrics integrated into the OSSF Benchmark are whether a tool marks the vulnerable code lines before the vulnerability is fixed and if they stop reporting it after the fix. However, if a tool marks all lines of a program as being vulnerable, it would get perfect score for the first metric. Therefore, meaningful comparison needs additional evaluation metrics. To mitigate this, we implemented and extended the benchmark measurements with the count of the number of flagged lines as well as the time required for detecting a vulnerability.

6   Conclusion

In this paper we presented the benchmarking results of a tool we created for the purpose of creating line level, explainable vulnerability predictions. For this purpose we used the OSSF CVE Benchmark, that not only provided an opportunity to test our method in a realistic environment, but to directly compare its capabilities to other, widely used, industry level tools.

We found that our method was more than capable of finding vulnerable lines, managing to find 60% of all vulnerabilities present in the examined dataset. We also showed that it is capable of finding vulnerabilities that other tools would likely miss, as it has a higher likelihood of finding issues belonging to CWEs, which the others find significantly less of.

However, it is limited by two factors. One is its high computation time, taking significantly longer to run, than any of the other examined tools. The other, is its high false positive rate. It flags over twice as many lines as its competitors.

In the future, we plan on reducing the time it takes for the method to run its checks, by heuristically reducing the number of examined lines, and possibly re-implementing it in a language more fit for fast calculations. Before these steps, it is most important to reduce its false positive rate, since we see that as the main limiting factor.

References

1. Alsaleh, M., Alomar, N., Alshreef, M., Alarifi, A., Al-Salman, A.: Performance-based comparative assessment of open source web vulnerability scanners. Sec. Commun. Netw. **2017**, 1–14 (2017)
2. Antunes, N., Vieira, M.: Comparing the effectiveness of penetration testing and static code analysis on the detection of sql injection vulnerabilities in web services. In: 2009 15th IEEE Pacific Rim International Symposium on Dependable Computing, pp. 301–306 (2009). https://doi.org/10.1109/PRDC.2009.54
3. Antunes, N., Vieira, M.: Benchmarking vulnerability detection tools for web services. In: 2010 IEEE International Conference on Web Services, pp. 203–210 (2010). https://doi.org/10.1109/ICWS.2010.76
4. Antunes, N., Vieira, M.: Assessing and comparing vulnerability detection tools for web services: benchmarking approach and examples. IEEE Trans. Serv. Comput. **8**(2), 269–283 (2015). https://doi.org/10.1109/TSC.2014.2310221
5. Austin, A., Williams, L.: One technique is not enough: a comparison of vulnerability discovery techniques. In: 2011 International Symposium on Empirical Software Engineering and Measurement, pp. 97–106 (2011). https://doi.org/10.1109/ESEM.2011.18
6. Ayewah, N., Pugh, W., Hovemeyer, D., Morgenthaler, J.D., Penix, J.: Using static analysis to find bugs. IEEE Softw. **25**(5), 22–29 (2008). https://doi.org/10.1109/MS.2008.130
7. Burato, E., Ferrara, P., Spoto, F.: Security analysis of the OWASP benchmark with julia. In: Proceedings of ITASEC 2017 (2017)

8. Dallmeier, V., Zimmermann, T.: Extraction of bug localization benchmarks from history. In: Proceedings of the Twenty-Second IEEE/ACM International Conference on Automated Software Engineering, ASE 2007, pp. 433–436. Association for Computing Machinery, New York (2007). https://doi.org/10.1145/1321631.1321702, https://doi.org/10.1145/1321631.1321702

9. El, M., McMahon, E., Samtani, S., Patton, M., Chen, H.: Benchmarking vulnerability scanners: an experiment on scada devices and scientific instruments. In: 2017 IEEE International Conference on Intelligence and Security Informatics (ISI), pp. 83–88 (2017). https://doi.org/10.1109/ISI.2017.8004879

10. Fonseca, J., Vieira, M., Madeira, H.: Testing and comparing web vulnerability scanning tools for sql injection and xss attacks. In: 13th Pacific Rim International Symposium on Dependable Computing (PRDC 2007), pp. 365–372 (2007). https://doi.org/10.1109/PRDC.2007.55

11. Ghaffarian, S.M., Shahriari, H.R.: Software vulnerability analysis and discovery using machine-learning and data-mining techniques: a survey. ACM Comput. Surv. (CSUR) 50(4), 1–36 (2017)

12. Goseva-Popstojanova, K., Perhinschi, A.: On the capability of static code analysis to detect security vulnerabilities. Inf. Softw. Technol. 68, 18–33 (2015)

13. Idrissi, S., Berbiche, N., Guerouate, F., Shibi, M.: Performance evaluation of web application security scanners for prevention and protection against vulnerabilities. Int. J. Appl. Eng. Res. 12(21), 11068–11076 (2017)

14. Joshi, C., Singh, U.K.: Performance evaluation of web application security scanners for more effective defense. Int. J. Sci. Res. Publi. (IJSRP) 6(6), 660–667 (2016)

15. Livshits, V.B., Lam, M.S.: Finding security vulnerabilities in java applications with static analysis. In: USENIX security symposium, vol. 14, pp. 18–18 (2005)

16. M. Parizi, R., Qian, K., Shahriar, H., Wu, F., Tao, L.: Benchmark requirements for assessing software security vulnerability testing tools. In: 2018 IEEE 42nd Annual Computer Software and Applications Conference (COMPSAC), vol. 01, pp. 825–826 (2018). https://doi.org/10.1109/COMPSAC.2018.00139

17. Mburano, B., Si, W.: Evaluation of web vulnerability scanners based on owasp benchmark. In: 2018 26th International Conference on Systems Engineering (ICSEng), pp. 1–6 (2018). https://doi.org/10.1109/ICSENG.2018.8638176

18. Mosolygó, B., Vándor, N., Antal, G., Hegelűs, P., Ferenc, R.: Towards a prototype based explainable javascript vulnerability prediction model. In: 1st International Conference on Code Quality, ICCQ 2021, pp. 15–25 (2021)

19. Pashchenko, I., Dashevskyi, S., Massacci, F.: Delta-bench: Differential benchmark for static analysis security testing tools. In: 2017 ACM/IEEE International Symposium on Empirical Software Engineering and Measurement (ESEM), pp. 163–168 (2017). https://doi.org/10.1109/ESEM.2017.24

20. Pistoia, M., Chandra, S., Fink, S.J., Yahav, E.: A survey of static analysis methods for identifying security vulnerabilities in software systems. IBM Syst. J. 46(2), 265–288 (2007). https://doi.org/10.1147/sj.462.0265

21. Shi, H.z., Chen, B., Yu, L.: Analysis of web security comprehensive evaluation tools. In: 2010 Second International Conference on Networks Security, Wireless Communications and Trusted Computing. vol. 1, pp, 285–289 (2010). https://doi.org/10.1109/NSWCTC.2010.72

22. Suteva, N., Zlatkovski, D., Mileva, A.: Evaluation and testing of several free/open source web vulnerability scanners (2013)

A Line-Level Explainable Vulnerability Detection Approach for Java

Balázs Mosolygó[1] , Norbert Vándor[1], Péter Hegedűs[1,2](✉) ,
and Rudolf Ferenc[1]

[1] Software Engineering Department, University of Szeged, Szeged, Hungary
hpeter@inf.u-szeged.hu
[2] FrontEndART Ltd., Szeged, Hungary

Abstract. Given our modern society's level of dependency on IT technology, high quality and security are not just desirable but rather vital properties of current software systems. Empirical methods leveraging the available rich open-source data and advanced data processing techniques of ML algorithms can help software developers ensure these properties. Nonetheless, state-of-the-art bug and vulnerability prediction methods are rarely used in practice due to numerous reasons. The predictions are not actionable in most of the cases due to their level of granularity (i.e., they mark entire classes/files to be buggy or vulnerable) and because the methods seldom provide explanation why a fragment of source code is problematic. In this paper, we present a novel Java vulnerability detection method that addresses both of these issues. It is an adaptation of our previous method for JavaScript that is capable of pinpointing vulnerable source code lines of a program together with a prototype-based explanation. The method relies on the word2vec similarity of code fragments to known vulnerable source code lines. Our empirical evaluation showed promising results, we could detect 61% and 41% of the vulnerable code lines by flagging only 43% and 22% of the program code lines, respectively, using two of the best detection configurations.

Keywords: Software security · Vulnerability prediction · Explainable prediction model · Empirical study

1 Introduction

Software systems have become a fundamental part of our every-day lives. They not only control critical infrastructure (power plants, air traffic, manufacturing)

This research was supported by the Ministry of Innovation and Technology of Hungary from the National Research, Development and Innovation Fund, financed under the TKP2021-NVA funding scheme and the framework of the Artificial Intelligence National Laboratory Program (MILAB). The research was partly supported by the EU-funded project AssureMOSS (Grant no. 952647). Furthermore, Péter Hegedűs was supported by the Bolyai János Scholarship of the Hungarian Academy of Sciences and the ÚNKP-21-5-SZTE-570 New National Excellence Program of the Ministry for Innovation and Technology.

O. Gervasi et al. (Eds.): ICCSA 2022 Workshops, LNCS 13380, pp. 106–122, 2022.
https://doi.org/10.1007/978-3-031-10542-5_8

or handle and store sensitive data (bank card details, health records, personal documents) but serve our convenience as well (smart TV, smart watches, smart homes, etc.).

The abundance of research results in the area promises a decent practical solution for managing bugs and security issues at the development phase (i.e. before the system goes public). Bug and vulnerability prediction models can be used during the development, even integrated within the CI/CD pipelines, to detect problematic or vulnerable code introduced by the developers on-the-fly. Having such an early alarming mechanism could help in fixing critical problems fast in an early phase, before malicious users even have the chance to exploit them.

In this paper, we focus on a line-level vulnerability detection method that is tailored to Java programs, which addresses both of the above mentioned short-comings of existing approaches. The proposed technique builds on, adapts and improves our very promising previous work [10] on detecting vulnerable lines in JavaScript programs together with a prototype based explanation. We use the project KB [14] manually validated vulnerability dataset containing hundreds of vulnerability fixing commits (that can be mapped to a CVE [9] entry) as a basis of creating a set of known vulnerable line repository (VLR). Using the word2vec [8] embedding technique on the lexical tokens of these lines, we build a golden set of vectorized features of vulnerable lines. Then, we scan the sub-ject systems line by line and determine the line in our golden set that is the most similar to the analyzed line. If the cosine distance is below an empirically established threshold, we declare the line to be vulnerable.

To adapt our JavaScript approach to Java, we had to perform the following steps:

- Create an entirely new VLR, a golden set of vulnerable Java lines;
- Adapt our code lexing approach to produce Java tokens and re-train the word2vec embeddings on a large Java corpus;
- Develop an approach for reducing the size of the VLR to maintain practical performance while keeping the prediction performance.

We ran an empirical evaluation on the created method, where we scanned 1282 commits' lines form 205 Java projects. Our method proved to be generalizable, meaning that we were able to adapt it to Java programs and re-run a simi-lar experiment to evaluate its performance. We found that our method works slightly worse for Java programs, but it could be improved by fine tuning the dictionary of tokens we take into consideration. It shows that different tokens play a major role in vulnerability prediction in the different languages, which is quite intuitive. We were able to reduce the large size of our Java VLR (from 10,000 to 3,200) to maintain practical applicability of the method without los-ing significant predictive power. In the two best setups, our line-level prediction model was able to identify 61% and 41% of the vulnerable code lines by flagging only 43% and 22% of the program code lines, respectively.

The remaining of the paper is organized as follows. In Sect. 4 we list the works related to our approach. Section 2 describes the methodology we used to build the prediction model. We present and explain the results of our empirical evaluation in Sect. 3. Section 5 lists the possible threats to validity of our work, while Sect. 6 concludes the paper.

2 Methodology

2.1 Background

In a previous work [10], we have created a method to effectively mark vulnerable lines in JavaScript programs. We used a simple word2vec based solution, where we took the average vectors of words found in code lines and checked whether there were similar code lines in a pre-constructed vulnerable line repository. The solution includes several rules that we created to refine the prediction, such as not leting the method mark lines that are only one word long, or preferring lines that consisted of more unique tokens.

In this paper, we present the results of our efforts to transfer our method to Java. Examining our findings both in terms of creating a valuable tool and gaining a deeper understanding of the complex structures of programming languages.

2.2 Motivation

Advantages of Java and Limits of JavaScript. Our JavaScript results, while promising, were not indicative of the true potential of our approach, since the available data was limited. JavaScript is not widely used for critical systems, as such, it contains relatively few known and documented vulnerabilities. This limited our abilities to provide our method with vulnerable lines to be used as prediction bases, and to run tests of the proper size.

Project KB [14] provides a large and validated knowledge base of vulnerabilities in Java programs.[1] Using this, a more realistic testing environment can be set up, making the results more likely to reflect the real capabilities of our approach.

Testing the Generalizability. Changing the examined language is a step towards understanding our method's limitations in terms of generalizability. Our approach does not clearly rely on any language specific properties of the examined JavaScript projects. Knowing how easily the model can be adapted, if it is even needed, can also show a direction for future improvements. Not relying on language specific information would keep a generalizable model flexible, which would be important to keep in mind.

However, if the method proves ineffective in its new application, the results it produces can still be used to push our progress forward. Failure in this case could be caused by the method using structural information yet unnoticed. If these hidden properties indeed exist, they could be used to augment our current method or be taken into account during later projects.

---

[1] https://sap.github.io/project-kb/.

2.3   Highlights of the Original Algorithm

In this section, we will discuss the method [10] we have developed for JavaScript in detail to introduce the terminology already established in our previous work. The process of vulnerability prediction can be broken down into 3 phases (for an overview, see Fig. 1), two of which do not need to be repeated every time.

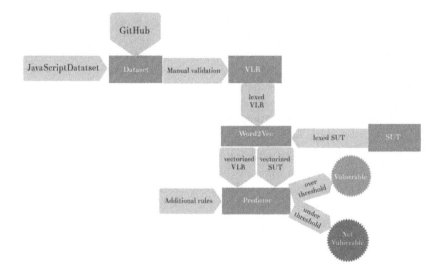

Fig. 1. Overview of our process

Phase 1. The first, and the most crucial step when it comes to getting accurate predictions is creating a word2vec model to be used to represent lines as vectors. This will be used to determine whether lines are similar to one an other. Word or token type count should be reduced to a point where it becomes manageable, since the complexity of code in term of words used can vary greatly. We used ANTLR[2] as a tokenizer, which allowed us to create the corpora for training word2vec models with different levels of abstraction. We used the GitHub Java Corpus [1] for training the word2vec model as a representative sample of Java code from open source projects.[3]

Phase 2. As mentioned before, our method looks for similarities between lines that are known to be vulnerable and the line that is being processed. To do this, we need a set of lines that are known to be vulnerable to serve as a ground truth. So naturally, the next step is to create a Vulnerable Line Repository or VLR for short that will serve as the basis of our prediction. As mentioned in Subsect. 2.2, we used the manually curated data published in project KB for this purpose.

---

[2] https://www.antlr.org/.
[3] https://groups.inf.ed.ac.uk/cup/javaGithub/.

This data set contains 1,282 commits from 205 open-source Java projects, which fix 624 publicly disclosed vulnerabilities (i.e. CVEs). The testing environment was set up by randomly splitting up the vulnerability database so that 90% of it would go in the VLR and 10% could be used for testing.

The knowledge base does not directly contain the vulnerable lines we need, only the projects and commits that contain their fixes. To extract the information we need, we simply clone the repository, checkout to the given commit, get its parent, and using the `git diff` command get the lines that have been removed or changed. We ignore any lines that originate from test files or that are one token long. Assuming that only the given vulnerability has been fixed in a commit, this heuristic would collect all lines that contributed to the vulnerable behavior of the code. To minimize the chance of a commit inducing other changes next to vulnerability fixes, we looked through every commit to check if they were merges or containing additional code changes other than vulnerability fixes based on their commit messages. After removing the duplicate lines, our VLR contained around 10,000 vulnerable lines.[4]

Phase 3. Once finished with the preparation, we can apply our method for predictions. This is done by taking a file from the System Under Test (SUT) and comparing each of its lines' word2vec representation to those in the VLR. A line's word2vec value is determined by the average of its words' vectors.

Using this distance, we can calculate a confidence value that will be used to decide whether a line should be marked vulnerable or not. The confidence value is calculated as follows:

$$Conf(line_{code}) = 1 - min_e(cos(\boldsymbol{v}(line_{code}), \boldsymbol{v}(line_{VLR_e})))$$

Using the confidence value a prediction can already be made. For this however, a threshold value is required to decide which line to be considered vulnerable. We will refer to this threshold as the method's *trip value*. The confidence value of the method will fall between 0 and 1, so it naturally follows that the trip value will also be within this range.

Nonetheless, we do not use this confidence score directly to make the prediction as our previous empirical evaluations showed, that this alone produces lots of false positives. Therefore, we have created multiple so called "rules", which can be used to decrease the false positive rate of our method. They are not specific to JavaScript, therefore they can be applied in this new environment without major modifications. The rules are applied after the initial prediction phase, and modify the base confidence score to decrease the method's false positive rate.

We have tested all of our previous rules [10], from which we kept the three most efficient ones: **no_one_word_line**, **prefer_complex**, and **surrounded**. The rules are applied by taking the average of the rules' score and the word2vec prediction's values, while the `no_one_word_line` rule is applied as a direct filtering or in combination with every other rule. The application of `prefer_complex` rule and the `surrounded` rule together did not produce productive results, therefore it will not be discussed.

---

[4] https://doi.org/10.5281/zenodo.5761680.

2.4   Changes to Adjust Our Method to the New Language

During the first tests we ran in the new environment, it became clear that the method as it was in JavaScript needs adjustments to work well in Java.

Using the adapted model, we examined a reduction in the model's ability to properly determine similarity between lines. Lines that, to the human eye, have no connection have started getting matched as being close to one another. The reason for this behavior was an increase in the average lines' complexity that got lost during the pre-processing stage of prediction. Java code tends to be more verbose, therefore more readable to human eyes. Our simple method of comparing the averages of lines' words was not prepared for the sudden increase in token count, especially without any change in the amount of unique tokens. Even a task as simple as printing out a string to the default output takes 9 tokens in Java, as opposed to the 6 in JavaScript. This was a drawback in our original case since even though the line became more complex and verbose, our model did not gain any extra information. To address this issue, we had to investigate our first research question:

RQ1: Does extending the dictionary used by the word2vec model help in capturing the nuances of the language at hand?

Our VLR in JavaScript contained a few hundred lines and the files examined were also relatively short. In this new setting however, the size of our knowledge base grew to over 10 times of its previous size. The examined files also increased in size, while retaining the same vulnerable line count. Not only is it more difficult to find the lines we are looking for, but it takes significantly more time since our method is essentially a matching algorithm with an $O(N * M)$ time complexity, where N is the number of lines in the SUT and M is the size of the VLR. Reducing the time it takes to create predictions is crucial not only for the development of the method but for its usability as well. To increase the performance without changing the fundamentals of our algorithm, we had to reduce the size of the VLR. This however, can not be done by simply removing some lines randomly, since that might impact performance. Therefore, we faced our second research question:

RQ2: Is it possible to reduce the size of the VLR without losing predictive power?

Reducing the Size of the VLR. The problem of the overly large VLR as mentioned in Subsect. 2.4 causes significant slowdown. To combat this, we aimed to decrease the size of the VLR without significantly reducing the amount of information it contains. We did this by removing lines that are not likely to take productive part in the prediction process.

We created a second repository of lines, this time saving those that were not vulnerable. This was done by collecting the lines that replaced the vulnerable ones in fix commits. Since these lines were created for removing issues, they can be considered to be non-vulnerable. Simply adding random lines from the repositories would have not been a good strategy as they may contain yet unknown vulnerabilities. This risk is present with the fixing lines as well since they may have some hidden flaws, which only get uncovered later in the project development, however the probability of this should be minimal.

Once the new repository was set up, we used its contents to eliminate lines from the VLR that were too similar to a non-vulnerable lines. This should not only reduce the VLR size but may decrease the amount of false positives the method generates as the lines that are very similar to a non-vulnerable line cannot trigger a false prediction anymore.

New Tokens in the Lexer. Introducing new tokens that are general enough to appear regularly but do not inflate the dictionary is challenging. For a start, we used the tokens with which the method performed the best in JavaScript (adapted to Java). Our additions to an otherwise standard lexing method were special string literals, which aim to differentiate between cases where the content of the string is not necessarily relevant to its function, and cases where its value directly influences functionality as it would be the case with strings containing SQL commands, for example.

In Java the original set of tokens did not prove to be satisfactory when it comes to capturing enough of the lines' content to allow for meaningful predictions. We expanded the tokens that may abstract too much information. The most common token was without question the `Identifier` token. Identifiers are used commonly in every language, but in Java's object oriented environment most of the functions are created through classes, methods, and in general variables, all parsed into the token `Identifier` once the lexing is done.

To overcome the issue, we have introduced 4 sub-classes of identifiers to preserve as much of the functionality as possible, without too much of a dictionary size explosion. These are the `VariableIdentifier`, `MethodIdentifier`, `ObjectIdentifier`, and `ArrayIdentifier`.

Since unlike in C++ for example, certain operations can only be executed on a specific subset of objects, we used the token following an `Identifier` instance to determine its type. An `Identifier` will be classified as a `MethodIdentifier` if its following token is a (. Similarly, `ObjectIdentifiers` and `ArrayIdentifiers` need to be followed by a . and a [, respectively. The `VariableIdentifier` tokens were harder to extract, we identified them by their next token being in the possibilities displayed in Table 1. This heuristic does not guarantee that we will be able to classify every `Identifier`, however, it introduces significant variety that our method leverages to produce results of a higher quality.

Table 1. Tokens we use to identify a VariableIdentifier

=	+=	-=	&=
*=	/=	|=	≙
%=	«=	»=	»>=
++	-		

2.5   Metrics Measured

In this section, we will briefly discuss the metrics we measured to evaluate our models. Table 2 contains a short description for all of them.

Table 2. Our measures and their short descriptions

`file_lines`	The total number of lines
`flagged_lines`	The number of lines flagged as vulnerable
`vuln_lines`	The number of lines confirmed to be vulnerable
`flagged_vuln_lines`	The number of confirmed vulnerable lines flagged as vulnerable
`%_flagged`	The percentage of `file_lines` flagged as vulnerable (i.e., efficiency)
`%_is_vuln`	The percentage of `flagged_lines` confirmed to be vulnerable (i.e., precision)
`%_vuln_flagged`	The percentage of `vuln_lines` being flagged (i.e., recall)

It is important to mention that our goal was not necessarily to find all vulnerable lines, rather to decrease the amount of lines that need to be checked, while still touching most if the issues.

2.6   Overview

In this section, we have discussed the method we have used previously in the context of JavaScript, and the one we have introduced here to increase the performance of the method in the context of Java. Taking these additional steps was necessary as we wanted to answer a third research question:

RQ3: Can the performance of our previous method for JavaScript be reproduced in Java?

3   Results

In this section, we discuss the results of the empirical evaluation of our proposed method with the changes mentioned in Sect. 2.

3.1   The Original Method for JavaScript

At first, as mentioned before we have tried to port the method as it was originally published in the context of JavaScript vulnerability detection without any major modifications. We used the parameters that performed best in the previous environment to test whether additional changes to the method were at all required. The results were less than ideal, see the method variant with the **O_** prefix (O as in Original) in Table 3.

We hypothesized that the reason for these results is the method's inability to correctly process the lines it is comparing. This could be because of the dictionary not allowing for an expressive enough representation. Java being a more verbose language than JavaScript leads to longer, more complex lines, and as such the gap between our lexed lines' information content and the original may increase. To address this, we increased the dictionary's size as described in Sect. 2.4 to decrease the reduction in information content between the processed and unprocessed lines.

During this initial run, we also encountered a major issue with the approach. Namely, its time complexity increased rapidly as the VLR's or the SUT's size increased. As the SUT's size cannot be influenced during the method run, the only way to speed up the process was to reduce the size of the VLR. Ideally, this reduction should occur without losing important information. We used a heuristic to collect the VLR's content as described in Sect. 2.4 so that we are able to remove certain lines that the heuristic wrongly added to the VLR, leading to a possible decrease in our method's false positive rate.

3.2   The Augmented Dictionary

The poor initial performance of our model as mentioned in Sect. 3.1 showed that we needed to increase our method's ability to process the lines' content accurately. Since the most common token as mentioned in Sect. 2.4 was `Identifier`, we chose to allow for more variety within them. Our new tokens have helped our method create more accurate predictions, as can be seen in Table 3 with the method variant having the **L_** prefix. Here, **L_** denotes lower similarity value. (See Sect. 3.3)

Since the new dictionary has lead to a clear improvement over the original version we started off using, we took it as our baseline during the tests for the reduction methods. As we will discuss in Sect. 3.3, the reduction created a significantly smaller VLR that was identical in predictive power than the full version. As a result of that, the original prediction (with the new tokens without VLR reduction) is not represented separately.

The improvement in performance in our opinion can be attributed to the increased understanding our method gains as the result. We hypothesize that a correctly extended dictionary leads to a better representation and as a result a more accurate prediction. Lines containing more of their original informational content should help us pair lines that are truly similar in function. The drawback, however, is that choosing an overly excessive dictionary might lead to an unnecessary increase in model size and complexity, which would in turn lead to increased prediction times. Balancing the dictionary's and in turn the model's complexity to keep the lexed lines as close to the original ones as necessary, while keeping the dictionaries size to a minimum could lead to further improvements in predictive performance without too much sacrifice on the usability front.

Based on the experiences, we can answer our first research question:

RQ1: Increasing the size and therefore complexity of the dictionary when lexing and creating the word2vec model increases the methods performance drastically. This is the case because the lexed lines created using our original dictionary fail to capture the complexity of the new environment (i.e. Java language).

3.3 The Impact of the Reduced VLR

As mentioned in Sect. 2.4, our VLR has been generated based on a heuristic. We ignored lines from files that can not contain relevant information, such as non-java files or even test files. However, chances of including lines that are not truly vulnerable should not be ignored. Adding non-vulnerable lines to the VLR may increase the method's false positive rate, and due to the time complexity of the matching algorithm any unnecessary inclusions should be avoided.

Table 3. The results produced by the method with different levels of reduction and using different filtering rules

method_variant	flagged_lines	vuln_lines	flagged_vuln_lines
O_nr	92973	21066	2087
L_nr	37439	4934	3385
H_nr	60006	16556	1907
O_no	79331	21066	1643
L_no	31865	4934	3012
H_no	50620	16556	1600
O_pc	57839	21066	1311
L_pc	20844	4934	2296
H_pc	63254	16556	1794
O_srd	42366	21066	1045
L_srd	16664	4934	2032
H_srd	8945	16556	518

method_variant	%_flagged	%_is_vuln	%_vuln_flagged
O_nr	40.64	2.24	9.91
L_nr	50.79	9.04	68.6
H_nr	33.67	3.18	11.52
O_no	34.68	2.07	4.03
L_no	43.23	9.45	61.04
H_no	28.41	3.16	9.66
O_pc	25.28	2.27	6.22
L_pc	28.28	11.02	46.53
H_pc	35.5	2.84	10.84
O_srd	18.52	2.47	4.96
L_srd	22.6	12.19	41.18
H_srd	5.02	5.79	3.13

To deal with both of these issues, we created a process, described in Sect. 2.4, to decrease the size of the VLR by eliminating lines that are likely to contain patterns not related to vulnerabilities.

Before any steps were taken to reduce its size, the VLR contained over 70,000 lines. Most of these, however, were identical, so a simple elimination of those elements greatly reduced its size. After this initial step, the non-vulnerable line based reduction process could be started. It works similarly to the prediction method, we check if any of the VLR's lines are close to the non-vulnerable ones, and if so, they are removed from the VLR. Two lines are considered close, if the distance between them is smaller than a predefined value, which we simply call the similarity value. Two separate tests were carried out, one with a similarity value of 0.01 and one with 0.1.

After the removal of repeated lines, the VLR was reduced to around 10,000 lines, and using the non-vulnerable lines, its size was further decreased to 3,200 and 350, respectively. Results of testing for both reduction methods can be seen in Table 3. The **L** prefix shows that the results belong to the test instance with the VLR given as a result of using a similarity value of 0.01. Similarly, the **H** prefix refers to a run using a VLR generated with a 0.1 similarity value.

The results of runs with the improved dictionary and original VLR mentioned in Sect. 3.2 are not represented separately, since their results were identical with the lower similarity value runs. Meaning that using the VLR consisting of 3,200 lines is nearly equivalent to the full 10,000 line version.

Therefore, we can answer our second research question.

RQ2: It is possible to significantly reduce the size of the VLR without losing the method's prediction performance. With a relatively high reduction ratio, the VLR is reduced to a third of its original size, yet the predictions based on it are practically equivalent with the original VLR.

The results produced by the high similarity value VLR, however, marks few lines, and even those are not usually correct. Applying that significant reduction already impacts the prediction power of the method.

3.4   Overview

We have attempted to recreate our previous success in JavaScript into a new environment, in order to both test our methods generalizability and to gain access to the more extensive datasets available for Java. The initial results were not ideal, however, we have fine-tuned our approach to get results very close to that we got for JavaScript.

We have created a method for Java that is capable of finding a large portion of the vulnerabilities in a given system. This shows that our method is generalizable, as it could be adjusted to a different language with minor modifications achieving comparable performance.

We have also found that the size of the VLR we use can be significantly reduced, while preserving the prediction performance.

We were able to show that while the base approach with word2vec similarity might perform slightly worse in this context, selecting the appropriate dictionary is crucial and boosts performance, similarly to the rules already established.

Considering the conclusions above, we can answer our third and possibly most important research question:

RQ3: Although adopting the original algorithm without modifications performed slightly worse in the context of Java vulnerable line prediction, with small adjustments in the considered tokens and enhancing rules, we could achieve a comparable results to that observed in the context of JavaScript.

4   Related Works

While our approach to predicting vulnerabilities using machine learning is unique, there are already a number of related studies using other methods. We can group the works based on the granularity of their proposed vulnerability detection methods: file, class, and function-level. There are much fewer works targeting line-level prediction (mostly for bug prediction); to the best of our knowledge ours is the first line-level prediction model addressing vulnerability detection.

4.1   File-Level Predictions

Shin et al. [16] investigated three metrics - complexity, code churn, and developer activity - to see whether they are useful at detecting vulnerabilities. In their empirical case study, they looked at two widely used open-source projects: the Mozilla Firefox web browser and the Red Hat Enterprise Linux kernel. The results indicate that the metrics are discriminative and predictive of vulnerabilities, with the model using all three metrics predicted over 80% of vulnerabilities with a false positive rate of less than 25%.

In one of their other works, Shin et al. [17] found that faults (or defects) have some similarities to vulnerabilities that may allow developers to use traditional fault prediction models and metrics for vulnerability prediction. They again used the Mozilla Firefox web browser to conduct an empirical study, where 21% of files have faults, and 3% of files have vulnerabilities. Both of their models provided similar results: the fault prediction model had a recall of 83% and a precision of 11% at classification threshold 0.6, and the vulnerability prediction model had a recall of 83% and a precision of 12% at classification threshold 0.5. They concluded that, while both models behaved similarly, and traditional fault prediction metrics can substitute for vulnerability prediction models, they still require significant improvement.

Jimenez et al. [6] created VulData7, an extensible dataset and framework automatically collected from software archives. The dataset contains all reported vulnerabilities of four security-critical open-source systems: the Linux Kernel,

WireShark, OpenSSL and SystemD. The framework provides the vulnerability report data (description, CVE and CWE number, etc.), the vulnerable code instance and the corresponding patches, when available. Since this is a lot of data, additional processing is required before it can be used to predict vulnerabilities.

In their work, Neuhaus et al. [11] introduced Vulture, a tool that automatically mines existing vulnerability databases and version archives, and maps past vulnerabilities to components by relying on the dependencies between them. In their approach, a component is a header-source pair for c++ and a .java file for Java. They used an SVM for classifying the dependencies and function calls between the different components. Their predictor correctly predicted about half of all vulnerable components, and about two thirds of all predictions were correct.

4.2   Class-Level Predictions

Siavvas et al. [18] conducted a study investigating the relationship between software metrics and vulnerability types. They studied 100 widely-used Java libraries and calculated a range of software metrics and quantified them through static analysis. They found that these metrics may not be sufficient indicators of specific vulnerability types but are capable of differentiating between security-specific and quality-specific weaknesses. They also found that there are certain metrics which could be used to search for security issues and that between a number of those issues there might exist some important interdependencies.

Basili et al. [2] used object-oriented design metrics described by Chidamber and Kemerer [3] to predict fault-prone classes. With these metrics they could make predictions in the early phases of the software life-cycle using a statistical approach. In contrast, our approach is mainly based on machine learning.

Palomba et al. [12] built a specialized bug-prediction model that they used on classes with code smells. They evaluated how much these code smells contributed towards bugs, and found that components affected by the smells were more bug-prone. To achieve this, they used several prediction models, and found that the best results were using the Simple Logistic model.

In their work, Sultana [19] proposed a vulnerability prediction model based on traceable patterns by examining Apache Tomcat, Apache CXF and three stand-alone Java web applications. Traceable patterns are similar to design patterns, but they can be automatically recognized and extracted from the source code. In their study, they compared the performance of these patterns and traditional software metrics, concluding that patterns have a lower false negative rate and higher recall in detecting vulnerable code than traditional metrics. Besides class-level predictions, the study also focuses on function-level predictions as well.

4.3   Function-Level Predictions

Giger et al. [5] performed experiments on 21 open-source Java systems with their model based on change- and source code metrics that are typically used in bug prediction. Their models reached a precision of 84% and recall of 88%. They also found that change metrics significantly outperform source code metrics.

Ferenc et al. [4] compared 8 different machine learning algorithms to determine the best one for predicting vulnerabilities in JavaScript functions. Their data set consisted of static source code metrics, vulnerability data from NVD[5] and patches obtained from GitHub.

Pascarella et al. [13] replicated a previous research on function-level bug prediction done by Giger et al. [5] on different systems, then proposed a more realistic approach. They found that the performance is similar to that of the replicated research when using the strategy of said research. However, when suing their more realistic approach, they experienced a dramatic drop in performance, with results close to that of a random classifier.

In their work, Saccente et al. [15] created Project Achilles, a Java source code vulnerability detection tool. They used the National Institute of Standards and Technology's Juliet Java Suite, which is a set containing thousands of examples of defective Java methods for several vulnerabilities. They implemented an array of Long-Short Term Memory Recurrent Neural Networks, to detect the vulnerabilities. Their tool employs various data preparation methods and can automatically extract functions from the source code. The result of running the tool is an n-dimensional vulnerability prediction vector. They found that this tool can achieve an accuracy higher than 90% for most of the vulnerabilities.

Li et al. [7] created the tool VulDeePecker, a deep learning-based vulnerability detection system that is capable of automatically extract and define features. They achieve this by defining so-called code gadgets: semantically related code lines that are not necessarily consecutive. First they extract library function calls, then generate backward slices from them. These slices then get assembled into code gadgets and transformed into a vector representation. They train a BLSTM neural network on the vectors, and use them to predict vulnerabilities by transforming the target source code into vectors and classifying them. With their tool, they managed to detect 4 vulnerabilities that were not reported in the NVD, only "silently" patched by the vendors.

4.4 Line-Level Predictions

Wattanakriengkrai et al. [20] found that, on average, only 1%–3% of lines are defective in a file. In their work they propose a framework called Line-DP to identify defective lines using a model-agnostic approach. In other words, they used a state-of-the-art explainable machine learning method, called LIME to identify so-called risky tokens and to provide information about why their model made a prediction. First, their framework builds a file-level model using code token features, then it searches for the risky tokens (code tokens that lead the file-level defect model to predict that the file will be defective). Any lines that contain risky tokens will be flagged as a defect. The authors created a case study of 32 releases of nine Java open-source systems. Their approach achieved a recall

---

[5] https://nvd.nist.gov.

of 61% and a false alarm rate of 47%, while needing around 10 s of processing time. These results are statistically better than the six baselines they compared their model to. Although their approach is similar to ours, they apply it to predict defects, while we specifically targeting vulnerability prediction.

5   Threats to Validity

In this section, we list the major threats to our work. For evaluating our method, we split the data randomly allowing commits of the same project to be present in both the VLR and testing set. The likelihood of this skewing our results is small, since the lexing of the source code will abstract away any project specific patterns, like identifier names or comments.

To derive a single vector for a whole line, we took the average of the word2vec vectors of the tokens in that line. This is a simple, yet reductive way of representing lines as it does not take into account the order of the tokens within the line. In our case, this does not pose a major threat as in programming languages the order of the tokens is relatively strict.

We build a repository of non-vulnerable lines to help us reduce the size of the VLR. However, there is a slight but non negligible chance of a non-vulnerable line being flawed, which only gets uncovered later in the project development (i.e. the fix for a vulnerability contains another vulnerability). Nonetheless, the probability of this should be minimal, therefore we do not expect any major effect of this threat on the final results.

6   Conclusions

In this paper, we presented an incremental work on our previous explainable method for line-level detection of vulnerabilities in JavaScript programs. Our current goal was to adapt the method to an entirely new context, namely to detect vulnerabilities in Java programs. Our replicated study in this new context addresses two issues of equal importance: i) to study and prove the generalizability of the method, and ii) to achieve a practically applicable tool for fine-grained vulnerability detection leveraging the rich data sources available in Java.

We found that adapting our previous method for Java line-based vulnerability detection as-is is feasible but leads to somewhat degraded performance. The major cause of this was the lack of expressiveness of our vocabulary used for the tokenization and word2vec embedding of the Java source code. Therefore, we extended the original vocabulary to better fit the new context and were able to improve the performance significantly. We faced another issue concerning practical applicability, the large size of the VLR slowed down the detection process. We proposed an enhancement of the algorithm, which reduces the size of the VLR, while keeping its prediction performance. We also revisited and fine-tuned the rules we developed for reducing false positive predictions. The explanation mechanism of the algorithm has not been changed, we can provide the most similar vulnerable line from the VLR to serve as a prototype-based explanation for a decision.

We ran an empirical evaluation using the 205 Java projects and 1282 vulnerability fixing commits contained in the project KB dataset. We used the dataset to build the VLR (using 90% of the records) and to test our method as well (on the remaining 10%). We were able to reduce the large size of our Java VLR (from 10,000 to 3,200) to maintain practical applicability of the method without loosing significant prediction power. In the two best setups, our line-level prediction model was able to identify 61% and 41% of the vulnerable code lines by flagging only 43% and 22% of the program code lines, respectively. We consider our experiment to be an overall success since we were able to – with only minor modifications – port our method from a vastly different environment to Java.

In the future, we plan to adapt the method to other languages as well and further study the effect of token vocabulary on the performance. Improvement and extension of the applied rules are also amongst our future plans.

References

1. Allamanis, M., Sutton, C.: Mining source code repositories at massive scale using language modeling. In: The 10th Working Conference on Mining Software Repositories, pp. 207–216. IEEE (2013)
2. Basili, V.R., Briand, L.C., Melo, W.L.: A validation of object-oriented design metrics as quality indicators. IEEE Trans. Softw. Eng. **22**(10), 751–761 (1996). https://doi.org/10.1109/32.544352
3. Chidamber, S.R., Kemerer, C.F.: A metrics suite for object oriented design. IEEE Trans. Softw. Eng. **20**(6), 476–493 (1994)
4. Ferenc, R., Hegedűs, P., Gyimesi, P., Antal, G., Bán, D., Gyimóthy, T.: Challenging machine learning algorithms in predicting vulnerable JavaScript functions. In: Proceedings of the 7th International Workshop on Realizing Artificial Intelligence Synergies in Software Engineering, pp. 8–14. IEEE Press (2019)
5. Giger, E., D'Ambros, M., Pinzger, M., Gall, H.C.: Method-level bug prediction. In: Proceedings of the 2012 ACM-IEEE International Symposium on Empirical Software Engineering and Measurement, pp. 171–180. IEEE (2012)
6. Jimenez, M., Le Traon, Y., Papadakis, M.: Enabling the continuous analysis of security vulnerabilities with VulData7. In: IEEE International Working Conference on Source Code Analysis and Manipulation, pp. 56–61 (2018)
7. Li, Z., et al.: VulDeePecker: a deep learning-based system for vulnerability detection. In: Proceedings 2018 Network and Distributed System Security Symposium (2018)
8. Mikolov, T., Chen, K., Corrado, G., Dean, J.: Efficient estimation of word representations in vector space. arXiv preprint arXiv:1301.3781 (2013)
9. MITRE Corporation: CVE - Common Vulnerabilities and Exposures (2020). https://cve.mitre.org/. Accessed 29 Apr 2020
10. Mosolygó, B., Vándor, N., Antal, G., Hegedűs, P., Ferenc, R.: Towards a prototype based explainable JavaScript vulnerability prediction model. In: 1st International Conference on Code Quality, ICCQ 2021, pp. 15–25 (2021)
11. Neuhaus, S., Zimmermann, T., Holler, C., Zeller, A.: Predicting vulnerable software components. In: Proceedings of the ACM Conference on Computer and Communications Security, pp. 529–540 (January 2007)

12. Palomba, F., Zanoni, M., Fontana, F.A., De Lucia, A., Oliveto, R.: Smells like teen spirit: improving bug prediction performance using the intensity of code smells. In: 2016 IEEE International Conference on Software Maintenance and Evolution (ICSME), pp. 244–255 (2016)
13. Pascarella, L., Palomba, F., Bacchelli, A.: Re-evaluating method-level bug prediction. In: 2018 IEEE 25th International Conference on Software Analysis, Evolution and Reengineering (SANER), pp. 592–601 (2018)
14. Ponta, S.E., Plate, H., Sabetta, A., Bezzi, M., Dangremont, C.: A manually-curated dataset of fixes to vulnerabilities of open-source software. In: Proceedings of the 16th International Conference on Mining Software Repositories (May 2019)
15. Saccente, N., Dehlinger, J., Deng, L., Chakraborty, S., Xiong, Y.: Project Achilles: a prototype tool for static method-level vulnerability detection of java source code using a recurrent neural network. In: 2019 34th IEEE/ACM International Conference on Automated Software Engineering Workshop (ASEW), pp. 114–121 (2019)
16. Shin, Y., Meneely, A., Williams, L., Osborne, J.A.: Evaluating complexity, code churn, and developer activity metrics as indicators of software vulnerabilities. IEEE Trans. Softw. Eng. **37**(6), 772–787 (2011)
17. Shin, Y., Williams, L.A.: Can traditional fault prediction models be used for vulnerability prediction? Empir. Softw. Eng. **18**, 25–59 (2011)
18. Siavvas, M., Kehagias, D., Tzovaras, D.: A preliminary study on the relationship among software metrics and specific vulnerability types. In: 2017 International Conference on Computational Science and Computational Intelligence - Symposium on Software Engineering (CSCI-ISSE) (December 2017)
19. Sultana, K.Z.: Towards a software vulnerability prediction model using traceable code patterns and software metrics. In: 2017 32nd IEEE/ACM International Conference on Automated Software Engineering (ASE), pp. 1022–1025 (2017)
20. Wattanakriengkrai, S., Thongtanunam, P., Tantithamthavorn, C., Hata, H., Matsumoto, K.: Predicting defective lines using a model-agnostic technique. IEEE Trans. Softw. Eng. **48**(5), 1480–1496 (2022)

Role of Serverless Computing in Healthcare Systems: Case Studies

Anisha Kumari[1], Ranjan Kumar Behera[2(✉)], Bibhudatta Sahoo[1],
and Sanjay Misra[3]

[1] Department of CSE, National Institute of Technology, Rourkela, India
[2] Department of CSE, Birla Institute of Technology, Mesra, Ranchi, India
ranjan.behera@bitmesra.ac.in
[3] Department of Information Technology, Ostfold University College,
Halden, Norway

Abstract. Recently, serverless architecture has gained popularity due
to its cost-effective policies, independent stateless functions, auto-scaling,
and simplified code deployment. It allows the developer to deploy and
run their applications without worrying about the underlying architecture. The healthcare services can be made available as a serverless application that consists of distributed cloud services achieving the various
requirements in the healthcare industry. The services offered may be
available on-premise on a cloud infrastructure to users and health service
providers. This paper presents four case studies that have been successfully adapted serverless architecture for health care systems, where the
health services are provided as functional units to various stakeholders.
We have also discussed various components of healthcare systems that
may require serverless services over the cloud infrastructure.

Keywords: Serverless computing · Function as a service · Healthcare
systems · HIPAA · Amazon lambda · Orchestration · OpenWhisk

1 Introduction

In the recent past decade, cloud computing has been emerging as one of the most
successful technology in the era of digital service over the Internet. Some of the
emerging public cloud computing providers includes Google cloud [8], Azure
platform of Microsoft [21], Amazon web Service [20], IBM cloud [19] etc. offer
a wide number of services over the Internet. OpenNebula [15], OpenStack [18],
Server-space, etc. are cloud management platforms allows the system administrators to create on-premises cloud infrastructures. Although it has number of
applications in various domain, it is associated with number of issues and challenges, especially when operational responsibility is handled by the developer.
Serverless computing is one of the recently developed cloud technology, which
migrate all configuration, provisioning and management responsibilities toward
the server side. Serverless framework has been categorized into container-based

O. Gervasi et al. (Eds.): ICCSA 2022 Workshops, LNCS 13380, pp. 123–134, 2022.
https://doi.org/10.1007/978-3-031-10542-5_9

and virtual machine based architecture [22]. In case of virtual machine, hardware is virtualized over an host operating system, whereas in container based serverless multiple separate environment is created so that multiple workload can be handled simultaneously on an host operating system. Container based serverless are found to be more popular in recent years [26]. Serverless computing has several advantages over the traditional cloud computing models by abstracting the management of underlying infrastructure [13]. However, the complexity associated with this infrastructure make more challenging to practically implemented by the normal user [1,21]. AWS Lambda is one of the most popular serverless tool that allow the users to build, deploy and run the application in serverless platform [11]. Developers are requited to upload the set of events corresponding to each stateless functions which can be used to trigger. Some of the example of event might be uploading a file to a bucket in Amazon S3 (Simple Storage Service) or HTTP calls made to a predefined endpoint created with the AWS API Gateway service. In serverless computing, FaaS platforms take over entire operational and computational responsibilities for resource management, scaling, function deployment, and monitoring. Developers can focus only on the business logic of functions, rather than expediting the application development. The serverless computing model focuses on revolutionizing the archetype and advancement of modern scalable applications, where developers can run event-driven code without managing or provisioning servers.

The technology and the service provided by healthcare sector has been growing at an exponential rate in the past few decades. Cloud computing and IoT has changed the way an healthcare operates [23]. It not only associated with health care management system or the keeping the medical records but also it deals with remote treatment of patient along with the constant monitoring. In the era of digital world, healthcare sector has been growing towards more patient-centric, data driven and more connectedness with each other. One of the major goal is to access and control the medical information and records any where anytime in the world. This is only possible, if the quick response can be provided over the cloud technology, which is the most popular trending platform in digital world. Cloud technology can be utilized to get the medical facilities over the Internet [4]. However, each of these services are required to be availed at greater response time with minimum cost. Serverless technology comes into the picture when the cost, auto-scaling services and faster response time are the major point of concern [11]. Serverless computing plays a major role in providing various service at an advanced level [7]. It can reduce electronic healthcare cost which includes, networking, hardware, software, proprietary licenses etc. It has been observed from many literature that bio-informatics sector is getting number of benefits in adopting serverless computing model [2,5,16]. Serverless has been emerging as a promising solution for maintaining digitized environment in healthcare sector where several healthcare services can be provided in low cost and faster response time.

Serverless provider may have various types of services based on the client requirement such as on-demand, on-reserve or the instance services. Healthcare sector popularly use on-demand service model of serverless which can handle the peak load at any point of time. It may be noted that different application in healthcare system like ECG, EEG, E-blood analysis etc. requires different pricing model. 'In this paper, we have presented four case studies in healthcare domain which are getting number benefits in adopting serverless frameworks. The first case study is related to Fast Healthcare Interoperability Resources (FHIR), which leverage various serverless services for managing and storing the health records and make them accessible faster in any corner of the world. The second case study is related to IoT based remote monitoring healthcare system, which allow the healthcare workers to diagnosis and monitor the patient remotely over the Internet. The third case study is RWE and data lakes, which allows the healthcare system to store and manage structured, un-structured, semi-structured data on a single repository. The fourth case studies is related to the how serverless architecture can be leveraged in healthcare startup solutions.

The case studies related to healthcare management system utilizing serverless framework as presented in this paper are motivated by the following points:

- Healthcare management systems has been transformed to the digitized sector in last few years, which essentially need a reliable, cost effective, and faster response solution for several health services. Serverless framework could be best choice for healthcare domain due to its pricing model, auto-scaling, enhanced agility features.
- Serverless technologies in healthcare can be a magic wand for applications that need to scale fast, be readily available and perform high-latency tasks in seconds.
- Serverless has been already applied in several real-time applications. However, compatibility of this novel technology with healthcare system needs to be examined more deeply.
- The case studies provided in this paper will definitely gives potential insight to the researchers as well as stake holders of healthcare regarding applicability of serverless in healthcare management system.

The rest of this paper is organized as follows: Sect. 1 describes the motivation toward this study. In Sect. 2, some of the background details of serverless computing have been discussed. Section 3 describes serverless computing for healthcare and its various components. Section 4 discusses various case studies of serverless application for healthcare system. Section 5 summarizes the conclusion and future work of the study.

2 Background Details

2.1 Serverless Computing

Serverless computing framework is one of the popular technology where the user can deploy and execute their application with a cost effective environment along with the faster response time. The term serverless does not mean that server is absent. Server is still there at the back-end. However, the user need not be worry about on which server the application is running. One of the major reason of its popularity is the migration of management and configuration responsibilities from the client side to the provider side. Clients are required to just upload their application in the cloud without bothering about the execution environment and the resource provisioning. Some of the notable features of serverless computing are the auto-scaling, billing per actual usages, quick deployment, very little involvement, support for diverse set of runtime, etc. Cloud providers are also responsible for constant monitoring, logging and security provision. The response time is way faster then other technology as the application is not associated with any specific server thereby it can run nearest server to the client. Serverless framework can be more suitable in healthcare sector due to its more effective pricing model. The billing is charge for the actual time the resources are utilized rather than for the resources that are provisioned.

2.2   FaaS

In serverless environment, every specific task is represented through the stateless function which are the unit of processing. Each of the functions are executed in an isolated environment may be in the form of container. The service provider are usually allocate and provision the resources to individual function rather than the environment. Therefore, an serverless application can be considered as the orchestration of functions which are independent and stateless. The user can get the service by triggering some events through the web API. User need not to be worry about resource configuration or the execution environment. The function in serverless platform is similar to the object in object oriented programming language or the functions in Functional programming concept.

FaaS service model of cloud plays an important role in providing health related service over the Internet. Each of the medical services can be bundled as a stateless function and can be executed anywhere in an isolated container. The function as a service are usually executed when an event is triggered. Developer needs to bundled the event details along with the business logic and upload into the server. Rest of the management, configuration and execution environment are taken care by the service provider.

2.3   Role of Cloud Technology in Healthcare

The use of cloud technology in the healthcare sector has been increased at an rapid pace in the past few years [24]. Some of the key features of cloud computing that helps in healthcare sector is High data availability, On-demand resource provisioned, Collaboration, Flexibility and scalability [14]. The cost effective and efficient IT services make the healthcare domain as healthTech. Many researchers, as well as experts, expect that cloud computing can change the face of information technology (IT), enhance health care offerings, and benefit fitness care studies. In particular, many researchers consider that cloud computing can reduce electronic health records (EHR) entire expenses, including hardware, software program, networking, personnel, and licensing prices, and therefore will inspire its adoption. Various informatics improvements have proven that cloud computing has the potential to triumph over these problems. Despite the various benefits associated with cloud computing programs for fitness care, there also are management, generation, safety, and felony issues to be pointed out.

One of the biggest challenge in healthcare sector is to provide security and storage to large volume of data which has been generated at an exponential rate over the past decade. The generated data should not only be stored but also be archived for several years based on the country's medical laws. Another challenge the healthcare industry faces is the sharing of medical information and its availability anywhere and anytime. Legal measures such as the Health Information Technology for Economic and Clinical Health Act (HITECH) [17] as part of the American Recovery and Reinvestment Act promote the emergence of health information exchange (HIE) to facilitate collaboration between health care organizations. As traditional IT systems in hospitals are so diverse with data sharing across hospital systems, it is even more challenging due to the lack of a quick and secure way to access data from external organization firewalls.

3   Serverless Computing for Healthcare and its Various Components

The serverless technology is based on contemporary services used to provide automation, scalability, flexibility, and availability. The computation .in the serverless platform relies on set of stateless functions which are deployed and executed on the physical machines or servers at the backend. The provisioning and maintaining of the infrastructure is abstracted from the application development and execution process. The abstraction of infrastructure management from clients is the key point for using the serverless paradigm by many fast-growing and agile health sector solutions. Depending on the serverless paradigm, large enterprises may develop, deploy and execute their business logic without bothering about configuration of infrastructure and the security. Serverless vendors like Microsoft azure, AWS Lambda, Google functions provides lot of services which can be leveraged for diverse requirement in healthcare management service. Some of the serverless components used in healthcare management system are shown in Fig. 1. Serverless infrastructure is one of the most suitable what to make web-based application which can be used to make user interface for patient portal at both front end and backend. AWS EC2 and S3 Buckets are the two storage services can be used to store huge amount of medical records in a secure manner. The authentication can be leveraged by using managed authentication services, such as AWS Cognito, while for the database, AWS Aurora Serverless can be utilized. The statistical result can be shown in a presentable form by using cloudwatch or the Datadog performance monitoring service. This leads to lower operational costs for building the portal, easier maintenance, and on demand scalability etc.

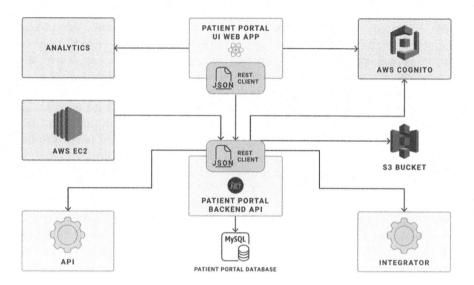

Fig. 1. Serverless architecture for healthcare management system

4   Case Studies

In this section, we have presented four case studies of healthcare management systems, which are heavily utilizing serverless framework. Some of the serverless components are used commonly in all the case studies and some of them are specifically meant for a particular use case. Each of the components are briefly discussed in this section.

4.1   Case Study I: Fast Healthcare Interoperability Resources (FHIR)

Amazon serverless cloud platform provides an efficient open source toolkit to provides various healthcare services popularly known as First Healthcare Interoperability Resources [6]. FHIR system is primarily use various serverless functions to provide APIs which can be used to access remote healthcare resources and facilities [12]. Various serverless services used in FHIR system is shown in Fig. 2. These services can be use in any mobile devices through which the stakeholder of healthcare sectors can avail the services. It also allows to integrate with existing digital services through a well-defined architectural design pattern. The serverless pattern deployed by Amazon's CloudFormation [25] tools can be used to provide services for FHIR request through APIS. The following components are provided to serve different kind of services as follows:

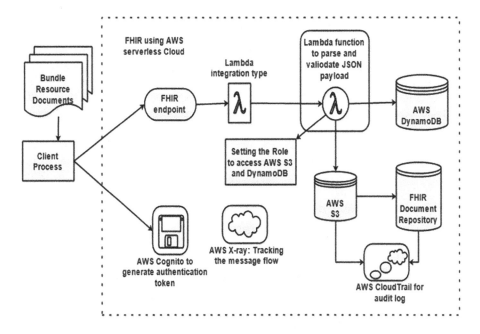

Fig. 2. Serverless configuration for FHIR system

- Amazon Cognito pools are used to provide authentication by verifying the user's identity and the group it belongs to.
- Amazon APIs are provided to routing the request towards the Lambda function which can be invoked by the event an trigger.
- Two very specified AWS Lambda functions are used in the serverless solution for FHIR. One of them is used to process the FHIR request by routing the path towards the storage services like Amazon S3 to store unstructured data, DynamoDB services to create, delete, update operation on healthcare data or to OpenSearch Service to indexing the search process for faster access by the stack holders. The other Lambda function is used to read the updates and make changes in the indexing component.
- The DynamoDB storage unit is used to store all the unstructured healthcare data. Whenever any updates are carried out the DynamoDB, the same is reflected back to the OpenSearch service. Sometimes Amazon's S3 is used to store binary data from healthcare resource such as X-ray or any ECG graphs etc. (Sivasubramanian, 2012).
- The indexing and the search process for the incoming request from FHIR APIs are provided by Amazon OpenSearch service.
- Various Key management services are used to encrypt all the storage components like S3, DynamoDB or the OpenSearch service.
- The CloudWatch service from the Amazon is used to log all API requests from the stakeholders of Healthcare system.

4.2 Case Study II: IoT Based Remote Monitoring System Using Serverless Architecture

Digital wearable devices such as smartwatches, digital blood pressure and weight scales have made it possible for patients to self-diagnose problems long before they become urgent cases that require emergency care [27]. However, self-diagnosis can be dangerous, and it is always preferable to have doctors view remote sensor data and perform diagnosis prior to clinic or hospital admittance. The challenge is to make such data available to doctors in real-time. The architecture for Integration of serverless framework with IoT based remote monitoring system is presented in Fig. 3.

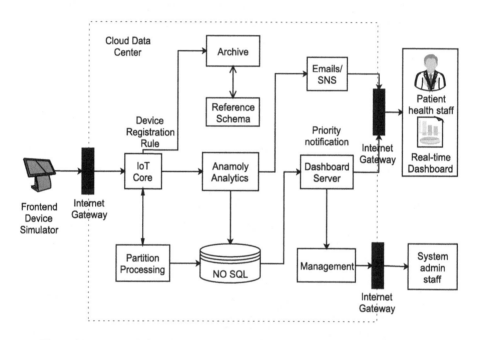

Fig. 3. Integration of IoT and serverless in remote health monitoring system

4.3 Case Study III: RWE and Data Lakes

We have all heard the phrase Real World Evidence in healthcare. This means evidence obtained from data gathered outside of randomized control trials - instead this is from data generated during regular clinical practice or real world practice [9]. In healthcare today, there is no shortage of this data, but it can be hard to glean meaningful insights from it. Think about the petabyte size data sets being generated by wearables, then factor in mobile apps, genomics, imaging and claims data to just name a few sources and you can see that the sky bound mountain of data is growing exponentially. It is also made up of data from various sources and in various formats. For example, you have the streaming data coming

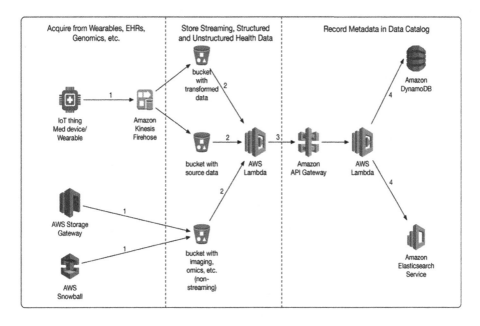

Fig. 4. An architecture of the features within a data lake

in from IoT including FitBits, Apple watches, and medical devices such glucose or heart monitors. Then, you have the structured data being generated from claims data and the unstructured data found in EMRs. The connectivity with various components in DataLake architecture for healthcare system is shown in Fig. 4.

On the public cloud, all of this data can be brought into a Real World Evidence platform with a data lake at the core. The platform stores metadata to identify where each piece of data came from and subsequent information about it. The architecture for your data lake can be built completely on serverless. If you are using AWS, for example, you can store it on S3 and invoke Lambda for your serverless to run your queries. Lambda can also write to a data catalog with metadata about the objects in your data lake. This kind of architecture lets you scale to any size, and when you're working with the kind of data healthcare stores, you'll need capacity. IAM (Identity Access Management) and other security protocols can be put in place to keep your data safe.

4.4 Case Study IV: Healthcare Startup Solution Using Serverless

A healthcare technology startup needs to create a highly scalable data gathering mechanism, which could leverage the power of data science and machine learning to create predictive insights [3,10]. Serverless architecture is found to be much more flexible for startup solution, which not only reduced the resources required to develop and maintain the product, but also it provides ample of opportunities to clients of having a highly modular and flexible product. It will always conformed to regional regulatory and data protection mechanisms with minimal effort. A sample healthcare system utilizing startup solution is shown in Fig. 5. GS Lab decided to use AWS serverless components, microservices and SAM (serverless application architecture), for the product. Although this architecture had been developed around for a couple of years, it has not been seriously implemented in real-time startup healthcare solution. The following AWS components can be leveraged to make the startup solution for healthcare system:

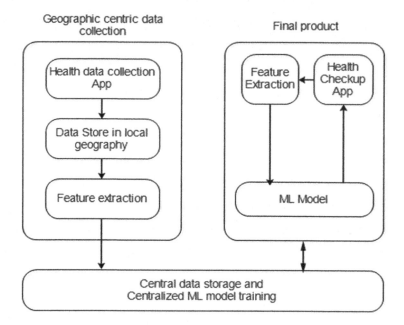

Fig. 5. A healthcare technology startup solution using serverless architecture

- The lambda function for almost all components (Lambda versioning is powerful when we have ML models as lambda).
- Kinesis service for feature extraction of the health data.
- AWS cloud formation templates.
- S3 for secure storage.
- RDS PostgreSQL for database needs.

5   Conclusion

Serverless is has been emerging as a promising solution for maintaining the digitized environment in the healthcare sector where several healthcare services can be provided at low cost and faster response time. In this paper, a survey on the serverless architecture for the healthcare system is presented along with the four case studies related to healthcare systems. In the present day, serverless architecture is found to be an efficient framework to provide various healthcare services. However, it poses a number of challenges in integrating IoT with the serverless healthcare system. As the serverless framework relies on a number of independent stateless functions, they failed to communicate with each other by exchanging data which is one of the major concerns in a healthcare management system. Another challenge in a serverless healthcare management system lies in maintaining the tradeoff between cost and deadline of various healthcare applications. Although it poses various challenges, it has been emerging as a potential tool for handling various services in the healthcare system. The identified research challenges may be considered as the scope of research in the era of the serverless computing in the healthcare system.

References

1. Aslanpour, M.S., et al.: Serverless edge computing: vision and challenges. In: 2021 Australasian Computer Science Week Multiconference, pp. 1–10 (2021)
2. Aubin, M.R., et al.: Helastic: on combining threshold-based and serverless elasticity approaches for optimizing the execution of bioinformatics applications. J. Comput. Sci. **53**, 101407 (2021)
3. Behera, R.K., Rath, S.K., Misra, S., Leon, M., Adewumi, A.: Machine learning approach for reliability assessment of open source software. In: Misra, S., et al. (eds.) ICCSA 2019. LNCS, vol. 11622, pp. 472–482. Springer, Cham (2019). https://doi.org/10.1007/978-3-030-24305-0_35
4. Chaudhary, S., Somani, G., Buyya, R. (eds.): Research Advances in Cloud Computing. Springer, Singapore (2017). https://doi.org/10.1007/978-981-10-5026-8
5. Crespo-Cepeda, R., Agapito, G., Vazquez-Poletti, J.L., Cannataro, M.: Challenges and opportunities of Amazon serverless lambda services in bioinformatics. In: Proceedings of the 10th ACM International Conference on Bioinformatics, Computational Biology and Health Informatics, pp. 663–668 (2019)
6. Eapen, B.R., Sartipi, K., Archer, N.: Serverless on FHIR: deploying machine learning models for healthcare on the cloud. arXiv preprint arXiv:2006.04748 (2020)
7. Elger, P., Shanaghy, E.: AI as a Service: Serverless Machine Learning with AWS. Manning Publications (2020)
8. Figiela, K., Gajek, A., Zima, A., Obrok, B., Malawski, M.: Performance evaluation of heterogeneous cloud functions. Concurrency Comput. Pract. Exp. **30**(23), e4792 (2018)
9. Iyengar, A., Kundu, A., Sharma, U., Zhang, P.: A trusted healthcare data analytics cloud platform. In: 2018 IEEE 38th International Conference on Distributed Computing Systems (ICDCS), pp. 1238–1249. IEEE (2018)
10. Jena, M., Behera, R.K., Dehuri, S.: Hybrid decision tree for machine learning: a big data perspective. In: Dehuri, S., Chen, Y.-W. (eds.) Advances in Machine Learning for Big Data Analysis, pp. 223–239. Springer, Singapore (2022). https://doi.org/10.1007/978-981-16-8930-7_9
11. Kumari, A., Sahoo, B., Behera, R.K., Misra, S., Sharma, M.M.: Evaluation of integrated frameworks for optimizing QoS in serverless computing. In: Gervasi, O., et al. (eds.) ICCSA 2021. LNCS, vol. 12955, pp. 277–288. Springer, Cham (2021). https://doi.org/10.1007/978-3-030-87007-2_20

12. Lehne, M., Luijten, S., Vom Felde Genannt Imbusch, P., Thun, S.: The use of FHIR in digital health-a review of the scientific literature. Stud. Health Technol. Inform. **267**, 52–58 (2019)
13. Lynn, T., Rosati, P., Lejeune, A., Emeakaroha, V.: A preliminary review of enterprise serverless cloud computing (function-as-a-service) platforms. In: 2017 IEEE International Conference on Cloud Computing Technology and Science (Cloud-Com), pp. 162–169. IEEE (2017)
14. Masrom, M., Rahimli, A., et al.: A review of cloud computing technology solution for healthcare system. Res. J. Appl. Sci. Eng. Technol. **8**(20), 2150–2153 (2014)
15. Milojičić, D., Llorente, I.M., Montero, R.S.: OpenNebula: a cloud management tool. IEEE Internet Comput. **15**(2), 11–14 (2011)
16. Niu, X., Kumanov, D., Hung, L.-H., Lloyd, W., Yeung, K.Y.: Leveraging serverless computing to improve performance for sequence comparison. In: Proceedings of the 10th ACM International Conference on Bioinformatics, Computational Biology and Health Informatics, pp. 683–687 (2019)
17. The US Department of Health and Human Services: Health information technology for economic and clinical health act (HITECH) (2009)
18. Rosado, T., Bernardino, J.: An overview of OpenStack architecture. In: Proceedings of the 18th International Database Engineering & Applications Symposium, pp. 366–367 (2014)
19. Sampé, J., Vernik, G., Sánchez-Artigas, M., García-López, P.: Serverless data analytics in the IBM cloud. In: Proceedings of the 19th International Middleware Conference Industry, pp. 1–8 (2018)
20. Sbarski, P., Kroonenburg, S.: Serverless Architectures on AWS: With Examples Using AWS Lambda. Simon and Schuster (2017)
21. Sewak, M., Singh, S.: Winning in the era of serverless computing and function as a service. In: 2018 3rd International Conference for Convergence in Technology (I2CT), pp. 1–5. IEEE (2018)
22. Shafiei, H., Khonsari, A., Mousavi, P.: Serverless computing: a survey of opportunities, challenges and applications. arXiv preprint arXiv:1911.01296 (2019)
23. Shashidhar, R., Abhilash, S., Sahana, V., Alok, N., Roopa, M.: IoT cloud: in health monitoring system. Int. J. Sci. Technol. Res. **9**(1), 227 (2020)
24. Sultan, N.: Making use of cloud computing for healthcare provision: opportunities and challenges. Int. J. Inf. Manage. **34**(2), 177–184 (2014)
25. Varia, J., Mathew, S., et al.: Overview of Amazon web services. Amazon Web Services, p. 105 (2014)
26. Xavier, M.G., Neves, M.V., Rossi, F.D., Ferreto, T.C., Lange, T., De Rose, C.A.: Performance evaluation of container-based virtualization for high performance computing environments. In: 2013 21st Euromicro International Conference on Parallel, Distributed, and Network-Based Processing, pp. 233–240. IEEE (2013)
27. Zamanifar, A.: Remote patient monitoring: health status detection and prediction in IoT-based health care. In: Marques, G., Bhoi, A.K., Albuquerque, V.H.C., K. S., H. (eds.) IoT in Healthcare and Ambient Assisted Living. SCI, vol. 933, pp. 89–102. Springer, Singapore (2021). https://doi.org/10.1007/978-981-15-9897-5_5

Securing Digital Transaction Using a Three-Level Authentication System

Moses Kazeem Abiodun[1] , Joseph Bamidele Awotunde[2](✉) ,
Abidemi Emmanuel Adeniyi[1] , David Ademuagun[1], and Dayo Reuben Aremu[2]

[1] Department of Computer Science, Landmark University, Omu-Aran, Nigeria
{moses.abiodun,adeniyi.emmanuel,ademuagun.david}@lmu.edu.ng
[2] Department of Computer Science, University of Ilorin, Ilorin, Nigeria
{awotunde.jb,aremu.dr}@unilorin.edu.ng

Abstract. In today's world, the rate at which people are transacting on the internet is rapidly increasing, but the majority of people are concerned with the security of the system. Shoulder-surfing, physical observation, keypad overlays, skimming attacks, etc. are the most common threats to the security of Personal Identification Number (PIN) verification. A lot of researchers have proposed several techniques for ensuring security, like Secure-PIN-Authentication-using QR Code (SPAQ), use of One-Time Password (OTP) received on a mobile phone, etc. However, we are still having hackers break into the systems. In order to overcome this threat, this study is proposing a three-level authentication system that will use PIN, OTP, and CAPTCHA at the same time. This will make it more difficult for attackers to succeed in their act and give users doing transactions online peace of mind.

Keywords: Security · CAPTCHA · Authentication · Transaction · SDG 4 · SDG 16

1 Introduction

In our world today, an authentication system is used to secure valuable things. The authentication system is used in the banking sector to secure the accounts and transactions of its customers. Through history, most of the implemented authentication systems have been hacked through. They have become vulnerable to hackers and fraudsters. A stronger authentication system is needed in our society today to strongly secure what is valuable to the people [1].

Also, according to research, people use common passwords and refuse to use complex passwords because they believe they will forget them. This makes the password they use very weak and vulnerable for an unauthorized user to break into.

What is required is a new authentication system that does not require any stressful effort from the user while also being highly secure. The method of identifying if

M. K. Abiodun and A. E. Adeniyi—Landmark University SDG 4 (Quality Education)
M. K. Abiodun—Landmark University SDG 16 (Peace and Justice, Strong Institution)
A. E. Adeniyi—Landmark University SDG 11 (Sustainable Cities and Communities)

someone or something is who or what they claim to be is referred to as authentication. The technology checks if a user's data matches that in a database of legitimate users or a data authentication server to offer a user access to the system [2].

Authentication started with the password in the 1960's. In the analog world, passwords have existed for a long time, but there is a popular narrative about the first digital or computer password. Fernando Corbató, an MIT (Massachusetts Institute of Technology) researcher who later became a professor, was one of the innovators of CTSS (Compatible Time-Sharing System), used to solve the problem of keeping a file private from another user by using a password to safeguard user records on the multi-user time-sharing system. Through history, the password system became weak and could easily be hacked, so other authentication systems had to be developed like the OTP (One Time Password), biometric authentication, certificate authentication, token-based authentication and many others. This is just to properly secure the private information and property of users and customers.

In this research work, a three-level authentication system that will involve the use of CAPTCHA ("Completely Automated Public Turing Test to Tell Computers and Humans Apart") system, OTP, and PIN (personal identification number) is proposed. This method will make it easier for people to authenticate their accounts, and at the same time, it will increase the security of the users' accounts by making it more difficult for unauthorized users to gain access to them.

Fig. 1. Workflow diagram of the three-level authentication

Figure 1 shows the workflow diagram for the implementation of the three level authentication system.

Using a single-factor authentication system puts you at risk and is not secure enough. Thus, the use of a three level authentication system will increase the security protection against attacks. The three-level authentication system combines three different means of authentication to form a more secure system for business transactions on the internet. The rest of the sections are as follows: Sect. 2 presents the review of related literature. Section 3 discusses the methodology used in carrying out the research. Section 4 describes the implementations. Section 5 summarizes the result of the research paper.

2   Literature Review

The method of ascertaining users who seek access to a device, system, or network is referred to as authentication. It is the electronic technique that permits a natural or legal person to be identified electronically. Authentication's overall purpose is to reduce the danger of fraud, particularly when someone deliberately misrepresents their identity or uses another person's credentials without permission. Access control is frequently used to verify a user's identification using credentials such as a username and password. Biometrics, IoT, and authentication apps are among the other technologies used to verify a user's identification [3].

Authentication has a long history that predates the first recorded writings that mention it. Since the birth of civilization, humans have utilized distinctive sounds or watchwords to "authenticate" one another. Roman troops utilized watchwords on a frequent basis. Over time, authentication has become more complicated. It's easy to verify someone's identification just by glancing at them when you know them well. As civilization became more difficult, people had to develop new techniques for authenticating strangers. Society has created personal identity numbers like Social Security numbers (SSN), passports, and other kinds of identification. Even strangers can use these analog forms of identification to verify each other's identity.

2.1 Factors of Authentication

There are four types of factors that can be utilized to verify that an internet customer is the certified owner of what he or she claims to be. These are:

What you know: these are the mental details known only to the genuine user and that should be kept secret, like the password, personal identification number (PIN), and security codes.

What you have: these are the things possessed by the genuine user, like photo ID, smart card, RFID, token, etc.

What you are: these are the distinct body features of a genuine user, like the face, palm, retina, fingerprint, Iris, and voice recognition.

Where you are: this is the data about the whereabouts of a genuine user, like the Internet Protocol (IP) address, Global Positioning System (GPS), etc.

2.2 Types of Authentication

(1) Password-based authentication.

Passwords are still the most widely used method of online authentication. This is understandable, considering that the only requirement is that everyone remember their login and password, rather than having to carry about a digital certificate, USB token, intelligent card, specialist hardware or software, and so on [4]. When it comes to password authentication, there are two parts to it. First, the suppliant will enter the username and then the password. A password can be defined as a private and secret combination of letters, numbers, or special characters known only by the suppliant. One of its strengths is that longer passwords with an accurate combination of characters are very difficult to break. But the problem is, people don't often make use of longer passwords because of fear of forgetfulness. They make use of simple passwords because they are easier to remember. Sadly, simpler passwords are weak and less reliable.

The issue with passwords is that:

(a) passwords can be forgotten if difficult to remember
(b) passwords are easily stolen if written down
(c) users may share passwords
(d) passwords are easy to guess or search if easy to remember [4]

(2) Multi-factor authentication.

To get access to a resource such as an app, an online account, or a VPN, a user must provide two or more verification factors. A good identity and access management (IAM) policy requires Multi-Factor Authentication (MFA). An MFA needs one or more extra verification criteria in addition to a login and password, which reduces the chances of a successful cyber-attack. MFA is a type of verification that entails knowing a customer through two or more approaches. Instances include programs produced by the customer's smartphone, Captcha tests, fingerprints, and facial recognition. MFA verification techniques and tools increase customer assurance by employing extra layers of security.

Although MFA offers an acceptable shield against most account hacks, it is not without errors [4, 5]. There are only three major types of authentication methods, which are:

The majority of the MFA authentication methodology is based on these three important pieces of data: The things you know (knowledge), e.g., your password or your PIN.

Things you own (possessions), such as an ID, an ATM card, or a smartphone.

The things you are (inherence), e.g. your biometrics like voice recognition or fingerprints.

(3) Certificate-based authentication.

The use of a digital certificate to identify a user, computer, or device before giving access to a resource, network, application, or other resource is known as certificate-based authentication. When it comes to user authentication, it is common practice to utilize it in conjunction with more traditional methods like username and password.

(4) Biometric authentication.

Businesses are finding it more difficult than ever to safeguard themselves and their customers from fraud and data breaches. Traditional authentication systems, such as passwords and knowledge-based authentication (KBA), are not only inconvenient but also hackable. Users who have more than 20 passwords to remember are irritated by forgotten credentials, closed accounts, and time-consuming reset processes. This frequently results in poor password hygiene. According to a PYMNTS report, almost 59 percent of users use the same password for several accounts, allowing attackers to inflict even more damage if a password is compromised. Passwords are the core cause of 80 percent of data breaches, according to the FIDO Alliance. Businesses are looking for stronger authentication methods and technology as more stories of cyber-attacks and sophisticated social engineering attempts emerge. Biometrics have the potential to improve security while also improving the user experience. According to Gartner, by 2022, 60% of major enterprises and nearly all medium-sized businesses will have reduced their reliance on passwords by half. Biometric authentication is becoming increasingly popular. ID R & D develops best-in-class speech biometric authentication and passive voice and facial liveness detection technologies, backed by extensive knowledge and a strong R & D emphasis. Stronger security, easier personalization, enhanced fraud protection, and a better user experience are all made possible by these technologies.

Biometrics verification is a kind of security that is founded on an individual's unique bodily features. In a couple of seconds, authorized properties in a database may be compared to biological traits. When placed on gates and doors, biometric authentication can be used to regulate physical access.

The following are some of the most common biometric authentication methods:

Facial recognition: matching a person's many facial characteristics in order to gain access to a database of approved faces. When comparing faces from different perspectives or when comparing people who seem identical, such as close relatives, face recognition might be inaccurate. Spoofing is prevented by facial recognition technology.

Fingerprint scanners are devices that compare the exceptional patterns on an individual's fingerprints. Most new scanners for fingerprints can now examine the vascular outlines in people's fingers. Undoubtedly, the most frequently used biometric technology for ordinary consumers, notwithstanding their frequent errors, is fingerprint scanners. This spike in popularity can be attributed to iPhones.

Voice identification examines how a speaker's speaking patterns create distinguishing forms and sound qualities. To identify users, a voice-protected device, like a password, usually uses predefined words.

Eye scanners include technology like iris recognition and retina scanners. Iris scanners shine a bright light into the eye and examine the colored ring surrounding the pupil for different patterns. Eye-based authentication may be inaccurate if a person wears spectacles or contact lenses.

(5) Authentication using tokens.

Token-based authentication systems allow users to enter their credentials once and receive a unique encrypted string of random characters in return. You can use the token to access protected systems instead of typing in your credentials again. The digital token proves that you have been allowed access previously. The Restful APIs that are utilized by many frameworks and clients are examples of token-based authentication use cases [5, 6].

2.3 Review of Related Literature

Kumar et al. [7] authentication method is based on a one-time password (OTP) entered through a registered personal device. The client and the server begin direct communication after the OTP is verified using the registered device interface. Near Field Communication (NFC), biometrics, and PIN are used in the authentication method [8] for financial transactions. To make a transaction, a smart phone app is used to enter the money, and then the receiver's information is retrieved using NFC. A picture of the sender will be taken, and after successful verification, a four-digit PIN will be used to finalize the transaction. This scheme's limitation is user discomfort. Virgile et al. [9] generate OTP and submit it to a cloud server using an app loaded on the phone. If the OTP comes from a trusted source, the user will be granted access by the registered MAC Address.

Ranasinghe et al. [10] described a technique in which the suggested device design functions as an RFID or NFC reader while also allowing fingerprint authentication. There are options for selecting data intake and output. Data is sent between the device and the NFC/RFID reader via RF signals after selection, although fingerprint authentication is performed first. The data exchange process can only begin after the validation step has been completed. The RFID/NFC reader has a power button, navigation buttons, a fingerprint scanner, and a display screen.

Hassan et al. [11] suggested a model called card-less in which the card is substituted by a fingerprint that utilizes a shuffling keypad method, in which a proximity sensor located on the terminal detects the user's finger and changes the keypad layout. Each time a user's finger is detected, a different layout is displayed. Mahansaria et al. [12] proposed a card-less NFC-enabled method. The mobile device connects with a terminal through NFC placed on the ATM device in this study. The user must first input his or her username and PIN. At the moment of registration, a PIN by default is created. The entered credentials are checked, and an OTP is generated if the authentication is successful. The NFC reader reads the OTP and the username, which is then certified by the server authenticating system, and lastly, a transaction is permitted after successful confirmation. In Card Emulation Mode, the provided concept works.

The authors in [13] proposed blockchain-based security and privacy in a multi-tenant environment, the proposed system was used to secured the cloud platform using Ganache and Meta-Mask schemes for creating dummy secure account for each cloud client. The proposed model revealed the importance of blockchain-based multi-tenancy in cloud computing platform. The model was able to secure the cloud environment by prevent an intruder from gaining access into the cloud database.

In [14], the authors proposed a model for the detection of intruders within the data-centric Internet of Medical Things (IoMT) environment using swarm-neural network. The model used swarm for feature selection and ANN was used for intrusion detection within the IoMT-based platform. The performance of the system was evaluated using NF-ToN-IoT dataset for IoT applications based on the telemetry, network, and operating systems data. The results of the proposed models revealed 89.0% accuracy over the ToN-IoT dataset. There are various security and privacy proposed models in various fields for the authentications and verifications of users to prevent cybersecurity and intruders' attacks within the systems [15–18].

3 System Design

The system design specifies the system's design, components, modules, interface, and data in order to meet specific criteria. There are many processes to be followed in this industry that are ensured during the design phase. The user can obtain a full grasp of how the system works thanks to the system design.

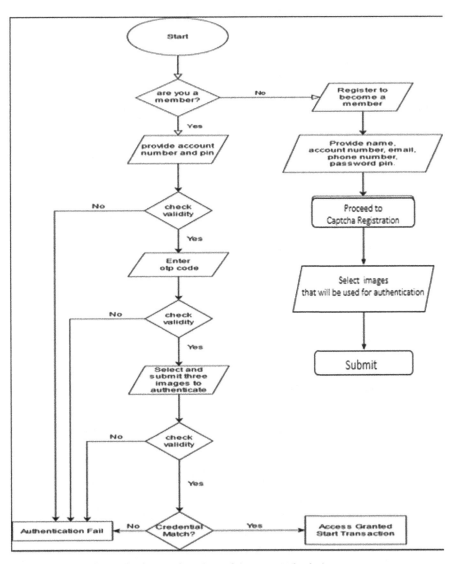

Fig. 2. The flowchart of the proposed solution

Figure 2 shows the step-by-step process of the proposed solution. The user goes to the address of the e-banking website platform, then starts the login process by entering their account number and pin. Unregistered users will have to start the registration process, in which they will have to provide their name, account number, email, phone number, pin code, and select the type of authentication they want. The registration for the 3-authentication method will be done on the registration form. After all the data has been submitted by the user, the user officially becomes a member of the e-banking platform.

As the user enters a valid account number and pin, the web browser goes through the validation phase and waits for authentication to be completed by the server. If authentication is correct, the user is led to the second authentication system, which is either the OTP or the Captcha authentication method. In the OTP authentication method, the user enters his email and then the OTP code is sent to the users email account. The code received will be used to authenticate the account. In the Captcha authentication method, the image recognition challenge will be presented to the user, and all the user has to do is to recognize and select the images chosen for verification. When the user has verified correctly, the user is granted access to his account.

When the user is verified correctly, the user will be granted access to the account and then E-transaction can start.

4   Results and Implementations

The Login Page:

Fig. 3. The login page for customers

Figure 3 is the very first page, which is the login page. This is where an official member of the e-banking platform will enter his account number and pin in order to gain access and start a transaction. An official member that inputs the correct credential will be taken to the next level of authentication, but a user trying to authenticate who is not a member will not be granted any access because their data is not stored in the database.

Instead, he will be advised to register to become an official member of the e-banking platform. When the user clicks on the Register text, it takes the user to another page, which is the page at which the user can register to become an official member of the e-banking platform. The Register text directs the user to the registration web page.

The Registration Page (Fig. 4):

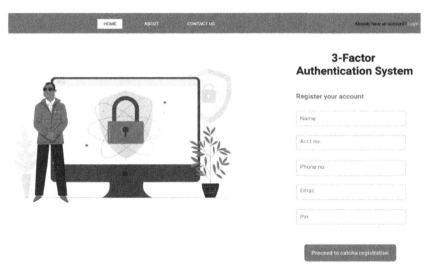

Fig. 4. The registration page

This is where a user intending to become a member of the e-banking platform can insert his data for registration. The user has to insert a username, his or her account number, email, phone number, and pin for authentication. And below all this is the option that allows the user to choose another authentication system for the security, safety, and protection of the account. When the user is done with the form, the user submits it by clicking "register", and after this, the user's data is now officially stored in the database, meaning the user has been assigned an account on the e-banking platform and can now login as an official member of the e-banking platform.

The OTP Authentication (Fig. 5):

Fig. 5. A page to submit OTP code

The OTP Authentication can come with the second level of authentication. The authentication is built in such a way that all the user has to do is to enter his/her email, and activate the OTP function by clicking Send OTP. By doing this, the OTP code (5 random digits) will be sent to the user's email, so the user fetches the code by checking his/her email accounts, and inputs the code into the new OTP page that requires the user to submit the OTP code. When the user inputs the OTP code and submit it, the authentication system checks the validity of the code. If it is correct, the user is granted access to the account. If it is not, the user is denied access.

The Captcha Authentication (Fig. 6):

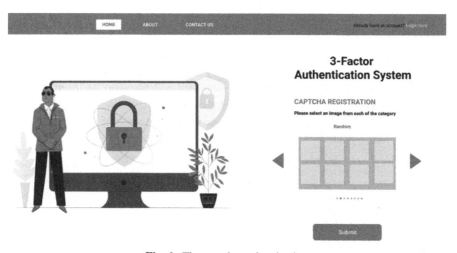

Fig. 6. The captcha authentication

The Captcha Authentication:

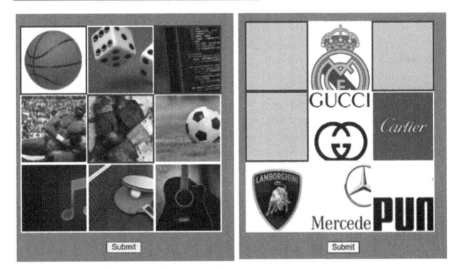

Fig. 7. Hobbies image dataset selected by user

Figure 7 is for the captcha authentication. A link was provided on the registration form that leads the user to select images from a different dataset of images that he or she would like to use to authenticate. It gives the user the freedom to select whichever image he or she would like in whichever dataset. The captcha authentication could also come as the second or third authentication. Therefore, during the request for captcha authentication IRC (image recognition challenge), nine random sets of images will be presented to the user, and all the user has to do is to recognize, select, and submit three images that the user has chosen for verification; when the user is verified correctly, the user is granted access to his account and he can now start transactions. But if the user is not verified correctly, he will be denied access to the account, securing the account from unauthorized users (Fig. 8).

Fig. 8. Access granted alert status

5   Result

The experimental results of the 3 level authentication are found to be a bit slower in the authenticating process. However, it is also found to be more reliable in comparison to a single authentication system. The process of authentication starts with registration, where a new user must register with the system and then get authenticated before he can request a service. The first level of authentication is the PIN, followed by OTP, and then CAPTCHA. The time complexity of the result for using a single method is faster than using all three methods. The sending of OTP took some time because of the network in some cases.

6   Conclusion

Securing an e-banking transaction account with a three-level authentication system was successfully implemented. The system has been able to perform its major function of securing a user's account from an unauthorized user using the PIN, OTP, and Captcha authentication. The three level authentication makes it difficult for hackers to attack the system and steal valuable data from customers. The study could be adopted by various organizations to use in securing an individual's account. Be it an online account or a computer-offline account. This method of authentication could be developed to accommodate more options in the future. In our future research work, we intend to add biometric options to enhance the security of files on the Internet.

References

1. Jang-Jaccard, J., Nepal, S.: A survey of emerging threats in cybersecurity. J. Comput. Syst. Sci. **80**(5), 973–993 (2014)
2. Awotunde, J.B., Jimoh, R.G., Folorunso, S.O., Adeniyi, E.A., Abiodun, K.M., Banjo, O.O.: Privacy and security concerns in IoT-based healthcare systems. Internet of Things **2021**, 105–134 (2021)
3. Abiodun, M.K., Awotunde, J.B., Ogundokun, R.O., Adeniyi, E.A., Arowolo, M.O.: Security and information assurance for IoT-based big data. In: Misra, S., Tyagi, A.K. (eds.) Artificial Intelligence for Cyber Security: Methods, Issues and Possible Horizons or Opportunities. SCI, vol. 972, pp. 189–211. Springer, Cham (2021). https://doi.org/10.1007/978-3-030-722 36-4_8
4. Dinesha, H.A., Agrawal, V.K.: Multi-level authentication technique for accessing cloud services. In: 2012 International Conference on Computing, Communication and Applications, pp. 1–4. IEEE (2012)
5. Rosner, G.L.: De-identification as public policy. J. Data Protection Privacy **3**(3), 250–267 (2020)
6. Hassan, M.A., Shukur, Z.: A secure multi factor user authentication framework for electronic payment system. In: 2021 3rd International Cyber Resilience Conference (CRC), pp. 1–6. IEEE (2021)
7. Kumar, S., Ganpati, A.: Multi-authentication for cloud security : a framework. Int. J. Comput. Sci. Eng. Technol. **5**(04), 295–303 (2014)
8. Adukkathayar A., Krishnan G.S., Chinchole, R.: Secure multifactor authentication payment system using NFC. In: The 10th International Conference on Computer Science & Education, pp. 349–354 (2015)
9. Virgile, K., Yu, H.: Securing cloud emails using two factor authentication based on password/apps in cloud computing. Int. J. Secur. Its Appl. **9**(3), 121–130 (2015)
10. Ranasinghe R.N.D., Yu, G.Z.: Rfid/nfc device with embedded fingerprint authentication system. In: 2017 8th IEEE International Conference on Software Engineering and Service Science (ICSESS), IEEE, pp. 266–269 (2017)
11. Hassan, A., George, L. Varghese, M.A., Sherly, K.: The biometric cardless transaction with shuffling keypad using proximity sensor. In: 2020 Second International Conference on Inventive Research in Computing Applications (ICIRCA), IEEE, pp. 505–508 (2020)
12. Mahansaria, D., Roy, U.K.: Secure authentication for atm transactions using nfc technology. In: 2019 International Carnahan Conference on Security Technology (ICCST), IEEE, pp. 1–5 (2019)
13. Adeniyi, E.A., Ogundokun, R.O., Misra, S., Awotunde, J.B., Abiodun, K.M.: Enhanced security and privacy issue in multi-tenant environment of green computing using blockchain technology. EAI/Springer Innovations Commun. Comput. **2022**, 65–83 (2022)
14. Awotunde, J.B., Abiodun, K.M., Adeniyi, E.A., Folorunso, S.O., Jimoh, R.G.: A deep learning-based intrusion detection technique for a secured IoMT system. Communications in Computer and Information Science, 2022, 1547 CCIS, pp. 50–62 (2021)
15. AbdulRaheem, M., et al.: An enhanced lightweight speck system for cloud-based smart health-care. Communications in Computer and Information Science, 2021, 1455 CCIS, pp. 363–376 (2021)
16. Awotunde, J.B., Misra, S.: Feature extraction and artificial intelligence-based intrusion detection model for a secure internet of things networks. Lecture Notes Data Eng. Commun. Technol. **2022**(109), 21–44 (2022)

17. Awotunde, J.B., Chakraborty, C., Adeniyi, A.E.: Intrusion detection in industrial internet of things network-based on deep learning model with rule-based feature selection. Wirel. Commun. Mob. Comput. **2021**(2021), 7154587 (2021)

18. Kumari, A., Behera, R.K., Shukla, A.S., Sahoo, S.P., Misra, S., Rath, S.K.: Quantifying influential communities in granular social networks using fuzzy theory. In: International Conference on Computational Science and Its Applications, pp. 906–917. Springer, Cham (2020)

International Workshop on Building Multi-dimensional Models for Assessing Complex Environmental Systems (MES 2022)

Supporting the EU Mission "100 Climate-Neutral Cities by 2030": A Review of Tools to Support Decision-Making for the Built Environment at District or City Scale

Anthony Robert Suppa[(✉)], Giulio Cavana, and Tiziana Binda

Interuniversity Department of Regional and Urban Studies and Planning (DIST),
Politecnico di Torino, Turin, Italy
{anthony.suppa,giulio.cavana,tiziana.binda}@polito.it

Abstract. Human activities are responsible for vast environmental impacts, including carbon emissions contributing to climate change. The urban environment is a main source of many of these impacts, and accordingly, the European Union has launched the "100 climate-neutral cites" mission to operationalize a carbon-free urban future. This paper investigates the various evaluation tools supporting the Decision-Makers (DMs) and stakeholders in their effort to achieve the carbon-neutral transition. Using the scientific database Scopus, we conducted a literature review focused on different keywords comprising widely used evaluation methods. The focus of the research is on different aspects and scales of the urban systems, considering the multi-dimensional nature of the decision problems at such scale. Specifically, the study presented here analyzes the way in which these methods deal with large scales, either with a bottom-up or a top-down approach, and how different categories of Key Performance Indicators (KPIs) and changes in the DMs system of values can influence their preferences. We find that Lifecycle Assessment (LCA) is the most used support tool at the district or city level, and most indicators focus on energy consumption and carbon emissions. A smaller share of studies reviewed are based on multi-domain evaluation methods.

Keywords: Climate-neutral cities · Low carbon · Energy transition · Urban regeneration · Decision-making tools · District · Neighborhood · Urban scale

1 Introduction

To advance the European Green Deal's climate neutrality pledge, the European Union (EU) recently launched the mission "100 climate-neutral cities by 2030 – by and for the citizens". The project envisages 100 cities (or districts thereof) with minimum population 50,000 as innovation hubs leading other cities ahead of the 2050 deadline. To participate, cities mitigate and offset all greenhouse gases (GHG) considered Scope 1 (direct emissions from buildings, industry, transport, waste treatment, agriculture, forestry, and other

O. Gervasi et al. (Eds.): ICCSA 2022 Workshops, LNCS 13380, pp. 151–168, 2022.
https://doi.org/10.1007/978-3-031-10542-5_11

activities within the city boundaries) and Scope 2 (GHG from grid-supplied energy). Also recommended is mitigation of Scope 3 emissions (out-of-boundary GHG arising from consumption within boundaries) [1].

For the mission to be successful, a key focus must be the building sector, which accounts for 40% of energy consumption and 36% of energy-related GHGs in the EU [2]. Supporting the transition in the building sector, the European Green Deal and Sustainable Europe Investment Plan will spend €1 trillion on climate action in the coming years [3], and the EU's Renovation Wave will foster deep renovation, double the annual energy renovation rate, and complete 35 million building renovations by 2030 [2].

There is no prescriptive path for a city to achieve climate neutrality, nor completed precedents of such cities. However, one can draw experience from substantial energy reduction in district or neighborhood examples. Among these are positive energy districts (PEDs), of which there are at least 60 projects in Europe in planning, implementation, or operational stages [4]. PEDs are districts or neighborhoods which produce more energy than they consume over the average course of the year, typically through locally produced renewable energy, thus reducing GHG from fossil fuel use [5].

As cities pursue climate neutrality through a series of district-level projects, they require support to develop and evaluate action plans [6]. The aim of this paper is thus to provide support for Decision Makers (DMs) in planning and policy implementation who seek strategies for zero-carbon buildings and neighborhoods, by reviewing literature on decision-making tools for the built environment at the district or city scale. Our approach includes a focus on decision-making inputs and Key Performance Indicators (KPIs) to provide DMs context required to use the decision-making tools and metrics to evaluate decisions. We focus on the building sector as it is the top energy consumer and emissions producer in the EU [2], and we consider other urban sectors such as transport and waste management as they arise within the built environment research.

With an estimated cost of €96 billion for the 100 cities participating in the new mission alone [1], it is essential to use decision-making tools to optimize climate-focused urban interventions. Research indicates that it is difficult for DMs to select among numerous retrofit and renewable energy system intervention scenarios, pointing to Multi-Criteria Analysis (MCA) as a basket of tools to make better decisions [7]. In addition to MCA, other decision-support tools such as Life Cycle Assessment (LCA), Life Cycle Costing (LCC), Cost-Benefit Analysis (CBA) and other methods can be used to assess intervention scenarios and justify decisions [8, 67, 70, 72].

This work investigates the following research questions, each of which referring to the built environment at the district or city scale:

Q1. On district- or city-level projects, how do studies deal with larger scale?
Q2. What are the decision-making support and evaluation tools used at district or city scale?
Q3. What are the KPIs and other inputs used with the decision-making tools?

This paper is structured as follows: Sect. 2 presents the research methodology; Sect. 3 discusses results to the research questions; and Sect. 4 provides conclusions.

2 Research Methodology

The literature review was conducted by using the database SCOPUS on March 16, 2022. We used different keywords to focus our review on decision-making tools for the building sector at the district or city scale. Specifically, the keywords used can be classified into four macro-groups: 1) "Decision-Making Tools", 2) "Building Sector", 3) "Climate Neutrality", and 4) "Scale of Intervention". In addition, we limited the research for the first three macro-groups to keywords, and for the last group regarding scale, we limited to article title. The keywords used for the different groups are:

1 Macro-group "Decision-Making Tools": ("Outranking" OR "Hedonic" OR "Stake-holder analysis" OR "SWOT" OR "Cost Benefit Analysis" OR "CBA" OR "Discounted Cash Flow Analysis" OR "DCA" OR "DCFA" OR "Contingent Valuation Method" OR "Discrete Choice Models" OR "Cost Effectiveness Analysis" OR "Risk Benefit Analysis" OR "Planning Balance Sheet" OR "Community Impact Evaluation" OR "Environmental Impact Assessment" OR "Strategic Environmental Assessment" OR "DPSIR" OR "NAIADE" OR "Evamix" OR "Lexicographic" OR "Cluster" OR "Analytic" OR "Input Output" OR "Concordance/discordance analysis" OR "Multiattribute Value Theory" OR "Multi-attribute Value Theory" OR "MAVT" OR "Multiattribute Utility Theory" OR "Multi-attribute Utility Theory" OR "MAUT" OR "Analytic Hierarchy Process" OR "AHP" OR "Analytic Network Process" OR "ANP" OR "Spatial Multicriteria Analysis" OR "SMCA" OR "SS-MCDA" OR "Dominance-based Rough Sets" OR "Non Additive Robust Ordinal Regression" OR "Choquet Integral" OR "ELECTRE" OR "PROMETHEE" OR "LCA" OR "LCC" OR "Life cycle" OR "Lifecycle" OR "ROI" OR "Return on investment" OR "SROI" OR "Social return on investment").
2 Macro-group "Building Sector": ("Built environment" OR "building" OR "dwelling").
3 Macro-group "Climate Neutrality": ("Energy" OR "efficiency" OR "efficient" OR "climate neutral" OR "carbon neutral" OR "zero carbon" OR "low carbon").
4 Macro-group "Scale of Intervention": ("District" OR "City" OR "Urban" OR "Neighborhood" OR "Neighbourhood" OR "Block" OR "precinct").

We used one comprehensive search string, using the "AND" operator to link macro-groups. We limited the search to peer-reviewed journals, yielding 249 results. Subsequently, we eliminated articles not relevant to the study in three steps. First, we removed articles deemed irrelevant based on title, resulting in 83 articles being excluded. Second, we read all abstracts and eliminated articles out of scope, excluding an additional 86 documents and resulting in 80 articles. Last, we read full articles, removing 24 further irrelevant papers, for a total of 56 articles reviewed in this work.

3 Results and Discussion

Of the 56 articles reviewed, the majority included Life Cycle Assessment (LCA), with 28 studies using LCA as the sole decision-making tool, and an additional seven studies using

LCA in combination with another tool. Energy Simulation (ES) was the second-largest category, with a total of seven studies using the tool. Figure 1 shows the percentage of studies reviewed by decision-making tool.

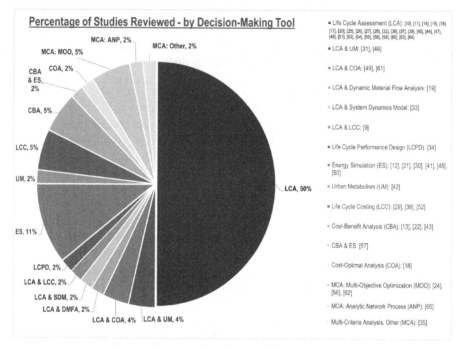

Fig. 1. Studies reviewed by decision-making tool

3.1 How Studies Deal with Greater Scale

Moving from models based on the building scale to larger scales, including district or city scale, requires strategies to deal with vastly greater building geometries and other parameters among hundreds or thousands of structures. In the studies reviewed, the strategies can be classified as geospatial and non-geospatial methods. As shown in Fig. 2, these methods can be further divided into approaches including archetype, sampling, individual building, scaling top-down data, and hybrid and other approaches. Most of the approaches can be considered "bottom-up" approaches, which analyze individual buildings and then extrapolate results to a greater scale, whereas the approach of scaling top-down data begin with macro-economic, national-level, or other aggregated data and apply downscaling ratios to arrive at the building level [67].

3.1.1 Geospatial Methods

Over 40% of reviewed studies used geospatial methods. Such methods usually rely on geographic information systems (GIS), enabling semi-automatic extraction of building geometry and other data, such as floor area, number of stories, building elevation, etc.

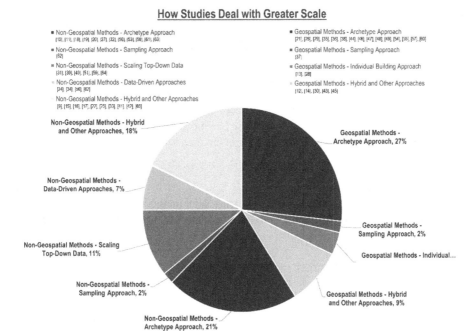

Fig. 2. How the studies reviewed deal with district or city scale.

Use of *building archetypes* was the most common single approach within the reviewed articles. The archetypes provide building characteristics to be used in the modelling such as construction materials, insulation values (U-values), glazing ratios, infiltration levels, and mechanical system efficiencies [47, 56]. Once the buildings in the GIS model are classified according to each archetype, the investigated characteristics are scaled to the real buildings. Archetypes in the reviewed studies are largely based on period of construction and building typology [35, 45, 47, 54, 59]. Different sources are used to define the archetypes such as the EU TABULA project [21, 48], national building libraries [53], and expert opinions and/or past studies [43, 45, 47, 54, 59].

The archetype approach is useful on very large scales, such as in [15] where 656,531 buildings were modelled across Barcelona. In another evaluation tool known as urban building energy modeling (UBEM), not reviewed in this work, research notes that upscaling building archetypes can average out inaccuracies of individual building models, with error ranges of 7–21% for heating loads and 1–19% for energy use intensity, deemed to be acceptable to guide decisions affecting multiple buildings [66].

The *individual building approach,* where each building is separately modelled using actual characteristics, was completed in two of the reviewed studies, and both on small district projects (8 and 4 buildings) [13, 27].

Next, a *sampling approach* was used as a single approach in one study [36] involving 1,092 in-person questionnaires with building residents in Xiamen, China, to retrieve building information, obtain energy bills, and ascertain occupant energy-saving awareness. The sample data were then normalized and scaled up across the city using GIS.

Finally, some studies adopted *hybrid and other approaches*. [44] used sampling in a hybrid approach to validate energy outcomes of geospatial archetype analysis. [12] used sampling energy bills in conjunction with data-driven analysis to create building clusters (similar to archetypes). In a study of urban heat island (UHI) effect and building energy demand, the researchers collected local climate zone data with GIS and subsequently used machine learning to compute optimal cool pavement solutions [14]. In a study on optimal selection of green roof areas across Seoul, South Korea [42], geospatial data was first used to help determine expected costs and benefits of green roofs on each building, before selecting optimal locations of green roofs in the city.

3.1.2 Non-geospatial Methods

About 57% of the studies reviewed used non-geospatial methods. In contrast to geospatial, non-geospatial methods often rely on statistical data instead of individual land parcel and building data [67]. These methods include archetype, sampling, scaling top-down data, and hybrid approaches.

Like its geospatial counterpart, the non-geospatial *archetype approach* uses building typologies for analysis, with sources such as expert opinion, statistics on the building stock, or reference buildings [67]. This is the most common approach of the non-geospatial methods, representing 12 of the reviewed studies. One study in Abu Dhabi, United Arab Emirates, [50] used an engineering consultant's report on the national building stock to create one average building archetype, then multiplied by 5,500 buildings to reach the total national amount of annual electricity consumption. In recent case studies from Norway [11, 19, 20], archetypes based on Norwegian Passive House standards were created and then multiplied by the 1,000 buildings in the Ydalir positive energy district. Reyna & Chester [52] used 16 reference buildings over three time periods, for a total of 42 building archetypes. They subsequently ran 42 LCAs and normalized them on a per-unit-area basis, multiplying these values by the area of each building archetype according to Los Angeles County Assessor statistics.

Another among non-geospatial methods is the *sampling approach*, used in one study as a single method [51] as well as in hybrid approaches. In Gonen, Turkey, researchers sampled 56 out of 300 buildings connected to an existing district heating system [51]. The sampled buildings were measured, surveyed, and/or the architectural drawings were studied to create an average set of building statistics to be modelled.

Four of the reviewed studies [23, 33, 55, 61] employed a *data-driven approach* to overcome the need for physical building models. Whereas classical modeling requires numerous building parameters as inputs into modelling software [33] (e.g. EnergyPlus or TRNSYS, as used in several of the bottom-up approaches mentioned above), if adequate consumption data are available for use in computational analysis, these can be used to create reliable estimation models for energy consumption [68]. In a study in the Netherlands [33], energy consumption data for 19 buildings, both from building energy management systems and statistical sources, were used to computationally create a life cycle performance design (LCPD) model. In Seoul, South Korea, researchers used clustering and evolutionary algorithm methods to analyze over 10^5 buildings with about 10^3 optimized future scenarios [23]. In a district project in Norway [55], researchers used computation with an evolutionary algorithm to solve the optimization of energy system selection with 1.66×10^{65} possibilities. In a district study in San Francisco [61], researchers used an evolutionary algorithm to determine thousands of optimal solutions.

Another non-geospatial approach was *scaling top-down data*, as seen in six of the reviewed studies. In a LCA study in Wuhan, China [58], the authors used data from national and provincial statistical yearbooks as inputs, scaling them to the city level to determine energy consumption at building material production, construction and demolition, and building operations. In a LCA and Urban Metabolism (UM) study comparing two Spanish cities [30], the authors used national and regional data and applied ratio-based downscaling based on the population and gross domestic product (GDP) in each city. In two district LCA projects in Australia [39, 50], the authors scaled statistical data to the local scale. Embodied energy of buildings was calculated based on energy intensities and floor areas, and operational energy was calculated from normalized per unit energy consumption and average per capita daily consumption. A study of cities in 84 countries around the world [38] scaled data related to heating and cooling degree days as well as population and income per capita to create city-level LCAs.

Finally, many of the non-geospatial methods adopted *hybrid or other approaches*, representing 10 of the studies reviewed. One study in Barcelona [40] combined resident interviews and energy bill data surveys to collect data, then applied data-driven analysis using clustering methods, generative topographic mapping and k-means, to obtain reference dwellings to represent different energy patterns and energy systems of the neighborhood. Both sample and scaled top-down data were used in a city-wide LCA study in Shenzhen, China [8]. A city-level study in Beijing creating a Life Cycle Dynamic model (LCDM) also used a combination of questionnaire surveys and field investigations plus top-down statistical data; econometric theory and system dynamics theory are used to process the data [32].

3.2 LCA and Related Decision-Making Tools

As noted, the majority of the analyzed papers use LCA, which aims at quantifying the environmental impacts of a system throughout different stages from beginning of life (BoL) to End of Life (EoL), avoiding the shift of impacts among different stages [65]. The LCA methodology is well defined, derived from Industrial Ecology [65], dating back to the 1970s [31], and used lately as a basis to evaluate the different dimensions of sustainability. These dimensions include social, economic, and environmental, and lead to the definition of the equation: LCSA = LCA + LCC + SLCA, where Life Cycle Costing (LCC) deals with the economic aspect assessment, Social Life Cycle Assessment (SLCA) deals with social aspects, and combined with LCA's analysis of environmental impacts, yield the total Life Cycle Sustainability Assessment (LCSA).

The LCA studies reviewed focus on three main aspects of the urban environment: energy intensity [15]; environmental impact, in terms of Global Warming Potential (GWP) and/or embodied carbon [27, 35, 36, 43, 52, 58, 59, 62], or as a wider spectrum of impacts, such as acidification of soil and water, eutrophication, photochemical ozone creation potential [17, 31, 54]) and the input-output of materials [19, 41].

The application of LCA at a scale greater than the building level dates back to 1996 [31], and has been applied to several studies both in evaluation of new construction of urban areas [46] and urban renovation analysis [10, 11, 25, 47, 53].

[46] use a LCA approach to compare six different scenarios for the planning of a new district of 100,000 m^2 in Granada, Spain, including 225 to 480 residential units. They consider the impact of the new dwellings by means of archetypes, as well as the impacts of road network and different land uses (leisure space, sport installation, school, commercial and social uses), identifying the best alternative in terms of carbon dioxide (CO_2) emissions and Embodied Energy (EE).

[53] focus on a city quarter of 1,148 buildings in Stuttgart, Germany, completing a LCA for all the residential buildings, or around 50% of the buildings in the district. The authors evaluate four different intervention scenarios in the district considering possible envelope interventions to reduce carbon emissions: (1) demolishing and reconstructing all the buildings, (2) an advanced retrofit of all the buildings, plus (3) and (4) with 12% of buildings replaced and the remaining refurbished, but with different priority sequences for the refurbishment. They performed a GHG calculation over 34 years (2016–2050) over the entire life cycle of the district (production stage, use stage, end-of-life stage), and conclude that the 80% reduction target of the German federal government in primary energy demand cannot be achieved with envelope refurbishment alone. Furthermore, 60% of GHG emissions during use stage can be avoided, but this figure is reduced when accounting for embodied emissions in refurbishment scenarios.

In another work evaluating retrofit scenarios, [47] ranked four intervention alternatives comprising increasingly high-performance solutions (status quo, envelope upgrades, low-carbon design and low-carbon materials, and low-carbon strategies combined with PV-panels) against three parameters: Embodied CO_2 emissions, Operational CO_2 emissions, Whole life cycle emissions at 1, 10, and 50 years after calculation.

[32] evaluate the energy consumption of material production of new residential construction, energy use for the operation and demolition of buildings, and the disposal of demolition waste. They combine LCA with a System Dynamics Model (SDM) to predict the newly built and demolished residences over the calculation period. The authors conclude that the majority of the energy consumption occurs in the operational stage (60% of the total energy consumption), with an increasing trend over the years. They note the possibility of reducing this figure by 6.6%-13.2% by lowering energy-intensive activities, such as heating, air conditioning, lighting, electric devices.

Another group of studies includes other sectors beyond the built environment, such as transport and mobility [26, 38, 39, 50], and infrastructure [14, 20, 57]. In their analysis of a suburban precinct in Adelaide (Australia), [50] include the total energy consumption embodied in the construction and maintenance of precinct objects, the total energy required for the operation of precinct objects and the total energy related to occupant travel, including commuting for work, school, and leisure. They propose two transportation scenarios: one assuming current modes of transportation; and another one assuming 30% of occupants switch to public transport. They found out that operational energy accounts for 32% of the total (of which HVAC accounts for 48.8%, appliances for 24%, and lighting 13.1%), while travelling energy reached 55% of the total, being the largest use of annual energy. A second transport scenario analyzed (30% of residents shifting to public transport) reduced precinct energy consumption by 6.3%.

Related to the previous study, [39] evaluate the two precincts depending on their geographical location and socio-economical composition, highlighting the significance of embodied carbon (both initial and recurrent) and travel related carbon, together accounting for 49.9% and 58% of the total. They also calculate carbon reductions in a scenario with increased public transport (15.1% and 30.4% in the inner and outer precinct respectively) and a scenario with a 90% increase in residential PV installation (81.7% and 75.7% in the outer and inner precincts respectively, with a 1.1% and 0.7% increase in embodied carbon).

With an approach including infrastructure, [14] apply the LCA method to capture the effect of Urban Heat Island (UHI) and climate change in cities considering the mutual relationship among buildings, vehicles and pavements.

[57] analyze five "synthetic" cities (Orlando, Phoenix, Austin, Seattle, and a fictitious "Maximum-Density Case"), studying embodied and operational energy for buildings, infrastructure (freshwater, wastewater, lighting) and transport (fuel use, parking, sidewalks, streets), and calculate energy performance per-capita. Furthermore, [20] evaluate different scenario for a pilot project in a neighborhood in Elverum, Norway. The parameters considered were mobility energy use in operation, area of PV panels, embodied emissions in building materials, emissions associated with vehicle production, travel distance per inhabitant and year, and the emission intensity of electricity. In this study, mobility is the largest GHG emission contributor (61% of the total), while PV panels are responsible for only 4% of total emissions.

In the evaluation of the LCA, several studies have highlighted the high percentage contribution of the operational energy consumption on the total environmental impacts [31, 32, 36, 39, 50, 53]. Indeed, several studies focus solely on Energy Simulation (ES) [12, 21, 29, 40, 44]. For instance, [21] analyze a neighborhood in Seville, Spain, proposing two intervention scenarios combining PV panel installation, substitution of heating and cooling systems, and implementation of specific energy efficiency measures, to prioritize possible areas of energy intensity reduction intervention. In [29], researchers use local weather station data to drive an ES, calculating energy consumption of a typical 30-storey building in Hong Kong and the resulting effect of UHI and Urban Moisture Island (UMI). They highlight a 96% increase in latent cooling demand due to UMI effect and UHI impact in a range of 45.7% - 104.2% increase in sensible cooling demand in urban areas compared to rural ones. In [40], the study combines data from a survey (resident questionnaire) and simulation models to evaluate tenants' behavior on energy consumption in a residential neighborhood to evaluate the impact of possible retrofit intervention on different socio-economically defined occupants.

Further combining methods from Industrial Ecology, some analogies can be drawn between Environmentally Extended Input-Output Analysis (EEIOA) and Material Flow Analysis (MFA) and UM. In particular, the first aims at including all monetary transaction in an economy to quantify the environmental impact of a product or service; the second has its goal in describing the input and output flows of materials [63].

With an approach focused on the urban scale, [30] combine LCA and UM to calculate construction materials, fossil fuels, energy, food beverages, as well as other flows in both Bilbao and Seville, Spain, estimating their impacts in terms of global warming, stratospheric ozone depletion, terrestrial acidification, freshwater eutrophication, marine eutrophication, fossil resource scarcity, human carcinogenic toxicity drawing specific insights related to different characteristics of the two cities. [45] use UM to combine

Environmental Input-Output (EIO) and LCA on the evaluation of flows in Los Angeles County, USA, quantifying GHG emissions related to electricity consumption, embodied energy due to buildings and roadways, water use, and waste flows. [41] calculate the impact of two recycling scenarios in Jakarta and Bandung, Indonesia, to compare the estimated flows of demolition materials during the time span of the calculation and the stocking capacity of two newly planned landfills. Table 1 provides a summary of LCA and related DM tools, including KPIs.

Table 1: Summary of LCA and related DM tools.

DM tool	KPIs most frequently observed in the literature	KPIs less frequently observed in the literature
Life Cycle Assessment (LCA)	• Carbon emissions ($kgCO_2$) • Energy consumption (kWh/GJ) *(Both of the above may include Embodied or Operational carbon / energy)*	• Eutrophication – Freshwater (kg_{PO4eq}) and Marine (kg_{Neq}) • Acidification of soil and water (kg_{SO2eq}) • Stratospheric ozone depletion ($kg_{CFC11eq}$) • Photochemical ozone creation ($kg_{ethyleneeq}$) • Water use (m^3) • Human toxicity ($kg_{1.4DCB}$) • Aquatic eco-toxicity (m^3)
Energy Simulation (ES)	• Operational energy consumption (kWh/GJ) • Operational carbon emissions ($kgCO_2$)	*n/a*
Urban Metabolism (UM)	• Embodied carbon ($kgCO_2$) and energy (PJ) • Disposed material (tonnes)	*n/a*

3.3 Cost-Based, Multi-criteria, and Other Tools for DMs

While LCA is the most widely used method to support decision making in district-wide energy upgrading, the literature review shows that other quantitative and qualitative evaluative methods are also common. In particular, quantitative economic evaluation methods found are Life Cycle Costing (LCC), Cost-Benefit Analysis (CBA), and Cost-Optimal Analysis (COA), whereas a range of methods falling under the umbrella term Multi-Criteria Analysis (MCA) include both quantitative and qualitative approaches.

Based on the literature review, it has emerged that the LCC method is the most widely used after the LCA method. This method of monetization, focusing on "global costs", is also used alongside LCA, as it estimates all costs related to the life cycle of the materials used in construction [9, 60]. Calculation of LCC of a building is based on adding up the investment, energy, maintenance and replacements costs minus the RV (Residual Value), and applying a discount rate to costs incurred in the future [69].

In the context of district-level energy retrofitting, LCC can be used to analyze potential scenarios to find the best energy solution from an economic standpoint. [28, 32]. In the redevelopment of a historic district in Visby, Sweden, [28] supported LCC using OPERA-MILP software (Optimal Energy Retrofit Advisory-Mixed Integer Linear Program), thus analyzing multiple strategies in terms of costs for each type of intervention.

Similar to a combination of LCA and LCC is Life-Cycle Performance and Design (LCPD), also used to evaluate the performance of an asset over its lifetime. The approach uses indicators of two main scopes – economic and environmental – and within each, develops specific KPIs for buildings, local energy systems, and other sectors [33].

Another method used to evaluate and support energy regeneration is Cost-Benefit Analysis (CBA). This method, unlike other financial methods such as Cost-Optimal Analysis, which calculates the investment cost, energy price, inflation, maintenance cost, and uses the discount rate [18], also considers the environmental and social co-benefits arising from the intervention [13, 22, 23, 56]. In a study analyzing installation of green roofs in Seoul [42], costs and benefits were calculated to find the optimal building locations for green roof installation, including socio-economic, energy, and environmental aspects, including bee habitats. The results show that 100 buildings were selected for the installation of green roofs, satisfying 92% of the demand imposed by existing green spaces [42].

A group of methods falls under the umbrella term Multi-Criteria Analysis (MCA), which can also be combined with cost-based methods. In one example, in a case study in Greece regarding the expansion of the electrical system where both methods are used to evaluate different scenarios to support the decision-maker [69]. MCA may consider not only quantitative but also qualitative aspects. In the article [34], the authors have classified four principal classes of MCA methods: (i) value measurement models (e.g., AHP, MAUT); (ii) goal, aspiration and reference level models (e.g., TOPSIS); (iii) outranking models (e.g., ELECTRE, PROMETHEE); and (iv) combination of models [34]. An example of the first type, Analytical Network Process (ANP) was used in Qingdao, China, to weight and score values of priorities related to architecture, planning, and design as well as construction management, including indicators related to building orientation, energy saving design, and building materials, among others [64].

The outranking method has been re-encountered in our bibliographic analysis. In detail, the study presented an application of the PROMETHEE multi-criteria method to outrank the different building energy retrofit alternatives at both the building and district levels, considering the citizen and municipality perspectives respectively [34]. In detail, different quantitative and qualitative criteria have been identified at the district and building level, moreover, alternatives have been defined. By performing sensitivity analysis and varying the weights of the various criteria, particularly the socio-economic ones, the preferential order of the alternatives is modified. The method demonstrates that the socio-economic part influences decision-making choices.

Another multi-criteria decision-making tool falling under the MCA umbrella, Multi-Objective Optimization (MOO) was used in studies [23, 55, 61]. MOO is a data-driven tool which can use computing power to process exponential possible outcomes. For example, [61] used MOO to maximize total fuel cycle efficiency, minimize life cycle cost, and minimize annual CO_2 emissions, finding tens of thousands of solutions that met their target criteria. Table 2 provides a summary of the other DM tools from the literature review, including KPIs.

Table 2: Summary of other DM tools commonly featured in the literature review.

DM tool	KPIs most frequently observed in the literature	KPIs less frequently observed in the literature
Life Cycle Costing (LCC)	• Investment cost (currency/ m^2) • Operations & maintenance cost (currency/ m^2)	• Payback period (years) • Net Present Value (currency)
Cost-Benefit Analysis (CBA)	Includes all KPIs as LCC, plus added co-benefits include: • Economic savings from energy reduction (currency/m^2)	*n/a*
Cost-Optimal Analysis (COA)	• Global cost (currency) • Carbon emissions (kgCO$_2$) • Payback period (years) • Energy savings compared to baseline (%)	• Net Present Value (currency)
Multi-Criteria Analysis (MCA), including Analytic Network Process (ANP)	• Energy savings (%) • Internal comfort / temperature (%)	• Costs – Investment, Replacement, Maintenance (currency) • Tax detraction (%) • Reliability / satisfaction with retrofit (%) • Social image & awareness (%)
Multi-Objective Optimization (MOO)	• Life cycle cost (currency) • Carbon emissions (kgCO$_2$)	• Total Fuel Cycle Efficiency (%) • Loss of Power Supply Probably (%)

4   Conclusions

Human activities are responsible for vast environmental impacts, with carbon emissions and climate change being chief among them. The urban environment is a main source of many of these impacts, and accordingly, the European Union has launched the "100 climate-neutral cites" mission to operationalize a carbon-free urban future.

While climate-neutral cities may be part of the solution to the climate problems we are experiencing, as Huovila et al. [59] note, cities require support to develop and evaluate action plans to transform into climate-neutral cities. Thus, this paper seeks to provide such assistance by reviewing the decision-making support and evaluation tools that facilitate this transition.

This paper employed a Scopus database search for key words in the macro groups Building Sector, Climate Neutrality, and Decision-Making Tools, and searching title for terms related to our target Scale of Intervention. This macro group approach allowed us to quickly narrow the results to articles within the scope of this review, excluding many irrelevant articles studies and providing a manageable quantity of articles to review. However, as a possible downside, relevant articles could have been excluded.

The review study shows that the most prevalent method among research in the built environment at the urban scale is LCA, which aims at quantifying the environmental impacts of a product from beginning of life (BoL) to End of Life (EoL) [65]. While we began this review with dozens of decision-making tools in mind, it is surprising to find that LCA is so dominant in the literature. However, this can be explained perhaps by the idea of searching for tools addressing carbon- and climate-neutral cities, as LCA seeks to quantify energy consumption and carbon emissions, and has been shown to work well in comparing pre- and post-intervention scenarios. While LCA provides a clear picture of energy, carbon, and several other environmental indicators, potential shortcomings of this tool are that it does not consider costs, nor co-benefits in the social domain. In theory, the extension of LCA to include social indicators, namely the complete life cycle sustainability assessment (LCSA) [65], would overcome this limitation, however we did not encounter any such applied case studies in this literature review.

We addressed scale in this review so that policy makers could contextualize decision-making at different scales, from the building to the district, ultimately extending to the climate-neutral city. The literature reveals challenges in measuring KPIs at scale, and notes numerous methods, both geospatial and non-geospatial, to address this. Previous work has referred to the two most common upscaling methods as the "building-by-building" and "archetype" approaches, noting that the former leads to more refined modelling of the building, at the cost of higher input data requirements and computational burdens [67]. We chose to classify these two methods as geospatial and non-geospatial archetypes, as both approaches begin with reference buildings, then upscaling based on building geometry from GIS in the former approach, or using statistical data in the latter. In either case, such a study uses averages based on construction eras and typologies, which necessitates simplification and thus some error. The geospatial methods reduce uncertainty by modeling with actual building parameters, such as surface area and volume. Other recent work attempts to further improve certainty with actual window to wall ratios, extracted automatically across urban areas from street view imagery using machine learning [73]. When aggregated at the city scale, archetype methods have been shown to provide overall results within acceptable error ranges [66].

While the research presented in this paper specifically focuses on the built environment, some of the studies analyzed also consider other aspects of the urban fabric, including the transport sector, infrastructure, water management and other material and energy flows. Our focus on the built environment might explain the finding that CO_2 emissions and energy-related indicators as the most common KPIs. Considering the

LCA studies reviewed, a minor number of these included other impact categories such as eutrophication and acidification of soil and water.

Additionally, if we consider wider criteria to evaluate urban interventions (such as in the framework of the triple bottom-line approach), neglecting some aspects of the evaluation could lead to distorted or suboptimal results as discussed in Sect. 3.3, where assigning a different weighing system to different social, economic and environmental criteria altered the ranking of urban scale retrofit intervention scenarios [34].

For future analysis, an in-depth exploration of methodologies related to a comprehensive framing of decision-making could be valuable, including social, environmental, and economic domains. Such an approach would focus on a deeper literature analysis of applications in the urban environment at different scales and on application in other fields, such as energy production, environmental risk and scenario analysis, and cultural heritage. Furthermore, the increasing availability of real-time data from monitoring systems and smart devices within the Internet of Things (IoT) paradigm could represent an untapped resource to develop realistic scenarios and support data-informed and holistic decision making [1, 71].

References

1. European Commission (EC): Proposed Mission: 100 Climate-neutral Cities by 2030 – by and for the Citizens. Report of the Mission Board for climate-neutral and smart cities. Publications Office of the European Union, Luxembourg (2020)
2. European Commission (EC): A Renovation Wave for Europe - greening our buildings, creating jobs, improving lives. COM (2020) 662 final. European Commission, Brussels (2020)
3. European Commission (EC): Sustainable Europe Investment Plan & European Green Deal Investment Plan. COM (2020) 21 final. European Commission, Brussels (2020)
4. Zhang, X., Penaka, S.R., Giriraj, S., Sánchez, M.N., Civiero, P., Vandevyvere, H.: Characterizing positive energy district (PED) through a preliminary review of 60 existing projects in Europe. Buildings 11(8), 318 (2021)
5. Ala-Juusela, M., Crosbie, T., Hukkalainen, M.: Defining and operationalising the concept of an energy positive neighbourhood. Energy Convers. Manage. 125, 133–140 (2016)
6. Huovila, A., et al.: Carbon-neutral cities: Critical review of theory and practice. J. Clean. Prod. 341, 130912 (2022)
7. Sibilla, M., Abanda, F.H.: Multi-criteria decision making optimisation framework for positive energy blocks for cities. Sustainability 14(1), 446 (2022)
8. Bottero, M., Dell'Anna, F., Morgese, V.: Evaluating the transition towards post-carbon cities: A literature review. Sustainability 13(2), 567 (2021)
9. Barbosa, R., Almeida, M., Briones-Llorente, R., Mateus, R.: Environmental performance of a cost-effective energy renovation at the neighbourhood scale—the case for social housing in Braga Portugal. Sustainability (Switzerland) 14(4), 1947 (2022)
10. Huang, B., et al.: Rethinking carbon–neutral built environment: Urban dynamics and scenario analysis. Energy and Buildings 255, 111672 (2022)
11. Lausselet, C., Brattebø, H.: Environmental co-benefits and trade-offs of climate mitigation strategies applied to net-zero-emission neighbourhoods. Int. J. Life Cycle Assess. 26(11), 2263–2277 (2021). https://doi.org/10.1007/s11367-021-01973-3
12. Yu, H., et al.: Prioritizing urban planning factors on community energy performance based on GIS-informed building energy modeling. Energy and Buildings 249, 111191 (2021)

13. Ascione, F., Bianco, N., Mauro, G.M., Napolitano, D.F., Vanoli, G.P.: Comprehensive analysis to drive the energy retrofit of a neighborhood by optimizing the solar energy exploitation – An Italian case study. J. Clean. Prod. **314**, 127998 (2021)

14. AzariJafari, H., Xu, X., Gregory, J., Kirchain, R.: Urban-scale evaluation of cool pavement impacts on the urban heat Island effect and climate change. Environ. Sci. Technol. **55**(17), 11501–11510 (2021)

15. Wang, J., et al.: Can buildings sector achieve the carbon mitigation ambitious goal: Case study for a low-carbon demonstration city in China? Environ. Impact Assess. Rev. **90**, 106633 (2021)

16. Nematchoua, M.K., Sadeghi, M., Reiter, S.: Strategies and scenarios to reduce energy consumption and CO_2 emission in the urban, rural and sustainable neighbourhoods. Sustain. Cities Soc. **72**, 103053 (2021)

17. Kaoula, D.: Towards a morpho-environmental neighbourhood optimization method: MENOM. Sustain. Cities Soc. **70**, 102880 (2021)

18. Fernandez-Luzuriaga, J., del Portillo-Valdes, L., Flores-Abascal, I.: Identification of cost-optimal levels for energy refurbishment of a residential building stock under different scenarios: Application at the urban scale. Energy and Buildings **240**, 110880 (2021)

19. Lausselet, C., Urrego, J.P.F., Resch, E., Brattebø, H.: Temporal analysis of the material flows and embodied greenhouse gas emissions of a neighborhood building stock. J. Ind. Ecol. **25**(2), 419–434 (2021)

20. Lausselet, C., Lund, K.M., Brattebø, H.: LCA and scenario analysis of a Norwegian net-zero GHG emission neighbourhood: The importance of mobility and surplus energy from PV technologies. Build. Environ. **189**, 107528 (2021)

21. Camporeale, P.E., Mercader-Moyano, P.: A GIS-based methodology to increase energy flexibility in building cluster through deep renovation: A neighborhood in Seville. Energy and Buildings **231**, 110573 (2021)

22. Yu, Z., et al.: Supportive governance for city-scale low carbon building retrofits: A case study from Shanghai. Climate Policy **21**(7), 884–896 (2021)

23. Song, J., Song, S.J.: A framework for analyzing city-wide impact of building-integrated renewable energy. Appl. Energy **276**, 115489 (2020)

24. Terés-Zubiaga, J., et al.: Cost-effective building renovation at district level combining energy efficiency & renewables – Methodology assessment proposed in IEA EBC Annex 75 and a demonstration case study. Energy and Buildings **224**, 110280 (2020)

25. Mastrucci, A., Marvuglia, A., Benetto, E., Leopold, U.: A spatio-temporal life cycle assessment framework for building renovation scenarios at the urban scale. Renew. Sustain. Energy Rev. **126**, 109834 (2020)

26. Lausselet, C., Ellingsen, L.A.-W., Strømman, A.H., Brattebø, H.: A life-cycle assessment model for zero emission neighborhoods. J. Ind. Ecol. **24**(3), 500–516 (2020)

27. Nault, E., Jusselme, T., Aguacil, S., Andersen, M.: Strategic environmental urban planning - A contextual approach for defining performance goals and informing decision-making. Build. Environ. **168**, 106448 (2020)

28. Milic, V., Amiri, S., Moshfegh, B.: A systematic approach to predict the economic and environmental effects of the cost-optimal energy renovation of a historic building district on the district heating system. Energies **13**(1), 276 (2020)

29. Shi, L., Luo, Z., Matthews, W., Wang, Z., Li, Y., Liu, J.: Impacts of urban microclimate on summertime sensible and latent energy demand for cooling in residential buildings of Hong Kong. Energy **189**, 116208 (2019)

30. González-García, S., Dias, A.C.: Integrating Lifecycle Assessment and Urban Metabolism at City Level: Comparison between Spanish Cities. J. Ind. Ecol. **23**(5), 1062–1076 (2019)

31. Nematchoua, M.K., Orosa, J.A., Reiter, S.: Life cycle assessment of two sustainable and old neighbourhoods affected by climate change in one city in Belgium: A review. Environ. Impact Assess. Rev. **78**, 106282 (2019)

32. Li, G., Kou, C., Wang, H.: Estimating city-level energy consumption of residential buildings: A life-cycle dynamic simulation model. J. Environ. Manage. **240**, 451–462 (2019)
33. Walker, S., Labeodan, T., Boxem, G., Maassen, W., Zeiler, W.: An assessment methodology of sustainable energy transition scenarios for realizing energy neutral neighborhoods. Appl. Energy **228**, 2346–2360 (2018)
34. Dirutigliano, D., Delmastro, C., Torabi Moghadam, S.: A multi-criteria application to select energy retrofit measures at the building and district scale. Therm. Sci. Eng. Prog. **6**, 457–464 (2018)
35. García-Pérez, S., Sierra-Pérez, J., Boschmonart-Rives, J.: Environmental assessment at the urban level combining LCA-GIS methodologies: A case study of energy retrofits in the Barcelona metropolitan area. Build. Environ. **134**, 191–204 (2018)
36. Yan, X., Cui, S., Xu, L., Lin, J., Ali, G.: Carbon footprints of urban residential buildings: A household survey-based approach. Sustainability (Switzerland) **10**(4), 1131 (2018)
37. Liu, L., Rohdin, P., Moshfegh, B.: Investigating cost-optimal refurbishment strategies for the medieval district of Visby in Sweden. Energy and Buildings **158**, 750–760 (2018)
38. Bergesen, J.D., Suh, S., Baynes, T.M., Musango, J.K.: Environmental and natural resource implications of sustainable urban infrastructure systems. Environ. Res. Lett. **12**(12), 125009 (2017)
39. Huang, B., Xing, K., Pullen, S.: Carbon assessment for urban precincts: Integrated model and case studies. Energy and Buildings **153**, 111–125 (2017)
40. Cipriano, X., Vellido, A., Cipriano, J., Martí-Herrero, J., Danov, S.: Influencing factors in energy use of housing blocks: a new methodology, based on clustering and energy simulations, for decision making in energy refurbishment projects. Energ. Effi. **10**(2), 359–382 (2016). https://doi.org/10.1007/s12053-016-9460-9
41. Surahman, U., Higashi, O., Kubota, T.: Evaluation of current material stock and future demolition waste for urban residential buildings in Jakarta and Bandung, Indonesia: Eembodied energy and CO2 emission analysis. J. Mater. Cycles Waste Manage. **19**(2), 657–675 (2017)
42. Gwak, J.H., Lee, B.K., Lee, W.K., Sohn, S.Y.: Optimal location selection for the installation of urban green roofs considering honeybee habitats along with socio-economic and environmental effects. J. Environ. Manage. **189**, 125–133 (2017)
43. Stephan, A., Athanassiadis, A.: Quantifying and mapping embodied environmental requirements of urban building stocks. Build. Environ. **114**, 187–202 (2017)
44. Torabi Moghadam, S., Coccolo, S., Mutani, G., Lombardi, P., Scartezzini, J.L., Mauree, D.: A new clustering and visualization method to evaluate urban heat energy planning scenarios. Cities **88**, 19–36 (2019)
45. Pincetl, S., et al.: Enabling future sustainability transitions: An urban metabolism approach to Los Angeles. J. Ind. Ecol. **18**(6), 871–882 (2014)
46. Roldán-Fontana, J., Pacheco-Torres, R., Jadraque-Gago, E., Ordóñez, J.: Optimization of CO2 emissions in the design phases of urban planning, based on geometric characteristics: A case study of a low-density urban area in Spain. Sustain. Sci. **12**(1), 65–85 (2017)
47. de Wolf, C., et al.: Life cycle building impact of a Middle Eastern residential neighborhood. Energy **134**, 336–348 (2017)
48. Delmastro, C., Mutani, G., Corgnati, S.P.: A supporting method for selecting cost-optimal energy retrofit policies for residential buildings at the urban scale. Energy Policy **99**, 42–56 (2016)
49. Balocco, C., Papeschi, S., Grazzini, G., Basosi, R.: Using exergy to analyze the sustainability of an urban area. Ecol. Econ. **48**(2), 231–244 (2004)
50. Huang, B., Xing, K., Pullen, S.: Life-cycle energy modelling for urban precinct systems. J. Clean. Prod. **142**, 3254–3268 (2017)
51. Aslan, A., Yüksel, B., Akyol, T.: Energy analysis of different types of buildings in Gonen geothermal district heating system. Appl. Therm. Eng. **31**(14–15), 2726–2734 (2011)

52. Reyna, J., Chester, M.: the growth of urban building stock: unintended lock-in and embedded environmental effects. J. Ind. Ecol. **19**(4), 524–537 (2015)
53. Harter, H., Weiler, V., Eicker, U.: Developing a roadmap for the modernisation of city quarters – Comparing the primary energy demand and greenhouse gas emissions. Build. Environ. **112**, 166–176 (2017)
54. Mastrucci, A., Marvuglia, A., Popovici, E., Leopold, U., Benetto, E.: Geospatial characterization of building material stocks for the life cycle assessment of end-of-life scenarios at the urban scale. Resour. Conserv. Recycl. **123**, 54–66 (2017)
55. Lu, H., Alanne, K., Martinac, I.: Energy quality management for building clusters and districts (BCDs) through multi-objective optimization. Energy Convers. Manage. **79**, 525–533 (2014)
56. di Turi, S., Stefanizzi, P.: Energy analysis and refurbishment proposals for public housing in the city of Bari Italy. Energy Policy **79**, 58–71 (2015)
57. Nichols, B.G., Kockelman, K.M.: Urban form and life-cycle energy consumption: Case studies at the city scale. J. Transp. Land Use **8**(3), 115–219 (2015)
58. Gong, Y., Song, D.: Life cycle building carbon emissions assessment and driving factors decomposition analysis based on LMDI-A case study of Wuhan city in China. Sustainability (Switzerland) **7**(12), 16670–16686 (2015)
59. García-Pérez, S., Sierra-Pérez, J., Boschmonart-Rives, J., Lladó, M.G., Romero, C.A.: A characterisation and evaluation of urban areas from an energy efficiency approach, using geographic information systems in combination with life cycle assessment methodology. Int. J. Sustain. Dev. Plan. **12**(2), 294–303 (2017)
60. Afshari, A., Nikolopoulou, C., Martin, M.: Life-cycle analysis of building retrofits at the urban scale-a case study in United Arab Emirates. Sustainability (Switzerland) **6**(1), 453–473 (2014)
61. Best, R.E., Flager, F., Lepech, M.D.: Modeling and optimization of building mix and energy supply technology for urban districts. Appl. Energy **159**, 161–177 (2015)
62. Stephan, A., Crawford, R.H., de Myttenaere, K.: Multi-scale life cycle energy analysis of a low-density suburban neighbourhood in Melbourne Australia. Build. Environ. **68**, 35–49 (2013)
63. Geng, J., et al.: Quantification of the carbon emission of urban residential buildings: The case of the Greater Bay Area cities in China. Environ. Impact Assess. Rev. **95**, 106775 (2022)
64. Wang, X., Zhao, G., He, C., Wang, X., Peng, W.: Low-carbon neighborhood planning technology and indicator system. Renew. Sustain. Energy Rev. **57**, 1066–1076 (2016)
65. Walzberg, J., Lonca, G., Hanes, R.J., Eberle, A.L., Carpenter, A., Heath, G.A.: Do we need a new sustainability assessment method for the circular economy? A critical literature review. Front. Sustain. **1**, 620047 (2021)
66. Reinhart, C.F., Davila, C.C.: Urban building energy modeling–A review of a nascent field. Build. Environ. **97**, 196–202 (2016)
67. Mastrucci, A., Marvuglia, A., Leopold, U., Benetto, E.: Life cycle assessment of building stocks from urban to transnational scales: A review. Renew. Sustain. Energy Rev. **74**, 316–332 (2017)
68. O'Neill, Z., O'Neill, C.: Development of a probabilistic graphical model for predicting building energy performance. Appl. Energy **164**, 650–658 (2016)
69. Diakoulaki, D., Karangelis, F.: Multi-criteria decision analysis and cost–benefit analysis of alternative scenarios for the power generation sector in Greece. Renew. Sustain. Energy Rev. **11**, 716–727 (2007)
70. Becchio, C., Ferrando, D.G., Fregonara, E., Milani, N., Quercia, C., Serra, V.: The cost-optimal methodology for the energy retrofit of an ex-industrial building located in Northern Italy. Energy and Buildings **127**, 590–602 (2016)
71. Bujari, A., Calvio, A., Foschini, L., Sabbioni, A., Corradi, A.: A digital twin decision support system for the urban facility management process. Sensors **21**, 8460 (2021)

72. Mirabella, N., Allacker, K., Sala, S.: Current trends and limitations of life cycle assessment applied to the urban scale: Critical analysis and review of selected literature. Int. J. Life Cycle Assess. **24**(7), 1174–1193 (2018). https://doi.org/10.1007/s11367-018-1467-3
73. Szczesniak, J.T., Ang, Y.Q., Letellier-Duchesne, S., Reinhart, C.F.: A method for using street view imagery to auto-extract window-to-wall ratios and its relevance for urban-level daylighting and energy simulations. Build. Environ. **207**, 108108 (2022)

Urban Metabolism: Definition of an Integrated Framework to Assess and Plan Cities and Territories

Vanessa Assumma[1]([⊠]) [iD] and Francesco Pittau[2] [iD]

[1] Interuniversity Department of Regional and Urban Studies and Planning, Politecnico di Torino, Viale Mattioli 39, 10125 Turin, Italy
vanessa.assumma@polito.it
[2] Department of Architecture, Built Environment and Construction Engineering (ABC), Politecnico di Milano, Via Ponzio 31, 20133 Milan, Italy
francesco.pittau@polimi.it

Abstract. The present paper deals with the role of sustainability assessment tools in tackling the increasing complexity and uncertainty of urban and territorial systems. Urban metabolism is ever more under the attention of Decision Makers and policy makers to deal with the current planning challenges, where climate change, environmental quality, social equity and justice, and governance represent very topical issues.

The paper focuses particularly on Life Cycle Assessment (LCA) and the family of Multicriteria Decision Analysis (MCDA) retained as suitable tools to design an integrated framework to envision sustainable, resilient and circular solutions with a multi-scaling approach, ranging from the product to the city and territory levels. This contribution represents a position paper of the authors which defines an integrated framework to explore urban metabolism and support real assessment and planning procedures for cities and territories transformations. This research work is addressed to planners, Decision Makers, technicians and freelances actively involved in planning and assessment procedures for ensuring a better quality of life.

Keywords: Life Cycle Assessment · Multicriteria Decision Analysis · Urban metabolism

1 Introduction

In the ongoing context of climate change, several and different variables, from environmental to economic, from social to political ones, are causing high uncertainty and ambiguity in the planning of sustainable cities and territories. The increasing population and of the quality of life have caused over time a systemic crisis in terms of accessibility to resources and thus causing a potential overcoming of Earth security margins (Rockström et al. 2009). Today, it is widely shared a global awareness about the need of (re)designing the planet boundaries and (re)thinking, on the one hand, the use of primary resources, and on the other hand, a new life for secondary materials. The decision-making problems, with particular focus on the urban and building scales, are dealing with important planning challenges. Actors and stakeholders are increasingly given attention to the quality of public and /or private interventions and also to the environmental impact which they could generate to the overall quality of life.

In the international context, many solicitations are counted over the latest years for a route change, spanning from the achievement of the 17 Sustainable Development Goals (SDGs), particularly the SD Goal 11 "Make cities and human settlements inclusive, safe, resilient and sustainable", the SD Goal 12 "Responsible consumption and production", and the SD Goal 13 "Climate Action", to the global reports on climate change (United Nations 2015; IPCC 2019, 2021), until to the 26th United Nation Climate Change Conference held in Glasgow (COP26) where some key issues were fixed to contrast at global warming, such as the creation of international sustainable standards on climate, environmental, social and governance issues (ESG) for businesses and related strategies, as well as the transition towards the net-zero economy (International Financial Reporting Standards - IFRS, 2021). On the one side, the put into practice of these key issues through a cascade adoption until to the local scale is a so urgent need. On the other side, an effort to detect these issues by the class of Decision Makers (DMs) and policy makers into their agendas as spatial interventions is more than ever required today.

Traditional and novel paradigms like sustainability, resiliency, or circularity emphasize the idea that urban systems and territories can be investigated through metabolic filters, since they can be conceived as living and evolving organisms that interact, evolves, adapts and respond across different spatial and temporal scales (Gunderson and Holling 2002). In this way it can be easier to understand their complexity and explore the interdependent relationships between the natural and human spheres. The concept of Urban Metabolism (UM) is not new in literature. It was firstly used to assess both industrialized systems and biological metabolic systems in terms of resource and waste flows from anthropogenic activities (Wolman 1965), influenced by ecological studies (Odum 1983) and was adapted over time and defined today as "the sum total of the technical and socio-economic process that occur in cities, resulting in growth, production of energy and elimination of waste" (Kennedy et al. 2007). UM is a very topical issue today and is interested by high margins of investigation and development. In this context, tools for sustainability assessment can effectively support policy design in the context of urban planning and management, thus promoting the "cradle to cradle" transition.

In light of the above-described context, this contribution represents a position paper of the authors which defines an integrated framework to support real assessment and planning procedures in the exploration of urban metabolism with respect to urban and territorial transformations with the aim to contribute to an extent of the state-of-the-art thinking. Moreover, the framework is finalized to help DMs, policy makers, planners and freelances to design greener and net-zero strategies.

The paper is organized into four sections: Sect. 2 is devoted to the description of the methodology, by focusing on some complex assessment tools for strategic environmental impact assessment; Sect. 3 defines a theoretical framework proposal that combines two specific assessment tools; Sect. 4 discusses the potentialities, the limits and opportunities of development and then concludes the paper with some future perspectives to prosecute this research work.

2 Complex Systems Analysis and Tools

The design of future cities and territories require ever more multidisciplinary and trans-disciplinary approaches to tackle their complexity and uncertainty. In this way, planners, and DMs can practice more easily traditional and novel paradigms within government agendas. It is certain that the environment health must be focal more than ever in policy decisions. Several methods and tools are deemed useful in this context to measure impact on the current state of the environment and its components, identifying the most valuable and most critical areas, and to predict possible futures by building alternative transformation scenarios.

Particularly, the paper focuses on two assessment tools which are considered the most suitable to be performed within strategic environmental impact assessment procedures: the Multicriteria Decision Analysis (MCDA) and the Life Cycle Assessment (LCA).

Both the methods can be employed to solve a wide range of complex problems with interdependences, that are often addressed through EIA and SEA procedures. On the one hand, MCDA can help DMs in dealing with uncertainty, subjectivity and multi-stakeholder participation (Linkov et al. 2011; Durbach and Stewart 2012), as well as in selecting the best sustainable solution, and providing a classification of the alternatives to the problem under investigation (Doumpos and Zopounidis 2004).

On the other hand, LCA is retained as a powerful technique for calculating both input and output flow of materials and energy over the course of their life cycle. Moreover, it is gaining importance within business models and, more generally, as decision supporting tool for the transition towards Circular Economy (CE) at various levels (Le Téno and Mareschal 1998; Ghisellini and Ulgiati 2020; Vázquez-Rowe et al. 2021; Hannouf et al. 2021) and addressing the complexity of metabolic processes and systems (Peponi et al. 2022).

The next sub-paragraphs provide an analysis on the concept of urban metabolism and also on both the tools, thus highlighting the strengths and weaknesses as well as potential implementations within integrated frameworks in the context of urban and territorial transformations.

2.1 Urban Metabolism

The UM definition, as stated in part in the introduction (Kennedy et al. 2007; Lucertini and Musco 2020) is intended as technical and socio-economic processes that characterise the cities functions. It can be conceptualized according to six elements: (i) complex system, that is mainly represented by urban and territorial settlements, (ii) material and energy inflows and outflows with respect to the system under investigation; (iii) economic-social interactions which may occur within the system and which are also influenced by outside relations with other systems, (4) economic driving forces that influence the rural-urban boundaries, (iv) inequalities which could be generated by the interactions, and (iv) adaptation and response to promote novel solutions able to rethink existing plans/programs/projects and envision urban planning and management strategies (Lucertini and Musco 2020).

Therefore, UM refers to a given system characterised by human presence, which constantly exchange flows of resources, energy, and information, thus contributing to its growth and development. However, a system must grow for guaranteeing a good functioning and equilibrium. This means that the resources consumption characterized the last century has significantly increased waste production and aggravated unbalances in the environment and its components (e.g. air, water, or soil, among others). This does not necessarily imply the annihilation of living creatures. It means that the metabolic processes of cities and territories have been altered and a recovery is required to ensure the survival and well-being of all living species.

Staring from the assessment of the complexity of metabolic processes associated to urban and territorial contexts, the shift to more sustainable and resilient planning and design models can be effectively supported. The expected result includes strategic guidelines and legislative suggestions, environmental mitigation and compensating initiatives, and best practices for a good Anthropocene (Bennett et al. 2016; Lucertini and Musco 2020).

Several frameworks and tools have been proposed in recent years, with the aim at encouraging beneficial interactions between disciplines and assisting Decision and Policy Makers in conceptualising and implementing as solutions of short-, medium- and long-term.

For example, in the paper (Mostafavi et al. 2014) an Integrated Urban Metabolism Analysis Tool (IUMAT) explores the dynamics occurring in urban and territorial systems from a spatial-temporal perspective and provides overall sustainability based on urban settlements typologies. The coupling of Circular Economy (CE) and Urban Metabolism (UM) in integrated and multidisciplinary frameworks is highly needed for operating in changing urban contexts (see Fig. 1) (Lucertini and Musco 2020).

An interesting conceptual framework is the Economy-Wide Material Flow Analysis (EW-MFA) that employs the Drivers-Pressures-Responses logic (as a simplified version of DPSIR tool) and the system dynamics approach between natural and human sides (Cárdenas-Mamani and Perrotti 2022), or even the combination of life cycle approach with dynamical modelling by considering a nested systems theory to support the improvement of building stocks (Stephan et al. 2022). GIS-based methods play a transversal role in dealing with complex spatial systems. The work (Montealegre et al. 2022) defines a bottom-up strategy to assessing food-energy-water systems (FEW) at district level, taking into account residential and non-residential morphology. The integration of many approaches, such as Life Cycle Thinking (LCT) and Machine Learning for Smart and regenerative urban places (SRUP).

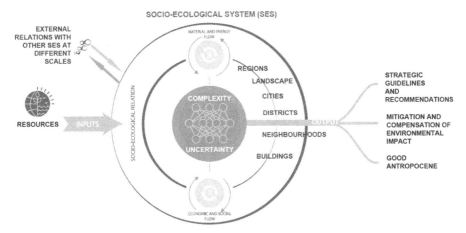

Fig. 1. Representation of urban metabolism with a multi-scale approach. Adapted from (Lucertini and Musco 2020)

2.2 Life Cycle Assessment and Regionalization of Impacts

In developed economies, the production, use, and disposal of goods along a value chain generate impacts and pressure on ecosystems and human wellbeing both at global and regional scale. LCA is a standard methodology for environmental impact accounting able to track the generation of pollutions and resource consumption and assess them from a systems perspective. The main objective of the analysis is identifying strategies for process improvement without shifting burdens along the life cycle. Recent emerging developments in LCA moved from a conventional attributional approach, mostly addressed to product development or company assessment, to a more cohesive approach to support policymakers in environmentally informed decisions or consumers in their responsive choices. Regionalization in LCA is a promising process which makes LCA more consistent for city planning and urban development (Bjorn et al. 2020). On one hand, "top-down" studies of national or transnational economies help to pinpoint crucial areas of consumption and drivers of environmental impacts in sustainable consumption and production, which could not be evaluated with a conventional attributional approach (see Fig. 2). For example, housing, mobility, and food – namely heating and cooling of buildings, car and air travel, and meat and dairy consumption - are responsible for the largest share of most environmental impacts in Europe (Tukker et al. 2008). On the other hand, more detailed "bottom-up" studies of single products or product groups can also help to determine submersed key drivers that may not be linked to the most commonly associated high impacts lifecycle stages (Garnett 2008).

Coupling LCA with material flow analysis (MFA) models is a consolidated approach in literature which allows building future scenarios and predict their environmental consequences and pressure on natural resources at a regional scale (Göswein et al. 2021). However, often the completeness in scope of regional LCA and combined LCA-MFA fails in simplifications and increasing uncertainties (Pittau et al. 2019). Recent studies have highlighted the contribution that system assumptions and value choices can

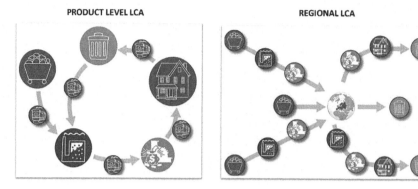

Fig. 2. The expanding nature of LCA from conventional product-based scope to regional-level assessments. Adapted from (Hellweg and Canals 2014)

make to overall uncertainty (De Schryver et al. 2013). Several quantitative uncertainty assessments and robustness analysis are available (Lloyd and Ries 2007) but are rarely implemented in practice (Galimshina et al. 2021). In some cases, rough estimates of input values can be enough to identify supply chain hotspots (Canals et al. 2011), but for other applications, such as product comparisons (Gregory et al. 2013), the demands for more accurate values are higher. LCA practitioners should always attempt to manage the decision-maker's expectations and clarify that LCA is not always a tool to provide a single answer, but rather one that permits comprehensive understanding of a problem and its possible solutions. Other studies have aimed at reducing uncertainties in LCA by mapping and assessing value chains and impacts through a regionalized approach (Yang et al. 2017; Yazdanbakhsh and Lagouin 2019). Regionalized assessments increase the accuracy by considering site-specific production conditions as well as differences in transport and the sensitivity of ecosystems. Impact-assessment methods often need a different geographical resolution, embracing the nature of the impact rather than political boundaries. However, acquiring spatial data constitutes a challenge. Although pilot research software systems are capable of doing this (Steubing et al. 2020), it has yet to be implemented in commercial LCA tools.

2.3 MCDA Within Multidisciplinary and Transdisciplinary Frameworks

Multicriteria Decision Analysis (here and after MCDA) is an umbrella term for techniques that can assist DMs and Policy Makers in solving complex situations characterised by uncertainty. This is the case of spatial problems affecting the environmental system and its key components at all scales, which often imply transformations and consequently impact, direct or indirect, cumulative, and/or synergic, resulting in a loss of natural and socio-economic capital. In this sense, the MCDA expanded its role within planning and environmental assessment procedures (i.e. Environmental Impact Assessment, Strategic Environmental Assessment, or Valuation for Ecological Incidence). The main motivation is that they can simultaneously consider numerous aspects of a decision problem. Second, they can take into consideration the preferences of real actors and stakeholders in a collaborative and transparent manner, which is another fundamental necessity to which public bodies are giving increasing attention (Fig. 3). The employment of MCDA can go beyond the monetary evaluation, such as the Cost-Benefit Analysis (CBA) or the Discount Cash-Flow Analysis (DCFA) and looking at hybrid evaluations to assess urban quality (Oppio and Dell'Ovo 2020), resilience in territorial scenarios (Assumma et al. 2020), the regeneration of critical areas (Bottero et al. 2021a), or even the ecological enhancement for animal species reintroduction (Treves et al. 2020), among others.

In an uncertain context where the policy decisions must consider the environmental impact, it is possible to state that the mentioned tools can be used whether supported by a multidimensional approach, as well as tools capable of addressing final users in the design of environmental mitigation and compensation actions to ensure a better quality of life for both present and next generations. This is a goal that MCDA can achieve.

This paragraph develops an analysis focused directly on the applications relevant in the field and emphasizing their ability or potentialities to be integrated or matched with other environmental assessment tools, such as the Life Cycle Assessment.

Table 1 collects exemplary MCDA applications. The selection was made by searching the Scopus database in March 2022. Specific contributions were selected according to the main scope of this paper and by combining specific keywords such as "multidisciplinary", "transdisciplinary", "decision-making process", "urban planning" and "management". In recent years, there has been an increasing trend in number of contributions that integrate MCDA with other methodologies, ranging from land use planning to landscape ecology, from site localisation to urban regeneration processes, from sustainability to resiliency assessment until circularity. The scope of this selection is to find those applications which highlight MCDA as a powerful tool being applied within multidisciplinary and transdisciplinary frameworks to solve complex spatial problems.

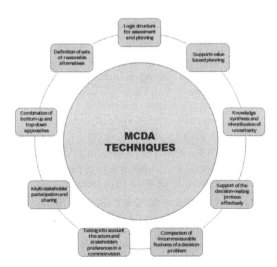

Fig. 3. MCDA techniques benefits from supporting decision-making process. Elaboration from (Marttunen 2010)

Table 1. Collection of exemplary MCDA applications within interdisciplinary and multidisciplinary frameworks

Author and Year	Structure	Field of application
(Miller et al. 2013)	Multicriteria Analysis and Geodesign to integrating livability and sustainability indicators into the overall planning process	Transportation policy and planning
(Evers et al. 2018)	Collaborative Modelling (CM) and MCDA within a Flood Risk Management framework (FRM) to favour the process-driven decision-making	Risk assessment and management
(Bottero et al. 2019)	Integration of A'WOT, DFCA and SROI to design strategies for the rural development of an island by taking into account social, economic, environmental and cultural features	Rural sustainable development
(Bottero et al. 2021.a)	Hybrid evaluation method including STEEP + SWOT Analysis, Stakeholders Analysis, Scenario Building and Multi-Attribute Value Theory to support the identification of the most suitable scenario of urban regeneration for a contaminated sited	Urban regeneration, Industrial Heritage
(Assumma et al. 2021)	Matching of SMARTER Ranking method through a AHP approach with a Lotka-Volterra cooperative model to predict scenarios of territorial resilience in a wine region	Landscape and urban planning
(Dell'Ovo et al. 2021)	GIS and MCDA for exploring the quality of open spaces in the context of COVID-19 pandemics	Urban design
(Vázquez-Rowe et al. 2021)	Coupling of MCDA, CBA and LCA to support the solution of a Building Information Modelling-based problem for a construction project	Education infrastructure

(continued)

Table 1. (*continued*)

Author and Year	Structure	Field of application
(Colucci et al. 2022)	Development of a European Interoperable Database for risk assessment of cultural assets. Integration of the SMARTER ranking method and factsheets to calculate a synthetic index of risk to support 3D GIS systems	Risk and Cultural Heritage management
(Voukkali and Zorpas 2022)	Assessment of urban metabolism through SWOT and AHP process	Urban metabolism
(Quagliolo et al. 2023)	Combination of InVEST modeling and A'WOT model to define the most suitable scenario to respond to flood risk in a Man and Biosphere area	Nature-Based Solutions

3   Integrated Evaluation Framework: A Methodological Proposal

Once having analysed the main characteristics of both the LCA and MCDA, it is possible to assert that they are suited for usage as independent tools as well as when integrated within multidisciplinary and transdisciplinary frameworks. In the case when they enter in synergy to solve the same decision problem, can effectively identify the most suitable solution. More in general, this synergy can handle the complexity and unpredictability of Socio-Ecological Systems (SES) (e.g., cities, rural settlements, or regions). Particularly, some specific cases are identified for implementing this synergy for urban revitalization and adaptive reuse (e.g. historic buildings, industrial sites, or villages, or rural accessibility), regeneration, growth, and cohesion (e.g. polluted sites, quarries, or landfills) as new opportunities for spatial planning (Biddau et al. 2020; Cotella and Vitale Brovarone 2021). Their integration can effectively assist DMs, as well as planners, public technicians and freelances for multiple purposes: i) knowledge and assessment studies for intervention site localisation; ii) selection of the best alternative solution; iii) designing the alternatives by considering the material and energy flow; iv) prioritizing winning policy recommendations for plans, programs, and projects, among others. It is provided below a scheme that illustrates the integration of both the tools proposed by the authors as a multi-scale hybrid dynamic model for a multi-scale impact assessment. As shown in Fig. 4, the integrated framework can effectively play the connecting role between planning and assessment procedures. From a practical point of view, the framework can be employed after the screening step (or *ex-ante* phase), once having acquired a comprehensive knowledge of territorial and decisional contexts. Therefore, it can be easily fixed the assessment goal and follow the *in-itinere* phase. The obtained information can be used to define the main criteria better representing the decisional problem and thus to be evaluated by MCDA, according to key actors and stakeholders' preferences, in order to select the best sustainable solution. It should be noted, however, that the solution of a decision problem through MCDA techniques such as Analytic Hierarchy Process (AHP) and Analytic Network Process (ANP) can provide the winning solution, even if the final decision to implement or not that solution is devoted to the DMs, since they detain the political power. Therefore, the evaluator should design the alternative evaluations and criteria selection according to the multidimensionality of a given decision problem, as well as the actors and stakeholders' *desiderata*. The alternatives design should be accompanied by a participatory approach, both bottom-up and top-down, with the purpose of converging towards sustainable policy decisions, including the economic development, social equity and environmental compatibility, and also other relevant components (i.e. technical, administrative-political, and cultural sustainability) (Bottero and Mondini 2009). In the case when the decision problem is explored with the desktop modality, the evaluator's sensitivity, as well as his/her ability to properly identify and blend a variety of driving forces, are required for scenarios building and planning.

In both the cases, the selection of the best solution will help the final users to define strategic and time-oriented recommendations and guidelines.

The LCA contribute to increase the awareness that an individual choice could have an impact on the environment and its components. It can effectively promote the transition towards a circular planning and design, ranging from the local to the regional scales. It can assess a set of alternatives, also complementary to a MCDA evaluation. For example, the alternatives can be contradistinguished using specific materials that can impact on the environment, or that can be recycled and (re)used in their second life in the production cycle. The LCA can address both planning and evaluation processes once the suitable alternative scenario is identified and monitor its performance over time (*ex-post* phase) by considering the material flow analysis and specific indicators.

Considering the scheme of the integrated framework (Fig. 4) we can combine the tools according to a multi-scalar approach, on the one hand, to explore the life and material flow and energy, and on the other hand, to identify the main characteristics of the problem under investigation and the cost-effectiveness ratio of the set of alternative scenarios under investigation.

Particularly, the authors identify some opportunities of employment of this framework. It could be useful in the context of spatial planning and management, for example for the revision of municipal plans, or urban regeneration projects, or even high-impact spatial projects, since these can increase the awareness of final users about the environmental impact entity generated by an intervention, as well as on the sensibilization of secondary material use for closing the cycles. An equitable context of investigation is environmental planning and management, with particular regard to the design and assessment of projects inspired by Nature-Based Solution approach (NBS) (Quagliolo et al. 2023). Last, but not least, the context of sustainable tourism planning could trigger interesting insights in terms of design of circular policies and actions, since projects and interventions developed in tourism destinations impact strongly on the environment, where local communities consensus could not be always reached (Cimnaghi and Mussini 2015; Mandić and Kennell 2021).

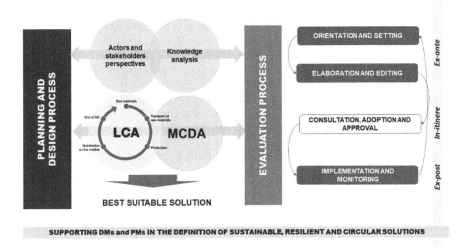

Fig. 4. Definition of the integrated framework combining LCA and MCDA (Own elaboration)

4   Conclusions

The resilient development of the society towards SDGs and the transition to net-zero carbon target by 2050 are challenging objectives which require a specific attention on current planning issues and understanding of complex mechanisms of urban metabolism. Life cycle integrated multi-criteria decision tools are fundamental instruments for sustainability assessment of urban and territorial development due to their ability to tackle the increasing complexity and uncertanties during the evaluation process.

This position paper aimed to identify an integrated framework to explore urban metabolism and define benefits and critical issues of applying integrated Life Cycle Assessment (LCA) and Multicriteria Decision Analysis (MCDA) for decision making. Outcomes from literature were reviewed and suitable tools, with spatial boundaries ranging from building to city/territory levels, discussed to evaluate sustainability, resiliency, and circularity within a multi-scaling approach. Regionalization and accuracy of data are currently the major limits of the integrated framework. Future advances in enhancing regional detail and broadening the assessment to economic and social aspects will make it more relevant for stakeholders involved in planning and assessment procedures.

References

Assumma, V., Bottero, M., Datola, G., et al.: Dynamic models for exploring the resilience in territorial scenarios. Sustain. **12**, 3 (2020). https://doi.org/10.3390/su12010003

Assumma, V., Bottero, M., De Angelis, E., et al.: A decision support system for territorial resilience assessment and planning: An application to the Douro Valley (Portugal). Sci. Total Environ. **756**, 143806 (2021). https://doi.org/10.1016/j.scitotenv.2020.143806

Bennett, E.M., Solan, M., Biggs, R., et al.: Bright spots: Seeds of a good Anthropocene. Front. Ecol. Environ. **14**, 441–448 (2016). https://doi.org/10.1002/fee.1309

Biddau, G.M., Marotta, A., Sanna, G.: Abandoned landscape project design. City, Territ. Archit. **7**, 1–17 (2020). https://doi.org/10.1186/S40410-020-00118-7/FIGURES/13

Bjorn, A., Chandrakumar, C., Boulay, A.M., et al.: Review of life-cycle based methods for absolute environmental sustainability assessment and their applications. Environ. Res. Lett. **15**, 083001 (2020). https://doi.org/10.1088/1748-9326/AB89D7

Bottero, M., Assumma, V., Caprioli, C., Dell'Ovo, M.: Decision making in urban development: The application of a hybrid evaluation method for a critical area in the city of Turin (Italy). Sustain Cities Soc **72**, 103028 (2021). https://doi.org/10.1016/j.scs.2021.103028

Bottero, M., Comino, E., Dell'Anna, F., et al.: Strategic assessment and economic evaluation: The case study of Yanzhou Island (China). Sustain. **11**, 1076 (2019). https://doi.org/10.3390/SU11041076

Bottero, M., Mondini, G.: Valutazione e sostenibilità. Piani, programmi, progetti. CELID, Torino (2009)

Canals, L.M.I., Azapagic, A., Doka, G., et al.: Approaches for addressing life cycle assessment data gaps for bio-based products. J. Ind. Ecol. **15**, 707–725 (2011). https://doi.org/10.1111/J.1530-9290.2011.00369.X

Cárdenas-Mamani, Ú., Perrotti, D.: Understanding the contribution of ecosystem services to urban metabolism assessments: An integrated framework. Ecol. Indic. **136**, 108593 (2022). https://doi.org/10.1016/J.ECOLIND.2022.108593

Cimnaghi, E., Mussini, P.: An application of tourism carrying capacity assessment at two Italian cultural heritage sites. J. Herit. Tour. **10**, 302–313 (2015). https://doi.org/10.1080/1743873X.2014.988158

Colucci, E., Matrone, F., Noardo, F., et al.: Documenting cultural heritage in an INSPIRE-based 3D GIS for risk and vulnerability analysis. J. Cult. Herit. Manag. Sustain. Dev., 1–302022). https://doi.org/10.1108/JCHMSD-04-2021-0068/FULL/HTML

Cotella, G., Vitale Brovarone, E.: Rethinking urbanisation after COVID-19: What role for the EU cohesion policy? Town Plan Rev. **92**, 411–418 (2021). https://doi.org/10.3828/TPR.2020.54

De Schryver, A.M., Humbert, S., Huijbregts, M.A.J.: The influence of value choices in life cycle impact assessment of stressors causing human health damage. Int. J. Life Cycle Assess. **18**, 698–706 (2013). https://doi.org/10.1007/s11367-012-0504-x

Dell'Ovo, M., Dezio, C., Oppio, A.: Bringing values at the center of policies for inner areas regeneration in the Covid-19 age. Territ - Sez Open Access, 43–51 (2021).https://doi.org/10.3280/TR2021-097-SUPPLEMENTOOA12926

Doumpos, M., Zopounidis, C.: A multicriteria classification approach based on pairwise comparisons. Eur. J. Oper. Res. **158**, 378–389 (2004). https://doi.org/10.1016/J.EJOR.2003.06.011

Durbach, I.N., Stewart, T.J.: Modeling uncertainty in multi-criteria decision analysis. Eur. J. Oper. Res. **223**, 1–14 (2012). https://doi.org/10.1016/J.EJOR.2012.04.038

Evers, M., Almoradie, A., de Brito, M.M.: Enhancing flood resilience through collaborative modelling and multi-criteria decision analysis (MCDA). In: Fekete, A., Fiedrich, F. (eds.) Urban Disaster Resilience and Security. TUBS, pp. 221–236. Springer, Cham (2018). https://doi.org/10.1007/978-3-319-68606-6_14

Galimshina, A., Moustapha, M., Hollberg, A., et al.: What is the optimal robust environmental and cost-effective solution for building renovation? Not the usual one. Energy Build. **251**, 111329 (2021). https://doi.org/10.1016/J.ENBUILD.2021.111329

Garnett, T.: Cooking up a storm Food, greenhouse gas emissions and our changing climate Cooking up a storm Food, greenhouse gas emissions and our changing climate Food Climate Research Network (2008)

Ghisellini, P., Ulgiati, S.: Circular economy transition in Italy. Achievements, perspectives and constraints. J. Clean. Prod. **243**, 118360 (2020). https://doi.org/10.1016/J.JCLEPRO.2019.118360

Gregory, J.R., Montalbo, T.M., Kirchain, R.E.: Analyzing uncertainty in a comparative life cycle assessment of hand drying systems. Int. J. Life Cycle Assess **18**, 1605–1617 (2013). https://doi.org/10.1007/s11367-013-0606-0

Göswein, V., Reichmann, J., Habert, G., Pittau, F.: Land availability in Europe for a radical shift toward bio-based construction. Sustain. Cities Soc. **70**, 102929 (2021). https://doi.org/10.1016/J.SCS.2021.102929

Gunderson, L.H., Holling, C.S.: Panarchy: Understanding transformations in systems of humans and nature (2002)

Hannouf, M.B., Assefa, G., Hannouf, M.B., Gates, I.: Cause-effect chains in S-LCA based on DPSIR framework using Markov healthcare model: an application to "working hours" in Canada. Int. J. Life Cycle Assess. **26**, 936–949 (2021). https://doi.org/10.1007/S11367-021-01900-6/FIGURES/7

Hellweg, S., Milà I Canals, L.: Emerging approaches, challenges and opportunities in life cycle assessment. Science **344**, 1109–1113 (2014). https://doi.org/10.1126/SCIENCE.1248361/SUPPL_FILE/HELLWEG-SM.PDF

IFRS - International Financial Reporting Standards. IFRS in your pocket 2021 (2021). https://www.iasplus.com/en/publications/global/ifrs-in-your-pocket/2021/at_download/file/IFRS%20in%20your%20pocket%202021.pdf. Accessed June 2022

IPCC: Global Warming of 1.5°C. An IPCC Special Report on the impacts of global warming of 1.5°C above pre-industrial levels and related global greenhouse gas emission pathways, in the context of strengthening the global response to the threat of climate change (2019)

IPCC: Summary for Policymakers SPM Summary for Policymakers Drafting Authors (2021). https://doi.org/10.1017/9781009157896.001

Kennedy, C., Cuddihy, J., Engel-Yan, J.: The changing metabolism of cities. J. Ind. Ecol. **11**, 43–59 (2007). https://doi.org/10.1162/JIE.2007.1107

Le Téno, J.F., Mareschal, B.: An interval version of PROMETHEE for the comparison of building products' design with ill-defined data on environmental quality. Eur. J. Oper. Res. **109**, 522–529 (1998). https://doi.org/10.1016/S0377-2217(98)00074-5

Linkov, I., Welle, P., Loney, D., et al.: Use of multicriteria decision analysis to support weight of evidence evaluation. Risk Anal. **31**, 1211–1225 (2011). https://doi.org/10.1111/J.1539-6924.2011.01585.X

Lloyd, S.M., Ries, R.: Characterizing, propagating, and analyzing uncertainty in life-cycle assessment: A survey of quantitative approaches. J. Ind. Ecol. **11**, 161–179 (2007). https://doi.org/10.1162/JIEC.2007.1136

Lucertini, G., Musco, F.: Circular urban metabolism framework. One Earth **2**, 138–142 (2020). https://doi.org/10.1016/J.ONEEAR.2020.02.004

Mandić, A., Kennell, J.: Smart governance for heritage tourism destinations: Contextual factors and destination management organization perspectives. Tour. Manag. Perspect. **39**, 100862 (2021). https://doi.org/10.1016/J.TMP.2021.100862

Marttunen, M.: Description of Multi-Criteria Decision Analysis (MCDA) (2010). http://environment.sal.aalto.fi/MCDA/. Accessed 17 May 2022

Miller, H.J., Witlox, F., Tribby, C.P.: Developing context-sensitive livability indicators for transportation planning: A measurement framework. J. Transp. Geogr. **26**, 51–64 (2013). https://doi.org/10.1016/J.JTRANGEO.2012.08.007

Montealegre, A.L., García-Pérez, S., Guillén-Lambea, S., et al.: GIS-based assessment for the potential of implementation of food-energy-water systems on building rooftops at the urban level. Sci. Total Environ. **803**, 149963 (2022). https://doi.org/10.1016/J.SCITOTENV.2021.149963

Mostafavi, N., Farzinmoghadam, M., Hoque, S.: A framework for integrated urban metabolism analysis tool (IUMAT). Build. Environ. **82**, 702–712 (2014). https://doi.org/10.1016/J.BUILDENV.2014.10.020

Odum, H.T.: Systems Ecology: An Introduction (Environmental Science and Technology: A Wiley-Interscience Series of Texts and Monographs) (9780471652779): Odum, H.T., Books (1983)

Oppio, A., Dell'Ovo, M.: Strategic Environmental Assessment (SEA) and Multi-Criteria Analysis: An Integrated Approach, pp. 47–63 (2020)

Peponi, A., Morgado, P., Kumble, P.: Life cycle thinking and machine learning for urban metabolism assessment and prediction. Sustain. Cities Soc. **80**, 103754 (2022). https://doi.org/10.1016/J.SCS.2022.103754

Pittau, F., Lumia, G., Heeren, N., Iannaccone, G., Habert, G.: Retrofit as a carbon sink: The carbon storage potentials of the EU housing stock. J. Cleaner Prod. **214**(2019), 365–376 (2019). https://www.sciencedirect.com/science/journal/09596526/214/supp/C. https://doi.org/10.1016/j.jclepro.2018.12.304

Quagliolo, C., Assumma, V., Comino, E., et al.: An integrated method to assess flood risk and resilience in the MAB UNESCO Collina Po (Italy). In: Lecture Notes in Networks and Systems (2023, in press)

Rockström, J., Steffen, W., Noone, K., et al.: A safe operating space for humanity. Nat. **461**(7263), 472–475 (2009). https://doi.org/10.1038/461472a

Stephan, A., Crawford, R.H., Bunster, V., et al.: Towards a multiscale framework for modeling and improving the life cycle environmental performance of built stocks. J. Ind. Ecol. (2022). https://doi.org/10.1111/JIEC.13254

Steubing, B., de Koning, D., Haas, A., Mutel, C.L.: The activity browser — An open source LCA software building on top of the brightway framework. Softw. Impacts **3**, 100012 (2020). https://doi.org/10.1016/J.SIMPA.2019.100012

Treves, A., Bottero, M., Caprioli, C., Comino, E.: The reintroduction of Castor fiber in Piedmont (Italy): An integrated SWOT-spatial multicriteria based approach for the analysis of suitability scenarios. Ecol. Indic. **118**, 106748 (2020). https://doi.org/10.1016/J.ECOLIND.2020.106748

Tukker, A., Emmert, S., Charter, M., et al.: Fostering change to sustainable consumption and production: An evidence based view. J. Clean. Prod. **16**, 1218–1225 (2008). https://doi.org/10.1016/J.JCLEPRO.2007.08.015

United Nations: Transforming Our World: the 2030 Agenda for Sustainable Development United Nations United Nations Transforming Our World: the 2030 Agenda for Sustainable Development. A/RES/70/1. United Nations (2015)

Vázquez-Rowe, I., Córdova-Arias, C., Brioso, X., Santa-Cruz, S.: A method to include life cycle assessment results in choosing by advantage (Cba) multicriteria decision analysis. A case study for seismic retrofit in peruvian primary schools. Sustain **13**, 1–18 (2021). https://doi.org/10.3390/su13158139

Voukkali, I., Zorpas, A.A.: Evaluation of urban metabolism assessment methods through SWOT analysis and analytical hierocracy process. Sci. Total Environ. **807**, 150700 (2022). https://doi.org/10.1016/J.SCITOTENV.2021.150700

Wolman, A.: The metabolism of cities. Sci. Am. **213**, 178–190 (1965). https://doi.org/10.1038/scientificamerican0965-178

Yang, Y., Heijungs, R., Brandão, M.: Hybrid life cycle assessment (LCA) does not necessarily yield more accurate results than process-based LCA. J. Clean. Prod. **150**, 237–242 (2017). https://doi.org/10.1016/J.JCLEPRO.2017.03.006

Yazdanbakhsh, A., Lagouin, M.: The effect of geographic boundaries on the results of a regional life cycle assessment of using recycled aggregate in concrete. Resour. Conserv. Recycl. **143**, 201–209 (2019). https://doi.org/10.1016/J.RESCONREC.2019.01.002

Assessing the Impacts of a Social Housing Project Through the Community Impact Evaluation (CIE) Methodology

Marta Bottero[✉] 🄳, Caterina Caprioli🄳, Giulia Datola🄳, and Nadia Caruso🄳

Dipartimento Interateneo di Scienze, Progetto e Politiche del Territorio, Politecnico di Torino, 10125 Torino, Italy

{marta.bottero,caterina.caprioli,giulia.datola,
nadia.caruso}@polito.it

Abstract. Housing policies concern complex and multidimensional decision problems, as far as they engage different stakeholders with different objectives and values. Moreover, these policies represent a significant effort in reaching social sustainability, with the aim of encouraging community engagement and the reduction of social inequalities. Within this context, an evaluation tool able to manage multidimensional impacts derived from these policies is required in order to assess the nature and the degree of these effects on the involved stakeholders. The present paper proposes the application of a mixed method, composed by the SWOT, the Stakeholders Analysis (SA), and the Community Impact Evaluation (CIE) to assess the multidimensional impacts and the overall impacts of the Ma.Ri. House project (Turin) on the different engaged stakeholders. The final result is a qualitative and multidimensional evaluation performed in the ex-ante phase that highlights the complexity and the multidimensionality of the interventions underlying which are the main effects of the proposes project.

Keywords: Community Impact Evaluation (CIE) · Social housing · Stakeholder Analysis (SA) · Multidimensional impacts · Decision-making supporting systems

1 Introduction

Public policies, known as the "welfare state" started to be less effective at the end of the 80s of the last century. This happens due to some limits of this system, spanning from the huge tax burden of public financing and the standardized measures applied in all contexts [1]. The overcoming of this model helps to change the role of states and their margin of intervention in the field of welfare measures, establishing new relationships with other subjects, including private ones. This new policy framework is known as "welfare society", where private entities, market actors, and nonprofit social enterprises work with public bodies in the direction of providing strategies specific to the area and territory where they are activated, as well as integrating different social actions, avoiding the adoption of separate interventions [2].

O. Gervasi et al. (Eds.): ICCSA 2022 Workshops, LNCS 13380, pp. 183–194, 2022.
https://doi.org/10.1007/978-3-031-10542-5_13

Housing policies have also followed a similar evolution. These measures were entirely managed by States during the 2WW reconstruction, but when public resources started to become limited, public and private partnerships have assumed even more strategic importance, built a closer relationship, and divided duties [3].

The impact assessment represents a good framework and tool to evaluate, in an *ex-ante, in itinere* and *ex-post* phase, a policy, project, plan, or program, in order to understand the stakeholders and resources involved in a process, as well as to trigger development processes whose effects can be measured in qualitative and quantitative terms. In the context of social housing policies and projects, the design of strategic actions is characterized by a multi-objective perspective and a multi-stakeholder view [4]. Consequently, it is necessary to rigorously set the design process, defining the objectives in an ex-ante phase and examining them in the medium term [4]. This allows the analyst to list, from the beginning, any externalities and effects affecting the local community system and the stakeholders involved in the process. The issue of externalities is crucial, whether positive or negative, in supporting social housing policies and strategies. However, their values are not always easily managed and assessed.

Housing policies are also engaged with the target of creating sustainable and inclusive cities and communities, as stated by the UN Sustainable Development Goals (SDGs) [5]. Thus, these interventions can contribute to achieve the social sustainability, through the promotion of community engagement and actions focused to reduce inequality, displacement, and poor quality of livability [6]. Therefore, the evaluation of the social impacts of physical elements and urban transformation is required [7].

Within this context, the present paper explores the potential of an integrated approach to evaluate the social impact of a social housing project in the city of Turin (Italy). The integrated approach adopts a SWOT Analysis, a Stakeholder Analysis (SA), and the Community Impact Evaluation (CIE) methodology. The novelty of the paper is related to the adoption and integration of CIE in the context of social housing assessment. In urban development and spatial planning, examples of CIE applications regard the evaluation of urban development projects [8–13], the estimation of costs and benefits for cultural built heritage conservation [14], and support for the design process [15]. Moreover, the framework proposed in this paper can be easily replicated and used for other decision-making problems, spanning from site to district/urban scale and from design projects to urban transformation programs.

2 Methodology

The present analysis proposes an integrated approach that adopts a SWOT Analysis, a SA, and CIE. The SWOT Analysis and the SA helped with the preliminary investigation of the context and the identification of the main stakeholders involved in the process. Then, the CIE methodology supports the evaluation of the multidimensional impacts (both positive and negative) generated by the project, as well as the impacts affecting the list of stakeholders previously detailed.

Developed around the 60s, the SWOT Analysis is a well-known technique aiming to analyze the strengths (S), the weaknesses (W), the opportunities (O), and the threats (T) of a complex problem [16]. The SWOT analysis aids in qualitatively identifying the drivers that can maximize strengths and opportunities while minimizing weaknesses and threats.

SA is a widely applied methodology in spatial planning, proper to list and map all the actors influenced or involved in the process analyzed [17]. SA is, therefore, able to highlight the interests and objectives of the stakeholders, based on their values and preferences [18]. The inclusion and comprehension of these different values and preferences, as well as the relations among the stakeholders, help to include them in the evaluation and/or design process from the first stages, eventually predicting outcomes and possible resolutions of conflicts [19]. From a practical standpoint, SA starts with listing and collecting the involved stakeholders and some of their characteristics, such as their level of intervention (national, regional, local), the category of actors to which they belong (political, bureaucratic, special interest, general interest, experts), and the resources they use (political, economic, legal, cognitive), as well as their roles and expectations [18, 19]. Among the various techniques for conducting SA, the present research adopts a Power-Interest Matrix [20, 21]. As the name suggests, this technique shows the different power and interest of the stakeholders concerning the project/plan/policy under analysis, thus providing information on the key-players, those to be satisfied or keep informed, and those to monitor.

CIE is a qualitative methodology that supports the preliminary evaluation of a project, plan, or policy [22]. The results obtained from the application of CIE represent not a resolution of a complex problem, but a suitable tool for conducting a preliminary analysis of a decision-making process by including the objectives of the project/plan analyzed, their impacts and benefits, with the stakeholders' views and aspirations. The development of CIE is essentially composed of the following steps [15]. Step 1 contains an overview of the project/plan/policy and the context of analysis, where the effects of the transformation could have an influence. Step 2 is devoted to listing and mapping all the stakeholders involved in the decision-making process or influenced by the intervention. According to this different inclusion of the stakeholders in the process (i.e., involved or influenced), the stakeholders are classified in CIE as active actors (who directly take actions and do the transformation) and passive subjects (who simply use or benefit from the good or service). In CIE, stakeholders are also mapped according to the time in which they are most relevant (in the short or medium-long term) and their spatial location (on-site and off-site). In Step 3, all the project/plan/policy objectives are listed and compared with the stakeholders' aims. This analysis is instrumental in the decision-making process to predict and evaluate the stakeholders' interests in an *ex-ante* phase of the project/plan/policy proposed. Following the classification proposed by Lichfield (1998), the objectives and stakeholders' interests are examined according to three categories of impacts generated by the project/plan/policy:

- monetary effects, classified as financial (F) that address the cost and revenues of the interventions, and fiscal (FIS) which include tax advantage both for individuals and for the public;
- non-monetary impacts, classified as social (SOC), environmental (ENV), and cultural (CUL);
- mixed impacts, which refer to the economic impacts (ECO).

The evaluation of these aforementioned impacts is conducted for each stakeholder and for each objective by filling in an intersection grid, called a coaxial matrix, on a qualitative scale.

3   Case Study

This paper analyses the case study of the Ma.Ri. House project, a new temporary house located in the periphery of the city of Turin (Italy) (Fig. 1).

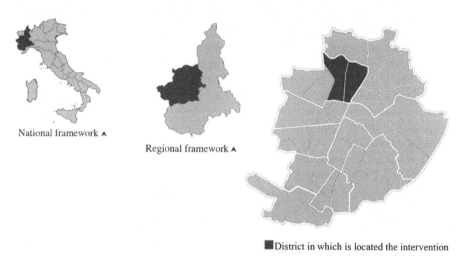

National framework ▲

Regional framework ▲

■District in which is located the intervention

Fig. 1. Territorial framework

The main objective of this project is to provide a temporary residence for both vulnerable people and those who need temporary accommodation for work or study reasons. The principal investor is Compagnia di San Paolo, a bank foundation that is involved in several regeneration projects with specific attention to the housing issue. Along with Compagnia di San Paolo, others collaborate in the realization of the project, such as the Municipality of Turin, the Caritas Diocesana, and Synergica, a social cooperative managing the building. The Ma.Ri. House aims at responding to a temporary housing need (18 months maximum), allocating spaces for families in emergency or housing stress, students, and temporary workers. Furthermore, the project hopes to respond to needs at the neighborhood and municipal level by creating a cultural hub. Therefore, the result will be the creation of a functional mix able to respond to diversified social needs, which allows to achieve financial equilibrium and the economic sustainability of the intervention.

4   Application

As specified in the methodological section, this research combines SWOT, SA, and CIE. The SWOT analysis has been first performed to examine the area of intervention, according to its strengths, weaknesses, opportunities, and threats. Figure 2 shows the SWOT analysis developed for the case study. Furthermore, this analysis can be used to help define actions that will highlight the strengths and opportunities while reducing the negative impact of the weaknesses and the threats.

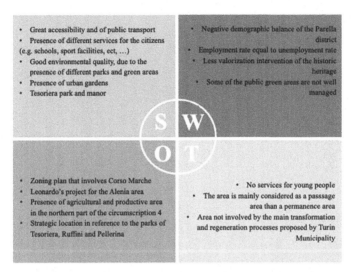

Fig. 2. SWOT analysis (elaborated from Mion, 2021)

Secondly, SA has been performed according to the power-interest matrix techniques. This analysis has been helpful in identifying the different stakeholders engaged in the project, as well as their objectives and position in relation to the project, categorizing them as "key players", "keep satisfied", "keep informed," and "minimal efforts". Figure 3 illustrates the developed power-interest matrix. As it is possible to see, the stakeholders Association Insieme per accogliere, Association Provincia Italiana dei Missionari di Nostra Signora delle Salette, Association Caritas of Turin, and the Social cooperative Synergica are identified as key players, according to their involvement in the financing of the project. Furthermore, SA is a fundamental step in developing the CIE in order to verify the different impacts on the various stakeholders.

The project Ma.Ri House is based on three general objectives, i.e., building temporary housing (1), accompanying people towards housing independence (2), and the creation of a cultural hub (3). These three objectives, respectively, refer to three fundamental dimensions, i.e., housing, social, and territorial. They share a common social view and various interconnected elements. The topic of housing deprivation, in fact, is not simply limited to the difficult access to the real estate market, but also to the reduced employment, social, and cultural opportunities in the city. For this reason, the project proposes affordable housing integrated with spaces for social gathering and personal empowerment in the same place.

The strategic vision of the three general objectives is put into place in the project through a set of specific goals, as it is possible to see in the two columns of Table 1. For example, different targeted people are considered in the development of the social

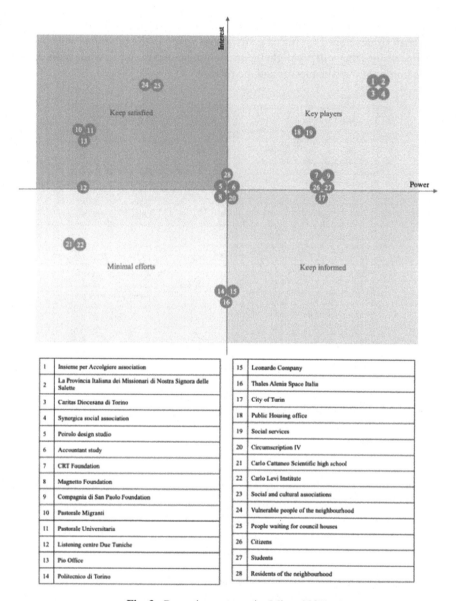

Fig. 3. Power interest matrix (Mion, 2021)

housing, i.e., fragile people, the citizens living in the deprived location, the off-site students, and the occasional workers.

According to CIE, once the objectives of the plan, project, or policy under investigation are identified, it is possible to classify and assess the different impacts (Table 1). Following the classification proposed by Coscia & De Filippi (2016) [23], the cluster divides the impacts into monetary and non-monetary. The sub-cluster consists of financial, fiscal, economic, social, cultural, and environmental impacts. The financial impact includes all the costs and revenues produced by the project, including those generated outside the transformation area. Examples of financial impacts in the Ma.Ri project are related to the capital investment for the building requalification and the implementation and promotion of socio-cultural initiatives. The fiscal impacts are the fiscal advantages connected to the project realization considering the current policy law. The present analysis does not consider the fiscal ones, thus the tax or fiscal benefits related to the project, since they are not relevant in the current phase of the investigation, as well as coherent with the objective of the developed analysis. The economic impacts collect the benefits that public and private stakeholders indirectly gain from the project as an externality. For example, the project can improve the existing building conditions in the area and increase the surrounding real-estate market values or create new job positions. The social impacts refer to social benefits generated by the project that involves the improvement of the sense of community, quality of life, and the citizens' well-being. The project can improve the social conditions through additional services and activities offered to neighbors, the creation of new social relationships and supportive networks, and the reduction of citizens living in a deprived state. The cultural impacts affect the developed of new cultural poles or enterprises, but they also experiment with new business models and the technical knowledge related to them. All these aspects can be achieved by the project, increasing the population's awareness of social topics and social interactions, as well as the experimentation with new business models grounded in a sharing economy. The environmental impacts consider all the positive and negative effects of the project on the environmental quality of the building and the surrounding areas. The renewal of an existing building is undoubtedly positive in terms of soil consumption and land take, as well as the reorganization of the public spaces and, particularly, the existing garden.

Then, analyzing the stakeholders involved, it is possible to state that above their different position in the power-interest matrix, they generally have similar views and objectives related to this project, considering all the three general project objectives equally important. Exemptions are those stakeholders with a very specific interest, such as, for example, schools that are more interested in the territorial dimension as an occasion to make and increase the network with citizens. Conversely, the three main foundations, which finance the project, aim for the complete realization of the project in all its dimensions. This analysis supports the following step of CIE, where the impacts are associated with the stakeholders influenced by them. In most cases, a single stakeholder is affected by many types of impacts, due to the strong connection between the project and social, cultural, and environmental aspects. The coaxial matrix represented in Table 2 shows both the partial and final qualitative evaluation of the impacts for each stakeholder and for each objective of the project, highlighting if the influences are positive or negative. The qualitative judgment follows a 7-point scale from very bad influence (red) to very positive influence (green). The final judgments are simply the summation of the partial judgments of each stakeholder. From Table 2, it is possible to clearly appreciate the financial losses of the key players in the project and the banking foundations. Conversely, many positive impacts generated by the project, particularly social, cultural, and environmental, effectively counterbalance the negative ones. The coaxial matrix additionally highlights how the housing objective is the most negative one in terms of financial expenses but also the most positive in terms of non-monetary impacts, since it contributes to ameliorating the well-being and quality of life of the citizens and the people living there, generating cultural innovations, and reducing the land take in the urban context. Instead, the second and third objectives aim to satisfy only one of the non-monetary impacts, i.e., the social dimension for the second objective and the cultural dimension for the third objective, respectively. Accompanying towards autonomy is specifically addressed to fragile people, creating social networks and supportive relationships, and avoiding marginalization. The realization of a territorial social aggregation center makes possible the development of opportunities for cultural growth, awareness, and promotion.

Table 1. Objectives – impacts matrix (elaborated from Mion, 2021)

OBJECTIVES		IMPACT TYPOLOGIES				
		MONETARY		NON-MONETARY		
General objectives	**Detailed objectives**	F	M	S	C	E
Building a temporary housing	A temporary residence for gray band population A temporary residence for people with a state of housing deprivation A temporary residence for off-site students with low-cost expenses A temporary residence for people with occasional work					
Accompanying towards autonomy	Accompanying paths towards housing autonomy Accompanying paths to work					
Creation of a territorial social aggregation center	Meeting points for the inhabitants of the neighborhood Services for guests and citizens with a view to sharing economy Raising population awareness about the housing problems in the city to counter prejudice					

Table 2. Final evaluation matrix with the co-axial matrix (elaborated from Mion, 2021)

	ACTORS	IMPACTS					OVERALL IMPACTS
		F	M	S	C	E	
PRIVATE	Association "Insieme per accogliere"						
	Association "Provincia Italiana dei Missionari di Nostra Signora delle Salette"						
	Association "Caritas" of Turin						
	Social cooperative "Synergica"						
	Design studio "Peirolo"						
	Financial advisor						
	Foundation CRT						
	Foundation Magnetto						
	Foundation Compagnia di San Paolo						
	Foundation "Office Pio"						
	Pastoral care of migrants						
	University pastoral care						
	Counseling office "Due Tuniche"						
	Polythecnic of Turin						
	Company "Leonardo"						
	Company "Thales Alenia Space"						
PUBLIC	Metropolitan City of Turin						
	Metropolitan City of Turin – Social housing sector						
	Metropolitan City of Turin – Social services						
	Metropolitan City of Turin – Circoscrizione IV						
	High school "Carlo Cattaneo"						
	Institute "Carlo Levi"						
CIVIL SOCIETY	Voluntary association and third sector realities						
	People experiencing housing stress						
	People in housing emergency						
	City users						
	University students						
	Neighborhood inhabitants						

OBJECTIVES

		F	M	S	C	E	
	Building a temporary housing						
	Accompanying towards autonomy						
	Creation of a territorial social aggregation center						

Legend

Very negative
Negative
Average negative
Neutral
Average positive
Positive
Very positive

5 Discussion and Conclusions

The aim of the present paper is to evaluate the multidimensional impacts provided by the Ma.Ri. House on both the key-players and the keep-informed stakeholders. Table 1 summarizes the CIE matrix with the co-axial matrix. The upper part of Table 2 addresses the different multidimensional impacts with their connections with the involved stakeholders. This part also highlights the nature of the overall impacts on the engaged stakeholders, according to the combination of the considered impacts. As an example, the overall impacts on the social cooperative "Synergica" are positive, due to the combination of negative financial impacts with positive and very positive social, cultural, and environmental impacts. Therefore, the performed analysis shows that the Ma.Ri. House should generate overall positive impacts on all the considered stakeholders, private, public, and civil society, considering all the impact clusters (monetary and non-monetary) and sub-clusters (economic, social, environmental, and cultural). As an example, the City of Turin, within its technical offices and the nearby high schools, should be engaged by multidimensional positive impacts, related to social, cultural, and environmental dimensions.

The lower part of Table 2 illustrates the impacts chain that connects the project objectives with all the considered impacts. More in detail, this chain represents the crossing between the different categories of impacts and the initial objectives of the Ma.Ri. House project. It aims at estimating both the nature and intensity of the impacts among the considered dimensions. Specifically, this part is helpful to understand how the different aspects of the project can interfere with the values of each stakeholder. It is possible to state that the most positive impacts concern the social, cultural, and environmental dimensions, according to the three project objectives (Table 2). Therefore, through this evaluation, it is possible to assess the Ma.Ri. House project within its complexity and multidimensionality, focusing on the nature and the degree of the generated impacts.

Moreover, beyond the results obtained by the performed evaluation, this paper generally investigates the role of evaluation tools in assessing the multidimensional impacts on the engaged stakeholders of housing intervention, with the perspective of achieving social sustainability, according to the objective stated by SDGs. Furthermore, this application illustrates the usefulness of the mixed and combined method in the *ex-ante* phase. In fact, the paper proposes a mixed-method based on the combination of SWOT, SA, and CIE. More in detail, the SWOT and the SA firstly permit the investigation of both the general and specific aspects of the intervention area according to its strengths and weaknesses, as well as the involved stakeholders within their resources and objectives. Secondly, CIE allows to evaluate the projects according to its multidimensionality, focusing on the several impacts that should be achieved by the projects according to both their degree and nature (positive or negative; monetary and non-monetary).

Moreover, this application demonstrates that the proposed mixed-method can also be performed and repeated for the monitoring phase of project impacts, in order to check if the initial actions are able to achieve the expected targets, or if it is necessary to intervene and correct some actions.

Furthermore, this application highlights the ability of the CIE evaluation to assess and manage complex decision problems through the assessment of a multidimensional set of impacts in relation to the involved stakeholders. This kind of evaluation contributes to supporting community engagement and the evaluation of the real needs of citizens, according to the main objective of creating sustainable cities and communities. However, the qualitative approach of CIE in assessing a policy, project, plan, or program can be, in some cases, a weakness. This is particularly true when referring to monetary benefits that can be easily assessed with other methods on a quantitative scale.

Considering this con of CIE, a future perspective of the proposed mixed-method could regard the integration of quantitative assessments and the evaluation of the financial impacts, supported, for example, by the Discount Cash Flow Analysis.

Acknowledgment. The present paper illustrates the results of a Bachelor course's thesis in Territorial, Urban, Environmental and Landscape Planning (Politecnico di Torino), developed by Martina Mion with the supervisions of Prof. Nadia Caruso and Prof. Marta Bottero. All the authors wish to thank Martina Mion for the data used in the present study.

References

1. Falletti, S.: L'evoluzione delle politiche sulla casa sociale: dal numero degli alloggi al welfare abitativo. Città metropolitana di Torino, Torino (2018)
2. Bravo, L.: La città del XXI secolo: dal welfare state alla welfare society. IN_BO Ric E Progett Per Territ La Città E l'architettura, 8–19 (2008). https://doi.org/10.6092/issn.2036-1602/1323
3. Saccomani, S.: Programmi complessi: una rilettura delle esperienze. In: Regione Piemonte. Valutare i programmi complessi. L'Artistica Editrice, Savigliano (2004)
4. Camoletto, M., Ferri, G., Pedercini, C., et al.: Social Housing and measurement of social impacts: Steps towards a common toolkit [Social Housing e misurazione degli impatti sociali: Passi avanti verso un toolkit comune]. Valori e Valutazioni **19**, 11–39 (2017)
5. Berisha, E., Caprioli, C., Cotella, G.: Unpacking SDG target 11.a: What is it about and how to measure its progress? City Environ Interact 14:100080 (2022). https://doi.org/10.1016/J.CACINT.2022.100080
6. Chan, E., Lee, G.K.L.: Critical factors for improving social sustainability of urban renewal projects. Soc. Indic. Res. **85**, 243–256 (2007). https://doi.org/10.1007/s11205-007-9089-3
7. Colantonio, A., Dixon, T.: Social sustainability and sustainable communities: Towards a conceptual framework. In: Urban Regeneration & Social Sustainability, pp. 18–36. Wiley-Blackwell, Oxford, UK (2011)
8. Bottero, M., Bragaglia, F., Caruso, N., et al.: Experimenting community impact evaluation (CIE) for assessing urban regeneration programmes: The case study of the area 22@ Barcelona. Cities **99**, 102464 (2020). https://doi.org/10.1016/j.cities.2019.102464
9. Daldanise, G.: From place-branding to community-branding: A collaborative decision-making process for cultural heritage enhancement. Sustainability **12**, 10399 (2020). https://doi.org/10.3390/su122410399
10. Della Spina, L., Ventura, C., Viglianisi, A.: A multicriteria assessment model for selecting strategic projects in urban areas. In: Gervasi, O., et al. (eds.) ICCSA 2016. LNCS, vol. 9788, pp. 414–427. Springer, Cham (2016). https://doi.org/10.1007/978-3-319-42111-7_32
11. Lami, I.M., Beccuti, B.: Evaluation of a project for the radical transformation of the Port of Genoa-Italy. Manag. Environ. Qual. An Int. J. **21**, 58–77 (2010). https://doi.org/10.1108/14777831011010865
12. Torre, C.M., Morano, P., Tajani, F.: Experimenting CIE and CBA in urban restoration. In: Gervasi, O., et al. (eds.) ICCSA 2017. LNCS, vol. 10406, pp. 639–650. Springer, Cham (2017). https://doi.org/10.1007/978-3-319-62398-6_45

13. Cerreta, M., Daldanise, G.: Community branding (Co-Bra): A collaborative decision making process for urban regeneration. In: Gervasi, O., et al. (eds.) ICCSA 2017. LNCS, vol. 10406, pp. 730–746. Springer, Cham (2017). https://doi.org/10.1007/978-3-319-62398-6_52

14. Lichfield, N.: Achieving the benefits of conservation. Built Environ. **23**, 103–110 (1997)

15. Dell'Anna, F., Dell'Ovo, M.: A stakeholder-based approach managing conflictual values in urban design processes. The case of an open prison in Barcelona. Land use policy 114:105934 (2022). https://doi.org/10.1016/j.landusepol.2021.105934

16. Humphrey, A.S.: SWOT Analysis for Management Consulting. SRI Alumni Assoc. Newsl. (2005)

17. Yang, J., Shen, G.Q., Ho, M., et al.: Stakeholder management in construction: An empirical study to address research gaps in previous studies. Int. J. Proj. Manag. **29**, 900–910 (2011). https://doi.org/10.1016/j.ijproman.2010.07.013

18. Dente, B.: Understanding policy decisions. In: Understanding Policy Decisions. SAST, pp. 1–27. Springer, Cham (2014). https://doi.org/10.1007/978-3-319-02520-9_1

19. Bottero, M., Assumma, V., Caprioli, C., Dell'Ovo, M.: Decision making in urban development: The application of a hybrid evaluation method for a critical area in the city of Turin (Italy). Sustain. Cities Soc. **71**, 103028 (2021). https://doi.org/10.1016/j.scs.2021.103028

20. Johnson, G., Scholes, K.: Exploring Corporate Strategy. Prentice Hall, London (1999)

21. Mendelow, A.L.: Environmental scanning - the impact of the stakeholder concept. Proc. Int. Conf. Inf. Syst., 407–417 (1981)

22. Lichfield, D.: Integrated planning and environmental assessment. In: Lichfield, N., Barbanente, A, Borri, D., Khakee, A., Prat, A. (eds.) Evaluation in Planning. The GeoJournal Library, vol 47, pp. 151–175. Springer, Dordrecht (1998). https://doi.org/10.1007/978-94-017-1495-2_8

23. Coscia, C., De Filippi, F.: The use of collaborative digital platforms in the perspective of shared administration. The MiraMap project in Turin (2016)

Assessing the Potential of a Disused Shopping Village by Comparing Adaptive Reuse Scenarios

Federica Cadamuro Morgante⬚, Marta Dell'Ovo$^{(\boxtimes)}$ ⬚, Luca Tamini⬚, and Alessandra Oppio⬚

Department of Architecture and Urban Studies (DAStU), Politecnico di Milano, Via Bonardi, 3, 20133 Milano, Italy
{federica.cadamuro,marta.dellovo,luca.tamini, alessandra.oppio}@polimi.it

Abstract. Unpredictable events can impact the Real Estate market on multiple fronts, influencing stakeholders' decisions regarding new investment criteria. Within uncertainty, a preliminary analysis strategically supports the Decision-Makers (DMs) in making a more conscious choice. Among the set of complex decisions, the present contribution investigates the topic of adaptive reuse of a disused commercial area where several potential scenarios are compared. Technical requisites in terms of sustainability, feasibility and flexibility are considered. The approach selected to support the investigation is the Multi-Criteria Decision Analysis (MCDA), a family of techniques that allows supporting decision-making processes characterized by multiple objectives to be pursued. Thus, several dimensions are assessed in order to select the most suitable function, namely Economic, Environmental and Social. A sensitivity analysis is moreover performed to measure the robustness of the final rank.

Finally, the applied methodology offers reflection opportunities on the future best reuse scenario for commercial assets in urban and peri-urban areas under Social Governance Criteria and circular economy lenses.

Keywords: Multi-Criteria Decision Analysis · Adaptive reuse · Feasibility analysis

1 Introduction

Major natural disasters resulting from climate and eco-systemic changes such as the COVID-19 pandemic of recent times, like the market inflation due to economic and political crises has resulted in a bitter uncertain panorama for investors. These events have redirected the trends of all markets, not only the Real Estate one, in pursuit of economic, social and environmental sustainability paradigms fostered by international policies that attempt to cope with new emergencies (i.e. the principle of the Circular Economy or to the so called Sustainable Development Goals in the 2030 Agenda) [1, 2].

Indeed, even in the Real Estate field, the combination of low predictability and major impact of all these events make them challenging when making property market

O. Gervasi et al. (Eds.): ICCSA 2022 Workshops, LNCS 13380, pp. 195–210, 2022.
https://doi.org/10.1007/978-3-031-10542-5_14

forecasts and evaluations. Meanwhile, other forces are pushing stakeholders towards new investment criteria, namely the digitalisation and the new evaluations standards of the Economic Social Governance Criteria – ESG. These two aspects are changing the needs and technical requisites of assets in term of sustainability and flexibility in "adaptive reuse" perspective.

The adaptive reuse concept is best described from the Department of Environment and Heritage – DEH as *"a process that changes a disused or ineffective item into a new item that can be used for a different purpose"*[3].

The adaptability criterion stems new opportunities for all involved actors along the lifecycle of the assets to better accomplish to a very concept of sustainability and to avoid land consumption derived from the shift of activities in new areas. Of particular concern, those assets related to industrial, productive or wholesale distribution activities are the most subjected to changes of production factors, technology advancement and consumers' behaviours that guide the entire economic supply chain, object of great concern for Decision Makers (DMs) about which regulative approaches to use [4].

Thus, more attention to this category would actively support future urban and peri-urban development strategies of cities that are no more centred but with sparse and continuous patterns.

Considering the framed topic of adaptive reuse of industrial and commercial assets, this research work attempts to draw an ad-hoc evaluative methodology in support to strategic reuse. Speculations are directly calibrated on a real case study of a disused commercial area, the Shopping Village "Le Acciaierie" in Lombardy Region, Italy, for which several alternative scenarios are considered.

In order to introduce and frame the methodology, the present article is structured in five main sections. Section 2 provides introductory material for the methodology application. After the description of the Italian Real Estate Market trends in major recent pandemic and economic shocks (and thus, providing food for thoughts for possible reuse scenarios), the methodological approach and used evaluative instruments are described. Section 3 introduces the case study under evaluation, by underling not only physical and locational characteristics but through legal, and planning constraints with the aim to refine the selection for the possible urban scenario at stake. Finally, Sects. 4 and 5 present the results of the analysis conducted and provide some future perspectives that could strengthen the methodology.

2   The "Adaptive Reuse": Challenges and Opportunities for Future Built Environment Transformation

2.1   The Real Estate Market Reaction to Uncertainty

Despite significant uncertainty on both the healthcare and political fronts due to last millennium events, Italy's economy and that of the Eurozone has continued to expand at high growth rates until the last 2022 first month's period. In Italy, the trend on real estate market investments has increased of about 17% with respect to 2020 (equal to 9.6 billion of Euros). However, this positive trends are attributed to foreign investors that occupy more than the 80% of investments transactions in the Italian territory [1, 5].

In term of asset class, especially pandemic phenomenon has fostered in the last years some already in act trend or unpredicted new ones.

Primarily, Italian offices asset has remained quite a good investment (especially for core activities) like the retail asset class, with particular reference to commercial buildings in-town. This last category has started to rise in Italian territory especially from the end of 2021, thanks to new few but huge foreign investments around Milan and Rome market stocks. However, as shown in Fig. 1, commercial buildings have seen a constant decrease in asset stock number (about 10% in the last three years) due to a transaction phase started well before the pandemic crisis and associated with the rise of the e-commerce and a decrease of the physical products stocks. Of particular concern, major negative impact has resulted on out-of-town assets, for big building dimension against the interest of investors for smaller size assets devoted to the sale of medium-high/luxury category products in the city centres (the so called in-town stock categories) that has better resisted the competition from e-commerce [1, 6].

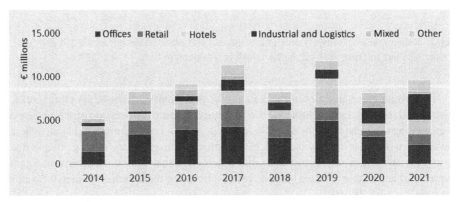

Fig. 1. Real estate investments in Italian territory per asset class between 2014 and 2021. Source: Colliers International, "Il mercato degli investimenti in Italia – Q4 2021".

On the contrary, logistics asset class continues to register a new record at the beginning of 2022: for the first time has become the first asset class on the Italian market, even more than the office category (ref. Figure 2). The attractiveness of investors for the sector began in 2014, with the perception of a diversified risk opportunity, deriving from the strengthening of the logistics activity due to e-commerce expansion and the trend has dramatically increased during pandemic restrictions [2, 7]. Still today, interest in this asset class is linked to the expansion of e-commerce that pushes investors to try to secure the best products or to develop some new in the areas deemed most strategic. Not by chance, technological advancement and new market targets that are oriented to client satisfaction for short delivery times has moved the attention from the centralization of warehouses for strategic distribution to European level, to that of proximity with small warehouses close to places of consumption. Data centres and Dark Stores (i.e. buildings designed as warehouses, but organized like a retail shop category), buildings type of high quality small size are increasing. However, large hubs (over 60,000 sqm) and intermediate size centres (around 20,000–30,000 sqm) still cover an important role [7, 8].

Therefore, the logistics demand is extremely heterogeneous in terms of size, space flex-ibility and location, which reflects the diversity of companies' nature and their specific needs for a high tech supply chain adaptation process.

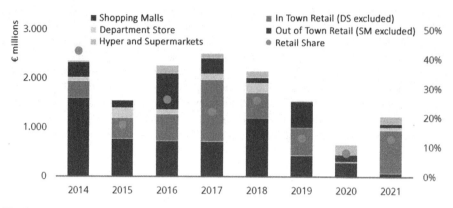

Fig. 2. Italian real estate investments in commercial and retail sector between 2014 and 2021. Source: Colliers International, "Il mercato degli investimenti in Italia – Q4 2021".

This preliminary analysis of the Italian real estate market focused on commercial, tertiary and industrial asset classes allows to better structure the decision problem aimed at evaluating the most suitable adaptive reuse for an ex former commercial area. Where the adaptive reuse, as already mention in the Introduction, is conceived as a process that changes a disused or ineffective item into a new item that can be used for a different purpose [3] and is able to find a balanced trade-off among the dimensions so to influence the final decision [9, 10].

Based on these premises the contribution proposes in the next sub-chapter an evalua-tion framework based on Multi-Criteria Decision Analysis (MCDA) to support the adap-tive reuse process decision guidelines. The MCDA has been considered has a suitable and coherent approach to support the decision process given its robust methodological structure and its application in other similar experimental researches [11–14].

2.2   The Evaluation to Support Adaptive Reuse Processes

This section describes the multi-criteria evaluation process adopted, aimed at identify-ing the most suitable adaptive reuse scenario to satisfy the economic, social and envi-ronmental needs that typically characterise complex investment decisions, such as the transformation of existing real estate complexes [7].

The Multi-Criteria Decision Analysis (MCDA) is a family of techniques that allows to support decision-making processes characterized by the presence of multiple objec-tives to be pursued [15, 16], mostly conflicting, and to anticipate the impact of alternative scenarios under a multi-dimensional perspective. It is also considered a strategic tool because alternatives are based on heterogeneous measures and with reference to different points of view by considering the stakeholders involved [17, 18]. The transparency of the process is ensured by the adoption of clear methodologies able to guide the DM in the different phases of the assessment, from the elicitation of the objectives to the final choice. The fundamental steps of the MCDA are briefly described below and presented in Fig. 3:

- Problem definition: elicitation of the objectives to be achieved and consequently structuring of the evaluation framework in criteria and sub-criteria;
- Design of alternatives: identification and/or generation of alternatives aimed at achieving previously identified objectives;
- Performance assessment: measurement of alternative scenarios considering the set of criteria and sub-criteria and their respective units of measurement;
- Standardization: normalization of units of measure (both qualitative and quantitative) into an a-dimensional scale between 0 and 1 (where 0 represents the worst performance and 1 the best);
- Weighting: assignment of weights to criteria and sub-criteria on the basis of their relative importance;
- Partial and final ranking: aggregation of weights and standardized scores, through compensatory or non-compensatory procedures, and display of partial and the overall results;
- Sensitivity analysis: validation of previously obtained results and validation of their robustness to changes.

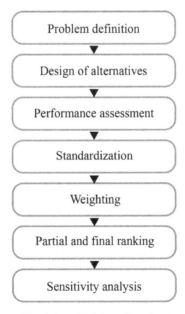

Fig. 3. Methodology flowchart

Within this context, alternatives have been assessed by considering a five-levels scoring system in order to highlight the ability of each alternative to achieve a specific objective, which in the evaluation process is represented by the criterion. The score was subsequently standardized through the use of increasing or decreasing linear functions, so as to specify the direction of preference (criterion/objective to maximize = benefit; criterion/objective to minimize = cost) by taking as reference Eq. (1) and (2):

$$Benefit\ criterion: \frac{score}{highest\ score} \qquad (1)$$

$$Cost\ criterion: -\frac{score}{highest\ score} + 1 \qquad (2)$$

The next step is the partial aggregation (with respect to each family of criteria) and the final aggregation of scores to obtain the overall ranking of alternatives developed by using the Weighted Sum Model (WSM), a compensative procedure.

Although this is a preliminary application of the MCDA, based on qualitative data, the results obtained can be considered a tool to support and guide the choices of potential investors and developers.

3 The Shopping Village "Le Acciaierie"

This chapter introduces the case study on which the methodology is tested. More precisely, the adaptive reuse problem under analysis concerns the identification of the best alternative reuse scenarios for a disused commercial area, the Shopping Village "Le Acciaierie" in Lombardy Region, Italy.

3.1 Case Study Description

The Shopping Village "Le Acciaierie" is a great disused commercial area of 58,000 sqm approximately in Cortenuova, a minor municipality of about 1,937 inhabitants of Bergamo Province, East to the Lombardy Region [19]. The area is located in a rural context independent from closest urban networks and it tangles the railway line Milano-Brescia, while is about four kilometers from the main highway that directly connects Brescia and Milano cities.

The commercial site includes several buildings of different use, linked together by a system of horizontal connections, and it is in a general abandoned state since 2014. Indeed, this area in Cortenuova municipality was interested by an urban transformation project in 2003, with the aim to provide a multifunctional shopping mall. The aforementioned project wrongly prompted the belief that the "more accessible and livable-decentralized position" of the site was preferable with respect to the congested suburban areas, once transformed into a place of social and work interactions.

On closer inspection of the site, the Shopping Village "Ex Acciaierie" includes mainly three buildings and a group of infrastructures that characterizes the commercial built environment (Fig. 4–5).

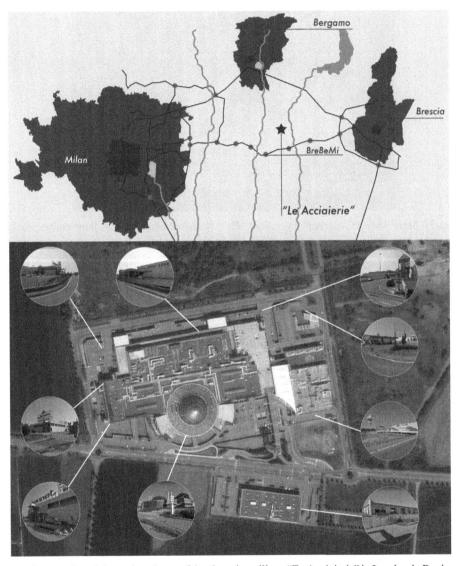

Fig. 4. Location of the analyzed area of the shopping village "Ex Acciaierie" in Lombardy Region and aerial view of the built complex.

The main one is the shopping mall of about 34,000 sqm plant. This building displays a scenic rounded façade with a laminated wood-glass dome that covers the circular-shape entrance hall with connective spaces, restaurants and bars. Sideways the hall there are

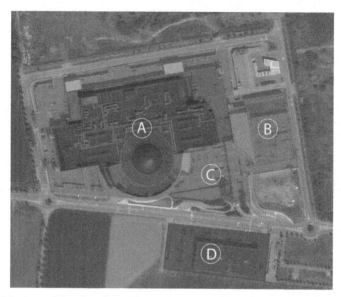

Fig. 5. Aerial view of the shopping village "Ex Acciaierie" complex with intervention areas: A – shopping mall; B – city park building; C – parking area; D – commercial building max Mercatone.

two wings on two floors respectively that host 152 shops together with a hypermarket of 8,600 sqm and other 18 supply activities spaces. The building structure, with the exception of the central square and the dome, is mainly in reinforced concrete and prefabricated technical elements.

East to the mall and the commercial area, the "City park" building offers several recreational activities: a multiplex cinema, a bowling alley, go-kart tracks, game rooms and various amenities for food services and recreational activities. The main body of the City park has a rectangular base (length of 97 m and width of 64 m) with a prefabricated reinforced concrete structure and an annex with a laminated wood roof.

Then, under the surface occupied by the mall, the basement area serves as a parking lot. The parking area is common to both the shopping mall and the City Park building. Similarly, the main structure is in prefabricated reinforced concrete pillars and beams.

Finally, the commercial building "Max Mercatone" is located separately south of the property lot, beyond the access street of the commercial area. This building in prefabricated reinforced concrete has a regular rectangular shape of about 3,950 sqm, including a ground floor (8 m of maximum external height) and an underground one. The industrial type structure with reinforced concrete pillars and beams is limited by an external wall in prefabricated panels.

3.2 Problem Definition

The area of the analyzed case study presented in Sect. 3.1 has remained inactive until today with the progressive worsening in the structure's conservation state due to the not-attracting location conditions and the special type of asset, like the most recent market and pandemic crises.

Currently, the property of the Shopping Village "Ex Acciaierie", the DM of the current research, has commissioned some technical and economic feasibility studies, while looking for possible new transformation scenarios that, in any case, will include the demolition of all the involved buildings, except the so called Max Mercatone one (Fig. 5). However, as the commercial area dimensions like the "non-ordinary" nature of these buildings from technological point of view, demolitions costs will be huge and of high impact for the surrounding context. For all these reasons, the scenarios of adaptive reuse need a solid and accurate methodology to provide a proper evaluation about possible intervention convenience from an economic-social-environmental sustainable point of view [20].

Given the complexity of the decision problem a solid set of criteria has been developed starting from the analysis of the context and consisting in urban and territorial investigations aimed at exploring strengths, weaknesses, opportunities and threats [21]. Three main dimensions have been identified and further divided in sub-criteria:

1. Economic dimension:

   1.1. Job opportunities, to measure the new jobs created by the alternative;
   1.2. Production of goods and services, to consider the services provided to the community;
   1.3. Initial investment, to estimate the initial cost to be incurred;
   1.4. Compatibility, to understand the impact of the new function within the territorial and social context;
   1.5. Compensations, to evaluate the capital to be paid to the Municipality.

2. Social dimension:

   2.1. Perception, to evaluate the negative impact of the new alternative perceived by the society;
   2.2. Externalities, to measure the attractiveness of the project;
   2.3. Specialized professionals, to understand if qualified operators are needed.

3. Environmental dimension:

   3.1. Renewable energy, to evaluate the sources of the energy consumed;
   3.2. Building re-use, to estimate the possibility to re-use the existing complex;
   3.3. New interventions, to consider under different perspectives the works required to activate the new function;
   3.4. Regreening, to measure the provision of new green spaces;
   3.5. Soil consumption, to assess if the alternative involves further consumption of agricultural land.

Each criterion is evaluated by assigning a score on a qualitative scale between 0 and 5, where 5 represents the highest value of performance, i.e., the highest ability of an alternative to achieve a given objective.

3.3 Scenarios of Adaptive Reuse

The identification of the most convenient adaptive reuse scenario is set as the final objective for the sake of ownership of the Shopping Village "Ex Acciaierie" case study. Hence, the property needs to identify the most profitable transformation of the abandoned asset while, as already mentioned, satisfying needs of economic social and environmental dimensions, which typically characterize complex investments decision such as the reuse of a multifunctional commercial asset.

With respect to the applied evaluation framework, after the final object definition, the methodology follows the identification of alternatives phase aimed at achieving the previously identified objectives.

In generating the alternatives, the case study under analysis has included the preliminary study of valorisation opportunities of the asset given the location context characteristics, the technical and legal constraints provided by zoning plans and a deep analysis of the real estate market trends from supply and demand sides.

The first condition to be assessed is represented by the legal and technical constraints provided by urban planning normative apparatus.

The Ex Acciaierie commercial centre is zoned under the *Piano di Governo del Territorio* - Territorial Zoning Plan of the Lombardy Region (from now on "PGT") within the "*Sistema funzionale del terziario e del commercio* - Tertiary and Commercial Sector System" that allows the establishment in the area of commercial activities like logistics. Then, the more specific technical norms that regulate the service and zones distribution in Cortenuova municipality specify the possibility to provide complementary activities like tertiary, directional, entertainment, health facilities, and wholesale commerce. Finally, except the already existing commercial area of the case study, no new commercial assets with an area exceeding 1,500 sqm are allowed with the Municipality's administrative boundaries [22, 23].

While considering the normative constraints and so the possible opportunities for the potential valorisation strategy to adopt, the analysis of the real estate market trends has been developed as it is possible to appreciate from the sub-chapter 2.

The normative apparatus and the analysis of the real estate market trend are finally addressed to the potentialities of the Shopping Village "Ex Acciaierie" case study characteristics and the territorial social-economic synergies.

The dimensional, functional and architectural characteristics of the abandoned commercial property would suggest an adaptive reuse with multifunctional activities set. However, commercial functions as a multi-functional shopping mall would not be capable to crowd out the competition of several close commercial centres and to come out as the primary choice of users over a 20–25 min' car accessibility distance, due to the limited catchment area in terms of small number of inhabitants and the vicinity with other major urban poles and competitors.

On the other hand, with a wider gaze, Bergamo Province can appear attractive in investors side for the overall size of the population and the proximity to the highway

North-West arteries, as well as to the Milan suburban area. The close A35 highway called "Brebemi" is increasingly developing as an infrastructure linked to logistic and service functions, while traffic flows decrease in intensity on weekends and during the summer months [24].

Finally, it would important to mention Lombardy Region's most recent regulatory provisions on urban development (PGT): the opening of new commercial polarities in these territorial contexts is discouraged, while favouring good practices of existing structures recovery [22].

All previous considerations reinforce the idea to propose an adaptive reuse of the case study, not oriented to a commercial function but to strategic assets that comply with supply chain changing processes that involve high quality technological spaces and sustainability criteria in terms of building performance and economic activities focused on social and environmental dimensions. Moreover, in line with Lombardy Region urban planning policies, the Municipality Council of Cortenuova issued in 2019 the Municipality policy deed for the functional reuse of the shopping centre "Le Acciaierie": "*Atto d'indirizzo comunale in merito alla riqualificazione e al riuso del centro commerciale Le Acciaierie*" [23]. The Act explicitly allows the implementation of any technical or administrative action aimed at the functional reuse of the property, coherently not only with the local PGT but also with the surrounding urban transformation process and emerging market opportunity (thus, including also other proposed functions as alternatives of a commercial use like the logistic one).

Thus, the MCDA analysis would attempt to compare and weight four possible alternative scenarios that include a logistic asset, a data centre, a recycling plant and a nuclear storage.

The logistic asset would appear to be a medium-large warehouse dedicated to different product categories for last-mile distribution. The warehouse could be equipped with automatic systems for storage management, like for picking and packing processes. The data centre or server farm would include all machinery and equipment for storing, processing or sharing large amounts of data. A good share of space is also devoted to supporting core activity systems that prevent blackouts like Uninterruptible Power Supply - UPS centres, cooling, fire extinguishing and security systems. While a recycling plant is intended (following the last EU Directive 98/2008) as a multi-function centre that could enable, through special types of machinery, the waste management, from waste selection and treating to its transformation or disposal. In line with other European cases [25], the recycling plant could also host other functions like offices, the staff canteen or even an Education Centre (museum). Finally, the alternative scenario with nuclear storage could represent a superficial storage system for intermediate-level-waste (ILW) and low-level-waste (LLW), considering the classification of the International Atomic Energy Agency [26]. The storage system physically represents a closed deposit where nuclear waste is temporarily hosted to wait for its radiological content to decay to lower levels and transfer it to other definite disposal centres.

4 Results

The alternatives have been evaluated by considering the set of criteria defined and their capability to meet each objective through the analysis of similar case studies. The results can be appreciated in Table 1.

Table 1. Performance matrix (where C: cost; B: benefit)

				Alternatives			
Criteria	Sub-criteria	C/B	Scale	Logistics	Data center	Recycling plant	Nuclear storage
1. Economic dimension	1.1 Job opportunities	B	0–5	5	1	3	2
	1.2 Production of goods and services	B	0–5	4	3	4	0
	1.3 Initial investment		0–5	2	3	4	5
	1.4 Compatibility	B	0–5	4	2	1	0
	1.5 Compensations	C	0–5	2	1	3	5
2. Social dimension	2.1 Perception	C	0–5	1	0	4	5
	2.2 Externalities	B	0–5	1	1	1	0
	2.3 Specialized professionals	C	0–5	1	3	2	5
3. Environmental dimension	3.1 Renewable energy	B	0–5	2	1	3	4
	3.2 Building re-use	B	0–5	3	4	2	2
	3.3 New interventions	C	0–5	2	5	2	5
	3.4 Regreening	B	0–5	1	2	2	4
	3.5 Soil consumption	C	0–5	1	0	1	0

Afterwards, performances have been standardized through the use of increasing or decreasing linear functions in relation to the need to maximize (benefit) or minimize (cost) the objective.

In order to obtain a complete ranking of the alternatives, an order of importance have been assigned to the criteria and sub-criteria. In accordance with DM a neutral scenario was selected, where the economic, social and environmental dimensions have equal importance (33, 3%) as well as the sub-criteria.

Figure 6 shows the ordering of the alternatives with respect to each criterion. From the graph illustrating the final ranking, the Logistics function maintains the top ranking with respect to the Economic and Social Dimension, with the Data Centre in second place followed by the Recycling plant and Nuclear Storage. The positions of the alternatives change with respect to the Environmental Dimension, where Nuclear Storage takes the first position, followed by Recycling Plant, Logistics, and finally Data Centre. In this last case, the distance between the first and last alternatives is not very significant, when compared to the partial orders related to the Economic and Social Dimension.

The final ranking confirms an order of preference where Logistics (60%) ranks first, immediately followed by Data Centre (50%). The result is stable, since validated by the sensitivity analysis (ref. Table 2), carried out by assuming three different scenarios, in which greater importance is assigned to the Economic Dimension *(scenario 1: Economic Dimension = 60%; Social Dimension = 20%; Environmental Dimension = 20%)*, to the Social Dimension *(scenario 2: Economic Dimension = 20%; Social Dimension = 60%; Environmental Dimension = 20%)* and to the Environmental Dimension *(scenario 3: Economic Dimension = 20%; Social Dimension = 20%; Environmental Dimension = 60%)*.

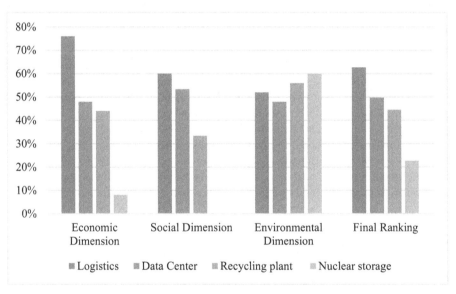

Fig. 6. Partial and final ranking

Table 2. Sensitivity analysis

	Alternatives			
	Logistics	Data center	Recycling plant	Nuclear storage
Scenario 1 economic	68%	49%	44%	17%
Scenario 2 social	62%	51%	40%	14%
Scenario 3 environmental	58%	49%	49%	38%

5 Conclusions

In the light of the urban and multi-criteria feasibility study, it is possible to direct the development of the Shopping Village "Le Acciaierie" property complex towards the conversion to a logistics function, envisaging the implementation of every technical/administrative action aimed at functional upgrading of the property, in a perspective of consistency with the surrounding urban framework and with market opportunities. With the concept of adaptive reuse, it is possible to introduce that of "demalling," conceived as the process that aims to transform a disused shopping centre into something new [27]. This approach can represent an opportunity of urban regeneration to enhance the urban quality of the Municipality where the building is located and, at the same time, a driving factor to promote economic development. In fact, the "demalling" also supports circular economy processes by reducing land consumption.

The analysis of the most suitable adaptive reuse alternative has been based on a robust and transparent methodology. As future perspectives, the research could be further detailed by introducing quantitate and monetary indicators in the evaluation to have a clear idea about the initial cost of the intervention. Moreover, since the decision taken will have an impact on several categories of stakeholders besides the current owner of the area, the generation of alternatives could be developed with a participatory process where round tables are organized to identify and elicit the values and objectives of the actors involved, both private and public.

References

1. Research and Reports | CBRE. https://www.cbre.it/it-it/research-and-reports. Accessed 12 Apr 2022
2. Logistics snapshot General Outlook (2021)
3. Department of the Environment and Heritage: Adaptive Reuse: Preserving our past, building our future, Camberra (2004)
4. Tamini, L.: What Future for Vacant Retail Spaces? Recent Experiences in Italy. In: Reactivation of Vacant Retail Spaces. SAST, pp. 37–75. Springer, Cham (2018). https://doi.org/10.1007/978-3-319-70872-0_2
5. Colliers | Research That Matters. https://www.colliers.com/it-it/research#sort=%40datez32xpublished%20descending. Accessed 12 Apr 2022

6. Rapporto 2021-Il mercato immobiliare della logistica in Europa e in Italia - Scenari Immobiliari (2021). https://www.scenari-immobiliari.it/shop/rapporto-2021-il-mercato-immobiliare-della-logistica-in-europa-e-in-italia/. Accessed 12 Apr 2022

7. Borsino Immobiliare della Logistica - WCG - World Capital Group. https://www.worldcapital.it/borsino-immobiliare-logistica/. Accessed 12 Apr 2022

8. Osservatorio Contract Logistics "Gino Marchet". https://www.osservatori.net/it/ricerche/osservatori-attivi/contract-logistics-gino-marchet. Accessed 12 Apr 2022

9. Rossitti, M., Oppio, A., Torrieri, F.: The financial sustainability of cultural heritage reuse projects: An integrated approach for the historical rural landscape. Sustainability **13**, 13130 (2021). https://doi.org/10.3390/SU132313130

10. Assumma, V., Bottero, M., de Angelis, E., Lourenço, J.M., Monaco, R., Soares, A.J.: A decision support system for territorial resilience assessment and planning: An application to the Douro Valley (Portugal). Sci. Total Environ. **756**, 143806 (2021). https://doi.org/10.1016/J.SCITOTENV.2020.143806

11. Dell'Anna, F., Dell'Ovo, M.: A stakeholder-based approach managing conflictual values in urban design processes. The case of an open prison in Barcelona. Land Use Policy **114**, 105934 (2022). https://doi.org/10.1016/J.LANDUSEPOL.2021.105934

12. Stival, C.A., Berto, R., Morano, P., Rosato, P.: Reuse of vernacular architecture in minor alpine settlements: A multi-attribute model for sustainability appraisal. Sustainability **12**, 6562 (2020). https://doi.org/10.3390/SU12166562

13. Cerreta, M., Elefante, A., la Rocca, L.: A creative living lab for the adaptive reuse of the morticelli church: The SSMOLL project. Sustainability **12**, 10561 (2020). https://doi.org/10.3390/SU122410561

14. Fabi, V., Vettori, M.P., Faroldi, E.: Adaptive reuse practices and sustainable urban development: Perspectives of innovation for european historic spa towns. Sustainability **13**, 5531 (2021). https://doi.org/10.3390/SU13105531

15. Roy, B.: Multicriteria Methodology for Decision Aiding. Springer, Boston (1996). https://doi.org/10.1007/978-1-4757-2500-1

16. Roy, B.: Paradigms and challenges. In: Multiple Criteria Decision Analysis: State of the Art Surveys. ISORMS, vol. 78, pp. 3–24. Springer, New York (2005). https://doi.org/10.1007/0-387-23081-5_1

17. Capolongo, S., Sdino, L., Dell'Ovo, M., Moioli, R., della Toree, S.: How to assess urban regeneration proposals by considering conflicting values. Sustainability (Switzerland) **11**, 3877 (2019). https://doi.org/10.3390/su11143877

18. Treves, A., Bottero, M., Caprioli, C., Comino, E.: The reintroduction of Castor fiber in Piedmont (Italy): An integrated SWOT-spatial multicriteria based approach for the analysis of suitability scenarios. Ecol. Ind. **118**, 106748 (2020). https://doi.org/10.1016/J.ECOLIND.2020.106748

19. Istat.it Popolazione e famiglie. https://www.istat.it/it/popolazione-e-famiglie?dati,%20last%20accessed%202022/04/05. Accessed 12 Apr 2022

20. Bottero, M., Datola, G.: Addressing social sustainability in urban regeneration processes. An application of the social multi-criteria evaluation. Sustainability (Switzerland) **12**, 7579 (2020). https://doi.org/10.3390/su12187579

21. Dell'ovo, M., Dell'anna, F., Simonelli, R., Sdino, L.: Enhancing the cultural heritage through adaptive reuse. A multicriteria approach to evaluate the castello visconteo in Cusago (Italy). Sustainability **13**, 4440 (2021). https://doi.org/10.3390/SU13084440

22. Piani di Governo del Territorio (PGT). https://www.regione.lombardia.it/wps/portal/istituzionale/HP/DettaglioRedazionale/servizi-e-informazioni/Enti-e-Operatori/territorio/pianificazione-comunale-e-provinciale/piani-governo-territorio-pgt/piani-governo-territorio-pgt. Accessed 12 Apr 2022

23. Documentazione PGT : Comune di Cortenuova (BG). http://m.comune.cortenuova.bg.it/doc umentazione_pgt.aspx. Accessed 12 Apr 2022
24. Osservatorio del traffico I Anas S.p.A. https://www.stradeanas.it/it/le-strade/osservatorio-del-traffico. Accessed 12 Apr 2022
25. Demo sites – Deep Purple – BBI Project. https://deep-purple.eu/demosites/. Accessed 11 May 2022
26. IAEA Safety Standards Classification of Radioactive Waste for protecting people and the environment No. GSG-1 General Safety Guide
27. Berta, M., Bottero, M., Bravi, M., Dell'Anna, F., Rapari, A.: The regeneration of a shopping center starts from consumers' preferences: a best-worst scaling application. In: Gervasi, O., et al. (eds.) ICCSA 2021. LNCS, vol. 12955, pp. 533–543. Springer, Cham (2021). https://doi.org/10.1007/978-3-030-87007-2_38

Spatial Econometric Analysis of Multi-family Housing Prices in Turin: The Heterogeneity of Preferences for Energy Efficiency

Federico Dell'Anna[(⊠)] [iD]

Interuniversity Department of Regional and Urban Studies and Planning,
Politecnico di Torino, Viale Mattioli 39, 10125 Turin, Italy
federico.dellanna@polito.it

Abstract. The positive impact of energy efficiency on property prices has been amply demonstrated in Europe by a large number of studies. However, much research has not considered the spatial nature of the data or has limited itself to considering it through fixed variables within econometric models based on hedonic price theory. To fill this gap in the literature, this study presents the spatial analyses by Geographically Weighted Regression (GWR) models of the Energy Performance Certificate (EPC) in Turin (Italy) using a dataset of apartments sales ads located in multi-family buildings. A number of models were created to study the interaction between energy class and age-related characteristics. The results indicate that the impact of EPC differs spatially and according to the age of construction of the buildings. The results are useful in the formulation of energy policies at the local scale, considering the location within the urban context, and the technological characteristics of the buildings according to the age of construction.

Keywords: Hedonic Pricing Method (HPM) · Ordinary Least Square (OLS) · Geographically Weighted Regression (GWR) · Energy Performance Certificate (EPC)

1 Introduction

In Europe, local governments are now interested in promoting the energy efficiency of buildings through targeted actions that require careful consideration of the economic resources allocated by the 2021 Recovery and Resilience Plans [1]. While the introduction of the Energy Performance Certificate (EPC), introduced by the European Directive on the Energy Performance of Buildings (EPBD) in 2002, is an important parameter for the definition of energy efficiency policies, it also represents one of the first actions at the European level to raise buyers' awareness of building energy consumption and environmental issues. In this regard, understanding potential buyers' perceptions of energy efficiency in terms of willingness to pay, through analysis of the residential real estate market, can support public actors in targeting policies on specific urban areas [2, 3]. Indeed, that energy consumption follows spatial patterns is obvious, as the building

© The Author(s), under exclusive license to Springer Nature Switzerland AG 2022
O. Gervasi et al. (Eds.): ICCSA 2022 Workshops, LNCS 13380, pp. 211–227, 2022.
https://doi.org/10.1007/978-3-031-10542-5_15

stock is not homogeneous, in terms of age of construction, structural and technological characteristics and, consequently, energy performance.

While this aspect has been investigated from the technological-energy point of view, it has been little explored from the economic one. Indeed, the positive impact of energy efficiency on house prices has been amply demonstrated in Europe by a large number of studies based on econometric models. However, few studies have considered the spatial nature of the data, often limiting themselves to considering it through fixed variables within models based on hedonic price theory.

In this context, the present study focuses on the analysis of a sample of multiple residential buildings in Turin (Italy) to investigate how building price varies with energy efficiency within municipal boundaries. Specifically, Geographically Weighted Regression (GWR) models were applied to study the spatial heterogeneity of building characteristics in terms of energy efficiency and the interaction of EPC with building age.

The paper is organized as follows. After the "Introduction," the "Research Background on EPC Investigation" section explores research in studies concerning applications of revealed preference methods in the energy sector. The "Methods" section presents the econometric models used. The case study, properties sample and initial descriptive analyses are presented in the "Application" section. The results are presented and discussed in the "Results" section. The "Conclusions" section summarizes the implications, limitations, and conclusions.

2 Research Background on EPC Investigation

One of the most widely used econometric approaches to analyzing the housing market is the hedonic pricing method (HPM) proposed by Rosen [4]. This method has been widely used in the field of analyzing consumer preferences for energy attributes of dwellings, by investigating the impact of sustainability certificates, such as the Building Research Establishment Environmental Assessment Method (BREEAM), the Leadership in Energy and Environmental Design (LEED), the Green Mark, and the Energy Performance Certificate (EPC).

The introduction of the EPC scheme [5], along with the Energy Performance Index (EPI), are the most widely used indicators in Europe in studies in this field of research to describe the energy performance of buildings. In 2012, Kok and Jennen proposed one of the first European studies to investigate the effect of EPC on real estate sales [6]. Rosen's theoretical explanation of HPM was applied to the office market in the Netherlands. The results show that non-green buildings are 6.5% lower than offices in the upper EPC class. Cajias and Piazolo [7] applied a hedonic price model to test the appreciation of a high EPC level in Germany. High prices are confirmed for buildings in high energy classes with a 32.8% increase in property value. In Italy, Fregonara et al. [8] and Dell'Anna et al. [9] used hedonic regression to study the impact of EPC in the Turin housing market. Both studies suggest that there is a green premium linked to energy class. However, other studies have shown that there was no positive relationship between the energy class and real estate prices. In Norway, Olaussen et al. [10] showed that there is no price premium guaranteed by a high EPC. In their view, the high price premium is related to the aesthetic quality of the buildings and not to better energy performance. Cerin et al. [11] did not find a relationship between EPC and high price in Swedish private buildings. However, this result is not confirmed by Högberg [12] who found a positive influence of energy performance improvements on selling prices in Stockholm in those same years. Thus, most of the literature consulted suggests that there is consumer willingness to pay for green buildings. Other studies have shown more moderate results, with minor or no effects of EPC. However, exploring this phenomenon in space could clarify why the impact of EPC is not significant or if uneven over the urban context.

One of the most highlighted issues in these studies refers to the need to improve the inclusion of spatial and temporal dimensions in the model, which are currently under-investigated [13–15]. The inclusion of fixed location variables partially solves the spatial problem, as they do not correctly delineate the distribution of the relationship between building characteristics and price, leading to biased coefficient estimates. Barreca et al. [16] investigated the influence of energy performance and different characteristics on property prices by performing spatial analyses on a sample of dwellings listed on the Turin housing market and on different subsamples. Exploratory Spatial Data Analyses (ESDA), Ordinary Least Squares (OLS) and Spatial Error Models (SEM) are applied first on the whole data sample and then on three different subsamples highlighting the presence of spatial effects in different submarkets. Marmolejo-Duarte et al. [17] applied a Geographically Weighted Regression (GWR) model to test the spatial heterogeneity of EPC ranking coefficients in the Barcelona metropolis (Spain). Their results found that energy efficiency is not a priority in some areas in relation to other residential and local attributes, making the coefficient for local EPC ranking erratic. McCord et al. [18] presented a spatial analyses of EPCs through GWR models using transaction data for the Belfast metropolitan area. The authors tested for spatial effects between EPCs and house prices through several spatial tests and through a series of models developed to test for the existence of spatial dependence and to determine if there are spatially correlated effects through autoregressive models. The authors showed that there are price differences in the spatial variation of EPCs with price effects consistent with building type and building age.

In line with the reviewed studies, this paper contributes to this recent literature that investigates the heterogeneity of the relationships between property characteristics, with a focus on energy performance and the interaction with building age, and sale or offer prices. Like other studies, we propose both traditional hedonic models based on the OLS method and local regression models based on the GWR to examine spatial differences in terms of the composition of the housing stock. The goal is to provide guidance to public decision makers to design energy policies in line with consumer behavior through maps showing the relationship between price, EPC, and age of building construction, following the McCord et al. [18] work.

3 Methods

According to the HPM approach, a property can be like a set of attributes, which can bring benefits to the consumer. These benefits are part of the hedonic price function, as shown in the Eq. (1):

$$P = f(x_1, x_2, ..., x_n) \tag{1}$$

where P is the market price, $x_1, x_2, ..., x_n$ are the property characteristics. The regression technique helps to find the relationship between the price and the different properties of the building. In the linear model, the form of the hedonic function is as follows (2):

$$y = \beta_0 + \beta_1 x_1 + \beta_2 x_2 + ... + \beta_n x_n + \varepsilon \tag{2}$$

where β_0 represents the intercept of the function, β_1 is the coefficient of the variable x_1, and ε is the stochastic error term.

In the linear model, the OLS method allows the determination of the function coefficients [19]. One of the limitations of OLS-based regression is that spatial autocorrelation and spatial dependency issues are not considered [20, 21] and a stationary process is usually assumed. In this setting, the parameters estimated by the model (β, ε) can only vary using different and independent subsamples. Under the assumption of dealing with a single sample, this problem was addressed by including the micro area (statistical or cadastral) as a dummy variable [22]. These approaches raise many questions, both from the point of view of sample size (which is never balanced for all areas) and from the point of view of stationarity and the application of the relevant estimates in institutional or market settings.

Some researchers have studied these effects by proposing the application of spatial regression models. Osland worked through the testing of various spatial models (Geographically Weighted Regression, semiparametric analysis, and mixed spatial Durbin model) as well as a discussion of the application and interpretation of diagnostic tests aimed at choosing the correct spatial specification [23]. Her comparative analysis shows that these spatially explicit models far outperform a traditional OLS model. Fotheringham et al. [24], Brunsdon and Fotheringham [25] proposed GWR as a spatial statistical technique that recognizes that traditional 'global' regression models may be limited when the elements influencing the dependent variable vary according to context. In the real estate context, the GWR model can capture the spatial heterogeneity of the real estate market, which is inevitably influenced by urban elements that are not uniformly distributed across urban space. The GWR model is based on a set of local linear models that is calibrated by considering data from a set of neighboring observations. The result is an estimate of the position characteristics for each observation in the model, as well as a single bandwidth parameter that provides insights into the geographical scale of the effects. A GWR model is specified as Eq. 3;

$$y_i = \beta_{i0} + \sum_{k=1}^{p} \beta_{ik} x_{ik} + \varepsilon_i i = 1, \ldots, n, \tag{3}$$

where y_i is the dependent variable at location i, β_{i0} is the intercept coefficient at location i, x_{ik} is the k-th explanatory variable at location i, β_{ik} is the k-th local regression coefficient for the k-th explanatory variable at location i, and ε_i represents the random error term associated with location i. GWR estimator for local parameter estimates become in matrix form as Eq. 4;

$$\hat{\beta}(i) = \left[X'W(i)X\right]^{-1}X'W(i)y \tag{4}$$

where X is a n by k matrix of explanatory variables, $W(i)$ is the n by n diagonal weights matrix that weights each observation according to its distance from the position i, $\hat{\beta}(i)$ is a k by 1 vector of coefficients, and y is a k by 1 vector of observations of the dependent variable.

The GWR model is advantageous in the analysis of spatial heterogeneity for two main reasons in housing market analysis. First, this method allows to test for spatial variation of parameters in the analysis of implicit house prices [26]. The GWR model also performs better than OLS in terms of explanatory power and predictive ability [27]. Secondly, the GWR model can provide detailed parameters of each sampling point and visualize the spatial pattern of the housing market using GIS (Geographic Information System) software to intuitively and clearly represent the spatial difference of marginal prices [28].

4   Application

The present study follows a multi-step methodology. First, data containing the prices and characteristics of properties were collected from immobiliare.it, the largest Italian site where real estate listings are collected, for the most part, from local agencies. The period considered refers to the years 2014 to 2021, representing a cross-sectional dataset of the Turin city area (Fig. 1). The data collection mainly concerned the multi-family building typology as it is the predominant housing type in the city, for a total of 79,347 observations. The second step was the definition of the explanatory variables. The data

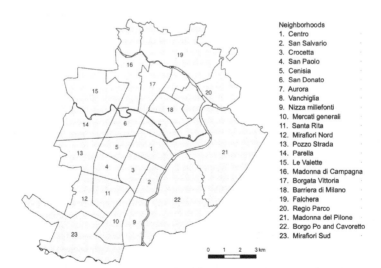

Fig. 1. Turin's neighborhoods.

were subsequently exported to SPSS© statistical software [29] to develop OLS models, and to MGWR© to calibrate GWR models [30].

In cases where there is one or more missing information within a statistical unit (e.g., a row in the data set), regression analysis involves eliminating it. Since many observations were missing some information of the features in the dataset, it was necessary to limit the number of variables to be considered in the hedonic model and to eliminate incomplete cases. In addition, since the research aims to investigate the spatial effect of the impact of energy performance, great attention was paid to the availability of EPC information for all observations. After eliminating incomplete records and outliers, the final dataset consisted of 25,245 sales announcements. As the spatial statistical analysis limits the analysis to spatially unduplicated data, it was not possible to include housing units located in the same building, and therefore with the same geographical coordinate. This limitation led to the selection of one transaction per geographical point. In addition, given the time required to calculate GWR models, 20% of the observations were randomly retained to develop the analysis, i.e., 5,899 observations.

The variables studied within the regression models relate to the structural characteristics of the apartment (floor area, dwelling level, maintenance status, EPC, age of construction, and year of advertisement publication). Some initial variables were transformed from their original scale to ordinal variables so that they could be included in the model. Initially expressed as a continuous variable, the housing level variable was categorized into a point scale as follows: −1 if the floor is basement or crawlspace; 0 if ground floor; 1 if floor is mezzanine, 1st or 2nd, 2 if floor 3rd or 4th, 3 if 5th floor or greater. Considering the data included in the database, the average number of floors is about 3 floors. A breakdown of the ordinal variable in this way should make it possible for the model to understand the consumers' appreciation of the different dwelling levels. The state of maintenance is composed of an ordinal variable ranging from 0 to 3, where 0 indicates an apartment in need of renovation, 1 in good condition, 2 renovated, 3 new/under construction). The market segment indicates the architectural quality of the property in which the apartment is located, and it is composed of an ordinal variable with 4 levels: 0 for economy class, 1 for medium class, 2 for high class, 3 for very high class. The continuous variable of year of construction was also reduced in age classes following TABULA classification which groups buildings based on the technological characteristics of the building envelope and thermal systems (before 1900, between 1901–1945, between 1946–1960, between 1961–1975, between 1976–1990, after 1990) [31]. The ordinal scale proposed by the European Commission was used to measure the impact of the energy label. In detail, the 12-level scale was reduced to 7, including levels above A in a single level, where 1 stands for properties in G and 7 in A. The proportions of the housing stock by EPC classification are quite similar to the Italian picture. It is worth noting, however, that houses with A and B classification represent the smallest portion of the Turin market (5.1%). The largest share of the market is covered by intermediate energy classes C to E (45.6%), and by buildings in classes F and G (49.3%). The spatial distribution of buildings categorized according to EPC makes it clear that the most efficient assets (class A-B) are scattered throughout the urban territory of the city of Turin, with a greater prevalence in the suburbs. On the other hand, the remaining building stock comprises the remaining classes and is spread throughout the city with a higher prevalence of the lowest classes (E-G) in the northern and southern part of the city (Fig. 2).

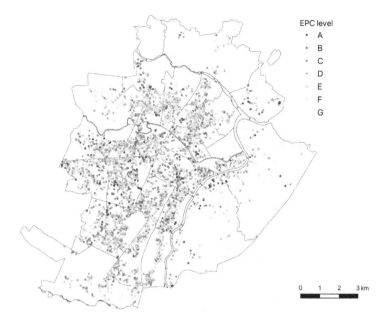

Fig. 2. Properties in the reduced sample categorized by energy class level.

Sample size across property attributes was studied to confirm representation within the dataset of sales transactions (Table 1). In terms of property age, the most recently built properties are the least representative, revealing that 9.4% of the sample data includes real estate properties built after 1990. Newer buildings (post-1960) account for 29.2% of the sample, while postwar housing accounts for 36.8%. This portion of the housing stock represents the phenomenon of building densification that occurred in Turin during the post-war recovery period.

Table 1. Sample representativeness according construction period.

Age	Frequency (No.)	% of total	Age	Frequency (No.)	% of total
Before 1900	588	10.0	Between 1961–1975	1564	26.5
Between 1901–1945	866	14.7	Between 1976–1990	158	2.7
Between 1946–1960	2169	36.8	After 1990	554	9.4

Table 2 presents a summary of the descriptive statistics of the data. The average price of the sample properties is 175,322 €, revealing a high variance (SD 173,627 €). The average floor size is 91.32 m^2, with an average EPC of 2.72, which is in line with the broader average residential range rated E.

Table 2. Descriptive statistics of variables.

Variables	Measure	Min	Max	Mean	SD
Price (€)[a]	Scale	14,900	2,250,000	175,322.64	173,627.621
Floor area (m^2)	Scale	28	1000	91.32	49.911
Dwelling level	Ordinal	− 1	3	1.63	0.970
Maintenance status[b]	Nominal	0	3	1.33	0.798
Market segment[c]	Nominal	0	3	1.42	1.007
EPC[d]	Ordinal	1	7	2.72	1.526
Before 1900[e]	Nominal	0	1	0.10	0.300
Between 1901–1945[e]	Nominal	0	1	0.15	0.354
Between 1946–1960[e]	Nominal	0	1	0.37	0.482
Between 1961–1975[e]	Nominal	0	1	0.27	0.441
Between 1976–1990[e]	Nominal	0	1	0.03	0.161
After 1990[e]	Nominal	0	1	0.09	0.292
Car parking	Scale	0	3	0.34	0.756
Lift[e]	Nominal	0	1	0.72	0.451
Year[f]	Ordinal	1	8	6.17	1.697

[a]Dependent variable

[b]Maintenance status (0 = To be restored; 1 = Good; 2 = Restored; 3 = New/Under construction)

[c]Market segment (0 = Low; 1 = Medium; 2 = High; 3 = Very high)

[d]Energy Performance Certificate (A = 7; B = 6; C = 5; D = 4; E = 3; F = 2; G = 1)

[e]1 Yes, 0 otherwise

[f]Advertising year (2014 = 1; 2015 = 2; 2016 = 3; 2017 = 4; 2018 = 5; 2019 = 6; 2020 = 7; 2021 = 8)

5   Results

5.1   Global Regression Model

The semi-logarithmic OLS model (Table 3) incorporates the EPC score and the age of construction of the buildings. The overall explanation of the model shows a relative performance (R^2) of 72.7%. All coefficients generally meet expectations in terms of sign and significance. The coefficient estimates show that floor area is the most influential feature (t = 83.646, p < 0.01), as expected. This means that a one-square meter increase in the commercial floor area of housing adds 0.9% value to the property. The results show that the top floors are worth more (coefficient 0.027). For architectural qualities, both the coefficients of property condition and maintenance status are positive and show percentage effects of 10.3% and 10.6% for a higher level, respectively. Increasing the energy class level leads to a 5% increase in property value. Regarding property age, the results show that older properties have more value - likely because older properties tend to be larger and of greater historical value ($\beta_{before900}$ = 0.211, t-value = 8.255, p-value < 0.01) than newer properties. In contrast, the coefficients for the other age groups are negative. The availability of a garage belonging to the housing increases the value of the property by 3%. The presence of an elevator inside the building adds a value of 23.6%. The variable referring to the year of publication of the advertisement, on the other hand, registers a negative coefficient value, reflecting the market trend that has characterized the Turin real estate market.

Table 3. OLS model results (dependent variable = ln price).

	β	SE	t-value	p-value	VIF
Intercept	29.431	5.965	4.934	0.000	
Floor area	0.009	0.000	83.646	0.000	1.274
Dwelling level	0.027	0.005	5.074	0.000	1.078
Maintenance status	0.103	0.007	14.346	0.000	1.312
Market segment	0.106	0.006	18.912	0.000	1.284
EPC	0.050	0.004	12.783	0.000	1.433
Before 1900	0.211	0.026	8.255	0.000	2.358
Between 1901–1945	− 0.061	0.025	− 2.459	0.014	3.069
Between 1946–1960	− 0.116	0.022	− 5.217	0.000	4.647
Between 1961–1975	− 0.116	0.022	− 5.257	0.000	3.792
Between 1976–1990	− 0.092	0.036	− 2.583	0.010	1.339
Car park	0.030	0.007	4.086	0.000	1.238
Lift	0.236	0.013	18.871	0.000	1.281
Year	− 0.009	0.003	− 3.201	0.001	1.012
R^2 = 0.727			SE = 0.3825		
Number of observations: 5,899			Mean dependent variable: 11.70		
VIF = Variance inflation factor			SE = Standard error		

The next model involves modifying the previous one by including interacting variables to examine the effects of EPC scores for each property age (Table 4). The interaction between age and EPC shows that properties prior to 1900 and constructed between 1901 and 1945 are positive. The remaining properties built after 1945 show a negative impact that is statistically insignificant. Interestingly, age classifications suggest that older (pre-1900) properties show a higher price effect ($\beta_{before900} = 0.099$, t $= 16.568$, p-value < 0.01), which may be explained by the fact that these properties are larger and have historic-architectural features that are valued in the market. These results may reflect the complex relationships in the market that can influence consumer preferences [32]. For example, an energy-efficient home located in a more desirable area may illustrate a high premium or discount due to the location effect, not the level of energy performance.

Table 4. OLS interactive model results for property age (dependent variable = ln price).

	β	SE	t-value	p-value	VIF
Intercept	34.897	6.086	5.734	0.000	
Floor area	0.009	0.000	81.958	0.000	1.273
Dwelling level	0.026	0.005	4.756	0.000	1.075
Maintenance status	0.145	0.007	22.102	0.000	1.060
Market segment	0.118	0.006	20.846	0.000	1.262
Before 1900 x EPC	0.099	0.006	16.568	0.000	1.240
Between 1901–1945 x EPC	0.030	0.006	5.057	0.000	1.289
Between 1946–1960 x EPC	0.006	0.004	1.314	0.189	1.465
Between 1961–1975 x EPC	0.003	0.005	0.629	0.529	1.408
Between 1976–1990 x EPC	0.006	0.010	0.607	0.544	1.072
Car park	0.050	0.007	6.882	0.000	1.165
Lift	0.249	0.012	19.984	0.000	1.222
Year	− 0.012	0.003	− 4.046	0.000	1.008
$R^2 = 0.715$			SE = 0.3911		
Number of observations: 5,899			Mean dependent variable: 11.70		
VIF = Variance inflation factor			SE = Standard error		

5.2 Local Regression Results

Consistent with other studies, OLS-based estimates have shown some important results on the green premium associated with effective properties. In this section, we explore the fluctuation of real estate market estimates in the urban environment. In detail, we test for the variable nature of EPCs as highlighted in Table 5. The first step of the GWR requires determining the value of the optimal bandwidth with iterations to obtain the minimum AICc. MGWR© software was used to calculate local parameter estimates [30]. The weighted matrix was formed using the adaptive bisquare function since the observations are not spatially uniformly distributed. The result of the iteration produced an AICc of 2284 with a bandwidth value of 504 neighbors. The GWR models showed better performance than OLS model, with $R^2 = 0.864$. The results reveal the existence of a clear heterogeneity and spatial variation by property construction era: properties built before 1900 show a negative price effect up to the median statistical value. While properties built between 1901 and 1975 reveal a negative price effect up to the third quartile, with a positive effect in the top value. Properties built between 1976 and 1990 show a consistent negative effect. These characteristics show distinct concentrations clustered in space presenting the complex picture of housing market composition. In terms of the effects of EPCs, the varying degree of impact on value ranges from a negative 2.85%, to the maximum effect positively affecting prices of 9.34% (Fig. 3). This is a noteworthy result as the average market coefficient for the OLS models suggests that there appears to be a uniform positive effect of 5% within the City of Turin market. In this sense, the OLS estimates may be misleading in terms of being a more truthful representation of the influence of EPC on market value. In terms of spatial variability, it is noteworthy that only the lowest value of the coefficient for EPCs is negative, while the bottom quartile shows a value of 3.4%. Focusing on the statistical-descriptive distribution of implied prices, the effects seem to be apparently premium-free at the lower end of the market. Instead, they appear to have a larger effect in the top quartile and the top value range (4.88 and 9.34 respectively).

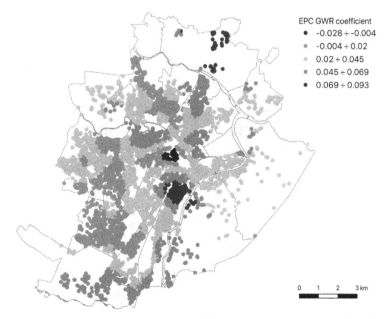

Fig. 3. Geographically Weighted Regression (GWR) energy performance certificate (EPC) level coefficients (equal interval classification of minimum and maximum value).

The results, as mentioned earlier, can be represented graphically using GIS. As noted in Fig. 3, the EPC coefficient appears to show differential price effects within the city of Turin. In Mirafiori, San Donato, southeast Aurora, and Barriera di Milano neighborhoods, and toward the southeast of the city center, energy efficiency appears to be a clear premium. The value of EPC coefficient, while positive, is small in the rest of the city. In contrast, there is only a small portion in the central part of the market area where energy efficiency seems to have a discount effect and is valued negatively in the market.

Further refining the GWR model to test the spatial interaction between structural characteristics for property age and EPC, we also show some heterogeneous effects of EPC (Table 6). Regarding the spatial interaction between property age and EPC score, pre-1900 properties show an effect on price ranging from –32% to 53%, with a negative effect observed only at the lowest value and a positive effect starting from the lowest quartile. Properties built between 1946 and 1960, and between 1961 and 1975 show a negative price effect at the lowest level. The coefficients become positive from the first quartile, also revealing a smaller range of impact than for older buildings. For properties built between 1901 and 1945, and between 1976 and 1990, the range of estimated coefficients is negative down to the first quartile. Examining the interactions between property age and EPC, some notable patterns emerge. The pre-1900 age category shows two distinct market geographies (Madonna di Campagna and Mirafiori Nord) where there appears to be a negative effect on market prices (Fig. 4), with a positive premium evident in the southwest (Mirafiori Sud).

Table 5. GWR model results.

	Minimum	Lower quartile	Median	Upper quartile	Maximum
Intercept	– 101.7108	41.1928	50.2950	60.6815	144.3426
Floor area	0.0054	0.0092	0.0106	0.0121	0.0160
Dwelling level	– 0.0493	0.0477	0.0583	0.0687	0.0994
Maintenance status	0.0469	0.0948	0.1170	0.1349	0.2181
Market segment	0.0313	0.0478	0.0643	0.0952	0.2132
EPC	– 0.0285	0.0346	0.0418	0.0488	0.0934
Before 1900	– 1.3641	– 0.3462	– 0.2539	0.2659	0.8528
Between 1901–1945	– 0.5154	– 0.3660	– 0.2792	– 0.2262	0.2031
Between 1946–1960	– 0.3751	– 0.2869	– 0.2414	– 0.2050	0.1910
Between 1961–1975	– 0.4159	– 0.2623	– 0.2291	– 0.1930	0.1856
Between 1976–1990	– 0.7354	– 0.3797	– 0.3228	– 0.2666	– 0.1756
Car park	0.0417	0.0557	0.0625	0.0781	0.1200
Lift	0.0724	0.1644	0.2005	0.2460	0.4267
Year	– 0.0664	– 0.0277	– 0.0220	0.0237	0.0558
$R^2 = 0.864$			Residual sum of squares = 429.944		
Number of observations: 5,899			Mean Dependent variable: 11.70		
AICc = 2248.62			Bandwidth = 504		

Interestingly, as noted in Table 6, the Before 1900 * EPC show the negative association at the lower end of the price distribution, signaling that these two respective neighborhoods are perhaps more socioeconomically disadvantaged. Buildings built between 1901 and 1960 show distinct areas recognizable in terms of positive prices in San Salvario, San Donato, Falchera, and the area to the west. The negative association is more pronounced in the north, downtown, and hillside areas, highlighting that EPCs for properties built between 1901–1945 include a price effect ranging from –9.24% to 11.6% (Table 6). For housing from the period between 1961 and 1975, the effect is positive starting at the lower quartile value, inferring that these properties tend to have a positive EPC effect in all price strata. In terms of spatial representation, there are also localized concentrations of both positive and negative effects with distinct enclaves in the west, north, south, and premiums, with more negative enclaves observed in the west of the city (Fig. 4). For properties built between 1976 and 1990, there is a premium in Aurora and Barriera di Milano, and between Parella and Campidoglio neighborhoods.

Table 6. GWR model results for testing the interaction between building age and EPC.

	Minimum	Lower quartile	Median	Upper quartile	Maximum
Intercept	– 111.1155	43.2291	53.9089	69.3565	129.6445
Floor area	0.0055	0.0092	0.0106	0.0121	0.0160
Dwelling level	– 0.0447	0.0491	0.0594	0.0687	0.0980
Maintenance status	0.0614	0.1269	0.1533	0.1736	0.2318
Market segment	0.0325	0.0508	0.0648	0.0963	0.2097
Before 1900 * EPC	– 0.3299	0.0476	0.0841	0.1557	0.5369
Between 1901–1945 * EPC	– 0.0924	– 0.0478	0.0331	0.0537	0.1160
Between 1946–1960 * EPC	– 0.0943	0.0266	0.0474	0.0633	0.0840
Between 1961–1975 * EPC	– 0.0484	0.0333	0.0390	0.0485	0.0710
Between 1976–1990 * EPC	– 0.1683	– 0.1037	0.0882	0.0972	0.1435
Car park	0.0428	0.0564	0.0648	0.0812	0.1411
Lift	0.0707	0.1874	0.2210	0.2590	0.4089
Year	– 0.0591	– 0.0314	– 0.0256	0.0219	0.0605

$R^2 = 0.855$	Residual sum of squares = 457.44
Number of observations: 5,899	Mean dependent variable: 11.70
AICc = 2533.99	Bandwidth = 504

Fig. 4. Geographically Weighted Regression (GWR) property age and energy performance certificate (EPC) level coefficients.

6   Discussion and Conclusions

The Energy Performance Certificate (EPC) is an important tool for improving the energy performance of buildings. It plays a central role in the context of the Energy Performance of Buildings Directive (EPBD), which requires Member States (MS) to take the necessary steps to establish a comprehensive certification system. This study contributes to the real estate literature by presenting an application of the hedonic pricing method (HPM) that evaluates the effect of EPC-derived energy labels on the value of the Turin real estate market through global and local regression models. The developed models demonstrated noteworthy results on the market price of energy performance, which are reflected in the spatial distribution of the estimated energy label coefficients. The OLS model highlighted the positive impact of the EPC, concluding that the higher the level, the greater the capitalized premium in the price of the property. OLS models also show that there is no increasing distribution of preferences with respect to age of construction: properties built before 1900 are more highly valued than those built from 1901 onward. A key finding demonstrated by the OLS model that makes EPC interact with building age is that consumers recognize the energy efficiency potential of buildings built before 1945. GWR models provide evidence of how prices of multifamily properties vary within city boundaries based on energy performance. Local models have shown that spatial variability in preferences is distributed across local scales based on short distances. The GWR model including the EPC label as an independent variable showed spatial variation for energy performance. Although the impact is positive on almost the entire city of Turin, with peaks of appreciation in the neighborhood of San Salvario and Rebaudengo north and Falchera. Only in the city center is an area identified where the impact of EPC is negative. Modifying the model specification by including interactive variables to examine the effects of EPC scores for each age, pre-1945 properties report statistically significant positive effects. Examination of the interactions between building age and EPC reveals some noteworthy topographic market structures. The pre-1900 age category shows two distinct market geographies where there appears to be a negative effect on market prices, with a positive premium evident on the rest of the city. Buildings constructed between 1901 and 1945 also show clusters with negative marginal prices. For housing from 1946–1975, the effect on prices is evident. Since the effect is positive from the lower quartile value onwards, it means that these buildings tend to have a positive EPC effect in all price strata.

These results are of particular interest to policymakers to ensure that differences in perceived value for EPC are aligned with energy efficiency policies [33, 34]. In fact, the results of the study could be useful to public policymakers in identifying areas and building types where energy efficiency operations in the building sector should be promoted through incentives and ad hoc policies to accelerate the green transition process.

Future research should include additional variables to be able to better reflect the energy performance of buildings such as the EPI. Indeed, the continuous variable describing energy efficiency could better match the continuous dependent variable of price, providing a more deterministic relationship.

References

1. Assumma, V., Datola, G., Mondini, G.: New cohesion policy 2021–2027: The role of indicators in the assessment of the SDGs targets performance. In: Gervasi, O., Murgante, B., Misra, S., Garau, C., Blečić, I., Taniar, D., Apduhan, B.O., Rocha, A.M.A.C., Tarantino, E., Torre, C.M. (eds.) ICCSA 2021. LNCS, vol. 12955, pp. 614–625. Springer, Cham (2021). https://doi.org/10.1007/978-3-030-87007-2_44
2. Oppio, A., Forestiero, L., Sciacchitano, L., Dell'Ovo, M.: How to assess urban quality: A spatial multicriteria decision analysis approach. Valori e Valutazioni **28**, 21–30 (2021)
3. Caprioli, C., Bottero, M., De Angelis, E.: Supporting Policy design for the diffusion of cleaner technologies: A spatial empirical agent-based model. ISPRS Int. J. Geo Inf. **9**, 581 (2020). https://doi.org/10.3390/ijgi9100581

4. Rosen, S.: Hedonic prices and implicit markets: Product differentiation in pure competition. J. Polit. Econ. **82**, 34–55 (1974). https://doi.org/10.1086/260169

5. European Commission: Directive 2002/91/CE, Energy Performance of Building Directive (EPBD). https://eur-lex.europa.eu/legal-content/EN/TXT/HTML/?uri=CELEX:32002L0091&from=EN. Accessed 18 May 2022

6. Kok, N., Jennen, M.: The impact of energy labels and accessibility on office rents. Energy Policy **46**, 489–497 (2012). https://doi.org/10.1016/j.enpol.2012.04.015

7. Cajias, M., Piazolo, D.: Green performs better: Energy efficiency and financial return on buildings. J. Corp. Real Estate **15**, 53–72 (2013). https://doi.org/10.1108/JCRE-12-2012-0031

8. Fregonara, E., Rolando, D., Semeraro, P.: Energy performance certificates in the Turin real estate market. J. Eur. Real Estate Res. **10**, 149–169 (2017). https://doi.org/10.1108/JERER-05-2016-0022

9. Dell'Anna, F., Bravi, M., Marmolejo-Duarte, C., Bottero, M., Chen, A.: EPC green premium in two different european climate zones: A comparative study between Barcelona and Turin. Sustainability. **11**, 5605 (2019). https://doi.org/10.3390/su11205605

10. Olaussen, J.O., Oust, A., Solstad, J.T.: Energy performance certificates – Informing the informed or the indifferent? Energy Policy **111**, 246–254 (2017). https://doi.org/10.1016/j.enpol.2017.09.029

11. Cerin, P., Hassel, L.G., Semenova, N.: Energy performance and housing prices. Sustain. Dev. **22**, 404–419 (2014). https://doi.org/10.1002/sd.1566

12. Högberg, L.: The impact of energy performance on single-family home selling prices in Sweden. J. Eur. Real Estate Res. **6**, 242–261 (2013). https://doi.org/10.1108/JERER-09-2012-0024

13. Fotheringham, A.S., Yang, W., Kang, W.: Multiscale Geographically Weighted Regression (MGWR). Ann. Am. Assoc. Geogr. **107**, 1247–1265 (2017). https://doi.org/10.1080/24694452.2017.1352480

14. Bloom, B., Nobe, M.C., Nobe, M.D.: Valuing green home designs: A study of energy star homes. J. Sustain. Real Estate **3**, 109–126 (2011)

15. Bisello, A., Antoniucci, V., Marella, G.: Measuring the price premium of energy efficiency: A two-step analysis in the Italian housing market. Energy and Buildings **208**, 109670 (2020). https://doi.org/10.1016/j.enbuild.2019.109670

16. Barreca, A., Fregonara, E., Rolando, D.: EPC labels and building features: Spatial implications over housing prices. Sustainability. **13**, 2838 (2021). https://doi.org/10.3390/su13052838

17. Marmolejo-Duarte, C., Chen, A., Bravi, M.: Spatial implications of epc rankings over residential prices. In: Mondini, G., Oppio, A., Stanghellini, S., Bottero, M., Abastante, F. (eds.) Values and Functions for Future Cities. GET, pp. 51–71. Springer, Cham (2020). https://doi.org/10.1007/978-3-030-23786-8_4

18. McCord, M., Lo, D., Davis, P.T., Hemphill, L., McCord, J., Haran, M.: A spatial analysis of EPCs in the belfast metropolitan area housing market. J. Prop. Res. **37**, 25–61 (2020). https://doi.org/10.1080/09599916.2019.1697345

19. Saavedra, L.A.: Tests for spatial lag dependence based on method of moments estimation. Reg. Sci. Urban Econ. **33**, 27–58 (2003). https://doi.org/10.1016/S0166-0462(01)00106-5

20. Krause, A.L., Bitter, C.: Spatial econometrics, land values and sustainability: Trends in real estate valuation research. Cities **29**, S19–S25 (2012). https://doi.org/10.1016/j.cities.2012.06.006

21. Anselin, L.: GIS research infrastructure for spatial analysis of real estate markets. J. Hous. Res. **9**, 113–133 (1998). https://doi.org/10.5555/jhor.9.1.e523670p713076p1

22. Goodman, A.C., Thibodeau, T.G.: Housing market segmentation. J. Hous. Econ. **7**, 121–143 (1998). https://doi.org/10.1006/jhec.1998.0229

23. Osland, L.: An application of spatial econometrics in relation to hedonic house price modeling. J. Real Estate Res. **32**, 289–320 (2010). https://doi.org/10.1080/10835547.2010.12091282

24. Fotheringham, A.S., Charlton, M.E., Brunsdon, C.: Geographically weighted regression: A natural evolution of the expansion method for spatial data analysis. Environ. Plan. A Econ. Space **30**, 1905–1927 (1998). https://doi.org/10.1068/a301905

25. Brunsdon, C., Fotheringham, A.S., Charlton, M.E.: Geographically weighted regression: A method for exploring spatial nonstationarity. Geogr. Anal. **28**, 281–298 (1996). https://doi.org/10.1111/J.1538-4632.1996.TB00936.X

26. Dell'Anna, F., Bravi, M., Bottero, M.: Urban green infrastructures: How much did they affect property prices in Singapore? Urban Forest. Urban Greening **68**, 127475 (2022). https://doi.org/10.1016/j.ufug.2022.127475

27. Wen, H., Jin, Y., Zhang, L.: Spatial heterogeneity in implicit housing prices: Evidence from Hangzhou, China. Int. J. Strateg. Prop. Manag. **21**, 15–28 (2017). https://doi.org/10.3846/1648715X.2016.1247021

28. Dell'Anna, F., Bottero, M., Bravi, M.: Geographically weighted regression models to investigate urban infrastructures impacts. In: Gervasi, O., et al. (eds.) ICCSA 2021. LNCS, vol. 12955, pp. 599–613. Springer, Cham (2021). https://doi.org/10.1007/978-3-030-87007-2_43

29. IBM Corp.: Released 2020. IBM SPSS Statistics for Macintosh. Version 27.0., Armonk (2017)

30. Oshan, T., Li, Z., Kang, W., Wolf, L., Fotheringham, A.: MGWR: A python implementation of multiscale geographically weighted regression for investigating process spatial heterogeneity and scale. ISPRS Int. J. Geo Inf. **8**, 269 (2019). https://doi.org/10.3390/ijgi8060269

31. Ballarini, I., Corgnati, S.P., Corrado, V.: Use of reference buildings to assess the energy saving potentials of the residential building stock: The experience of TABULA project. Energy Policy **68**, 273–284 (2014). https://doi.org/10.1016/j.enpol.2014.01.027

32. Dell'Anna, F., Marmolejo-Duarte, C., Bravi, M., Bottero, M.: A choice experiment for testing the energy-efficiency mortgage as a tool for promoting sustainable finance. Energ. Effi. **15**, 27 (2022). https://doi.org/10.1007/s12053-022-10035-y

33. Bragolusi, P., D'Alpaos, C.: The willingness to pay for residential PV plants in Italy: A discrete choice experiment. Sustainability **13**, 10544 (2021). https://doi.org/10.3390/SU131910544

34. Gabrielli, L., Ruggeri, A.G.: Developing a model for energy retrofit in large building portfolios: Energy assessment, optimization and uncertainty. Energy and Buildings. **202**, 109356 (2019). https://doi.org/10.1016/j.enbuild.2019.109356

Definition of an Integrated Theoretical Framework to Assess the NBS Suitability in Flood Risk Areas

Vanessa Assumma[1] , Carlotta Quagliolo[2]([⊠]) , Elena Comino[3] ,
and Giulio Mondini[1]

[1] Interuniversity Department of Regional and Urban Studies and Planning,
Politecnico di Torino, 10125 Torino, Italy
{vanessa.assumma,giulio.mondini}@polito.it
[2] Interuniversity Department of Regional and Urban Studies and Planning,
Politecnico di Torino and Università degli Studi di Torino, 10125 Torino, Italy
carlotta.quagliolo@polito.it
[3] Department of Environment, Land and Infrastructure Engineering,
Politecnico di Torino, 10129 Torino, Italy
elena.comino@polito.it

Abstract. Urban flood events are strongly affecting cities by compromising their whole system. Additionally, these events are becoming even more frequent due to the climate change effect. In this context, the urban and territorial planning require changing to plan the adaptation scenarios by considering the Nature-Based Solutions (NBS).

Consequently, this study aims to define an integrated theoretical framework to support decision makers, planners, technicians, freelances and public bodies in the assessment and design in the assessment of the more suitable NBS adaptation scenario. The proposed method includes InVEST modelling to quantify in biophysical terms the runoff mitigation effect due to NBS implementation. By combining this method with a novel extension of a tool of analysis and assessment: the D-A'WOT Analysis. This extension proposes the dynamic approach to the A'WOT to identify the dependent and independent variables that characterise a complex spatial system, as well as to solve the decisional problem by de-composing it in its simpler parts through a hierarchical approach. In this way, it can facilitate the identification of indicators which may support the identification of the most suitable alternative. The integration of the InVEST modelling and the multicriteria approach can trigger fruitful insights in the context of urban planning and design of site-specific interventions in priority areas and scaling up investments. On the one hand to contrast at flood risk and on the other hand to generate multiple benefits for a safer, sustainable and resilient quality of life.

Keywords: Nature-Based Solutions (NBS) · InVEST modeling · Decision-making

© The Author(s), under exclusive license to Springer Nature Switzerland AG 2022
O. Gervasi et al. (Eds.): ICCSA 2022 Workshops, LNCS 13380, pp. 228–237, 2022.
https://doi.org/10.1007/978-3-031-10542-5_16

1 Introduction

Today is widely shared a global awareness that the environment health is one of the main priorities of governmental agendas (United Nations 2015). The impact of anthropogenic activities in two centuries have led to the creation of an intergenerational debt (Mondini 2019) which must be extinguished to avoid an irreversible future for next generations (IPCC 2019). The increasing global temperatures, the draining of water bodies, the melting of glaciers and the consequent arise of sea levels, are revolutionizing the Nature's clock and causing an increase of unpredictable events. To mitigate and compensate the Man's mistakes, Nature-Based Solutions are retained ever more fundamental and thus helping the Socio-Ecological Systems (SES) to evolve, adapt and respond to perturbations (Gunderson and Holling 2002) in a more sustainable way.

The EU commission defines Nature-Based Solutions (NBS) as "[...] inspired and supported by nature, which are cost-effective, simultaneously provide environmental, social and economic benefits and help build resilience. Such solutions bring more, and more diverse, nature and natural features and processes [...] through locally adapted, resource-efficient and systemic interventions."[1]. NBS includes a wide range of interventions, their scale can vary in function of the biodiversity protection and their resilience, and these can be co-designed by local communities (Reid et al. 2018; Sutton-Grier et al. 2018; Watson et al. 2018; Keeler et al. 2019; Seddon et al. 2020; Dell'Anna et al. 2022). For example, NBS differ from Low Impact Development (LID), Sustainable Urban Drainage Systems (SUDS), Water Sensitive Urban Design (WSUD), and Blue-Green Infrastructure (BGI) because they can provide many benefits and co-benefits at multiple scale, where natural risk like floods can be mitigated and/or compensated (Qin et al. 2013; Martin-Mikle et al. 2015; Ahmed et al. 2017; Qi et al. 2020; O'Donnell et al. 2020; Quagliolo et al. 2021a; Alves et al. 2022).

Policy decisions needs to be ever more supported by suitable tools of analysis and assessment and bridge the gap between theorization and practice of novel paradigms such as the one of climate resilience.

The World Bank has developed a catalogue collecting NBS solutions to satisfy the increasing need of Decision and Policy makers to deliver infrastructures and services, and other interventions to the built environment, as well as to identify related investments (World Bank 2021).

The Global Program on Nature-Based Solutions for Climate Resilience financed by the partnership GFDRR (Global Facility for Disaster Reduction and Recovery) sustains low- and middle-income countries in the risk and vulnerability reduction through resilience building projects to respond at climate-change and natural disasters[2]. Particularly, specific projects are devoted to flood risk reduction with benefits such as the redirection drainage and storage infiltration of flood storm water, or the loss reduction of urban infrastructure, among others.

---

[1] European Commission: https://ec.europa.eu/info/research-and-innovation/research-area/env ironment/nature-based-solutions_en (Accessed: April 2022).

[2] Global Facility for Disaster Reduction and Recovery (GFDRR) https://www.gfdrr.org/en (Accessed April 2022). Global Program on Nature-Based solutions for climate resilience https:// naturebasedsolutions.org/projects (Accessed April 2022).

Amidst the tools available in the relevant literature, the InVEST modelling and MCDA models whether combined may trigger useful insights for NBS design and assessment, thus supporting the adaptation of urban and territorial systems to extreme events, such as the flood and heavy rains.

It is important to underline that the present paper (re)start from a previous article of some of the authors (Quagliolo et al. 2023 in press) which employ the combination of the InVEST modelling with the Multicriteria Decision Analysis (MCDA) in a pilot cases study. Thanks to the interesting results obtained by that first application, the present paper continues that research in order to define a theoretical evaluation framework able to support Decision and Policy Makers in the assessment and planning of complex spatial systems affected by flood risk areas which require priority interventions.

The paper includes the following sections: a Methodology section devoted to the development of a literature review on InVEST modelling and a novel MCDA technique called D-A'WOT Analysis; a Theoretical proposal section which takes into account the main features of both the methodologies in order to develop a novel model; and a conclusive section that recapitulates the utility of the novel framework and envisions the next steps of this research work.

2 Methodology

This section deals with the theorization of a novel multidisciplinary framework to tackle the complexity and uncertainty of urban and territorial problems. This paper focuses on the need of Decision Makers to find suitable interventions able to respond to the occurrence of urban flood events that could, on the one hand, damage cities and their socio-economic axis, and on the other hand perturbate the whole Socio-Ecological System (SES), leading this to its reorganization (Gunderson 2010). The proposed method, as already said, recalls the research work developed in the paper (Quagliolo et al. 2023) and defines more deeply its theoretical structure, thus proposing a novelty in the family of decision support systems.

Particularly, the InVEST modelling can help prioritisation of intervention areas for NBS implementation (Kadaverugu et al. 2020; Salata et al. 2021). Through the biophysical assessment, quantification of NBS effects to mitigate climate/natural hazards while increasing a range of related benefit (i.e. social and economic) could be performed by implementing different scenarios (Quagliolo et al. 2021b).

The MCDA can help Decision Makers in the solution of multidimensional problems by considering the actors and stakeholder preferences. They can represent the complementary piece, on the one hand of Cost-Benefits Analysis and/or Discount-Cash Flow (CBA and DCFA) because can deal with multiple elements, including the monetary ones. On the other hand, these are complementary of procedures of sustainability assessment, because can help in the identification and assessment of alternative solutions, and thus supporting the selection of the best scenario and in the impact of objectives and actions annexed (Bottero and Mondini 2009; Bottero et al. 2021).

2.1 InVEST Modeling

To help quantifying NBS biophysical effects and ecosystem services (ES) processes, various modelling tools have been developed to integrate many natural and human components (Francesconi et al. 2016). Among others, InVEST (Integrated Valuation of Ecosystem Services and Tradeoffs), ARIES (Artificial Intelligence for Ecosystem Services), SWAT (Soil and Water Assessment Tool) and LUCI (Land Utilization and Capability Indicator) are all freely downloadable software and require medium technical skills but a good knowledge of Ecosystem Services and their processes. Particularly, the modular InVEST tool simplify the process of mapping. This tool for integrated spatial evaluation assessment of ES was developed by the Natural Capital Project[3] (NatCap), a partnership between the Stanford University, University of Minnesota, The Nature Conservancy and the World Wildlife Fund to integrate ES value into decision making (www.naturalcapitalproject.org). Through the terrestrial, freshwater, coastal and marine Ecosystem Services maps, InVEST is specifically designed for urban planning evaluation, ranging from general environmental assessment to local scale evaluations and all the decisions are aimed at restoring and protecting the Natural Capital. One of the main advantages to InVEST employment is related essentially to the consistent format of data input and output of the models which facilitate their integration with other spatially explicit models for ecosystems assessment. Specifically, the Urban Flood Risk Mitigation (UFRM) model is a recent product (2019) of InVEST which focuses on urban areas' ability to reduce the runoff process due to extreme rainfall and flash flooding events. The UFRM model considers the potentiality of permeable green areas to mainly reduce runoff while slowing surface flows and creating space for water (as in floodplains or basins). The model output represents the amount of retained runoff per pixels assuming mainly the flood-prone areas due to the interaction between the permeable-impermeable surface layers (related to the land use type) and the soil drainage (depending on the soil characteristics).

Since the InVEST software works with spatial models, the elaboration of model inputs and outputs is conducted through the employment of GIS tools. The UFRM model solves the empirical representation of the hydrological aspects for estimating runoff production and retention ability in the study area (Sharp et al. 2020). By applying GIS-based approaches to elaborate model's production, the localization of the implementation NBS areas (opportunity spaces) is identified (Albert et al. 2020). Overall, the resulting spatial index provides a picture of the vulnerability pattern by presenting the biophysical assessment (Davies and Lafortezza 2019).

2.2 Multicriteria Techniques: The D-A'WOT Analysis

The techniques of Multicriteria Decision Analysis (MCDA) are well known to be suitable for dealing complex problems and considering the interests and expectations of multiple actors and stakeholders in a shared vision of potential urban and territorial transformation. The MCDA techniques are ever more considered within integrated assessment frameworks thanks to their flexibility and ability to consider both qualitative and quantitative features of a decision problem. Considering the MCDA classifications according

---

[3] Available at https://naturalcapitalproject.stanford.edu/software/invest.

to the weighting assignment (i.e. choice, description, ranking and sorting), the paper focuses on the ranking-based techniques. In fact, they can provide to the final users a clear classification of the alternatives based on the users' preferences and/or expertise. The A'WOT model was developed in the early 2000s by combining the Analytic Hierarchy Process (AHP) and the SWOT analysis (Kurttila et al. 2000; Kangas et al. 2001).

According to previous studies of some of the authors, we retain that the SWOT Analysis should be integrated by a dynamic approach, which can better support the resolution of decision problems characterized by interdependent relationships. For example, cities and territories are interested by physical and immaterial influences (e.g. transport infrastructures, or migration routes) and there are certain variables which are more influent than other variables, positive or negative. These could influence the design and the prioritization of policy interventions. Therefore, it is required a method capable to interpret the values and pressures and understand the dynamics that occur within the system.

According to the results obtained in a previous research work, the authors states that it is ever more required a dynamic approach for dealing with the complexity of spatial systems, and to analyze their general and site-specific features.

The A'WOT is thus extended by a dynamic approach, by substituting the conventional SWOT Analysis with the Dynamic SWOT Analysis (Bezzi 2005; Bevilacqua et al. 2019). If the classical SWOT Analysis takes a photograph of the elements of a decisional problem according to the strengths (S), weaknesses (W), opportunities (O) and threats (T), the Dynamic SWOT Analysis makes a step forward and assess the relationships between the same elements (Bezzi 2005). Therefore, we present this novel method as Dynamic A'WOT (or D-A'WOT).

The proposed extension is here contextualized in the field of risk analysis and management to help Decision Makers, and other bodies in the assessment and design of Nature-Based Solutions (NBS).

This technique combines the dynamic SWOT Analysis with the Analytic Hierarchy Process (AHP), on the one hand to identify the main elements which characterize a complex spatial problem and their influence relationships, and on the other hand, to assess their relevance in solving a complex problem, such as the identification of the most suitable NBS scenario to contrast at flood risk in critical areas.

The methodological steps which characterize the D-A'WOT Analysis are provided below:

1. Data collection to identify the main elements of the decision problem under investigation. In the case of complex spatial systems, it is useful to develop territorial knowledge analysis through GIS methods and enriched with information material such as main national, regional and data sources, plans and regulations in force, or local knowledge, among others;
2. Importing the elements in the SWOT Analysis: in this step it is possible to analyze the values and the pressures as endogenous and exogeneous factors of the complex spatial system, by clustering them according to the Strengths (S), Weaknesses (W), Opportunities (O) and Threats (T). It is possible to use the conventional "four quadrants" configuration, recent extensions like the STEEP and SWOT Analysis (Szigeti et al. 2011), infographics, etc. The configuration choice may depend also on the

amount of data and features to be highlighted. A useful step is the codification of each element of the SWOT Analysis in order to create a bridge with the subsequent step and thus facilitating its development. The SWOT Analysis can be designed by team groups (i.e. desktop modality), or built by participants who are close to the decisional problem and able to provide useful information (i.e. participatory modality). However, independently from the modality choice, the SWOT Analysis can deliver a photograph of the decision problem and embryonal objectives and strategies which will be explicated through scenario building tools (Amer et al. 2013);

3. Development of the D-SWOT Analysis: each codified element is imported within a matrix (e.g. Excel environment) and evaluated according to a quali-quantitative scale, where 0 means lack of influence between two elements, scores as $+1$ means positive interaction between two elements and $+2$ labels a very positive synergy between them, whereas the scores -1 and -2 label a limitation of an element with respect to another and a potential nullification (Bezzi 2005). Once having filled the matrix, it is possible to summarize the scores in rows and in columns thus obtaining the dependent and independent variables which are useful to select the most relevant criteria that will be considered in the core of the assessment process;

4. Structuring of the decision problem. The criteria and related sub-criteria (or indicators) are organized according to a hierarchical approach which is typical of the Analytic Hierarchy Process (AHP) and connected to a defined set of alternatives with the purpose of finding the most suitable scenario (Saaty 2004).

5. Evaluation. This step follows the conventional multicriteria procedure: i) hierarchical configuration of the criteria and sub-criteria; ii) pairwise comparisons at the level of criteria and then of sub-criteria; iii) aggregation of the final priorities; iv) synthesis into the global priorities.

6. Ranking of the alternative scenarios and final check. In this final step, the alternatives are ranked from the most relevant to the least relevant. Then, their stability is checked through the sensitivity analysis and according to the "what if" approach (Razavi et al. 2021).

3 Theoretical Proposal

As shown in Fig. 1, the integrated approach here presented is constituted by three stages: the *ex-ante, in-itinere* and *ex-post* evaluation. In the *ex-ante* and *in-itinere* phases, the physical-environmental and performance analysis have been developed through the employment of InVEST modelling integrated with GIS tools. Specifically, this method can help in the identification of the priority intervention areas, intended as those interested by high flood risk. From the *ex-ante* to the *in-itinere* phase, the physical performance analysis can quantify the biophysical effect related to the NBS implementation to reduce the runoff production derived from rainfall events.

The MCDA, developing in this paper the D-A'WOT as the combination of the D-SWOT Analysis and the AHP method, can integrate the physical environmental and performance analyses in the *ex-ante* and *in-itinere* phases on different features. First, the criteria identification can also derive from data elaborated with GIS, InVEST, as well as from D-SWOT Analysis. Second, the D-A'WOT assessment can accompany the three stages of the evaluation procedure and thus supporting the refinement of the NBS implementation. In this way, it is possible to deliver to Decision and Policy Makers an efficient-efficacy adaptation scenario. Moreover, the method can support the impact assessment of this scenario, positive and/or negative (e.g. increase of ecological connectivity, or financial availability) and providing in the *ex-post* phase, the scenario performance and helping the Decision and Policy Makers to identify potential mitigation and compensation actions.

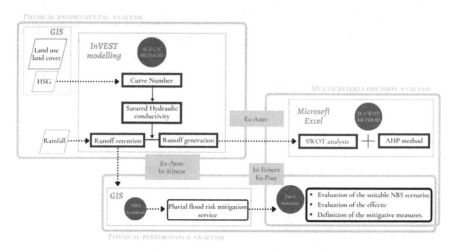

Fig. 1. Integrated theoretical framework

4   Future Perspectives of the Research

This paper has described a theoretical decision supporting framework that integrated the InVEST modelling with the MCDA in order to help Decision and Policy Makers in the assessment and design of NBS adaptation scenarios to contrast flood risk. It has underlined the value of NBS-based interventions within urban and territorial transformation and the potential benefits which may be generated for local community. It emerged also the need to implement them in policy decisions according to a systemic perspective (Lafortezza et al. 2018; Palomo et al. 2021).

Pros and cons of the individual methods are identified and reported as follows. Concerning the InVEST modelling, one limitation is that it synthesizes the hydrological urban aspects through a simple method (SCS-CN method). On the other hand, it allows to return numerical and quantifiable values in biophysical terms for the ecological measurement and for the flood reduction related to a given NBS intervention.

The D-A'WOT reunifies the analysis and the assessment phases in a unique method. This can help the users to manage and solve the decision problem since the early stages, until to its resolution. This can accompany both the planning and assessment along with the *ex-ante*, *in-itinere* and *ex-post* stages.

A limit of the D-A'WOT can be related to the difficulty of evaluating the influence relationships between numerous elements through the D-SWOT Analysis. Therefore, it is important to select a well and reasonable number of elements and supported by an expert knowledge.

The theoretical and methodological definition of this method, and the application developed in the previous work of the authors raised a number of reasonable perspectives to follow the next steps of this research.

As future perspective, the results of the D-A'WOT could be further extended with GIS methods, and thus making the methodological proposal of this paper even more integrated. Particularly, the dependent and independent variables obtained through the D-SWOT referred to a Socio-Ecological System (SES) and the set of weights obtained through the pairwise comparison method, will be combined and spatialized as suitability maps. In this way, the outputs of InVEST modelling and of the D-A'WOT can deliver as outcome the most suitable sites to localise the best NBS intervention, according to a SES perspective. The next steps of this research work will contribute to a practical advance of the Multicriteria Spatial Decision Support System (MCSDSS) (Malczewski 2006; Treves et al. 2020).

A future perspective for InVEST is to integrate the biophysical flood assessment with the economic estimation of flood damages to finally calculate the NBS cost-benefit analysis (Quagliolo et al. 2021a; 2021b).

The proposed extension has been theorized in the context of risk analysis and management, and it will apply to other issues which characterize the overall complexity of SES. Starting from the application in the paper (Quagliolo et al. 2023), this integrated framework will be applied to other similar territories interested by flooding criticalities. The local scale (i.e. Municipality or districts) will be considered in order to implement the concept of urban resilience related to flood risk.

It will be further explored the integration of specific dynamic models, such as System Dynamics Models and Lotka-Volterra cooperative models (Assumma et al. 2020) to predict potential evolution scenarios to tackle the climate change effect with socio-economic variables and the economic impact, positive or negative, which could be caused by a potential loss, as well as the possible benefits delivered by the NBS solution.

References

Ahmed, K., Chung, E.S., Song, J.Y., Shahid, S.: Effective design and planning specification of low impact development practices using water management analysis module (WMAM): case of Malaysia. Water **9**(3), 173 (2017). https://doi.org/10.3390/W9030173

Albert, C., et al.: Planning nature-based solutions: principles, steps, and insights. Ambio **50**(8), 1446–1461 (2020). https://doi.org/10.1007/s13280-020-01365-1

Alves, P.B.R., Djordjević, S., Javadi, A.A.: Understanding the NEEDS for ACTING: an integrated framework for applying nature-based solutions in Brazil. Water Sci. Technol. **85**, 987–1010 (2022). https://doi.org/10.2166/WST.2021.513

Amer, M., Daim, T.U., Jetter, A.: A review of scenario planning. Futures **46**, 23–40 (2013). https://doi.org/10.1016/j.futures.2012.10.003

Assumma, V., Bottero, M., Datola, G., et al.: Dynamic models for exploring the resilience in territorial scenarios. Sustainability **12**, 1–19 (2020). https://doi.org/10.3390/su12010003

Bevilacqua, C., Anversa, I.G., Cantafio, G., Pizzimenti, P.: Local clusters as "building blocks" for smart specialization strategies: a dynamic SWOT analysis application in the case of San Diego (US). Sustainability **11**, 1–25 (2019). https://doi.org/10.3390/su11195541

Bezzi, C.: Teoria e metodi. Rendiamo dinamica la SWOT. RIV Rass Ital di valutazione (2005). https://doi.org/10.1400/66625

Bottero, M., Assumma, V., Caprioli, C., Dell'Ovo, M.: Decision making in urban development: the application of a hybrid evaluation method for a critical area in the city of Turin (Italy). Sustain. Cities Soc. **72**, 103028 (2021). https://doi.org/10.1016/j.scs.2021.103028

Bottero, M., Mondini, G.: Valutazione e sostenibilità. Piani, programmi, progetti. CELID, Torino (2009)

Davies, C., Lafortezza, R.: Transitional path to the adoption of nature-based solutions. Land Use Policy **80**, 406–409 (2019). https://doi.org/10.1016/j.landusepol.2018.09.020

Dell'Anna, F., Bravi, M., Bottero, M.: Urban Green infrastructures: how much did they affect property prices in Singapore? Urban For Urban Green **68**, 127475 (2022). https://doi.org/10.1016/j.ufug.2022.127475

Francesconi, W., Srinivasan, R., Pérez-Miñana, E., et al.: Using the soil and water assessment tool (SWAT) to model ecosystem services: a systematic review. J. Hydrol. **535**, 625–636 (2016). https://doi.org/10.1016/j.jhydrol.2016.01.034

Gunderson, L.: Ecological and human community resilience in response to natural disasters. Ecol. Soc. **15**, 29 (2010). https://doi.org/10.5751/ES-03381-150218

Gunderson, L.H., Holling, C.S.: Panarchy: understanding transformations in systems of humans and nature (2002)

IPCC: Global Warming of 1.5 °C. An IPCC Special Report on the impacts of global warming of 1.5 °C above pre-industrial levels and related global greenhouse gas emission pathways, in the context of strengthening the global response to the threat of climate change (2019)

Kadaverugu, A., Nageshwar Rao, C., Viswanadh, G.K.: Quantification of flood mitigation services by urban green spaces using InVEST model: a case study of Hyderabad city, India. Model. Earth Syst. Environ. **7**(1), 589–602 (2020). https://doi.org/10.1007/s40808-020-00937-0

Kangas, J., Pesonen, M., Kurttila, M., Kajanus, M.: A'wot: Integrating the AHP with Swot Analysis, pp. 189–198 (2001). https://doi.org/10.13033/isahp.y2001.012

Keeler, B.L., Hamel, P., McPhearson, T., et al.: Social-ecological and technological factors moderate the value of urban nature. Nat. Sustain. **21**(2), 29–38 (2019). https://doi.org/10.1038/s41893-018-0202-1

Kurttila, M., Pesonen, M., Kangas, J., Kajanus, M.: Utilizing the analytic hierarchy process (AHP) in SWOT analysis - a hybrid method and its application to a forest-certification case. For. Policy Econ. **1**, 41–52 (2000). https://doi.org/10.1016/s1389-9341(99)00004-0

Lafortezza, R., Chen, J., van den Bosch, C.K., Randrup, T.B.: Nature-based solutions for resilient landscapes and cities. Environ. Res. **165**, 431–441 (2018). https://doi.org/10.1016/J.ENVRES.2017.11.038

Malczewski, J.: GIS-based multicriteria decision analysis: a survey of the literature. Int. J. Geogr. Inf. Sci. **20**, 703–726 (2006). https://doi.org/10.1080/13658810600661508

Martin-Mikle, C.J., de Beurs, K.M., Julian, J.P., Mayer, P.M.: Identifying priority sites for low impact development (LID) in a mixed-use watershed. Landsc. Urban Plan. **140**, 29–41 (2015). https://doi.org/10.1016/J.LANDURBPLAN.2015.04.002

Mondini, G.: Valutazioni di sostenibilità: dal rapporto Brundtland ai Sustainable Development Goal. J. Valori e Valutazioni **23**, 129–138 (2019)

O'Donnell, E., Thorne, C., Ahilan, S., et al.: The blue-green path to urban flood resilience. Blue-Green Syst **2**, 28–45 (2020). https://doi.org/10.2166/BGS.2019.199

Palomo, I., Locatelli, B., Otero, I., et al.: Assessing nature-based solutions for transformative change. One Earth **4**, 730–741 (2021). https://doi.org/10.1016/J.ONEEAR.2021.04.013

Qi, Y., Chan, F.K.S., Thorne, C., et al.: Addressing challenges of urban water management in chinese sponge cities via nature-based solutions. Water (Switz.) **12**, 1–24 (2020). https://doi.org/10.3390/w12102788

Qin, H.-P., Li, Z., Fu, G.: The effects of low impact development on urban flooding under different rainfall characteristics. J. Environ. Manage. **129**, 577–585 (2013). https://doi.org/10.1016/j.jenvman.2013.08.026

Quagliolo, C., Assumma, V., Comino, E., et al.: An integrated method to assess flood risk and resilience in the MAB UNESCO Collina Po (Italy). In: Lecture Notes in Networks and Systems (2023, in press)

Quagliolo, C., Comino, E., Pezzoli, A.: Nature-based simulation to address climate change-related flooding. Preliminary insights on a small-sized Italian city. In: Gervasi, O., et al. (eds.) ICCSA 2021. LNCS, vol. 12955, pp. 544–553. Springer, Cham (2021). https://doi.org/10.1007/978-3-030-87007-2_39

Quagliolo, C., Comino, E., Pezzoli, A.: Experimental flash floods assessment through urban flood risk mitigation (UFRM) model: the case study of Ligurian coastal cities. Front. Water **3**, 1–16 (2021). https://doi.org/10.3389/frwa.2021.663378

Razavi, S., Jakeman, A., Saltelli, A., et al.: The future of sensitivity analysis: an essential discipline for systems modeling and policy support. Environ. Model. Softw. **137**, 104954 (2021). https://doi.org/10.1016/J.ENVSOFT.2020.104954

Reid, H., Bourne, A., Muller, H., et al.: A framework for assessing the effectiveness of ecosystem-based approaches to adaptation. Resil. Sci. Adapt. Clim. Change **2018**, 207–216 (2018). https://doi.org/10.1016/B978-0-12-811891-7.00016-5

Saaty, T.L.: Decision making—the analytic hierarchy and network processes (AHP/ANP). J. Syst. Sci. Syst. Eng. (2004). https://doi.org/10.1007/s11518-006-0151-5

Salata, S., Ronchi, S., Giaimo, C., et al.: Performance-based planning to reduce flooding vulnerability insights from the case of Turin (North-West Italy). Sustainability **13**, 1–25 (2021)

Seddon, N., Chausson, A., Berry, P., et al.: Understanding the value and limits of nature-based solutions to climate change and other global challenges. Philos. Trans. R Soc. B **375**, 1–12 (2020). https://doi.org/10.1098/RSTB.2019.0120

Sharp, R., Douglass, J., Wolny, S., et al.: InVEST 3.9.0. User's Guide. The Natural Capital Project (2020). https://storage.googleapis.com/releases.naturalcapitalproject.org/invest-userguide/latest/index.html. Accessed 12 Apr 2021

Sutton-Grier, A.E., Gittman, R.K., Arkema, K.K., et al.: Investing in natural and nature-based infrastructure: building better along our coasts. Sustainability **10**, 523 (2018). https://doi.org/10.3390/SU10020523

Szigeti, H., Messaadia, M., Majumdar, A., Eynard, B.: STEEP analysis as a tool for building technology roadmaps. In: eChallenges Conference Proceedings, Florence, pp 1–12 (2011)

Treves, A., Bottero, M., Caprioli, C., Comino, E.: The reintroduction of Castor fiber in Piedmont (Italy): an integrated SWOT-spatial multicriteria based approach for the analysis of suitability scenarios. Ecol Indic **118**, 106748 (2020). https://doi.org/10.1016/J.ECOLIND.2020.106748

United Nations: Transforming Our World: the 2030 Agenda for Sustainable Development United Nations United Nations Transforming Our World: the 2030 Agenda for Sustainable Development. A/RES/70/1. United Nations (2015)

Watson, J.E.M., Evans, T., Venter, O., et al.: The exceptional value of intact forest ecosystems. Nat. Ecol. Evol. **24**(2), 599–610 (2018). https://doi.org/10.1038/s41559-018-0490-x

World Bank: A Catalogue of Nature-Based Solutions for Urban Resilience (2021)

Quagliolo, C., Assumma, V., Comino, E., Mondini, G., Pezzoli, A.: An integrated method to assess flood risk and resilience in the MAB UNESCO Collina Po (Italy). In: International Symposium New Metropolitan Perspectives. Lecture Notes in Networks and Systems, 25–27 May 2022, Reggio, Calabria (2023, in press)

International Workshop on Models and Indicators for Assessing and Measuring the Urban Settlement Development in the View of ZERO Net Land Take by 2050 (MOVEto0 2022)

Ecosystem Services for Planning Impacts Assessment on Urban Settlement Development

Angela Pilogallo[1] , Lucia Saganeiti[2]([⊠]) , Lorena Fiorini[2] ,
and Alessandro Marucci[2]

[1] Laboratory of Urban and Regional Systems Engineering (LISUT), School of Engineering,
University of Basilicata, Viale dell'ateneo Lucano 10, 85100 Potenza, Italy
angela.pilogallo@unibas.it
[2] Department of Civil, Building-Architecture and Environmental Engineering, University of
L'Aquila, Via G. Gronchi, 18, 67100 L'Aquila, Italy
{lucia.saganeiti,lorena.fiorini,alessandro.marucci}@univaq.it

Abstract. At global level, land-use changes induced by urban growth processes
are considered to be one of the most relevant threats to the conservation of natural
habitats, their biodiversity and capacity to provide ecosystem services for human
well-being. While in the academic field there is a growing interest in the methodological framework of ecosystem services, in the practice of urban and territorial
planning there is a need for new methods and tools to support the assessment
of planning choices' sustainability. The aim of this work is to propose a method
to evaluate the effects of expansion forecasts set in the urban plan (PRG) of the
Municipality of Perugia. The comparison between the state of art and the forecast
scenario highlights the degradation increase especially along the interface between
urban settlements and agricultural areas, and the relevant habitat quality decrease
in urban green areas and in complex agricultural systems close to built-up areas. In
spite of the limitations related to the subjectivity of the parameterization of input
values, the approach shows potential for the assessment of urbanization processes
and for supporting the evaluation of planning choices.

Keywords: Urban growth · Ecosystem services · Habitat quality

1 Introduction

Worldwide, urbanization processes are one of the greatest threats to ecosystem services'
and biodiversity conservation. Different development dynamics, the speed of growth of
settlements and the specificities of the several contexts lead to increased threats and pressures having negative impacts in terms of reduction and fragmentation of natural habitats
[1], depleting their ability to provide ecosystem services and to constitute suitable sites
for trophic resources supply and reproduction of wild animal and plant species [2].

In this perspective, it is extremely important for planners to dispose of methodologies
and tools to understand and quantify the effects following the implementation of urban
and territorial plans on natural systems and their capacity to provide ecosystem services

[3]. This consideration constitutes the background to the present work, which intends to evaluate the impact due to the full implementation of expansion forecasts of Perugia's urban plan (Piano Regolatore Generale - PRG) in force.

According to Umbria Regional Law no. 31/97, the PRG is divided into a structural and an operational part, assigning to the latter the task of identifying and regulating urban planning forecasts in the methods, forms and limits established in the structural part, specifying its contents and identifying territorial transformations.

The operational part also includes the zones' delimitation, detailing their use and implementation methods in the "Technical standards for implementation" (Testo Unico Norme di Attuazione - TUNA). This identifies areas destined for the completion of building fabric and the expansion of urban aggregates.

On this basis the zoning vectorization was performed, which allowed the spatialization of threats posed by further surfaces' artificialization, increase in settlement pressure and the infrastructural development of new areas.

In particular, for the purposes of this work these threats were implemented within the InVEST Habitat Quality model [4] in order to verify how the levels of cumulative degradation and environmental quality change following the full implementation of the plan forecasts.

For this reason, two scenarios were compared using the informative layers of the Urban Atlas as a basis for land use. The first is the state of art: threats assume an increasing value according to the current urbanization density. The second is the scenario of the full implementation of the expansion forecasts: the mainly residential expansion areas (Zone C) provided within the plan replace the current urban aggregates, leading to an increase in urbanization density.

In the context of this work, the basic assumption is that habitat quality is significant for the total capacity to deliver ES and is therefore a proxy for biodiversity level [5] and overall environmental performance [6].

The paper is structured as follows. The first paragraph describes the study area, illustrating the main characteristics of settlement system of the Perugia Municipality.

The "materials and methods" section describes the preparatory phases of the layers used to simulate the effects of zoning, the datasets used, the functioning of the "Habitat Quality" software of the InVEST suite with relative input data and informative layers.

The second section of the paper concerns the discussion of the results both in terms of mapping cumulative degradation and habitat quality, and in terms of changes in ES considered for each land use class affected by urban growth.

Finally, conclusions report the most relevant highlights showing the contribution that this approach can make to the assessment of expected impacts following different plan choices.

2   Study Area

This work, within the Integrated Project LIFE IMAGINE UMBRIA (LIFE19 IPE/IT/000015) – "Integrated MAnagement and Grant Investments for the N2000 NEtwork in Umbria", focuses on the territory of the Municipality of Perugia, in central Italy, which covers approximately 450 km^2.

Over the last decade, the demographic trend has been more or less constant, with a resident population of around 165 000 000 inhabitants at 31/12/2020 [7].

The overall settlement system is characterized by four main macro-components.

The first is represented by the historic nucleus which, despite its most significant expansion towards the Genna valley, has preserved the characteristics of the compact settlement.

The second macro-component is made up of the system of secondary centers located beyond the Genna valley, which are characterized by considerable complexity due to the overlapping and intertwining of urban and rural structures and functions.

The urban centers along the Tiber valley, which constitute the third macro-component, have different specificities. They are in fact urban aggregates that have developed quite compactly around pre-existing historical settlements.

Finally, the last component is diffuse urbanization consisting of small residential and productive areas set in a disorderly and fragmented way in the rural and natural landscape.

The negative impacts on habitats and ecosystems of high fragmented aggregates and the poor socio-economic efficiency of low-density settlements [8, 9] have led the Umbria Region to search for settlement planning and design models oriented to favor settlement aggregation and preserve the significant landscape heritage [10].

As it emerges from the contribution published in the ISPRA report in 2021 [11], the region of Umbria and the province of Perugia in particular, have an index of settlement dispersion (urban sprinkling) equal to 0.66 (in a range of values between 0 and 1 where 0 indicates dispersed settlement and 1 compact settlement).

In order to obtain an overall picture in terms of the effects of urbanization on natural systems and to avoid the "island effect" linked to the assessment of habitat quality, the elaborations were carried out at a supra-municipal scale including the municipalities of Passignano sul Trasimeno, Magione, Corciano, Panicale, Piegaro, Marsciano, Deruta, Torgiano, Bettona, Bastia Umbra and Valfabbrica. For all of them, the informative layers of the Urban Atlas were available.

3   Materials and Methods

The aim of this work is to compare the impacts due to the full implementation of Perugia's urban plan with those due to the distribution of the existing settlement system in terms of habitat quality.

To this end, the methodology is essentially structured in two successive steps: the construction of a synthesis vector layer showing the zoning of the municipal territory of Perugia according to what foreseen in the PRG; the execution of the "Habitat Quality" model with reference to the two phases before and after the implementation of Zone C and therefore the increase in building and housing density.

3.1   Dataset Building: The PRG Mosaic

The PRG mosaic is a product of the Life SUN project (ref) developed in order to have a strategic vision on the territorial transformation forecasts. In fact, the mosaic of PRG forecasts is a procedure of elaboration and standardization of the urban planning tools in force on the territory of the Umbria Region. PRG mosaic has been defined by Fiorini et al. [12] as PTM - Planning Tool Mosaic. A PTM contains the summary of the contents of individual municipal planning tools, using a unified legend obtained from the interpretation of the zone assignments indicated in the source documents. In this way, the zoning of n plans that flow together into PTMs are welded into a single layer accompanied by a single database. Of course, it would also be possible to prepare a simply spatial PTM, maintaining the original synoptic items of the individual plans, but this would compromise the searchability of the device relative to the macroscopic effect deriving from the summary of the indications of the individual municipalities [12]. The standardization procedures of the General Regulatory Plans in the PTM:

- the coding of the graphics and symbolisms to be used to identify the homogeneous zones, the restricted areas, and the land use destinations through the creation of a standard legend;
- defining technical and informatics characteristics of the documentation through the organization and naming of the folders and files;
- defining characteristics of the basic cartography formats to be used for the works.

A strategic level assessment tool was critical to moving forward with the proposed analyses.

3.2 Habitat Quality

Although the result is not immediately convertible into a bio-physical quantity, Habitat Quality (HQ) is recognized as a useful tool for investigating the spatial heterogeneity of the impact of urbanization on ecosystems [1].

The HQ model belongs to the InVEST software suite and it assumes that areas with greater habitat quality grade is characterized by higher biodiversity and relevant environmental values [13]. Its implementation produces two maps: habitat degradation (D_{xj}) and quality (Q_{xj}).

Habitat degradation (D_{xj}) represent the cumulative impact depending on several threats. According to the following formula, it is a function of both habitat sensitivity (S_{jr}) and threats characteristics, i.e. the weight w_r and the impact i_{rxy} of the threat r in cell x originating in y and distant d_{xy}:

$$D_{xj} = \sum_r \sum_y \left(\frac{w_r}{\sum_r w_r} \right) r_y i_{rxy} \beta_x S_{jr}$$

where β_x (varying from 0 to 1) is the accessibility degree of grid cell x.

Habitat sensitivity (S_{jr}) ranges from 0 to 1 and represents the intensity to which the habitat type is affected by each threat: higher values mean that the habitat type is heavily degraded by threats [14].

The HQ is instead dependent from the suitability of each Land Use class to provide adequate conditions for biodiversity persistence (H_j) [15] and from the degradation level (D_{xj}):

$$Q_{xj} = H_j\left(1 - \left(\frac{D_{xj}^z}{D_{xj}^z + k^z}\right)\right)$$

where z and k are numeric constant parameters.

On the basis of these brief model descriptions, it can be stated that the key aspects affecting the execution of HQ model are basically three: the definition of threats, the assignment of habitat suitability and the compilation of the sensitivity matrix.

The definition of threats depends on the purpose of the work: some authors [5, 15, 16] use the model in order to maximize the efforts of long-term biodiversity conservation policies and therefore consider agricultural lands and imperviousness soils to be among the threats. Others [18, 19] use the model to assess the relationships between the loss of ecosystem services and factors representative of socio-economic development, such as population and gross domestic product (GDP). In works and case studies strictly related to urban and spatial planning, it is common to attribute threats only to anthropic territorial components such as infrastructures, urban aggregates, production areas, extraction sites and landfills [19, 20].

As can be seen from Table 1, this is the approach chosen for this work as well. The highly detailed format of the Urban Atlas also allowed for the differentiation of threats posed by urban areas on the basis of building density. In particular, three types of urban areas were considered, characterized by increasing values of both weight and distance of impact of threat. The first type (Urban Areas 1) includes isolated structures, construction sites and discontinuous very low density urban fabric. Urban Areas 2 comprises low and medium density urban areas; the third (Urban Areas 3) consists of dense and continuous urban aggregates.

Table 1. The threats factors and related parameters.

Threat	Max_Dist	Weight	Decay
Urban Areas 1	0.6	0.75	Exponential
Urban Areas 2	1.0	0.80	Exponential
Urban Areas 3	1.5	0.85	Exponential
Industrial areas	1.0	0.90	Exponential
Dump	1.0	0.80	Exponential
Road networks	0.6	0.75	Exponential
Railways	0.75	0.60	Exponential

Concerning the habitat suitability (H_j), the highest values were assigned to the land use classes corresponding to wetlands and freshwaters, forests and herbaceous vegetation associations; intermediate values were assigned to the semi-natural classes (including arable land, permanent crops, pastures, complex and mixed cultivation patterns) in which the presence of herbaceous, tree and shrub vegetation is relevant, but the impact of anthropic activities is not negligible.

Table 2. Habitat suitability and sensitivity matrix.

Land Use class	Habitat suitability	Urban Areas 1	Urban Areas 2	Urban Areas 3	Industrial areas	Dump	Road networks	Railways
Continuous urban fabric	0.1	0.22	0.24	0.25	0.58	0.51	0.47	0.41
Disc. dense urban fabric	0.15	0.25	0.28	0.32	0.59	0.53	0.48	0.43
Disc. medium density urban fabric	0.20	0.31	0.34	0.37	0.58	0.54	0.49	0.45
Disc. low density urban fabric	0.25	0.36	0.39	0.42	0.61	0.56	0.52	0.47
Disc. very low density urban fabric	0.30	0.42	0.45	0.48	0.62	0.57	0.56	0.48
Isolated structures	0.35	0.35	0.36	0.37	0.38	0.37	0.35	0.34
Industrial, commercial, public, military and private units	0.1	0.30	0.34	0.38	0.56	0.54	0.54	0.49
Fast transit roads and associated land	0.1	0.28	0.34	0.38	0.54	0.53	0.53	0.52
Other roads and associated land	0.15	0.37	0.40	0.43	0.52	0.50	0.52	0.51
Railways and associated land	0.15	0.38	0.41	0.44	0.54	0.51	0.53	0.52

(*continued*)

Table 2. (*continued*)

Land Use class	Habitat suitability	Urban Areas 1	Urban Areas 2	Urban Areas 3	Industrial areas	Dump	Road networks	Railways
Port areas	0.1	0.39	0.42	0.45	0.55	0.52	0.54	0.53
Airports	0.1	0.39	0.42	0.45	0.55	0.52	0.54	0.53
Mineral extraction and dump sites	0.2	0.25	0.28	0.32	0.59	0.53	0.48	0.43
Construction sites	0.30	0.36	0.39	0.42	0.61	0.56	0.52	0.47
Land without current use	0.3	0.45	0.49	0.54	0.72	0.69	0.47	0.47
Green urban areas	0.5	0.71	0.73	0.75	0.81	0.59	0.75	0.68
Sports and leisure facilities	0.25	0.46	0.49	0.54	0.65	0.61	0.68	0.65
Arable land	0.6	0.68	0.71	0.74	0.81	0.79	0.67	0.65
Permanent crops	0.7	0.73	0.75	0.79	0.80	0.74	0.82	0.79
Pastures	0.7	0.77	0.79	0.82	0.87	0.86	0.88	0.86
Complex and mixed cultivation patterns	0.75	0.71	0.75	0.78	0.79	0.83	0.72	0.70
Forests	1.0	0.91	0.93	0.95	0.98	0.97	0.89	0.83
Herbaceous vegetation associations	0.9	0.86	0.89	0.92	0.93	0.88	0.84	0.54
Open spaces with little or no vegetation	0.7	0.76	0.78	0.81	0.89	0.86	0.83	0.81
Wetlands	1.0	0.85	0.88	0.96	0.96	0.91	0.90	0.87
Water	0.85	0.81	0.83	0.91	0.87	0.88	0.72	0.71

As already explained, for the purposes of this work it was not useful to differentiate between land-use classes characterized by the presence of intensive agricultural practices and more conservative ones as proposed in other works [21–24]. Finally, land-use classes related to urban areas and infrastructures were associated the lowest habitat suitability values. Again, for urban areas, values differ on the basis of building density: lower density (Urban Areas 1) corresponds to slightly higher values than dense and compact settlements (Urban Areas 3).

The last step is to compile the sensitivity matrix (Table 2), considering the relative impact of each threat on every land use class. The criterion used for the assignment of these values reflects the assignment of habitat suitability, considering the greater impact occurring on the more vulnerable land use classes.

4 Results and Discussion

Running the model results in two maps, degradation and habitat quality, which provide different information. While habitat degradation map highlights areas where a relevant cumulative impact occurs by different threats, habitat quality also depends from the suitability, i.e. from its intrinsic environmental value. In other words, quality depends on the specific habitat characteristics and threats extent, degradation is particularly useful to evidence parts of a territory where there is a risk of natural values deterioration [5].

As can be seen from Fig. 1 related to the "State of art" scenario, the areas characterized by the greatest degradation correspond to the most densely populated areas and those with the largest industrial areas.

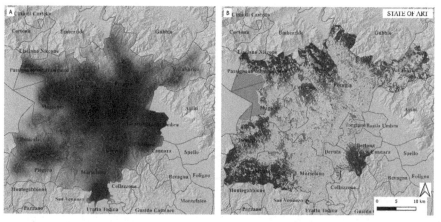

Fig. 1. Outcomes related to the "State of art" scenario: A) Habitat Degradation; B) Habitat Quality

Conversely, areas with quality values close to 1 coincide with areas that are mainly forested or characterized by the presence of herbaceous vegetation associations.

Figure 2 shows the impacts due to the full implementation of urban growth forecasts set out in the PRG. It is possible to notice an increase of areas with maximum degradation values, especially near the built-up area of Perugia. In the interface areas, at the border between urbanised urban settlements and semi-natural land use classes, an increase in the spatial continuity of most degraded areas can also be observed.

In order to facilitate the interpretation of the results and the comparison between the two scenarios, the Habitat Quality maps have been reclassified into five classes

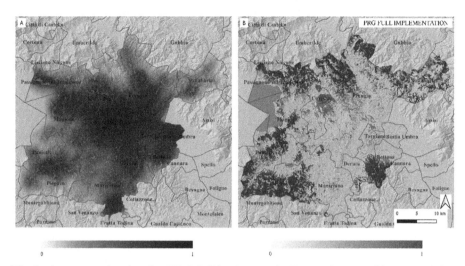

Fig. 2. Outcomes related to the "PRG Full implementation" scenario: A) Habitat Degradation; B) Habitat Quality

from "very low" to "very high". The following graph (Fig. 3) shows that in the forecast scenario areas characterized by lower quality levels increase to the detriment of all other classes.

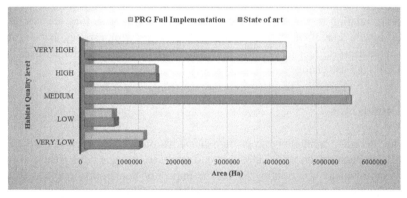

Fig. 3. Comparison between the two scenarios in terms of areas classified into five Habitat Quality levels

Further considerations can be made by assessing the habitat types most affected by the impact of urban growth. To this end, the Table 3 shows the percentage changes in both Quality and Degradation for each natural or semi-natural land use class present within the study area.

Confirming the previous highlights, the decrease in environmental value concerns almost all natural and semi-natural land use classes and especially urban green areas. The decrease in open spaces and in complex cultivation patterns is instead negligible.

Table 3. Variations in Habitat Quality and Degradation for each Land Use class

Land Use class	Habitat Quality variation (%)	Habitat Degradation variation (%)
Arable land	−0,0345%	3,09%
Permanent crops	−0,0032%	4,86%
Pastures	−0,0255%	3,82%
Complex and mixed cultivation patterns	0,0000%	23,39%
Forests	−0,0040%	3,90%
Herbaceous vegetation associations	−0,0027%	5,31%
Open spaces with little or no vegetation	0,0000%	4,68%
Green urban areas	−1,0546%	2,03%
Wetlands	−0,0013%	7,17%
Water	−0,0022%	3,05%

The changes in degradation are much more significant, particularly in complex cultivation patterns, herbaceous vegetation associations and permanent crops.

Finally, it should be also noted that changes in Quality and Degradation also concern the classes relating to surface water and wetlands, even though they are not directly affected by the spatial transformations simulated. This demonstrates that the model succeeds in capturing an increase in pressures acting on natural habitats even in the absence of land use changes.

5   Conclusions

In the last decades, conflicts between human and natural resources has intensified [25]. Globally, processes such as urbanization and land-use changes have advanced in frequency and intensity contributing to rise the impact of human disturbance on natural habitats [26] threatening long-term human well-being [27] and negatively affecting the livability of urban spaces [28–30].

In order to achieve sustainable development, there is need to comprehensively understand and assess the health of complex ecosystems [31] and to better integrate these evaluations into planning processes [32–34].

This paper proposes an innovative approach for assessing planning choices related to urban expansion processes on the basis of their influence on the capacity of ecosystems to provide ecosystem services for human well-being and biodiversity conservation.

The effort of this work is in fact to formulate a methodological proposal that allows in a spatially explicit way to quantify the impact resulting from the full implementation of expansion forecasts provided by the urban plan of the Perugia Municipality.

To this aim, impacts were assessed using the Habitat quality model which provides a proxy of overall environmental values of the territory [19], showing how increasing artificial surfaces, rising urban density and changes in the land use pattern affect the ability of ecosystems to provide appropriate conditions for biodiversity persistence.

The results show that the proposed approach provides useful insights to govern urban growth phenomena by limiting disorderly urban sprawl [35] and to explain the trade-offs between natural habitats and urbanization needs [36] by orienting planning choices towards areas where the expected impacts are lower. This constitutes an innovative aspect of this research, which operationally integrates the methodological framework of ecosystem services with urban planning, supporting an ex-ante evaluation of processes and thus fostering a more balanced combination between urban growth needs and ecosystem functionality.

Some limitations are related to the subjectivity of the parameterization of the model input values and the extent to which the assignment of these sets affects the result. One of the most important aspects to address in future research development is certainly the selection of threats, which, as pointed out in the description of method, is affected by subjectivity. In this regard, it could be useful to carry out a sensitivity analysis in order to check how much the choice of threats and their parameterization affect the resulting variations in Habitat Quality values.

Future research developments will therefore be oriented towards making more rational the values setting, so that the methodology can be replicated in other urban contexts without affecting results accuracy.

Acknowledgment. The analysis described in this paper are developing within the Integrated Project LIFE IMAGINE UMBRIA (LIFE19 IPE/IT/000015 - Integrated MAnagement and Grant Investments for the N2000 NEtwork in Umbria).

References

1. Bai, L., Xiu, C., Feng, X., Liu, D.: Influence of urbanization on regional habitat quality: a case study of Changchun City. Habitat Int. **93**, 102042 (2019). https://doi.org/10.1016/J.HAB ITATINT.2019.102042
2. Fan, X., Xinchen, G., et al.: The spatial and temporal evolution and drivers of habitat quality in the Hung River Valley. Land **10**(12), 1369 (2021). https://doi.org/10.3390/land10121369
3. Pilogallo, A., Scorza, F.: Ecosystem services multifunctionality: an analytical framework to support sustainable spatial planning in Italy. Sustainability. **14**, 3346 (2022). https://doi.org/10.3390/su14063346
4. Terrado, M., Sabater, S., Chaplin-Kramer, B., Mandle, L., Ziv, G., Acuña, V.: Model development for the assessment of terrestrial and aquatic habitat quality in conservation planning. Sci. Total Environ. **540**, 63–70 (2016). https://doi.org/10.1016/j.scitotenv.2015.03.064
5. Sallustio, L., et al.: Assessing habitat quality in relation to the spatial distribution of protected areas in Italy. J. Environ. Manage. **201**, 129–137 (2017). https://doi.org/10.1016/J.JEN VMAN.2017.06.031
6. Pilogallo, A., Scorza, F., Murgante, B.: An ecosystem services-based territorial ranking for Italian provinces. In: Gervasi, O., et al. (eds.) ICCSA 2021. LNCS, vol. 12955, pp. 692–702. Springer, Cham (2021). https://doi.org/10.1007/978-3-030-87007-2_49

7. Istituto nazionale di statistica (ISTAT): Istat.it Popolazione e famiglie. https://www.istat.it/it/popolazione-e-famiglie. Accessed 06 December 2019
8. Manganelli, B., Murgante, B., Saganeiti, L.: The social cost of urban sprinkling. Sustainability 12(6), 2236 (2020). https://doi.org/10.3390/su12062236
9. Romano, B., Fiorini, L., Zullo, F., Marucci, A.: Urban growth control DSS techniques for de-sprinkling process in Italy. Sustainability. 9, 1852 (2017). https://doi.org/10.3390/su9101852
10. Marucci, A., Fiorini, L., Zullo, F., Dato, C.D., Tomei, V., Romano, B.: Vision and project to retrofit the "urban dust" scenario: simulation in the region of Umbria, Central Italy. J. Urban Plan. Dev. 147, 04021030 (2021). https://doi.org/10.1061/(ASCE)UP.1943-5444.0000722
11. Munafò, M. (a cura di): Consumo di suolo, dinamiche territoriali e servizi ecosistemici Edizione 2021 Report SNPA 22/21 (2021)
12. Fiorini, L., Zullo, F., Marucci, A., Di Dato, C., Romano, B.: Planning tool mosaic (Ptm): a platform for Italy, a country without a strategic framework. Land. 10, 279 (2021). https://doi.org/10.3390/land10030279
13. Chu, L., Sun, T., Wang, T., Li, Z., Cai, C.: Evolution and prediction of landscape pattern and habitat quality based on CA-Markov and InVEST model in hubei section of three gorges reservoir area (TGRA). Sustainability 10(11), 3854 (2018). https://doi.org/10.3390/su10113854
14. Linlin, W., Sun, C., Fan, F.: Estimating the characteristic spatiotemporal variation in habitat quality using the InVEST model—a case study from Guangdong–Hong Kong–Macao Greater Bay Area. Remote Sens. 13(5), 1008 (2021). https://doi.org/10.3390/rs13051008
15. Nelson, E., et al.: InVEST 3.6.0 User's Guide. The Natural Capital Project (2018)
16. Sun, X., Jiang, Z., Liu, F., Zhang, D.: Monitoring spatio-temporal dynamics of habitat quality in Nansihu Lake basin, eastern China, from 1980 to 2015. Ecol. Indic. 102, 716–723 (2019). https://doi.org/10.1016/J.ECOLIND.2019.03.041
17. Di Febbraro, M., et al.: Expert-based and correlative models to map habitat quality: which gives better support to conservation planning? Glob. Ecol. Conserv. 16, e00513 (2018). https://doi.org/10.1016/J.GECCO.2018.E00513
18. Li, F., Wang, L., Chen, Z., Clarke, K.C., Li, M., Jiang, P.: Extending the SLEUTH model to integrate habitat quality into urban growth simulation. J. Environ. Manage. 217, 486–498 (2018). https://doi.org/10.1016/J.JENVMAN.2018.03.109
19. Aneseyee, A.B., Noszczyk, T., Soromessa, T., Elias, E.: The InVEST habitat quality model associated with land use/cover changes: a qualitative case study of the Winike Watershed in the Omo-Gibe Basin, Southwest Ethiopia. Remote Sens. 12, 1103 (2020). https://doi.org/10.3390/rs12071103
20. Arcidiacono, A., Ronchi, S., Salata, S.: Managing multiple ecosystem services for landscape conservation: a green infrastructure in Lombardy Region. Procedia Eng. 161, 2297–2303 (2016). https://doi.org/10.1016/j.proeng.2016.08.831
21. Nematollahi, S., Fakheran, S., Kienast, F., Jafari, A.: Application of InVEST habitat quality module in spatially vulnerability assessment of natural habitats (case study: Chaharmahal and Bakhtiari province, Iran). Environ. Monit. Assess. 192, 1–17 (2020). https://doi.org/10.1007/S10661-020-08460-6/TABLES/5
22. Scorza, F., Pilogallo, A., Saganeiti, L., Murgante, B., Pontrandolfi, P.: Comparing the territorial performances of renewable energy sources' plants with an integrated ecosystem services loss assessment: a case study from the Basilicata region (Italy). Sustain. Cities Soc. 56, 102082 (2020). https://doi.org/10.1016/j.scs.2020.102082
23. Scorza, F., Pilogallo, A., Saganeiti, L., Murgante, B.: Natura 2000 areas and sites of national interest (SNI): measuring (un)integration between naturalness preservation and environmental remediation policies. Sustain. 12, 2928 (2020). https://doi.org/10.3390/su12072928

24. Muzzillo, V., Pilogallo, A., Saganeiti, L., Santarsiero, V., Murgante, B., Bonifazi, A.: RES and habitat quality: ecosystem services evidence based analysis in basilicata area. In: Bevilacqua, C., Calabrò, F., Della Spina, L. (eds.) NMP 2020. SIST, vol. 178, pp. 1714–1721. Springer, Cham (2021). https://doi.org/10.1007/978-3-030-48279-4_162

25. Nolè, L., Pilogallo, A., Saganeiti, L., Scorza, F., Santos, L., Murgante, B.: Habitat degradation: a comparative study between Tomar (PT) and Potenza (IT). In: Gervasi, O., et al. (eds.) ICCSA 2020. LNCS, vol. 12253, pp. 645–654. Springer, Cham (2020). https://doi.org/10.1007/978-3-030-58814-4_51

26. Lu, X., Zhou, Y., Liu, Y., Le Page, Y.: The role of protected areas in land use/land cover change and the carbon cycle in the conterminous United States. Glob. Chang. Biol. **24**, 617–630 (2018). https://doi.org/10.1111/GCB.13816

27. Xu, L., Chen, S.S., Xu, Y., Li, G., Su, W.: Impacts of land-use change on habitat quality during 1985–2015 in the Taihu Lake Basin. Sustainability **11**, 3513 (2019). https://doi.org/10.3390/su11133513

28. John, J., Chithra, N.R., Thampi, S.G.: Prediction of land use/cover change in the Bharathapuzha river basin, India using geospatial techniques. Environ. Monit. Assess. **191**, 1–15 (2019). https://doi.org/10.1007/S10661-019-7482-4/TABLES/10

29. Tratalos, J., Fuller, R.A., Warren, P.H., Davies, R.G., Gaston, K.J.: Urban form, biodiversity potential and ecosystem services. Landsc. Urban Plan. **83**, 308–317 (2007). https://doi.org/10.1016/j.landurbplan.2007.05.003

30. McPhearson, T., Andersson, E., Elmqvist, T., Frantzeskaki, N.: Resilience of and through urban ecosystem services. Ecosyst. Serv. **12**, 152–156 (2015). https://doi.org/10.1016/J.ECOSER.2014.07.012

31. Albert, C., Von Haaren, C.: Implications of applying the green infrastructure concept in landscape planning for ecosystem services in Peri-urban areas: an expert survey and case study. Plan. Pract. Res. **32**, 227–242 (2017). https://doi.org/10.1080/02697459.2014.973683

32. Sarra, A., Nissi, E.: A spatial composite indicator for human and ecosystem well-being in the Italian urban areas. Soc. Indic. Res. **148**(2), 353–377 (2019). https://doi.org/10.1007/s11205-019-02203-y

33. Cortinovis, C., Geneletti, D.: A performance-based planning approach integrating supply and demand of urban ecosystem services. Landsc. Urban Plan. **201**, 103842 (2020). https://doi.org/10.1016/J.LANDURBPLAN.2020.103842

34. Staiano, L., Camba, G.H., Sans, P.B., Gallego, F., Texeira, M.A., Paruelo, J.M.: Putting the Ecosystem Services idea at work: applications on impact assessment and territorial planning. Environ. Dev. **38**, 100570 (2021). https://doi.org/10.1016/j.envdev.2020.100570

35. Ronchi, S.: Ecosystem services for planning: a generic recommendation or a real framework? Insights from a literature review. Sustainability **13**(12), 6595 (2021). https://doi.org/10.3390/su13126595

36. Dupras, J., Alam, M.: Urban Sprawl and ecosystem services: a half century perspective in the Montreal Area (Quebec, Canada). J. Environ. Policy Plan. **17**, 180–200 (2014). https://doi.org/10.1080/1523908X.2014.927755

37. Shoemaker, D.A., BenDor, T.K., Meentemeyer, R.K.: Anticipating trade-offs between urban patterns and ecosystem service production: scenario analyses of sprawl alternatives for a rapidly urbanizing region. Comput. Environ. Urban Syst. **74**, 114–125 (2019). https://doi.org/10.1016/J.COMPENVURBSYS.2018.10.003

International Workshop on Modelling Post-Covid Cities (MPCC 2022)

Sustainable Urban Mobility Planning and Walkability in the Post Pandemic era. Assessing the Role of Urban Enclaves

Ginevra Balletto[1]([✉]), Mara Ladu[1], and Federico Camerin[2]

[1] Department of Civil, Environmental Engineering and Architecture, University of Cagliari, 09100 Cagliari, Italy
{balletto,mara.ladu}@unica.it
[2] Departamento de Urbanística y Ordenación Territorial (GIAU+S), University UVA of Valladolid/University UPM of Madrid, Madrid, Spain
fcamerin@iuav.it

Abstract. The process of economic, social, and cultural development leads to relevant changes in urban areas. Urban transformations usually generate a series of public and private real estate compounds which constitute real obstacles to urban walkability. The growing attention towards the sustainable development goals established on a global scale introduced new contents in urban redevelopment policies, aimed at favoring higher levels of accessibility in the consolidated fabric, particularly that of the pedestrian type. In addition, the recent pandemic has recently reassessed the role of pedestrian mobility as a primary way of moving instead of using other means of transport. As a result, urban walkability has moved at the core of the sustainable city paradigm. More precisely, issues related to accessibility and walkability should be considered when addressing the obstacle generated by those sites that can be properly defined 'urban enclaves', especially when abandoned or under redevelopment. These conditions may encourage the gradual reopening of these areas for citizens. Within this framework, the Sustainable Urban Mobility Plan (SUMP) can represent a strategic tool for identifying the critical aspects to face for the creation of a new network of pedestrian routes aimed at improving urban walkability. The objective of this study is to define a set of principles and criteria, both tangible and intangible, for calculating the proximity index (PI). The PI may consequently drive urban regeneration projects also through the design of new paths for crossing the enclaves to improve urban permeability and, therefore, the level of walkability (This paper is the result of the joint work of the authors. In particular: Sect. 1 and 3 have been written by M. Ladu; Sect. 2 by F. Camerin; Sect. 4 and 5 by G. Balletto and M. Ladu.).

Keywords: Sustainable mobility · Walkability · Urban enclaves

1 Introduction

The current health crisis has made even more evident specific problems affecting contemporary urban areas. Various levels of government have addressed them to promote

© The Author(s), under exclusive license to Springer Nature Switzerland AG 2022
O. Gervasi et al. (Eds.): ICCSA 2022 Workshops, LNCS 13380, pp. 257–266, 2022.
https://doi.org/10.1007/978-3-031-10542-5_18

sustainable development models. Environmental crisis and, more precisely, atmospheric pollution, stands out because it influences the health condition of people [1, 2], so it requires new urban planning paradigms based on the theories of the 15 min City [3] and the Proximity and Health City [4]. These solutions, in turn, bring the challenges related to walkability and accessibility back to the center of the recent urban debate.

Mobility plays a fundamental role in this context as it is the result of a complex phenomenon of economic and social interaction between various territorial-scaled activities and the transport system, which responds to a derived need. The latter is generated by the physical form and the organizational and functional structure of the territory.

Within this framework, if mobility represents the potential ability to travel, accessibility is the measure of this attitude and represents an interaction between people, goods and activities located in different places. Accessibility has historically been defined as the degree of ease with which an individual can reach a spatially distant place using a specific transport system [5]. It means that accessibility depends on four main factors:

- characteristics of the individual;
- distribution of activities on the territory;
- place of departure and arrival; and
- transport system that connects a specific area to the other located in the territory.

Until the 1990s, accessibility was linked to a dual concept that led to the recognition of the transport system as the main response to the demand for local mobility. From the 1990s, web technology and, in general, ICT systems, have led to major changes in the ways of relating and using activities located in the territories, transforming the consolidated dual paradigm (spatial proximity-physical mobility) into a tripolar system (spatial proximity-physical mobility-digital connection) [6]. The pandemic has then increased the value of digital connection systems in guaranteeing adequate accessibility to primary services and more. At the same time, the need to ensure inclusive, safe, healthy, and sustainable cities has brought attention back to open spaces and sustainable urban mobility, including slow and pedestrian mobility. The health crisis has indeed highlighted the need of individuals to move on foot to reach the main urban facilities

Fig. 1. The walkability as a transversal element of the tripolar system of accessibility (spatial proximity- physical mobility-digital connection). Author: Ladu M. (2022).

[7], making pedestrian mobility a transversal element of the tripolar system (spatial proximity-physical mobility-digital connection) (see Fig. 1).

Within this framework, the Urban Sustainable Mobility Plan (SUMP) may represent a stimulating planning tool for achieving the Proximity City, guaranteeing higher levels of pedestrian accessibility and, therefore, quality of urban life. The promotion of urban walkability, to achieve also by expanding bike and pedestrian paths to reduce vehicular traffic, contributes not only to decrease air pollution levels but also to responding to the need for healthier lifestyles. Despite this growing awareness, a significant obstacle to the realization of the urban walkability project is represented by the public or private real estate sites often unused [8]. Due to their size and architectural features, these areas represent impenetrable places, a sort of real enclave in the urban fabric.

Starting from these assumptions and the analysis of the potential role that the Urban Sustainable Mobility Plan (SUMP) plays to face the new challenges of the sustainable city in Italy, this paper proposes a methodology for calculating an index aimed at measuring the degree of transformability of urban enclaves. It is believed that the attribution of the degree of transformability can prove to be functional to the definition of urban planning strategies aimed at improving and increasing the existing pedestrian network.

After the first section (Introduction), the rest of the paper is organized as follows: second section: Literature review, dedicated to an in-depth study of the concept of urban enclaves, especially in reference to the case of the military settlements (Sects. 2); third section: Materials, wherethe opportunities of the Sustainable urban mobility plan and the most relevant aspects of a recent planning experience in Italy are discussed (Sects. 3); fourth section: Method, which focuses on a methodological proposal to improve urban walkability through the Proximity Index (PI) (Sects. 4); Results and Conclusions are drawn in the fifth section, where the main research results carried out are presented, together with the future developments of the study (Sects. 5).

2   Urban Enclaves. The Case of the Military Settlements

Enclave is a term derived from the French eclaver, i.e. "to close with a key", and from the vulgar Latin inclavare, "to lock up". It defines closed and sheltered spaces that can be possibly opened with an entrance from the outside to the inside and vice versa. Due to their condition and position, enclaves maintain a close relationship with their surrounding context. The notion of enclave, which is significantly reviewed by Aiello [9], is often applied to research on gated communities. In this field of study, enclaves are pretty much defined by the presence of "gates, walls, and guards" [10]. From a spatial planning point of view, this definition can be quite literally applied to a specific kind of enclave in urban environments, i.e. military settlements, which are large land-consuming spaces immured. Their relevant presence in the Italian cities relied on the need to provide accommodation and training areas for soldiers since the Italian Unification. The realization of these settlements followed specific architectural and urban schemes according to an international debate among military engineers [11]. The condition of enclosures was also characterized by their location at the border of the 19th-century Italian city centers and their condition of a large piece of land excluded from the real estate dynamics. These factors have strongly contributed to making them drivers of urbanization patterns over decades. As a matter of fact, urban historians [12, 13] claimed that quartering usually overcame planning rationales due to national security needs and provided ad hoc enclosures that have been both physical and conceptual barriers that separate the military from civil society. It is in this sense that military settlements cannot be considered only topographical locations in the city, but the military interacts with the local population, even though the latter is usually forbidden to enter the military enclosure.

The end of the Cold War and the dissolution of the Soviet Union in 1991 was a pivotal event that implied strong geopolitical changes and territorial repercussions such as the Forced Army's reorganization and rationalization. As a result, thousands of military settlements have faced closure since the 1990s [14]. The conversion of former defense sites became a significant challenge in terms of urban regeneration that took decades to complete due to a variety of factors [15]. In particular, once abandoned, military enclosures may lose their meaning as immured spaces for fostering new mobility patterns. Behind the perimetral wall, the morphology of military sites is made up of precise layouts. Wide-open and green areas for circulation and training give military enclosures the potential value for developing new urban mobility planning schemes on the basis of slow-mobility routes. This, in turn, may improve urban permeability and thus the level of walkability. The same opportunities may be tied to other public-owned sites that, like military sites, show similar architectural and urban planning schemes that give them the status of proper "urban enclaves" (see Fig. 2 and 3).

Fig. 2. Abandoned "Tommaso Salsa" barracks as urban enclave, Treviso (IT). Source: photo by F. Camerin.

Fig. 3. Abandoned "Tommaso Salsa" barracks as urban enclave, Treviso (IT). The perimeter wall of the military site. Source: photo by F. Camerin.

The focus of this study is precisely on the appropriateness of the regeneration of such sites with the aim of providing useful tools to guide the proximity city project.

3   The Opportunities of the Sustainable Urban Mobility Plan

In Italy, the Sustainable Urban Mobility Plan (SUMP) is a strategic planning tool based on the principles of integration, participation, monitoring, and evaluation drafted to meet the demand of mobility for people and goods. The SUMP aims to ensure the right to mobility, without burdening, as far as possible, in terms of air and noise pollution, traffic and road accidents. It is a tool that contributes significantly to improving the quality of life and the environmental performance of urban areas in order to ensure a healthier urban system within an overall framework of sustainable economic and social development. In contemporary times, characterized by a return to the principles of the Walkable City, the SUMP can represent a strategic planning tool to support the realization of new scenarios of walkability.

The case of Modena stands out within recent experiences of sustainable urban mobility planning (see Fig. 4). Here was made an attempt to ensure the integration of the two forms of active urban mobility, i.e. walking and cycling. More precisely, the creation of a new network of pedestrian paths was highly integrated with the cycle paths' one. Another relevant aspect of this experience concerns the ability to recognize the strong interactions between mobility systems and urban development issues. The SUMP [16] was developed in full synergy with the local development plan (LDP) of the Municipality of Modena. This approach is at the base of the sustainable urban planning that tends to manage the demand for mobility, coordinate development policies, contain land consumption, and pursue urban quality.

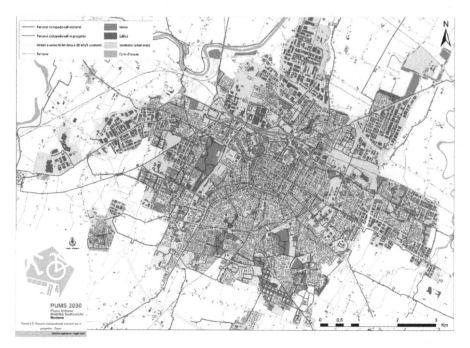

Fig. 4. Existing and planned pedestrian and cycle paths, SUMP, City of Modena (July, 2020). Source: https://www.comune.modena.it/servizi/mobilita-e-trasporti/pums/documenti-pums

Considering the obstacles generated by the urban enclaves in the development of a Walkable City, the authors argue that the SUMP should become a strategic tool to highlight and address these critical issues, especially regarding the positive externalities that the opening of pedestrian and/or cycle paths could generate in the urban environment. These types of interventions affect urban morphologies so may contribute to transform immured sites into opportunities for mobility [17]. The creation of new networks of pedestrian and/or cycle paths ensures higher levels of urban walkability, as well as proximity to urban facilities, in line with the 15-min city paradigm [18, 19].

4   A Methodological Proposal to Improve Urban Walkability: The Proximity Index (PI)

The need to guide design choices aimed at creating new pedestrian paths within the city led the authors to develop a methodology for calculating the proximity index [20]. It required the definition of a series of indicators to evaluate the positive externalities generated by the opening of a pedestrian and cycle path within an enclave.

The method used is based on the Deming Cycle framework [21] which allows a continuous monitoring process and result.

In particular, the method is divided into the following phases (see Fig. 5): i) Plan: phenomenon observation (survey and analysis of urban enclaves) and goal definition;

ii) Do: desk analysis and dataset evaluation to define a set of indicators and index construction (PI); iii) Check: comparison of the results (values of the PI associated with each enclave) and intervention priority assessment; iv) Act: promotion of urban regeneration policies (definition of a time schedule of interventions according to the priorities identified by the PI).

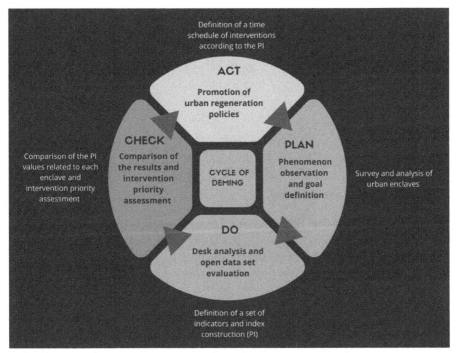

Fig. 5. Methodological framework based on the Deming Cycle. Authors: Balletto G., Ladu M. (2022).

The five indicators we are proposing are fundamental to represent the characteristics of a single building or public real estate complex (intrinsic characteristics), and those of its context (extrinsic characteristics):

1) Attractiveness indicator (A): this is given by the product between the number of functions located in the context and the weight (w_a) from 1 to 10, which increases as the variety of functions increases;

2) Uniqueness indicator (Un): this is given by the product between the number of potentially feasible crossings in the enclave and the weight (w_{un}) from 1 to 10, which reaches the maximum value if there are no alternative crossings in the immediate vicinity and there is no possibility of make new ones;

3) Usability indicator (Us): this is defined as the degree of difficulty in walking the crossing, determined by the physical characteristics of the space to be crossed,

whether it is open or closed. It assumes a value between 1 and 10 (w_{us}), where 1 represents the maximum degree of difficulty and 10 the minimum degree of difficulty.

4) Satisfaction indicator (S): this is given by the product between the number of inhabitants who would benefit from the opening of the crossing in the neighborhood and the weight (w_s) from 1 to 10;

5) Feasibility indicator (F): this is defined as the degree of technical and economic difficulty in making the crossing. It assumes a value between 1 and 10, where 1 represents the maximum degree of difficulty and 10 the minimum degree of difficulty (w_f).

The Proximity Index (PI) is given by the sum of these indicators, according to the following formula:

$$PI = \sum_{i=5}^{n} Ii/50 \tag{1}$$

where: $I_i = A, Un, Us, S, F$ for $i = 1, 2,3,...5$ and, consequently, $0 \leq PI \leq 1$.

5 Results and Conclusions

The analysis of the indicators of attractiveness (A), uniqueness (Un), usability (Us), satisfaction (S), and feasibility (F), appropriately weighted, and the subsequent calculation of the Proximity Index (PI), provide an assessment of the degree of transformability of the urban enclaves in relation to the possibility of creating a network of pedestrian paths. More precisely, after selecting sites having the characteristics of "urban enclaves'", the PI assigns a different degree of priority of intervention to each of these parts of the city. It defines a hierarchy in terms of positive externalities that can be generated by the progressive opening of the immured sites for the construction of pedestrian and / or cycle paths. In this sense, the PI represents a useful tool to support the decision-making process in the implementation of urban regeneration projects aimed at pursuing the model of Proximity City.

Moreover, this index may stimulate the introduction of temporary and/or transitory interventions in urban governance. As a matter of fact, the indicator referring to the feasibility informs about the possibility of creating new pedestrian crossings in certain urban enclaves, even before defining an overall redevelopment scheme for the entire site. It is believed that such transitory interventions, aimed at promoting urban walkability, can increase the attractiveness of the property, give it a new identity, and facilitate the choice of new uses.

The present study recognizes the role of the SUMP as a strategic tool to integrate the issues concerning the regeneration of urban enclaves within the more complex framework of objectives to achieve through the sustainable urban mobility planning. In line with this renewed perspective, the SUMP could indicate the most critical enclaves and the related proximity indexes to guide the realization of a new network of pedestrian paths, in line with the provision of the local development plan.

The next steps of this study can be the following: choosing an urban setting for the application of the proposed methodology; tests on urban enclaves, also taking into consideration the scenarios proposed by the planning tools in force, as the local plan and the Metropolitan Strategic Plan [22]; and defining a time schedule of interventions according to the priorities identified by the PI and the offer of local public transport (LPT).

Acknowledgments. The authors Balletto G. and Ladu M. took part in the following research activities: Strategic Plan of the Metropolitan City of Cagliari, commissioned to the Temporary Business Association (ATI), constituted by Lattanzio Advisory and Lattanzio Communication in 2019: Luigi Mundula (PI) University of Cagliari, "Investigating in the relationships between knowledge-building and design and decision-making in spatial planning with geodesign—CUP F74I19001040007—financed by Sardinia Foundation—Annuity 2018'". Professor Michele Campagna (PI) University of Cagliari: Italian National Institute for Urban Planning (INU) and Jane's Walk Festival. Balletto G.: City organizer for Cagliari, Cagliari Accessibility Lab, interdepartmental center of the University of Cagliari. This paper is part of the research carried out by Mara Ladu for the following research scholarships under the supervision of prof. Ginevra Balletto: "The role of the public real estate for the governance of the Metropolitan City of Cagliari" (n.13_2020); "Research and cataloguing of abandoned real estate assets within the Metropolitan City of Cagliari" (n.44_2020).

Federico Camerin has participated as co-author within the research project "La Regeneración Urbana como una nueva versión de los Programas de Renovación Urbana. Logros y fracasos".

This project is co-funded by the Spanish Ministry of Universities in the framework of the Recovery, Transformation and Resilience Plan, by the European Union – NextGenerationEU and by the Universidad de Valladolid.

References

1. Murgante, B., et al.: Health hazard scenarios in Italy after the COVID-19 outbreak: A methodological proposal. Scienze Regionali, 1–27 (2021)
2. Murgante, B., et al.: A methodological proposal to evaluate the health hazard scenario from COVID-19 in Italy. Environ. Res. **209**, 112873 (2022)
3. Balletto, G., Pezzagno, M., Richiedei, A.: 15-minute city in urban regeneration perspective: Two methodological approaches compared to support decisions. In: Gervasi, O., et al. (eds.) ICCSA 2021. LNCS, vol. 12953, pp. 535–548. Springer, Cham (2021). https://doi.org/10.1007/978-3-030-86976-2_36
4. Ladu, M., Balletto, G., Borruso, G.: Sport and smart communities. Assessing the sporting attractiveness and community perceptions of Cagliari (Sardinia, Italy). In: Proceedings of the International Conference on Computational Science and Its Applications, pp. 200–215. Springer, Cham (2019, July)
5. Dalvi, M.Q., Martin, K.M.: The measurement of accessibility: Some preliminary results. Transportation **5**(1), 17–42 (1976)
6. Ladu, M., Milesi, A., Balletto, G., Borruso, G.: Urban enclaves and accessibility. The role of walkability in sustainable urban mobility planning. In: Proceedings of the En SUPTM 2022: 1st Conference on Future Challenges in Sustainable Urban Planning & Territorial Management, 17–19 Jan 2022. https://repositorio.upct.es/handle/10317/10585 (2021)
7. Campisi, T., Ignaccolo, M., Inturri, G., Tesoriere, G., Torrisi, V.: Evaluation of walkability and mobility requirements of visually impaired people in urban spaces. Res. Transp. Bus. Manag. **40**, 100592 (2021)

8. Rusci, S.: La città senza valore: Dall'urbanistica dell'espansione all'urbanistica della demolizione. FrancoAngeli, Milan (2021)
9. Aiello, G.: From wound to enclave: The visual-material performance of urban renewal in bologna's manifattura delle arti. West. J. Commun. **75**(4), 341–366 (2011)
10. Low, S.M.: The edge and the center: Gated communities and the discourse of urban fear. Am. Anthropol. **103**(1), 45–58 (2001)
11. Turri, F., Zamperini, E.: The military engineers and hygiene in barracks in the second half of the 19th century. In: Carvais, R., et al. (eds.) Nuts and Bolts of Construction History. Culture, Technology and Society, vol. 3, pp. 309–316. Picard, Paris (2012)
12. Insolera, I.: Insediamenti militari e trasformazioni urbane. In: Antonelli, G., Grispo, R. (eds.) Esercito e città. Dall'Unità agli anni Trenta. Tomo II, pp. 663–676. Ministero per i beni culturali e ambientali, Rome (1989)
13. Savorra, M., Zucconi, G.: Spazi e cultura militare nella città dell'Ottocento. Città e Storia **4**(2). Croma, Rome (2009)
14. BICC: Study on the Re-use of Former Military Lands. Bonn International Center for Conversion, Germany (1997)
15. Touchton, M., Ashley, A.J.: Salvaging Community. How American Cities Rebuild Closed Military Bases. Cornell University Press
16. City of Modena. PUMS https://www.comune.modena.it/servizi/mobilita-e-trasporti/pums/cose-il-pums
17. Balletto, G., Ladu, M., Milesi, A., Borruso, G.: Methodological approach on disused public properties in the 15-minute city perspective. Sustainability **13**(2), 593 (2021)
18. Scorza, F., Fortunato, G., Carbone, R., Murgante, B., Pontrandolfi, P.: Increasing urban walkability through citizens' participation processes. Sustainability. **13**(11), 5835 (2021)
19. Meng, L.I.: The planning strategies of a 15-minute community life circle based on behaviors of residents. Urban Plann. Forum **1**, 111–118 (2017)
20. Balletto, G., Ladu, M., Milesi, A., Camerin, F., Borruso, G.: Walkable city and military enclaves: Analysis and decision-making approach to support the proximity connection in urban regeneration. Sustainability **14**(1), 457 (2022)
21. Walton, M.: The deming management method: The bestselling classic for quality management! Penguin (1988)
22. Palumbo, M.E., Mundula, L., Balletto, G., Bazzato, E., Marignani, M.: Environmental dimension into strategic planning. The case of metropolitan city of Cagliari. In: Proceedings of the International Conference on Computational Science and Its Applications, pp. 456–471. Springer, Cham (2020). https://doi.org/10.1007/978-3-030-58820-5_34

City Form, Mobility and University Students in Post Pandemic Era

Ginevra Balletto[1]([⊠]), Tiziana Campisi[2], Giuseppe Borruso[3], Italo Meloni[1], and Beatrice Scappini[1]

[1] Department of Civil, Environmental Engineering and Architecture, University of Cagliari, 09100 Cagliari, Italy
{balletto,imeloni,eatricescappini}@unica.it
[2] Faculty of Engineering and Architecture, University of Enna Kore, Cittadella Universitaria, 94100 Enna, Italy
tiziana.campisi@unikore.it
[3] Dipartimento di Scienze Economiche, Aziendali, Matematiche e Statistiche "Bruno de Finetti", University of Trieste, Trieste, Italy
giuseppe.borruso@deams.units.it

Abstract. The relationships between the shape of the city, proximity and mobility have always been the subject of study for urban planning and urban geography, however more oriented towards finding treatments than causes to be solved. What role does centrality and urban attractiveness determine in consideration of daily actions and therefore of access to the main services? The urban mobility of university students is the focus of this paper while the aim is to develop a methodological proposal to build an index of centrality (Uni_City Index) of the Italian Universities as a function of a set of open data indicators of innovation, socio-economic, mobility and land use to support city–university integrated policy actions in the context of post-pandemic recovery and the recent energy crisis.

Keywords: City form · City of proximity · Mobility · University students · Post pandemic city

1 Introduction

What is the relationship between the shape of the city and mobility? Is it a relationship of mutual cause and effect?

The question of the relationship between the shape of the city and mobility has always been the subject of study for urban planning and urban geography. The mobility of university students is the focus of the paper while the objective is to develop a methodological proposal to build a centrality index of the University as a function of a set of socio-economic indicators, mobility, innovation and land use to support policy actions integrated city–university.

The rest of the paper is organized as follows: first section: Introduction and Literature review (paragraphs 1.1 and 1.2); Sect. 2: Materials and Method and discusses the topic (paragraphs 2.1 and 2.2); Sect. 3: case study (paragraphs 3); Sect. 4: Results and Discussion, reports and discusses the main research results carried out (paragraphs 4); Conclusions are drawn in the Sect. 5, where the major findings are presented, together with the future developments of the research (paragraphs 5).

1.1 The University and the City

The relationship between cities and their universities is not a trivial one, and a particular attention needs to be put onto the functions played by cities as providers of services. From an urban and economic geography point of view, in fact, a university as a service can be seen as a higher order service provided by cities as market centers, attracting users from both the city itself and a 'regional', wider hinterland, given the relative scarcity of places in a territory where such an activity is provided and carried on [1]. Universities therefore play a role both on a local community, and on a wider community of users from a regional hinterland but also from other parts of the national and international contexts. From a Christallerian point of view, universities play their role as city serving activities, dedicated to the local community, and city forming ones, operating on a wider range of regional and national/international users, and therefore characterizing the city and its functions as a higher order center, competing with other national and international ones [2].

However, within cities, university campuses can play a territorialization role, that of transforming an urban and regional territory, also having different impacts on different sites within a same city—region—i.e., with nodal roles played by different major campuses and agglomerations of facilities in different parts of a city. University campuses and cities can be considered as nodes of a transport network with profound similarities even if of different rank and potential for generating and attracting travel [3, 4]. In fact, university campuses can be considered a small urban model in which to study and adopt more efficient sustainability strategies than the widespread university model. More generally, universities are a development factor for society and encourage the economy of the territories in which they are located [5], through a continuous process of innovation:

- for the diffusion of training for young people in a nation increasingly characterized by a population over 65 that needs generational change;
- for the commitment in research and for the ideas they produce, potentially capable of optimizing the choices and strategies to be implemented in the context both from a territorial and economic point of view;
- for the circuits they generate at national, European and World levels in which cities, with their activities, could usefully enter;
- for the economic, social, artistic-cultural value they produce and make available to the communities to which they belong.

The location choices of universities, the contribution in terms of increasing the cultural offer of a city, the ability to attract students and staff, the indirect economic impact generated by the needs of the latter and the increase in jobs, are all examples of how the multiple roles and functions of a university are closely linked with the transformations of an entire city or individual neighborhoods. Although universities are seen as an increasingly fundamental presence for the growth of a territory, the choices and actions carried out by a university do not always have entirely positive implications. The presence or, even more so, the opening of a university center brings with it inevitable social, urban and economic changes in which it is located, leading to the so-called "studentification" of the area [6].

The areas located near a university are in fact often subject to the increase in demand for houses for rent or for sale for students. Also in these areas, moreover, the commercial offer is moving towards activities that contribute to spatially reproducing a certain model of "university life". Both the negative impact on access to homes by resident families and—and above all—the negative effects that accompany the transformation of a neighborhood into a "university neighborhood" often generate conflicts between students and the resident population; conflicts that arise around the use of public space, the different rhythms of life, habits and behaviors related to nightlife.

In recent years, the city–university combination and the common goal of attracting a growing number of students has also become evident in the boom in private university residences (the so-called PBSA—Purpose Built Student Accommodation) [7].

On the one hand, the construction of this type of residences makes it possible to increase and diversify the supply of beds, in the face of a sector of public residences which, in an era of cuts and austerity policies, is unable to adequately satisfy the 'increase in demand'; on the other hand, the construction of residences or the conversion of former industrial buildings are often an integral part of urban regeneration projects.

Furthermore, numerous international and national universities have set environmental, social and economic objectives such as the reduction of the carbon footprint, the use of green technologies, the design according to principles oriented towards the balance between man and the environment, the use of systems green transport, the reduction of collective costs and the progressive reduction of social injustices [8–11].

A systematic and non-systematic type of student travel behavior emerges from the city–university framework in Italy. In other words, the presence of university students is strictly connected both to the concept of commuting [12] and to city users [13] depending on the period of stay in the cities and campuses.

In particular, the definition of city users includes those who move to a city to use its public and private services for: buying entertainment, tourism, bureaucratic procedures, etc. Instead, the concept of commuter includes workers or students who move daily from their place of residence to reach that of their business/study building-area.

This difference makes it possible to underline the trend of travel demand and the relative frequency (for example temporality and frequency) as well as the possibility of implementing a series of actions/activities within the university cities (for example travel habits). Furthermore, the demand for mobility of university students affects in some cases the travel habits of a city and in others increases the need to enhance public transport LPT and multimodality, within the framework of student economic availability.

It is no coincidence that many universities have closed agreements with mobility service companies for the creation of ad hoc services and rates for students, often free to encourage the use of public transport or shared mobility (cars, bikes or scooters.) [14, 15] with respect to the use of the private vehicle [16, 17].

1.2 University, Mobility, and Covid-19

The COVID-19 epidemic has disrupted daily life very quickly. Transport is one of the sectors most affected by the pandemic and for this reason, the changing demands of users in its various segments need to be carefully examined in order to undertake effective post-pandemic transport policies [18]. In particular, after the lockdown there was a reduction in the use of public transport and an increase in private transport, especially by workers and university students. In addition, several studies have shown that COVID-19 has caused an increase in the use of e-scooters/hoverboards and active travel modes [19, 20]. Some Action Plans are based on a context analysis, a road map model and make use of the use of ICT tools capable of improving the capacity of decision makers and university mobility managers in order to plan the best mobility solution sustainable. The integration of student mobility in the Sustainable Urban Mobility Plans (SUMP) allows the development of a long-term strategy based on services dedicated to students and the spread of multimodality. The students' mobility must be ensured, and, at the same time, it must be acceptable, accessible, affordable, and available, always verified in the proximity city model [21–24]. Furthermore, universities with or without campuses are able to generate a significant number of trips. From the Travel Demand Management (TDM) strategies of the nineties focused only on employees, we have moved on to the mobility managers of the years, introducing policies that are also and above all student-oriented, with the aim of improving the university's sustainability standards. Furthermore, universities with or without campuses are able to generate a significant number of trips [25]. From the Travel Demand Management (TDM) strategies of the nineties focused only on employees, we have moved on to the mobility managers of the years, introducing policies that are also and above all student-oriented, with the aim of improving the university's sustainability standards. If on the one hand the presence of a university campus brings benefits to the cities that host them, on the other there are still some critical issues connected to the demographic decline and the lack of mobility/connection services for some regions. This forecast scenario will have a decisive impact on many Italian universities, given their poor ability to attract foreigners, and considering that the majority of students enrolled are not only Italian but also mostly from the province in which the university has legal office [26]. Several studies in the literature have focused on the accessibility of campus areas by analyzing the modes of transport available to students [27], others have focused on travel habits and frequency [28].

In addition, various actions to support and protect the mobility of university students have been carried out in Italy by the ERSU (Regional Agency for the Right to University Education) with a 50% discount on the cost of the urban and extra-urban transport season ticket. o reduction of train fares or actions such as in Fig. 1.

The recent pandemic has put a stop to student mobility, nearly emptying entire university towns of their temporary inhabitants. However, since September 2021, the private rental market has registered a new increase in demand, which has led to an aggravation of the problem of the lack of affordable rooms already registered before the pandemic in some of the most attractive destinations for students. Particular attention was paid in the recent pandemic phase to the psycho-social aspects connected to movement and to the sensations of stress, fear and anxiety in moving [29, 30]. The main difficulties

Mode of transport	Action	City and Integration of interventions with SUMP
Local Public Transport	Discount for urban and extra-urban buses	Camerino_no SUMP Bologna_SUMP2019 (integration of the activities in the proposal) Catania_SUMP2020 being drafted Turin_SUMP2011 not definited Rome (metropolitan) _PUMS2020 being drafted Trento_SUMPS2020 being drafted Brescia_SUMP2018 not definited Perugia_SUMP2019 (integration of the activities in the proposal)
Shared Mobility	Discounted rates (50% reduction) for booking car-sharing and bike sharing cars	Perugia_SUMP2019 (integration of the activities in the proposal) Palermo_SUMP2019 Enna_SUMP2020 being drafted
Rent and Parking	Facilities relating to bike rental, guarded parking for bicycles, bicycle repairs and auto repairs	Bologna_SUMP2019 (integration of the activities in the proposal)
Car pooling	Creating an APP	Perugia_SUMP2019 (integration of the activities in the proposal) Cagliari_SUMP2021 (integration of the activities in the proposal)

Fig. 1. Mode of transport, action and integration with SUMP (Authors: T. Campisi and G. Balletto, 2022).

encountered in the home-university journey concern traffic congestion, excessive crowding of public transport and their absence or low frequency, regularity and punctuality, especially after the lockdown due to the recent pandemic. In the post-pandemic phase, there was a vigorous acceleration of local administrations in the initiatives aimed at promoting active and sustainable mobility [31], intervening in a regulatory framework in the process of evolution (and which can still be improved).

The gradual exit from the most critical phase of the infections of the first wave has stimulated various reorganization initiatives necessary to continue the social distancing, in view of the resumption of the spread of the virus (as promptly occurred after the summer) but, at the same time, able to go beyond the temporary or exceptional nature of the measures and guarantee safe travel for millions of people in the future by alternative means. Despite the technical, legal and administrative challenges, the measures have been implemented demonstrating in some cases how local authorities can be responsive and agile in times of need, as well as the fact that existing avenues to promote active travel do not always require substantial economic funding, no complex planning or lengthy administrative processes. Furthermore, once the effectiveness of the policies adopted for the critical phase has been assessed, it is possible that the temporary measures may be permanent. In any case, administrative innovation and the experience of cooperation between structures and entities may be useful in the future for long-term strategic planning paths. The theme of student mobility involves about eighty Italian universities-cities, for a total of 566 faculties, with different spatial distribution: scattered and/or concentrated, producing positive and negative externalities in the context [32].

2   Materials and Methods

2.1   University as an Urban Centrality

More generally, universities belong to the main urban hierarchies that can be associated with the theory of central places [33]. The Italian university system can therefore be summarized as in Fig. 2.

N	Type	Italian Region Distribution
76	State Universities	30% (north) 35,68%(central region) 34,32%(south region)
19	Not State Universities (legally recognized)	73% (north) 6%(central region) 21%(south region)
11	Telematic universities (not statal and legally recognized)	27% (north) 63%(central region) 10%(south region)

TOT= 97 University

Fig. 2. Overview of universities in Italy (elaboration: T. Campisi; G. Balletto, 2022) [34].

It is worth noting that universities represent important elements in the organization of territory and particularly in providing services to urban areas. The idea is that higher education institutions, as universities and research centers, can have an effect on cities on two different scales or points of view. From the point of view of the concept and functions played, the presence of a university characterizes a city has holding a higher hierarchical position in the rank of cities, in terms of the superior services provided: i.e., all the municipalities host primary, schools some municipalities offer secondary schools, few municipalities host universities. That helps in adding value to cities and metropolitan areas in providing services that characterize them in city forming activities.

A second scale and point of view is related to the spatial and local effect that universities can have in the different buildings and campuses within—or around—a certain city [35–37], remembering that students are the main supporters of the 15 min city. In particular, according to Badii et al. (2021) urban centrality in the 15 min city can be represented through the following dimensions [34]: Housing viability (H); Govern Services (G); Safety Services (SS), Culture and Cults Services (CCS); Environmental Quality (EQ); Slow Mobility Services (SMS), Fast Mobility Services (FMS), Sport Services (SS); Economy/sustainability (E/S); Food Services (FS); Health Services (HS); Education Services and Entertainment Services (EES).

However, it should be noted that the University as a central place of higher rank helps to hierarchize the city that hosts it [38], regardless of the form and distribution of the University [39]. Specifically, the University has its own or directly connected—intrinsic—characteristics that contribute to the formation of the relative role of 'central place' which in turn is inserted in the urban spatial context with its own characteristics, extrinsic with respect to the central place of the University and therefore own from the city [40]. Therefore, the attractiveness or marginality of the University can be understood as a combined result of its intrinsic and extrinsic characteristics [41–43]. In particular, the characteristics:

1) Intrinsic (own and directly connected to the University): University ranking, number of students compared to the resident population, number of the spin-offs or youth entrepreneurship, student housing;
2) Extrinsic (own and directly connected to the city): Socio-economic, public transport, cycle paths, pedestrian areas, outdoor sports and food and pleasure services.

In fact, in the last 30–20 years university campuses have spread to various Italian regions, bringing a series of benefits from an economic and social point of view, but above all to compensate for the low level of extrinsic characteristics, representative of the urban system and therefore to limit the negative externalities deriving from student mobility [44]. Furthermore, the development of urban planning and sustainable mobility of SUMPs still neglects university students [45] although they constitute the most versatile segment of the population in accepting innovation applied to sustainability [4].

2.2 Methodology

The method used to construct the University centrality index as a function of intrinsic (University and innovation) and extrinsic (socio-economic, mobility and land use in urban system) characteristics is based on the framework of the Deming Cycle [46] to ensure a continuous monitoring process and result. In particular, the method is divided into the following phases: i) Plan: observation of the phenomenon (Mobility of university students) and goal definition; ii) Do: desk analysis and open dataset, index construction (Uni_City); iii) Check: comparison results—objective; iv) Act: university—city policy.

Furthermore, in agreement with Kang et al. (2021), the importance of the diversity of activities (i.e. that serve different primary functions), both temporal (i.e. that attracts people at different times of the day) and both spatial (i.e. that attracts people from different neighborhoods is highlighted) which play important roles in promoting urban life in large cities through for example the use of mobility data and the spread of crowdsourcing [47].

Below is the summary scheme of the method used (Fig. 3).

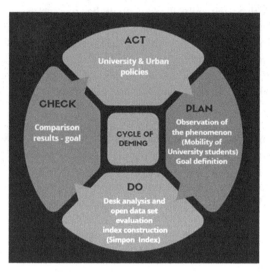

Fig. 3. Framework of methodology based on the cycle of Deming. (Source: Balletto G., 2022).

In particular, the construction of the index, called Uni_City Index, derives from the application of the Simpson formula to the whole set of selected intrinsic and extrinsic characteristics. The Simpson diversity index, in fact, is used in statistics in the case of populations with a finite number of elements and is widely applied in ecology to represent ecological environmental diversity and by analogy it has been transposed to the urban context [48, 49], in this case of the characteristics intrinsic and extrinsic that represent the combined centrality of the University and the city to which it belongs.

$$Uni\_City\ Index = 1 - log \sum_{j} \frac{Nj(Nj - 1)}{N(N - 1)}$$

where Nj indicates the number of j-th "species"

$$N = \sum Nj$$

The Simpson index finds a wide application in ecology to represent environmental ecological diversity and by analogy it has been transposed to the university and urban system and specifically, it refers to the diversity of central locations [50, 51].

3 Case Study

What is the relationship In this context, the case study is aimed at the first test of the phases of the Deming diagram (Fig. 3) by comparing it in pairs of cities hosting medium-sized

(Cagliari and Trieste) and small (Enna and Aosta) universities, excluding the cities with large universities that deserve a different approach by virtue of national and international hierarchies. The data set was built on open indicators and published annually (Figs. 4, 5 and 6) [52].

	University and innovation	Badii et al (2021)	Cagliari	Trieste	Enna	Aosta
Intrinsic Characteristic	University ranking_2020	CCS	86.7	92	74.8	72.4
	N. of university students_2018	CCS	25450	15239	5284	1071
	N. of graduates (25-29 years) 2020	CCS - E/S	590	1000	233.7	492.5
	Youth employment rate_2020	E/S	477.6	880.5	248	840.6
	Youth entrepreneurship (% companies under 35) 2020	E/S	211.4	235.9	852.9	377.3
	Rent (% of rent on average income) 2020	H	785.1	575.5	931.0	799.6
	Gap rents between center suburbs (%) 2020	H	957.1	883.9	857.1	600

Fig. 4. Data set of international characteristics of University of Cagliari, Trieste, Enna and Aosta (Italy) (Balletto G., 2022).

	Socio-economic, Mobility and Land use	Badii et al (2021)	Cagliari	Trieste	Enna	Aosta
Extrinsic Characteristic	Labor Market Areas (LMA) N of Municipality_2019	E/S	42	6	4	35
	Area of LMA (Kmq)_2019	E/S	2459.52	212.5	512.17	1627.21
	Population of the LMA_2019	E/S	505533	231445	24551	77677
	Average income_2019	E/S	25681	23118	20268	24257
	Local Public Transport (LPT) offer Km / inhabitant_2020	FMS	4.05	56.22	15.03	13.1
	Car motorization rate_2020	FMS	68	54	70	64
	Motorcycle motorization rate for _2020	FMS	10	21	12	12
	Passengers, LPT year, per million_2020	FMS	32	70	0.2	12.5
	Passenger public transport (trips / person / year, 2020	FMS	147.15	200.37	41.52	11.2
	Cycle paths eq. meters / 100 thousand inh._2010	SMS- EQ	6.05	2.15	9.1	0.26
	Bar, disco, take away every 10 thousand / pop 15-35 years_2020	FS	779.5	427.7	80.5	561.1

Fig. 5. Data set of extrinsic characteristics of University of Cagliari, Trieste, Enna and Aosta (Italy) (Balletto G., 2022).

	Cagliari	Trieste	Enna	Aosta
Simpson Index (SI)	0.0915	0,137	0.444	0.244
1-SI	0.91	0.86	0.56	0.75

Fig. 6. Simpson Index (SI) and (1-SI) of Cagliari, Trieste, Enna and Aosta (Italy).

4   Results and Discussion

In the context of post-pandemic recovery strategies and actions aimed at achieving the sustainable development goals, this study presents the first results of ongoing research relating to the identification of a representative index of the interrelationship between universities and their urban environment, in support of integrated university–city policy actions.

The UniCity Index aims to focus on the evaluation of the centrality level of universities—and therefore the attractiveness of the "university-city" system—based on intrinsic and extrinsic features that characterize the universities and the cities in which they are located. The establishment of a university, in fact, certainly has an impact on the city that concerns not only the urban planning, but also the system of economic and social relations of its territory.

The intrinsic and extrinsic characteristics selected in this first step of investigation refer to the available indicators, persistent and stable over time, belonging to the fields of culture and education, economy, livability, environment, and mobility. These indicators are identified in the literature as representative of the complexity and diversity of an urban area, with reference to the concept of the 15 min city, and can be classified in the following dimensions [34]:

– Culture Services (CCS). Indicators of culture and education's quality related to the attractiveness of educational and cultural services.
– Economy/Sustainability (E/S). Indicators of economic sustainability related to average income, unemployment rate, entrepreneurship, presence of activities and services.
– Housing viability (H). Indicators of livability and housing quality of the area related to the incidence of housing costs.
– Environment Quality (EQ). Indicators of environmental quality based on pollution reduction factors such as cycle paths and networks.
– Fast Mobility Services (FMS). Mobility-related indicators for medium and long-distance travel (public transport, motorization rate for cars and motorcycles).
– Slow Mobility Services (SMS). Indicators related to active mobility for short-distance journeys (cycle paths).

The methodology applied for the index definition, based on the Deming Cycle framework, can also be used in the following steps to add more factors and details to the model in case other types of data, additional or alternative to those used in the case study, become available.

More specifically, the index relates the characteristics of the university itself or directly connected to it, which concur to define it as a 'central place', with the characteristics of its urban context, therefore external to the university but still influencing it. Through its application on four cities that host medium-sized universities (Cagliari and Trieste) and small universities (Enna and Aosta), the Uni_City Index highlights the tendency of the university-city system to develop greater attractiveness (index value tending to 1) or marginality (index value tending to 0). The results show that the university-city system is more cohesive and interdependent in the case of medium-sized cities such as Cagliari (0.91) and Trieste (0.86) while it is weaker in the case of Enna (0.56) and Aosta (0.75).

As its value increases, the index shows that universities and urban areas that host them are increasingly linked by a continuous exchange of resources, knowledge and human capital and therefore they are two ecosystems that cannot ignore a strong physical, economic and social interdependence. This happens above all when universities have no central campus, but rather university buildings are scattered around the city, as in the cases of Cagliari, Trieste and Aosta, which "permeate the city representing crucial hubs of a complex urban network" [53] by which, at the same time, they are influenced.

The characteristics selected for the construction of the set of indicators take into account simultaneously the intrinsic attractiveness of the university, determined by factors such as its ranking, the number of students, the cost of renting for university students, and the extrinsic one linked to the components of the city and in particular its socio-economic system, urban mobility and land use. The combination of these features highlights how the centrality of universities is configured not only in terms of innovation of the educational services offered but also in terms of actions and relationships that universities trigger and establish with their urban surroundings, generating socio-economic impacts, on the urban mobility system and on the land use of the city itself. Qualifying itself as a real urban space, the university is a system able to extend its area of influence to the surrounding context and at the same time to be influenced by the latter [54].

This relationship of mutual dependence relates in particular to the aspects of accessibility and urban mobility, since the attractiveness of universities also depends on the urban planning choices of the urban areas in which they are located, the organization of services related to mobility and therefore the degree of accessibility of the places.

The diffusion of universities and university buildings open to public use (libraries, cultural centers) or intended for mixed functions (residential, commercial) points out that a greater permeability allows the university to become a real piece of the city [55], which can help to compensate for the limited performance of an urban system or, conversely, can benefit from the positive results of its urban surroundings.

Enhancing the proximity between universities and the urban environment, today, seems fundamental both in the post-pandemic context and even more in the framework of a possible energy crisis, which inevitably requires a rethinking of urban space and its distribution with the aim of enhancing the construction of a network of central, accessible, and livable places.

5 Conclusions

The development and spatial distribution (concentrated and/or widespread) of universities over the years has increased the spread of services and activities in their vicinity. They have also led to a different demand for mobility characterized not only by residents but also by commuters with reference to university students. In particular, the attractiveness of universities depends not only on the educational offer for students but also on the characteristics of cities, in terms of connections, quality of life and cost of living. Specifically, urban planning of the areas and on the optimization of services and in particular on transport and therefore on the degree of accessibility of the places.

In recent years, universities and local administrations have focused on environmental, social and economic impacts and this must also be pursued in the post-pandemic phase to avoid the increase in the use of private vehicles and therefore the related road congestion phenomena.

Several intrinsic and extrinsic indicators were considered for a preliminary assessment of the universities with particular reference to the comparison between two medium-sized and two small university towns.

After selecting a set of extrinsic intrinsic indicators, the Simpon's index commonly used to measure biodiversity, i.e. the diversity of living beings in a given place -, allowed us to measure the diversity of anthropogenic elements such as schools, commerce, mobility and transport, etc. The future prospects of this research are to extend to the main University Italian cases.

References

1. Christaller, W.: Die zentralen Orte in Süddeutschland. Fischer, Jena (1933)
2. Sombart, W.: Der moderne Kapitalismus. Lipsia (1902)
3. Göçer, Ö., Göçer, K.: The effects of transportation modes on campus use: a case study of a suburban campus. Case Stud. Transp. Policy 7(1), 37–47 (2019)
4. Papantoniou, P., et al.: Developing a sustainable mobility action plan for university campuses. Transp. Res. Procedia 48, 1908–1917 (2020)
5. Moos, M., Revington, N., Wilkin, T., Andrey, J.: The knowledge economy city. Gentrification, studentification and youthification, and their connections to universities. Urban studies 56(6), 1075–1092 (2019)
6. Haghighi, F.: Study. Be silent. Die: indeterminate architecture and the dispositive of studentification. J. Cult. Res. 22(1), 55–72 (2018)
7. Reynolds, A.: Geographies of purpose built student accommodation: exclusivity, precarity and (im) mobility. Geogr. Compass 14(11), e12543 (2020)
8. Kalayci Onac, A., Cetin, M., Sevik, H., Orman, P., Karci, A., Gonullu Sutcuoglu, G.: Rethinking the campus transportation network in the scope of ecological design principles: case study of Izmir Katip Çelebi University Çiğli Campus. Environ. Sci. Pollut. Res. 28(36), 50847–50866 (2021). https://doi.org/10.1007/s11356-021-14299-2
9. Mendoza-Flores, R., Quintero-Ramírez, R., Ortiz, I.: The carbon footprint of a public university campus in Mexico City. Carbon Manage. 10(5), 501–511 (2019)
10. Mota, J.C., Sá, F.M.E., Isidoro, C., Pereira, B.C., Azeiteiro, U.D.M., Davim, J.P.: Bike-friendly campus, new paths towards sustainable development. In: Higher Education and Sustainability, pp. 223–245. CRC Press (2019)

11. Palumbo, M.E., Mundula, L., Balletto, G., Bazzato, E., Marignani, M.: Environmental dimension into strategic planning. The case of metropolitan city of Cagliari. In: International Conference on Computational Science and Its Applications, pp. 456–471). Springer, Cham (2020, July)

12. Simpson, D.B., Burnett, D.: Commuters versus residents: the effects of living arrangement and student engagement on academic performance. J. Coll. Stud. Retent.: Res. Theory Pract. **21**(3), 286–304 (2019)

13. Balletto, G., Borruso, G., Murgante, B., Milesi, A., Ladu, M.: Resistance and resilience. a methodological approach for cities and territories in Italy. In: International Conference on Computational Science and Its Applications, pp. 218–229. Springer, Cham (2021, September)

14. Campisi, T., Torrisi, V., Ignaccolo, M., Inturri, G., Tesoriere, G.: University propensity assessment to car sharing services using mixed survey data: the Italian case study of Enna city. Transp. Res. Procedia **47**, 433–440 (2020)

15. Torrisi, V., Ignaccolo, M., Inturri, G., Tesoriere, G., Campisi, T.: Exploring the factors affecting bike-sharing demand: evidence from student perceptions, usage patterns and adoption barriers. Transp. Res. Procedia **52**, 573–580 (2021)

16. Campisi, T., Tesoriere, G., Ignaccolo, M., Inturri, G., Torrisi, V.: A behavioral and explanatory statistical analysis applied with the advent of sharing mobility in urban contexts. Outcomes from an under thirty-age group perspective. In: International Conference on Innovation in Urban and Regional Planning, pp. 633–641. Springer, Cham (September 2021)

17. Nguyen-Phuoc, D.Q., Amoh-Gyimah, R., Tran, A.T.P., Phan, C.T.: Mode choice among university students to school in Danang, Vietnam. Travel Behav. Soc. **13**, 1–10 (2018)

18. Bagdatli, M.E.C., Ipek, F.: Transport mode preferences of university students in post-COVID-19 pandemic. Transp. Policy **118**, 20–32 (2022)

19. Torrisi, V., Campisi, T., Inturri, G., Ignaccolo, M., Tesoriere, G.: Continue to share? An overview on Italian travel behavior before and after the COVID-19 lockdown. In: AIP Conference Proceedings, vol. 2343, no. 1, p. 090010. AIP Publishing LLC (March 2021)

20. Barbarossa, L.: The post pandemic city: challenges and opportunities for a non-motorized urban environment. An overview of Italian cases. Sustainability **12**(17), 7172 (2020)

21. Balletto, G., Ladu, M., Milesi, A., Camerin, F., Borruso, G.: Walkable city and military enclaves: analysis and decision-making approach to support the proximity connection in urban regeneration. Sustainability **14**(1), 457 (2022)

22. Caselli, B., Carra, M., Rossetti, S., Zazzi, M.: Exploring the 15-minute neighborhoods. An evaluation based on the walkability performance to public facilities. Transp. Res. Procedia **60**, 346–353 (2022)

23. Balletto, G., Pezzagno, M., Richiedei, A.: 15-Minute city in urban regeneration perspective: two methodological approaches compared to support decisions. In: Gervasi, O., et al. (eds.) ICCSA 2021. LNCS, vol. 12953, pp. 535–548. Springer, Cham (2021). https://doi.org/10.1007/978-3-030-86976-2_36

24. Ladu, M., Balletto, G., Borruso, G.: Sport and smart communities. Assessing the sporting attractiveness and community perceptions of Cagliari (Sardinia, Italy). In: International Conference on Computational Science and Its Applications, pp. 200–215. Springer, Cham (July 2019)

25. Vale, D.S., Pereira, M., Viana, C.M.: Different destination, different commuting pattern? Analyzing the influence of the campus location on commuting. J. Transp. Land Use **11**(1), 1–18 (2018)

26. Cattaneo, M., Horta, H., Malighetti, P., Meoli, M., Paleari, S.: Universities' attractiveness to students: the Darwinism effect. High. Educ. Quart. **73**(1), 85–99 (2019)

27. Cattaneo, M., Malighetti, P., Morlotti, C., Paleari, S.: Students' mobility attitudes and sustainable transport mode choice. Int. J. Sustain. High. Educ. **19**, 942–962 (2018)

28. Canale, A., Campisi, T., Tesoriere, G., Sanfilippo, L., Brignone, A.: The evaluation of home-school itineraries to improve accessibility of a university campus through sustainable transport modes. In: International Conference on Computational Science and Its Applications, pp. 754–769. Springer, Cham (July 2020)

29. Campisi, T., Basbas, S., Al-Rashid, M.A., Tesoriere, G., Georgiadis, G.: A region-wide survey on emotional and psychological impacts of COVID-19 on public transport choices in Sicily, Italy. Trans. Transp. Sci. **12**, 34–43 (2021)

30. Abdullah, M., Ali, N., Dias, C., Campisi, T., Javid, M.A.: Exploring the traveler's intentions to use public transport during the COVID-19 pandemic while complying with precautionary measures. Appl. Sci. **11**(8), 3630 (2021). https://doi.org/10.3390/app11083630

31. Balletto, G., et al.: Sport-city planning. A proposal for an index to support decision-making practice: principles and strategies. In: Gervasi, O., et al. (eds.) ICCSA 2021. LNCS, vol. 12952, pp. 255–269. Springer, Cham (2021). https://doi.org/10.1007/978-3-030-86973-1_18

32. Villani, P., et al..: Mobilità, modelli insediativi ed efficienza territoriale. Franco Angeli (2001)

33. Fischer, K.: Central places: the theories of von Thünen, Christaller, and Lösch. In: Foundations of location analysis, pp. 471–505. Springer, New York, NY (2011)

34. Badii, C., et al.: Computing 15MinCityIndexes on the basis of open data and services. In: Gervasi, O., et al. (eds.) ICCSA 2021. LNCS, vol. 12956, pp. 565–579. Springer, Cham (2021). https://doi.org/10.1007/978-3-030-87010-2_42

35. Vazzoler, N., Roveroni, S.: Luoghi Centrali e Spazi Pubblici. La Costruzione di Reti di Prossimità. EUT Edizioni Università di Trieste, Trieste (Italy) (2016). https://www.openstarts.units.it/bitstream/10077/12792/1/Vazzoler_Roveroni_131-145.pdf

36. Moreno, C., Allam, Z., Chabaud, D., Gall, C., Pratlong, F.: Introducing the "15-Minute City". Sustainability, resilience and place identity in future post-pandemic cities. Smart Cities **4**(1), 93–111 (2021)

37. Li, Z., Zheng, J., Zhang, Y.: Study on the layout of 15-minute community-life circle in third-tier cities based on POI: Baoding City of Hebei Province. Engineering **11**(9), 592–603 (2019)

38. Abiodun, J.O.: Urban hierarchy in a developing country. Econ. Geogr. **43**(4), 347–367 (1967)

39. Berry, B.J., Garrison, W.L.: The functional bases of the central place hierarchy. Econ. Geogr. **34**(2), 145–154 (1958)

40. The Geography of Transport Systems. https://transportgeography.org/

41. Capponi, A., Vitello, P., Fiandrino, C., Cantelmo, G., Kliazovich, D., Sorger, U., Bouvry, P.: Crowdsensed data learning-driven prediction of local businesses attractiveness in smart cities. In 2019 IEEE Symposium on Computers and Communications (ISCC), pp. 1–6. IEEE (June 2019)

42. Hidayati, I., Tan, W., Yamu, C.: Conceptualizing mobility inequality mobility and accessibility for the marginalized. J. Plan. Lit. **36**(4), 492–507 (2021)

43. Balletto, G., Pezzagno, M., Richiedei, A.: 15-Minute city in urban regeneration perspective: two methodological approaches compared to support decisions. In International Conference on Computational Science and Its Applications. Springer, Cham, pp. 535–548 (2021)

44. Perry, D.C., Wiewel, W.: From campus to city. The university as developer, vol. 1. Taylor & Francis Ltd. (2005). ISBN 10: 076561541X

45. Sgarra, V., Meta, E., Saporito, M.R., Persia, L., Usami, D.S.: Improving sustainable mobility in university campuses. The case study of Sapienza University. Transp. Res. Procedia **60**, 108–115 (2022)

46. Walton, M.: The Deming management method. The bestselling classic for quality management! Penguin (1988)

47. Kang, C., Fan, D., Jiao, H.: Validating activity, time, and space diversity as essential components of urban vitality. Environ. Plan. B **48**(5), 1180–1197 (2021)

48. Comer, D., Greene, J.S.: The development and application of a land use diversity index for Oklahoma City, OK. Appl. Geogr. **60**, 46–57 (2015)
49. Balletto, G., Ladu, M., Milesi, A., Borruso, G.: A methodological approach on disused public properties in the 15-Minute city perspective. Sustainability **13**(2), 593 (2021). https://doi.org/10.3390/su13020593
50. Borruso, G., Porceddu, A.: A tale of two cities: density analysis of CBD on two midsize urban areas in Northeastern Italy. In: Murgante, B., Borruso, G., Lapucci, A. (eds.) Geocomputation and Urban Planning Studies in Computational Intelligence, vol. 176. Springer, Berlin/Heidelberg (2009)
51. Borruso, G.: Il ruolo della cartografia nella definizione del central business district. Prime note per un approccio metodologico. Bollettino A.I.C, 271–287 (2006). https://www.openstarts.units.it/bitstream/10077/12342/1/Borruso.pdf. Accessed 20 March 2022
52. Il Sole 24 Ore. https://lab24.ilsole24ore.com/qualita-della-vita-generazioni/; https://lab24.ilsole24ore.com/ecosistema-urbano/; https://lab24.ilsole24ore.com/indiceSportivita/index.php; https://www.censis.it/formazione/la-classifica-censis-delle-universit%C3%A0-italiane-edizione-20212022
53. Dilorenzo, P., Stefani, E.: Università e città. Il ruolo dell'università nello sviluppo dell'economia culturale delle città. Fondazione CRUI (2015). https://www.crui.it/images/allegati/pubblicazioni/2015/crui_universita_citta_digital.pdf
54. Fedeli, V., Cognetti, F.: Università come nodo dello sviluppo urbano. Riflessioni a partire dal caso milanese. In: XIII Conferenza Italiana di Scienze Regionali. Torino (2011). https://re.public.polimi.it/retrieve/handle/11311/608705/238752/COGNETTIFEDELIaisre.pdf
55. Barioglio, C., De Rossi, A., Durbiano, G., Gabbarini, E.: Verso un'università della città: il caso studio del Masterplan per i campus del Politecnico di Torino. Eco Web Town **17**, 198–209 (2018). http://www.ecowebtown.it/n_17/pdf/17_05_1.pdf

International Workshop on Ecosystem Services: Nature's Contribution to People in Practice. Assessment Frameworks, Models, Mapping, and Implications (NC2P 2022)

Spatial Features of a Regional Green Infrastructure and Identification of Ecological Corridors: A Study Related to Sardinia

Federica Isola⬤, Sabrina Lai(✉)⬤, Federica Leone⬤, and Corrado Zoppi⬤

Dipartimento di Ingegneria Civile, Ambientale e Architettura (DICAAR),
University of Cagliari, Cagliari, Italy
{federica.isola,sabrinalai,federicaleone,zoppi}@unica.it

Abstract. This study aims at assessing the relationship between the spatial frame-work of the characteristics of a regional green infrastructure (RGI) and the ecological corridors of a regional network of protected areas. The spatial layout of the regional infrastructure is identified based on the potential supply of seven ecosystem services (intrinsic value of biodiversity, habitat quality, nature-based recreation potential, agricultural and forestry value, regulation of land surface temperature, and carbon storage and sequestration), whereas ecological corridors are detected through a methodological approach which builds on resistance-based models. The maps of the RGI characteristics and of the ecological corridors are overlaid and their correlations are assessed through a regression model. Such methodological approach is applied into the spatial context of the Sardinia Region. Finally, relevant planning implications concerning the implementation of planning policies to improve the effectiveness of the regional network of protected areas through the enhancement of the features related to the RGI are proposed and discussed, as well as the exportability of the methodological approach.

Keywords: Ecological corridors · Green infrastructure · Ecosystem services

1 Introduction

Green Infrastructures (GIs) are broadly defined, both in the literature [1] and in policy documents [2], as multifunctional and interconnected networks of green areas, be they natural, semi-natural, or even artificial, that provide a wide range of benefits to humans. Two main characteristics here stand out, that is, multifunctionality and connectivity [3].

As for the first, GIs are regarded as a means for pursuing environmental, social, and economic goals, especially within urban contexts [4]. Because they pursue such different goals, GIs must implement several functions and deliver various ecosystem services (ESs). Multifunctionality is a distinctive trait of GIs, although at the urban scale GIs are often being designed and implemented with one specific main function in mind [5].

© The Author(s), under exclusive license to Springer Nature Switzerland AG 2022
O. Gervasi et al. (Eds.): ICCSA 2022 Workshops, LNCS 13380, pp. 285–297, 2022.
https://doi.org/10.1007/978-3-031-10542-5_20

As for the second characteristic, i.e., connectivity, Ecological corridors (ECs) are the edges of green infrastructures (GIs) identified as networks whose nodes are areas characterized by relevant concentrations of ecosystem services (ESs) and environmental quality. ECs enhance the flows of wild species across the network and facilitate biological exchange processes. Negative impacts manifest as consequences of degradation or destruction of natural ecosystems [6]. Several environmental and landscape features characterize the potential of a GI's ECs to improve genetic exchange and biological flows across the network, such as presence, location and size of natural and anthropic barriers, spatial continuity, and supply of ESs supporting behavioral characteristics of species, such as food catching opportunities, suitable habitats, etc. [6]. Such potential is effectively represented by the concept of connectivity, which associates the movement of species through GI networks to the suitability to such flows of their linear edges, designated as ecological corridors [7].

This study discusses the relationship between the ECs and the capacity of GIs to supply ESs. Methodological approaches to identify GIs as providers of ESs and ECs as linear structures connecting the nodes of a GI are proposed in the second section, and, in the following section, implemented into the case study of a GI, represented by the regional network of protected areas, and related ECs, concerning the regional context of Sardinia. In the fourth section, the spatial taxonomy of the regional GI (RGI) and the ECs map are overlaid, and the correlations between the spatial features of the RGI and of the ECs are detected through a regression model; moreover, planning implications are highlighted.

2 Materials and Methods

2.1 Study Area

The island of Sardinia, among the largest islands of the Mediterranean Sea, is taken as a spatial context particularly suitable to implement the methodological approach of this study since GI features and ESs supply can be analyzed and assessed in a straightforward way, due to the clear-cut identification of the regional borders. In this study, ECs are considered as linear elements connecting the regional natural protected areas (NPAs), which are identified according to the classification defined by Lai et al. [8] and include natural regional parks, public woods, permanent oases of faunal protection, Ramsar sites and Natura 2000 Sites (N2Ss) (Fig. 1).

2.2 Data

Because multifunctionality is here considered as the landscape's capacity to supply multiple ESs, seven ESs, chosen across the provisioning, regulating and cultural groups, were modeled and mapped. The seven chosen ES are as follows.

- Intrinsic, non-use value of biodiversity (Conservation value, Consval), cultural ES.
- Ecosystems' capacity to provide habitats for animal and vegetal species (Natural value, Natval), regulating or supporting ES depending on the classification scheme.

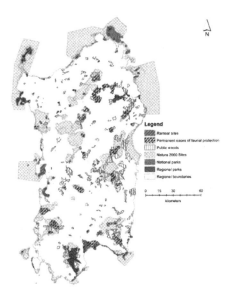

Fig. 1. The regional system of Sardinian NPAs.

- Ecosystems' attractiveness for recreational activities (Recreation value, Recrval), cultural ES.
- Ecosystems' support to sustaining sense of place, cultural identity, and heritage values (Landscape value, Landsval), cultural ES.
- Ecosystems' capacity to provide food, fibers, timber (Agriculture and forestry value, Agrofor), provisioning ES.
- Ecosystems' capacity to regulate local climate (Land Surface Temperature, LST), regulating ES.
- Ecosystems' capacity to regulate global climate (Carbon capture and storage, CO2Stor), regulating ES.

2.3 Methodology

The methodological approach of this study develops as follows. First, the characteristics of the Sardinian RGI are identified; next, ECs are detected on the basis of a resistance-based map. Finally, the maps of the RGI characteristics and of the ecological corridors are overlaid and their correlations are assessed through a regression model.

The Sardinian RGI. Natval and CO2Stor were mapped using two InVEST tools[1], i.e., "Habitat quality" and "Carbon Storage and Sequestration", respectively. As for Recrval, the conceptual model ESTIMAP [9], developed by a group of researchers working at the JRC, was applied; moreover, a plugin developed by Ndossi and Avdan [10] for retrieving the Land Surface Temperature was applied to summer satellite images. As regards the other variables, Consval and Landsval were mapped following Lai and Leone's methods [11]; the first relies on data from a regional monitoring project that assessed the presence of habitats of community interest, protected under the European Directive 92/43/EEC, while the second on data concerning environmental and cultural landscape assets subject to legally binding protection under the provisions of the Regional Landscape Plan (RLP). Furthermore, Agrofor was mapped following the methodology developed by Lai *et al.* [12], where land value is taken as a proxy for agricultural and forestry production. All of the ES were mapped on a regular, squared grid whose cell size equals 300 m; moreover, each ES was normalized in the [0–1] interval, so as to obtain comparable values, where 1 corresponds to the maximum supply of each ES. This entails that, as far as the LST is concerned, temperature values retrieved in Kelvin from the model were not only normalized, but also inverted, so that 1 corresponds to the lowest temperature, and 0 to the highest one. Finally, the elevation was retrieved from a digital terrain model available from the Regional (Sardinian) geoportal.

The identification of the ECs.[2] Spatial connectivity is generally assessed through models that map resistance, which comprise least-cost-path (LCP) models that identify ECs as connections between spatial parcels, detected as habitat locations, featured by the least resistance to movement of species. The map of connectivity is drawn through a four-step methodological approach, originally proposed by Cannas [14, 15] and structured into four steps.

First, a vector map representing the regional spatial taxonomy of the habitat suitability is identified, by means of the 2008 regional land cover map of Sardinia, and of the values of the habitat suitability identified, in species-specific terms, by a study commissioned by the Autonomous Region of Sardinia [16].

Secondly, a vector map representing the regional spatial taxonomy of the ecological integrity is drawn through Burkhard *et al.*'s studies [17], where the capacity of land-cover classes to supply supporting ESs is assessed through an expert-based approach.

Thirdly, the resistance regional spatial taxonomy is defined based on an article by LaRue and Nielsen [18] through the following steps. First, two raster maps are derived

---

[1] InVEST is a suite of tools that allows for developing spatially explicit assessments of various ecosystem services. Developed by the Natural Capital Project, it is freely available from https://naturalcapitalproject.stanford.edu/software/invest, last accessed 2022/03/21.

[2] A detailed description of the procedure for the identification of ECs can be retrieved from Chapter 3 by Lai *et al.* [13].

from the vector maps of the habitat-suitability and of the ecological-integrity indexes; secondly, two raster maps are generated from such raster maps, by mapping the inverse of the habitat-suitability and of the ecological-integrity indexes; thirdly, an ordinal scale, which identifies the resistance scores ranging between 1 and 100, is used to order the two raster maps, building on a report by the European Environment Agency [19]; finally, a (total) resistance map is defined by summing up the resistance scores of the two raster spatial taxonomies identified in the third phase.

The ECs connecting the regional NPAs are identified by means of the Tool "Linkage Pathways" (LPT) of the GIS Toolbox "Linkage Mapper". LPT adopts the Cost-Weighted Distance (CWD) as the reference variable to detect ECs through an LCP-related model [20]. Data used by LPT are the raster resistance map defined in the third step and the vector map of the regional NPAs. The linear path of the ECs and the CWD raster map are the outputs made available by LPT.

The regression model to detect the correlations between the RGI and the ECs.
The spatial taxonomy of the RGI based on the supply of the seven types of ESs above described is overlaid on the ECs connecting the regional NPAs. Patches are included in ECs if their CWD is included in the first two deciles of the CWD distribution. The CWD of a patch i which belongs to the EC connecting two elements, A and B, of the NPAs vector map is detected as follows:

$$CWD_i = CWD_{iA} + CWD_{iB}, \tag{1}$$

where CWD_{iA} CWD_{iB} are the CWDs between patch i and the core areas A and B.

A multiple linear regression is used to assess the correlations between the CWD of patches included in ECs and the normalized supply of ESs, which characterize the Sardinian RGI. The regression operationalizes as follows:

$$ECWD = \beta_0 + \beta_1 Consval + \beta_2 Natval + \beta_3 Recrval + \beta_4 Landsval$$
$$+ \beta_5 Agrofor + \beta_6 LST + \beta_7 CO2Stor + \beta_8 Altd + \beta_9 Aut, \tag{2}$$

where dependent and explanatory variables are identified by the overlays of ECs and patches providing ESs:

- ECWD is the CWD of a patch included in an EC.
- Consval, Natval, Recrval, Landsval, Agrofor, LST, CO2Stor are seven values representing the potential supply of as many ecosystem services, as per Sect. 2.2.
- Altd is a control variable related to the altitude of a patch included in an EC.
- Aut is a control variable which controls for spatial autocorrelation.

The regression estimates account for the marginal effects of the covariates on the CWD of patches included in ECs. A multiple regression model is used since no priors are recognized as regards the influence of the variables which identify the ESs which characterize the Sardinian RGI on ECWD [21], and, as a consequence, a local linear approximation of the unknown surface which generally represents the n-dimensional relational phenomenon related to the dependent variable and covariates of model (2) is the most suitable way to detect information on such influence [22].

The altitude-related variable controls for systematic differentials in the impacts of different ecosystem services on CWD due to elevation. A spatially lagged variable, Aut, calculated using GeoDa[3], is used to control for spatial autocorrelation. Lastly, the p-values of the coefficients of the covariates are references to implement hypothesis tests to assess their estimates' significance, e.g., at 5%. As per the regression results reported in Table 1, the estimates of the two control variables' coefficients are significant and they highlight negative effects on the patches' performance.

3 Results

The outcomes of the implementation of the methodology described in the previous section are shown in the following three subsections.

3.1 The Spatial Taxonomies of the Supply of Ecosystem Services

The spatial layout of the supply of the seven chosen ESs is provided in Fig. 2, together with an eightieth map that provides the sum of the seven normalized ESs.

Consval is null in approximately 66% of the island's land mass, where no habitats of community interest have been identified and monitored; areas taking non-null values are mostly, but not exclusively, located within Natura 2000 sites and highly spatially clustered in their immediate surroundings.

As for Natval, a mere 3.44% of the island takes null values. High values mostly concern the island's largest forests, and regional and national natural protected areas.

Recrval is null in a negligible part of the island. The spatial patterns of Recrval are similar to Natval's ones, except for the coastal area, where Recrval takes high values.

Landsval equals 0 in 61.18% of the region. Among non-null values, the maximum value spatially dominates, mainly because of the presence of the main environmental assets protected under the under the RLP.

Agrofor is null in around 34.1% of the island; approximately 47.3% takes low values (Agrofor $\leq$ 0.33), while only 14.1% takes mid values (0.33 < Agrofor $\leq$ 0.66), and a mere 4.5, clustered along the two main plains, takes high values (0.66 < Agrofor $\leq$ 1).

LST in summer mostly (59.9%) takes mid normalized values (0.33 < LST $\leq$ 0.66), whereas 38.7% of the island is characterized by low normalized values (0 < LST $\leq$ 0.33), meaning that the surface temperature is hot, and a mere 1.4% takes high nor-malized values (0.66 < LST $\leq$ 1), hence it is cooler than the rest of the island.

CO2Stor is null in around 2.2% of the island. No clear spatial pattern emerges, except for low and very low values, coinciding with urban areas and inland waters.

Finally, the total value map provides a simple overview of the level of multifunctionality through the multiple ecosystem services landscape index (MESLI) [23], i.e., the sum of the seven normalized ESs values.

---

[3] GeoDa is an open-source software program developed by L. Anselin and his team; it is freely available from https://geodacenter.github.io/ [last accessed: 2022/03/21].

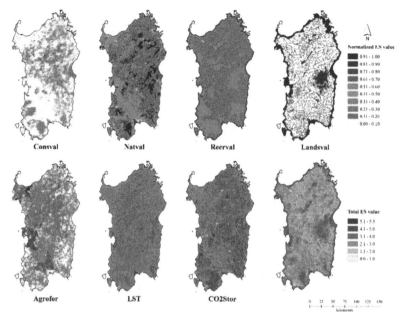

Fig. 2. Spatial distribution of the seven components of the Sardinian RGI, and of the sum of their normalized values.

3.2 The Ecological Corridors Connecting the Sardinian Natural Protected Areas

The raster map of the CWD values and the spatial identification of the ECs connecting the regional network of the Sardinian NPAs are the two outputs obtained through the implementation of the methodological approach described in Sect. 2.3. The ECs are identified by patches with CWD values lower than the second decile of the CWD distribution. Figure 3 shows the identification of ECs by patches with CWD values lower than the second decile.

3.3 Regression Results

The regression outcomes (Table 1) show the marginal effects of the supply of the seven ecosystem services on CWD of patches, and, by doing so, they identify a hierarchy of ESs in contributing to their inclusion in the spatial system of ECs.

Consequently, the assessment of the estimates of the other explanatory variables can be easily implemented, and, in so doing, the hierarchy of the supply of the seven ecosystem services can be straightforwardly identified, in terms of their contribution to the inclusion of patches in the ECs' spatial system.

The estimates of the coefficients of the seven explanatory variables are significant with respect to the p-value test described above and entails the following.

First, three out of the seven ESs have a negative impact on CWD, or, they increase the eligibility of a patch to be included in an EC, everything else being equal. These covariates are LST, Agrofor and Landsval. The largest impact is related to LST, which, on average, shows a 1% decrease in CWD associated to a 10% decrease in LST, whereas the marginal effects of Agrofor correspond to a 3.9‰. The estimated coefficient of the dichotomous variable Landsval indicates that a relevant increase in the supply of landscape assets is associated to a 1.6‰ decrease in CWD.

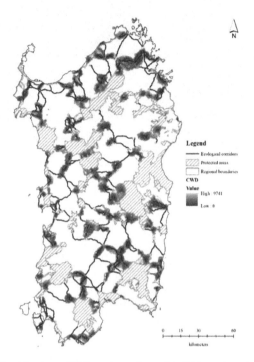

Fig. 3. The spatial identification of ECs and patches with CWD values lower than the second decile

Secondly, the variable Consval shows a positive impact on CWD which can be considered almost irrelevant, since even a 100% increase in conservation value would be associated to a very low increase in CWD (lower than 1‰).

Finally, Natval, Recrval and CO2Stor show positive marginal effects on CWD: on average, a 10% increase in the variables is associated to 3.08‰, 8.54‰ and 2.90‰ increases in CWD, respectively.

Therefore, the estimates of the model put in evidence that the supply of ESs related to ecosystems' capacity of providing home to animal and plant species (Natval), leisure-related and recreational opportunities (Recrval) and capture and storage capacity of carbon dioxide are the most problematic in order to identify ECs throughout the Sardinian RGI. On the other hand, mitigation of LST, agricultural and forestry production, and landscape assets are the most effective ESs to implement connections between NPAs through ECs.

Table 1. Regression results.

Explanatory variable	Coefficient	Standard deviation	t-statistic	p-value	Mean of the explanatory variable
Consval	8.918	44.2792	6.777	0.000	0.118
Natval	300.073	35.4105	23.516	0.000	0.395
Recrval	832.710	64.1078	2.159	0.031	0.403
Landsval	−151.722	22.1392	−6.853	0.000	0.290
Agrofor	−377.346	37.8409	−9.972	0.000	0.195
LST	−1,023.733	65.4963	−15.621	0.000	0.431
CO2Stor	282.343	50.3026	5.613	0.000	0.543
Altd	0.930	0.0355	26.213	0.000	356.766
Aut	0.541	0.0022	245.322	0.000	5595.630

Dependent variable: ECWD: Mean: 4,925,323 km; Standard deviation: 2,866.858 km; Adjusted R-squared: 0.530.

4 Discussion and Conclusions

The regression outcomes show that three out of the seven ESs, that is LST, Agrofor and Landsval, contribute to increase the eligibility of a patch to be part of an EC.

In relation to LST, a decrease in CWD values is associated to a decrease in LST. The reason of this behavior can be related to the presence of agricultural areas, which are likely to negatively impact connectivity [24] since they may possibly reduce the flow of species within ECs. In particular, the main sources of negative impacts generated by agricultural land uses are physical barriers such as fences and hedges, cultivation techniques and methods, and the use of herbicides, pesticides, and fertilizers. Moreover, both intensive and extensive agriculture can exert relevant impacts on LST due to low and dense vegetation that prevents evapotranspiration and reduces air circulation and downwind cooling [25].

Agrofor, as well as LST, is influenced by the presence of agricultural areas that represent a potential obstacle to the flow of species. The higher the productive potential, which is related to crop type, site elevation, and geographical location, the higher the decrease in connectivity. On the other hand, the presence of forest areas shows positive effects on connectivity, since it is associated to a decrease in CWD values. One of the main causes of habitat loss are changes in forest covers [26], which reduce the habitat areal size and increase habitat fragmentation.

As regards Landsval, regression results show that an increase in the supply of landscape assets entails a decrease in CWD values. In this study, patches characterized by the presence of landscape assets associated to more restrictive rules under the provisions of the Sardinian RLP show the highest values of Landsval. Among such landscape assets, the RLP includes the coastal strip, lakes, reservoirs, wetlands, rivers, and creeks. Rivers are especially effective in enabling connectivity by protecting wildlife through riparian formations and floodplain woods and by providing water resources and food. Riparian formations and floodplain woods represent preferential corridors for several terrestrial and semiaquatic species, such as reptiles and amphibians, and birds [27].

In conclusion, a number of recommendations concerning policies aimed at strengthening the spatial frame of ECs are implied by the outcomes of this study; such policies focus on lowering land surface temperature, boosting forestry coverage and increasing the quantity and spatial dimension of the landscape assets protected under the provisions of the Sardinian RLP.

Policies that promote afforestation are the most effective in lowering the land surface temperature [28], and hence increasing the LST variable used in this study, in non-urbanized zones, such as rural areas. Consequently, combining the regression outcomes related to the marginal effects expressed by the coefficients of Agrofor and LST, afforestation is the leading policy recommendation concerning the strengthening of ECs, which effectively addresses both lowering land surface temperature and boosting forestry coverage, even if transitions to forestry are frequently hindered by the strong cultural bond which characterize the relation between farmers and agriculture and by the high-rents of arable land [29, 30].

The presence of landscape assets is also relevant to improve the ECs that enable linkages between protected areas. Protected landscape assets can be either man-made or natural, and the stricter the conservation policy is, the higher Landsval. Therefore, policy makers could act in two directions: first, raising the levels of statutory provisions in case of already protected landscape features; second, amplifying the types of landscape features that are subject to such protection regime. This is especially important in case of linear goods and assets, such as tree lines, hedgerows and drywalls that have been proven to be key to support connectivity within landscapes [31], higher levels of biodiversity [32], and species' movement. New landscape features such as line trees and hedgerows, which incidentally are also recognized as integral parts of local identities in many cultures (among many: [33]), should therefore be treated as protected landscape assets in a future, updated, version of the RLP.

The methodology here applied, which combines assessment of multifunctionality in terms of ES provision and identification of ECs based on LCP approaches, can be applied in other contexts and re-adjusted as needed. For instance, the selection of ESs to be assessed, as well as the choice of models used to assess the spatial distribution of their provisioning areas, can be appropriately re-considered and tailored to local distinctive aspects, data availability, and modelers' expertise.

Acknowledgments. The study was implemented within the Research Program "Paesaggi rurali della Sardegna: pianificazione di infrastrutture verdi e blu e di reti territoriali complesse" [Rural landscapes of Sardinia: Planning policies for green and blue infrastructure and spatial complex networks], funded by the Autonomous Region of Sardinia under the 2017 call for "Projects related to fundamental or basic research" of the year 2017. Federica Isola, Sabrina Lai, Federica Leone, and Corrado Zoppi collaboratively designed this study, and jointly written the Introduction. Individual contributions are as follows: S.L.: 2.1, 2.2, "The Sardinian RGI" in 2.3, and 3.1. F.I. and F.L.: "The identification of the ECs" in 2.3, 3.2 and 4; C.Z.: "The regression model to detect the correlations between the RGI and the ECs" in 2.3 and 3.3; S.L. and C.Z.: 4.

References

1. Benedict, M.A., McMahon, E.T.: Green infrastructure: smart conservation for the 21st century. Renew. Resour. J. **20**(3), 12–17 (2002)
2. European Commission: Green infrastructure (GI)—Enhancing Europe's natural capital. Communication from the Commission to the European Parliament, the Council, the European Economic and Social Committee and the Committee of the Regions (2013). https://eur-lex.europa.eu/resource.html?uri=cellar:d41348f2-01d5-4abe-b817-4c73e6f1b2df.0014.03/DOC_1&format=PDF. Accessed 21 Mar 2022
3. Liquete, C., et al.: Mapping green infrastructure based on ecosystem services and ecological networks: a Pan-European case study. Environ. Sci. Policy **54**, 268–280 (2015). https://doi.org/10.1016/j.envsci.2015.07.009
4. Madureira, H., Andresen, T.: Planning for multifunctional urban green infrastructures: promises and challenges. Urban Des. Int. **19**, 38–49 (2014). https://doi.org/10.1057/udi.2013.11
5. Meerow, S.: The politics of multifunctional green infrastructure planning in New York City. Cities **100**, 102621 (2020). https://doi.org/10.1016/j.cities.2020.102621
6. D'Ambrogi, S., Gori, M., Guccione, M., Nazzini, L.: Implementazione della connettività ecologica sul territorio: il monitoraggio ISPRA 2014 [Ecological connectivity implementation in practice: ISPRA's 2014 monitoring]. Reticula **9**, 1–7 (2015). http://www.isprambiente.gov.it/it/pubblicazioni/periodici-tecnici/reticula/Reticula_n9.pdf. Accessed 21 Mar 2022
7. Baudry, J., Merriam, H.G.: Connectivity and connectedness: functional versus structural patterns in landscapes. In: Schreiber, K.-F. (ed.) Connectivity in Landscape Ecology. Proceedings of the 2nd International Seminar of the "International Association for Landscape Ecology". Münster 1987. Münsterche Geographische Arbeiten 29, 23–27. Ferdinand Schöningh, Paderborn, Germany (1988). ISBN 978-35-067-3229-3. ISSN 0176-1064
8. Lai, S., Leone, F., Zoppi, C.: Land cover changes and environmental protection: a study based on transition matrices concerning Sardinia (Italy). Land Use Policy **67**, 126–150 (2017). https://doi.org/10.1016/j.landusepol.2017.05.030
9. Zulian, G., Paracchini, M.L., Maes, J., Liquete, C.: ESTIMAP: Ecosystem services mapping at European scale. JRC Technical Report EUR 26474 ENG. Publications Office of the European Union, Luxembourg (2013). https://doi.org/10.2788/6436
10. Ndossi, M.I., Avdan, U.: Application of open source coding technologies in the production of Land Surface Temperature (LST) maps from Landsat: a PyQGIS Plugin. Remote Sens. **8**, 413 (2016). https://doi.org/10.3390/rs8050413
11. Lai, S., Leone, F.: Bridging biodiversity conservation objectives with landscape planning through green infrastructures: a case study from Sardinia, Italy. In: Gervasi, O., et al. (eds.) ICCSA 2017. LNCS, vol. 10409, pp. 456–472. Springer, Cham (2017). https://doi.org/10.1007/978-3-319-62407-5_32
12. Lai, S., Isola, F., Leone, F., Zoppi, C.: Assessing the potential of green infrastructure to mitigate hydro-geological hazard. Evidence-based policy suggestions from a Sardinian study area. TeMA J. Land Use Mobility Environ. Special Issue 1/2021, 109–133 (2021). https://doi.org/10.6092/1970-9870/7411
13. Lai, S., Isola, F., Leone, F., Zoppi C.: Green Infrastructure and Regional Planning: An Operational Framework. FrancoAngeli, Milan, Italy (forthcoming)
14. Cannas, I., Lai, S., Leone, F., Zoppi, C.: Green infrastructure and ecological corridors: a regional study concerning Sardinia. Sustainability **10**(4), 1265 (2018). https://doi.org/10.3390/su10041265
15. Cannas, I., Zoppi, C.: Ecosystem services and the natura 2000 network: a study concerning a green infrastructure based on ecological corridors in the metropolitan city of Cagliari. In:

Gervasi, O., et al. (eds.) ICCSA 2017. LNCS, vol. 10409, pp. 379–400, Springer, Cham (2017). https://doi.org/10.1007/978-3-319-62407-5_27

16. AGRISTUDIO, CRITERIA, TEMI: Realizzazione del Sistema di Monitoraggio dello Stato di Conservazione degli Habitat e delle Specie di Interesse Comunitario della Regione Autonoma della Sardegna. Relazione Generale, Allegato 1b: Carta dell'Idoneità Faunistica" [Implementation of the Monitoring System Concerning the Conservation Status of Habitats and Species of Community Interest of the Autonomous Region of Sardinia. General Report, Attachment 1b: Habitat Suitability Map]. MIMEO (2011). Unpublished work

17. Burkhard, B., Kroll, F., Müller, F., Windhorst, W.: Landscapes' capacities to provide ecosystem services—a concept for land-cover based assessments. Landsc. Online **15**, 1–22 (2009). https://doi.org/10.3097/LO.200915

18. LaRue, M.A., Nielsen, C.K.: Modelling potential dispersal corridors for cougars in Midwestern North America using least-cost path methods. Ecol. Model. **212**, 372–381 (2008). https://doi.org/10.1016/j.ecolmodel.2007.10.036

19. EEA (European Environment Agency): Spatial Analysis of Green Infrastructure in Europe. EEA Technical Report no. 2/2014, Publications Office of the European Union, Luxembourg (2014). https://doi.org/10.2800/11170

20. McRae, B.H., Kavanagh, D.M.: User Guide: Linkage Pathways Tool of the Linkage Mapper Toolbox—Version 2.0—Updated October 2017 (2017). https://github.com/linkagescape/linkage-mapper/files/2204107/Linkage_Mapper_2_0_0.zip. Accessed 21 Mar 2022

21. Zoppi, C., Argiolas, M., Lai, S.: Factors influencing the value of houses: estimates for the City of Cagliari, Italy. Land Use Policy **42**, 367–380 (2015). https://doi.org/10.1016/j.landusepol.2014.08.012

22. Wolman, A.L., Couper, E.: Potential consequences of linear approximation in economics. Fed. Reserve Bank Econ. Q. **11**(1), 51–67 (2003)

23. Pilogallo, A., Scorza, F.: Ecosystem services multifunctionality: an analytical framework to support sustainable spatial planning in Italy. Sustainability **14**(6), 3346 (2022). https://doi.org/10.3390/su14063346

24. Gregory, A., Spence, E., Beier, P., Garding, E.: Toward best management practices for ecological corridors. Land **10**, 140 (2021). https://doi.org/10.3390/land10020140

25. Lai, S., Leone, F., Zoppi, C.: Policies to decrease land surface temperature based on land cover change: an assessment related to Sardinia, Italy. In: La Rosa, D., Privitera, R. (eds.) Innovation in Urban and Regional Planning—Proceedings of the 11th INPUT Conference, vol. 1, Lecture Notes in Civil Engineering (LNCI) book series no. 146, pp. 101–109. Springer International Publishing, Basilea, Svizzera (2021)

26. Santos, J.S., et al.: Delimitation of ecological corridors in the Brazilian Atlantic Forest. Ecol. Indic. **88**, 414–424 (2018). https://doi.org/10.1016/j.ecolind.2018.01.011

27. Sánchez-Montoya, M.M., Moleón, M., Sánchez-Zapata, J.A., Tockner, K.: Dry riverbeds: corridors for terrestrial vertebrates. Ecosphere **7**(10), e01508 (2016). https://doi.org/10.1002/ecs2.150

28. Lai, S., Leone, F., Zoppi, C.: Land surface temperature and land cover dynamics. A study related to Sardinia, Italy. TeMA J. Land Use Mobility Environ. **13**(3), 329–351 (2020). https://doi.org/10.6092/1970-9870/7143

29. Howley, P., Buckley, C., O'Donoghue, C., Ryan, M.: Explaining the economic 'irrationality' of farmers' land use behaviour: the role of productivist attitudes and non-pecuniary benefits. Ecol. Econ. **109**, 186–193 (2015). https://doi.org/10.1016/j.ecolecon.2014.11.015

30. Hyytiainen, K., Leppanen, J., Pahkasalo, T.: Economic analysis of field afforestation and forest clearance for cultivation in Finland. In: Proceedings of the International Congress of European Association of Agricultural Economists, Ghent, Belgium, 26–29 August 2008 (2008). https://doi.org/10.22004/ag.econ.44178

31. Kollányi, L., Máté, K.: Connectivity analysis for green infrastructure restoration planning on national level. Proc. Fábos Conf. Landsc. Greenway Plan **5**(1), 30 (2016). https://scholarwo rks.umass.edu/fabos/vol5/iss1/30. Accessed 21 Mar 2022

32. Lenoir, J., Decocq, G., Spicher, F., Gallet-Moron, E., Buridant, J., Closset-Kopp, D.: Historical continuity and spatial connectivity ensure hedgerows are effective corridors for forest plants: evidence from the species–time–area relationship. J. Veg. Sci. **32**, e12845 (2021). https://doi. org/10.1111/jvs.12845

33. Gravsholt Busck, A.: Hedgerow planting analysed as a social system—interaction between farmers and other actors in Denmark. J. Environ. Manage. **68**(2), 161–171 (2003). https://doi. org/10.1016/S0301-4797(03)00064-1

The Provision of Ecosystem Services Along the Italian Coastal Areas: A Correlation Analysis Between Environmental Quality and Urbanization

Giampiero Lombardini[1]($\boxtimes$) ⓘ, Angela Pilogallo[2] ⓘ, and Giorgia Tucci[1] ⓘ

[1] University of Genoa, dAD, Stradone Sant'Agostino 37, 16123 Genoa, Italy
{giampiero.lombardini,giorgia.tucci}@unige.it
[2] University of Basilicata, Viale dell'Ateneo Lucano 10, 85100 Potenza, Italy
angela.pilogallo@unibas.it

Abstract. Over the course of its urban history, the Italian peninsula has seen an increasing concentration of population, economic activities and urbanization processes along its coastal areas. Many of Italy's large cities and main metropolitan areas are located along the coast or retain a strong and direct connection with it. In addition, in recent decades there has been growing anthropic pressure due to increasingly intense tourist activity. The aim of this work is to investigate the relationship between overall ecosystem services' provision, assumed as a comprehensive measure of territorial environmental performances, and urbanization processes along the Italian coastal municipalities. The work started with the assessment of a selected set of ecosystem services successively combined into a synthetic index representative of the overall environmental values: the Multiple Ecosystem Services Landscape Index (MESLI). The intensity of this index was then correlated with several synthetic indicators (geographic, morphological, socio-economic and territorial indicators) descriptive of urbanization processes. The results show that more intensively urbanised areas are generally characterized by lower environmental performances. On the other hand, the variability of correlation ratios suggests that the settlement quality (shape, density...) plays an important role in depleting or protecting the overall ecosystem services provision. Equally relevant is the morphology of coastal strips, which evidently influences both settlements' morphology and ecosystem services' distribution and quality.

Keywords: Ecosystem services · Urbanization · Spatial correlation · Settlement morphology

1 Introduction

Since the 1980s, the scientific community has shared the thesis that the world has entered a new geological era, known as the Anthropocene, in which the exploitation of environmental resources, increased urbanization and the activities of human beings are significantly and irreversibly changing spatial structures, ecosystems and climate on planet

O. Gervasi et al. (Eds.): ICCSA 2022 Workshops, LNCS 13380, pp. 298–314, 2022.
https://doi.org/10.1007/978-3-031-10542-5_21

Earth, triggering a process of extinction and a new biotic transition. Human action has altered between 50 and 75% of the earth's surface to make room for cultivated fields and cities, cementing natural areas, promoting soil erosion, destroying biodiversity and polluting the atmosphere, thus dominating 90% of the earth's ecosystems. To cope with the complex global situation, EU challenges have set goals for sustainable development by promoting actions that provide ecosystem services.

In recent decades, the concept of 'ecosystem service' (EC) has become widely established because of its ability to summarize "the multiple benefits provided by ecosystems to humankind" (MEA, 2005) [1], i.e. the multiplicity of values and functions performed by the presence of natural areas within an urbanized context. The role of ecosystem services is crucial, as they directly or indirectly influence and sustain human life and well-being in terms of health, access to primary resources, livelihoods, etc.

Today, the topic of ECs is strongly intertwined with scientific research and the increasing amount of European funding for green infrastructure [2], renaturation strategies [3] or urban greening in cities [4].

In the following study, the scope of the research is the 628 Italian maritime coastal municipalities (small islands have been excluded), located along the approximately 7,914 km of national coastline, which - due to its extension and vulnerability - represents an area of high environmental risk. In the course of its urban evolution, in fact, Italy has seen a growing concentration of population, economic activities and urbanization processes along its coasts. Many of the great Italian cities, starting with the capital Rome and other large centers such as Genoa, Naples, Palermo, Messina, Venice, arise along the coast or in direct connection with it. Today, the balance of the coastal territory is labile and complex and depends on a number of morphological, natural and anthropic factors. Attention to ecosystem services therefore becomes vital in order to promote quality of life and environmental well-being, while attempting to mitigate the anthropic effect on this territory.

The Italian coasts have been affected in recent decades by a profound social and urban change. While in some areas important productive activities have been consolidated with the related industrial plants and port areas, in most of the other cases, the coastal areas have transformed into areas with a strong tourist component, with a very intense urbanization process. This double opportunity that has been created in the labor markets has led to a strong attraction of the population towards coastal areas to the detriment of inland areas. The high degree of urbanization that is on average noticeable has led to a general deterioration of the environmental qualities of coastal centers, especially those with a stronger seaside vocation. On the other hand, the strong patrimonial value recognized to the coastal areas themselves has over time increased environmental protection actions and environmental conservation policies (even if with different levels from area to area).

The work that we intend to present here starts from a synthetic analysis of the ecological qualities of the Italian coastal municipalities, evaluated through a synthetic indicator of the quality of the supply of ecosystem services – the Multiple Ecosystem Services Landscape Index (MESLI) - in order to investigate the relationship between ecosystem services' provision and urbanization processes in the municipalities of the Italian coastal strip.

2 Materials and Methods

The MESLI index is a synthetic indicator relevant to the joint supply of multiple SEs and significant of the environmental performance of different ecosystems. It is therefore both representative of the number of ES provided and of their intensity. The value of this indicator, detected on the basis of the most recent land use map created as part of the Corine-Copernicus project, containing a spatially detailed analysis of the ecosystemic qualities of the Italian coastal territory.

The methodology used provides a spatially continuous distribution of the MESLI index, resulting in a raster that maintains the same resolution as the Corine Land Cover, CLC (100 m). Once this analysis was carried out, we moved to a correlation analysis between the quality of the MESLI indicator and other synthetic indicators (at the municipal level) that are able to represent the urbanization process: morphology of the settlement (calculated through shape indicators), intensity of urbanization (ratio between artificial surfaces and natural areas), population density, income per capita. Another group of indicators was then summarized through some indicators that represent the level and intensity of the protection policies of natural areas, the morphology of the territory, the quality of the landscape, the presence and quality of territorial assets. Once these indicators were collected, we moved to spatial correlation analysis to evaluate the possible relationships between the quality of ecosystem services and the urbanization process. Generally speaking, the more urbanized areas are inversely correlated to those where the MESLI indicator is lower, but this does not always happen, and this is an indication of how the quality of urbanization (shape, density, etc.) play an important role. Another relevant element is the relationship between the morphology of the coastal territory (coastal plains, coastal hills or mountains) which evidently affects both the forms of the settlement and the distribution and quality of the SEs.

The methodology used is therefore articulated in the following three steps: the capacity assessment to provide ecosystem services through MESLI Index [5] assumed as the dependent variable; the dataset building related to the selected predictive factors; the correlation analyses whose outcomes are presented in Sect. 3.

2.1 The Assessment of Ecosystem Services Provision

The approach of multifunctionality, to be intended as the ability to jointly provide multiple ecosystem services, is becoming consolidated in urban and territorial planning practice as it is capable of expressing an overall measure of environmental performance provided by a territorial area [6].

The main hypothesis of this work is that assessing multifunctionality by means of a synthetic index can be an innovative and integrated way to deepen the link between the ensemble of environmental values expressed by a territorial unit, and factors representing the intensity and characteristics of urbanization processes.

In the multitude of approaches and conceptualizations that characterize the scientific literature on multifunctionality [7], we refer to the framework proposed by Holting et al. [8, 9] who define abundance as one of the three dimensions of multifunctionality. In particular, we assume the MESLI index as a measure of the intensity of joint supply of multiple ecosystem services. Selected as being simultaneously relevant for both the number of ES provided and their intensity [10] and robust regardless of the used spatial scale [11], it constitutes a synthetic index based on the sum of the standardized ES indicators [12]. The comparison and overall measurement of multiple ES biophysical assessments always entails the need to normalize non-comparable quantities. On the basis of "proximity-to-target" methodology, this index performs a normalization with respect to the minimum "low performance benchmark" and maximum "target" values.

In the present work, we assigned them on the basis of the minimum and maximum values assumed by each ecosystem service considering the historical series that includes all dates for which a CLC map is available (2000–2006–2012–2018).

Considering the Italian territory as a reference area, we selected ten indicators of ecosystem services considered most significant. According to the Common International Classification (CICES v5.1) [13], this set belongs to 5 classes ("Regulation of chemical composition of atmosphere", "Pollination", "Maintaining nursery populations and habitats", "Control of erosion rates", "Regulation of the chemical condition of freshwaters") for Regulation & Maintenance ecosystem services, and 2 classes ("Cultivated terrestrial plants grown for nutritional purposes", "Ground water for drinking") for Provisioning ecosystem services.

For details about the models, informative layers and basic assumptions considered for mapping each ecosystem service, please refer to the published work [13–15].

The result is a raster information layer (Fig. 1) with a resolution of 100 m (equal to the pixel size of Corine Land Cover maps) depicting a measure of overall environmental quality by means of values ranging between 0 and 6.

As can be seen, the highest values are distributed along the main Italian mountain chains, which are characterized by mostly forested and highly vegetated land covers, low anthropic pressure and geomorphological factors that have contributed to limiting the development of human settlements and the spread of urbanization processes.

On the other hand, the lowest values characterize the Po Valley and the Southern part of Sicily Island where a highly fragmented settlement and production system, the massive adoption of intensive cultivation practices and the high density of road infrastructure contribute with different weights to determine low environmental performance [16–18].

As far as coastal areas are concerned, the overall picture shows a high variability of MESLI values that tends to reward the Tyrrhenian side and, to a lower extent, the Apulian peninsula. A not-negligible variability is observed also in function of urbanization intensity: correspondences in fact emerge between areas characterized by medium-low values and the main coastal metropolitan cities.

Precisely in order to interpret more specifically the MESLI variability along the coastal strips, index values were spatially aggregated at the municipal scale. This statistical spatial analysis allowed the Italian coastal municipalities to be classified on the basis of the MESLI index mean value (Fig. 2).

The ultimate goal is to obtain a dependent variable to be studied through correlation analysis, with geographic, morphological, socio-economic and territorial factors descriptive of urbanization processes.

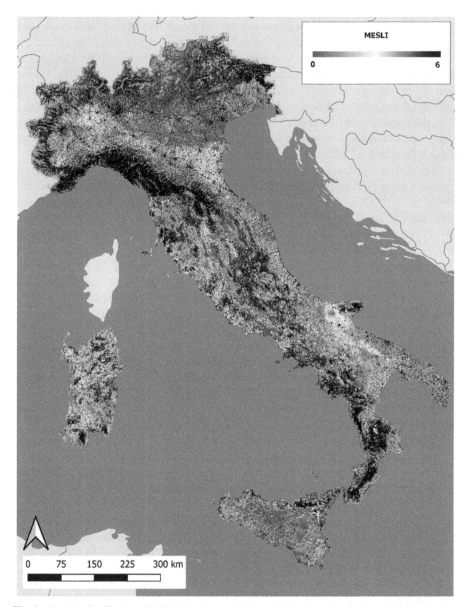

Fig. 1. Spatial distribution of MESLI index to 2018. In black, the urbanized areas related to the same year.

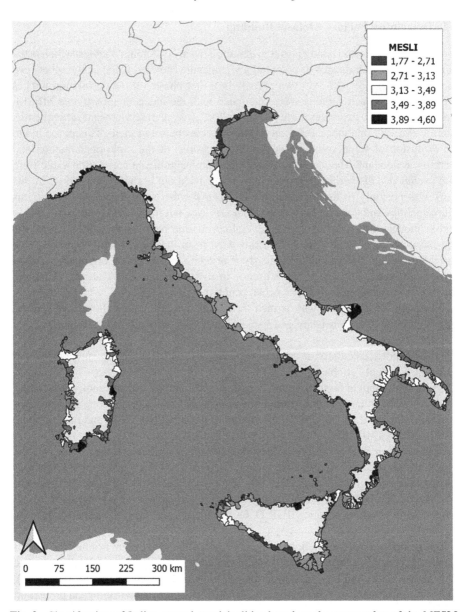

Fig. 2. Classification of Italian coastal municipalities based on the mean value of the MESLI index.

2.2 Descriptive Factors' Dataset Building

The work was started by taking into consideration twenty different variables, which in the literature had been indicated as potentially significant. The correlation analysis between the variables was divided into two phases. In a first phase, all the correlation indices (Pearson's P) of each variable were calculated with the independent variable MESLI, which synthetically expresses the level of supply of ecosystem services and subsequently, later, to evaluate this index between all the variables between them. This phase led to the exclusion of some variables as proxy expressions of the same phenomenon and therefore redundant. The variables that showed an insignificant correlation value were also excluded. This verification procedure was carried out because the purpose of this work was not only to find correlations between the urbanization rate of the various Municipalities and the supply of ecosystem services, but it was also (and above all) to find a "model" that could express a general correlation between the MESLI indicator and the most significant variables. In this way, from the initial twenty variables, the variables relating to social phenomena (type of demographic curve, population growth rate), environmental (such as the presence of hydrogeological risk areas), economic (income level, economic profile of urban centers).

Once the MESLI index was defined for all 628 coastal municipalities case studies, a table was drawn up consisting of 13 selected variables divided into 5 categories:

- **MESLI index,** calculated as described in Sect. 2.1 (which is subsequently considered the independent variable);
- **Geomorphological factors,** summarize the main geographical and geological connotations of the municipalities through the indices that represent the roughness (roughness) of the territory (ROUGH), the energy of the relief (RELIEF) and the territorial morphology (MORPHO);
- **Urbanization and population factors,** highlight the demographic trend and the urbanization process affecting the coastal municipalities through the indices that represent the demographic trend (DEMO), the territorial density (DENS), the degree of urbanization (D_URB), the of occupation of the houses (in turn expression of the level of the tourism sector) (BUILD_OCC), the average age of the building stock (BUILD_AGE);
- **Environmental factors**, define the characteristics linked to the environmental-natural heritage present on the coastal territory through the indices that represent the presence of natural areas and the value in terms of biodiversity of the territory (ENV_BIO), the incidence of natural surfaces (ENV_NAT); the degree of environmental protection (ENV_PROT);
- **Economic factors**, indicate the main characteristics of the economic sector, specifically the tourism sector and the quality of services through the indices that represent the weight of the tourist accommodation facilities (TOUR), the presence of cultural assets (HERIT).

In particular:

- ROUGHNESS (**ROUGH**) is the variable that expresses the degree of natural roughness of the soil which varies from a very low value (close to zero) for mainly flat territories, up to a maximum value of 12 for those areas characterized by continuous slope variations: it was calculated through the geomorphological analysis algorithm which systematizes the 40×40 meter cells of the DTM of the territory of each Municipality; it is calculated on the basis of data updated to 2018 from satellite surveys;
- RELIEF ENERGY (**RELIEF**) is the variable that is the expression of the difference between the minimum altitude above sea level of the Municipality territory (normally equal to zero) and the maximum altitude; it is calculated on the basis of data updated to 2018 from satellite surveys and DTM;
- the **MORPHO** variable represents the geomorphology of the soil: it is a variable with ordinal values and helps to define the type of coastal landscape that characterizes the territory (plain, coastal hills, coastal mountains, etc.);
- the **DEMO** variable is the coefficient that expresses the demographic growth or decrease rate of the resident population of coastal Municipalities; it was calculated by comparing the resident population in each municipality in 1951 and the resident population in 2020;
- DENSITY (**DENS**) is the coefficient that measures the number of inhabitants per square kilometer (inhab/km^2); the value is obtained by dividing the number of inhabitants of the municipal area by the surface of the area itself. It is calculated on the basis of data relating to the number of inhabitants updated to 2020;
- URBANIZED AREA (**D_URB**) indicates the quantity of occupied land / built surface and represents the degree of urbanization of the territory. The value is obtained as the ratio between the first five categories of the CORINE legend and the surface of the total territory of each Municipality. It is calculated on the basis of CORINE data updated to 2018 (Copernicus Project);
- the OCCUPIED BUILDINGS variable (**BUILD_OCC**) is the ratio of occupied to unoccupied dwellings within each municipality; it is therefore the variable that measures the incidence of the tourist phenomenon in its physical manifestation (this is because in areas with a strong tourist vocation many settlements are occupied by seasonal and non-permanent residents) and is calculated on the basis of data updated to 2018;
- the **BUILD_AGE** variable is the data calculated as a ratio that relates the share of buildings built in an era prior to 1945 and those built after that year: it therefore represents the level of urbanization intensity recorded since the post-war period to date (very variable in individual territorial contexts): the variable is calculated on the basis of data updated to 2018;
- NATURAL AREAS (**ENV_BIO**) indicate the quantity of natural spaces recognized as such by the European Directive Nature 2000 and include sites of naturalistic interest with particular biodiversity values. It is calculated on the basis of the official Natura 2000 site map;
- the variable **ENV_NAT** is an environmental indicator that considers the level of naturalness of the territory of each Municipality; the variable is taken from the CORINE land cover map, considering the first 5 classes of the classification;

- the variable **ENV_PROT** was calculated as a percentage of the area with the identification of specific environmental protection actions within each municipality added to the protected areas by law (i.e. the quantity of spaces subject to landscape and protection restrictions ecological); the variable was calculated on the basis of the data provided by the National Cartographic Portal of the EUAP areas;
- the **TOUR** variable, is a complex indicator that associates the incidence of available "touristic beds" at the level of tourist accommodation with certified certification of cultural quality. The beds, in particular, indicate the capacity of the accommodation establishments in the Municipality, i.e. the quantity of beds registered in the hotel structures, in the non-hotel structures (campsites, tourist villages, mixed forms of campsites and tourist villages, rental accommodation managed in an entrepreneurial form, agro-tourist accommodation, youth hostels, holiday homes, mountain huts), bed and breakfasts and private accommodation. The data are collected by Istat at a national level annually. The data entered in the table were extrapolated from the Istat reports "Capacity of reception exercises" of the year 2020;
- the **HERIT** variable is a complex indicator that expresses the amount of cultural, artistic, historical, architectural heritage recognized in the municipal area, that is, the Municipalities characterized by the presence of at least one Unesco site, or a village certified by the "One of Most beautiful villages in Italy", or Orange Flags of the Touring Club Association, or that insist in a National Park, or that have been the Capital of Culture, or with at least 10.000 visitors a year to a museum, a monument or a site archaeological, state or non-state, as well as being recognized as a BLUE FLAG (which is the data relating to the certification of the environmental quality of beaches in coastal locations, recognized all over the world, as a valid eco-label relating to sustainable tourism in seaside and lake tourist locations).

2.3   The Correlation Analyses

In a second phase, we proceeded with the construction of a correlation matrix between the 13 significant variables and the MESLI variable as the guiding variable. The results of this analysis are shown in the correlation table (Fig. 3) and show an overall significant level of correlation. In particular, the variables that express the degree of naturalness and protection of the environment and biodiversity are positively correlated with the MESLI index, while urbanization and other variables that somehow measure the nature of the urban phenomenon have assumed values of negative correlation.

The correlation analysis performed did not take into consideration the potential effect of spatial self-correlation, since for the type of variables selected and for the spatial distribution (linear type) of the 628 analysis cases, this influence was not considered significant. In any case, a first simple observation of the spatial distribution of some variables highlights how the recognition of the areas with greater environmental protection (variables ENV_PROT and HERIT) is positively correlated with the MESLI index: that is, it occurs that in the areas where policies are already implemented of environmental protection and enhancement, the production of ecosystem services is on average much better, and this regardless of the degree of urbanization (at least within certain limits).

The second phase of this correlation analysis then concentrated on the construction general correlation equation. This exercise was possible through an estimate of the correlation parameters which led to a further selection of variables, excluding the less significant ones and those that still had local correlation residues. The model results are contained in the Table 1 below.

	MESLI	ROUGH	RELIEF	MORPHO	DEMO	DENS	D_URB
MESLI	1	0,39	0,45	-0,26	-0,07	-0,32	-0,38
ROUGH	0,39	1	0,70	-0,57	-0,16	-0,06	-0,06
RELIEF	0,45	0,70	1	-0,58	-0,17	-0,14	-0,21
MORPHO	-0,26	-0,57	-0,58	1	0,12	0,03	0,06
DEMO	-0,07	-0,16	-0,17	0,12	1	0,09	0,15
DENS	-0,32	-0,06	-0,14	0,03	0,09	1	0,77
D_URB	-0,38	-0,06	-0,21	0,06	0,15	0,77	1
BUILD_OCC	-0,18	-0,14	-0,08	0,17	0,10	0,34	0,24
BUILD_AGE	0,24	0,43	0,26	-0,24	-0,19	0,19	0,10
ENV_BIO	-0,12	0,18	-0,06	-0,03	-0,03	0,09	0,16
ENV_PROT	0,23	0,38	0,24	-0,07	-0,09	-0,04	-0,08
HERIT	0,02	0,15	-0,10	0,13	-0,02	0,20	0,27
TOUR	0,03	-0,06	-0,10	0,07	-0,03	-0,12	-0,05
ENV_NAT	0,57	0,75	0,69	-0,48	-0,13	-0,17	-0,22

	BUILD_OCC	BUILD_AGE	ENV_BIO	ENV_PROT	HERIT	TOUR	ENV_NAT
MESLI	-0,18	0,24	-0,12	0,23	0,02	0,03	0,57
ROUGH	-0,14	0,43	0,18	0,38	0,15	-0,06	0,75
RELIEF	-0,08	0,26	-0,06	0,24	-0,10	-0,10	0,69
MORPHO	0,17	-0,24	-0,03	-0,07	0,13	0,07	-0,48
DEMO	0,10	-0,19	-0,03	-0,09	-0,02	-0,03	-0,13
DENS	0,34	0,19	0,09	-0,04	0,20	-0,12	-0,17
D_URB	0,24	0,10	0,16	-0,08	0,27	-0,05	-0,22
BUILD_OCC	1	0,10	-0,03	-0,01	-0,10	-0,39	-0,20
BUILD_AGE	0,10	1	0,03	0,16	0,15	-0,11	0,29
ENV_BIO	-0,03	0,03	1	0,13	0,18	0,03	0,02
ENV_PROT	-0,01	0,16	0,13	1	0,25	0,11	0,33
HERIT	-0,10	0,15	0,18	0,25	1	0,19	0,17
TOUR	-0,39	-0,11	0,03	0,11	0,19	1	0,08
ENV_NAT	-0,20	0,29	0,02	0,33	0,17	0,08	1

Fig. 3. The correction matrix of the 13 selected variables.

This equation was obtained with the WLS method which is a generalization of the OLS method, ien which each observation is assigned a different weight based on its variance. In this way, however, the model, by construction, is homoscedastic (with constant variation). The main descriptive statistics of this model are those shown in the following Table 2:

Table 1. Model estimation of selected variables (*90%; ** 95%; *** 99%).

Variable		Coefficient	St error	T value	p-value	Significance level	
Constant		2,70060	0,0720646	37,47	2,42e-161	***	
BUILD_AGE	0,00219784	0,000620497		3,542	0,0004	***	
ROUGH	− 0,0939089	0,0235140		− 3,994	0,0004	***	
ENV_NAT	0,00949767	0,000879793		10,80	5,20e-25	***	
l_RELIEF	0,0874246	0,0159386		5,485	6,03e-08	***	
D_URB	− 0,00802733	0,000674949		− 11,89	1,60e-29	***	
Sq ROUGH	0,00641952	0,00201655		3,183	0,0015	***	

Table 2. Descriptive statistics of the model.

Residual sum of squares	2380,571	S.E. of regression	1,961
R-Square	0,519	R-Squared adjusted	0,514
F (6, 619)	111,512	P-Value	4,17e-95
Log-Likehood	− 1306,344	Akaike criteria	2626,688
Schwartz Criteria	2657,763	Hannan-Quinn	2638,762

3   Results and Discussions

The estimate model thus elaborated led to the conclusion that the MESLI index is conditioned on the one hand by the urbanization rate (which can be interpreted as a combination
of the urbanized surface and the share of natural areas within each Municipality) and by
the other from some morphological characteristics of the soil, in particular the roughness
and the energy of the relief. This result can be interpreted as the fact that different coastal
morphological typologies have, in the absence of urbanization, different potentialities
in terms of production of ecosystem services. These diversified initial conditions are
then altered in a more or less intensive way by the rate of urbanization and by the forms
of the built territory. In some environmental contexts (mainly the very "rough" coastal
mountain) urbanization is in turn conditioned by the initial orographic conditions, so it
tends to take on more compact forms, with less occupancy of built-up land. This further strengthens the trend recorded by the model of a correlation between production of
ecosystem services and urbanization.

The model developed also allows for some interesting spatial evaluations. In fact, the Municipalities that are characterized by a greater supply of ecosystem services are distributed along the Italian coasts in different ways. The coastal regions where the greatest ecosystem capacities are concentrated are in fact located along all the coasts of Sardinia, along the northern coasts of the Tyrrhenian Sea (Ligurian Sea), south of Naples (Cilento) and then in Calabria and Puglia and finally along the coasts northern Sicily. These spatial differences are rather independent of the level of urbanization reached in the different places but are strongly correlated instead with the measures and actions of environmental protection and with the cultural recognition of the most valuable coastal landscapes which has also allowed a certain conservation of the ecosystem potential.

Another interesting element is the rather evident correlation between the MESLI indicator and the type of geomorphological structure of the coastal areas. Municipalities that arise in mountain or coastal hill situations, as well as coastal natural areas such as lagoons and river mouths is another element that proves favorable to the supply of ecosystem services and, conversely, limiting the urbanization process.

The model also makes it possible to interpret the statistical significance of the correlations existing between the MESLI indicator and the other variables. The following graphs show the plot of the values of the MESLI index with each of the most significant variables, where linear correlation functions are recorded for the variables that refer to urbanization, to the conditions of the natural environment (biodiversity) and at the time of construction of the buildings. The correlation between the MESLI index and the morphological variable of the roughness is of the polynomial type and that with the variable energy of the relief (RELIEF) is of the logarithmic type. This means that the relationship between the production of ecosystem services and the morphology of the land is never linear but follows other more complex, but no less robust behavioral laws.

The estimated relationship between the MESLI index and the degree of urbanization reveals not only the fairly predictable circumstance that where the higher the urbanization rate and the lower the ecosystem services produced, but more specifically that there are different urbanization situations that affect different way on the production of ecosystem services. These situations can probably be traced back to general climatic factors and to the different settlement morphologies (degree of compactness of the settlements, presence of low-density housing areas, degree of connectivity of the settlement network, fragmentation conditions of the urban fabric, configurational aspects of the settlement model). The study carried out shows that it would be interesting to investigate the potentially existing relationships between the urban form and the production of ecosystem services. In fact, a part or similarity of urban form probably corresponds to similar performances also in terms of production of ecosystem services.

The following graphs show the estimate of the correlation functions between the various significant variables in the model (Fig. 4, variables relating to urbanization processes and the environment; Fig. 5, variables relating to the morphology of the sites).

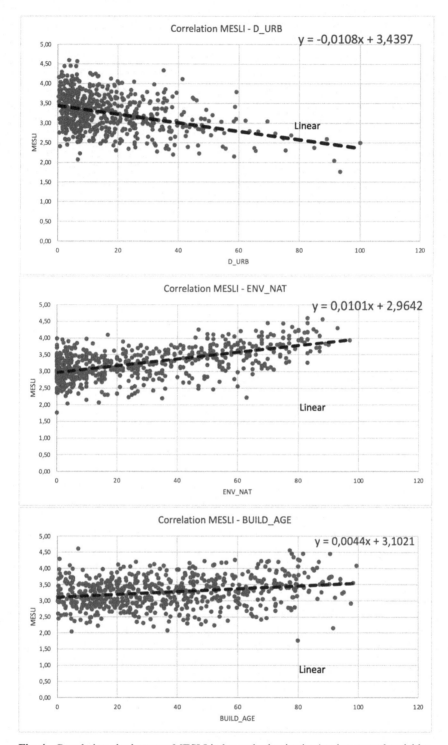

Fig. 4. Correlation plot between MESLI index and urbanization/environmental variables.

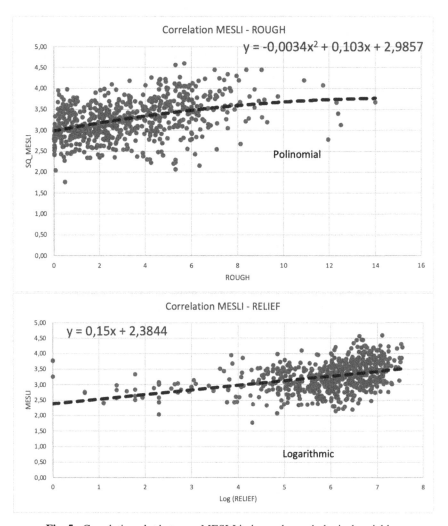

Fig. 5. Correlation plot between MESLI index and morphological variables.

As a last consideration, we can take a look at the spatial distribution of the MESLI values in relation to the urbanization indicators, which shows a negative correlation sign (Fig. 6). There are coastal regions where, notwithstanding even average high levels of urbanization, there is still a good (in some cases) very good production of ecosystem services (this is the case of Liguria, some areas of Sardinia and northern Sicily). In other cases, however, the production of ecosystem services is lower even in the presence of weak urbanization processes. This situation highlights how other factors, not so closely linked to urbanization, contribute to define good performance in the production of ecosystem services. The role played by morphology and general environmental conditions emerges (widespread presence or not of wooded areas, types of plant cover, exposure, climatic and micro-climatic factors).

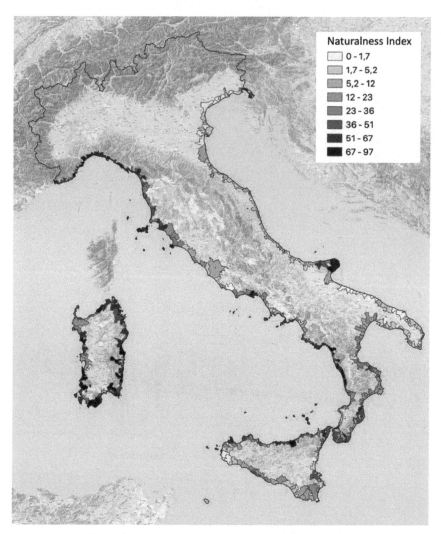

Fig. 6. Degree of naturality in the Italian Coastal Municipalities.

4   Conclusions

The research conducted led to focus on the conditions in the supply of ecosystem services in a very specific area: that of coastal areas. The results produced started from the hypothesis that an inverse (but not linear) correlation could exist between the degree of urbanization and the production of ecosystem services. In order to try to grasp other potential correlations, the field of observation has also been extended to geomorphological, socio-economic variables (trying to produce proxy variables that effectively describe the process of strong tourist activity that interests most of the coastal municipalities Finally, indicators were also considered that represented a first approximation of the heritage values of the territory, expressed through the recognition of the areas subject to environmental protection (together with other variables relating to the level of presence of historical values).

The results led to the conclusion that there is a significant level of correlation not only between the MESLI index (used to obtain a spatial synthesis of the level of production of ecosystem services) and the main urbanization indicators, but that there is also a set of variables that they refer to the geomorphological conditions that express an effective synthesis between the potentialities in the production of ecosystem services and the conditioning to urbanization processes.

The study presented here can only be an initial work that must be verified and deepened with furthermore specific studies. It confirms the findings of previous studies [19] about the interest in considering the relationship between the production of ecosystem services and forms of the urbanized territory (compactness, density, fragmentation, uses).

References

1. Millennium Ecosystem Assessment (MEA): Ecosystems and Human Well-Being: Biodiversity Synthesis. World Resources Institute, Washington (2005)
2. Moretti, B., Tucci, G.: A Landscape Infra-structure Research. Roma Tuscolana Pilot Project. ListLab, Trento (2022)
3. Sdino, L., Rosasco, P., Lombardini, G.: The evaluation of urban regeneration processes. In: Della Torre, S., Cattaneo, S., Lenzi, C., Zanelli, A. (eds.) Regeneration of the Built Environment from a Circular Economy Perspective Research for Development, pp. 47–57. Springer, Cham (2020). https://doi.org/10.1007/978-3-030-33256-3_6
4. Sabbion, P., Tucci, G.: City Greening, il mutamento del paesaggio urbano tra estetica e salubrità. Ri-Vista Res. Landsc. Des. 15(1), 32–45 (2017). https://issuu.com/dida-unifi/docs/ri-vista_01_2017
5. Rodríguez-Loinaz, G., Alday, J.G., Onaindia, M.: Multiple ecosystem services landscape index: A tool for multifunctional landscapes conservation. J. Environ. Manage. 147, 152–163 (2015). https://doi.org/10.1016/j.jenvman.2014.09.001
6. Pilogallo, A., Scorza, F.: Ecosystem services multifunctionality: an analytical framework to support sustainable spatial planning in Italy. Sustainability, 14, 3346 (2022).https://doi.org/10.3390/su14063346
7. Mastrangelo, M.E., Weyland, F., Villarino, S.H., Barral, M.P., Nahuelhual, L., Laterra, P.: Concepts and methods for landscape multifunctionality and a unifying framework based on ecosystem services. Landsc. Ecol. 29(2), 345–358 (2013). https://doi.org/10.1007/s10980-013-9959-9
8. Hölting, L., Beckmann, M., Volk, M., Cord, A.F.: Multifunctionality assessments – more than assessing multiple ecosystem functions and services? A quantitative literature review. Ecol. Indic. 103, 226–235 (2019). https://doi.org/10.1016/J.ECOLIND.2019.04.009
9. Hölting, L., et al.: Measuring ecosystem multifunctionality across scales. Environ. Res. Lett. 14 (2019). https://doi.org/10.1088/1748-9326/AB5CCB
10. Stürck, J., Verburg, P.H.: Multifunctionality at what scale? A landscape multifunctionality assessment for the European Union under conditions of land use change. Landsc. Ecol. 32(3), 481–500 (2016). https://doi.org/10.1007/s10980-016-0459-6
11. Shen, J., Li, S., Liang, Z., Liu, L., Li, D., Wu, S.: Exploring the heterogeneity and nonlinearity of trade-offs and synergies among ecosystem services bundles in the Beijing-Tianjin-Hebei urban agglomeration. Ecosyst. Serv. 43, 101103 (2020). https://doi.org/10.1016/j.ecoser.2020.101103

12. Haines-Young, R., Potschin, M.: Common International Classification of Ecosystem Services (CICES) V5.1 Guidance on the Application of the Revised Structure. (2018)
13. Pilogallo, A., Scorza, F.: Regulation and maintenance ecosystem services (ReMES): a spatial assessment in the Basilicata region (Southern Italy). In: Gervasi, O., et al. (eds.) ICCSA 2021. LNCS, vol. 12955, pp. 703–716. Springer, Cham (2021). https://doi.org/10.1007/978-3-030-87007-2_50
14. Pilogallo, A., Scorza, F.: Mapping regulation ecosystem services (ReMES) specialization in Italy. J. Urban Plan. Dev. **148**, 04021072 (2021)https://doi.org/10.1061/(ASCE)UP.1943-5444.0000801
15. Pilogallo, A., Scorza, F., Murgante, B.: An ecosystem services-based territorial ranking for Italian provinces. In: Gervasi, O., et al. (eds.) ICCSA 2021. LNCS, vol. 12955, pp. 692–702. Springer, Cham (2021). https://doi.org/10.1007/978-3-030-87007-2_49
16. Murgante, B., Balletto, G., Borruso, G., Saganeiti, L., Scorza, F., Pilogallo, A., Dettori, M., Castiglia, P.: Health hazard scenarios in Italy after the COVID-19 outbreak: a methodological proposal. Sci. Reg. **20**, 327–354 (2021). https://doi.org/10.14650/101721
17. Murgante, B., Balletto, G., Borruso, G., Saganeiti, L., Pilogallo, A., Scorza, F., Castiglia, P., Arghittu, A.: A methodological proposal to evaluate the health hazard scenario from COVID-19 in Italy. Environ. Res. **209**, 112873 (2022)
18. Romano, B., Zullo, F.: Half a century of urbanization in southern European lowlands: a study on the Po valley (Northern Italy). Urban Res. Pract. **9**, 109–130 (2016). https://doi.org/10.1080/17535069.2015.1077885
19. Lai, S., Lombardini, G.: Regional drivers of land take: a comparative analysis in two Italian regions. Land Use Pol. **56**, 262–273 (2016). https://doi.org/10.1016/j.landusepol.2016.05.003

Multiscale Planning Approach in the Analysis and Proposition of Ecosystem Services

Camila Fernandes de Morais[iD], Tiago Augusto Gonçalves Mello[iD], and Ana Clara Mourão Moura[(⊠)] [iD]

Escola de Arquitetura, Laboratório de Geoprocessamento, Universidade Federal de Minas Gerais (UFMG), Rua Paraíba 697, Belo Horizonte, Brazil
anaclara@ufmg.br

Abstract. In the Brazilian context, urban regulations prioritize built environment guidelines over the management – in terms of conservation, creation and optimization – of open green areas. Based on the characterization, analysis, and proposition of possible strategies, this paper discusses the importance and the usage potentialities of the vegetation cover in cities, as well as the repercussions of its absence. The study considered three landscape planning scales (regional, urban, and local) in order to comprehend their relation, and to present possibilities for the enhancement of environmental quality from a large to a day-to-day perspective. The investigation results in a summary of green-sensitive design strategies, as well as in urban instruments, interventions, and parameters at the local scale; all likely to improve urban characteristics regarding green infrastructure.

Keywords: Urban green areas · Green infrastructure · Urban and environmental planning

1 Introduction

The identification and the management of the Ecosystem Services (ES) are few of the greatest challenges in contemporary urban planning [1]. The ES correspond to the functions, processes, and benefits related to ecological resources. They are essential to human well-being, to productive regimes, and for climate regulation [2]. To deal with collateral effects of urban growth and protect ecological resources, systemic evaluations, coordinated efforts, and tangible measures are demanded [3]. Hence, biodiversity richness can be assessed in cities, since it can provide a great range of opportunities, and services [4].

Another fundamental concept is known as Green Infrastructure (GI), and regards the vegetation cover – especially in the urban context. It comes from a holistic perspective of the landscape elements, based on landscape ecology principles, such as structure, function, and change [5]. GI consists in the connection of permeable and multifunctional vegetated fragments – preferably arboreal, that restructures the landscape mosaic. It allows the maintenance or restoration of natural and cultural processes, and the achievement of a dynamic, sustainable and resilient balance of the urban ecosystem [6–8].

O. Gervasi et al. (Eds.): ICCSA 2022 Workshops, LNCS 13380, pp. 315–327, 2022.
https://doi.org/10.1007/978-3-031-10542-5_22

However, it needs to be critically planned, implemented, and monitored. Effective planning depends on a systemic, and transdisciplinary approach, based on the consideration of abiotic, biotic, and cultural aspects and conditions of the place [9].

The concept can also be applied at different scales. At the private scale (individual urban lots), it occurs as the green-design strategies, such as green roofs, gardens, rainwater retention etc.; At the local scale (neighborhoods), as road afforestation of roadsides, rain gardens etc.; at the urban scale (municipality), through ecological corridors that connect existent parks or rainwater-related structures, draining paving; And at the regional scale (landscape and territories), with the conservation and maintenance of forests and other ecological elements [8, 10].

In terms of planning, the landscapes of the Brazilian cities are limited to morphometric guidelines, such as Floor Area Ratio, Maximum Heights, Setbacks and Land Use Ratio[1] [11]. From the beginning of the 20th Century, the Brazilian urban parameterization associated with land zoning has been used as the main planning instruments [12]. What is done in a segmented, individual way at the lot scale, constitutes the urban landscape as it is reproduced all over the cities. This process generates massified and meaningless landscapes [13]. Beyond that, the urban legal instruments created in big cities are remarkably copied to smaller places, with few or no adaptation to the local specificities. Since generally there is a lack of regulations that consider environmental-related aspects even in metropolises, it can be said that, ultimately, green areas are not considered in planning strategies.

The private sector maximizes the occupation of urban settlements. These actions, associated with the neglect of the environmental quality at the urban scape, the lack of monitoring, and the low government budget destined to the creation, conservation and qualification of open green areas, enhance the situation [14].

In this sense, this paper argues about the importance of the creation and adequate distribution of green areas in the Brazilian urban context, which can result in more resilient, equilibrated and qualified spaces. The improvement of the urban normative linked to urban development, and the consideration of the existence of functional typologies and providers of ES are, then, essential. The aim of the investigation was to discuss the importance of the vegetation cover in urban landscapes based on the characterization, analysis, and proposition of green strategies, by considering its usage potentialities at different planning scales.

2 Methodology

The conceptual approach of the study is aligned with the UN's Sustainable Development Goals (SDGs), especially the SDGs 6, 13, 14, 15 – related to the biosphere (regarding land and water ecosystems, hydrology and climate systems); and the SDGs 11 and 17, related to sustainable cities and partnerships. Those are goals objectively linked to environmental quality enhancement, carbon sequestration, and the promotion of green areas. At the regional scale, the concept is addressed in a broad perspective, and the main goal is to enhance environmental quality in general. At the urban and local scales,

---

[1] Known as Utilization Coefficient in literal translation, it is a Brazilian building guideline that limits the constructed area to the area of the urban lot in which it will be settled.

the chosen concept regards ecological, landscape, and recreational processes, aiming at the aesthetic, functional and environmental quality of the open green spaces.

The methodology is supported by a contemporary trend of planning, that parts from the macroscale – from a context analysis, to the main object of study. Although the database used, and consequently the results achieved, present different temporal-spatial cutouts, the articulation of these landscape[2] scales is relevant since each of them is related to specific planning mechanisms and attributes.

The case study areas are placed in the Minas Gerais State, Brazil. It starts in from Iron Quadrangle region (regional scale approach), passes through Belo Horizonte city (urban scale), and finally gets to the Centro-Sul administrative unit (local scale) (Fig. 1). In this paper, the study is presented briefly, and the third step – which consists in the local scale investigations, is highlighted, due to the proposed strategies related to ES.

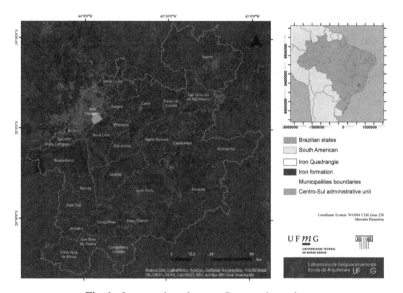

Fig. 1. Iron quadrangle area. Source: the authors.

The Iron Quadrangle is extremely expressive in terms of environmental quality, and is characterized by the presence of physical, cultural, and natural resources – such as geological and geomorphological features, hydrological potential, paleontological and historical sites etc. Classified as Special Biological Importance Area [15], the region is considered a priority in terms of biodiversity conservation in Minas Gerais State. The local attributes of its forests and natural fields are relevant for the protection of the wild life, especially the endemic species – rare and endangered [16].

Belo Horizonte city is the capital of the Minas Gerais State and one of the biggest metropolises in Brazil. In general, the largest cities' decisions in terms of planning tend to impact smaller settlements guidelines [13]. In this sense, studying this area is strategically

---

[2] In this study, landscape is understood as the result of human and natural interactions; where cultural expressions are produced.

interesting in terms of technical repercussions. Moreover, the comprehension of the urban environment is essential for local scale propositions.

The Belo Horizonte's Centro-Sul Administrative Unit is the sector of the city with the most evident integration with the Iron Quadrangle landscape. Beyond that, it was a methodological strategy to propose green parameters for a context already consolidated in terms of human transformation, as it has the potential of being placed as a reference for other studies in Brazil.

The goal was to propose ecosystems services (instruments, parameters and design interventions) to the study area, considering some SDG (Sustainable Development Goals) and working in multiscale approach (Fig. 2).

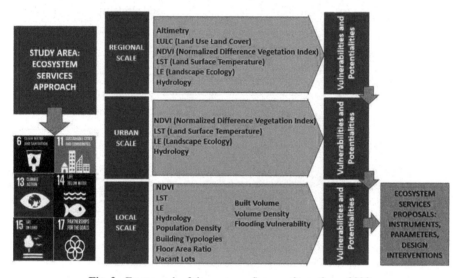

Fig. 2. Framework of the process. Source: the authors, 2022.

The dataset used at the environmental analysis was related to natural and human aspects and their correlation. To select the variables, principles of potentialities, cultural values and conflicts of interests were considered, since those processes interfere and reproduce in the territory dynamics. In all landscape scales the following information were studied: green cover (NDVI and Landscape Ecology metrics); biomes, protected areas, land use and land cover, hydrology (drainage density, rainwater recharge potential, hydrological importance, and watercourse typologies); land surface temperature; topography; slope; etc. At the local scale only, considering the proposition phase of the investigation, social aspects such as population density, built volume, risks and vulnerabilities etc. were also analyzed. The map set produced did not always follow the color ramp standards commonly adopted in cartography, because it was a methodological choice to use contrasting chromatic patterns to favor the reading of colorblind users (Fig. 3).

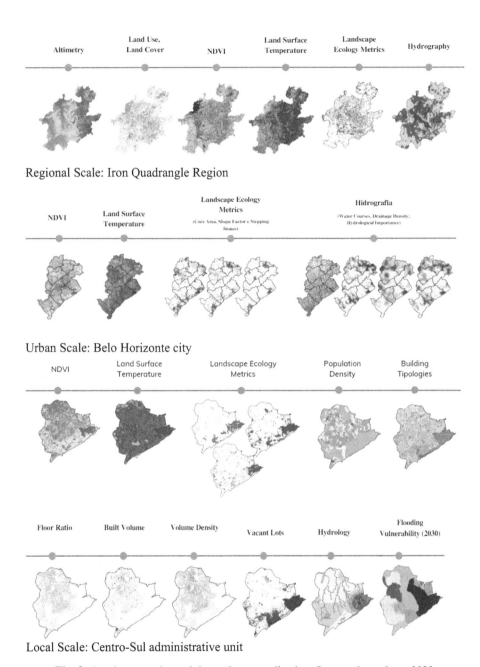

Fig. 3. Landscape scales and the study map collection. Source: the authors, 2022.

The characterization of the vegetation cover was held by calculating NDVI with Landsat-8 v.2's red (B4) and near infrared (B5) registers for 2014 and 2020 scenarios. The Landscape Ecology metrics applied were Core Area, Shape Factor, and Stepping Stones, aiming at the evaluation of the green fragments in terms of dimensions, density, isolation, distance, connectivity and shape complexity. Both analyses were conducted critically in order to comprehend spatial patterns and recurrent dynamics, since it conditions ecological processes. The main goal was to identify the better conditions to create, increase or conserve green areas at the regional and urban scales [17].

The physical conditions, such as topography, slope and biomes, were investigated with the objective to comprehend their correlation and how they condition or interfere on regional and urban dynamics, i.e., natural limits to urban sprawl; remarkable elements of the landscape; etc. Land use and land cover were analyzed to identify land conflicts in areas of environmental importance. Land Surface Temperature were also investigated in 2014 and 2020 to favor the reading of urban transformations and its consequences over the territory; and of the relation of the arboreal vegetation with thermal load, urban surfaces and urbanization itself.

The hydrology analysis was conducted with the use of different data layers constructed both for this research and on previous studies on the Iron Quadrangle region. The drainage density is considered as an important morphometric parameter of analysis of river basins, once it considers factors such as rainfall regime, relief, rainwater infiltration capacity, erosion resistance and so one [18]. It was modeled by the calculation of hydrology of the area, followed by spatial concentration analysis. The rainwater recharge potential is associated with the likelihood of the land to recharge aquifers by the infiltration of water in general.

Is considered an important analysis parameter, since the process favors the hydrological cycle – related itself to hydric protection and water availability. The model was constructed by Camargos *et al.* [19] with the use of different variables, such as slope, geology-related contamination risk, land use and land cover, etc. The methodology utilized was a Multicriteria Analysis by Weights of Evidence. The hydrological importance was estimated by using a Combinatory Analysis of the previous datasets – drainage density and rainwater recharge potential. Before the map algebra operation, the spatial model indicated low to high hydrological importance zones in the area. The data were also used to study Belo Horizonte's characteristics in terms of hydrology.

For the local scale, beyond the previous present information, the city hall dataset [20] were also observed i.e., built volume, building typologies, vacancies and flood risk. Geoprocessing methods were also utilized to calculate the Floor Area Ratio and the volumetry of the built environment, which indicated the effect of the current building guidelines over the landscape.

3   Development

The environmental analysis enabled the identification of the potentialities and the vulnerabilities of the study areas, by giving information for planning-related aspects, as well as for the proposition of strategic actions. It was possible to design procedures related to the reduction and contention of environmental threats linked to the characteristics of the place. Since the analysis motivated the survey of proposals, it is a projection of the territory's reality as well as a plan based on the desired landscape. The purposes are linked to the generation of a more sustainable and resilient scenario for the city.

The association or the overlaying of all information were primordial for the identification of the existing conflicts, activities and processes in the Iron Quadrangle in general, and in Belo Horizonte in particular. At the regional context, it was possible to reaffirm the importance of conservation for the management of existing resources, since Federal Protected Areas showed to be located in areas of extreme interest in terms of water availability, for example. At the urban scale, it was also observed that the conservation of open green spaces is not an organic, spontaneous process, since the expressive fragments of arboreal vegetation were generally located in protected areas. These observation enforces the urgency of protecting other zones in the Iron Quadrangle region and in Belo Horizonte, since the natural resources, such as mineral goods and vegetation cover, are under constant pressure from the private sector.

The ideas cited in this study can guarantee the vegetation presence, which are significant for the landscape, for urban ambiance, to achieve climate regulations etc. They can serve as an environment policy guide, as economic, sustainable, risk reduction, and resource protection features were considered. It was also considered that those open green areas need to be connected to a multifunctional net that can integrate leisure, cultural, functional facilities etc., with the potential of improving life-quality of communities. The application of each of the proposals implies the commitment of the understanding of the place in order to comprehend existing capacities. It reinforces the importance and the relevance of the multiscale approach.

The proposed instruments, parameters, and design interventions are present in a summary (Fig. 4), containing information i.e., its name; description; impact; category (traditional or not conventional – in the Brazilian context); involved stakeholders; tax incentive possibilities; known benefits defended by specialists – identified by icons; an illustration in an urban context; and a zoning map indicating the most suitable areas in the

Instruments, Parameter or Design Intervention:
Community Garden

Urban Impact: Short Term

Category: Not conventional in the Brazilian context

Stakeholder: Local government and/or private sector

Tax Incentive Possibility: Tax benefits to qualified designs; government incentive to the construction and maintenance; long term usage allowance.

Description: Creation of an open green are in an urban vacancy that can be shared by citizens. The owner – or group of owners – is allowed to register it in the City Hall as a collective use space, and, in return, receives governmental incentives to maintain the space. The managers are responsible for the construction and maintenance of the area.

Benefits: Pocket parks can contribute to the improvement of air quality, to the reduction of heat concentrations, the rainwater retention, the access to food – vegetables, spices etc., to the enhancement of nature contact, and, ultimately, to neighborhood encounters. Each one allows an experience with its own arrangement, aesthetics, use and colors. They area spaces that carry culture within the city, as they are the spatial expression of a specific group (Castro, 2014).

Example: West Side Communitty Garden - Manhattan, New York

Illustration:

Source: West Side Rag >> 7 Walks in 7 Days:
A Garden in the Middle of the City

Fig. 4. Summary example – community garden proposition. Source: Morais, 2022.

Centro-Sul administrative unit to receive the intervention. The zoning developments were held by overlaying the most important information – regarding each of the proposals, of the produced map set. Regional, urban and local scale data, its correlations and influences were interpreted and used at this moment (Fig. 5). General information of all proposals is indicated in Table 1 [21].

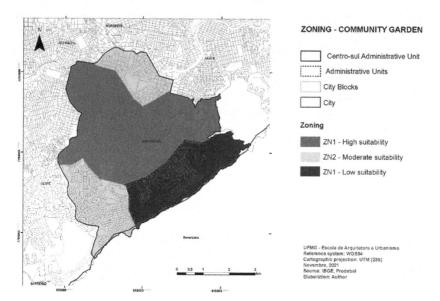

Fig. 5. Zoning example – community parks suitability. Source: Morais, 2022.

Table 1. General information of all proposals.

Instruments, parameter or design intervention	Proposal	Benefits
Vertical gardens	Green structures in building facades	Ecological, microclimate, landscape
Green roofs	Vegetated areas above residential, industrial, commercial or public houses or buildings. Vegetation can be undergrowth, shrub or arboreal. The roof can be adopted in an extensive type (with ecological function); Semi-intensive (green roof with design) and Intensive (garden type park). The implementation of green roofs on existing roofs is important to create ecological green corridors, as the multiplication of these roofs can connect urban centers with natural areas around cities	Ecological, rainwater retention, microclimate, landscape, leisure

(continued)

Table 1. (*continued*)

Instruments, parameter or design intervention	Proposal	Benefits
Minimum permeability ratio	Permeable area of urban lots that must be on natural soil and partially vegetated with shrub and/or robust vegetation. The calculation of the Minimum Permeability Ratio must consider not only the size of the lot, but also the drainage capacity of the soil (soil type). In this sense, the most fragile areas in terms of soil typology (less draining) should have a higher permeability rate. For areas where it is not possible to practice permeability, depending on the occupation density and/or infrastructure saturation due to occupation, it is necessary to proportionally add to the permeability rate other forms of capturing rainwater, such as a green roof. Ex: 30% permeability rate + 10% other initiative	Ecological, geological risk, microclimate, landscape, leisure
Community gardens	Creation of a green area on a parcel of urban land that can be shared by a group of people. The owner is allowed to register it with the city hall as a collective space and, in return, receives government incentives to requalify and maintain the space and rent the space for collective use. The group is responsible for the consolidation and maintenance of the space	Ecological, rainwater retention, microclimate, landscape, leisure
Linear parks	Linear areas of vegetation covering rivers and streams, acting as a biological conduit for wildlife, contemplating the function of leisure areas, urban mobility (such as bicycle paths) and still being able to recover and requalify areas of the city, as well as enabling the preservation of cultural heritage	Ecological, geological risk, rainwater retention, microclimate, landscape, leisure
Vegetated volume	Creation of minimum vegetated volume (arboreal vegetation) proportional to the area of the lot and the built volume, implanted in the back of the lots, so that the multiplication in all the backyards creates a kind of green corridor through the city	Ecological, geological risk, rainwater retention, microclimate, landscape

(*continued*)

Table 1. (*continued*)

Instruments, parameter or design intervention	Proposal	Benefits
Urban ecological corridors	Linear open spaces that connect non-linear areas or large patches of natural spaces, constituting systems of spaces planned, designed and managed for multiple purposes, including ecological, recreational, cultural, aesthetic and productive, compatible with the concept of sustainability	Ecological, geological risk, rainwater retention, microclimate, landscape
Green sidewalks	Streets with intense urban afforestation. These would be more restricted streets, favoring the transit of pedestrians and cyclists. Afforestation should give preference to native vegetation that promotes urban biodiversity. The streets must be composed of other resources of green infrastructure, such as rain gardens, porous pavements, vegetated ditches etc	Ecological, rainwater retention, microclimate, landscape
Rainwater reservoirs	Delay in the access of rainwater to the drainage network, making the runoff in and out of the reservoir compatible with the infrastructure capacity. The reservoir dimensioning criterion must consider that the outlet condition cannot be worse than the lot would have in its "natural" condition, that is, before human alterations	Rainwater retention, microclimate
Rain gardens	Rain gardens at lower levels, which can be projected onto streets or buildings, to receive water from surface runoff from impermeable areas	Ecological, geological risk, rainwater retention, microclimate, landscape
Vegetated drainage/runoff ditches	Devices made up of depressions excavated in the ground, whose purpose is to collect rainwater from surface runoff to be temporarily stored. The ditches are vegetated, configuring linear gardens. They can be implemented in common areas along blocks, streets, avenues, roads, parallel to public transport roads/tracks, in parking lots, on property boundaries etc	Ecological, geological risk, rainwater retention, microclimate, landscape
Detention basins	Vegetated depression that receives water during the rainy season, reducing surface runoff and consequently delaying the entry of rainwater into the drainage system	Ecological, rainwater retention, microclimate, landscape, leisure

Source: Morais, 2022.

4 Results and Conclusions

The characterization and environmental analysis at the three landscape scales made it possible to identify the potentialities and vulnerabilities of the study areas and the viability for the implementation and qualification of the green areas. It also served as a subsidy to propose instruments, interventions and urban parameters that generate distributed, and no longer concentrated, environmental quality.

The adopted methodology of environmental analysis in different scales of landscape presented satisfactory results, since it allowed to approach urban planning in an articulated way, integrating and connecting the proposals in the different scales, and understanding the importance of an integrated planning. It also made it possible to think about the most satisfactory and coherent planning actions and proposals for each planning scale, considering the different actors involved and realizing that each scale fulfills specific functions related to planning.

Therefore, the temporal and spatial effects on the urban landscape are different and associated with the nature of the proposals and scales. Actions on a regional scale will be perceived over a longer period of time, as the actions are spatially larger, and therefore will have a broad temporal and spatial effect. On the other hand, at the local scale, actions are spatially more restricted, with more immediate spatial and temporal effects, functioning as "urban surgeries" and acting as mitigating actions for the most urgent processes. Although they present different spatial and temporal results, it is essential that the scales of approach are worked in an articulated way.

The analysis and proposition at different scales also allowed us to understand how actions and legislation related to urban planning need to be integrated, articulated and compatible with the specifics of each landscape scale.

In proposing instruments, interventions and green urban parameters, we sought to give visibility to the possibilities of actions, integrating different functions (principle of multifunctionality), and contemplating the possibility of action for the different actors – public power, private initiative and civil society. The proposals also contemplated short-term and long-term actions and considered the different environmental and social benefits involved, such as improved climate, drainage, leisure areas, etc. The proposals started from the concept of green infrastructure in order to mitigate the problems caused by the traditional urbanization models that, in general, do not contemplate the structure and processes that occur in the landscape.

Regarding the need to improve environmental quality, changes are necessary at different planning scales (regional, urban, and local) to change the current scenario, considering the influencing factors in each of them. The planning and implementation need to occur in an integrated and articulated way, considering actions in different temporal spaces, conditioned and coherent with each planning scale.

The proposal of parameters and the zoning indication for the Centro-Sul administrative unit, based on environmental analysis, can serve as a starting point for future studies in the discussion of the need and strategies for implementation and maintenance of urban green areas.

Investigations with the application of geoprocessing are also methodological contributions, as the study organizer proposes steps, application models, collections and data integrations with reproducible criteria applicable to other areas of study, if these areas have the same quality of collections of data. All work that involves geoprocessing is a methodological contribution, as it is a set of methods and techniques that will result in the proposition of a framework, whose intention is to collaborate not only with the study itself, but also with the possibility of applicability of the model in other case studies.

Acknowledgments. The authors thank CNPq support through the project 401066/2016-9 and FAPEMIG PPM-00368-18.

References

1. Steffen, W., et al.: Planetary boundaries: guiding human development on a changing planet. Science, **347**, 6223 (2015). https://doi.org/10.1126/science.1259855
2. dos Monteiro, M.S.: Serviços Ecossistêmicos como diretriz para o planejamento urbano: uma análise da Área Metropolitana do Rio de Janeiro. Dissertação apresentada ao Programa de Pós-graduação em Engenharia Civil da PUC-Rio de Janeiro (2016)
3. Zaman-Ul-Haq, M., Saquib, Z., Kanwal, A., Naseer, S., Shafiq, M., Akhtar, N., Bokhari, S.A., Irshad, A., Hamam, H.: The trajectories, trends, and opportunities for assessing urban ecosystem services: a systematic review of geospatial methods. Sustainability **14**, 1471 (2022). https://doi.org/10.3390/su14031471
4. Convention on Biological Diversity – CBD, Secretariat: Cities and Biodiversity Outlook: Action and Policy (2013)
5. Yu, K., Padua, M.: The Art of Survival – Recovering Landscape Architecture. The Images Publishing Group Pty, Victoria (2006)
6. Benedict, M.A., Mcmahon, E.T.: Green Infrastructure – Linking Landscapes and Communities. Island Press, Washington (2006)
7. Ahern, J.: Green infrastructure for cities: the spatial dimension. In: Novotny, V., Brown, P. (eds.) Cities of the Future – Towards Integrated Sustainable Water Landscape Management, pp. 267–283. IWA Publishing, London (2007)
8. de Vasconcellos, A.A.: Infraestrutura verde aplicada ao planejamento da ocupação urbana. 1edn., Appris, Curitiba (2015)
9. Herzog, C.P., Rosa, L.Z.: Infraestrutura Verde: Sustentabilidade e resiliência para a paisagem urbana. Revista LABVERDE **1**, 92–115 (2010)
10. Pellegrino, P.R.M., Moura, N.C.B.: de. Estratégias para uma infraestrutura verde [S.l: s.n.] (2017)
11. Moura, A.C.M.: Landscape design or parameterization? Recent tendencies in geotechnologies for representing and planning urban territory. DisegnareCon, **11**, 3–10 (2013)
12. Gonçalves, F.S.: Parâmetros Ambientais para o Ordenamento Territorial Municipal e Proposta para o Estado do Rio Grande do Sul. Tese (Doutorado) – Universidade Federal do Rio Grande do Sul. Instituto de Geociências. Programa de Pós-Graduação em Geografia, Porto Alegre (2017)
13. Nogueira, R.H.: Os (des)caminhos da linguagem coletiva nas paisagens urbanas brasileiras: a forma urbana modelada pela norma. Dissertação de mestrado, Escola de Arquitetura – Universidade Federal de Minas Gerais, Belo Horizonte (2018)
14. Silva, M.M.A., Bezerra, M.C.L.: Ecológico: possibilidades de suporte ao Sistema de Áreas Verdes Urbano na construção de cidades mais saudáveis. Trabalho Inscrito na Categoria de Resumo Expandido ISBN 978-65-86753-30-1. I Congresso Latino-americano de desenvolvimento sustentável (2021)

15. Fundação Biodiversitas: Quadrilátero Ferrífero: Avanços do conhecimento nos últimos 50 anos. In: Biodiversidade em Minas Gerais. Segunda Edição. Belo 2020. 1st edn., p. 480, 3i Editora Horizonte, Belo Horizonte (2005)
16. ALBERTI, G. A. VICTORINO, H.S. Detecção da expansão da barragem de rejeitos Maravilhas II (MG) por Subtração Simples de Bandas e Análise de Componentes Principais – Instituto Nacional de Pesquisas Espaciais – INPE, São José dos Campos - SP, 2015. Anais XVII Simpósio Brasileiro de Sensoriamento Remoto – SBSR, João Pessoa-PB, Brasil, INPE, pp. 4883–4890 (2015)
17. Forman, R.T.T., Godron, M.: Landscape Ecology. Wiley, New York (1986)
18. Horton, R.E.: Erosional development of streams and their drainage basins: hydrophysical approach to quantitative morphology. Bull. Geo. Soc. Am. **56**(3), 275–370 (1945)
19. Camargos, L.M., Moura, A.C.M., Rezende, C.: Análise multicritérios na identificação de classificação de importância hídrica no quadrilátero ferrífero – MG. Anuário do Instituto de Geociências – UFRJ, **43**(3), 23–34 (2020)
20. Prefeitura De Belo Horizonte; Waycarbon; Ela-Kas: Análise de vulnerabilidade às mudanças climáticas do município de Belo Horizonte: resumo para os tomadores de decisão. Prefeitura de Belo Horizonte (2016)
21. Morais, C.F.: Parametrização da qualidade ambiental urbana em diferentes escalas de paisagem. Monografia de conclusão de curso (Graduação em Arquitetura e Urbanismo) – Escola de Arquitetura. Universidade Federal de Minas Gerais, Belo Horizonte (2022)

International Workshop on New Mobility Choices For Sustainable and Alternative Scenarios (NEWMOB 2022)

Users' Socio-economic Factors to Choose Electromobility for Future Smart Cities

Ankit R. Patel[1]([✉]) [iD], Giovanni Tesoriere[2] [iD], and Tiziana Campisi[2]([✉]) [iD]

[1] Department of Industrial Electronics, ALGORITMI Research Center,
University of Minho, Guimaraes, Portugal
majorankit@gmail.com
[2] Faculty of Engineering and Architecture, University of Enna Kore, Enna, Italy
{giovanni.tesoriere,tiziana.campisi}@unikore.it

Abstract. Recently, governments worldwide have sought solutions on how to lower carbon emissions. One of the more preferable options is the daily use of electromobility for various types of transportation. Clearly, reforming the different kinds of urban mobility is a far from simple task for policymakers; and from the perspective of users, there are many socioeconomic factors that are responsible. A preliminary literature search was conducted into the issues related to environmental protection, consumer awareness and knowledge of e-mobility, and purchasing behaviour. We have focused on these factors to take advantage of the usefulness of electromobility and provide a holistic overview, which will ultimately be the impetus for developing future smart cities. The study results may be a good base from which to build future discussions regarding the need for bottom-up analysis of e-mobility demand and standardisation, whilst taking into consideration the interests of various communities, including individual users, policymakers, and other industry-related stakeholders.

Keywords: Choice of vehicle · Electric vehicles (EVs) · Smart cities · Socio-economic barriers · User demand

1   Introduction

Over the past few decades, transport has become integral to human life. Smart mobility is necessary because of the increase in urbanisation, public awareness of the environment, and numerous other socioeconomic factors. Thus, in order to provide hassle-free transportation solutions, governments worldwide have become actively involved in smart mobility solutions. Electrical advances are accelerating these efforts and electric vehicles (EVs) will consequently become the solution to all daily transportation methods in future smart cities. This achieves traditional mobility goals (e.g., travel costs, user-friendliness, etc.) and is vital to reach sustainable development goals (SDGs) as defined by the United Nations, to become more accessible, inclusive, sustainable, and multimodal. In general, the transition to clean and smart mobility is based on four key pillars: (i) a more efficient transport system, (ii) low and zero emission vehicle, (iii) new business models and services for transport, and (iv) multi-modality and inter-modality- integration of all possible transport modes. Research and innovation play a key role in developing, testing, and bringing to market next-generation solutions in these four areas. In addition, the long-term potential of disruptive innovations needs to be explored. Particular attention should not only be paid to infrastructure and modal choices, but also to assessing the socio-economic parameters that influence the choices of users, whether as drivers, passengers, or operators of electric transport services.

User adoption of electric vehicles [1,2] has vastly increased over the past decade and has seen incredible sales growth regardless of the economic crisis caused by the COVID-19 pandemic [3]. Flexible government financial incentives have changed people's mindsets (for example, in Norway the government incentive to purchase an EV is USD8800, whereas in the USA it is USD6000 [4]). Moreover, during COVID-19 public transportation saw a decline in demand, with EVs becoming the most convenient mode of transport. Overall, over the past two years sales of EVs have surged from 43% to 108%; this is significant when global vehicle sales increased by only 4.7% [5].

Even given the remarkable growth in the EV sector, the industry is still facing challenges at all levels in the successful deployment of electric transportation [6,7]. One reason is because of the gap between electricity production and its generous distribution to the end user [8]. Other reasons include charging infrastructure availability [9–11], government subsidies on new EV purchases [12,13], intelligent battery swapping technology [14,15], and many others not yet available in many countries. There is also the possibility that people's awareness and rate of acceptance [16,17] is lower in EVs compared to conventional vehicles [18]as a result of socioeconomic barriers.

Infrastructure is now one of the main reasons for the success of any revolution; this also applies to the field of electromobility. The evolution of recharging infrastructures and the reduction of waiting times as well as the spread of public and shared electric transport are topics that have been addressed by several authors recently [19–21]. However, less attention has been paid to the role of socioeconomic factors in the success of electromobility. Such factors usually centre around the daily lives of users, which influences the adoption of new mobility technologies. This is crucial in the context of smart cities, where all components (e.g., transportation, home, other utilities, etc.) have been user-centric.

Current and future electromobility solutions require a shift in people's minds. Furthermore, daily advancements in technology and various electric mobility types (e.g., e-scooter, e-rickshaw, e-bus, e-port, e-rail, etc.) raise new socioeconomic challenges. This raises questions about the types of challenges faced when deploying electromobility on roads. A key future topic is how smart cities, and their transportation systems respond to the present concerns. Thus, the aim of this paper is to provide new informative knowledge on social influence and economic impact in the context of choosing electromobility.

In this paper, Sect. 2 includes social influential factors affecting electromobility choices. Section 3 describes how economic factors affect electromobility choices during a purchase. Finally, Sect. 4 concludes the paper with a future direction.

2   Social Factors Affecting to Choose Electromobility

Societal barriers are equally as important as technical challenges in successfully deploying electromobility at every level. It is a direct indication of the level of acceptance by society and, therefore, agencies and policymakers can plan accordingly for the future implementation of EVs on the road. The various factors which affect this are shown in Fig. 1.

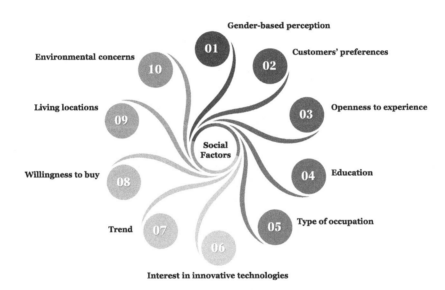

Fig. 1. Social factors

2.1   Gender-Based Perception

An idiosyncrasy to the new technological innovations, especially in terms of electromobility, is that adoption may differ between men and women [22]. For example, charging locations, vehicle usage in urban and rural areas, driving range per battery charge, etc. Without an awareness of these important issues, the sales, and services of EVs may be affected. Therefore, for the accessibility of vehicles to all end-users, it is crucial to understand gender behaviour [23,24].

2.2 Customers' Preferences

Electric vehicles have gained increased attention over the past decade, which has facilitated the diverse preference-based decision-making capabilities of the vehicle purchase, which has made the vehicles more 'personalised', and these preferences vary over time [25]. In the profitability race of original equipment manufacturers (OEMs), recent results show that vehicle body type also plays a significant role in vehicle choice [26]. Electromobility is the future of personal transportation, and therefore vehicle charging is a prime concern of users. Consequently, charging infrastructure should be made affordable and payments accessible to all users with access through all payment gateways [27,28]. Choice of brand is one of the prime reasons for the purchase of electric vehicles [29].

2.3 Openness to Experience

Car-sharing provides a more affordable and sustainable transportation option for making cities smart. Thus, users experience a more open environment of mobility, and a new path will consequently be revealed for choosing electromobility as a key fleet [30,31]. Moreover, the type of experience felt by users before and after using EVs also matters when choosing a new vehicle [32,33].

2.4 Education

EVs are a relatively new consumer technology. Therefore, to understand all of its benefits will take time. Over the past five years, EVs have changed personal transportation; yet, this has not paved the way for full utilisation by customers. One reason why adoption of EVs is not seen as a viable option is education. It is apparent that consumers who are more educated prefer hybrid vehicles for routine use [34]. Studies show that in the Netherlands, Sweden, and Norway, those with a higher level of education prefer EVs [23].

2.5 Type of Occupation

There are many influential factors when choosing EVs, yet there has been little focus on the type of occupation of the user. There is a disparity in the various results, for example, in Thailand [35] and South Korea [36] people with a higher income tend to adopt EVs, while in India [37] those who have a lower income tend to buy EVs. This clearly indicates the socio-geographical impact on the choice of electromobility.

2.6 Interest in Innovative Technologies

Continuous developments in state-of-the-art innovative technologies attract users to purchase EVs as their first vehicle of choice. These technologies include fast charging, various payment gateways, and connected cars. Users who have a greater interest in technology and want to experience their vehicle's features are more willing to choose EVs than other users [38,39]. Additionally, leveraging these features will be helpful for comprehending user experiences.

2.7   Trend

To better understand user adoption of EVs, we must also understand current market trends. This is due to the influential factor of dispersal of new technology [40]. People largely adopt new products based on their lifestyles and market trends [41].

2.8   Willingness to Buy

The psychology of users and policy concerns are also influential factors. Therefore, by knowing user preferences, the OEMs can provide user-centric features in the EVs [42]. These factors change geographically. For example, in Indonesia users are greatly affected by emotions, vehicle functionality, identity of the car, and ownership [43]. Whereas, Indian consumers have faith in new technology [44], and South Korean consumers have strong environmental concerns during the purchase of EVs [45].

2.9   Living Locations

The market growth of electromobility is highly dependent on the location of users. It is particularly important that the purchasing power of urban and rural users is different, for various reasons. This includes availability of charging facilities, incentives from central and state governments, government policies, education, income level, willingness to pay more for charging, etc. Various preference levels have been observed in rural and urban users, especially in terms of the ownership of the vehicle and charging profiles [46].

2.10   Environmental Concerns

The key responsibility of any revolution in the mobility sector should be to ensure the needs of the environment. Recent years have witnessed the awareness of users towards electromobility in regard to environmental concerns. The aforementioned social and environmental confluence will be the game changer for automotive transportation in paving the way for the widespread adoption of EVs [47]. Indian [48] and Australian [49] consumers are pro-environment and have a greater sense of adaptive behaviour when choosing EVs. In the USA, because of federal policies towards sustainability, customers have a deeper interest in environmental and legal matters [50].

3   Economic Factors Affecting to Choose Electromobility

An economy acts as a bridge between customers and policymakers and includes various factors which directly or indirectly affect the infrastructure, policy, finance, and technical variability to formulate user preferences [25]. The active involvement of various economic factors are shown in Fig. 2.

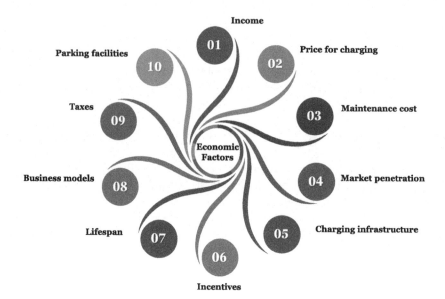

Fig. 2. Economic factors

3.1 Income

There is sufficient evidence that there is a connection between the choice of vehicle and user income [51]. For example, countries such as France and Germany, where a large number of users are in a higher income bracket, opt for EVs [52]. Conversely, in Ireland [53] and India [54] the first preference of users is EVs regardless of income level.

3.2 Price for Charging

Whenever we are thinking of purchasing EVs, the first question we come across is what the vehicle will cost. There are four main purchase factors: Owner of the vehicle, charging points, prospective EV buyers, and distribution companies [55]. It is important to manage the smart charging of electric vehicles according to the tariff rate and attitude of the customers [56,57].

3.3 Maintenance Cost

In electromobility, the high cost of maintenance is due to the batteries, and users are always keen to know the life expectancy of the batteries. Depending upon the cost analysis, user trends towards purchasing EVs will increase [58].

3.4 Market Penetration

By knowing the consumer adoption rate and purchasing behaviour, one can predict EV penetration. The rate of EV penetration characterises the future market share of electromobility [59]. For example, the EV penetration rate in the Netherlands is higher than in Germany [60]. This demonstrates the willingness of users to buy EVs and provide sustainable mobility for upcoming generations.

3.5   Charging Infrastructure

Commercial success, as well as the wide adoption of electromobility, is highly dependent on the charging infrastructure. This is crucial as the needs of most users revolve around affordable, easy to use, and easy access charging infrastructure. In addition, charging infrastructure locations provide information on which to base future policies and power network services [61]. In the field of charging facilities, technological developments have been seen in recent times, for example, mobile charging [62], two-charging station charging method [27], etc. Providing consumers with friendly charging facilities at users' doorsteps will increase the EV adoption rate [63].

3.6   Incentives

Recent years have witnessed the increased adoption of electromobility. However, there is a huge gap between traditional vehicles and electromobility. One of the easiest ways to bridge the gap between them is to provide financing with a loan at a low interest rate. To promote and increase the market share of electric vehicles, many incentives are provided to consumers. This is necessary because the technology is relatively new, and consumers can be hesitant in their purchasing behaviours. Various studies in Norway [13], Australia [64], and the USA [65] have shown that providing sufficient incentives increases users' belief towards buying electric vehicles.

3.7   Lifespan

An important user concern is in regard to the vehicle's lifespan. A longer vehicle lifespan provides both the users and manufacturing companies with ease-of-use access to electromobility. Current versions of electric vehicles have a lifetime driving distance in the range of 100,000 to 300,000 km, which is expected to increase to 150,000 to 350,000 km in the future through high performance batteries [66]. To boost battery lifespan, various techniques have been applied; for example, the ultracapacitor based method [67], thermally modulated lithium iron phosphate batteries which have the capacity to operate at a temperature of 60 °C [68], etc.

3.8   Business Models

New business models in electromobility should also foster the needs of the customer. Therefore, the interaction between the various business models (such as vehicle sharing, e-mobility services, or mobility shops) has been measured. This will help customers to define their interest in new mobility solutions and allow companies to decide where to invest their money for providing future innovative solutions [69].

3.9 Taxes

To encourage people to buy electric vehicles, governments should think about providing tax benefits. What kind of financial mechanisms can be used so that consumers will benefit from the mileage tax [70]? Tax locations also matter in the case of electromobility, for example, at the domestic supply side or at the public charging station end.

3.10 Parking Facilities

As the size of the electromobility market increases with time, a crucial question is where will users park their vehicles? One of the simplest answers is to park the vehicle near existing charging facilities. However, it is not enough only to add new users into the electromobility sector. Therefore, to persuade people to purchase a vehicle, parking facilities must have incentives and policies to promote the technology and user awareness. For example, managed parking and charging at parking lots using solar power generation [71], enough prior information provided for the use of information technology [72], optimal residential parking slots information [73], etc. Additionally, it has been noticed that consumer preference for charging locations matters. Consumers prefer to charge first at home, then at work, and then at other destinations and service stations [74].

4   Discussion and Conclusion

Although there has been widespread acceptance of electromobility in recent years, much of the focus has not been on choice elements, such as societal and economic factors. In the paper, we have discussed the various socio-economic factors which are key when a consumer purchases an electric vehicle. Broadly speaking, the user plays a central role in the transformation of going from purchasing a conventional vehicle to adopting an electric vehicle. Thus, the factors that affect the understanding of the socio-economic situation of users is crucial.

It is important to define the holistic view of these socio-economic factors in future studies. This could be in terms of understanding user perceptions of electric transformation of vehicles and how we can build up future, liveable, smart cities. To define socio-economic factors more concisely, a user study would be a preferable choice.

Future research steps should focus on an in-depth survey related to the definition of potential users of electric vehicles: whether they are potential buyers of vehicles (cars, scooters...) or potential managers of transport services with electric vehicles, especially vehicles related to public and/or shared transport such as taxis or DRT. This will provide an insight into the various criteria of different users in different geospatial locations.

Acknowledgments. The authors acknowledge financial support from the MIUR (Ministry of Education, Universities and Research [Italy]) through a project entitled WEAKI TRANSIT: WEAK-demand areas Innovative TRANsport Shared services for

Italian Towns (Project code: 20174ARRHT/CUP Code: J74I19000320008), financed with the PRIN 2017 (Research Projects of National Relevance) program. We authorize the MIUR to reproduce and distribute reprints for Governmental purposes, notwithstanding any copyright notations thereon. Any opinions, findings, and conclusions or recommendations expressed in this material are those of the authors and do not necessarily reflect the views of the MIUR. Conflicts of Interest: The authors declare no conflict of interest.

References

1. Jabeen, F., Olaru, D., Smith, B., Braunl, T., Speidel, S.: Acceptability of electric vehicles: findings from a driver survey. In: Proceedings of 35th Australasian Transport Research Forum (ATRF), pp. 1–15, Perth, Australia (2012). https://trid.trb.org/view/1224115

2. Lioutas, V., Adamos, G., Nathanail, E.: How ready are Greek consumers to use electric vehicles? In: Nathanail, E.G., Adamos, G., Karakikes, I. (eds.) CSUM 2020. AISC, vol. 1278, pp. 760–769. Springer, Cham (2021). https://doi.org/10.1007/978-3-030-61075-3_74

3. Marie R.B., Dale, H., Nic, L.: Update on electric vehicle uptake in European cities. In: International Council on Clean Transportation, Working Paper 2021-37, pp. 1–18 (2021). https://theicct.org/publication/update-on-electric-vehicle-uptake-in-european-cities/. Accessed 13 Mar 2022

4. If you build it, they will come: Lessons from the first decade of electric vehicles. https://blogs.worldbank.org/transport/if-you-build-it-they-will-come-lessons-first-decade-electric-vehicles. Accessed 13 Mar 2022

5. Global EV sales for 2021. https://www.ev-volumes.com/. Accessed 13 Mar 2022

6. Sreeram, K., Preetha, P.K., Pooranchandran, P.: Electric vehicle scenario in India: roadmap, challenges, and opportunities. In: Proceedings of IEEE International Conference on Electrical, Computer and Communication Technologies (ICECCT), Coimbatore, India, pp. 1–7 (2019). https://doi.org/10.1109/ICECCT.2019.8869479

7. Ona, E., Suzanna, L.: Barriers to widespread adoption of electric vehicles: an analysis of consumer attitudes and perceptions. Energy Policy **48**, 717–729 (2012). https://doi.org/10.1016/j.enpol.2012.06.009

8. Ghazale, H., Mohammad, K., Shahidehpour, M.: Accelerating the global adoption of electric vehicles: barriers and drivers. Electr. J. **28**(10), 53–68 (2015). https://doi.org/10.1016/j.tej.2015.11.011

9. Sun, X.-H., Yamamoto, T., Morikawa, T.: Charge timing choice behavior of battery electric vehicle users. Transp. Res. Part D Transp. Environ. **37**, 97–107 (2015). https://doi.org/10.1016/j.trd.2015.04.007

10. Levinson, R.S., West, T.H.: Impact of public electric vehicle charging infrastructure. Transp. Res. Part D Transp. Environ. **64**, 158–177 (2018). https://doi.org/10.1016/j.trd.2017.10.006

11. Funke, S.Á., Sprei, F., Gnann, T., Plötz, P.: How much charging infrastructure do electric vehicles need? A review of the evidence and international comparison. Transp. Res. Part D Transp. Environ. **77**, 224–242 (2019). https://doi.org/10.1016/j.trd.2019.10.024

12. Rudolph, C.: How may incentives for electric cars affect purchase decisions? Transp. Policy **52**, 113–120 (2016). https://doi.org/10.1016/j.tranpol.2016.07.014

13. Bjerkan, K.Y., Nørbech, T.E., Nordtømme, M.E.: Incentives for promoting battery electric vehicle (BEV) adoption in Norway. Transp. Res. Part D Transp. Environ. **43**, 169–180 (2016). https://doi.org/10.1016/j.trd.2015.12.002
14. Raj, N., Suri, M., Deepa, K.: Integration of battery charging and swapping using metaheuristics: a review. In: Tomar, A., Malik, H., Kumar, P., Iqbal, A. (eds.) Machine Learning, Advances in Computing, Renewable Energy and Communication. LNEE, vol. 768, pp. 247–258. Springer, Singapore (2022). https://doi.org/10.1007/978-981-16-2354-7_23
15. Jatschka, T., Oberweger, F.F., Rodemann, T., Raidl, G.R.: Distributing battery swapping stations for electric scooters in an urban area. In: Olenev, N., Evtushenko, Y., Khachay, M., Malkova, V. (eds.) OPTIMA 2020. LNCS, vol. 12422, pp. 150–165. Springer, Cham (2020). https://doi.org/10.1007/978-3-030-62867-3_12
16. Campisi, T., Ticali, D., Ignaccolo, M., Tesoriere, G., Inturri, G., Torrisi, V.: Factors influencing the implementation and deployment of e-vehicles in small cities: a preliminary two-dimensional statistical study on user acceptance. Transp. Res. Procedia **62**, 333–340 (2022). https://doi.org/10.1016/j.trpro.2022.02.042
17. Bühler, F., Cocron, P., Neumann, I., Franke, T., Krems, J.F.: Is EV experience related to EV acceptance? Results from a German field study. Transp. Res. Part F Traffic Psychol. Behav. **25**, 34–49 (2014). https://doi.org/10.1016/j.trf.2014.05.002
18. Hackbarth, A., Madlener, R.: Consumer preferences for alternative fuel vehicles: a discrete choice analysis. Transp. Res. Part D: Transp. Environ. **25**, 5–17 (2013). https://doi.org/10.1016/j.trd.2013.07.002
19. Kaya, Ö., Alemdar, K.D., Campisi, T., Tortum, A., Çodur, M.K.: The development of decarbonisation strategies: a three-step methodology for the suitable analysis of current EVCS locations applied to Istanbul, Turkey. Energies **14**(10), 2756 (2021). https://doi.org/10.3390/en14102756
20. Campisi, T., Cocuzza, E., Ignaccolo, M., Inturri, G., Torrisi, V.: Exploring the factors that encourage the spread of EV-DRT into the sustainable urban mobility plans. In: Gervasi, O., et al. (eds.) ICCSA 2021. LNCS, vol. 12953, pp. 699–714. Springer, Cham (2021). https://doi.org/10.1007/978-3-030-86976-2_48
21. Acampa, G., Campisi, T., Grasso, M., Marino, G., Torrisi, V.: Exploring European strategies for the optimization of the benefits and cost-effectiveness of private electric mobility. In: Gervasi, O., et al. (eds.) ICCSA 2021. LNCS, vol. 12953, pp. 715–729. Springer, Cham (2021). https://doi.org/10.1007/978-3-030-86976-2_49
22. Hanson, S.: Gender and mobility: new approaches for informing sustainability. Gend. Place Cult. **17**(1), 5–23 (2010). https://doi.org/10.1080/09663690903498225
23. Sovacool, B.K., Kester, J., Noel, L., de Rubens, G.Z.: The demographics of decarbonizing transport: the influence of gender, education, occupation, age, and household size on electric mobility preferences in the Nordic region. Glob. Environ. Chang. **52**, 86–100 (2018). https://doi.org/10.1016/j.gloenvcha.2018.06.008
24. Caperello, N., TyreeHageman, J., Kurani, K.: Engendering the future of electric vehicles: conversations with men and women. In: Proceedings of 5th International Conference on Women's Issues in Transportation (WIIT), Paris, France, pp. 427–437 (2014). https://escholarship.org/uc/item/4fv7x1qv
25. Liao, F., Molin, E., van Wee, B.: Consumer preferences for electric vehicles: a literature review. Transp. Rev. **37**(3), 252–275 (2017). https://doi.org/10.1080/01441647.2016.1230794
26. Higgins, C.D., Mohamed, M., Ferguson, M.R.: Size matters: how vehicle body type affects consumer preferences for electric vehicles. Transp. Res. Part A Policy Pract. **100**, 182–201 (2017). https://doi.org/10.1016/j.tra.2017.04.014

27. Patel, A.R., Trivedi, G., Vyas, D., Mihaita, A.S., Padmanaban, S.: Framework for user-centered access to electric charging facilities via energy-trading blockchain. In: Proceedings of 24th International Symposium on Wireless Personal Multimedia Communications (WPMC), Okayama, Japan, pp. 1–6 (2021). https://doi.org/10.1109/WPMC52694.2021.9700475

28. Anderson, J.E., Lehne, M., Hardinghaus, M.: What electric vehicle users want: real-world preferences for public charging infrastructure. Int. J. Sustain. Transp. **12**(5), 341–352 (2018). https://doi.org/10.1080/15568318.2017.1372538

29. Vongurai, R.: Factors affecting customer brand preference toward electric vehicle in Bangkok, Thailand. J. Asian Financ. Econ. Bus. **7**(8), 383–393 (2020). https://doi.org/10.13106/jafeb.2020.vol7.no8.383

30. Schlüter, J., Weyer, J.: Car sharing as a means to raise acceptance of electric vehicles: an empirical study on regime change in automobility. Transport. Res. F Traffic Psychol. Behav. **60**, 185–201 (2019). https://doi.org/10.1016/j.trf.2018.09.005

31. Tiziana, C., Matteo, I., Giovanni, T., Giuseppe, I., Vincenza, T.: The evaluation of car-sharing to raise acceptance of electric vehicles: evidences from an Italian survey among university students. SAE Technical Paper, 2020-24-0021, pp. 1–10 (2020). https://doi.org/10.4271/2020-24-0021

32. Jensen, A.F., Cherchi, E., Mabit, S.L.: On the stability of preferences and attitudes before and after experiencing an electric vehicle. Transp. Res. Part D Transp. Environ. **25**, 24–32 (2013). https://doi.org/10.1016/j.trd.2013.07.006

33. Roberson, L.A., Helveston, J.P.: Electric vehicle adoption: can short experiences lead to big change? Environ. Res. Lett. **15**(9), 0940c3 (2020). https://doi.org/10.1088/1748-9326/aba715

34. He, L., Chen, W., Conzelmann, G.: Impact of vehicle usage on consumer choice of hybrid electric vehicles. Transp. Res. Part D Transp. Environ. **17**(3), 208–214 (2012). https://doi.org/10.1016/j.trd.2011.11.005

35. Kongklaew, C., et al.: Barriers to electric vehicle adoption in Thailand. Sustainability **13**(22), 12839 (2021). https://doi.org/10.3390/su132212839

36. Javid, R.J., Nejat, A.: A comprehensive model of regional electric vehicle adoption and penetration. Transp. Policy **54**, 30–42 (2017). https://doi.org/10.1016/j.tranpol.2016.11.003

37. Bansal, P., Kumar, R.R., Raj, A., Dubey, S., Graham, D.J.: Willingness to pay and attitudinal preferences of Indian consumers for electric vehicles. Energy Econ. **100**, 105340 (2021). https://doi.org/10.1016/j.eneco.2021.105340

38. Anthony Jnr., B.: Integrating electric vehicles to achieve sustainable energy as a service business model in smart cities. Front. Sustain. Cities **3**, 1–12 (2021). https://doi.org/10.3389/frsc.2021.685716

39. Kotilainen, K., Mäkinen, S.J., Valta, J.: Sustainable electric vehicle - prosumer framework and policy mix. In: 2017 IEEE Innovative Smart Grid Technologies - Asia (ISGT-Asia), Auckland, New Zealand, pp. 1–6 (2017). https://doi.org/10.1109/ISGT-Asia.2017.8378406

40. Rasouli, S., Timmermans, H.: Influence of social networks on latent choice of electric cars: a mixed logit specification using experimental design data. Netw. Spat. Econ. **16**(1), 99–130 (2016). https://doi.org/10.1007/s11067-013-9194-6

41. Jung Moon, S.: Integrating diffusion of innovations and theory of planned behavior to predict intention to adopt electric vehicles. Int. J. Bus. Manage. **15**(11), 88–103 (2020). https://doi.org/10.5539/ijbm.v15n11p88

42. Ye, F., Kang, W., Li, L., Wang, Z.: Why do consumers choose to buy electric vehicles? A paired data analysis of purchase intention configurations. Transp. Res. Part A Policy Pract. **147**, 14–27 (2021). https://doi.org/10.1016/j.tra.2021.02.014

43. Febransyah, A.: Predicting purchase intention towards battery electric vehicles: a case of Indonesian market. World Electr. Veh. J. **12**(4), 240 (2021). https://doi.org/10.3390/wevj12040240

44. Irfan, M., Ahmad, M.: Relating consumers' information and willingness to buy electric vehicles: does personality matter? Transp. Res. Part D Transp. Environ. **100**, 103049 (2021). https://doi.org/10.1016/j.trd.2021.103049

45. Lashari, Z.A., Ko, J., Jang, J.: Consumers' intention to purchase electric vehicles: influences of user attitude and perception. Sustainability **13**(12), 6778 (2021). https://doi.org/10.3390/su13126778

46. Lee, R., Brown, S.: Social & locational impacts on electric vehicle ownership and charging profiles. Energy Rep. **7**, 42–48 (2021). https://doi.org/10.1016/j.egyr.2021.02.057

47. Krause, R.M., Carley, S.R., Lane, B.W., Graham, J.D.: Perception and reality: public knowledge of plug-in electric vehicles in 21 U.S. cities. Energy Policy **63**, 433–440 (2013). https://doi.org/10.1016/j.enpol.2013.09.018

48. Verma, M., Verma, A., Khan, M.: Factors influencing the adoption of electric vehicles in Bengaluru. Transp. Dev. Econ. **6**(2), 1–10 (2020). https://doi.org/10.1007/s40890-020-0100-x

49. Smith, B., Olaru, D., Jabeen, F., Greaves, S.: Electric vehicles adoption: environmental enthusiast bias in discrete choice models. Transp. Res. Part D Transp. Environ. **51**, 290–303 (2017). https://doi.org/10.1016/j.trd.2017.01.008

50. Debnath, R., Bardhan, R., Reiner, D.M., Miller, J.R.: Political, economic, social, technological, legal and environmental dimensions of electric vehicle adoption in the United States: a social-media interaction analysis. Renew. Sustain. Energy Rev. **152**, 111707 (2021). https://doi.org/10.1016/j.rser.2021.111707

51. Sovacool, B.K., Kester, J., Noel, L., de Rubens, G.Z.: Income, political affiliation, urbanism and geography in stated preferences for electric vehicles (EVs) and vehicle-to-grid (V2G) technologies in Northern Europe. J. Transp. Geogr. **78**, 214–229 (2019). https://doi.org/10.1016/j.jtrangeo.2019.06.006

52. Ensslen, A., Paetz, A.-G., Babrowski, S., Jochem, P., Fichtner, W.: On the road to an electric mobility mass market—how can early adopters be characterized? In: Fornahl, D., Hülsmann, M. (eds.) Markets and Policy Measures in the Evolution of Electric Mobility. LNM, pp. 21–51. Springer, Cham (2016). https://doi.org/10.1007/978-3-319-24229-3_3

53. McCoy, D., Lyons, S.: Consumer preferences and the influence of networks in electric vehicle diffusion: an agent-based microsimulation in Ireland. Energy Res. Soc. Sci. **3**, 89–101 (2014). https://doi.org/10.1016/j.erss.2014.07.008

54. Rastogi, A., Thomas, R.G., Digalwar, A.K.: Identification and analysis of social factors responsible for adoption of electric vehicles in India. Curr. Sci. **121**(9), 1180–1187 (2021). https://doi.org/10.18520/cs/v121/i9/1180-1187

55. Kenneth, N.J.J., Logenthiran, T.: A novel concept for calculating electricity price for electrical vehicles. In: Proceedings of 2017 IEEE PES Asia-Pacific Power and Energy Engineering Conference (APPEEC), Bangalore, India, pp. 1–6 (2017). https://doi.org/10.1109/APPEEC.2017.8308963

56. Nour, M., Said, S.M., Ali, A., Farkas, C.: Smart charging of electric vehicles according to electricity price. In: Proceedings of 2019 International Conference on Innovative Trends in Computer Engineering (ITCE), Aswan, Egypt, pp. 432–437 (2019). https://doi.org/10.1109/ITCE.2019.8646425

57. Kämpfe, B., et al.: Preferences and perceptions of bidirectional charging from a customer's perspective – a literature review and qualitative approach. In: Liebl, J. (ed.) Electrified Mobility 2019: Including Grid Integration of Electric Mobility, pp. 177–191. Springer, Wiesbaden (2022). https://doi.org/10.1007/978-3-658-32471-1_16

58. Hagman, J., Ritzén, S., Stier, J.J., Susilo, Y.: Total cost of ownership and its potential implications for battery electric vehicle diffusion. Res. Transp. Bus. Manage. **18**, 11–17 (2016). https://doi.org/10.1016/j.rtbm.2016.01.003

59. Vibhor, T., Paulus, A., Dilum, D.: Public attitudes towards electric vehicle adoption using structural equation modelling. In: Proceedings of 2019 World Conference on Transport Research (WCTR), Mumbai, India, pp. 1615–1634 (2019). https://doi.org/10.1016/j.trpro.2020.08.203

60. van Heuveln, K., Ghotge, R., Annema, J.A., van Bergen, E., van Wee, B., Pesch, U.: Factors influencing consumer acceptance of vehicle-to-grid by electric vehicle drivers in the Netherlands. Travel Behav. Soc. **24**, 34–45 (2021). https://doi.org/10.1016/j.tbs.2020.12.008

61. Lee, R., Brown, S.: Evaluating the role of behavior and social class in electric vehicle adoption and charging demands. iScience **24**(8), 102914 (2021). https://doi.org/10.1016/j.isci.2021.102914

62. Daniel, F., Filip, C., Maria, S.R., Constantin, F.: New mobile charging station for urban and resort areas. In: Proceedings of 2019 Electric Vehicles International Conference (EV), Bucharest, Romania, pp. 1–6 (2019). https://doi.org/10.1109/EV.2019.8892866

63. Abdullah-Al-Nahid, S., Khan, T.A., Taseen, M.A., Aziz, T.: A consumer-friendly electric vehicle charging scheme for residential consumers. In: Proceedings of 2020 International Conference on Smart Grids and Energy Systems (SGES), Perth, Australia, pp. 893–897 (2020). https://doi.org/10.1109/SGES51519.2020.00164

64. Broadbent, G., Metternicht, G., Drozdzewski, D.: An analysis of consumer incentives in support of electric vehicle uptake: an Australian case study. World Electr. Veh. J. **10**(1), 11 (2019). https://doi.org/10.3390/wevj10010011

65. Wee, S., Coffman, M., La Croix, S.: Do electric vehicle incentives matter? Evidence from the 50 U.S. states. Res. Policy **47**(9), 1601–1610 (2018). https://doi.org/10.1016/j.respol.2018.05.003

66. Cox, B., Bauer, C., Mendoza Beltran, A., van Vuuren, D.P., Mutel, C.L.: Life cycle environmental and cost comparison of current and future passenger cars under different energy scenarios. Appl. Energy **269**, 115021 (2020). https://doi.org/10.1016/j.apenergy.2020.115021

67. Alobeidli, K., Khadkikar, V.: A new ultracapacitor state of charge control concept to enhance battery lifespan of dual storage electric vehicles. IEEE Trans. Veh. Technol. **67**(11), 10470–10481 (2018). https://doi.org/10.1109/TVT.2018.2871038

68. Yang, X.-G., Liu, T., Wang, C.-Y.: Thermally modulated lithium iron phosphate batteries for mass-market electric vehicles. Nat. Energy **6**(2), 176–185 (2021). https://doi.org/10.1038/s41560-020-00757-7

69. Knoppe, M.: E-mobility generates new services and business models, increasing sustainability. In: Subic, A., Wellnitz, J., Leary, M., Koopmans, L. (eds.) Sustainable Automotive Technologies 2012, pp. 275–281. Springer, Heidelberg (2012). https://doi.org/10.1007/978-3-642-24145-1_36

70. Davis, L.W., Sallee, J.M.: Should electric vehicle drivers pay a mileage tax? Environ. Energy Policy Econ. **1**, 65–94 (2020). https://doi.org/10.1086/706793

71. Anil, K.M., Charan, T.S., Pradeep, K.Y.: Optimal charging schedule for electric vehicles in parking lot with solar power generation. In: Proceedings of 2018 IEEE Innovative Smart Grid Technologies - Asia (ISGT Asia), Singapore, pp. 611–615 (2018). https://doi.org/10.1109/ISGT-Asia.2018.8467916
72. Babic, J., Carvalho, A., Ketter, W., Podobnik, V.: Evaluating policies for parking lots handling electric vehicles. IEEE Access **6**, 944–961 (2018). https://doi.org/10.1109/ACCESS.2017.2777098
73. Abdelhak, B., Hamid, O., Mohamed, N.: Optimal sizing of electric vehicle charging stations in residential parking. In: Proceedings of 47th Annual Conference on the IEEE Industrial Electronics Society (IECON), Toronto, Canada, pp. 1–6 (2021). https://doi.org/10.1109/IECON48115.2021.9589453
74. Lavieri, P., Carmen, B.D.: Electric vehicle uptake and charging - a consumer-focused review. In: Technical Report of Large-Scale Network and System Integration of Electric Vehicles: A Techno-Economic Perspective, pp. 1–55 (2021). https://doi.org/10.13140/RG.2.2.17678.08009

A Holistic Approach to SUMP Strategies and Actions in the Post-pandemic and Energy Crisis Era

Ines Charradi[1] , Tiziana Campisi[2]([✉]) , Giovanni Tesoriere[2] ,
and Khaled Ben Abdallah[1]

[1] Higher Institute of Transport and Logistics of Sousse, University of Sousse, Sousse, Tunisia
[2] Faculty of Engineering and Architecture, University of Enna Kore, 94100 Enna, Italy
tiziana.campisi@unikore.it

Abstract. Since its first appearance, the COVID-19 pandemic has disrupted urban mobility in cities. Governments around the world have tried to implement various actions to limit the spread of this virus. As a result, a significant amount of research on sustainable urban mobility has been published since 2020. The spread of the virus has led to changes in transport supply and demand, which is represented by policy makers and users. In fact, the literature reviewed is classified into two broad categories:

(i)   User studies: analysis of modal choice before and after the pandemic.
(ii) Policy makers' studies: analysis of government actions to promote public transport (bus, train), soft mobility (cycling, walking) and micro-mobility (especially electric scooters) and rationalization of private car use.

Therefore, this manuscript analyses the relationship between urban mobility and COVID-19 through a holistic review of the literature published from 2020 until 2022. The main objective of the research aims at identifying new trends in research and recommendations in the field of sustainable urban mobility. While the COVID-19 pandemic represents an opportunity for governments to rethink the mobility system, this synthesis helps to clarify the vision of policy makers in developing post-pandemic urban mobility recovery plans and developing or updating Sustainable Urban Mobility Plans (SUMPs) in line with sustainable development goals and also taking into account the recent energy crisis.

Keywords: Sustainable mobility · SUMPs · COVID-19 pandemic · Energy crisis

1   Introduction

In general, an event such as a crisis causes disruptions that affect the functionality of infrastructure, services and travel patterns of citizens.

In the context of the COVID-19 pandemic, there is no direct impact on infrastructure, but rather on demand and mobility patterns.

© The Author(s), under exclusive license to Springer Nature Switzerland AG 2022
O. Gervasi et al. (Eds.): ICCSA 2022 Workshops, LNCS 13380, pp. 345–359, 2022.
https://doi.org/10.1007/978-3-031-10542-5_24

These events threaten the sustainability of urban mobility not only in the short term but also in the long term. Therefore, cities have accelerated their efforts to take emergency measures to rebuild and maintain urban mobility through the implementation of resilient and sustainable alternatives.

These alternatives are related both to transport infrastructure (roads, railways, ports and airports) but also to mobility services and energy and digital infrastructure.

Technological development can foster a country's resilience and contribute to the process of reducing greenhouse gas emissions and should always be correlated with political strategies aimed at aligning economic opportunities with minimising environmental impact. Digital technology, for example, can directly and indirectly contribute to reducing a significant share of overall emissions.

The current demographic trends and the agglomeration development have underlined the need for real adaptation, resilience and mitigation actions.

According to the UN 2030 Agenda and the G7 and G20 goals, a sustainable infrastructure system must respect individual characteristics, improve the lives of communities in economic and social terms, and enhance the landscapes concerned.

The Sustainable Development Goal (SDG) directly related to infrastructure is known as SDG 9; however, it is clear that the impacts go far beyond this and relate to gender issues (SDG 5), inequality reduction (SDG 10), sustainable cities (SDG 11), access to clean water and energy (SDGs 6 and 7) and responsible production and consumption (SDG 12).

Therefore, acting on infrastructure generates very strong impacts on the 2030 Agenda.

The energy crisis, exacerbated even more by the recent events of the war in Ukraine, has undoubtedly created a very strong shock on all fronts, especially energy. However, despite the drama of the moment, it is clear that there is a greater need to accelerate the European Green Deal. If completed as planned, it should reach net zero in 2050.

Achieving this goal, starting today with a strong commitment to increase renewable energy production, also goes in the direction of making Europe energy independent, thus also supporting the goal of overcoming the energy crisis.

Consequently, these short-term measures are triggering a sustainable transition that continues even after the end of the pandemic. Indeed, crisis management requires emergency actions by urban mobility planning represented by the Sustainable Urban Mobility Plan (SUMP) and long-term perspectives that align with the Sustainable Development Goals (SDGs).

1.1 The Evolution of Strategies Introduced by SUMPs in the Era of the COVID Pandemic and the Energy Crisis

The Sustainable Urban Mobility Plan (SUMP) is about improving the accessibility of urban areas and ensuring sustainable mobility and transport within the urban area and its periphery. Indeed, much research has been published since 2020 that describes, analyses and recommends various actions taken by public authorities in different regions of the world. These actions cover urban infrastructure design, new trends in urban mobility, and strategic planning for the SUMP. In order to plan resilient cities that are able to maintain their functioning with the minimum amount of contamination, it is essential to prioritize post-COVID urban plans that are inclusive and low-carbon.

The main urban characteristics of the European cities most affected by the pandemic, namely Italy, Germany and the United Kingdom, were analysed by a study conducted by [1]. This study found the impacts resulting from urban connectivity by public transport. these impacts correlated with the speed of virus spread but also with population size, density and urban morphology.

Another research investigated the urban planning trends during the pandemic, considering the strategies for a better and sustainable transportation and the new development of urban parks. In fact, a new approach to resilient urban planning based on seven aspects is recommended, namely; density, inclusiveness, public spaces, public health system, movement of goods and people, migration of populations, tourism and travel. [2].

In addition, the situation related to the pandemic, highlights the importance of public space, green networks and soft mobility also supported by the Sustainable Development Goals. [3] analyses the results of integrating urban planning and projects through the design of public space along blue and green networks in the United Kingdom. The resulting model of cooperation is based on a responsible, inclusive and sustainable strategy for building and networking new resilient urban spaces, green infrastructure and new forms of sustainable mobility.

In the same context, the organization of space plays a decisive role in the orientation of people's behaviours. [4] Recommends that the planning of spaces where Parklets can be implemented should be included in the guidelines of urban planning strategies in Italy. A new initiative accelerated by the COVID-19 pandemic in the city of Rotterdam, Holland and initially concluded in the context of the local climate agreement and the study conducted by [5] describes the governance process for this city's transition. This transition is based on inclusive, zero-emission and shared mobility in 2030. Thus, local policies prioritize bicycling, walking, car sharing and public transport in line with urban mobility systems in developed countries based on integrated policies that include individual, private and public transport.

Obviously, the updating of the current SUMPs is strongly recommended in order to achieve sustainable and intelligent mobility. This objective is achieved through the active participation of citizens in the implementation of sustainable mobility actions.

A study by [6] showed the actions needed for a new post-pandemic vision of SUMP in Latin America and the Caribbean region. This study emphasised that the promotion of cycling requires the development of the necessary infrastructure in terms of bicycle lanes and parking.

Likewise, it is recommended that the necessary public spaces be developed to encourage walking. In addition, modes of transport are re-evaluated in terms of necessity and usability.

Similarly, a study conducted by [7] proposed developing walking and cycling paths and improving the connectivity of transit stations and car parks to contribute to the resilience of urban mobility in Turkey.

Finally, a study by [8] highlighted how the COVID-19 pandemic represents a window of opportunity for sustainable mobility in Germany and other jurisdictions. This study states that individuals can actively participate in the transformation towards sustainability by changing their travel habits and lifestyle. Table 1 summarises the main SUMP-related contributions:

Table 1. Classification of contributions by aspect of SUMP

Infrastructure development	New trends in urban mobility	Strategic planning for SUMP
[1–6, 10]	[3, 5, 8]	[9–11]

Source: Authors elaboration

Since 2022, some literature studies have analysed the measures adopted in the various cities of the world due to the COVID-19 emergency in terms of urban mobility and assess which have been the most effective, verifying their effects both in the short and long term. In particular, it was conducted on some cities located in Europe and in North and South America, analysing and comparing the most effective measures adopted [12]. Due to the difficulties brought about by the COVID-19 pandemic, there is a need to provide road users with a range of appropriate services and infrastructure to discourage the use of private vehicles with combustion engines.

For some years now, several scientific works have focused on the problems and stresses of the contemporary city, mainly due to natural and health factors as well as climate change and the COVID19 pandemic [13–15]. Some work has integrated the aspect of health security into the SUMP in order to promote safer mobility by assessing accidents, risk perception, the location of possible vaccination hubs and generally taking into account health emergencies [9–16]. Therefore, the evolution of the strategies to be intruded in the next SUMP will have to identify factors and possible mitigation actions considering both the behavioural aspect of the transport demand subjected to the above-mentioned scenarios and to consider previous policy and planning actions in order to make further modifications and decisive choices. In this context, literature suggests that in many countries there is still a need to create or implement an adequate network of public charging infrastructure and to facilitate the establishment of private charging stations.

In particular, an analysis of some of the European Sustainable Urban Mobility Plans (SUMP) and the transport offerings related to several cities was recently carried out. The comparison revealed factors and criteria that allow for exemplification in the development and adaptation of the planning and design concept [17]. In addition to increased infrastructure and services, the deployment of intelligent transport systems (ITS) and info mobility systems is crucial. Research conducted by [18] laid the foundations for the definition of Key Performance Indicators (KPIs) to measure and monitor the impact of technologies on the development of smart cities and promote sustainable mobility approaches, addressing the urban planning and transport mobility issues of modern society. The Fig. 1 summarise the challenges and the results on short and long terms of the sustainable urban mobility planning.

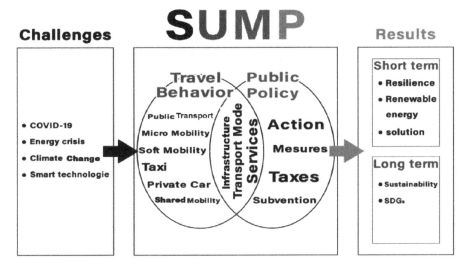

Fig. 1. Summary of challenges and results of SUMP. (Source: Authors elaboration)

With these events in mind, this paper aims to analyse the literature of the last two years with regard to transport demand and modal choices and compare the results with the actions implemented by planners and politicians.

The following paragraphs show summary tables comparing the literature and the discussion and conclusion paragraph suggests the criticalities and possible improvement actions and also the limitations of the research are underlined and the next research steps are announced.

2 Literature Review

This paragraph shows a comparison of literature acquired on google scholar considering the recent literature from 2020 until today and related to the two categories related respectively to the behaviour of the transport demand (users) and to the political choices implemented and actions promoted through the creation and evolution of planning tools such as SUMPs.

2.1 Mobility User Trends

With the intention of limiting the spread of the virus, cities around the world have instituted restrictive measures that vary from social distancing, telecommuting, distance education, travel barriers, and lockdown. This situation has caused a sense of fear and anxiety among citizens, which has resulted in a change in daily travel patterns [19]. Indeed, through the variation in travel demand and modal choice, users seek safe and healthy means of transportation [9].

For example, a high number of citizens have stopped commuting to work due to shifts to remote work and online education [20]. Also, leisure-related travel has been reduced as meeting places such as restaurants and movie theatres are closed [21]. In contrast, travel for basic necessities has not seen a major change as these are vital trips for anyone exposed to shocks especially the COVID-19 pandemic [22]. Thus, the analysis of new travel patterns facilitates the updating of urban mobility policies [23]. At the end of the above, there is an interaction relationship between changes in travel patterns and public policies stimulated by the coronavirus pandemic. As evidenced by [24], before imposing restrictions on public transport, it is necessary to understand users' modal choice. In this respect, a large number of papers have been published from 2020 onwards analysing modal choice and intention to use transport means [25] in different regions of the world with the aim of helping public authorities to formulate new urban mobility policies.

Some work has been based on travel surveys, others on smart card systems and mobile travel data such as Google and Apple like described on Table 2:

Table 2. Summary of main finding from previous modal choice research

References	Main outcome	Data source	Country
[19]	Reduction of travel distance Low-income people are more likely to use public transport	L	South Korea
[21]	Reduction of bus and train use Increase of walking activities	S	Greece
[25]	Increase of the use of personal motorized vehicles Reduction in the use of public transport Reduction of national air transport	S	New Zealand-Australia
[26]	PT is the choice for long journeys Reduced use of carpooling services people without cars prefer to buy electric vehicles rather than cars	S	China
[22]	Reduction in leisure travel Modal choice depends on socio-economic status Increasing car use for long trips Decreasing carpooling rates Increasing feeling of fear of PT	S	China
[27]	Increased teleworking Increase in the use of shared mobility and active transport Lack of equity in public transport increase of car use	S	USA

(continued)

Table 2. (*continued*)

References	Main outcome	Data source	Country
[27]	The rate of car use was tripled Reduction of the emission rate linked to transport following the decline in the number of trips at the beginning of the pandemic	S	Canada
[23]	High perception of risk of contamination in PT Interactivity between behaviour change and public policy	S	Japan
[24]	Low-income users are more likely to use public transport Women are more likely to use public transport because authorities do not allow women to drive cars Car owners have not changed their travel habits	S	Pakistan
[29]	Reduction of non-essential travel Older people tend not to travel	S	India
[30]	Overall decrease in mobility for all commercial activities Increase in residence-to-park trips Decrease in traffic and accidents	L, G	Germany
[30]	Overall decrease in mobility except for residential mobility Reduction of traffic and accidents	L,G	Qatar
[31]	Walking and driving have not been affected by the pandemic The spread of the virus is linked to travel to the market and to work Restrictive measures are not effective enough	G, A	Turkey

Source: Authors elaboration
Notes: A = Apple mobility report; G = google mobility report; L = local agencies; S = survey

It is clear that there is a consensus on the new trend of using individual modes of transport at the expense of collective modes.

Indeed, there is a significant reduction in the use of buses and trains, which is related to the decrease in the need to travel and the fear of contamination in closed areas [32]. A study conducted by [33] finds that there is a decline in public transport use in Zagreb-Croatia, but it is less proportional than that recorded in other EU member countries.

In African cities, the crisis has significantly affected the mobility of people. While changes in mobility differ among governments, the number of public transport trips made in African cities declined by an average of 40% in April 2020 compared to the pre-COVID-19 period. In contrast, low-income users, who are more likely to use public transport [19], have not changed their travel patterns [34], because their mode choices are limited [23].

Hence the need to develop a transport system that is equitable, inclusive, and reduces disparities in accessibility among residents of a region regardless of socioeconomic background, that encourages citizens to regain confidence in public transport [21], and that helps promote sustainable development [27].

In this sense, society is becoming increasingly dependent on the car in the post-pandemic phase given the personal sense of safety and non-contact that the car provides [27]. However, [26] states that the purchase intention of two-wheeled electric vehicles is higher than that of automobiles.

However, it is still dependent on the development of smart infrastructure and charging stations in China.

In addition, there is a trend of walking and biking as non-contact modes of travel. [35, 36] study the trend of shared bike usage during the coronavirus period.

Thus, this alternative mode of transportation reduces the fear of contamination that is likely to occur in crowded public transportation. It also preserves health, social distancing, reduces polluting emissions and traffic congestion.

Therefore, the shift towards active transport promotes modal transition in the long term [37]. It is clear that bicycle sharing requires less investment in infrastructure development and capital than public transport [38]. In this respect, this situation represents opportunity for public authorities to reformulate their strategies for sustainable and resilient urban mobility planning.

In addition, the evolution of micromobility, including the supply of electric scooters, has been a kind of alternative to public transport for short trips in urban areas.

These new intelligent modes of travel have also been supported by government measures. In order to analyse the effectiveness of e-scooters even in the post-pandemic phase [39] studies the diffusion of electric scooters in Italian cities and proposes to elaborate a GIS containing the origins and destinations as well as the areas of implementation of shared e-scooter systems in order to promote its use at the community level.

2.2 Public Policy Aspects

Policies put in place in response to the COVID-19 crisis help promote the use of public transport, encourage the deployment of low-carbon transport modes, promote walking and cycling where possible, and limit the use of private motorized cars.

Table 3. Summary of main research on shifts in travel patterns in responding to new public policy measures

Public transport (bus, train, metro)	Soft mobility (cycling, walking)	Micro mobility (e-scooter)	Private car
[7, 32, 33, 40–42] [43–53]	[20, 35–38, 54–59, 69]	[39, 60–68, 70]	[25, 26, 28, 70]

Source: Authors elaboration

The Table 3 summarizes key research on changing travel patterns in response to new government measures during the pandemic.

These policies must be consistent with the Sustainable Development Goals as they relate to long-term climate change reduction.

Similarly, these actions must interact with changes in user behaviour during the pandemic. It is obvious that these measures differ according to the objectives and urban characteristics of the region of implementation. As evidenced by the COVID Mobility Works platform, which is dedicated to collecting, synthesizing and sharing mobility initiatives that facilitated citizens' travel during the pandemic. The Table 4 shows examples of various actions carried out by different regions.

Table 4. Example of public policies for urban mobility implemented during the COVID pandemic 19 [71]

Purpose	Action	Cities
Public health	17 km walkway implemented	Mexico city-Mexico
	Active and family street	Quebec-Montreal Canada
Equity	CARTA allows rides to use expired passes	South Caroline-USA
	TriMet opens virtual application for low-income fare program	Oregon Portland-USA
Safety	Adds 150 km of bicycle lanes	Rome-Italy
	Temporary transformation of car lane into space for bicycles	Utrecht-Netherlands
Public engagement	Collaborative services to smooth demand at peak hours	Ile de France
Moving people	Launches app to show passengers bus occupancy levels	Catalonia-Spain
	Free use of bicycles through the bike citizens app	Stuttgant-Germany

In addition, the World Bank Transport Group recommends improving governance, financing and capacity building, supporting non-motorised and active modes, improving the existing public transport system, and supporting modal shift from private vehicles to high-capacity transport systems in Africa. [72]. The increase in the price of fuel affects everyone and not just those who use a private vehicle with a combustion engine. It is enough to consider the "last mile" to understand why: the goods arrive in the places where we buy them by trucks and vans, to get them moving, fuel is needed, they often have to travel long distances and all this partly affects those who carry them, partly about who sells them and, above all, about who buys them. Those who suffer the greatest burden of this mechanism are the less well-off classes. When the fuel increases, it always ends up like this: the worst damage is always suffered by those who have no room to make ends meet. hence the need to rethink the entire supply chain by integrating the Block Chain in order to reduce the total cost and improve the quality of services. Some states have reduced excise duties on fuels (such as Italy).

Others are considering different energy sources and implementing measures that may discourage the use of cars by using bikes, skates and scooters instead As in Tunisia, which has reduced subsidies for petroleum products and increased car taxes in order to limit the use of private vehicles.

3   Discussion and Conclusions

In this context, when defining the incentive measures to be adopted, a fair balance should be sought between subsidy or tax relief policies and fiscal policies (taxes or permits) in order to keep the public budget constraint as balanced as possible. Some examples of measures to decarbonise transport and mobility can be related to:

- the differentiation of tariffs of managed services (airports, motorways, railways) on the basis of vehicle emissions and tax recovery on the same basis;
- the strengthening of Green Public Procurement to use rewarding or disincentive criteria in public (procurement code) and private tenders;
- incentives for urban public transport vs. private transport as mobility in cities and penalties for car use (eco pass style or road pricing).

In conclusion, this study established that a holistic approach is needed in research and publications related to understanding the factors and strategies driving the evolution of sustainable mobility considering the recent criticalities produced by the COVID19 pandemic and the growing energy crisis.

Our systematic review and analysis of the literature of the last two years highlighted that the covid-19 pandemic has led to changes in travel choices and perceptions of transport use. Trends in walking, cycling and private car use are expressed by feelings of fear of contamination on congested public transport. In order to limit car dependency, promote active mobility and significantly reduce GHG emissions, cities are being asked to rethink urban planning through the design of "15-min cities". This type of planning represents an effective solution to reduce congestion, ensure equity of access to services and strengthen the attractiveness and sense of belonging to cities. In this regard, public policymakers must take advantage of changing modal choices to promote intermodality and shared mobility by integrating new service modes such as MAAS to make it easier for citizens to move around and to make mobility more sustainable and economical. Similarly, urban mobility planning strategies should prioritize the provision of bicycle lanes and pedestrian sidewalks.

Thus, public authorities are called to invest more in transport strategies centred on intelligent transport systems (IT), new Internet of Things (IOT) technologies and technologies based on artificial intelligence (AI) in order to promote the concept of smart cities. In this same context, to face the dependence on fossil fuels accelerated by the energy crisis that emerged from the war in Ukraine, the strategies must include renewable alternatives accompanied by the implementation of new charging stations.

These new strategies promote planning for urban mobility that is sustainable in the face of climate change and resilient to disruption.

In the end, the success of sustainable and smart cities depends on the interaction between transport demand and supply in close connection with energy and smart technology developments. Therefore, future research must not only define actions to mitigate impacts but also maximise these correlations in order to generate sustainable and more resilient actions and strategies.

References

1. AbouKorin, S.A.A., et al.: Role of urban planning characteristics in forming pandemic resilient cities. Case study of COVID-19 impacts on European cities within England, Germany and Italy. Cities **118**, 103324 (2021). https://doi.org/10.1016/j.cities.2021.103324
2. Raj, S.A., et al.: Impact of Covid-19 in shaping new resilient urban planning approach. IOP Conf. Ser.: Mater. Sci. Eng. **1114**, 012040 (2021). IOP Publishing. https://doi.org/10.1088/1757-899X/1114/1/012040
3. Ravagnan, C., et al.: Sustainable mobility and resilient urban spaces in the United Kingdom. Practices and proposals. Transp. Res. Proc. **60**, 164–171 (2022). https://doi.org/10.1016/j.trpro.2021.12.022
4. Campisi, T., et al.: Evolution of sustainable mobility and urban space planning: exploring the factors contributing to the regeneration of car parking in living spaces. Transp. Res. Proc. **60**, 76–83 (2021). https://doi.org/10.1016/j.trpro.2021.12.011
5. Loorbach, D., et al.: Transition governance for just, sustainable urban mobility: an experimental approach from Rotterdam, the Netherlands. J. Urban Mob. **1**, 100009 (2021). https://doi.org/10.1016/j.urbmob.2021.100009
6. Lozano, D.L.A., et al.: Sustainable and smart mobility evaluation since citizen participation in responsive cities. Transp. Res. Proc. **58**, 519–526 (2021). https://doi.org/10.1016/j.trpro.2021.11.069
7. Özden, A., et al.: Urban mobility in COVID-19: how we adapted to change and how should we respond. Acad. Platform J. Nat. Hazards Dis. Manage. **1**(2), 96–109 (2020)
8. Schmidt, K., et al.: COVID-19 – A window of opportunity for the transition toward sustainable mobility? Transp. Res. Interdisc. Persp. **10**, 100374 (2021). https://doi.org/10.1016/j.trip.2021.100374
9. Spadaro, I., et al.: Sustainable urban mobility plan and health security. Sustainability **13**(8), 4403 (2021). https://doi.org/10.3390/su13084403
10. Valenzula-Levi, N., et al.: Housing and accessibility after the covid-19 pandemic: rebuilding for resilience, equity and sustainable mobility. Transp. Policy **109**, 48–60 (2021). https://doi.org/10.1016/j.transpol.2021.05.006
11. Torrisi, V., Garau, C., Ignaccolo, M., Inturri, G.: "Sustainable urban mobility plans": key concepts and a critical revision on SUMPs guidelines. In: International conference on computational science and its applications, pp. 613–628. Springer, Cham (2020)
12. Suraci, D.: New urban mobility strategies after the COVID-19 pandemic. In: Smart and sustainable technology for resilient cities and communities, pp. 61–71 (2022)
13. Moraci, F., Errigo, M. F., Fazia, C., Campisi, T., Castelli, F.: Cities under pressure: strategies and tools to face climate change and pandemic. Sutainability **12**(18), 7743 (2020). https://doi.org/10.3390/su12187743
14. Medina-Rioja, R., et al.: Grace under pressure: resiliency of quality monitoring of stroke care during the COVID-19 pandemic in Mexico City. Front. Neurol. **13**, 831735 (2022). https://doi.org/10.3389/fneur.2022.831735

15. Kyriazis, A., Mews, G., Belpaire, E., Aerts, J., Malik, S.A.: Physical distancing, children and urban health: the COVID-19 crisis' impact on children and how this could affect future urban planning and design policies. Cities Health, S83–S88 (2020). https://doi.org/10.1080/23748834.2020.1809787

16. Alemdar, K.D., Kaya, Ö., Çodur, M.Y., Campisi, T., Tesoriere, G.: Accessibility of vaccination centers in COVID-19 outbreak control: a GIS-based multi-criteria decision making approach. ISPRS Int. J. Geo-Inf. **708**, 10 (2021). https://doi.org/10.3390/ijgi10100708

17. Campisi, T., Cocuzza, E., Ignaccolo, M., Inturri, G., Torrisi, V.: Exploring the factors that encourage the spread of EV-DRT into the sustainable urban mobility plans. In: International conference on computational science and its applications, vol. 12953, pp. 699–714. Springer, Cham (2021). https://doi.org/10.1007/978-3-030-86976-2_48

18. Torrisi, V., Garau, C., Inturri, G., Ignaccolo, M.: Strategies and actions towards sustainability: Encouraging good ITS practices in the SUMP vision. In: AIP Conference Proceedings, vol. 2343, p. 090008. AIP Publishing LLC (2021). https://doi.org/10.1063/5.0047897

19. Kim, S., et al.: Changes in car and bus usage amid the COVID-19 pandemic: relationship. Transp. Geo. **96**, 103168 (2021). https://doi.org/10.1016/j.jtrangeo.2021.103168

20. Campisi, T., Tesoriere, G., Trouva, M., Papas, T., Basbas, S.: Impact of teleworking on travel behaviour during the COVID-19 era: the case of Sicily, Italy. Transp. Res. Proc. **60**, 251–258 (2022). https://doi.org/10.1016/j.trpro.2021.12.033

21. Baig, F., et al.: Changes in people's mobility behavior in Greece after the COVID-19 outbreak. Sustainability **14**(6), 3567 (2022). https://doi.org/10.3390/su14063567

22. Chen, X., et al.: Exploring essential travel during COVID-19 quarantine: evidence. Transp. Policy **111**, 90–97 (2021). https://doi.org/10.1016/j.tranpol.2021.07.016

23. Ding, H., et al.: Dynamic associations between temporal behavior changes caused by the COVID-19 pandemic and subjective assessments of policymaking : a case study in Japan. Trans. Policy **110**, 58–70 (2021). https://doi.org/10.1016/j.tranpol.2021.05.014

24. Abdullah, M., et al.: Public transport versus solo travel mode choices during the COVID19 pandemic: self-reported evidence from a developing country. Transportation engineering **5**, 100078 (2021). https://doi.org/10.1016/j.treng.2021.100078

25. Thomas, F.M.F., et al.: Commuting before and after COVID-19. Transp. Res. Interdisc. Persp. **11**, 100423 (2021). https://doi.org/10.1016/j.trip.2021.100423

26. Luan, S., et al.: Exploring the impact of COVID-19 on individual's travel mode choice. Transp. Policy **106**, 271–280 (2021). https://doi.org/10.1016/j.tranpol.2021.04.011

27. Shamshiripour, A., et al.: How is COVID-19 reshaping activity-travel behavior? Evidence from a comprehensive survey in Chicago. Transp. Res. Interdisc. Persp. **7**, 100216 (2020). https://doi.org/10.1016/j.trip.2020.100216

28. DeWeese, J., et al.: Travel behaviour and greenhouse gas emissions during the COVID-19 pandemic : a case study in a university setting. Transp. Res. Interdisc. Persp. **13**, 100531 (2021). https://doi.org/10.1016/j.trip.2021.100531

29. Pawar, D.S., et al.: Modelling work- and non-work-based trip patterns during transition to lockdown period of COVID-19 pandemic in India. Travel Behav. Soc. **24**, 46–56 (2021). https://doi.org/10.1016/j.tbs.2021.02.002

30. Jaekel, B., et al.: Transport impacts in Germany and State of Qatar: an assessment during the firt wave of COVID-19. Transp. Res. Interdisc. Persp. **13**, 100540 (2022). https://doi.org/10.1016/j.trip.2022.100540

31. Kartal, M.T., et al.: The relationship between mobility and COVID-19 pandemic: daily evidence from an emerging country by causality analysis. Transp. Res. Interdisc. Persp. **10**, 100366 (2021). https://doi.org/10.1016/j.trip.2021.100366

32. Subbarao, S.S.V., Kadali, R.: Impact of COVID-19 pandemic lockdown on the public transportation system and strategic plans to improve PT ridership: a review. Innov. Infra. Sol. **7**(1), 1–14 (2021). https://doi.org/10.1007/s41062-021-00693-9

33. Naletina, D., et al.: Public transportation during the COVID-19 pandemic in the city of Zagreb. Intereulaweast (2021). https://doi.org/10.22598/iele.2021.8.2.2
34. Politis, I., et al.: COVID-19 lockdown measures and travel behavior: the case of Thessaloniki, Greece. Transp. Res. Interdisc. Persp. **10**, 100345 (2021). https://doi.org/10.1016/j.trip.2021.100345
35. Jobe, J., et al.: Bike share responses to COVID-19. Transp. Res. Interdisc. Persp. **10**, 100353 (2020). https://doi.org/10.1016/j.trip.2021.100353
36. Padmanabhan, V., et al.: COVID-19 effects on shared-biking in New York, Boston, and Chicago. Transp. Res. Interdisc. Persp. **9**, 100282 (2020). https://doi.org/10.1016/j.trip.2020.100282
37. Teixeira, J.F., et al.: The link between bike sharing and subway use during the COVID-19 pandemic: the case-study of New York's Citi Bike. Transp. Res. Interdisc. Persp. **6**, 100166 (2020). https://doi.org/10.1016/j.trip.2020.100166
38. Wang, H., et al.: Bikeshare and subway ridership changes during the COVID-19 pandemic in New York City. Transp. Policy **106**, 262–270 (2021). https://doi.org/10.1016/j.tranpol.2021.04.004
39. Fistola, R., et al.: Micro-mobility in the "Virucity" the effectiveness of e-scooter sharing. Transp. Res. Proc. **60**, 464–471 (2022). https://doi.org/10.1016/j.trpro.2021.12.060
40. Fridrisek, P., et al.: COVID-19 and suburban public transport in the conditions of the Czech Republic. Transp. Res. Interdisc. Persp. **13**, 100523 (2021). https://doi.org/10.1016/j.trip.2021.100523
41. Patlins, A., et al.: Adapting the public transport system to the COVID-19 challenge ensuring its sustainability. Transp. Res. Proc. **55**, 1398–1406 (2021). https://doi.org/10.1016/j.trpro.2021.07.125
42. Rasca, S., et al.: Impacts of COVID-19 and pandemic control measures on public transport ridership in European urban areas – the cases of Vienna, Innsbruck, Oslo, and Agder. Transp. Res. Interdisc. Persp. **10**, 100376 (2021). https://doi.org/10.1016/j.trip.2021.100376
43. Parker, M.E.G., et al.: Public transit use in the United States in the era of COVID-19: transit riders' travel behavior in the COVID-19 impact and recovery period. Transp. Policy **111**, 53–62 (2021). https://doi.org/10.1016/j.tranpol.2021.07.005
44. Kamga, C., et al.: Slowing the spread of COVID-19: Review of "Social distancing" interventions deployed by public transit in the United States and Canada. Transp. Policy **106**, 25–36 (2021). https://doi.org/10.1016/j.tranpol.2021.03.014
45. Li, T., et al.: Assessing regional risk of COVID-19 infection from Wuhan via high speed rail. Transp. Policy **106**, 226–238 (2021). https://doi.org/10.1016/j.tranpol.2021.04.009
46. Jenelius, E., et al.: Impacts of COVID-19 on public transport ridership in Sweden: analysis of ticket validations, sales and passenger counts. Transp. Res. Interdisc. Persp. **8**, 100242 (2020). https://doi.org/10.1016/j.trip.2020.100242
47. Vichiensan, V., et al.: COVID-19 countermeasures and passengers' confidence of urban rail travel in Bangkok. Sustainability **13**(16), 9377 (2021). https://doi.org/10.3390/su13169377
48. Adamkiewicz, Z., et al.: The outbreak of COVID-19 pandemic in relation to sense of safety and mobility changes in public transport using the example of Warsaw. Sustainability **14**(3), 1780 (2022). https://doi.org/10.3390/su14031780
49. Basu, R., et al.: Sustainable mobility in auto-dominated Metro Boston: challenges and opportunities post-COVID-19. Transp. Policy **103**, 197–210 (2021). https://doi.org/10.1016/j.tranpol.2021.01.006
50. Scorrano, M., et al.: Active mobility in an Italian city: mode choice determinants and attitudes before and during the COVID-19 emergency. Res. Transp. Econ. (2021). https://doi.org/10.1016/j.retrec.2021.101031

51. Dai, J., et al.: Improving the subway attraction for the post-COVID-19 era: the role of fare-free public transport policy. Transp. Policy **103**, 21–30 (2021). https://doi.org/10.1016/j.tranpol. 2021.01.007
52. Ceder, A.: Syncing Sustainable Urban Mobility with Public Transit Policy Trends Based on Global Data Analysis. Natureportfolio (2021). https://doi.org/10.1038/s41598-021-93741-4
53. Shaheen, S., et al.: Future of public transit and shared mobility: scenario planning for COVID19 recovery. Inst. Transp. Stud. (2021). https://doi.org/10.7922/G2NC5ZGR
54. Carboni, A., et al.: Active mobility perception from an intersectional perspective: insights from two European cities. Transp. Res. Proc. **60**, 560–567 (2022). https://doi.org/10.1016/j. trpro.2021.12.072
55. Cerasoli, M.A.: An antifragile strategy for Rome post-COVID mobility. Transp. Res. Proc. **60**, 338–345 (2022). https://doi.org/10.1016/j.trpro.2021.12.044
56. Campisi, T., et al.: Anxiety, fear and stress feelings of road users during daily walking in COVID-19 pandemic: Sicilian cities. Transp. Res. Proc. **10**, 62 (2022). https://doi.org/10. 1016/j.trpro.2022.02.014
57. Harrington, D.M., Hadjiconstantinou, M.: Changes in commuting behaviours in response to the COVID-19 pandemic in the UK. J. Transp. Health **24**, 101313 (2022). https://doi.org/10. 1016/j.jth.2021.101313
58. Vučinić, M., Vučićević, M., Nenadović, K.: The COVID-19 pandemic affects owners walking with their dogs. J. Vet. Behav. **48**, 1–10 (2022). https://doi.org/10.1016/j.jveb.2021.10.009
59. Nguyen, M.H., Pojani, D.: The emergence of recreational cycling in Hanoi during the COVID19 pandemic. J. Transp. Health **24**, 101332 (2022). https://doi.org/10.1016/j.jth.2022. 101332
60. Dias, G., et al.: The role of shared e-scooter systems in urban sustainability and resilience during the COVID-19 mobility restrictions. Sustainability **13**(13), 7084 (2021). https://doi. org/10.3390/su13137084
61. Campisi, T., Basbas, S., Skoufas, A., Tesoriere, G., Ticali, D.: Socio-eco-friendly performance of e-scooters in Palermo: preliminary statistical results. In: International conference on innovation in urban and regional planning, p. 64 (2021). https://doi.org/10.1007/978-3-030-86976-2_46
62. Dean, M.D.-G.: Shared e-scooter trajectory analysis during the COVID-19 pandemic in Austin, Texas. Transp. Res. Rec. (2022). 03611981221083306
63. Hosseinzadeh, A.: Analyzing the impact of COVID-19 pandemic on micromobility transportation. In International conference on transportation and development, pp. 52–60 (2021)
64. Latinopoulos, C.P.: Planning for e-scooter use in metropolitan cities: a case study for Paris. Transp. Res. Part D: Transp. Environ. **100** (2021). https://doi.org/10.1016/j.trd.2021.103037
65. Glavic, D., Trpkovic, A., Milenkovic, M., Jevremovic, S.: The e-scooter potential to change Urban mobility—belgrade case study. Sustainability **13**(11), 5948 (2021). https://doi.org/10. 3390/su13115948
66. Almannaa, M.H.: Perception analysis of E-scooter riders and non-riders in Riyadh, Saudi Arabia: survey outputs. Sustainability **13**(2) (2022). https://doi.org/10.3390/su13020863
67. Bagdatli, M.E.C., Ipek, F.: Transport mode preferences of university students in post-COVID19 pandemic. Transp. Policy, **118**, 20–32 (2022). https://doi.org/10.1016/j.tranpol. 2022.01.017
68. Campisi, T., Akgün-Tanbay, N., Nahiduzzaman, M., Dissanayake, D.: Uptake of e-Scooters in Palermo, Italy: Do the Road Users Tend to Rent, Buy or Share?. In: International Conference on Computational Science and Its Applications, vol. 12953, pp. 669–682. Springer, Cham (2021). https://doi.org/10.1007/978-3-030-86976-2_46
69. Campisi, T., et al.: Factors influencing the implementation and deployment of e-vehicles in small cities: a preliminary two-dimensional statistical study on user acceptance. Transp. Res. Proc. **62**, 333–340 (2022). https://doi.org/10.1016/j.trpro.2022.02.042

70. Van Der Drift, S., Wismans, L., Olde Kalter, M.J.: Changing mobility patterns in the Netherlands during COVID-19 outbreak. J. Location Based Services, **16**(1), 1–24 (2022)
71. COVID Mobility Works: (2022). https://www.covidmobilityworks.org/find-responses?actors=public-sector-action. Accesed 4 October 2020
72. World Bank Group Transport: Mobilité urbaine et Covid-19 en Afrique (2020)

A Design Method for Pedestrian Areas by a Simplified Approach to Predict the Future Traffic Scenarios

Mauro D'Apuzzo[1]([⊠]) [iD], Giuseppe Cappelli[1,2], Azzurra Evangelisti[1] [iD], and Daniela Santilli[1]

[1] University of Cassino and Southern Lazio, Via G. Di Biasio 43, 03043 Cassino, Italy
{dapuzzo,giuseppe.cappelli1,daniela.santilli}@unicas.it,
giuseppe.cappelli@iusspavia.it
[2] University School for Advanced Studies, IUSS, Piazza della Vittoria n.15, 27100 Pavia, Italy

Abstract. The interest in sustainable mobility and active modes has increased in the last years. A strong measure to encourage citizens towards sustainable transport choices is to promote and enlarge pedestrian areas, that appears to be the most radical and feasible measures against the modal choice towards transit and private traffic because of a reduction of noise and air pollution levels but also because of a dramatic decrease of the safety risk of vulnerable users. However, the design of a new pedestrian area will have an impact on future vehicular traffic flows that need to be evaluated. In this paper a simplified method to predict the future traffic scenarios following the establishment of a pedestrian area is presented. Results by this method have been compared with those provided by a conventional traffic demand model and a sensitive analysis employing different assignment techniques has been carried out. It is believed that the use of this method may help urban road designers and city planners in identifying critical traffic scenarios induced by new pedestrian areas and in studying suitable countermeasures to reduce traffic congestion in surrounding areas.

Keywords: Pedestrian area design · Sustainable mobility · Simplified methods

1 Introduction

In the past years, interest into sustainable mobility and active modes has increased [1] and Governments have set goals to increase active mode share [2]. In 2015, the governments of 193 UN member countries approved the Agenda 2030 for Sustainable Development, whose essential elements are 17 objectives: the theme of sustainable mobility, which falls under objectives 3 (Health and well-being), 9 (Business, innovation and infrastructures) and 11 (Sustainable cities and communities) [3].

The realization of pedestrian areas is one of the many ways of applying sustainable mobility and it is the most radical and feasible measure for a defined reason: because it prohibits the transit of public and private traffic [4]: only vulnerable users (in particular pedestrian and cyclist, except for vehicles that carry out an emergency service or used by disabled people) are allowed, changing so the actual paradigm which is vehicular center-based [5]. Pedestrian areas are mostly located in the city center or in strategical urban areas, where the main social and economical activities are located: according to the literature, the 60% of pedestrians use pedestrian areas for leisure purposes [6].

Although the environmental aspects are of primary importance, the major impacts in terms of road safety [7] must not be neglected because this also leads to an increase of the number of pedestrian and consequentially to a reduction of private cars, as it has been shown in Pontevedra, Spain [8]. In addition to a reduction of air pollutants and noise pollution levels in the areas where this measure is envisaged, there is also a drastic reduction in the risk [9], associated with any accidents since the exposure factor with vehicular traffic plays a secondary role [10]. To assess the pedestrian safety, it is essential not only to focus on the vehicle-pedestrian accidents, but also on pedestrian-pedestrian conflicts [11], bearing in mind the pedestrian attitudes and perceptions [12]. However, it is worth to be highlighted that the interactions with cyclists, who travel at a higher speed, and the increasingly use of electric scooters (increasingly present in all European cities) have risen several concerns among urban managers.

In order to simulate this type of interventions, performing software tools are required since it is necessary to predict a realistic future traffic scenario and evaluate the corresponding safety impacts [13]. Due to the high complexity of creating and managing these traffic demand models, in this article a simplified method, which can be useful for road designers and managers, is proposed. The novelty of the proposed method is to estimate both new distribution and magnitude of the flow rates modified by the construction of a pedestrian area, starting from the identification of the inhibited maneuvers and relative flow rates, without the use of traffic simulation software.

2   Framework of the Method

2.1   Description of the Method

The best way to predict the citizens' habits and attitudes to move, in order to design or redevelop our cities by promoting interventions that push towards sustainable mobility choices, is to develop a travel demand model, i.e., a mathematical model that is able to capture of the features describing trips (purpose, departure time, origin, destination, mode and route).

Following these premises, if one is interested in study a typical worst case urban traffic scenario (early morning peak-hour due to commuting traffic) one of the most well-known approaches, is based on a four-stage model that describes the total travel choice as a succession of partial choices. The model can be represented by the following relation (Eq. 1) [14]:

$$d^i(h, s, o, d, m, k) = n^i(o)p^i(x/osh)p^i(d/osh)p^i(m/dosh)p^i(k/mdosh) \qquad (1)$$

where:

- $n^i(o)$pi(x/osh) is the generation model.
- $p^i(d/osh)$ is the distribution model.
- $p^i(m/dosh)$ is the modal choice model.
- $p^i(k/mdosh)$ is the route choice model.

The generation model provides the number of significant trips (and therefore the demand flow) made in the period h for the reason s by the generic user belonging to category i with origin in the area o. The generation model expressed by relationship (1) consists of the following terms:

- $n^i(o)$ is the number of people belonging to category i.
- $p^i(x/osh)$ is the percentage (probability) of users moving.

The distribution model, on the other hand, makes it possible to estimate the percentage of trips made by users belonging to category i who, starting from the area or for reason s in period h, go to destination d. The modal choice model allows to estimate the percentage of individuals belonging to category i who, moving from the origin or destination d, for the reason s, in the time period h, choose the mode of transport m. The route choice model allows to determine the percentage (probability) of individuals of category i who, moving between o and d, for the reason s, in the time slot h and with the mode m, choose the path k.

These methods of forecasting the transport demand are very time consuming to develop since they require a huge amount of data from Census and from traffic counts and survey. Especially for small cities and municipalities where this modelling effort is not already available, it can be useful to seek for alternative engineered approaches to evaluated future traffic scenarios. For this reason, a simplified method was created and can be summarized in the fundamental steps listed below.

- In a preliminary stage, road nodes near the pedestrian area where a modification of the traffic rules or a suppression of one or more accesses has occurred and related inhibited manoeuvres, need to be identified. It is necessary also to detect those manoeuvres (and therefore the relative flow rates for which traffic counts exist) which, due to this change in traffic, in the ex-post scenario, they will be inhibited.
- For each inhibited maneuver it is necessary to identify at least two alternative routes consistent with the traffic rules in the new traffic scenario.
- For each of these new routes it is necessary to calculate the relative travel time by means of a typical internet-based on-line navigation program.

- Following the identification of the main nodes and alternative routes for the inhibited maneuvers and the related travel times, it is necessary to understand what the distribution of the initial inhibited flow will be on these new routes that are created in the ex-post scenario.
- Flow distribution can be preliminarily estimated by re-arranging in an increasing order the travel times (Tt) corresponding to decreasing flow rates related the j^{*th} alternative route (see Fig. 1). Ad a matter of fact, it is essential to remember that shorter travel times should correspond to greater flow rates.

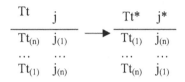

Fig. 1. Index correspondence scheme

- The calculation of the distribution of the flow rates of the inhibited maneuvers is performed assuming an inverse proportionality with the travel time (Eq. 2) and the entire procedure is managed on an iterative basis in order to provide a stable estimation of the traffic flows:

$$F_{kj} = F_k \frac{Tt_{kj^*,i}}{\sum_{j*} Tt_{kj^*,i}} \tag{2}$$

where:

F_{kj} is the inhibited flow due to the inhibited manoeuvre k^{th} on a specific ordered alternative route j^* [veic. eq/h].
F_k is the total inhibited flow due to the inhibited maneuver k^{th} [veic. eq/h].
$Tt_{kj^*,i}$ is the travel time corresponding to the specific ordered alternative routes j^* due to the inhibited maneuver k^{th} [min];
i is the value of the iteration.

Within the specific iteration step, the inhibited flow rates must then be added to basic or pre-existing flows (that represent the actual scenario, derived from traffic counts or traffic simulations) and so it is possible to calculate the new travel times. With these new times a new distribution of the inhibited flow rates has been recalculated in the next iteration step. In the picture below (Fig. 2), a flow chart of the computational procedure is conveniently reported.

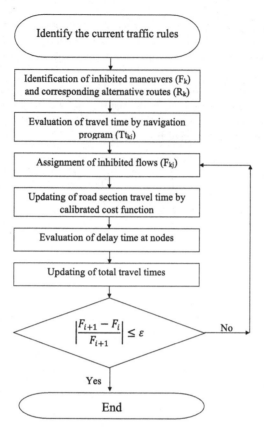

Fig. 2. Flow chart of the simplified method for the evaluation of redistributed flows.

2.2 Description of the Assignment Method

The process of allocating given number of trips to the transportation network is usually referred to as traffic assignment [14, 15].

In this study references are made to five types of traffic assignment: the first is expressed by equation (Eq. 2); the other four (which will be described in the followings) are the *User Equilibrium Assignment* (UE), *System Optimum Assignment* (SO), *All Or Nothing Assignment* (AON) [16], *User Equilibrium/System Optimum Assignment neglecting free flow travel times*.

The problem of the *User Equilibrium Assignment* is equivalent to the minimization of the following nonlinear equation:

$$V_k(F_{kj}) = \sum_{j=1}^{n} \int_{0}^{F_{kj}} Tt_{kj} dF_{kj} \tag{3}$$

where:

$V_k(F_{kj})$ is the total volume between the origin and the destination of the inhibited maneuver k^{th} on a specific alternative route j [veh];

F_{kj} is the inhibited flow due to the inhibited maneuver k^{th} on a specific alternative route j [veh. eq/h].

Tt_{kj} is the travel time of the inhibited maneuver k^{th} on a specific alternative route j [h].

The travel time in (3) can also be expressed as:

$$Tt_{kj} = Tt_{0,kj} + a_{kj}F_{kj} \tag{4}$$

where:

$Tt_{0,kj}$ is the travel time of the inhibited maneuver k^{th} on a specific alternative route j in the free flow conditions [h];

a_{kj} is a proportionality coefficient expressed as in the following equation [h^2/veh]:

$$a_{kj} = \frac{Tt_{0,kj}^2}{F_k} \tag{5}$$

After solving the integral in Eq. (3), it is possible to solve the system (6):

$$\begin{cases} \min : V_k(F_{kj}) = \sum_{j=1}^{n}\left(Tt_{0,kj}F_{kj} + a_{kj}\frac{F_{kj}}{2}^2\right) \\ F_k = \sum_{j=1}^{n} F_{k,j} \end{cases} \tag{6}$$

where:

F_k is the total inhibited flow due to the inhibited maneuver k^{th} [veh. eq/h].

Regarding the second assignment method, the problem of the *System Optimum Assignment* is equivalent to the minimization of the following nonlinear equation:

$$V_k(F_{kj}) = \sum_{j=1}^{n} F_{kj}Tt_{kj}(F_{kj}) \tag{7}$$

And the final system to resolve, follow the same step to solve the system (6):

$$\begin{cases} V_k(F_{kj}) = \sum_{j=1}^{n} F_{kj}\left(Tt_{0,kj} + a_{kj}F_{kj}\right) \\ F_k = \sum_{j=1}^{n} F_{k,j} \end{cases} \tag{8}$$

As it can be easily observed by examining the equation's set (8) if the alternative routes are only two, the expressions provide a closed-form solution with a perfect balance between unknown flows and number of equations. However, if the number of alternative paths is greater than two, it is necessary to introduce additional conditions on unknown traffic flow by making use of the following relationship (9):

$$F_{kj} = F_k\frac{a_{kj^*,i}}{\sum_{j^*} a_{kj^*,i}} \tag{9}$$

where $a_{kj*,i}$ is the same proportionality coefficient expressed as in the Eq. (5) in this chapter [h^2/veh]: it is essential to arrange in an increasing order this coefficient corresponding to decreasing flow rates related the j*th alternative route (see Fig. 3). In fact, it is essential to remember that shorter travel times correspond to greater flow rates.

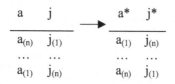

Fig. 3. Index correspondence scheme

It was also seen that it is possible to make a further simplification, which is to neglect travel times as, especially in urban areas, this amount are exceptionally low and negligible quantities. By making use of this simplification, the two assignment approaches (UE and SO) tend to perfectly coincide.

In the *All or Nothing Assignment* users follow the path which present the minimum cost and so the minimum travel times. This model does not appear to be very realistic, especially in nearly saturated road networks, because only one path is chosen, and it ignores the fact that travel times are function of link volume and capacity.

3   Case Study

3.1   Description of the Study Area

The study was conducted in the city of Cassino, an average Italian city with about 36497 inhabitants (Census data) [17] in the Province of Frosinone (Lazio). The city area is mainly flat and without a historic centre: it is still possible identify an urban centre, where the main commercial, administrative and legal activities are located. The city centre is thus characterized by a strong incidence in terms of vehicular flows, which share road areas with consistent cycle-pedestrian flows. These flows are generated by the presence of many attractive activities in the urban centre [8, 12]. Other attractive poles are universities and numerous schools (from kindergartens to secondary schools). It is therefore evident that mobility and the remarkable demand for transport are a central problem in the Municipality and especially in the city centre area.

3.2   Comparison of Flows Before and After the Calibration Phase

The calibration phase is a fundamental step in this analysis. Different traffic counts are available (referring to periods before the Covid-19 pandemic) intersections, which play a strategic role in the urban centre.

With reference to the analysis, 30 traffic zones and 10 external centroids are provided with 14907 trips in a daily basis.

Particular attention was paid to the choice and definition of the cost functions. A BPR function was chosen for the cost functions associated with the links:

$$T_{cur} = T_0\left(a + \frac{F^b}{C}\right) \tag{10}$$

where:

T_{cur} is the time travel with the network charged [s].
T_0 is the travel time with the network un-charged [s].
F is the actual flow [veh/h].
C is the capacity [veh/h].

With references to the cost function of the intersection, modified BPR formula was chosen, that is the one defined by Lohse [18]:

$$T_{cur} = \begin{cases} T_0\left(a + sat^b\right)sat \le sat_{crit} \\ T_0\left(a + sat_{crit}{}^b\right) + abT_0\left(sat_{crit}{}^{b-1}\right)\left(sat - sat_{crit}\right)sat > sat_{crit} \end{cases} \tag{11}$$

where:

sat is the ratio F/C [dimensionless].
sat_{crit} is the critic degree of saturation [dimensionless].

For the calibration of the origin-destination (OD) matrix, 46 traffic counts for the morning time window (07:15–08:15) of a typical weekday are used and the traffic demand model is calibrated with the Visum software. Regarding the TPr procedure, the Equilibrium assignment Bi-conjugate Frank Wolfe (BFW) method has been adopted, and for the calibration the Lohse procedure has been used.

Taking as an example this morning time window (07:15–08:15) of a typical weekday, in the pre-calibration phase there is a low agreement between the estimated flows by the forecast transport model (Fig. 4) and the traffic counts available. Therefore (as can be seen in Fig. 5) following the calibration phase, a satisfying correlation between flows estimated with the forecast model and counts on the intersections has been obtained.

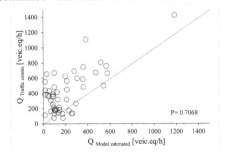 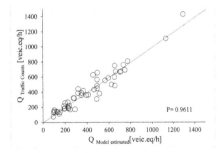

Fig. 4. Comparison of flows before the calibration phase in the morning time window (07:15–08:15) of a typical weekday (P = 0.7068).

Fig. 5. Comparison of flows after the calibration phase in the morning time window (07:15–08:15) of a typical weekday (P = 0.9611).

3.3 Ex-Post Scenario and Redistribution of Flows

The Municipality of Cassino, through the indications of the PUT (Urban Traffic Plan) has provided for the establishment of a Zone 30 (in the city centre) which encloses the pedestrian area inside, built with a partial pedestrianization of Corso Della Repubblica (see Fig. 6).

The adoption of this new traffic rule is likely to generate a strong perturbation in the flow of vehicles. Although there is no direct interaction within the pedestrian area between vulnerable users and vehicles, but there is an indirect interaction which has strong consequences in the surrounding areas (roads) and which can reverberate even at unpredictable distances, to congest roads and itineraries that in the current situation don't present problems, and to unload others.

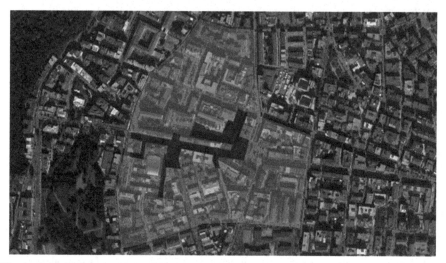

Fig. 6. A detail of the study area: in green the pedestrian area and in red the Zone 30 in the ex-post scenario. Source: Google Maps pluging in [19]. (Color figure online)

It is necessary to analyse the new routes that will be chosen by drivers to carry out a certain manoeuvre that will be suppressed due to the establishment of the new pedestrian area.

As an example, the current or ex-ante condition (Fig. 7) and the condition of the project or ex post (Fig. 8) have been correspondingly represented. In the condition of the current scenario, in order to be able to travel from point A to point B, or from B to A, road users choose a very direct route, such as to minimize travel times and therefore the cost of transport. In the project scenario, however, with the operation of the pedestrian area and the change in the traffic rules for some roads, road users will be forced to follow alternative routes to carry out their trips between points A and B. Among the possible alternative itineraries, users will choose those with shorter travel times.

Fig. 7. Two routes to carry out trips between point A and B in the ex-ante condition. Source: Google Maps pluging in [19].

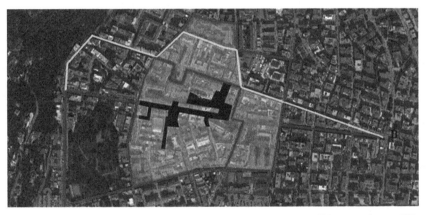

Fig. 8. In the ex-post condition, for the trips between A and B, users will have to choose different paths and will experience different travel times. Source: Google Maps pluging in [19].

4   Results

Following the identification of new itineraries that will affect the road network surrounding the pedestrian area, a comparison between the flows estimated by the proposed simplified method and those provided by a traffic demand model is conveniently reported (Fig. 9). This comparison allows to understand how reliable this simplified method can be compared to the canonical use of traffic simulation software.

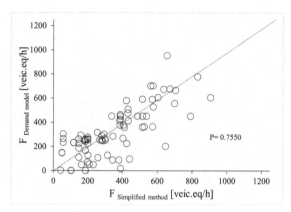

Fig. 9. Comparison between the flows estimated with the simplified method and the flows of the demand model.

A sensitivity analysis has been performed by applying the four assignment methods. In Fig. 10 the comparision between the simplified approach with the UE assignment and the demand model is shown, and in Fig. 11 the SO assignment is implemented in this simplified approach. In Fig. 12 it is possible to notice the results of the *All or Nothing Assignment* Method and in Fig. 13 the UE/SO collapsed Assignment when free flow travel times are neglected.

As it can be observed, the best agreement has been shown by the first proposed simplified Assignment Method that is based on travel time, but good results are also obtained with *User Equilibrium* and *System Optimum Assignment* and also with *User Equilibrium/ System Optimum Assignment neglecting free flow travel times*. The worsts assignment method appears to be the *All or Nothing Assignment* because of its somehow unrealistic hypothesis in a typically congested urban environment.

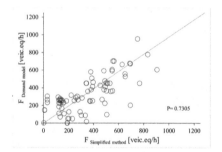

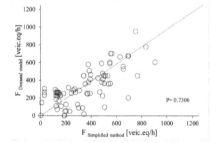

Fig. 10. Comparison of flows between the simplified approach with the User Equilibrium Assignment and the demand model (P = 0.7305).

Fig. 11. Comparison of flows between the simplified approach with System Optimum Assignment and the demand model (P = 0.7306).

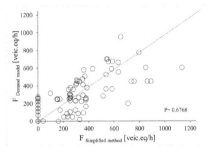 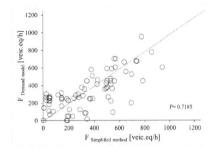

Fig. 12. Comparison of flows between the simplified approach with All or Nothing Assignment and the demand model (P = 0.6768).

Fig. 13. Comparison of flows between the simplified approach with User Equilibrium/ System Optimum Assignment neglecting free flow travel times and the demand model (P = 0.7185).

5 Conclusions

Following the recent attention paid to sustainable mobility in urban areas, an increasing focus on the design of new pedestrian areas implies the need of new methodological approaches that can be easily used by municipal managers. In this connection a simplified approach to give a comprehensive method to understand the future traffic scenario after the establishment of a new pedestrian area impacting on local vehicular traffic conditions has been presented in this paper.

It is believed that due to the high complexity of developing and handling travel demand models, a simplified method to predict the future traffic scenario after the establishment of the pedestrian area, may represent an effective tool for roads managers and designers in promoting policies based on sustainable mobility.

A travel demand model has been conveniently developed and calibrated and corresponding future traffic scenarios have been compared with results provided by the aforementioned simplified approach employing five different assignment methods. The benchmarking among these different assignment approaches employed within the simplified methodology highlighted that the five methods are almost equivalent in terms of implementation process, but, as it is possible to see, the worst method is that based on too simplified assumptions on route decision processes (the *All or Nothing* approach) than cannot be employed in a congested road network such that of an urban city.

In the future, it is planned to carry out analysis on different peak-hour time period, in order to gain a more refined prediction of the future traffic scenarios on a daily pattern basis. The calibration of the proposed simplified method highlighted two critical aspects that need to be carefully taken into consideration: the first is the overestimation of the vehicle flows (which in the design phase could be an advantage) and the second is the choice of an adequate amount of alternative routes which affects the estimation of traffic flow.

However, it is believed that this method can also be used in a planning phase of the urban road network allowing city roads designers and managers to make decisions about road safety and to understand how to prioritize interventions and allocate funds in urban areas.

References

1. Ton, D., Duives, D.C., Cats, O., Hoogendoorn, S.P.: Cycling or walking? Determinants of mode choice in the Netherlands (2019)
2. Programme, Pan-European: Fourth high-level meeting on transport, health and environment. Retrieved from Paris Declaration. World Health Organisation & United Nations, Paris (2014)
3. United Nations. The 17 Goals (2015). https://sdgs.un.org/goals
4. Santilli, D., D'Apuzzo, M., Evangelisti, A., Nicolosi, V.: Towards sustainability: new tools for planning urban pedestrian mobility. Sustainability 13(16), 9371 (2021)
5. Hubert, M., Corijn, E., Neuwels, J., Hardy, M., Vermeulen, S., Vaesen, J.: From pedestrian area to urban and metropolitan project: assets and challenges for the centre of Brussels (new edition). BSI Synopsis (2020)
6. Basbas, S., Campisi, T., Canale, A., Nikiforiadis, A., Gruden, C.: Pedestrian level of service assessment in an area close to an under-construction metro line in Thessaloniki, Greece. Transp. Res. Procedia 45, 95–102 (2020)
7. D'Apuzzo, M., Santilli, D., Evangelisti, A., Nicolosi, V.: A conceptual framework for risk assessment in road safety of vulnerable users. In: Gervasi, O., et al. (eds.) ICCSA 2021. LNCS, vol. 12958, pp. 542–556. Springer, Cham (2021). https://doi.org/10.1007/978-3-030-87016-4_39
8. Jiao, J., He, S., Zeng, X.: An investigation into European car-free development models as an opportunity to improve the environmental sustainability in cities: the case of Pontevedra. In: Papers of Canadian International Conference on Humanities & Social Sciences, pp. 84–91 (2019)
9. D'Apuzzo, M., Santilli, D., Evangelisti, A., Pelagalli, V., Montanaro, O., Nicolosi, V.: An exploratory step to evaluate the pedestrian exposure in urban environment. In: 20th International Conference on Computational Science and Applications (ICCSA 2020), ICCSA 2021, University of Cagliari, Italy, 1–4 June 2020, pp. 645–657 (2020)
10. D'Apuzzo, M., Santilli, D., Evangelisti, A., Di Cosmo, L., Nicolosi, V.: Towards a better understanding of vulnerability in pedestrian-vehicle collision. In: Gervasi, O., et al. (eds.) ICCSA 2021. LNCS, vol. 12958, pp. 557–572. Springer, Cham (2021). https://doi.org/10.1007/978-3-030-87016-4_40
11. Gruden, C., Campisi, T., Canale, A., Tesoriere, G., Sraml, M.: A cross-study on video data gathering and microsimulation techniques to estimate pedestrian safety level in a confined space. In: IOP Conference Series: Materials Science and Engineering, vol. 603, no. 4, p. 042008. IOP Publishing (2019)
12. Amprasi, V., Politis, I., Nikiforiadis, A., Basbas, S.: Comparing the microsimulated pedestrian level of service with the users' perception: the case of Thessaloniki, Greece, coastal front. Transp. Res. Procedia 45, 572–579 (2020)
13. Highway Safety Manual (HCM): American Association of State Highway and Transportation Officials (AASTHO) (2010)
14. Cascetta, E.: Transportation Systems Analysis: Models and Applications. Springer, New York (2001). https://doi.org/10.1007/978-0-387-75857-2
15. Sheffi, Y.: Urban Transportation Networks: Equilibrium Analysis with Mathematical Programming Methods. Prentice-Hall, New Jersey (1984)
16. Thomas, R.: Traffic Assignment Techniques. Avebury Technical Publication, England (1991)

17. ISTAT: Basi territoriali e variabili censuarie. https://www.istat.it/it/archivio/104317. Accessed Apr 2021

18. Schnabel, W., Lohse, D.: Grundlagen der Straßenverkehrstechnik und der Verkehrspla-nung, vol. 2. Verlag für Bauwesen, Berlin (1997)

19. QGIS.org. QGIS Geographic Information System. QGIS Association (2022). http://www.qgis.org

International Workshop on Privacy in the Cloud/Edge/IoT World (PCEIoT 2022)

Sensitive Information Detection Adopting Named Entity Recognition: A Proposed Methodology

Lelio Campanile$^{(\boxtimes)}$, Maria Stella de Biase, Stefano Marrone, Fiammetta Marulli, Mariapia Raimondo, and Laura Verde

Department of Matemathics and Physics, Università degli Studi della Campania "L. Vanvitelli", Caserta, Italy
{lelio.campanile,mariastella.debiase,stefano.marrone,fiammetta.marulli, mariapia.raimondo,laura.verde}@unicampania.it

Abstract. Protecting and safeguarding privacy has become increasingly important, especially in recent years. The increasing possibilities of acquiring and sharing personal information and data through digital devices and platforms, such as apps or social networks, have increased the risks of privacy breaches. In order to effectively respect and guarantee the privacy and protection of sensitive information, it is necessary to develop mechanisms capable of providing such guarantees automatically and reliably. In this paper we propose a methodology able to automatically recognize sensitive data. A Named Entity Recognition was used to identify appropriate entities. An improvement in the recognition of these entities is achieved by evaluating the words contained in an appropriate context window by assessing their similarity to words in a domain taxonomy. This, in fact, makes it possible to refine the labels of the recognized categories using a generic Named Entity Recognition. A preliminary evaluation of the reliability of the proposed approach was performed. In detail, texts of juridical documents written in Italian were analyzed.

Keywords: Named entity recognition · Sensitive information · Data privacy · Anonymization · Information extraction

1 Introduction

With the fervent expansion of Internet usage, trillions of data circulate in the virtual world every day: a critical part of this data is constituted by *sensitive information*. In particular, there are four types of sensitive data and some examples for each type are given below. *Personal Information*, including: name, surname, date of birth, address, religious orientation. *Network Identity Information* such as: IP address, MAC address or social media account. *Secret Information and Credentials*, for example: digital certificates, private key, combo login password. *Financial Information*, which includes: bank account information, credit card number, digital currency [9].

The loss of a single sensitive data, among many, and its malicious use can be a source of damage to personal image, generation and dissemination of fake news, virtual theft to the detriment of companies and financial losses. Two are the main factors that determine the leakage of information: data structure and type of breach. It is easier to extract data, to be used in malicious way, in structured data such as databases. On the other hand, documents such as emails, text messages, social networks posts and newspaper articles[1], which are characterized by the use of Natural Language (NL), are defined as *unstructured data*. These types of documents are irregular and do not follow a predetermined pattern. Furthermore, the features of NL reside in the syntactic and semantic rules that vary according to language nationality. Although not easily processed by software, unstructured data falls within the categories of sensitive information and therefore are vulnerable to malicious attacks.

In the light of this, each country felt the need to establish data protection regulations[2]. In the People's Republic of China (PRC), the three main pillars of the personal information protection framework are the Personal Information Protection Law (PIPL), the Cybersecurity Law (CSL), and the Data Security Law (DSL). The Act on the Protection of Personal Information (APPI) regulates privacy protection issues in Japan. To safeguard privacy also in healthcare, the U.S. has adopted the Health Insurance Portability and Accountability Act (HIPAA). Also, the General Data Protection Regulation (GDPR), for European Union (EU) Member States, proposes a unified law for the processing and the circulation of sensitive data.

The GDPR allows the collected personal data to be used and processed only for the purpose stated in the consent statement [5,6]. In many cases, the purposes do not involve training a Machine Learning (ML) model. However, the principle of purpose limitation does not apply if the personal data is anonymized [4]. Several studies discussed the use of Named Entity Recognition (NER) to automatic annotate and anonymize sensitive data [14–17].

In this study, we propose a methodology that can automatically detect sensitive data from textual documents to support their obfuscation and preserve people's privacy. Linguistic processing was performed on these documents, appropriate entities were automatically recognized through the use of a NER to select the data to obfuscate. However, the recognition of such entities is not always reliable, especially for Italian. The categorization of Italian texts, in fact, is not very specific in contrast to texts written in English. Our aim is to improve the recognition of these entities based on the context domain, perfecting the sensitive information detection. Preliminary experimental tests were performed to assess the proposed methodology. A corpus of juridical documents from the Italian Court of Cassation (Corte di Cassazione) were processed.

The paper consists of the following sections: Sect. 2 presents an overview of the state of the art, the issues related to data privacy and the proposed solutions. Section 3 and Sect. 4 describe the steps of the proposed methodology and show

---

[1] https://www.mongodb.com/unstructured-data.
[2] https://www.dlapiperdataprotection.com/index.html.

its application to the legal domain. Section 5 explains how the methodology was evaluated and discusses the results. The article ends with an observation on the future plan.

2 Related Works

Many researchers worked to solve privacy protection problems and many techniques have been developed, such as Anonymization (not only for text [21]), Perturbation [12], Condensation [1], Randomization [3] and Fuzzy based methods [2]. The work in [20] demonstrates that the anonymization of information does not affect the *quality* of the data. In particular, anonymization can be implemented in four different ways: suppression, tagging, random substitution and generalization. The research in [13] discusses, applies and evaluates these methods to present an anonymization for documents written in Portuguese, with the aim to remove sensitive information from unstructured documents.

Suppression and tagging (both evaluated in [23], too) are used to replace the sensitive information; on the contrary, random substitution (analyzed in [10]) and generalization are used to replace sensitive information by textual expression. Their anonymization system uses the NER module to detect possible entities of relevance for the considered documents. Indeed, NER is one of the pre-processing stages of Natural Language Processing (NLP). Its goal is tagging entities in the text. There are several pre-trained libraries to recognize entities like spaCy[3] and Natural Language Processing Tool Kit (NLTK).

The concept of data quality is introduced as the problems to be settled, however, are closely linked to the purpose of using sensitive data. The systematic review in [11] classifies and discusses four categories of purpose in anonymization: data secondary usage, re-identification risk, effects on information extraction and inadequacy of current methods for heterogeneous documents. The availability of digital documents and the access to these is crucial in different fields. On the one hand, the research needs datasets to perform model training for machine learning, data exploration, qualitative and quantitave analysis. On the other hand, companies request analysis on financial, legal and clinical sensitive documents. Because of these needs, anonymization is necessary to comply with the regulations and therefore to allow a second usage of the data. In the medical field, in order to balance privacy protection and data value preserving, [19] proposes a pseudonymization approach and [8] shows that the k-anonimity algorithm degrades test coverage of Database-centric applications (DCAs).

Another observation should be made, as shown in [7]: an anonymization process can give different results depending on the application dataset. Therefore, since the data quality can invalidate the analysis, it would be necessary to carefully tailor the extraction methodology to the available data. Linked to this problem, attention can be placed on a field as delicate as the medical one: the legal field. The documents produced at each legal sentence are full of sensitive data.

---

[3] Here a demonstration of entities with spaCy https://explosion.ai/demos/displacy-ent.

Information extraction becomes more difficult to apply with current methodologies. In fact, although there are legal formulas recited during the sentences, the entities with the same syntactic tags have different semantic functions. Therefore, a deeper and more sensitized analysis of linguistic rules is necessary.

The approach followed in [22] uses Support Vector Machines (SVMs) to identify legal concepts and then NER to identify entities such as locations, organizations and dates. Other works use the concept of *context window*. In text sense, a context window is the set of words that compose the neighborhood of a given tagged word. The work in [27] proves that the choice of a proper fixed value for the context window size positively impacts on the overall performance of word segmentation; the same cannot be said for a higher one. This study focuses on Chinese linguistics, which is very different from the Italian and English one, and for this reason it is necessary to carry out tests to support or refute the goodness of using the context window. Here comes back the problem of tailoring the methodology on data, in particular on languages. An example is given in [18], where a pre-trained NER could not properly recognize tag in Dravidian language group, and the authors developed a NER trained on customized entities.

Considering the goals, issues and techniques analyzed in the literature, this work wants to get more than a well-performing NER customized on the rules of the Italian language in legal domain. This paper aims to focus on the information extraction phase preceding the application of anonymization. The goal is to provide a methodology disconnected from the choice of the next step to apply, be it a tagging step or a suppression one.

3   Methodology

The proposed methodology can automatically detect sensitive information in textual documents to support data obfuscation and, consequently, preserve the confidentiality and privacy of the subjects. Linguistic features are extracted from these textual documents and appropriate entities are identified. The aim is to optimize the detection of entities based on the domain of interest, in order to improve the classification of that entity as sensitive information.

As indicated in Fig. 1, to contextualize the detection of entities within a specific domain in Italian, a Domain Taxonomy (DT) is defined through an unsupervised word embedding model, aimed at assessing the words distributions, word

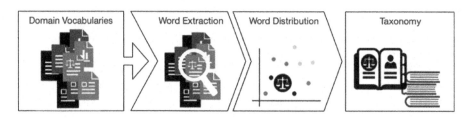

Fig. 1. Domain taxonomy definition

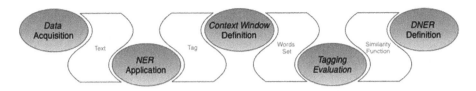

Fig. 2. Methodology phases

frequencies and words pattern co-occurrences. This taxonomy was constituted by the main entities recognized by the main NLP toolkits for Italian. For each entity are also defined subcategories that specify the domain. The main category "PER", for example, that indicates the category of people, has a series of subcategories such as, for example, minor, relative, adopted or adopter.

As shown in Fig. 2, the proposed methodology consists of several phases. Starting from the acquisition of data, a first level NER is applied, which returns labeled entities. Then, a context window is defined, in order to optimize the recognition of the obtained tags, leveraging the domain knowledge. Finally, the methodology provides the application of a specialized NER.

The first phase is data acquisition, within which textual documents to be evaluated are collected. Then, a pre-trained NER is applied to the textual documents in order to highlight entities with appropriate tags. NER is a fundamental step in NLP for the information extraction, necessary to classify entities in texts according to a list of predefined tags.

Three are the main NLP toolkits that allow to apply NER: spaCy, NLTK[4] and StanfordNLP[5]. In this work, spaCy has been adopted due to its ease of use within Python and reliability in the entities extraction [24,25]. In fact, spaCy provides pre-trained models for several languages, including Italian.

Unfortunately, this toolkit has a gap between the list of recognized tags in English and the list of possible tags for Italian. Table 1 shows the comparison between the tags provided for English[6] and Italian[7] models.

In particular, Italian pre-trained models have only four categories of possible tags (LOC, MISC, ORG and PERSON) in contrast to the eighteen categories provided by the English ones. The exiguous number of tags recognized in Italian inevitably generates a loss of specificity. In fact, a word that in English could be categorized as Geopolitical entity (GPE), in Italian would fall into the Miscellaneous entities (MISC) group. Therefore, one of the objectives to be achieved in this work is the improvement of the entities recognition for the Italian language.

To this aim, the next step of the methodology is the definition of context windows for the previously tagged words, in order to optimize the estimation of the entity tag. The choice of context is crucial to support correct entity recogni-

---

[4] https://www.nltk.org.

[5] https://nlp.stanford.edu/projects/project-ner.shtml.

[6] The English model *en_core_web_lg* is available at https://spacy.io/models/en.

[7] The Italian model *it_core_news_lg* is available at https://spacy.io/models/it.

tion. The context window, constructed by centering the word to be estimated, determines which contextual neighbours are considered. Several experimental tests were performed to define the suitable value for the window size, since it is fundamental to select the most appropriate size for the context window.

Table 1. spaCy tag comparison between English and Italian

Tag	Description	English	Italian
CARDINAL	Numerals that do not fall under another type	✓	✗
DATE	Absolute or relative dates or periods	✓	✗
EVENT	Named hurricanes, battles, wars, sport events, etc.	✓	✗
FAC	Buildings, airports, highways, bridges etc.	✓	✗
GPE	Countries, cities, states	✓	✗
LANGUAGE	Any named language	✓	✗
LAW	Named document made into law	✓	✗
LOC	Non-GPE locations	✓	✓
MISC	Miscellaneous entities	✗	✓
MONEY	Monetary values, including unit	✓	✗
NORP	Nationalities or religious or political groups	✓	✗
ORDINAL	"first", "second", etc.	✓	✗
ORG	Companies, agencies, institutions, etc.	✓	✓
PERCENT	Percentage, including "%"	✓	✗
PERSON	People, including fictional	✓	✓
PRODUCT	Objects, vehicles, foods etc.	✓	✗
QUANTITY	Measurements, as of weight or distance	✓	✗
TIME	Times smaller than a day	✓	✗
WORK_OF_ART	title of book, songs, etc.	✓	✗

The successive phase of the methodology consists in comparing the labeled entities obtained from the application of the NER with the entities defined in DT.

The accuracy of each tag was evaluated through a *similarity function*. In this study, the similarity function D has been defined taking into account lexical, semantic and taxonomy measures. Words that have a similar characters sequence are lexically similar. On the other hand, if the words are lexically different, but they express the same concept, then they are semantically similar. Additionally, it is possible to obtain another measure evaluating the semantic similarity of a given word in comparison to the words in the DT.

Several methods can be used to calculate the lexical, semantic and taxonomy similarities. Appropriate metrics and algorithms, such as for example Levenshtein distance, Latent Semantic Analysis (LSA) or Lesk similarity, are computed to estimate the grade of similarity [26]. The function D is defined as follows:

$$D(w_c, w_{DT}) = p_L * L + p_C * C + p_K * K \tag{1}$$

with

$$L = \sum_{i=1}^{n_l} l_i(w_c, w_{DT}) \quad C = \sum_{i=1}^{n_c} c_i(w_c, w_{DT}) \quad K = \sum_{i=1}^{n_k} k_i(w_c, w_{DT}) \tag{2}$$

where w_c and w_{DT} indicate, respectively, the words of the context window and the words of the DT, while L, C and K are the sum of similarity metrics (l_i, c_i and k_i), respectively, for the lexical, semantic and taxonomy similarities, and p_L, p_C and p_K are the corresponding weights for the three measures.

A linear constraint placed on the definition of the function is that each weight takes on a value in the range $[0, 1]$. The similarity function D is applied to each word w_c in the context window to evaluate its similarity to the words of the DT. Therefore, assuming that the DT has cardinality M, a value vector v of size M is obtained for each word of the context window, containing the results of the function D. It is worth reminding that the DT consists of different N categories and that each word of the DT belongs to exactly one category.

To associate a category to each w_c, the average of all calculated distances between the w_c among the same category of the DT is computed, obtaining a vector $\tilde{v}$ of size N, i.e., the number of categories. Each number of this vector indicates how much the w_c is "near" to the category.

In order to decide the category, the N values of the vector are compared to a threshold value, α. This value has been found experimentally and a rule-based approach was applied to associate w_c to a specific category, as shown in Algorithm 1. Each value $\tilde{v}_i$ in $\tilde{v}$ is compared to the threshold. If only one value exceeds α, then the corresponding category is associated to the w_c. If several values exceed the threshold, the category corresponding to the largest $\tilde{v}_i$ is chosen. By doing so, each w_c with a specific associated category becomes a sentinel word w_s.

Algorithm 1. The rule-based adopted approach.

Require: $\alpha > 0$
  if $v_i \geq \alpha$ **then**
    $w_c \leftarrow w_s$ ▷ Algorithm for the definition of w_s.
  else
    $w_c \leftarrow Not\ \ Considered$
  end if

The sentinel word, which was assigned a specific DT-subcategory, will improve the classification of w_t. But several w_s could be included in the considered context window. In this case, to support the definition of the sub-category of the w_T, the DT-subcategory of w_s that achieved the best $\tilde{v}_i$ and had the same category of the w_T was chosen.

Finally, the methodology provides the application of a Domain NER (DNER), which consists in the definition of a specialized context window-based NER. Such a DNER is applied to selected textual documents to perform a second tagging evaluation to assess the reliability of the methodology.

4   Case Study

In order to evaluate the reliability of the proposed approach, preliminary experimental tests were performed. Appropriate documents concerning legal domain were considered. In detail, recent sentences selected from archive of the Italian Court of Cassation (Corte di Cassazione) were processed.

The dataset was composed by 29 civil judgments on divorce, separation or succession of property. All documents are written in Italian. The average number of words per document is 896, whilst the total number of words in the whole dataset is 26001.

An open-source NLP toolkit was used in the first step of our experiments. In detail, spaCy pre-trained model[8] for Italian was adopted. This model was trained by using data selected from four database: UD Italian ISDT v2.8[9], an Italian corpus annotated according to the Universal Dependencies (UD) annotation, obtained by the conversion from Italian Stanford Dependency Treebank (ISDT); WikiNER[10], a learning multilingual named entity recognition from Wikipedia; Lemmatization Lists[11], a dataset of several lemma/token pairs; and Explosion fastText Vectors[12]. As said in Sect. 3, for the Italian language, this tool returns data annotated with the following Named Entity (NE) classes: LOC, PER, ORG, MISC.

A DT was defined for this juridical sector, according to the approach described in [14]. For each one of the main categories, several subcategories were identified. As an example, Table 2 shows the subcategories of the PER category in the considered domain.

For each subcategory, a number of useful words were collected for the recognition of the subcategory itself. Taking into account "AVVOCATO" (i.e., lawyer), Table 3 shows some of the words gathered to identify this subcategory, like "Avv.", "Avvocato", "Difensore".

The application of the pre-trained NER to the legal documents considered led to the identification of 2378 labels. An average of 82 labels were identified for each document. We focused on the PER category because it was the predominant one in our documents, thus it was the best one to work on to check the effective optimization of the labeling.

---

[8] https://spacy.io/models/it#it_core_news_lg.

[9] https://github.com/UniversalDependencies/UD_Italian-ISDT.

[10] https://figshare.com/articles/dataset/Learning_multilingual_named_entity_recognition_from_Wikipedia/5462500.

[11] https://github.com/michmech/lemmatization-lists/.

[12] https://spacy.io/.

Table 2. PER category

Category	Subcategory
PER	GIUDICE
	INABILE
	RAPPRESENTANTE INCAPACI
	RAPPRESENTANTE CAPACI
	INCAPACE
	MINORENNE
	PARENTE
	PARTE
	ADOTTATO
	ADOTTANTE
	AVVOCATO

Table 3. Recognition of AVVOCATO subcategory

Subcategory	Word
AVVOCATO	Avv.
	Avvocato
	difensore
	difeso
	legale
	patrocinante
	patrocinato
	patrocinio
	rappresentante
	rappresentato
	patrocinatore

As indicated in Table 4, the amount of recognized words, in all documents, labeled as PER category was 957, each document has an average of 33 PER labels.

For each document a version annotated by domain experts was available to evaluate the correctness of the identified categories. For the annotated documents, 1715 entities were individuated, an average of 59 entities were recognized for each document. Relating to the PER category, 814 were the labeled entities, with an average of 28 per document.

An opportune context window was chosen. The size of the window used in the analysis was 5, which has been found by experimental tests. By choosing this size, the results obtained from the application of the DNER were of 86 words for which a specific subcategory was identified and used as label. This means that about a 10% of the PER labels could be specialized to a specific subcategory.

Table 4. Case study: results achieved for the recognition of PER category.

	Total PER words	Average per document
NER	957	33
Domain expert	814	28

5 Conclusions

Nowadays, the increasing opportunities to capture and share sensitive information and data have increased the risks of privacy violations. Therefore, techniques and countermeasures to preserve and protect sensitive data of people are necessary. Data anonymization can play a critical role to protect privacy of people obscuring sensitive information to avoid the identification of the subject.

This paper presents a methodology to automatically anonymize personal data. This methodology is able to extract linguistic features, from textual documents, necessary to identify opportune entities fundamental to recognize personal data. In detail, an automatic NER was used to detect the main entities in these documents. Then, an opportune domain taxonomy has been defined and used to improve the categorization of these entities.

Preliminary experimental tests were performed to evaluate the reliability of the proposed approach. Juridical documents from the Italian Court of Cassation (Corte di Cassazione) were processed. Appropriate entities were extracted by using the pre-trained NER provided by spaCy, an open-source NLP toolkit. An opportune DT was defined to improve the recognition of categories.

Our future plans will include an improvement of the proposed methodology considering other similarity metrics. Additionally, this is a preliminary study, in which only some aspects of the proposed approach were evaluated. Further aspects of the proposed methodology will be analyzed, not only in the juridical domain, but even in other sector such as healthcare or financial.

Acknowledgement. The work of Maria Stella de Biase is granted by PON Ricerca e Innovazione 2014/2020 MUR—Ministero dell'Università e della Ricerca (Italy)—with the Ph.D. program XXXVI cycle. The work of Mariapia Raimondo is granted by INPS—Istituto Nazionale di Previdenza Sociale (Italy)—with the PhD program XXXVI cycle.

The work of Fiammetta Marulli is granted by the project "Attrazione e Mobilità dei Ricercatori" Italian PON Program (PON_AIM 2018 num. AIM1878214-2). The work of Laura Verde is granted by the "Predictive Maintenance Multidominio (Multidomain predictive maintenance)" project, PON "Ricerca e Innovazione" 2014–2020, Asse IV "Istruzione e ricerca per il recupero"-Azione IV.4-"Dottorati e contratti di ricerca su tematiche dell'innovazione" programme CUP: B61B21005470007.

The research leading to these results has received funding from the projects "ANDROIDS" and "WAIILD TROLS" funded, respectively, by the programs V:ALERE 2019 and V:ALERE 2020 of the Università della Campania "Luigi Vanvitelli".

References

1. Aleroud, A., Yang, F., Pallaprolu, S.C., Chen, Z., Karabatis, G.: Anonymization of network traces data through condensation-based differential privacy. Digit. Threat. Res. Pract. **2**(4), 1–23 (2021). https://doi.org/10.1145/3425401

2. Ashok, V.: Fuzzy-based methods for privacy-preserving data mining, pp. 348–353 (April 2011). https://doi.org/10.1109/ITNG.2011.68

3. Batmaz, Z., Polat, H.: Randomization-based privacy-preserving frameworks for collaborative filtering. Procedia Comput. Sci. **96**, 33–42 (2016). https://doi.org/10.1016/j.procs.2016.08.091

4. Biesner, D., et al.: Anonymization of German financial documents using neural network-based language models with contextual word representations. Int. J. Data Sci. Anal. **13**(2), 151–161 (2022)

5. Campanile, L., Iacono, M., Levis, A.H., Marulli, F., Mastroianni, M.: Privacy regulations, smart roads, blockchain, and liability insurance: putting technologies to work. IEEE Secur. Priv. **19**(1), 34–43 (2020)

6. Campanile, L., Iacono, M., Marulli, F., Mastroianni, M.: Privacy regulations challenges on data-centric and IoT systems: a case study for smart vehicles. In: IoTBDS, pp. 507–518 (2020)

7. Ferrández, Ó., South, B.R., Shen, S., Friedlin, F.J., Samore, M.H., Meystre, S.M.: Generalizability and comparison of automatic clinical text de-identification methods and resources. In: AMIA Annual Symposium Proceedings, vol. 2012, p. 199. American Medical Informatics Association (2012)

8. Grechanik, M., Csallner, C., Fu, C., Xie, Q.: Is data privacy always good for software testing? pp. 368–377 (November 2010). https://doi.org/10.1109/ISSRE.2010.13

9. Guo, Y., Liu, J., Tang, W., Huang, C.: Exsense: extract sensitive information from unstructured data. Comput. Secur. **102**, 102156 (2021). https://doi.org/10.1016/j.cose.2020.102156. https://www.sciencedirect.com/science/article/pii/S0167404820304296

10. Kang, J.S.: An improvement of privacy-preserving scheme based on random substitutions (March 2022)

11. Langarizadeh, M., Orooji, A., Sheikhtaheri, A.: Effectiveness of anonymization methods in preserving patients' privacy: a systematic literature review. Stud. Health Technol. Inf. **248**, 80–87 (2018)

12. Liu, L., Thuraisingham, B.: The applicability of the perturbation model-based privacy preserving data mining for real-world data, pp. 507–512 (January 2007). https://doi.org/10.1109/ICDMW.2006.155

13. Mamede, N., Baptista, J., Dias, F.: Automated anonymization of text documents, pp. 1287–1294 (July 2016). https://doi.org/10.1109/CEC.2016.7743936

14. Martinelli, F., Marulli, F., Mercaldo, F., Marrone, S., Santone, A.: Enhanced privacy and data protection using natural language processing and artificial intelligence. In: 2020 International Joint Conference on Neural Networks (IJCNN), pp. 1–8. IEEE (2020)

15. Di Martino, B., Marulli, F., Graziano, M., Lupi, P.: PrettyTags: an open-source tool for easy and customizable textual multilevel semantic annotations. In: Barolli, L., Yim, K., Enokido, T. (eds.) CISIS 2021. LNNS, vol. 278, pp. 636–645. Springer, Cham (2021). https://doi.org/10.1007/978-3-030-79725-6_64

16. Di Martino, B., Marulli, F., Lupi, P., Cataldi, A.: A machine learning based methodology for automatic annotation and anonymisation of privacy-related items in textual documents for justice domain. In: Barolli, L., Poniszewska-Maranda, A., Enokido, T. (eds.) CISIS 2020. AISC, vol. 1194, pp. 530–539. Springer, Cham (2021). https://doi.org/10.1007/978-3-030-50454-0_55
17. Marulli, F., Verde, L., Marrone, S., Barone, R., De Biase, M.S.: Evaluating efficiency and effectiveness of federated learning approaches in knowledge extraction tasks. In: 2021 International Joint Conference on Neural Networks (IJCNN), pp. 1–6. IEEE (2021)
18. Melinamath, B.: Rule based methodology for recognition of Kannada named entities. Int. J. Latest Trends Eng. Technol. (IJLTET) **3**, 50–58 (2014)
19. Neubauer, T., Riedl, B.: Improving patients privacy with pseudonymization. Stud. Health Technol. Inf. **136**, 691–696 (2008). https://doi.org/10.3233/978-1-58603-864-9-691
20. Panackal, J., Pillai, A.: Adaptive utility-based anonymization model: performance evaluation on big data sets. Procedia Comput. Sci. **50**, 347–352 (2015). https://doi.org/10.1016/j.procs.2015.04.037
21. Perero-Codosero, J., Espinoza-Cuadros, F.M., Gómez, L.: X-vector anonymization using autoencoders and adversarial training for preserving speech privacy. Comput. Speech Langu. **74**, 101351 (2022). https://doi.org/10.1016/j.csl.2022.101351
22. Quaresma, P., Gonçalves, T.: Using linguistic information and machine learning techniques to identify entities from juridical documents. In: Francesconi, E., Montemagni, S., Peters, W., Tiscornia, D. (eds.) Semantic Processing of Legal Texts. LNCS (LNAI), vol. 6036, pp. 44–59. Springer, Heidelberg (2010). https://doi.org/10.1007/978-3-642-12837-0_3
23. Samarati, P.: Protecting respondents' identities in microdata release. IEEE Trans. Knowl. Data Eng. **13**, 1010–1027 (2001). https://doi.org/10.1109/69.971193
24. Schmitt, X., Kubler, S., Robert, J., Papadakis, M., LeTraon, Y.: A replicable comparison study of ner software: Stanfordnlp, nltk, opennlp, spacy, gate. In: 2019 6th International Conference on Social Networks Analysis, Management and Security (SNAMS). pp. 338–343. IEEE (2019)
25. Spring, R., Johnson, M.: The possibility of improving automated calculation of measures of lexical richness for EFL writing: a comparison of the LCA, NLTK and SpaCy tools. System **106**, 102770 (2022)
26. Vijaymeena, M., Kavitha, K.: A survey on similarity measures in text mining. Mach. Learn. Appl. Int. J. **3**(2), 19–28 (2016)
27. Xu, W., Nong, G.: A study for extracting keywords from data with deep learning and suffix array. Multimedia Tools Appl. **81**(5), 7419–7437 (2022). https://doi.org/10.1007/s11042-021-11762-7

Evaluating the Impact of Data Anonymization in a Machine Learning Application

Lelio Campanile[1], Fabio Forgione[2], Michele Mastroianni[3], Gianfranco Palmiero[2], and Carlo Sanghez[2(✉)]

[1] Dip. Matematica e Fisica, Università degli Studi della Campania "L. Vanvitelli", Caserta, Italy
lelio.campanile@unicampania.it
[2] GAM Engineering srlu, Caserta, Italy
{fforgione,gpalmiero,csanghez}@gameng.it
[3] Università degli Studi di Salerno, Salerno, Italy
michele.mastroianni@unisa.it
https://www.gameng.it

Abstract. The data protection impact assessment is used to verify the necessity, proportionality and risks of data processing. Our work is based on the data processed by the technical support of a Wireless Service Provider. The team of WISP tech support uses a machine learning system to predict failures. The goal of our the experiments was to evaluate the DPIA with personal data and without personal data. In fact, in a first scenario, the experiments were conducted using a machine learning application powered by non-anonymous personal data. Instead in the second scenario, the data was anonymized before feeding the machine learning system.

In this article we evaluate how much the Data Protection Impact Assessment changes when moving from a scenario with raw data to a scenario with anonymized data.

Keywords: Risks · DPIA · Privacy · WISP · Unwanted modification of data · Illegitimate access to data · Data disappearance · GDPR

1 Introduction

The data protection impact assessment (DPIA) is a procedure aimed at describing the processing, assessing its necessity and proportionality, and facilitating the management of risks to the rights and freedoms of individuals deriving from the processing of their personal data. There are some contexts in which it is necessary to make use of personal data in order to provide a service.

O. Gervasi et al. (Eds.): ICCSA 2022 Workshops, LNCS 13380, pp. 389–400, 2022.
https://doi.org/10.1007/978-3-031-10542-5_27

Article 35 of the GDPR (General Data Protection Regulation) prescribes that *Where a type of processing in particular using new technologies..... is likely to result in a high risk to the rights and freedoms of natural persons* the controller shall carry out a Data Protection Impact Assessment (DPIA), which aims to conduct a systematic risk assessment in order to identify privacy threats and impose technical and organizational controls to mitigate those threats. Article 35 prescribes that DPIA shall in particular be required in the case of:

- a systematic and extensive evaluation of personal aspects relating to natural persons which is based on automated processing, including profiling, and on which decisions are based that produce legal effects concerning the natural person or similarly significantly affect the natural person;
- processing on a large scale of special categories of data referred to in Article 9(1), or of personal data relating to criminal convictions and offenses referred to in Article 10;
- systematic monitoring of a publicly accessible area on a large scale.

Consider the case of a wireless internet service provider that wants to predict the failures of customer equipment: there is no way to avoid collecting customer personal data. In fact, the technical support of a wireless service provider normally has access to the MAC address of the customer's device, the geolocalization of the customer's device, personal and administrative data of individuals, but also, theoretically, the time slots of greatest use of the network, the favorite streaming service providers, the device most bandwidth consuming, etc. Technical support has all the data to profile customers or to know if a customer is home or not. In short, the risks for individuals are high.

The main purpose of technical support of a wireless service provider is to offer the best possible connection. The biggest challenge here is to predict device failures using both field data such as weather conditions, wind, humidity and personal data such as customer preferred streaming services, location of radio antennas, number of device connected etc.

Industry best practices indicate a need to take action before a blocking radio failure, but to take action sooner you need to somehow predict failure. Furthermore, best practices indicate two ways to reduce the risk: data anonymization and data encryption.

Failure prediction systems that rely on machine learning are already available, but the problem here is that these systems need access to personal data. Such systems are based on machine learning applications need personal data during training and they need personal data during the prediction phase.

However, there are solutions that mitigate the risk through data anonymization, data disruption or encryption, but performance in terms of failure prediction degrades significantly. Preservation of privacy in data mining and machine learning is the absolute prerequisite in the above scenarios.

This paper is the continuation of the research begun with [3], and the actual work is to assess the risk in a scenario where personal data was neither anonymized nor encrypted. Next, we measure the risk of the same scenario after applying different anonymization and encryption techniques on the data.

The research questions the paper aims to answer are:

RQ1: is there an effective reduction in risk for individuals?

RQ2: among the methods of anonymization, which is the one that guarantees the best performance in terms of failure prediction with moderate risk for individuals?

The goals of this research are to perform a risk assessment in order to reduce illegitimate access to data and to reduce unwanted data changes.

This paper is organized as follows: the Sect. 2 presents related works, in the Sect. 3 is presented the methodology we use in order to ensure pseudonimization and anonymization of data; in Sect. 4 is described the case study, while in Sect. 5 are discussed the results of the DPIA analysis. Section 6 concludes the paper.

2   Related Works

In [1] are highlighted threats and vulnerabilities of the emerging technologies (IoT - Internet of Things, Cloud Computing, and AI - Artificial Intelligence), as well as the techniques of risk mitigation as stated in the outlining standards and regulations. A comparison was then made between the three technologies and the international standards (OWASP - Open Web Application Security Project, NIST - National Institute of Standards and Technology, ISO - International Organization for Standardization, and GDPR). The study shows that, while in the case of cloud technology the standards are able to effectively support the developers in order to obtain compliance, for the case of IoT and AI there's still a lot of work to be done on standards. An interesting systematic literature review is [6], in which 159 research paper have been analyzed and a thematic analysis to all identified risks has been performed and ten noticeable DPIA assessment methodologies have been identified.

Some authors use the methodologies suggested by National Authorities to perform privacy assessment. The work of Georgiou et al. [7] deals with DPIA performing in health sector, using the CNIL-PIA methodology [5] proposed by the French privacy authority (Commission Nationale de l'Informatique et des Libertés - CNIL). This paper focuses on the first steps of the methodology, and in particular about the purpose of processing and the evaluation of the organization's GDPR compliance level and of the gaps that must be filled-in (Gap Analysis). Also in [2] is used the CNIL-PIA methodology to perform a risk assessment analysis related to the use of pseudonimization in blockchain.

In this paper, is used the tool PIA created by CNIL to evaluate the risks and their related mitigation techniques. In [8] in order to perform DPIA, is used the guideline redacted by Information Commissioner's Office (ICO) [10], the UK independent authority set up to uphold the information rights for public interest.

On the other side, other authors developed ad-hoc methodologies and tools to deal with DPIA. In [13], a methodology is proposed to perform DPIA for healthcare information systems, due to the specific constraints posed by the heterogeneous and highly sensitive nature of data and software use in hospitals. The methodology proposed uses as the starting point the Record Of Processing Activities (ROPA), stated as mandatory by Art. 30 of GDPR, and a specialized tool to perform DPIA has been developed. Also in [11] the ROPA is seen as the starting point to perform risk assessment, and the methodology proposed is based on ontologies and use of AI tools. In [12] is proposed a framework specialized in the context of Public Administration information to perform assessment.

3   Methodology

Our methodology was based on the Data Protection Impact Assessment. The DPIA is a process designed to identify risks arising out of the processing of personal data and to minimize these risks as far and as early as possible [4]. Although the DPIA is often used to demonstrate GDPR compliance, in our work we used that process to check how good the data anonymization solutions were.

The first step was to perform a preliminary Data Protection Impact Assessment on the raw data. In our case the raw data included a data set with 43,780 rows x 25 columns.

The columns included personal data:

– MAC address of the Customer Premise Equipment
– Customer ID
– name of Customer
– ZIP code of costumer
– geo-localization of radio device in customer's house

The second step was to mitigate the risks related to data breach. For this purpose, We used several good practices in terms of data obfuscation [9]:

– **Attribute suppression**: refers to the removal of the personal part from data. We simply deleted the columns with personal data from the data set.
– **Pseudo-anonymization by HASH**: refers to the replacement of personal data with anonymous data. We simply used a hash function on strings containing personal data. The new value was used instead of the old one.
– **Generalization**: refers to the converting personal data in an range of values. We simply grouped personal values in order to keep the rough information, but accepting the loss of detail.

- **Generalization and k-anonymity**: refers to the converting data in an range of values as seen before, but in this case we deliberately deleted those samples that had no other k-similar. We did not use K-anonymization due to the size of our data set.

In order to achieve an anonymous data set from the raw data set using the attribute suppression, one possible choice is to delete all columns that include personal data from the data set. As an alternative, is possible to anonymize the data set replacing all characters of the columns containing personal data with the 'x' character.

Another technique to mitigate risks, is the pseudo-anonymization of the columns containing personal data, applying a hash function directly to those data.

Finally, another useful technique is using the generalization. In order to operate in that way, it is possible to eliminate the last octet present in the 'MAC' column, and group the values present in the 'CUSTOMER CODE' column into groups of 500, eliminating the last two digits from the ZIP code present in raw data and considering only the first letter present in the values of the 'DEVICE NAME' column.

The raw data set was represented by 25 columns. Of these 25 columns, some contain personal data: the customer code and the device name of the customer, ZIP code of the customer, geo-localization of the customer's device, MAC address of the router and MAC of the customer's access point, name and surname of the customer, etc. The source of the data was represented by about 2000 radio devices connected by radio frequency.

We evaluated the performance in terms of predicting failures and in terms of the time required to process data from the devices. Obviously the machine learning model provides the best performance with the raw data set.

The best performance using the anonymous data set was obtained by applying hashing techniques, but the code is too much time consuming. The point here is that the anonymization of raw data is done on small Linux servers with low-power ARM processors.

In order to improve the performance of the fault prediction system, then, we decided to spread the computational load across multiple ARM servers. Consequently, to distribute the load between the servers running the machine learning application, we have to send the data to the servers and sending the data to the servers increases the likelihood that the data is somehow corrupted, stolen, modified, and so on.

The idea of using more powerful ARM processors was ruled out due to the higher impact in terms of power consumption of the solution.

In the case study, the focus was to achieve DPIA from raw data set and DPIA from the modificated data set.

4   Case Study

In this section we describe the case study on which is based our work.

Before continuing, it is advisable to clearly distinguish the problem to be addressed, the testbed and the expected results for each step of the methodology.

The problem to be addressed is the processing of personal data done by the fault prediction system based on artificial intelligence.

The testbed was the machine learning system and the personal data coming from Flyber's customers.

The methodology involved first evaluating the DPIA with personal data and then evaluating the DPIA with anonymous data. The expected results were to have a significant reduction in the risk of compromising user privacy.

Flyber is a Wireless Internet Service Provider (WISP) based on Teverola, Italy, that offers its customers free technical support to solve problems related to the quality of signal reception. Since the technology is wireless over open bands, the quality of the connection depends mainly on radio interference.

To check the health status of the Customer Premise Equipments (CPE), Flyber adopts a monitoring system that produces a daily report with 25 fields. The monitoring system produces information on a lot of personal data: MAC Address of the customer's device, GPS coordinates of the customer's device, customer name, etc.

Internet Service Providers technical support needs personal data to predict potential anomalies, there is no way to gather this stuff. To monitor radio quality and to prevent failures Flyber uses a machine learning application.

To avoid the disclosure of personal data, the machine learning application uses an anonymous data set. There are several aspects that determines the need of DPIA: systematic monitoring, evaluationg and predicting internet usage, data processed on a large scale, etc. Because of the above criteria, DPIA must be required.

The DPIA allowed us to assess the risk to individuals in the event of a data compromise, the impact of the data compromise, and the likelihood of adverse events. It should be noted that Flyber already used a fault monitoring system based on artificial intelligence [3].

The first version of the fault monitoring system included a single ARM Linux Appliance capable to manage data from more than 1000 radio devices. In the work [3], it is already explored the impact of adopting anonymization in a real-word application, but in that case our experiments were focused on computing performance and accuracy and computing performance was limited to the single ARM Linux server.

In order to boost performance we deployed a new architecture based on multiple computational devices. Now the updated fault monitoring system includes a cluster of four ARM Linux Appliance capable to manage data from more than 2000 radio devices for 0,5 GB of data per second. Because more and more ARM Linux server and because the need to transfer data outside the single system, the likelihood of risk got higher.

5   Results

This section shows the privacy risks, taking into account existing or planned controls. The diagrams allow us to have a global and synthetic view on the controls effects on the risks they address. This section shows risk mapping as well in order to compare the positioning of the risks hem, before and after application of the complementary controls.

In order to perform the risk assessment, we use the PIA tools developed by CNIL, the French data protection authority.

The fault prediction procedure using raw data set is divided into three steps:

- The first step is to save the raw data on the monitoring server.
- The second step is to send the raw customer data to the machine learning application.
- The third step is fault prediction through the machine learning model.

If the prediction system indicated a problem, then the system sent an e-mail to technical support with the data of the problem encountered and opened a ticket.

According to definition "a threat is a *Procedure comprising one or more individual actions on data supporting assets*", in our work we considered the following threats:

- Saving the raw data on the server.
- Sending the raw data to the AI application.
- Feeding and running the machine model.

The risk overview Fig. 1, produced by PIA, shows the relationships between impacts, threats, sources of threats and security measures implemented at this stage. We assessed the levels of risk and likelihood of the events according to the methodology of the French Data Protection Authority (CNIL).

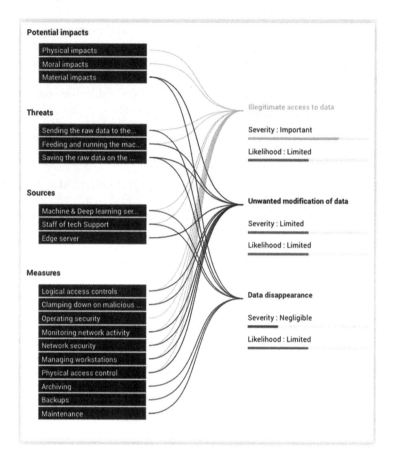

Fig. 1. Risk overview with raw data.

The framework comprises three guides [5]:

– the first guide sets out the approach,
– the second guide contains facts that could be used for formalizing the analysis,
– the third guide provides knowledge bases. This guide is a catalog of controls aimed at complying with the legal requirements and treating the risks.

We have come to the following conclusions to according to the above knowledge bases.

Unwanted Modification of Data

In the event of unwanted modification of data, we consider the risk **limited** in relationship to material impacts (outdated data or loss of access to temporary services), while on the moral side we have not assessed any particular critical issues.

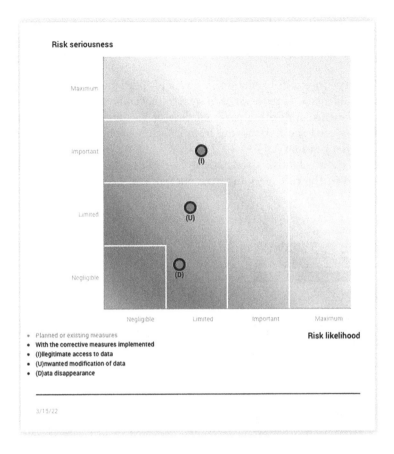

Fig. 2. Risk mapping with raw data.

Illegitimate Access to Data
In the event of illegitimate access to data, we have considered the severity level of the risk to be **important** due to potential property damage/theft.

Data Disappearance
In the event of Data disappearance, we considered the risk level to be **Negligible**.

We considered the likelihood of threats **limited**: the data are stored on servers suitably protected by both logical and physical controls.

In the Fig. 1) are shown the risk overview in case of raw data without anonymization. In the Fig. 2 is shown the risk mapping without encryption.

The fault prediction procedure using anonymous data set is divided into four steps:

- The first step is to save the raw data on the edge ARM Linux server.
- The second step is to delete any personal data from the raw data on the edge ARM Linux server.

- The third step is to send the data set to the machine learning application.
- The final step is fault prediction through the machine learning model using only anonymous data set.

In order to reduce risk likelihood in terms of illegitimate access to data and unwanted modification of data we used several methods of Data anonymization.

As a consequence of deleting personal data or hashing personal data we have significantly reduced the risk moving from a scenario where risk was important to a **limited** risky scenario.

In Fig. 3 is shown the risk assessment in case of raw data with anonymization. In Fig. 4 is shown the risk mapping with encryption.

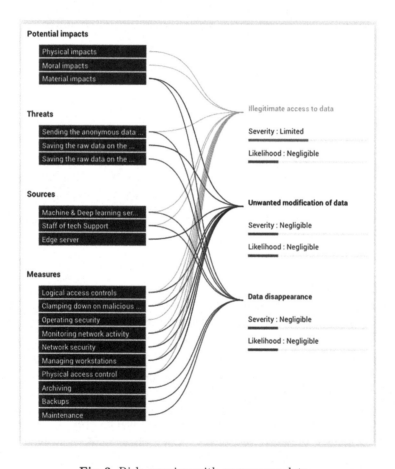

Fig. 3. Risk overview with anonymous data.

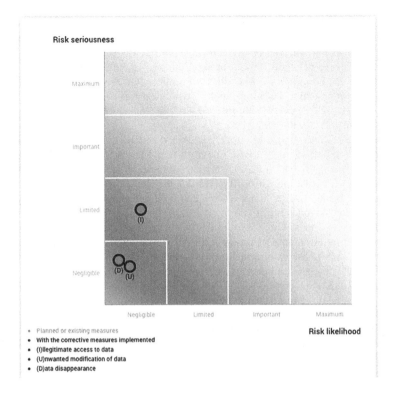

Fig. 4. Risk mapping with anonymous data.

6   Conclusion and Future Works

In this study has been studied the impact of obfuscation techniques on personal data in order to mitigate the data breaches risks on personal data. The CNIL-PIA methodology on privacy risk assessment, and the related tool PIA, has been used to show the impact of those techniques and to show which could be the better way to obtain GDPR compliance in personal data used by learning machine tools to perform technical activities. The results show that some techniques are really effective in that direction. In future work, we aim to explore with better detail the obfuscation techniques.

References

1. Attar, R.A., Al-Nemri, J., Homsi, A., Qusef, A.: Risk assessment for emerging domains (IOT, cloud computing, and AI). In: 2021 IEEE Jordan International Joint Conference on Electrical Engineering and Information Technology (JEEIT), pp. 120–127 (2021). https://doi.org/10.1109/JEEIT53412.2021.9634156

2. Campanile, L., Cantiello, P., Iacono, M., Marulli, F., Mastroianni, M.: Risk analysis of a GDPR-compliant deletion technique for consortium blockchains based on pseudonymization. In: Gervasi, O., et al. (eds.) ICCSA 2021. LNCS, vol. 12956, pp. 3–14. Springer, Cham (2021). https://doi.org/10.1007/978-3-030-87010-2_1

3. Campanile, L., Forgione, F., Marulli, F., Palmiero, G., Sanghez, C.: Dataset anonimyzation for machine learning: an ISP case study. In: Gervasi, O., et al. (eds.) ICCSA 2021. LNCS, vol. 12950, pp. 589–597. Springer, Cham (2021). https://doi.org/10.1007/978-3-030-86960-1_42

4. Cantiello, P., Mastroianni, M., Rak, M.: A conceptual model for the general data protection regulation. In: Gervasi, O., et al. (eds.) ICCSA 2021. LNCS, vol. 12956, pp. 60–77. Springer, Cham (2021). https://doi.org/10.1007/978-3-030-87010-2_5

5. French Data Protection Authority (CNIL). Privacy Impact Assessment (PIA) - Knowledge Bases (2018). https://www.cnil.fr/sites/default/files/atoms/files/cnil-pia-3-en-knowledgebases.pdf

6. Georgiadis, G., Poels, G.: Towards a privacy impact assessment methodology to support the requirements of the general data protection regulation in a big data analytics context: a systematic literature review. Comput. Law Secur. Rev. **44**, 105640 (2022) https://doi.org/10.1016/j.clsr.2021.105640

7. Georgiou, D., Lambrinoudakis, C.: Data protection impact assessment (DPIA) for cloud-based health organizations. Future Internet **13**(3) (2021). https://doi.org/10.3390/fi13030066

8. Henriksen-Bulmer, J., Faily, S., Jeary, S.: DPIA in context: applying DPIA to assess privacy risks of cyber physical systems. Future Internet **12**(5) (2020). https://doi.org/10.3390/fi12050093

9. Hosseinzadeh, S., et al.: Diversification and obfuscation techniques for software security: a systematic literature review. Inf. Softw. Technol. **104**, 72–93 (2018) https://doi.org/10.1016/j.infsof.2018.07.007

10. Information Commissioner's Office (ICO). Data protection impact assessments (2018).   https://ico.org.uk/for-organisations/guide-to-data-protection/guide-to-the-general-data-protection-regulation-gdpr/accountability-and-governance/data-protection-impact-assessments/

11. Di Martino, B., Mastroianni, M., Campaiola, M., Morelli, G., Sparaco, E.: Semantic techniques for validation of GDPR compliance of business processes. In: Barolli, L., Hussain, F.K., Ikeda, M. (eds.) CISIS 2019. AISC, vol. 993, pp. 847–855. Springer, Cham (2020). https://doi.org/10.1007/978-3-030-22354-0_78

12. Szczepaniuk, E.K., Szczepaniuk, H., Rokicki, T., Klepacki, B.: Information security assessment in public administration. Comput. Secur. **90**, 101709 (2020) https://doi.org/10.1016/j.cose.2019.101709

13. Todde, M., Beltrame, M., Marceglia, S., Spagno, C.: Methodology and workflow to perform the data protection impact assessment in healthcare information systems. Inf. Med. Unlocked **19**, 100361 (2020) https://doi.org/10.1016/j.imu.2020.100361

On IoT Localization Architectures Comparison and Privacy Concerns in the Healthcare Sector

Antonio Scarfò[(✉)] [iD]

Department of Information of Computer Science, University of Salerno, 84084 Fisciano, Italy
ascarfo@unisa.it

Abstract. Nowadays, localization is one of the most interesting and used application in IoT domain. It promises to gain more and more relevance, especially in the healthcare market, thanks to the optimization of the operations that localization-aware applications allow to achieve. The paper presented has the aim to provide a high-level review of some significant use cases of localization applications in the healthcare industry and highlight their peculiarities in a framework of evaluation. That helps to select the most suitable localization architecture, given the requirements of a use case. Among the parameters that are part of the framework of evaluation, the paper gives special relevance to the privacy concerns, that are tightly related to the IoT-based applications in the sector of healthcare. The work is introduced by a brief description of the IoT topics, the guiding question, and the main elements which are taken into consideration to evaluate the cases selected. These elements define the main criterion to select the cases in the literature. A brief description of the cases selected is reported. And the final part of the review consists of a very concise comparison of the cases, leveraging the key elements of evaluation framework defined.

Keywords: IoT · Localization · Privacy · Comparison · WiFi · BLE · RFID · Indoor · Healthcare · 802.15.4

1 Introduction

The availability of new technologies in IoT sector opens the doors to new use cases aimed to optimize operations through a pervasive interaction among sensors and the real word. In the healthcare sectors, for instance, the continuous and the real time monitoring of patients allow to save lives, improve treatments fulfillments, and optimize the logistic. Emerging use cases require new communication technologies that can connect a multitude of smart things from the world of "perception", randomly, in mobility fashion, and with low power consumption. This is especially true for localization aware applications where the mobility is mandatory and, often, low energy consumption is also a basic requirement. The localization aware applications are getting a more and more relevant role in the IoT sector. A report of Market&Market shows that applications based on GPRS will record a 12.9% CAGR of market growth from 2016 to 2023. Specifically,

© The Author(s), under exclusive license to Springer Nature Switzerland AG 2022
O. Gervasi et al. (Eds.): ICCSA 2022 Workshops, LNCS 13380, pp. 401–418, 2022.
https://doi.org/10.1007/978-3-031-10542-5_28

m-Heath market is forecasted to record a CAGR of 30% from 2021 to 2030 by Global Market Insight Institute. This impressive growth of localization application is related with the benefits that is possible to achieve in terms of processes optimization, according to [1]. This sector will leverage more and more localization features as well as IoT healthcare technologies will evolve and will be adopted. This comes really clear in the current pandemic period, where monitoring people form remote and trace them is key to contain the infection and monitor the status of the patients. This paper analyzes four cases of localization aware application based on different methods, to highlining differences, peculiarities, and provide a guide to select the most suitable architecture against the use case requirements, giving a special relevance to the privacy concerns related with.

Localization requires multidiscipline contributes and involve the complete IoT stack, including devices, communication protocols, algorithms and computational resources, data collection and analytics. To provide the background useful to create the framework of reference of relevant parameters, following are summarized the most common methodologies and methods used to localize a target [2].

- Proximity vs Localization: proximity returns the distance between the target and another object whereas localization provides coordinates of the target in a reference system (anchors). Proximity could be a part of a localization system.
- Devices-free vs devices-based localization, device-based localization uses devices as a target whereas in device-free targets that are not equipped with a device.
- Architecture models: in anchor-based the architecture leverages a well-known reference system. In anchor-free, the architecture does not leverage a well-known reference system.
- Methodology of calculation:

  – range-based uses target-sensor geometrical distance calculation.
  – range-free uses indirect methods based on hop count between anchors and targets.

- Range-based required hardware and is not simple to deploy whereas range-free do not needs of special hardware and it is cost efficient but less accurate.

  Among the localization techniques, following a summary of the most used.

- Time based, based on signal propagation information

  – ToA or ToF, Time of Arrival or of Flight, is based on time of propagation of the signal and time stamps, it requires tightly synchronization among anchors-targets.
  – DToA, Difference of Time of Arrival, is based on Difference of Time of Arrival of the signal at anchors, it limits the need of synchronization at transmitters.
  – RToF, Return Time of Flight, is an evaluation of distance between two targets based on round-trip time of the signal, it requires a moderate synchronization.

- Angle Based, based on trigonometrical evaluation.

  - AoA, Angle of Arrival, uses array of antennas to evaluate the angle of arrival, it leverages the difference of time of arrival on adjacent antennas.
  - PoA, Phase of Arrival, based on phase difference of the signal received in adjacent antennas of an array, it could be used to estimate distances or improve accuracy of RSSI, ToF, TDoA.

- Signal energy based.

  - RSSI, Received Signal Strength Indicator, based on signal power received.

- Other elements

  - CSI, Channel State Information, enrich RSSI with information about subchannel amplitude and phase information (CIR + CFR), it improves accuracy.
  - Fingerprinting, mathematical algorithms to compare real time RSSI/CSI information with an offline measurement data set. Often used with AI algorithms.
  - Likelihood function, this is an estimator statistical function, it depends on condition changing and have tradeoff with accuracy vs granularity of samples.
  - Artificial Neural Network (Multi-Layer Perceptron), mostly used to train RSSI.
  - K-Nearest Neighbors, used to obtain k-nearest matches with known location in the RSSI online measures.
  - Support Vector Machine, a method to gain classification and regression, used for ML and statistical analysis with high accuracy, can be used for localization on RSSI online/offline measures.
  - Dead Reckoning, try to predict the position of targets using information like historical information, accelerometers and so on.
  - Hybrid methods, a combination of methods to increase accuracy and robustness.

The picture Fig. 1 reports pro and cons of the most used localization techniques.

Technique	Advantages	Disadvantages
RSSI	Easy to implement, cost efficient, can be used with a number of technologies	Prone to multipath fading and environmental noise, lower localization accuracy, can require fingerprinting
CSI	More robust to multipath and indoor noise,	It is not easily available on off-the-shelf NICs
AoA	Can provide high localization accuracy, does not require any fingerprinting	Might require directional antennas and complex hardware, requires comparatively complex algorithms and performance deteriorates with increase in distance between the transmitter and receiver
ToF	Provides high localization accuracy, does not require any fingerprinting	Requires time synchronization between the transmitters and receivers, might require time stamps and multiple antennas at the transmitter and receiver. Line of Sight is mandatory for accurate performance.
TDoA	Does not require any fingerprinting, does not require clock synchronization among the device and RN	Requires clock synchronization among the RNs, might require time stamps, requires larger bandwidth
RToF	Does not require any fingerprinting, can provide high localization accuracy	Requires clock synchronization, processing delay can affect performance in short ranger measurements
PoA	Can be used in conjunction with RSS, ToA, TDoA to improve the overall localization accuracy	Degraded performance in the absence of line of sight
Fingerprinting	Fairly easy to use	New fingerprints are required even when there is a minor variation in the space

Fig. 1. Advantages and Disadvantages of Different Localization Techniques [2]

Localization techniques are tightly related to wireless communication protocols, to complete the background, a summary of the most used wireless protocols and localization methodologies are reported. The Table II of [2] reports the most important telecommunication protocols and their characteristics in terms of throughput, coverage, scalability, energy consumption. The Table I of [10] shows the relations among telecommunication protocols and localization techniques, including some key parameters like accuracy, scalability, costs.

2   Previous Works and Methodology

Researching in engines like IEEE, Research Gate, Direct Science, does not return relevant papers about comparison among real cases based on heterogeneous methods to localize things/people in healthcare sector. Whereas it is possible to find several works about localization methods and localization performance improvement, and comparison among them. This is, likely, due to the complexity to compare heterogeneous architectures. The keywords used to search previous works were: IoT, Localization, Indoor, Case, Healthcare.

The methodology adopted to select and compare real use cases about localization in healthcare domain is explained in the following points:

- Create a framework of evaluation. A set of parameters, that are relevant for the most common use cases, is created to compare the cases selected.
- Select the cases. To be as relevant as possible, the cases selected from literature leverage different methods and methodologies to localize targets. All of them include applied tests in real or nearly real world.
- Analysis. The cases selected were analyzed trying to esteem the parameters that are part of the framework of evaluation. When the parameters are not deducible from the analysis of the cases, their esteem has been completed using data from the literature.
- Comparison. A comparison was carried out from the cases analysis according to the framework of evaluation. This comparison can be used as a guide to select the most suitable architecture of localization, given the requirements of a use case.

The methodology is designed to be the easily appliable and open to be extended including more cases or parameters.

3   Evaluation Parameters and Cases Selection

The parameters selected are the most common for the use cases of localization: Range of coverage, Latency, Accuracy, Power consumption/Energy Efficiency, Scalability, Costs, Privacy. Given a solution, these parameters define its scope of the applications.

Given the framework of evaluation, it is the moment of select the cases. The purpose of the review is comparing applied cases of localization in healthcare industry, to respond the question: "What is the most suitable method to fulfill a given use case of localization in healthcare applications domain?". The research was carried out to find heterogeneous cases.

The first criterion was restricting the set of articles to select as following:

- Restricting the research to IEEE Explorer engine
- Restricting the research to IEEE journals
- Restricting the research to the last 10 years of publication.

Then, the key words used were: indoor, localize/localization, healthcare. Fifty-five articles emerged and, in that basket, five experimentations were selected, which leverage different localization methodologies.

4   Privacy Perspectives

Localization applications in healthcare domain often have the final aim to trace patients and transmit data related to his vitals. That entails serious issues of privacy and security. Indeed, according to GDPR regulation [11, 22], data related to health status are specifically defined as sensitive because of the compromission of this information could have significant impact on the rights of the patients. The personal health data are among the most priced in the dark web due to the high level or returns that is possible earn from them. Fundamentally, according to [12, 21], the risks related to the privacy are: illegitimate access to data and diffusion, unwanted data changing, data cancellation. Risk management models take in consideration the process of collect, transmit, memorize, and use data. Each process could be object of privacy risks coming from both humans and not humans. The model of risk analysis in Fig. 2, from [12], is taken in consideration in the following part of the document.

Risks	Impacts on data subjects	Main risk sources	Main threats	Existing or planned measures	Severity	Likelihood
Illegitimate access to personal data						
Unwanted change of data						
Disappearance of data						

Fig. 2. Risk analysis model [12]

All cases taken in consideration relay on wireless telecommunication protocols that are used also to localize targets through many methods, where devices that equip the target are used to collect and transmit data. Protocols and devices are exposed to several privacy risks, according to the model of Fig. 3, is possible to categorize in:

- Edge attacks, that are the attacks to the devices in the perception layer.
- Network attacks, that are the attacks to the elements devoted to collect and transmit the information coming from perception layer.

Often, in the domain of the analysis, devices are limited in resources of computation to save energy, this could entail limitations in apply complex algorithms for authentication and encryption. On the other hand, general purpose devices, like smartphones, are more exposed to be attacked due to both the commercial operation systems and the presence of many and not always secure applications.

The Fig. 4, [14, 18] summarizes the attacks that can threat the edge and the network layers of an IoT infrastructure. Finally, the Fig. 5 reports the correlation between threats and risks of a IoT infrastructure, according to the risk model aforementioned, which is used to evaluate the cases selected.

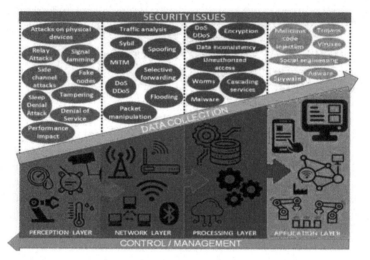

Fig. 3. Layers and typologies of attacks [17]

EDGE ATTACKS	PRIVACY IMPACTS	NETWORK ATTACKS	PRIVACY IMPACTS
Hardware Trojan	Leak personal data, data manipulation	Side channel attacks	Access to security parameters
Node replication	Unreal data generation, inpersonification, access to security parameters	Collision attacks:	Service blocking (eg sensor battery drain)
		Fragmentation attacks	Service issues
Denial of Service (DoS) attacks	Block of services	Routing attacks	
Sleep deprivation		Hello Flood	Service issues
Battery draining		Gray Hole	Service issues
Outage attacks		Sybil attack	Unreal data transmission
Physical attack	Leak security parameters, device cloning, unreal data	Worm Hole	Lack of information
Malicious node	Possible entry point for an excalation phase	Selective forwarding	Service issues
Side channel attack	Leak of information even about security parameters	Eavesdropping	Observation of data related to the sensors and also security parameters
Eavesdropping	Leak of data related to the sensors and also security parameters	Inject malicious packets	Unreal data transmission
Tag Counterfeiting	Unreal data transmission	Dos attacks	Service issues, service blocking
Tag cloning	Unreal data trasmission of an device associated person	Desynchronized attack	N - usually result in service preformance issues or service break
		Spoofing	Unreal data transmission
Tag Tracking	Leak of data related to the sensor localization	Sinkhole	Service issues, preparation for other attacks
Tag Inventorying	Sensitive data leakage	Man in the middle attack	Observation of sensitive data, unreal data trasmission

Fig. 4. Edge attacks and privacy impacts - networks attacks and privacy impacts

Finally, looking at the whole architecture, the most likely targets of the attackers are the points where data are stored and visualized. Access to the data storage open the doors to gain the access to all data available. The magnitude of the impact of an attack to a datastore is certainly higher than an attack to the edge or to the network of the architecture. Attack the edge and the network of the architecture can result in trace a person, corrupt/leak some data, denial a little piece of the service, but, also, access to the infrastructure and moving gradually to the datastore in datacenter, in cloud or in the edge. The focus of the analysis is limited to the edge and to the network because of the cases do not report the processing and application layers architectures.

Risks	Main risk sources	Main Threats
Illegitimate acces to personal data	Non Human	Hardware Trojan
	Non Human	Node replication
	Human	Physical Attack
	Non Human	Eavesdropping
	Human & Non Human	Tag cloning
	Non Human	Tag Tracking
	Human & Non Human	Tag Inventorying
	Non Human	Network Eavesdropping
	Non Human	Network Side channel attacks
	Non Human	Network Sinkhole
	Non Human	Network Worm Hole
	Non Human	Man in the middle attack

Risks	Main risk sources	Main Threats
Unwanted change of data	Non Human	Hardware Trojan
	Non Human	Node replication
	Human	Physical Attack
	Non Human	Eavesdropping
	Human & Non Human	Tag Counterfeiting
	Non Human	Sybil attack
	Non Human	Inject malicious packets
	Non Human	Spoofing
	Non Human	Man in the middle attack

Risks	Main risk sources	Main Threats
Disappearance of data	Non Human	Hardware Trojan
	Non Human	Tag Counterfeiting
	Non Human	Network Worm Hole

Fig. 5. Risk analysis for IoT privacy

To protect edge and network layers what is fundamental to protect security and privacy are [18]:

- Strong authentication methods.
- Strong encryption other methods.
- Robust key/certificate management system.
- Decouple device ID and people identity.
- Hardening Operating System of the employed devices.

The methodology used to evaluate the privacy aspects of the cases selected is based on risk qualitative analysis according to the risk model aforementioned.

5 A Brief Description of the Cases Selected

In this section are described four use cases about localization in healthcare industry, taken from the literature. The cases are based on different architectures and use different methods of localization.

5.1 Case 1. "An IoT-Aware Architecture for Smart Healthcare Systems"

The purpose of this case, described in [3], is to create a solution able to provide insights about patients and environmental conditions in a healthcare budling, within a robust, optimized, and low power HMS (Health Management System). Key goals:

- Tracking the patients' paths to allow a fast first aid in case of emergencies.

- Collecting vitals samples in time and space, to provide insights for decisions support.

The authors chose to use a hybrid solution, 802.15.4 and RFID, with the aim to reduce energy consumption as much as possible. The architecture is composed by:

- Host Terminal (HT), the mobile devices for patients, supporting both RFID Tag and 802.15.4 radios, with sensors for vitals and a battery to enable RFID-BAP (battery-assisted passive). The battery is used to send alarms via 802.15.4 in wakeup mode.
- Low Power Router Reader (LPRR), devices equipped with an RFID reader, an 802.15.4 transceiver, and some environmental sensors. LPRRs act as anchors localizing the HTs and collecting data. LPRR are scattered in the budling with the appropriate density to detects patient in rooms. LPRR upload data in WSN fashion.
- IoT Smart Gateway, a server that receive and elaborate locally data from LPRRs.
- A central server that memorizes data and provide post elaboration/http interface to the users.

The architecture is shown in Fig. 1-Fig. 2-Fig. 3 of [3]. The system uses a CoAP protocol, which use http interface to provide insights to the doctors. The HT, usually passive, can generate alarms, proactively, in the case that vitals/movements are anormal. The Table I of [3] shows the comparison of power consumption among protocols used, to give the idea how the dual radio approach at HT (with 802.15.4 sleeping most of the time except for emergencies) could improve power consumption if compared with a full 802.15.4 based architecture. The result of experimentation points out a wakeup range of 11 mt in RFID, 13 mt of coverage in fully passive mode, 22 mt of coverage in BAP mode. It is very interesting that BAP mode recorded 0.025 mA of current consumption, which is three order of magnitude less than 802.15.4, with the same range of coverage when devices are set up for indoor operation (22 mt). Finally, the architecture provides quite real time insightful information, asking for three orders of magnitude less of energy than a WSN architecture, assuring comparable range of coverage as shown in Fig. 6 and Table III of [3]. The scalability of the model is related to the scalability, in terms of people-things/mt^2, of RFID and of 802.15.4. Accuracy is not discussed because the aim of the work is tracking with approximation. The devices used are not directly available on the market but easily makable.

Privacy consideration. In this case, the utilization of ah-hoc target, could reduce the security vulnerabilities compared to commercial targets. Like all systems aimed to save energy, RFID is subject to several kind of attacks due to the lack of resources of computation. These systems, even if is more secure if compared with the past generation of tags, has several weaknesses [16]. Main risks coming from the possibility to compromise the tag, eavesdropping and rouge scanning attacks. That could result in privacy risks for data transmitted, for data authenticity and data observation. Anyway, the short range of the RFID technology reduce the possibility to attack the devices, the attacker should be very near to the target.

802.15.4 is a protocol that shows issues in term of security, the most important are Denial of Services attacks, attacks aimed to decrypt frames and reply attack [15]. The needs to save energy is a limitation to use all security features of the protocol.

Given the sensitivity of the data transmitted and the weakness of the protocol used, the architecture proposed left doubt about the privacy robustness. To improve the privacy, several counter measures are needed. Mostly, the personal information of the patients must be separated and anonymized by the data transmitted from the edge.

5.2 Case 2. "A Novel Architecture Using iBeacons for Localization and Tracking of People Within Healthcare Environment"

The purpose of the case, described in [4], is tracking patients and devices in a hospital, and provide insights related to the patient caring and the asset management.

The architecture is based on BLE iBeacon and RSSI technique to localize targets. To improve the accuracy of the centroid - RSSI a smoothing filter and an improved Least Square Estimation are used. The authors have chosen BLE because it is a very widespread technology, accurate and energy efficient. They discarded WiFi and RFID. Like reported by [8, 9], WiFi would require many APs to achieve accuracy of some meters, whereas RFID is accurate but requires dense infrastructure due the short range achievable. The architecture, reported in Fig. 3 of [4], involves some anchors in fixed and well-known positions, determined in previous works to achieve the optimal signal coverage. The practical maximum distance between the anchor and devices is claimed to be under 10 m. The mobile device should be a wearable, but a smartphone was used for the tests. It collects anchors RSSI signals along the path. This information is integrated with other parameters, accelerometer and gyroscopes information, to improve the accuracy and add on real time insights about patient conditions.

A phase of positioning and calibrating is needed (fingerprinting), then the data are collected by the application and sent to server via 4G/WiFi. A server elaborates information sent by smartphone to provide position. The server acts also as beacon manager, but it is not explained in which way it manages the bacons in term of communication protocols. In the experimentation, the beacons are four vertices of a parallelogram of 20 mt^2, there were 12 people, 16 computers, 32 chairs and tables, 2 WiFi routers. The devices were at 1.2 mt of height. The results, reported by Fig. 5 of [4], show that the system can achieve 37 cm of maximum error and 12.5 cm of average error. RSSI accuracy is really improved by LSE method.

Some words related to our metrics: the architecture presents a good cost given the commercial devices used, the coverage is quite limited and rely on BLE capabilities. The improved LSE returns good results, but nothing is said about the latency related to post elaboration. The energy consumption of BLE is one of the best technologies on the market.

Privacy consideration. This case leverage two wireless technologies BLE and WiFi/4G, this entails to expose the architecture to the weakness of both protocols. The architecture leverage on ad-hoc targets and, generally, reduce the privacy risks compared to a localization method based on smartphone application. Contiki is an operative system that is prone to several CVEs, mostly related to DDoS attacks. BLE [13] is a system that has been really improved in the recent past with the integration features to address parity, authentication, and encryption schemes, reducing the threats in security and privacy. Given that the target exchanges only distance information with anchors, (aggregation and elaboration are performed by the central architecture) the risks related the privacy at edge and at network are low as well as the impact resulting. 4G protocol has some weakness in terms of security and privacy, it can receive sinkholes attacks via DNS and redirect packets. What is more critical is that the target device is a smartphone, that has a more extended attack surface compared to ad-hoc target devices. On the other hands, a smartphone has more capacity of computation and memory to adopt strong authentication and encryption algorithms. That, anyway, requires more energy. Further, WiFi Router [17], even using WPA3, allows the attackers to perform side-channel attacks, downgrade attacks, passphrase brute-force attacks and even DoS attacks.

5.3   Case 3. "Indoor Localization Using 802.11 WiFi and IoT Edge Nodes"

The purpose of the case, described in [5], is to create a system that provides localization of patients and medical staff in real time. The accuracy requested is at room level. The system, called LoCATE, is based on WiFi, with APs already deployed at the site, and Edge Nodes that are ad-hoc devices. The Authors chose ad-hoc devices instead of smartphone because of, often, healthcare's organization do not have smartphone policies. The idea to experiment a framework that provides localization services based on 802.11 via RSSI, which is notoriously one of the less accurate methods of localization, takes in primary consideration costs of the infrastructure. In fact, WiFi infrastructures are in place in almost all healthcare organizations. The Edge Nodes are built on a Raspberry Pi Zero with USB WiFi dongles, powered via a rechargeable lithium battery pack which grants 6/8 h of autonomy. Edge nodes operates in monitor mode (beaconing) when they scan for AP, and in upload mode when they communicate to a central serve a considerable change of position. The experimentation was done at James Madison University where a survey of 1/2/4 min for channel hopping took place to find most of the APs (4 min allows to discover all AP) from four different spots. The Fig. 1 of [5]. shows the architecture. The software took one minute to scan and elaborate signals, which results in a near real time localization. A trimming could improve the accuracy, but it is not impacting so much if compared with the average error recorded.

The results, reported in Table 1 of [5], show that coherent measurements are achievable, even if, some incongruent values are also present. The authors relate that incongruence with the presence of barriers. Anyway, errors could reach 60% against the expected distance. The AP that recorded the worst measures are the ones which have obstacles interposed with the spot.

To give a reference regarding Wifi localization based on RSSI, the [7] claims to achieve a mean of error of 3.7 mt and using a denser solution of APs per square meters achieves 1.5 mt mean of error (18AP per 100 mt^2). The proposed model is very rough in terms of accuracy and in terms of variance of the measures. The time required to discover the APs could be an insurmountable limitation that restricts drastically the scope of the application to some static scenarios. The architecture is largely available, often already in place and not complex. There is not information about scalability.

Privacy consideration. In this case, the authors given some indication about how to manage security and privacy concerns, recognizing the sensitiveness of the data managed. The authors take in consideration the risks related to the data transmission and the attacks like spoofing or side-channel. They want to avoid the tracking of the devices and the patients path reconstruction. To reduce these risks, they employ an AES-128-GCM for authentication and encryption and 802.1x to authenticate the devices.

Anyway, the analysis seems to be uncomplete, indeed the device based in Raspberry Pi is prone to some attacks that could result in unauthorize access and in denial of service [19]. Further, as already mentioned in the previous case, WiFi has several security concerns still.

5.4   Case 4: "DeFi: Robust Training-Free Device-Free Wireless Localization with WiFi"

The purpose of the case, described in [6], is to create an architecture based on commercial WiFi devices to provide localization information both devices-free and training-free. Devices-free method of localization is very suitable for healthcare industry because carrying on devices or wearable sensors could be inconvenient for elder and children. The methodology proposed to implement devices-free model leverage the distortion and the fluctuation of transmitted signals to establish the location of the target. Usually, that is achieved via both mathematical methods and machine learning algorithms. These methodologies use time consuming and labor-intensive offline learning activities, which are prone to environmental changes. The approach proposed, called DeFi, is aimed to avoid learning activities, estimating the target location by refining the angle-of-arrival (AoA) of the signal reflected by the target, using just out of shelf APs. To achieve that object is basic to identify the reflection paths of the signal from the transmitter to the receivers. To do that, it is needed to have N antennas to discriminate N-1 reflection paths and, empirically, eight antennas are required in almost of all real cases. Given that commercial APs hardly are equipped with eight antennas, CSI (available on new models of APs) have a key role because it provides the phase shift information from the subchannel, and this allows to simulate more antennas. Even ten time more than the physical antennas installed. In this way it is possible estimate both AoA and the related ToF. The Fig. 1 and Fig. 2 of [6], shows the geometry of the AoA method and the paths of the signal. The implementation consists in three steps.

- Calibration, a phase of calibration is required to eliminate random phase across sub-channels, drift by Sampling Time Offset. Commercial AP are imperfect in hardware and loosely synchronized in the transmitter - receiver pairs.
- Estimation of AoA via the MUSIC algorithms to extract key signal parameters.
- A joint AoA and ToF estimations to refine the evaluation.

Given the three steps above, the phases to estimate AoA are following summarized:

- Identify and eliminate static paths (background). Using the high correlation of samples of static paths is possible eliminating background.
- Separate out the target reflection path from the motion path via a likelihood criterion. To identify direct reflection path, a target reflection paths refinement is needed. It is possible assuming that direct path is the shortest one and has the minimum ToF. Also, direct reflection path produces the smaller variation of AoA compared to other paths. By a likelihood criterion, the reflection paths are separated out from the motion

412   A. Scarfò

paths, and it is possible leverage the informative AoA estimation of the target direct reflection path to estimate the target location.

- Make the evaluation of AoA reliable, even in challenging conditions, via a particles filter. Due to the complex signal propagation characteristics, it is possible that large errors in the AoA estimations are recorded, that leads to poor target location estimation. The Particles Filter is a Bayesian filter which estimates the posterior probability distribution function (Fig. 6).

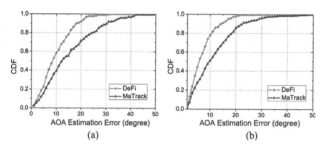

Fig. 6. AoA methods estimation of error in CDF in laboratory (a) and lobby (b) [6]

The model depicted is extended to all receivers and the target position is estimated thought the intersection of the probability distribution function of each receiver.

In the experimentation were involved a lobby (36 mt^2) and a laboratory (48 mt^2) with chairs, desks, and computers. One mini pc, equipped with an AP, operated as transmitters and four APs were used as receivers. Transmitter sent packets every 1 ms on channel 132 of the 5 GHz spectrum, and the receivers provide CSI information that are elaborated by a server. The server applies all concepts above descripted and perform a triangulation. Also, the impact of receivers was evaluated increasing from two (that is the desiderata) to four, it returns a reduction of median localization error of 13%. Finally, the number of particles impacts as well, 100 particles needed to get the saturation in localization error. In conclusion, in the lobby, the system returns a mean error of 0.47 mt with a variance of 0.07 mt. Figure 6 of [6] shows the cumulative distribution functions of the localization errors that results from tests in laboratory (a) and lobby (b).

The experimentation is well arranged and complete in the analysis of parameters. Anyway, no information is given about complexity of calculation and its latency, scalability, and range of coverage to face a real environment with many people. Concerning costs, the devices used are out of shelf but an high density is required in the test. The power consumption is practically zero given the lack of devices. Further works should analyze multi targets in a noisier environment.

Privacy consideration. In this case there are not issues related to edge of the networks. Indeed, there are not devices to be identified and traced and there are not sensitive data to be transmitted. Consequently, the approach does not require authentication and encryption. Even if the attackers could track a target, leverage the weakness of WiFi, them should discover the link between the path of the target and the people related with. Also, tracking a target is not so simple because the location of the target is obtained by a complex analysis of many signals coming from all the receivers. The architecture is prone to all the weakness of WiFi and to risks related with. Giving the opportunity to the attacker to reduce the performance and denial the service, manipulate the signal and corrupt data. As mentioned, almost all anchors should be compromised localize the target.

6 Comparison

The final part of the survey is aimed to compare the cases selected. To make the reading easy, the Fig. 7 reports a synthesis of the analysis done with some notes related to the framework of reference defined. The scale of evaluation is created on the base of the measures reported by cases, normalized in a scale of 0–10. For the KPIs not included in the description of the cases, we take in account the estimation reported in the Table I of [10] and in the the Table II of [2].

Following a brief description of the parameters of evaluation of their meaning.

Case	Object	Method	Note
1	Patient/assets tracing, vitals recording, emergency alerts with localization	Hybrid: 802.15.4 + RFID • Devices based (ad hoc) • Proximity • No post elaboration • RFID scalability • RFID coverage (11mt) • Costs in average • Power consumption the best • Accuracy less than the avg (mt) • Latency no reported	To use when is required: high energy efficiency, accuracy in meters, coverage in meters, average market costs and no latency.
2	Patients/assets localization, localization for emergency alerts	BLE iBeacons, Out of Shelf beacon • Device based (Smartphone) • RSSI device-anchors distance • Post elaboration LSE+Smoothing filter • BLE scalability • BLE coverage (mt) • Costs in average • Power consumption better than avg • Accuracy the best (cm) • Latency not reported but existing	To use when is required: high accuracy (in cm), good energy efficiency, average market costs, coverage of meters is acceptable, dense infrastructure is acceptable, latency is not required in very real time.
3	Localization of patients and medical staff in real time	802.11 OFS • Devices based (ad hoc Raspberry) • RSSI • Post Elaboration No • WiFi scalability • WiFi Coverage the best (x100mt) • Costs better than the avg • Power consumption less of the average • Accuracy the worst (mt) • Latency 1 min	To use when is required: large coverage, high scalability, low costs, accuracy is acceptable in tens of meters, power consumption is not a problem, one minute of latency
4	Localization of patients	802.11 OFS • Devices free • RSSI • Post Elaboration No • Scalability to be investigated more • Coverage less than the avg • Costs the worst due the infrastructure • Power consumption the best • Accuracy better than the avg (cm) • Latency not reported but likely impacting	To use when is required: zero power consumption, zero cost of devices, accuracy in tens of meters, coverage acceptable in ten of meters, cost of infrastructure above the average.

Fig. 7. Summary of the cases analysis

- Range of coverage – reported by the cases, it means how many infrastructural devices are used by square meters. The lower the better.
- Latency – not reported by cases, it means how match time is needed to have the localization once it has been measured. The case 3 asks minutes to prepare the measure because of the multi-hopping action to discover all reachable APs Even if, in a real case, it could be a too long time to consider the solution applicable, it does not impact on latency, indeed once the multi-hopping is completed the localization is available in real time The case 4 could require of a consistent post elaboration time. The case 2 asks for some post elaboration, less than the case 4 and more than the case 1 and 3. The case 3 takes 1 min to export the position of the target. To take in consideration this scenario a score of 10 is given to the case with no post elaboration, zero to the case 4, 5 to the case 2. The lower the better.
- Accuracy – reported by each case, it means the average error to localize the target. The lower the better.
- Power consumption/Energy Efficiency – not reported by all cases, it means how much energy is needed to feed mobile devices. It is complex to compare the cases because of the measurements are not directly comparable. The [23] reports a comparison among WiFi, BLE and 802.15.4. Assuming that most of the time the device target is in sleeping, then it is in beaconing mode and sometimes it transmits/receives data mode. BLE is the most energy efficient technology, 802.15.4 absorbs about 145% more electricity than BLE, and, finally, WiFi requires five time more of energy compared to BLE. The power consumption of the case 4, device-free, is esteemed almost zero. The authors of the case 1 claim to achieve three orders of magnitude less than 802.15.4 using RFID in BAP mode. The lower the better.
- Scalability - not reported by cases. Scalability means how many targets are sustainable for square meters. About the case 4, it is very hard to talk about scalability, [20] shows that it is possible to manage multi-target scenarios with 80% of error about present entities. On the other hand, it is possible estimate how many targets WiFi and BLE can manage but, at the same time, these technologies are prone to interferences and obstacles, so even in these cases is not too easy esteem in term of number of target detectable/error measured. More research is required to have a precise evaluation, so, we assume this parameter according to [10]. The higher the better.
- Costs – this is related to the costs of the solutions. To esteem the cost of architecture selected, are taken in consideration both the costs of the targets and the cost of the infrastructure used for the implementation. To normalize the cost of the infrastructure, it is normalized by per square meters. The lower the better.
- Privacy – the privacy evaluation is threated apart. A qualitative evaluation is provided on the base of the security risks related to both edge and network, the likelihood of the attacks and the consequences of the attacks.

To make the comparison as more readable as possible, all metrics are reported in the higher the better fashion even if the metrics are naturally evaluable as the lower the better, these are converted in complement of ten.

The Fig. 8 shows the comparison among the cases selected by the means of a radar.

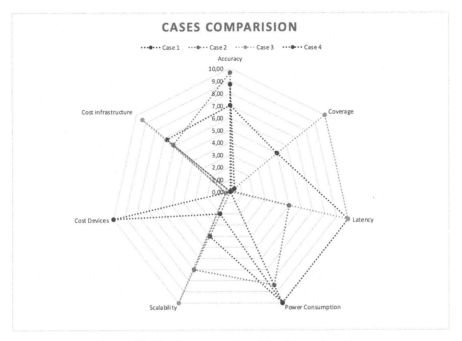

Fig. 8. Cases comparison by radar graph

The case 1 has the best compromise. This is a solution suitable for case where accuracy is acceptable in meters and the power consumption is key. The cost of the devices, generally, is affordable, even if it is poor compared with the other cases. The case 2 is excellent for accuracy and power consumption. The limited coverage does not affect the costs of the infrastructure. Latency and scalability are around the average and devices are generally affordable. The case 3 is clearly suitable for use cases that require low cost, high coverage but accuracy and power consumption should be not a key factor. The case 4 provide the very intriguing opportunity to localize people in devices-less fashion. This is a real step forward in terms of power consumption and easiness of adoption. The solution works very well in term of accuracy and, of course, in term of power consumption and cost of devices. The cost of infrastructure is poor compared to the other cases because a high density of APs is required, but WiFi device could be found already in place in many network infrastructures. Anyway, that solution needs of a complex post elaboration phase that is not evaluated in the case neither in term of costs nor of latency. To complete the evaluation, it should be investigated the scalability of the system, in other words, how the solution behaves in a multitarget scenario. In the end, the case 2 seems to be the most balanced solution because of do not has important weaknesses.

Consideration on privacy. From the privacy perspective we can split the risks in two categories, risk from network and risk form edge both reported by Fig. 4. About the edge, the case 1 is the most exposed because of the weakness of both the RFID protocol and the tag. Also, a successful attack to the RFID tag results immediately in accessing to the vital data of the patients and tracking the path of the target. The case 2 leverage a smartphone device, that has weakness related to the operative system and to the Apps installed. The case 3 leverage a Raspberry target that is prone to unauthorized accesses to the device and to denial of service. The case 4 do not use any target device. The attacks to the network can target both the anchors and the target devices. In the second case, the attacks can be risky for the privacy in terms of data exfiltration, device tracking, denial of the service, data manipulation. Attacking the anchors hardly affect the privacy. Indeed, to collect data about a target entail the corruption a significant number of anchors. Instead, attacks to the anchors, and to edge as well, can result very impactful as a first step to access centralized data. Among the protocol used, the WiFi results exposed to attacks also because of its wide range of coverage that allow the attackers to avoid being near the target. The protocol could be prone to device tracking, brute-force, side-channel, denial of service and so on. BLE is prone to several attacks, but recent developments have improved its security, especially regarding to the tracking of the device, but it remains prone to eavesdropping and man in the middle attacks. 802.15.4 is prone to denial of service, frame decrypt and reply to attacks. The case 4, that does not use target devices, is less prone to privacy risks because of it does not transmit data at all, even tracking the target entail a complex attack to the infrastructure. Finally, WiFi seems to be the protocol most exposed to be attacked and risky for the privacy as well as RFID is the weakest device prone to consequences about privacy.

7 Conclusions and Future Works

Even if the comparison among the four cases selected is not simple to yield, by the mean of a framework of key parameters it emerges clear when the solutions investigated are suitable. In this moment in time, BLE based architecture seems to be the most balanced even in terms or privacy risks. WiFi based architecture is excellent for coverage, costs, and latency but is weak for accuracy, power consumption and privacy. RFID based architecture is something in the middle, excellent for power consumption and latency, weak for privacy and in the middle for the other parameters. Device free architectures are very promising from the perspective of energy consumption and accuracy, but some elements require of further investigation, the impact of a complex post elaboration phase effort for latency and costs, and accuracy in multi-targets scenarios. The most real risks in term of privacy are related to device tracking, data observation/corruption and limitation of service. Risks that coming from the attacks to devices are more likely and impact on a single target. The attacks to the networks could involve many targets and are mostly oriented to denial of services. A most critical and likely scenario is when attackers use edge and network to escalate towards the datacenter.

The analysis of the cases selected leaves some point of further investigation to provide a more complete scenario. It is possible split the improvement in two typologies:

- Vertical improvement: further investigation about the parameters that are not clearly threated by the case. For instance, the behavior of the architecture in terms of scalability and latency in a multi-target environment as well as the costs/time required by post elaboration computations. It is also possible to provide a set of suggestions to improve the cases analysis is another important domain of further studies.

- Horizontal improvement: extend the framework with more parameters and extend the number of cases analyzed, adding solutions tested in actual environments that employ other and different architecture to localize targets.

This approach improves the analysis done and provide the opportunity to extend the scope of the analysis and its applicability in terms of use case requirements.

References

1. Mckinsey Digital: Unlocking the potential of the Internet of Things, 1 June 2015|Report. https://www.mckinsey.com/business-functions/mckinsey-digital/our-insights/the-internet-of-things-the-value-of-digitizing-the-physical-world. Accessed 15 May 2022
2. Zafari, F., Gkelias, A., Leung, K.K.: A survey of indoor localization systems and technologies. IEEE Commun. Surv. Tutor. **21**(3), 2568–2599 (2019). https://doi.org/10.1109/COMST.2019.2911558
3. Catarinucci, L., et al.: An IoT-aware architecture for smart healthcare systems. IEEE Internet Things J. **2**(6), 515–526 (2015). https://doi.org/10.1109/JIOT.2015.2417684
4. Nguyen, Q.H., Johnson, P., Nguyen, T.T., Randles, M.: A novel architecture using iBeacons for localization and tracking of people within healthcare environment. In: Global IoT Summit (GIoTS), pp. 1–6 (2019). https://doi.org/10.1109/GIOTS.2019.8766368
5. Salman, A., El-Tawab, S., Yorio, Z., Hilal, A.: Indoor localization using 802.11 WiFi and IoT edge nodes. In: IEEE Global Conference on Internet of Things (GCIoT), pp. 1–5 (2018). https://doi.org/10.1109/GCIoT.2018.8620162
6. Zhang, L., Gao, Q., Ma, X., Wang, J., Yang, T., Wang, H.: DeFi: robust training-free device-free wireless localization with WiFi. IEEE Trans. Veh. Technol. **67**(9), 8822–8831 (2018). https://doi.org/10.1109/TVT.2018.2850842
7. Zhang, L., Wang, H.: 3D-WiFi: 3D localization with commodity WiFi. IEEE Sens. J. **19**(13), 5141–5152 (2019). https://doi.org/10.1109/JSEN.2019.2900511
8. Mainetti, L., Patrono, L., Sergi, I.: A survey on indoor positioning systems. In: 22nd International Conference on Software Telecommunications and Computer Networks (SoftCOM) (2014)
9. Van Haute, T., et al.: Performance analysis of multiple Indoor Positioning Systems in a healthcare environment. Int. J. Health Geogr. **15**(1), 13–15 (2016)
10. Stojanovic, D., Stojanovic, N.: Indoor localization and tracking: methods, technologies and research challenges. Facta Universitatis Ser. Autom. Control Robot. **13**, 57–72 (2014)
11. Homepage page Regulation EU. https://www.privacy-regulation.eu/. Accessed 14 May 2022
12. Homepage CNIL PIA. https://www.cnil.fr/sites/default/files/atoms/files/cnil-pia-3-en-knowledgebases.pdf. Accessed 14 May 2022
13. Cäsar, M., Pawelke, T., Steffan, J., Terhorst, G.: A survey on Bluetooth Low Energy security and privacy. In Computer Networks **205**, 108712 (2022). https://doi.org/10.1016/j.comnet.2021.108712. ISSN 1389-1286
14. Ahmadi, P., Islam, K., Maco, T., Katam, M.: Survey on internet of things security issues and applications. In: International Conference on Computational Science and Computational Intelligence (CSCI), pp. 925–934 (2018). https://doi.org/10.1109/CSCI46756.2018.00182
15. Reziouk, A., Laurent, E., Demay, J.: Practical security overview of IEEE 802.15.4. In: International Conference on Engineering & MIS (ICEMIS), pp. 1–9 (2016). https://doi.org/10.1109/ICEMIS.2016.7745382

16. Garcia-Alfaro, J., Herrera-Joancomartí, J., Melià-Seguí, J.: Security and privacy concerns about the RFID layer of EPC Gen2 networks. In: Navarro-Arribas, G., Torra, V. (eds.) Advanced Research in Data Privacy. SCI, vol. 567, pp. 303–324. Springer, Cham (2015). https://doi.org/10.1007/978-3-319-09885-2_17

17. Zahariev, P., Hristov, G., Kinaneva, D., Chaisricharoen, R., Georgiev, G., Stoilov, P.: A review on the main characteristics and security vulnerabilities of the wireless communication technologies in the Industry 4.0 domain. In: Joint International Conference on Digital Arts, Media and Technology with ECTI Northern Section Conference on Electrical, Electronics, Computer and Telecommunications Engineering (ECTI DAMT & NCON), pp. 514–517 (2022). https://doi.org/10.1109/ECTIDAMTNCON53731.2022.9720331

18. Abdul-Ghani, H.A., Konstantas, D.: A comprehensive study of security and privacy guidelines, threats, and countermeasures. J. Sens. Actuator Netw. **8**, 22 (2019). https://doi.org/10.3390/jsan8020022

19. Sainz Raso, J., Martin, S., Diaz, G., Castro, M.: Security vulnerabilities in Raspberry Pi–analysis of the system weaknesses. IEEE Consum. Electron. Mag. **8**, 47–52. https://doi.org/10.1109/MCE.2019.2941347

20. Seifeldin, M., Saeed, A., Kosba, A.E., El-Keyi, A., Youssef, M.: Nuzzer: a large-scale device-free passive localization system for wireless environments. IEEE Trans. Mob. Comput. **12**(7), 1321–1334 (2013). https://doi.org/10.1109/TMC.2012.106

21. Di Martino, B., Mastroianni, M., Campaiola, M., Morelli, G., Sparaco, E.: Semantic techniques for validation of GDPR compliance of business processes. In: Barolli, L., Hussain, F.K., Ikeda, M. (eds.) CISIS 2019. AISC, vol. 993, pp. 847–855. Springer, Cham (2020). https://doi.org/10.1007/978-3-030-22354-0_78

22. Campanile, L., Cantiello, P., Iacono, M., Marulli, F., Mastroianni, M.: Risk analysis of a GDPR-compliant deletion technique for consortium blockchains based on pseudonymization. In: Gervasi, O., et al. (eds.) ICCSA 2021. LNCS, vol. 12956, pp. 3–14. Springer, Cham (2021). https://doi.org/10.1007/978-3-030-87010-2_1

23. Kazeem, O., Akintade, O., Kehinde, L.: Comparative study of communication interfaces for sensors and actuators in the cloud of internet of things. Int. J. Internet Things **6**, 9–13 (2017). https://doi.org/10.5923/j.ijit.20170601.02

TruthSeekers Chain: Leveraging Invisible CAPPCHA, SSI and Blockchain to Combat Disinformation on Social Media

Meriem Guerar[1,3]([envelope])[iD] and Mauro Migliardi[1,2,3][iD]

[1] University of Padua, Padua 35131, Italy
{meriem.guerar,mauro.migliardi}@unipd.it
[2] Centro per l'Ingegneria delle Piattaforme Informatiche (CIPI), Genova 16145, Italy
mauro.migliardi@cipi.unige.it
[3] Cybertooth, Joint CIPI Gruppo SIGLA CyberSecurity Lab, Genoa, Italy
https://www.unipd.it, https://cybertooth.grupposigla.it/index.html

Abstract. Disinformation has become a worrisome phenomenon at a global scale, spreading rapidly thanks to the growth of social media and frequently causing serious harm. For instance, it can perplex and manipulate users, fuel scepticism on crucial issues such as climate change, jeopardize a variety of human rights, such as the right to free and fair elections, the right to health, to non-discrimination, etc.

Among the most used tools and techniques to spread disinformation are social bots, deep-fakes, and impersonation of authoritative media, people, or governments through false social media accounts. To deal with these issues, in this paper, we suggest TruthSeekers Chain, a platform which add a layer on top of the existing social media networks where I) the feed is augmented with new functionalities and reliable information retrieved from a blockchain II) a bot screening mechanism is used to allow only human generated content and engagement to be posted, III) the platform is open to integration of 3rd-party content verification tools helping the user to identify the manipulated or tampered content and IV) a self sovereign identity model is used to ensure accountability and to contribute building a reliable portable reputation system.

Keywords: Fake news · Social Media · Reputation system · SSI · NFT · CAPTCHA · Blockchain

1 Introduction

During the last decade disinformation and fake news proved to be serious threats to democracies and to the freedom of citizens. Disinformation is defined as a subset of information that can be false, inaccurate, or misleading intentionally designed, published, and promoted for causing public harm or making a profit [1]. It is a force undermining citizens' faith in democratic institutions by

O. Gervasi et al. (Eds.): ICCSA 2022 Workshops, LNCS 13380, pp. 419–431, 2022.
https://doi.org/10.1007/978-3-031-10542-5_29

distorting free and fair elections and, through the amplification of social division, resentment, and fear, often resulting in fomenting violence and repression. Furthermore, disinformation is a danger for a range of economic, social and cultural rights [2]. The COVID-19 pandemic as well as the Russian invasion of Ukraine intensified disinformation related challenges and problems. In all cases, the role of social media platforms as major vectors of such disruptive phenomena has been questioned, especially after scandals such as Cambridge Analytica's misuse of data from Facebook [4], and court cases such as United States of America versus Internet Research Agency [5].

It is clear that a comprehensive and reliable solutions to fight fake news spreading and disinformation in social media networks is needed. Although several solutions have been proposed in the literature, either they focus on a specific content authenticity or they provide completely new platforms for social media content verification (e.g., [6,24]). In the mentioned solutions, users have to check the veracity of each social media post separately which is unrealistic and time consuming. Aside from the fact that consumers must seek for the truth across numerous platforms and repeat the process for each piece of content, information about the source and its trustworthiness is unknown, and the verification process is available only to specific groups (e.g., accredited journalists). To the best of our knowledge, TruthSeekers Chain (TSC) is the first platform that augment the content of existing social media with reliable information and offer content verification and network analysis as features to the users while browsing their favorite social media feed. In addition, thanks to TSC design and Self-Sovereign Identity model (SSI), TSC is the first platform that can provide its members a set of verifiable credentials that links their real identity with their social media accounts and provides a portable social reputation score based on the user's behavior in multiple social media networks. Furthermore, TSC is also the first platform that offers the tokenization of evidence or social media contents by creating NFTs (Non-Fungible Tokens) and provides a marketplace for trading them. This way, TSC members can both prove ownership and monetize their evidence or content.

The objectives targeted by TSC vision are as follow: 1) leveraging beyond-state-of-the-art technological framework such as Self-Sovereign Identity, blockchain, Machine Learning-based tools and bots screening to increase trust and to ensure transparency and accountability; 2) create open and easy to use platform with transparent algorithms dedicated to content ordering ; 3) aggregate content from multiple social networks in one place where verification and social network analysis tools can be applied; 4) Build a portable decentralized social reputation system; 5) stop bot-generated content; 6) track content, the users and their engagement (individual or group); 7) create incentive mechanisms to share and verify contents; 8) build a censorship-resistant platform; 9) design algorithms based on the content veracity rather than the user's engagement; 10) access multiple social media networks with a single login.

2 Related Work

The state of the art includes multiple blockchain-based solutions that aim at fighting fake content/news. However, most existing solutions focused on the authenticity of a specific content (e.g., image, video, article, document). So, the users of social media have to register in multiple platforms (e.g., Prover [7], Truepic [17], Po.et [14], D.tube [15], OriginalMy [16]) in order to verify the authenticity of a content and have to pay to use some of them.

EUNOMIA project [21] introduced a new decentralized social media platform with emphasis on trust instead of likes. The content is considered trustworthy if a high number of users vote that the content is trustworthy without using any mechanism to distinguish between human users and bots. Users need to rely on some undefined external tool to determine by themselves whether the content has been posted and/or voted by a human or a bot. Unlike EUNOMIA [21], TSC aims at fighting the fake news spreading in the existing dominant social media networks, keeping the interaction mechanism such as like/dislike to allow users to express their opinion but at the same time holding them accountable for their actions. In addition, TSC leverages a bot screening mechanism that prevents bots from posting or engaging with social media content.

SocialTruth project [20] integrates its content verification services which provide a specific type of content analytics (e.g. for text, image, video) and verification-relevant functionality (e.g. emotional descriptors, social influence mapping) with various platforms such as web search, journalist tools and a browser add-on. In order to check a content, users give an input to the Social-Truth search bar such as the URL of the content or website and get feedback regarding its type, source, trustworthiness etc. Unlike TSC, the content verification can be performed only by experts connected in a p2p network. So, the SocialTruth users have to trust the decision taken by unknown experts and have to verify each content in social media separately.

Recently, a project called WeVerify [24] is developing cross-modal disinformation detection and content verification tools. Similar to SocialTruth [20], WeVerify allows only professionals (journalists/Fact checkers) to verify and determine the reliability of the content without providing the users details about professionals and their reputation. So a leap of faith is required as users cannot check the level of trustworthiness of the people involved.

Trive [26] is a browser extension plugin, built on Ethereum. When a user browses a website, Trive plugin changes the story opacity based on how true/false it is. After the verification process performed by researchers and verifiers, a randomly selected group of 10 witnesses decide whether the content is true or false. Trive users have to pay to use the platform and it is not known whether the involved entities in the verification process are experts or not.

The main difference between the above-mentioned solutions and TSC is that their performance depends on results of verification and validation process, and that they don't take the threat posed by bots into consideration. It is known that the verification of content requires time, and it is not always obvious to find evidence and to prove whether the content/news is true or false. So, by the time the verification results are provided, the fake news might be already widespread. In contrast to above mentioned projects, TSC doesn't depend on the content verification results to combat the spreading of fake news, it relies instead on the user's accountability and on bot screening mechanism among others to increase the level of trust in content recorded in the blockchain. TSC front-end will offer the users all the necessary information about the content, its sources, their reputation, and the evidence while browsing their favorite social media feed. In addition, it allows both experts and non-expert to contribute to check the content veracity by sharing their opinion and resources in a secure and transparent way. The expert's statements, votes, opinions will be highlighted. Furthermore, TSC provides a portable decentralized social reputation profile based on the user's behavior on multiple social media platforms. Besides the reputation system, different incentive mechanisms are used to encourage good and deter bad behaviour. Hence, TSC proposes a different approach to fight fake news spreading that completes the efforts performed by the existing projects (e.g., WeVerify, Truly Media, SOMA, etc.) in designing content verification platforms and tools. The users would be able to access these tools while browsing their feeds to check the veracity of content as well as accessing the verification results of the other identified members. The TSC incentive mechanisms and reputation system are designed to encourage the users to engage only with the likely true content. This have a direct impact on the spreading of fake news in the existing social media where content sorting algorithms are based on the user's engagement regardless its veracity.

3   Truth Seekers Chain Concept

Truth Seekers Chain is an open ecosystem that aims at mitigating fake news spreading and the impact of tampered-with content posted on social media by increasing the user's awareness on the consequences of the engagement with likely fake contents and encouraging them to verify and engage with likely true content. TSC allows the users to access multiple social media networks with a single and passwordless login. The main idea is to aggregate news, facts, claims, and media content in one place where verification and social network analysis tools can be applied and multiple independent verifiers around the world can compete to check its veracity. On the other hands, TSC aims to return control back to the users by enabling them to select the way they want to see the posts in their feeds. By defaults, the posts which are likely true based on the users votes and the attached evidence to it will be on top. This feature protects users from micro-targeting and the algorithms used by TSC are transparent to the users.

In order to increase trust and to ensure transparency and accountability, TSC relies on cutting-edge technologies in the range of distributed ledgers, incorporating Self-sovereign identity and blockchain technology as well as an invisible mechanism for bots screening (i.e., Invisible CAPPCHA [18] or ascCAPTCHA [19]). The latter allows only actions performed by humans to be transferred to existing social media networks or recorded in the blockchain. When a user submits a post to the blockchain, it is important to note that it's the content hash which will be recorded in the blockchain and not the content itself, hence the amount of blockchain storage needed is limited. By using the Self-sovereign identity (SSI) model, the user's identity, and its related claims such as ID, diploma, social reputation are directly and autonomously managed by the user through their SSI mobile wallet. To login, the users are required to present verifiable credentials with the following attribute: full name, photo, country and optionally a certificate of expertise from well-known trusted institutions (e.g. government, universities, etc.). TSC will link these attributes to the user's social media accounts accessed through the platform. To the best of our knowledge, TSC is the first platform that links user's social media accounts to the user real identity and provides a portable decentralized social reputation profile based on the user's behavior on multiple social media platforms.

The main user-side component of the system is TSC User Interface (TSC-UI). Through TSC-UI, users will have a view of their favorite social networks contents augmented with information derived from the blockchain (see Fig. 1). This augmentation will relate to the source (e.g., social reputation, membership and digital badges) as well as information related to post/content (e.g., whether the post hash has been recorded in the blockchain, rebuttals, sharings, endorsements by experts and non-experts and all the links to directly access the details and evidence). Furthermore, TSC is designed to be interoperable with third party's services such as Expert-Based and ML-based content verification tools, whose results can be accessed by all the members without leaving the platform. Besides, users will also be able to upload evidence on InterPlanetary File System (IPFS), rate evidence, participate in campaigns, tokenize pieces of evidence and sell them, and leverage social network analysis tools to visualize the network of users interacting with the content to have global views on the intention behind the viral spreading of a given content. The results will be displayed in the form of a network graph.

Hence, TSC saves user's time spent in reading fake news that might be posted by bots or looking for the truth from different places and unknown sources. Furthermore, one of TSC main feature is the fact that it increases the level of trust in content recorded in the blockchain even before its validation by verifiers. This is mainly due to two factors: i) Accountability and ii) bot screening mechanism. If the author submit his post to the blockchain through TSC, this means that content has been submitted by a real human and that he accepts full responsibility of his action. Since this will have a direct impact on his reputation, users will likely submit posts that they believe represent the truth.

4   Truth Seekers Chain Architecture

The TSC Architecture is depicted in the Fig. 2. It consists of seven core components, TSC UI, SSI mobile wallet, MetaMask, Bot screening mechanism, IPFS, blockchain and smart contracts. As well as two other components that allow

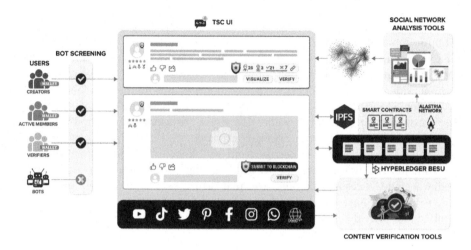

Fig. 1. TruthSeekers Chain overall concept.

TSC to interact with existing social media networks (i.e., social media API) and integrate external tools (i.e., open API).

TSC UI: the user interface is the main contact point for users, since all the user's interactions pass through it. The users will be able to sign up using the SSI model and interact with the system. The user's feed from the various social media platforms will be displayed in separate tabs and depending on whether the post is on-chain or not, users will have different options. For instance, the user can visualize the network using social network analysis tools only if the content (its hash) is already on-chain. The front-end is currently available as a Proof of concept and the final version will be developed using NextJS framework.

SSI Mobile Wallet: the mobile wallet is a mobile application that handles cryptographic keys and offers the potential to store and manage identity data in the form of verifiable credentials. Each verifiable credential is a representation of data which is cryptographically tamper-proof and traceable to its origin. Using this wallet, the user will be able to select some of these credentials to sign up to TSC. The credentials required by TSC are full name, photo, country and optionally certificate of expertise. For PoC implementation, we will use Trinsic ID wallet [8] or Alastria ID wallet [9].

Metamask: Metamask is a popular crypto wallet that will be used for managing rewards (TSC tokens) and NFTs. It is available as a browser extension or a mobile app [11].

Bot Screening Mechanism: Any action performed by the users will be filtered by a fully transparent bot screening mechanism, called invisible CAP-PCHA [18] or ascCAPTCHA [19] depending on the device. The rationale behind a CAPPCHA is that the bot as a piece of code cannot perform a physical task. Since all social media networks requires users interaction with touchscreen or the keyboard, Invisible CAPPCHA leverages this natural interaction (e.g., post a content, write a comment, tap like/dislike/share/submit to the blockchain button, etc.) to distinguish between humans and bots (see Fig. 3). In fact, such physical interactions cause micro-movements of the mobile device or generate a sound wave when the user taps on the keyboard. These can be detected easily by the microphone [19] or motion sensors such as the accelerometer [18,22,23].

Smart Contracts: smart contracts will be responsible for identity management, reputation management, incentive management and content tracking. Any changes will be recorded in the blockchain in the form of transactions. For smart contracts development, we decided to use Truffle. The smart contracts are written in Solidity programming language and will be deployed in Alastria red B Network [10] which is a public-permissioned Blockchain network that uses the Hyperledger Besu technology, IBFT 2.0 consensus algorithm and it's managed by Alastria partners. It is important to note that the gas price in Alastria network is zero, the users don't need to pay anything for using TSC. We use web3.js library, which is an Ethereum Javascript API, that allows us to make requests to an individual Ethereum node with JSON-RPC in order to read and write data to the network.

Blockchain: the public-permissioned blockchain will be responsible for storing all the information that allows tracking of the contents/evidence, their sources, user's reputation profile, user's engagement with content and NFT trading. For instance, the link to social content, votes, like/share of content, IPFS hash of the content, etc. We selected a public-permissioned blockchain network that uses hyperledger besu technology (i.e., Alastria red B) to ensure data immutability, transparency and accountability. The Interaction with the hyperledger besu node is carried out via JSON-RPC API.

IPFS: IPFS is both a protocol and a peer-to-peer network for storing and sharing data in a distributed file system. All data that cannot be stored in the blockchain due to size will be stored in IPFS (e.g., , resources and evidence, NFT metadata, etc.), while the IPFS hash will be recorded in the blockchain to ensure the data integrity. The communication to IPFS is carried out via HTTP-RPC API.

Social Media API: it is a set of programmatic endpoints that allows TSC to communicate and exchange data with social media networks. Twitter API [12] for instance, can be used to find and retrieve, engage with, or create a variety of different resources such as Tweets, Users, Direct Messages, Trends, etc.

Open APIs: it is an open API that allows the integration of third-party content verification and social media analysis tools in TSC.

5   Comparison and Discussion

The verification of content requires time and it is not always obvious to find evidence and to prove whether the content/news is true or fake. The performance of existing solutions depends on the results of the verification and validation process. So, by the time the verification results are provided, the fake news might be already widespread. Besides, the fact that the users have to search for the truth across multiple platforms and repeat that for each content is extremely

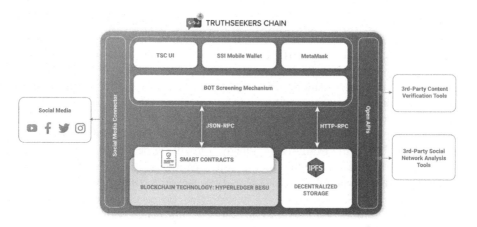

Fig. 2. TruthSeekers Chain architecture.

time-consuming, information about the source and its credibility is often scarce if not unavailable and sometimes the verification process is limited only to specific groups (e.g., accredited journalists). Furthermore, in all the solutions currently available, users will have to play the role of intermediary between existing social networks and content verification platforms. So, in the case in which the users do not fulfil this role, there is no real impact of these content verification platforms in combating the spreading of fake content.

In contrast, using TSC platform, users will be able to access multiple social media content with a single login and to see information about the content authenticity and the credibility of the person who posted them while browsing their favourite social media feed. These pieces of information help the user in differentiating between fake and true content from the very beginning. If expert or ML based verification tools are available, they can be used to detect deep fake or whether the content has been tampered with. When the verification results are available, they will be available in all the media networks accessed through TSC, users don't need to look for them. On the other hands, involving the users in the verification process saves the journalists and fact-checkers a lot of time. The users might witness an event or have an information which journalists don't have. In addition, the tools used by Truly Media for instance don't require high skills, any user can use them and the results would be available to journalists, fact-checkers and the other members. Furthermore, the users can filter the feed to see only posts that have been proved to be true or are from authors with a high reputation score, etc. This feature address Micro-targeting issue because the users take back control on what they see. Hence, TSC saves journalists time spent in the verification process as well as user's time spent in reading fake content or looking for the truth from different places and unknown sources.

Social bots represent a serious threat as they automatically produce content and mimic human social media behavior to influence the perception of reality and attempt to manipulate public opinion. Therefore a bot screening mechanism is crucial to combat fake news spreading. However, one of the big challenges that the existing solutions face today is to determine whether the content has been posted by a human or bot. In TSC, any user's input will be filtered by a fully transparent bot screening mechanism based on the physical nature of humans. Bot screening mechanism will reduce significantly the spreading of fake content, however this alone is not enough, as humans are also contributing in spreading fake news. Other mechanisms are built in TSC to achieve this goal: accountability and a fully historical reputation based on the blockchain, increasing the user's awareness to the consequences of his actions and limiting the fast gut-reaction by asking for explanations, linking to verification and analysis tools, incentivizing honest behavior and seeking for the truth through a rewarding system and competitions. These mechanisms aim at reducing the user's arousal, the engagement with fake contents/news and thus decreasing the visibility of such content in existing social media networks.

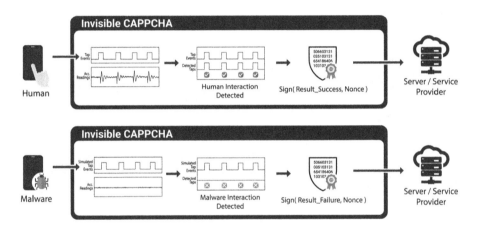

Fig. 3. Invisible CAPPCHA concept.

6 Security and Privacy Analysis

TruthSeekers Chain platform as any other digital system is potentially vulnerable to cyber-attacks. In this section we analyse the security of TSC against the most common attacks and we discuss its privacy.

6.1 Distributed Denial of Service (DDOS)

Using an effective CAPTCHA mechanism [3,22,23,25] prevents DDoS attacks because only humans would be able to pass the challenge and thus, prevent any attacking machines or zombified computers from passing this security checkpoint.

As we mentioned in the previous section, any user interaction with the TSC platform will be filtered by a fully transparent bot screening mechanisms [18,19].

TSC uses Invisible CAPPCHA [18] or ascCAPTCHA [19] depending on the device to filter disruptive traffic and prevent bots from abusing social media networks APIs (e.g., Twitter API) and spreading the fake news. Unlike the traditional CAPTCHA methods [3], these mechanisms allow users to interact with the online services without the need to solve any challenge which makes them fully transparent and thus very usable.

6.2   Malicious Actors

TSC discourage malicious actors from giving unfair feedbacks (e.g., vote fake for a true content or provide low rating to a verifier to destroy the reputation of the user who created them) by incentivizing the users to act honestly. It rewards the users for their good behavior by offering them TSC tokens (ERC20 utility tokens) and increasing their reputation score and punishes them otherwise. In addition, TSC periodically checks the amount of likely fake news posted, shared or liked by each member, if the amount is higher than a threshold, the user's actions will appear in TSC platform but will not be transferred to existing social media networks to prevent the spreading of their posts or the posts that they engaged with. Unlike the existing social media networks, TSC sorts the posts in the user's feed based on their veracity, users' votes and the amount of evidence attached to it, rather than the users' engagement with it. So the risk of fake news going viral in TSC is culled; on the contrary, a permanent, blockchain attested proof of participating the spreading of fake news will be attached to the user's social reputation profile.

TSC also offers to the users the possibility to participate in campaigns by contributing in the verification process and earning an amount of cryptocurrency in Ether. So, the users are more likely to act honestly to get the reward and have this behavior stored in their blockchain-saved, permanent history.

It is important to mention that the TSC members can only vote or rate once the resources that don't belong to them and cannot evaluate their own resources. Furthermore, as the login to TSC is linked to the users real identities it is not possible to create false accounts to accrue votes.

6.3   Sybil Attack

In this type of attack, the attacker creates many accounts (Sybils) to perform malicious activities in social network. For example, it can create phantom feedback in the system, spread fake news, ruin the reputation of honest users, etc. TSC is resilient to this attack because the users can not have multiple identities issued by a trusted third party (e.g., Government) unlike email accounts. Thanks to SSI model and TSC design, all the user's social media accounts accessed through the platform will be automatically linked to the users real identity information shared through their SSI mobile wallet.

6.4   Whitewashing Attack

The attacker behaves maliciously and after receiving negative ratings, he creates a new account to neutralize his reputation score. Although the user can have several social media accounts, in our system these accounts will refer to the same individual. To sign in, the users have to present verifiable credential which include information about their real identity signed by trusted entity such as the government. TSC links all their user's social media accounts accessed through TSC to their real identity. Thus, their social reputation score based on their behavior in all their social media networks accessed through TSC is permanent and cannot be neutralized.

6.5   51% Attack

TSC smart contracts will be deployed in the Alastria red B network which uses Proof-of-Authority consensus (IBFT 2.0). Thus, the security against 51% attack depends on the Validator nodes. When the consortium selects these nodes, they have to ensure that these nodes will not collude and collaborate among them to make decisions that will adversely affect the rest of the nodes. The number of not fully trusted nodes should be less than one third of the total number of Validator nodes.

6.6   Data Privacy

The user personal information requested by TSC like full name, photo and country are not considered sensitive information. Actually, these pieces of information and others are required also by the traditional social media platforms. However, traditional social platform do not verify whether they are correct or not. This allows some users to create accounts with fake data or use other person's data. Fortunately, using SSI model, TSC can ensure that the user's information are correct by verifying the signature of the verifiable credential issuer. By using TSC, users agree to share these pieces of information and accept responsability for their actions as in the real world.

Regarding the user's social media accounts, TSC also ensures that the registered social accounts (i.e., account ID) belong to a specific user. In order to access the existing social media accounts through TSC, users are required to authorize TSC to read and write data (e.g., get timeline, transfer like, post content, etc.) in their social media on their behalf without sharing their usernames and passwords using Oauth protocol [13]. If TSC successfully receives the access token after the users' authorization, this means that the users have successfully signed in to their social media accounts and they are the rightful owners of these accounts.

7 Conclusion

Modern social media are public platforms where anyone, including news organizations, can post anything without being accountable and where fact-checking is extremely time-consuming. Furthermore, it is left to users to separate humans from bots, and fake news from truth inside their social feeds. In this paper, we proposed TruthSeekers Chain, an open platform that fights fake news spreading and helps users in recognizing fake news and tampered content. Using Truth-Seekers Chain, users can I) access their feeds from multiple social media networks with a single login; II) adopt a transparent algorithm for the selection of what they see; III) contribute in the verification process as an expert or non-expert IV) monetize and prove ownership of their evidence or media content and finally V) they can receive a portable social reputation profile that can be used in other context and platforms. Journalists and fact-checkers can also benefit from the TSC platform, they would have access to resources that can help them in their investigation and they can as well buy NFTs that represent ownership of media files to use them in their blogs and articles. Involving the users in the verification process will save them a lot of time. In future work, we plan to provide a detailed description of TSC main components, its internal mechanisms, a Proof of Concept implementation and some preliminary experiments.

Acknowledgments. This project has received funding from the European Union's Horizon 2020 research and innovation program under grant agreement No. 957228 (TruBlo) and has also received financial support from Gruppo SIGLA s.r.l.

References

1. European Commission, Directorate-General for Communications Networks, Content and Technology. A multi-dimensional approach to disinformation: report of the independent high level group on fake news and online disinformation. Publications Office (2018). https://data.europa.eu/doi/10.2759/0156
2. Colomina, C., Sánchez Margalef, H., Youngs, R.: The impact of disinformation on democratic processes and human rights in the world (2021)
3. Guerar, M., Verderame, L., Migliardi, M., Palmieri, F., Merlo, A.: Gotta CAPTCHA 'Em all: a survey of 20 years of the human-or-computer dilemma. ACM Comput. Surv. **54**(9), 192 (2022). https://doi.org/10.1145/3477142
4. Hu, M.: Cambridge Analytic as Black Box. Big Data Soc. **7**(2), 2053951720938091 (2020)
5. Bastos, M., Farkas, J.: Donald Trump is my President!: The internet research agency propaganda machine. Social Media Soc. **5**(3), 2056305119865466 (2019)
6. TrulyMedia. https://www.truly.media. Accessed 14 Mar 2022
7. Prover. https://prover.io. Accessed 14 Mar 2022
8. Trinsic Wallet. It's like your physical wallet, but digital. https://trinsic.id/trinsic-wallet/. Accessed 14 Mar 2022
9. Alastria Wallet. https://github.com/alastria/alastria-wallet. Accessed 14 Mar 2022
10. Alastria Network. https://alastria.io/en/la-red/. Accessed 14 Mar 2022
11. A crypto wallet & gateway to blockchain apps. https://metamask.io/. Accessed 15 Mar 2022

12. Twitter API. https://developer.twitter.com/en/docs/twitter-api. Accessed 15 Mar 2022
13. Oauth 1.0 Wokflow. https://www.ibm.com/docs/en/tfim/6.2.2.7?topic=overview-oauth-10-workflow. Accessed 15 Mar 2022
14. Po.et Github. https://github.com/poetapp/documentation. Accessed 14 Mar 2022
15. D.tube Github. https://d.tube/. Accessed 14 Mar 2022
16. OriginalMy. https://originalmy.com/. Accessed 15 Mar 2022
17. Berkhead, S.: Truepic app lets journalists instantly verify images, videos. Int. J. Netw. (2017)
18. Guerar, M., Merlo, A., Migliardi, M., Palmieri, F.: Invisible CAPPCHA: a usable mechanism to distinguish between malware and humans on the mobile IoT. Comput. Secur. **78**, 255–266 (2018). https://doi.org/10.1016/j.cose.2018.06.007
19. Di Nardo Di Maio, R., Guerar, M., Migliardi, M.: ascCAPTCHA: an invisible sensor CAPTCHA for PCs based on acoustic side channel. In: 2021 44th International Convention on Information, Communication and Electronic Technology (MIPRO), pp. 482–487 (2021). https://doi.org/10.23919/MIPRO52101.2021.9597134
20. Choraś, M., Pawlicki, M., Kozik, R., Demestichas, K., Kosmides, P., Gupta, M.: SocialTruth Project Approach to Online Disinformation (Fake News) Detection and Mitigation. In: <i>Proceedings of the 14th International Conference on Availability, Reliability and Security</i> (<i>ARES '19</i>), vol. 68, pp. 1–10. Association for Computing Machinery, New York (2019). https://doi.org/10.1145/3339252.3341497
21. Toumanidis, L., Heartfield, R., Kasnesis, P., Loukas, G., Patrikakis, C.: A prototype framework for assessing information provenance in decentralised social media: the EUNOMIA concept. In: Katsikas, S., Zorkadis, V. (eds.) e-Democracy 2019. CCIS, vol. 1111, pp. 196–208. Springer, Cham (2020). https://doi.org/10.1007/978-3-030-37545-4_13
22. Guerar, M., Merlo, A., Migliardi, M.: Completely automated public physical test to tell computers and humans apart: a usability study on mobile devices. Future Gen. Comput. Syst. (2017). https://doi.org/10.1016/j.future.2017.03.012
23. Guerar, M., Migliardi, M., Merlo, A., Benmohammed, M., Messabih, B.: A completely automatic public physical test to tell computers and humans apart: a way to enhance authentication schemes in mobile devices. In: Proceedings of the 2015 International Conference on High Performance Computing Simulation (HPCS), pp. 203–210 (2015). https://doi.org/10.1109/HPCSim.2015.7237041
24. Marinova, Z., et al.: Weverify: wider and enhanced verification for you project overview and tools. IEEE Int. Conf. Multim. Expo Worksh. **2020**, 1–4 (2020). https://doi.org/10.1109/ICMEW46912.2020.9106056
25. Guerar, M., Verderame, L., Migliardi, M., Merlo, A.: 2GesturePIN: securing PIN-based authentication on smartwatches. In: 2019 IEEE 28th International Conference on Enabling Technologies: Infrastructure for Collaborative Enterprises (WETICE), pp. 327–333 (2019). https://doi.org/10.1109/WETICE.2019.00074
26. Mondrus, D., McKibbin, M., Barnetson, M.: Trive Whitepaper. https://trive.news/Whitepaper.0.2.6x.pdf. Accessed 14 Mar 2022

AKMA for Secure Multi-access Edge Computing Mobility in 5G

Gizem Akman[1,2]([📧]) [ID], Philip Ginzboorg[3] [ID], and Valtteri Niemi[1,2] [ID]

[1] University of Helsinki, Helsinki, Finland
{gizem.akman,valtteri.niemi}@helsinki.fi
[2] Helsinki Institute for Information Technology (HIIT), Helsinki, Finland
[3] Huawei Technologies, Helsinki, Finland
philip.ginzboorg@huawei.com

Abstract. Multi-Access Edge Computing (MEC) extends the cloud computing capabilities to the edge of the 5G network. The current 3rd Generation Partnership Project (3GPP) and European Telecommunications Standard Institute (ETSI) specifications about MEC cover connectivity between a mobile user and a MEC host, including security, but they do not extend to application-level security and privacy issues. We solve the problem of creating a secure and privacy-preserving communication channel between a mobile user and a distributed MEC application. The solution is limited to the case where the mobile network remains the same during communication. The solution is based on the 3GPP AKMA for authentication and key sharing. It includes protocols for (1) registering the user to the main server of the application, (2) updating the user information and shared keys with the main server of the application, (3) using the application in the MEC host in the static case, (4) using the application in MEC host while moving.

Keywords: MEC · 5G · AKMA · MEC mobility · Security · Privacy

1 Introduction

The Fifth Generation (5G) mobile network is developed to have reliable, energy-efficient, and high capacity service with low latency. 5G can offer reliability and delay-critical services [11]. Ultimately, the 5G is expected to have data rates up to 10 Gbps, service level latency below 1 ms, ubiquitous connectivity of 100%, improved battery life by reducing the energy consumption by 90%, and support for 300,000 devices within a single cell [11,16,17].

Internet of Things (IoT) is a growing ecosystem with massive interconnections of heterogeneous physical objects, and the number of IoT devices is increasing exponentially. Thus, these devices generate a large amount of data. However, IoT devices are resource-constrained. They have low battery power, low storage capacity, small processing power, and limited communication capacity [11,12]. Therefore, IoT applications require a decentralized local service for location awareness, reliability, low latency [11], and access to centralized cloud computing facilities for data processing and storing [12].

Cloud computing-based services support IoT applications in providing computing resources and storage. However, cloud computing can cause latency issues, jitter, service interruption, and a single point of failure, which is inconvenient, especially for time-sensitive IoT services [11,17]. Multi-access Edge Computing (MEC) is developed to extend the capabilities of cloud computing to the edge of the mobile network and provide improved Quality of Service (QoS) and Quality of Experience (QoE) [6,12]. In order to do this, MEC hosts are deployed to the edge of the mobile network.

Together with 5G technology, MEC provides proximity, very low latency, high bandwidth, location awareness, real-time responsiveness, security and privacy protection, proximate data outsourcing, and mobility support [11,12,17]. Examples of IoT applications that can benefit from MEC supported by 5G include Ultra High Definition (UHD) video streaming, Augmented Reality (AR), Virtual Reality (VR), Mixed Reality (MR), tactile internet, Machine Type Communication (MTC), Machine-to-Machine (M2M), Unmanned Aerial Vehicles (UAV), Vehicle-to-Everything (V2E), Intelligent Transportation Systems (ITS), serious gaming, factory automation, healthcare, smart grid, smart home, smart city, smart retail, and smart agriculture [11,16,17].

The application instance in the device of the user may relocate from one MEC host to another when the user moves within the network [7]. The source MEC host is the MEC host where the user is initially connected to and provided services. The target MEC host is where the user is being relocated.

MEC applications can be sensitive to User Equipment (UE) mobility or not. For example, suppose the purpose of the MEC application is to process the traffic in the local MEC host. Then, it is not sensitive to UE mobility because the service can continue rapidly after the handover without disrupting the service. However, if the service requires continuous connectivity between the device and MEC applications, the MEC application becomes sensitive to the UE mobility and requires seamless handover to another MEC host [8]. In order to provide seamless relocation, it is necessary to transfer the user context (i.e., user-specific application state) associated with the device along with the application instance between the source and target MEC hosts to continue providing services without interruption [7,19]. The user context transfer can happen in three ways: device application-assisted state transfer, MEC-assisted state transfer, and application self-controlled state transfer [7]. MEC orchestrator, which has an overview of the MEC system, selects a new host for relocation and initiates the transfer of an application instance from the source MEC host to the target MEC host [8,13].

Considering that MEC applications process data related to users, share secret keys, and store private data, relocating the services between different MEC hosts might introduce security and privacy issues [21]. Therefore, UE mobility should be handled while maintaining security and privacy. For example, it is necessary to run authentication with the target MEC application, and authorization should be provided before relocation. Otherwise, unauthorized UE may start using the

MEC application, or the UE may share its information with the unauthorized MEC application [3].

The problem we are addressing in this paper is how to secure communication between the MEC application client in UE and the MEC application in the MEC host, both when the user is static and when the user is mobile but is still connected to the mobile network of the same Mobile Network Operator (MNO). Our contribution is a secure and privacy-friendly solution for using the MEC application by static and mobile users. The solution includes the following protocols: (A) registration of the user to the main server of the application, (B) updating the user information and shared keys with the main server of the application, (C) usage of the application in the MEC host in the static case, (D) usage of the application in MEC host in the mobile case. We use the 3rd Generation Partnership Project (3GPP) Authentication and Key Management for Applications (AKMA) service for authentication and key sharing.

We continue below with background information and related work in Sect. 2. The system model is explained in Sect. 3 and the solution that includes four protocols is presented in Sect. 4. Then, the solution is analyzed in Sect. 5. The paper ends with the conclusion and future work in Sect. 6.

2   Background and Related Work

In this section, we give additional background about the MEC framework and AKMA service and summarize the related work.

2.1   MEC Framework

European Telecommunications Standard Institute (ETSI) initiated MEC standardization in 2014 [13]. The framework of MEC consists of three levels [8]: MEC system, MEC host, and network.

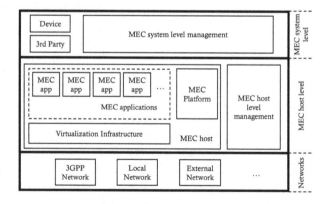

Fig. 1. MEC Framework, adapted from [8]

The MEC system level includes the MEC orchestrator and user application. Network can be the 3GPP, local, or external network. The MEC host-level has MEC host and MEC host-level management. The MEC host is deployed to the edge of the mobile network, which includes a MEC platform, MEC applications, and virtualization infrastructure. Overall MEC framework is shown in Fig. 1.

2.2   AKMA Service

Authentication and Key Management for Applications (AKMA) is a service in the 5G system to support authentication and security protection between the UE and applications. AKMA is using similar principles, e.g., those of Generic Bootstrapping Architecture (GBA) in the legacy mobile networks, while adapting to the architectural changes in the 5G system to meet the requirements for scenarios related to the Internet of Things [9]. The authentication and key agreement rely on the credentials and identities of the mobile subscriber, which are pre-established with Mobile Network Operator (MNO) for 5G access [10]. The AKMA service will help mutual authentication between UE and applications [9].

The key for AKMA, K_{AKMA}, is derived from the shared key that results from the primary authentication between the UE and the 5G mobile network. In addition, an identifier A-KID is assigned to the user to identify the key K_{AKMA}. Another application-specific key K_{AF} is derived from K_{AKMA} by UE and mobile network [10]. The key K_{AKMA} and A-KID are updated with every primary authentication, but the lifetime of K_{AF} depends on the policy of the MNO. For example, after K_{AKMA} is renewed, K_{AF} can still be used until the lifetime of K_{AF} expires, or the application session ends. Then, a new K_{AF} will be derived from the new K_{AKMA} [1].

2.3   Related Work

Niewolski et al. [14] propose a solution using a token-based authentication framework for the 5G MEC system. However, they do not consider the case where the user is mobile. The articles [4,5] propose third-party authentication for securing the MEC application mobility with different approaches for the state transfer of the MEC application during mobility, such as token-based and federated state transfer. The solution of Sanchez-Gomez et al. [20] uses Pre-Shared Key Extensible Authentication Protocol Method (EAP-PSK) to authenticate of the user and MEC application for both static and mobile users.

3   System Model

Our system model can be illustrated by the following scenario: Alice travels to another city in her home country. Assume she is in Finland and she travels from Helsinki to Tampere. On the way to Tampere, Alice uses a MEC application APPIFY, which could be an application, e.g., for video streaming, AR, or mobile gaming. Since Alice stays in her country, it is very likely that MNO will not change during her trip. However, MEC coverage is only local, unlike MNO coverage. Alice would need to change several MEC hosts between Helsinki and Tampere, therefore, several MEC application servers. Nonetheless, she wants to continue using APPIFY with the benefits of MEC services, like low latency and high bandwidth. Additionally, she wants to protect her information from outsiders and the other parties in the network unless the information is needed to get the service. This information can be, e.g., the name of APPIFY, the content of her communication with APPIFY, and her identifiers.

The system model includes the following entities: the User Equipment (UE), Mobile Network Operator (MNO), MEC Hosts, MEC applications, and the main server of the application. Figure 2 presents the settlement of these entities in the system model.

Alice is the user who possesses the user equipment UE, and she uses the application APPIFY. This application has a main server that can be reached through the internet. In addition to this, the application server of APPIFY resides in MEC hosts. APPIFY in the MEC host is synchronized with its main server. Alice connects to the APPIFY in the MEC host and gets the service there instead of the main server for the benefits of multi-access edge computing.

The MEC hosts are deployed in the network of MNO. There are only two MEC hosts in our illustration of the system model, presented in Fig. 2. However, the number of MEC hosts with an APPIFY server is not limited to two. It should also be noted that there could be several other MEC application servers in MEC hosts other than APPIFY.

As shown in Fig. 2, Alice is on the move, and her connection is regularly transferred from one base station to another. The connection also eventually changes between two MEC hosts depending on the coverage.

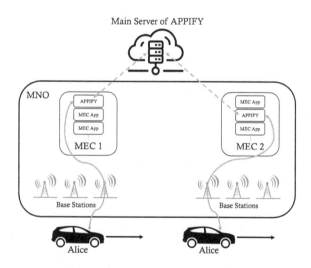

Fig. 2. System model

4   Solution

This section presents a solution that adapts AKMA for the purpose of maintaining security and privacy for the MEC applications that are used by both static and mobile users.

Alice is a subscriber of MNO, and she uses an application called APPIFY. The application APPIFY appears in the solution as the main server of APPIFY (S-APPIFY) and the APPIFY in the MEC host (M-APPIFY). Alice uses AKMA to authenticate herself to APPIFY.

S-APPIFY has public encryption and secret decryption key pair (EK, DK). The users of APPIFY use this EK to encrypt their identifiers. S-APPIFY also has a key K_{MAIN}, which is used to protect the privacy of the application identifier of the user against MNO. ID-APPIFY is the identifier of S-APPIFY and is known by MNO. The MNO has a key K_{MNO}, which is used during the generation of the user identifier that identifies Alice to S-APPIFY during AKMA. In addition, Alice has her identifier Subscription Permanent Identifier (SUPI) for MNO and identifier–password pair (Alice13, psw) for APPIFY.

Our solution consists of four protocols: A, B, C, and D. Protocols A and B are executed between Alice and the S-APPIFY. Protocol A is used to add a new user or register a new trusted device. Protocol B is for renewing EK and shared keys. This protocol is also run to establish a secure connection between Alice and S-APPIFY for the purpose of providing service to Alice from the main server. Protocol C is executed between Alice and M-APPIFY when Alice wants to start using services provided by APPIFY in the MEC host. Protocol D is used when Alice is moving and uses APPIFY in the MEC host, but the serving MEC host and M-APPIFY change.

In Protocols A and B, a Transport Layer Security (TLS) connection is established between Alice and the main server of APPIFY. Alice uses a verification key of a root certificate in the TLS connection set-up to verify the certificate of the main server. This is a well-known procedure and will not be discussed in this paper.

A secure channel between Alice and MEC host [2], e.g., a TLS or Datagram Transport Layer Security (DTLS) connection, is established in Protocols C and D. This secure channel establishment is based either on a certificate of the MEC host or, alternatively, on a pre-shared key PSK method with a key that results from AKMA between Alice and MEC [3]. This paper will not discuss further the details of the secure channel between Alice and MEC.

Next, we explain the protocols of our solution.

4.1   Protocol A: Signing Up

Protocol A is run when a new user wants to sign-up, or a registered user wants to add a new trusted device. In this context, a new device means a new SUPI. Protocol A runs between Alice and S-APPIFY through MNO. The protocol is explained step by step below, and the communication flow is shown in Fig. 3.

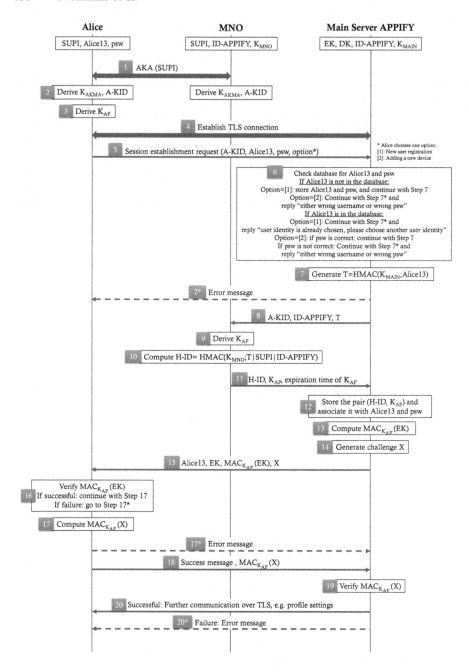

Fig. 3. Communication flow of Protocol A

1. Alice runs Authentication and Key Agreement (AKA) with MNO. (If an existing and valid shared key K_{AUSF} is stored, this step can be skipped.)
2. After AKA is completed, Alice and MNO (Authentication Server Function (AUSF) in MNO) compute K_{AKMA} from the shared key K_{AUSF}, which is agreed in AKA, and generate the AKMA Key Identifier (A-KID) [1].
3. Alice derives K_{AF} for APPIFY, according to AKMA specifications.
4. Alice establishes a TLS connection to S-APPIFY.
5. Alice sends session establishment request with the parameters A-KID, Alice13, psw, and the selected option to S-APPIFY through the secure channel. The options are (1) New user registration and (2) Registering a new device. Recall that a new device means a new SUPI.
6. S-APPIFY checks the database for Alice13 and psw.
    If Alice13 is not found in the database:
        If Option (1) is selected, then S-APPIFY stores Alice13 and psw to the database, and the protocol continues with Step 7,
        If Option (2) is selected, then the protocol continues with Step 7* with the message "either wrong username or wrong psw".
    If Alice13 is found in the database:
        If Option (1) is selected, then the protocol continues with Step 7* with the message "user identity is already chosen, please choose another user identity",
        If Option (2) is selected, we still have two cases:
            If psw is correct: The protocol continues with Step 7;
            If psw is not correct: The protocol continues with Step 7* with the message "either wrong username or wrong password".
7. S-APPIFY generates T=$HMAC_{K_{MAIN}}$(Alice13).
7*. S-APPIFY sends an error message and the protocol is aborted.
8. S-APPIFY sends A-KID, ID-APPIFY, and T to MNO.
9. MNO derives K_{AF} according to AKMA specifications.
10. MNO also computes H-ID=$HMAC_{K_{MNO}}(T \mid SUPI \mid \text{ID-APPIFY})$.
11. MNO sends H-ID, K_{AF}, and the expiration time of K_{AF} to S-APPIFY.
12. S-APPIFY stores the pair (H-ID, K_{AF}) and associates it with Alice13 and psw. It should be noted that MNO can enable the authentication of Alice to S-APPIFY without learning the identifier Alice13.
13. S-APPIFY computes $MAC_{K_{AF}}(EK)$.
14. S-APPIFY generates a challenge X to later verify that Alice has the shared key.
15. S-APPIFY sends Alice13, EK, $MAC_{K_{AF}}(EK)$, and X to Alice over the TLS channel.
16. Alice verifies $MAC_{K_{AF}}(EK)$.
    If the verification is successful: The protocol continues with Step 17.
    If the verification is a failure: The protocol continues with Step 17*.
17. Alice computes $MAC_{K_{AF}}(X)$.
17*. Alice sends an error message to S-APPIFY, and the protocol is aborted.
18. Alice sends $MAC_{K_{AF}}(X)$ to S-APPIFY along with the success message.

19. S-APPIFY verifies $MAC_{K_{AF}}(X)$.
   If the verification is successful: The protocol continues with Step 20.
   If the verification is a failure: The protocol continues with Step 20*.
20. Further communication continues over TLS; for example, the profile settings can be updated.
20*. S-APPIFY sends an error message to Alice and the protocol is aborted.

4.2 Protocol B: Signing In

Protocol B is run when the user and its devices are already registered, and the user wants to connect to the main server. The user can renew the shared keys or use APPIFY from the main server. Protocol B runs between Alice and S-APPIFY and includes MNO. The protocol is explained step by step below, and the communication flow is shown in Fig. 4.

1. Alice runs AKA with MNO. (If an existing and valid K_{AUSF} is stored, this step can be skipped.)
2. Alice and MNO compute K_{AKMA} and generate the AKMA Key Identifier (A-KID).
3. Alice derives K_{AF} for APPIFY.
4. Alice establishes a TLS connection to S-APPIFY.
5. Alice sends session establishment request with A-KID, Alice13, and the selected option to S-APPIFY through the secure channel. The options are (1) Renewing EK and (2) Signing into the main server. In both options, K_{AF} is updated.
6. S-APPIFY checks the database for Alice13.
   If Alice13 is found in the database: The protocol continues with Step 7,
   If Alice13 is not found in the database: The protocol continues with Steps 14–17 and then goes to Step 19*.
7. S-APPIFY finds the H-ID(s) related to the identity Alice13. Note that Alice may use the application from several different devices, and there would be different H-IDs for each device.
8. S-APPIFY generates $T=HMAC_{K_{MAIN}}(Alice13)$.
9. S-APPIFY sends A-KID, ID-APPIFY, and T to MNO.
10. MNO derives K_{AF}.
11. MNO also computes H-ID$=HMAC_{K_{MNO}}(T \,|\, SUPI \,|\, \text{ID-APPIFY})$.
12. MNO sends H-ID, K_{AF}, and the expiration time of K_{AF} to S-APPIFY.
13. S-APPIFY checks if the H-ID sent by MNO matches any existing H-ID(s) found in Step 7.
   If H-ID matches: The protocol continues with Step 14,
      If there is an existing K_{AF}, update it.
      If there is no existing K_{AF}, save it.
   If H-ID does not match: The protocol continues with Steps 14–17 and then goes to Step 19*.
14. S-APPIFY generates a challenge X.
15. S-APPIFY sends X to Alice over the TLS channel.

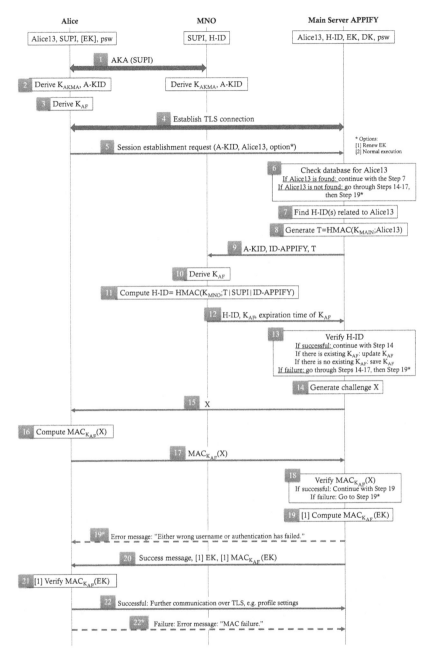

Fig. 4. Communication flow of Protocol B

16. Alice computes $MAC_{K_{AF}}(X)$.
17. Alice sends $MAC_{K_{AF}}(X)$ to S-APPIFY.
18. S-APPIFY verifies $MAC_{K_{AF}}(X)$.

   <u>If the verification is successful:</u> The protocol continues with Step 19.

   <u>If the verification is a failure:</u> The protocol continues with Step 19*.

19. If Option (1) is chosen, S-APPIFY computes $MAC_{K_{AF}}(EK)$. Otherwise, skip this step.

19*. Error message "Either wrong username or authentication has failed." is sent by S-APPIFY, and the protocol is aborted.

20. S-APPIFY sends the success message to Alice. If Option (1) is chosen, S-APPIFY also sends EK and $MAC_{K_{AF}}(EK)$.

21. If Option (1) is chosen, Alice verifies $MAC_{K_{AF}}(EK)$.

   <u>If the verification is successful:</u> The protocol continues with Step 22.

   <u>If the verification is a failure:</u> The protocol continues with Step 22*.

   If Option (2) is chosen, the protocol continues with Step 22.

22. Further communication continues over TLS; for example, the profile settings can be updated.

22*. Alice sends an error message "MAC failure." to the main server of APPIFY, and the protocol is aborted.

4.3   Protocol C: Connecting to Application in MEC Host

Protocol C is run when Alice has up-to-date keys for the main server and wants to use M-APPIFY. The entities, MNO, MEC, M-APPIFY, and S-APPIFY, participate in this protocol. Protocol C is explained step by step below, and the communication flow is shown in Fig. 5.

At the beginning of the protocol, Alice has her identities SUPI for MNO and Alice13 for APPIFY. She also has psw, public key EK of S-APPIFY, and K_{AF}. MNO knows the SUPI of Alice and has saved K_{AKMA} and A-KID relating to the SUPI. S-APPIFY has public key EK and saved Alice13, psw, H-ID, and K_{AF} in the database. MEC and M-APPIFY do not have any information on the user.

1. Alice and MEC establish a secure connection, e.g., DTLS connection.
2. Alice generates a random X. Then, she encrypts X and her identifier Alice13 by using the public key of S-APPIFY EK: $E_{EK}(Alice13, X)$.
3. Alice sends the ID-APPIFY and $E_{EK}(Alice13, X)$ to MEC through the secure channel.
4. MEC notices the identifier of S-APPIFY and forwards the message $E_{EK}(Alice13, X)$ to M-APPIFY.
5. M-APPIFY forwards $E_{EK}(Alice13, X)$ to S-APPIFY.
6. S-APPIFY decrypts $E_{EK}(Alice13, X)$ with its secret key DK. Then, S-APPIFY checks the database for Alice13.

   <u>If Alice13 is in the database:</u> S-APPIFY gets the related identifiers and keys, e.g., K_{AF}.

   If there is existing K_{AF}, the protocol continues with Step 7.

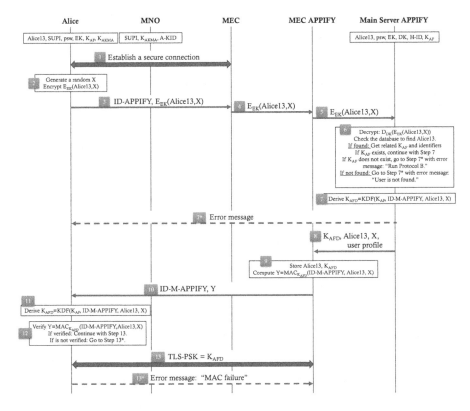

Fig. 5. Communication flow of Protocol C

If there is no existing K_{AF}, the protocol continues with Step 7*
with the error message: "Run Protocol B."

If Alice13 is not in the database: The protocol continues with Step 7*
with the error message: "User is not found."

7. S-APPIFY derives a new key $K_{AFD}=\mathrm{KDF}(K_{AF}, \mathrm{ID\text{-}M\text{-}APPIFY}, \mathrm{Alice13},$
   $X)$, where the ID-M-APPIFY is the identifier of M-APPIFY.

7* The error message is sent and the protocol is aborted.

8. S-APPIFY sends K_{AFD}, Alice13, X, and the user profile of Alice13 to
   M-APPIFY.

9. M-APPIFY stores Alice13 and K_{AFD}. Then, it computes
   $\mathrm{Y}=MAC_{K_{AFD}}(\mathrm{ID\text{-}M\text{-}APPIFY}, \mathrm{Alice13}, \mathrm{X})$.

10. M-APPIFY sends ID-M-APPIFY and Y to Alice through MEC.

11. Alice derives $K_{AFD}=\mathrm{KDF}(K_{AF}, \mathrm{ID\text{-}M\text{-}APPIFY}, \mathrm{Alice13}, \mathrm{X})$ after receiving
    ID-M-APPIFY.

12. Alice computes $MAC_{K_{AFD}}(\mathrm{ID\text{-}M\text{-}APPIFY}, \mathrm{Alice13}, \mathrm{X})$ and verifies
    whether it matches Y.

    If the verification is successful: The protocol continues with Step 13.

    If the verification is a failure: The protocol continues with Step 13*.

13. Alice and M-APPIFY establish a TLS connection with a pre-shared key method (TLS-PSK), where the key is K_{AFD}. Communication proceeds securely with this key.

13*. Error message: "MAC Failure." is sent, and the protocol is aborted.

Application may have a time limit that defines how long a user remains signed in for S-APPIFY and M-APPIFY. After that time, the user is kicked out, which means the TLS connection is dropped.

Alice may want to use the same M-APPIFY after some time, assuming that the time limit is not over. In this case, the following steps are followed.

Is the TLS connection still on?

Yes: Protocol C continues with Step 13.

No: Is K_{AFD} is still valid?

Yes: TLS session resumption [18] is run with the key K_{AFD}, and Protocol C continues with Step 13.

No: Alice needs to start Protocol C from Step 1. If Alice does not have K_{AF} stored, she first needs to run Protocol B to renew the key K_{AF}.

4.4 Protocol D: Changing the MEC Host

Protocol D is run when Alice, who is actively using M-APPIFY, i.e., the parties are in Step 13 of Protocol C, is also moving. Let us recall the case where Alice travels from one city to another in the same country, say from Helsinki to Tampere. While she moves, the MEC host that provides services to Alice changes. During this trip, MNO might or might not change. This paper focuses on the case where MNO does not change and leaves the extension to the roaming case for future work.

There may be no available MEC host with M-APPIFY near where the user is moving to. In this case, Alice continues to be served through S-APPIFY, and Protocol B is run. This can be enhanced by an option where the source M-APPIFY informs the main server about losing connection to Alice13. We do not explain this option further and leave it for future work.

When Alice is moving, and she is about to leave the service area of the MEC host, MEC Orchestrator (MEO), finds the target MEC host and the target M-APPIFY [8]. Protocol D is explained step by step below, and the communication flow is shown in Fig. 6.

0. Protocol starts when there is an existing connection between Alice and source M-APPIFY resulting from Protocol C, i.e., Step 13.
1. When MEO determines the target MEC host, MEO provides this information to the source MEC host. Then, source MEC notifies source M-APPIFY that the connection of Alice13 is being transferred to another MEC host and M-APPIFY.
2. Source M-APPIFY sends Alice13, K_{AFD}, and the target MEC host information to S-APPIFY. Source M-APPIFY also sends the service state information of Alice13. This is the same state information that was mentioned in the Introduction, in Sect. 1.

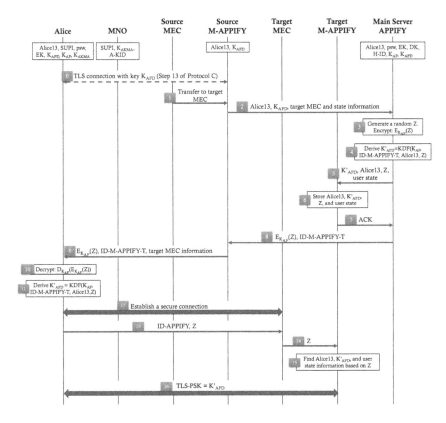

Fig. 6. Communication flow of Protocol D

3. S-APPIFY generates a random Z. Then, it encrypts Z with K_{AF}: $E_{K_{AF}}(Z)$.
4. S-APPIFY derives the key K'_{AFD}=KDF(K_{AF}, ID-M-APPIFY-T, Alice13, Z), where ID-M-APPIFY-T is the identifier of the target M-APPIFY.
5. S-APPIFY sends K'_{AFD}, Alice13, Z, user profile, and service state information of Alice13 to the target M-APPIFY.
6. Target M-APPIFY stores Alice13, K'_{AFD}, Z, user profile, and service state information of Alice13.
7. Target M-APPIFY sends an acknowledgment to S-APPIFY that it received the message.
8. S-APPIFY sends $E_{K_{AF}}(Z)$ and ID-M-APPIFY-T to the source M-APPIFY.
9. Source M-APPIFY sends $E_{K_{AF}}(Z)$, ID-M-APPIFY-T, and the target MEC host information to Alice.
10. Alice decrypts $E_{K_{AF}}(Z)$ with K_{AF} to retrieve Z.
11. Alice derives K'_{AFD}=KDF(K_{AF}, ID-M-APPIFY-T, Alice13, Z).
12. Alice establishes a secure connection with the target MEC host, e.g., DTLS connection.
13. Alice sends Z with ID-APPIFY to the target MEC host.
14. Target MEC host forwards Z to the target M-APPIFY.

15. Target M-APPIFY checks the database for Z and finds related Alice13, K'_{AFD}, and the user information.
16. Target M-APPIFY initiates a TLS-PSK connection with Alice with the key K'_{AFD}.

When the TLS connection between Alice and target M-APPIFY is established successfully, target M-APPIFY continues with providing the services to Alice instead of source M-APPIFY. Note that until this happens, Alice has been receiving services from the source M-APPIFY. The TLS connection with source M-APPIFY is terminated when the TLS connection with target M-APPIFY is established. If the connection with source M-APPIFY is lost before the connection with target M-APPIFY is established, the service continues with the main server.

5   Analysis

Our solution uses 3GPP AKMA for the authentication and key sharing between the user Alice and the main server of the application S-APPIFY in Protocol A (Sect. 4.1) and Protocol B (Sect. 4.2). The shared key resulting from AKMA is used later in Protocol C (Sect. 4.3) and Protocol D (Sect. 4.4) when Alice wants to get service from the M-APPIFY. It is appropriate to adapt the AKMA system to our solution because AKMA is created in 5G to support applications, and APPIFY is one such application. MNO already verifies the identity of the user during the subscription and already authenticates the user during the network access. Therefore, AKMA is using the capability of MNO to help the user and S-APPIFY authenticate each other.

Moreover, AKMA is a better option for the authentication and key sharing between Alice and S-APPIFY compared to, e.g., a solution where S-APPIFY creates a random key and sends it back to Alice. If one of the parties loses the shared key, the synchronization of the keys between these parties requires less effort with AKMA.

It is natural to use usernames and passwords for accessing the applications. However, when Alice uses AKMA, she does not need to enter her password for the application all the time she uses the application. This also decreases the chance of the password being compromised.

In our solution, secure communication channels are established between the parties, which protects the integrity and confidentiality of the messages sent. The channel between Alice and MNO is secured after the Authentication and Key Agreement (AKA) is run.

In Protocols A and B, a TLS connection is established between Alice and the main server of APPIFY before she sends her identifiers and password. This way, Alice can be sure that she is talking to the correct server. Moreover, these identifiers and passwords would not be visible to outsiders, and neither to MNO.

Protocols C and D focus on the usage of APPIFY in MEC hosts. Therefore, there should also be a secure connection between Alice and MEC, e.g., DTLS.

The handshake can be based on a pre-shared key (resulting from AKMA) or a certificate. 3GPP defines usage of AKMA in their technical documents [3]. We do not discuss how to secure the connection between the user and MEC further.

3GPP studies focus on the authentication between Alice and MEC host and Alice and MEC system. In this paper, we focus on authentication at the application level. We use AKMA to provide mutual authentication between the user and the main server of the application. As a product of AKMA, the user and the main server of the application share a key. Another key, derived from the shared key, is then used to secure the connection between the user and the MEC application, e.g., TLS-PSK in Protocols C and D. This newly derived key depends on the MEC application. Therefore, every time the user wants to connect to a MEC application in a different MEC host, a new key can be derived from the shared AKMA key without the need to run AKMA each time. In addition, since the same key is not used with different entities, the key is less likely to be compromised.

The TLS connection between Alice and M-APPIFY protects the communication from outsiders and honest-but-curious entities of the system model, e.g., MNO and MEC host. These honest-but-curious entities would like to learn as much as possible without interfering with the communication protocol [15]. In order to preserve the privacy of the user, MNO and MEC should not learn anything related to the user that is not needed for providing services.

Privacy of the user is preserved against MNO with our solution. Therefore, MNO only learns that Alice uses S-APPIFY since AKMA is run between these two entities. However, MNO cannot know whether or when Alice is using M-APPIFY.

MNO cannot learn the identifier of Alice for APPIFY, Alice13, and her password, because these are sent to S-APPIFY in Protocols A and B after the TLS connection is established. Similarly, in Protocols C and D, Alice first establishes a secure connection with MEC and then sends her identifier, which is also encrypted with the public encryption key of the main server. This latter encryption protects the privacy of the identifier against honest-but-curious MEC hosts.

We have introduced H-ID to AKMA to prevent MNO from learning the identifier Alice13 during the authentication. S-APPIFY sends the keyed hash of Alice13 instead of Alice13 itself to MNO, and MNO binds A-KID and SUPI to the keyed hash of Alice13. Therefore, neither MNO nor S-APPIFY can link SUPI and Alice13.

In addition, the communication between Alice and S-APPIFY continues over the TLS channel in Protocols A and B, so MNO cannot see the data sent between the two parties. In Protocols C and D, the secure channel between Alice and MEC and the TLS channel between Alice and M-APPIFY prevents MNO from seeing the content sent between Alice and M-APPIFY.

Regarding the TLS channel between Alice and M-APPIFY in Protocols C and D, we introduce a derived key K_{AFD} instead of K_{AF} as a pre-shared key. Since MNO knows the key K_{AF} but not the derived one, MNO would not be able to decrypt the communication channel. Therefore, MNO cannot learn the content of the communication of Alice with either S-APPIFY or M-APPIFY.

Privacy of the user is also preserved against MEC. Alice sends her identifier Alice13 after encrypting it with the public encryption key of the main server. Also, the TLS connection between Alice and M-APPIFY prevents MEC from learning the content of the messages between Alice and M-APPIFY. Therefore, MEC cannot learn the identifiers of Alice or the details of the services she gets from M-APPIFY.

6   Conclusion and Future Work

Multi-access edge computing (MEC) is an emerging technology in 5G. We solve the problem of creating a secure and privacy-preserving communication channel between the user and MEC application in the local MEC host when the user moves from the source MEC host to another target MEC host. The scope of the paper is restricted to the case where the source and the target MEC hosts belong to the same MNO.

One limitation of our study is that AKMA is not yet deployed. Therefore, observing the limits of AKMA in practice and experimenting with our solution are left for future work. Two other topics for future work are the formal verification of our solution and extending the scope to the roaming situation where the source and the target MEC hosts belong to different MNOs.

Acknowledgements. The authors would like to thank Mohsin Khan for his helpful comments.

References

1. 3GPP. Authentication and key management for applications (AKMA) based on 3GPP credentials in the 5G system (5GS). Technical Specification TS 33.535 V17.4.0, 3GPP (2021)
2. 3GPP. Security aspects of enhancement of support for enabling edge applications. Technical Specification TS 33.558 V0.3.0, 3GPP (2021)
3. 3GPP. Study on security aspects of enhancement of support for edge computing in the 5G Core (5GC). Technical Report TR 33.839 V17.1.0, 3GPP (2021)
4. Ali, A., Lin, Y.D., Li, C.Y., Lai, Y.C.: Transparent 3rd-party authentication with application mobility for 5G mobile edge computing. In: 2020 European Conference on Networks and Communications (EuCNC), pp. 219–224. IEEE, Dubrovnik (2020). https://doi.org/10.1109/EuCNC48522.2020.9200937
5. Ali, A., Rahman Khan, S., Sakib, S., Hossain, M.S., Lin, Y.D.: Federated 3GPP mobile edge computing systems: a transparent proxy for third party authentication with application mobility support. IEEE Access 10, 35106–35119 (2022). https://doi.org/10.1109/ACCESS.2022.3162851
6. Ali, B., Gregory, M.A., Li, S.: Multi-access edge computing architecture, data security and privacy: a eview. IEEE Access 9, 18706–18721 (2021). https://doi.org/10.1109/ACCESS.2021.3053233

7. ETSI. Application Mobility Service API. Group Specification GS MEC 021 V2.2.1, ETSI (2022)
8. ETSI. Framework and Reference Architecture. Group Specification GS MEC 003 V3.1.1, ETSI (2022)
9. Huang, X., Tsiatsis, V., Palanigounder, A., Su, L., Yang, B.: 5G authentication and key management for applications. IEEE Commun. Stand. Magaz. **5**(2), 142–148 (2021). https://doi.org/10.1109/MCOMSTD.001.2000024
10. Lei, W., et al.: 5G security system design for all ages. In: 5G System Design, pp. 341–390. Springer, Cham (2021). https://doi.org/10.1007/978-3-030-73703-0_6
11. Liu, Y., Peng, M., Shou, G., Chen, Y., Chen, S.: Toward edge intelligence: multiaccess edge computing for 5G and Internet of Things. IEEE Internet Things J. **7**(8), 6722–6747 (2020). https://doi.org/10.1109/JIOT.2020.3004500
12. Liyanage, M., Porambage, P., Ding, A.Y., Kalla, A.: Driving forces for multi-access edge computing (MEC) IoT integration in 5G. ICT Express **7**(2), 127–137 (2021). https://doi.org/10.1016/j.icte.2021.05.007
13. Nencioni, G., Garroppo, R.G., Olimid, R.F.: 5G multi-access edge computing: security, dependability, and performance. arXiv:2107.13374 [cs] (2021)
14. Niewolski, W., Nowak, T.W., Sepczuk, M., Kotulski, Z.: Token-based authentication framework for 5G MEC mobile networks. Electronics **10**(14) (2021). https://doi.org/10.3390/electronics10141724
15. Paverd, A., Martin, A., Brown, I.: Modelling and Automatically Analyzing Privacy Properties for Honest-But-Curious Adversaries. Technical Report (2014)
16. Ranaweera, P., Jurcut, A., Liyanage, M.: MEC-enabled 5G use cases: a survey on security vulnerabilities and countermeasures. ACM Comput. Surv. **54**(9), 1–37 (2022). https://doi.org/10.1145/3474552
17. Ranaweera, P., Jurcut, A.D., Liyanage, M.: Survey on multi-access edge computing security and privacy. IEEE Commun. Surv. Tutor. **23**(2), 1078–1124 (2021). https://doi.org/10.1109/COMST.2021.3062546
18. Rescorla, E.: The Transport Layer Security (TLS) Protocol Version 1.3. Internet-Draft draft-ietf-tls-rfc8446bis-03, IETF (2021, work in progress)
19. Sabella, D.: MEC federation and mobility aspects. In: Multi-access edge computing: software development at the network edge. TTE, pp. 245–279. Springer, Cham (2021). https://doi.org/10.1007/978-3-030-79618-1_8
20. Sanchez-Gomez, J., Marin-Perez, R., Sanchez-Iborra, R., Zamora, M.A.: MEC-based architecture for interoperable and trustworthy internet of moving things (2022). https://doi.org/10.1016/j.dcan.2022.03.028
21. Tabatabaee Malazi, H., et al.: Dynamic service placement in multi-access edge computing: a systematic literature review. IEEE Access **10**, 32639–32688 (2022). https://doi.org/10.1109/ACCESS.2022.3160738

International Workshop on Psycho-Social Analysis of Sustainable Mobility in The Pre- and Post-Pandemic Phase (PSYCHE 2022)

Modelling of Interactions Between Pedestrians and Vehicular Traffic to Promote Active Mobility: The Case of San Benedetto Neighbourhood in Cagliari (Italy)

Vincenza Torrisi[1]([⊠]) [iD], Chiara Garau[2]([⊠]) [iD], Antonio Barbagallo[1] [iD],
Pierfrancesco Leonardi[1] [iD], and Matteo Ignaccolo[1] [iD]

[1] Department of Civil Engineering and Architecture, University of Catania,
Viale Andrea Doria, 6, 95125 Catania, Italy
vtorrisi@dica.unict.it
[2] Department of Civil and Environmental Engineering and Architecture,
University of Cagliari, 09129 Cagliari, Italy
chiara.garau@unica.it

Abstract. The COVID-19 has significantly led to changes in the mobility needs and in user travel behavior, due to the measures adopted to reduce the spread of the virus. While on the one hand this has resulted in a reduction in the number of trips, on the other this has entailed an increase in the use of the private car, considered as the safest form of transportation in urban contexts. Thus, administrations and policy makers have to promote actions and strategies to encourage soft mobility (i.e. walking and cycling), viewed as solutions to reduce transport emissions and ensure social distancing. This often implies the need for a redesign of urban spaces as pedestrians experience uncomfortable or unsafe situations about the surrounding environment. Within this framework, the paper proposes a methodological framework to evaluate the interactions between pedestrians and vehicular traffic using a microsimulation approach. The analyzed case study concerns a road intersection within the S. Benedetto neighbourhood in Cagliari (Italy). A scenario assessment has been performed through the computation of several performance indicators related both to private transport (i.e. level of service and emissions) and pedestrian users (i.e. density; speed and crossing time). The comparative analysis of results demonstrates that this research approach could represent a flexible and effective tool in guiding administrations through the decision-making process during the planning and development of projects for redevelopment of urban spaces and the promotion of soft mobility. Further research will focus on an extended study area, by modelling the behaviour of different categories of pedestrians and introducing in-field data.

Keywords: VISSIM/VISWALK · Microsimulation · Active mobility · Redesign urban spaces · Level of service · Emissions · Pedestrian evaluation · Smart City

1   Introduction

Cities represent a key to conduct Europe towards sustainable, climate-friendly and healthy mobility. Nearly 3 out of 4 Europeans live in urban areas and there, road mobility is responsible for 23% of EU greenhouse gas emissions [1]. In Italy it is significant how dependent it is on the car, which accounts for 80% of total passenger traffic [2].

The emergency due to COVID-19 and the measures taken to limit the spread of the virus have represented a concrete possibility to redeem urban spaces dedicated to people, safer roads and less pollution [3–5]. The lockdown imposed to tackle the health crisis has resulted in the consistent spread of previously underdeveloped activities such as smart working, e-commerce and distance learning, significantly changing people's mobility needs. In Italy, 33% of citizens have changed their preferences in terms of frequency and travel times and type of vehicle; private cars and walking are the most used solutions in the post COVID-19 and 51% of citizens have limited their daily trips for personal activities [6–9]. The reduction in the number of trips during the lockdown phase led to a significant reduction in pollutants as reported by the ICOS - Integrated Carbon Observation System - which analyzed the effects of the lockdown for the containment of COVID-19 on CO^2 emissions in seven European cities. This study showed that in the busiest metropolises the blocking of mobility led to CO^2 emissions reduced by up to 75% [10].

Since the transport sector in Europe accounts for about a quarter of greenhouse gas emissions [11], it is essential to adopt strategies and actions with a view to planning sustainable urban mobility. Achieving zero-emission mobility in cities will only be possible through the joint efforts of local policies supported by national and European measures [12, 13]. In line with the *Avoid, Shift, Improve* principles to be implemented to reduce the use of private cars, specific measures must be adopted, including:

– support smart working and proximity services [14, 15];
– expand and differentiate entry times (i.e. in workplaces, schools, public and private services, etc.) to reduce peak hours and make the best use of the spaces and services available [16, 17];
– promote Sharing Mobility (i.e. car sharing, bike sharing, scooter sharing and electric micro mobility) and MaaS services [18–20];
– foster the integration of Intelligent Transport System technologies and the use of big-data [21, 22];
– improve local public transport services, adapt the vehicle fleet towards electrification, implement innovative mobility services, integrating them with other modes of transport [23, 24];
– promote the Limited Traffic Zones and Low Emission Zones [25, 26].

From the perspective of Sustainable and Smart Cities, the redevelopment of urban spaces is essential to encourage soft mobility (i.e. walking and cycling) and move from a car-oriented to a human-centered vision. Pedestrian networks must be designed to be able to move safely without obstacles and to stop pleasantly within urban areas. With the aim of minimizing the dangers induced by motorized traffic, priority should be given to speed reduction, which contributes considerably to lowering the number of accidents and risks. [27–30]. Moreover, in accordance with the SUMPs guidelines, developed both at the European and national level [31–33]. The interventions to encourage soft mobility and made it safer could be represented by the limitation of vehicle traffic and the extension of Restricted Traffic Areas (ZTL) with Traffic Calming areas, or the establishment of 30 km/h zones in historical centres [34]. It would be more profitable to adopt predictive analysis tools that allow to measure and quantify the impacts of different scenarios and to provide decision support for administrations.

Within this context, the paper deals with the concepts of sustainable and active mobility and the goal of the work is to present a methodological approach for analyzing the interactions of pedestrians with other traffic components. Specifically, a microscopic modeling has been carried out based on Wiedmann's psycho-social theoretical model. The case study concerns the San Benedetto neighborhood in Cagliari (Italy), presenting the microsimulation of a road intersection at Piazza San Benedetto and focusing on a specific pedestrian crossing. Using a microsimulation software, several alternative design scenarios have been modeled, with variations in terms of both transport supply and mobility demand. Qualitative and quantitative assessments have been carried out based on computed performance indicators related to vehicles and pedestrians.

The paper is structured in five sections: Sect. 2 illustrates the methodological framework based on the use of a microsimulation model to assess the interactions between vehicles and pedestrians; Sect. 3 presents the case study to which the methodology has been applied. The section contains territorial information on the San Benedetto neighbourhood and infrastructural details about the modelled road intersection with related simulated scenarios. Section 4 shows the results of the simulations of various scenarios in terms of levels of service, emissions and pedestrian parameters (i.e. density, speed and crossing time). Moreover, it provides a discussion about the comparison of the results for the different performed scenarios. Finally, Sect. 5 provides conclusions and paves the way for further in-depth research on this work, aimed at analyzing and evaluating strategies and actions to promote sustainable mobility and encourage soft mobility.

2 Methodological Approach

The evaluation of the interactions between pedestrians and vehicular traffic is addressed through a microsimulation model, to simulate the behaviour of the individual units in relation to the configuration of the road geometry and the presence of elements within the urban space.

Figure 1 shows the methodological framework, which is characterized by two phases: the first one is constituted by the model reconstruction, considering both the transport supply and the mobility demand, and the second one is represented by the scenario evaluation through the computation and assessment of several indicators.

The model reconstruction has involved these 3 main steps:

1.1 the identification of the study area, in this specific case coinciding with a road intersection with a focus on the pedestrian crossing and related data acquisition which is the basis of the two subsequent steps;

1.2 the transport supply modelling which provides for the construction of the road network graph, essentially consisting of links (i.e. lanes with relative widths and travel directions) and nodes (i.e. connectors representing the turning manoeuvres), on which the priority rules have been defined. In this regard, two different traffic conditions have been modelled, the first one more consistent with the state of affairs in which pedestrians stop before crossing, giving priority to vehicles; and the second one in favor of pedestrians, who are given priority at the intersection. The priority rules have been modelled through the Vissim software with the Viswalk add-on [35], by placing the conflict areas at the intersections generated between the road and the crossing links. The conflict areas have been set to "Red-Green" for pedestrians in the case of vehicles priority and "Green-Red" to model pedestrians' priority. Moreover, the geometrical infrastructural elements concerning pedestrians (i.e. sidewalks and crossing) have been modelled considering variations in the road geometry;

1.3 the transport demand modelling, with the vehicular and pedestrian flows. Vehicle flows have been simulated based on the Wiedemann 74 model and pedestrian flows in accordance with the social force model. Considering that variations in transport supply (e.g. road geometry) can consequently influence the demand, it has been carried out a sensitivity analysis by varying the values of flows, both pedestrian and vehicular, respectively. This sensitivity analysis serves to determine the robustness of the simulation model by examining which results may be affected by changes in some variables (i.e. in this case the flows) [36]. However, for the correct determination of the mobility demand, the estimates should be validated with in-field surveys.

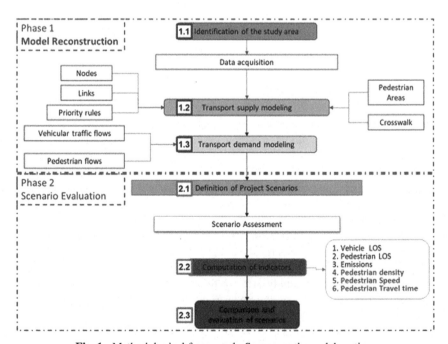

Fig. 1. Methodological framework. Source: authors elaboration.

After this first phase, it has been necessary to identify the node at which to perform node evaluations. This second phase envisages the following steps:

2.1   the definition of various alternative scenarios, with variations both in terms of transport supply and demand;
2.2   the identification and choice of certain nodes at which to calculate several evaluation parameters for the scenario assessment in accordance with [37, 38]; specifically, it concerned the calculation of levels of service (LOS) which represents a measurement of the quality of vehicular and pedestrian traffic; in addition the estimation of emissions (i.e. CO, NOx, VOC), relating to vehicular traffic, and a pedestrian assessment in terms of density, speed and crossing time.
2.3   the analysis and comparison of the indicators relating to the various hypothesized scenarios.

3   Case Study

The methodological approach has been applied to the study area located within the San Benedetto neighbourhood in Cagliari (Sardinia), in the southern part of the region. San Benedetto is a central district of the Sardinian municipality with a high population rate (i.e. more than 5,000 inhabitants per square kilometer). It is characterized by commercial services, public and private activities (e.g. schools, bus stops, shops, churches, post offices and banks). This work focuses on the area corresponding to *San Benedetto Square*. It consists of a roundabout where the main streets of the district converge. Dante Alighieri *Road* represents the main road that crosses the neighbourhood along the north-south direction (Fig. 2a).

Fig. 2.   (a) Delimitation of the neighbourhood boundaries of San Benedetto; (b) street-view of the pedestrian crossing. Source: Author elaboration from Google Earth.

What emerges from the analysis of this area is that the concept of public space, and in the case of a square (i.e. San Benedetto Square), is completely distorted. In fact, the square is not used as a meeting place, but it constitutes a road infrastructure that is a roundabout, in which roads are characterized by high vehicular flows.

The analysis presented in this paper consisted of the microsimulation of a pedestrian crossing located in Dante Alighieri Road near the intersection with San Benedetto square (Fig. 2b). The choice to model this crossing is motivated by the fact that it is characterized by a high pedestrian transit and at the same time by an intense interaction with other traffic components (i.e. private vehicles, public transport and bicycles).

Using simulation software, it has been possible to carry out an accurate analysis of the road intersection. In the PTV Vissim/Viswalk software, the pedestrian crossing has been first modelled by entering all the information relating to the transport supply. For this purpose, to model the state of affairs referred to March 2022, an online survey has been carried out using the Google Street View tool, to detect the number and width of road lanes, the travel directions, the dimensions of the pedestrian crossing and adjacent sidewalks. Subsequently, the transport demand has been modelled. In the absence of in-field traffic measurements, therefore, variable pedestrian and vehicular flows have been simulated to perform sensitivity analysis when these input data vary. Furthermore, two different traffic regulation conditions have been identified (in accordance with Table 1). The first condition attributes the priority rule to vehicles penalizing pedestrians, in which cars do not respect the right of way of pedestrians at the crossing. The second condition, on the other hand, attributes the priority rule to pedestrians, in which the cars strictly comply with this rule. For each of these conditions, the percentage of pedestrian flow has been varied (see Table 1) to evaluate the impact on the simulation results.

The outputs that have been taken into consideration for the research study are: the pedestrian density, the pedestrian speed and travel time of the crossing, the level of service relating to both the pedestrian and vehicular traffic. In addition, emissions associated with private traffic and public transport have been estimated. In our case, they have been calculated with the COPERT model which allows to estimate the emission values of these pollutant CO, NOx and VOC.

Table 1 summarizes the seven scenarios that have been performed in the microsimulation model, derived from the combination of variations in both the transport demand and supply. In the four scenarios (i.e. from 1.1 to 1.4) the priority rules (alternatively for vehicles and pedestrians) and the pedestrian hourly flow (between 200 ped/h and 400 ped/h in each crossing direction) have been varied. Subsequently, for the scenario 2.1 and 2.2 a variation of the road geometry with narrowing of the pedestrian crossing has

Table 1. Scenarios description with supply and demand combinations

Scenario	N. Tpr lanes	Crosswalk length	Vehic/h	Ped/h	Priority rules
1.1	2	18 m	675	200	Vehicles
1.2	2	18 m	675	400	Vehicles
1.3	2	18 m	675	200	Pedestrian
1.4	2	18 m	675	400	Pedestrian
2.1	1	13 m	675	200	Pedestrian
2.2	1	13 m	675	400	Pedestrian
2.3	1	13 m	450	400	Pedestrian

been assumed. Finally, in the last scenario 2.3, a modal shift from private transport in favour of pedestrian mobility has been hypothesized.

4   Results and Discussion

4.1   Scenarios 1.1 and 1.2: Priority to Vehicles

A first step of the analysis has been to model the current state of the pedestrian crossing, simulating that pedestrians give priority to vehicles before entering the crosswalk. This occurs due to various factors, e.g. the lack of adequate lateral visibility. The following Fig. 3 shows how, during the simulation, pedestrians stop on the sidewalk threshold waiting for no more vehicles to be able to cross later.

Fig. 3. 3D simulation showing pedestrians waiting at the sidewalk of the crosswalk

With the priority rule to vehicles, two scenarios have been modelled: the scenario 1.1 with a pedestrian flow of 200 pedestrians per hour and the scenario 1.2 with 400 pedestrians per hour in each crossing direction. Specifically, Table 2 reports the obtained results from the performed simulations, both in terms of vehicular indicators and pedestrian ones. The Highway capacity manual (HCM) defines 6 values of level of service, from the best A to the worst F, depending on the generated delay. As it emerges from the analysis, by increasing the pedestrian demand it is registered an increase in the pedestrian density and in the travel time of the crosswalk. From the comparison of Table 2 by increasing the pedestrian flow there is an increase in density equal to 89% and a decrease of 3% in speed. Furthermore, even by increasing the number of pedestrians, this has no impact in terms of level of service, i.e. always maintaining a service level equal to A for vehicles. In terms of emissions, there is also no significant increase since vehicles are not subject to stop and go phenomena because they have the priority. In fact, the sum of the total emissions for scenario 1.1 is equal to 161.82 g and for scenario 1.2 it is 162.18 g. This information is also provided in accordance with ANPA's "Local Air Emission Inventory Guidelines" and forms the basis for the calculation of pollutant concentrations in the macro-sector of transport, and to analyze which threshold values are exceeded.

460   V. Torrisi et al.

Table 2. Simulation results of scenarios 1.1 and 1.2 with private vehicles priority rules

Scenario 1.1. - 200 ped/h and vehicles priority

Type lane	LOS (vehic)	LOS (ped)	CO [g]	NOx [g]	VOC [g]
Tpr 1	LOS A	LOS A	80,195	15,603	18,586
Tpr 2	LOS A	LOS A	31,894	6,205	7,392
Tpb	LOS A	LOS A	1,1366	0,266	7,392
Bike	LOS A	LOS A	–	–	–
Total	**LOS A**	**LOS A**	**113,454**	**22,074**	**26,294**
Pedestrian evaluation			*Density [ped/m²]*	*Speed [km/h]*	*Travel time [s]*
			0,0162	2,94	24,85

Scenario 1.2. - 400 ped/h and vehicles priority

Type lane	LOS (vehic)	LOS (ped)	CO [g]	NOx [g]	VOC [g]
Tpr 1	LOS A	LOS A	80,266	15,617	18,602
Tpr 2	LOS A	LOS A	32,001	6,226	7,417
Tpb	LOS A	LOS A	1,445	0,281	0,335
Bike	LOS A	LOS A	–	–	–
Total	**LOS A**	**LOS A**	**113,712**	**22,124**	**26,354**
Pedestrian evaluation			*Density [ped/m²]*	*Speed [km/h]*	*Travel time [s]*
			0,0307	2,85	25,90

4.2   Scenarios 1.3 and 1.4: Priority to Pedestrians

The second modelled condition requires vehicles to give priority to pedestrians during the crossing (Fig. 4). In practice, this is achieved by trying to make this pedestrian crossing more visible, e.g. making a two-color marking, increasing the vertical and horizontal signs near the crossing, or transforming it into a raised crosswalk. With these design measures, drivers will be encouraged to give priority to pedestrians, increasing road safety and ensuring that pedestrians do not feel like "guests" in the surrounding urban spaces.

Fig. 4. 3D simulation showing vehicles waiting for pedestrians to cross.

Tables 3 shows the results of the simulations carried out respectively with 200 and 400 pedestrians per hour and per crossing direction. It should be noted that following the continuity of the pedestrian path, the crossing time decreases. On the other hand, there is a worsening in terms of vehicular emissions due to continuous stop and go phenomena. Furthermore, it is found that the vehicular level of service remains equal to A with 200 pedestrians per hour even if they have the priority at crossing; while there is a downturn (i.e. level of service equal to C) when the pedestrian demand is increased to 400 pedestrians per hour. By comparing Table 3, by doubling the pedestrian flow, the total emission levels increase from 241.81 g for scenario 1.3 to 530.75 g for scenario 1.4. Looking at the level of service for the lanes of private transport, as previously highlighted it is reduced, by passing from LOS A to LOS B and LOS C on the two lanes.

Table 3. Simulation results of scenarios 1.3 and 1.4 with pedestrians' priority rules

Scenario 1.3. - 200 ped/h					
Type lane	*LOS (vehic)*	*LOS (ped)*	*CO [g]*	*NOx [g]*	*VOC [g]*
Tpr 1	LOS A	LOS A	120,205	23,388	27,859
Tpr 2	LOS A	LOS A	45,607	8,873	10,570
Tpb	LOS A	LOS A	3,727	0,725	0,864
Bike	LOS A	LOS A	–	–	–
Total	**LOS A**	**LOS A**	**169,539**	**32,986**	**39,292**
Pedestrian evaluation			*Density [ped/m^2]*	*Speed [km/h]*	*Travel time [s]*
			0,0136	3,58	19,78
Scenario 1.4. - 400 ped/h					
Type lane	*LOS (vehic)*	*LOS (ped)*	*CO [g]*	*NOx [g]*	*VOC [g]*
Tpr 1	LOS C	LOS A	295,694	57,531	68,530
Tpr 2	LOS B	LOS A	72,352	14,077	16,768
Tpb	LOS A	LOS A	4,066	0,791	0,942
Bike	LOS A	LOS A	–	–	–
Total	**LOS C**	**LOS A**	**372,112**	**72,399**	**86,241**
Pedestrian evaluation			*Density [ped/m^2]*	*Speed [km/h]*	*Travel time [s]*
			0,0243	3,46	20,43

4.3 Scenarios 2.1 and 2.2: Crossing Narrowing and Priority to Pedestrians

The second step of the analysis focused on the effects that would occur assuming to narrow the pedestrian crossing and widening the sidewalk, suppressing one of the two vehicle lanes and diverting the traffic flow only to ones. As can be seen from Table 4, having reduced the length of the pedestrian path, the crossing travel time is reduced. Moreover, the pedestrian density decreases as the sidewalk has been widened. From the comparison of scenarios 2.1 and 2.2, with the new geometric road configuration, doubling the number of pedestrians, the level of service drastically worsens, passing from A to F. Total emissions also undergo a sharp increase, from 266, 86 g in scenario 2.1 against 1372.08 g in scenario 2.2. From the point of view of pedestrian evaluations, comparing the two scenarios, there is a 74% increase in pedestrian density and a 7% decrease in pedestrian speed.

Table 4. Simulation results of scenarios 2.1 and 2.2 with narrowing crossing and pedestrians' priority rules

Scenario 2.1. - 200 ped/h					
Type lane	*LOS (vehic)*	*LOS (ped)*	*CO [g]*	*NOx [g]*	*VOC [g]*
Tpr 1	LOS A	LOS A	184,185	35,836	42,687
Tpb	LOS A	LOS A	2,912	0,567	0,675
Bike	LOS A	LOS A	–	–	–
Total	**LOS A**	**LOS A**	**187,097**	**36,402**	**43,361**
Pedestrian evaluation			*Density [ped/m^2]*	*Speed [km/h]*	*Travel time [s]*
			0,0105	3,53	15,82
Scenario 2.2. - 400 ped/h					
Type lane	*LOS (vehic)*	*LOS (ped)*	*CO [g]*	*NOx [g]*	*VOC [g]*
Tpr 1	LOS F	LOS A	956,270	186,055	221,625
Tpb	LOS A	LOS A	5,704	1,110	1,322
Bike	LOS A	LOS A	–	–	–
Total	**LOS F**	**LOS A**	**961,975**	**187,165**	**222,947**
Pedestrian evaluation			*Density [ped/m^2]*	*Speed [km/h]*	*Travel time [s]*
			0,0184	3,29	17,21

4.4   Scenario 2.3: Modal Shift, Crossing Narrowing and Priority to Pedestrians

Evaluating the results of scenario 2.2, in which pedestrian flows have been increased, as road safety conditions have also been improved thanks to the restriction of pedestrian crossing, it is reasonable to hypothesize a modal shift from private motorized mobility. In fact, following the elimination of one of the two private traffic lanes, drivers may no longer be inclined to travel along this road section. Therefore, they could first choose another route or secondly, opt for another transport mode (e.g. public transport, cycling, walking).

In this view, a final new scenario has been defined and modelled (i.e. scenario 2.3), in which the vehicular flow decreases by approximately 25%.

From Table 5, it emerges that a decrease in vehicular flow corresponds to an improvement in the level of service, which passes from F in scenario 2.2 to C in scenario 2.3. In addition, there is also a clear improvement in the reduction of emissions, with a total of 404.57 g.

Table 5. Simulation results of scenario 2.3 with modal shift, mobility demand of 400 pedestrians per hour and pedestrians' priority rules

Scenario 2.3. - 400 ped/h Shift modale					
Type lane	*LOS (vehic)*	*LOS (ped)*	*CO [g]*	*NOx [g]*	*VOC [g]*
Tpr 1	LOS C	LOS A	276,060	53,711	63,980
Tpb	LOS A	LOS A	7,562	1,471	1,753
Bike	LOS A	LOS A	–	–	–
Total	**LOS C**	**LOS A**	**283,622**	**55,183**	**65,732**
Pedestrian evaluation			*Density [ped/m^2]*	*Speed [km/h]*	*Travel time [s]*
			0,0185	3,28	17,33

4.5 Scenario Comparison Results

This section presents a comparative analysis of the obtained results for all simulated scenarios: 1.1 and 1.2 with the schematization of the intersection according to the state of affairs and with priority to vehicles; 1.3 and 1.4 with priority to the pedestrians; 2.1 and 2.2 with a geometric variation characterized by the reduction of the crossing width and the elimination of a transit lane; 2.3 similar to 2.2 but with a reduction of vehicles from 500 veic/h to 400 veic/h. Attention has been paid to the effects deriving from changes in terms of transport demand (i.e. increase in pedestrian flow and modal shift) and transport supply (i.e. road geometric variations).

The graph relating to the level of service represented in Fig. 5 shows that in scenarios where pedestrians stop to give way to vehicles, decreases in the vehicle level of service are not recorded, despite the increase in pedestrian flow. The situation is different in the scenarios where vehicles stop to give way to pedestrians. In fact, by increasing the pedestrian flow, the level of service is lowered to level C. The worst result is obtained when the carriageway is narrowed by eliminating a private traffic lane, when the level of service assumes the value F. Therefore, to balance the simulated improvements in favour of pedestrians and return to service level C it is essential to hypothesize a modal shift, by reducing vehicular flows.

By observing the graph of the total emissions (Fig. 6), it presents approximately the same trend as the graph of the level of service, since, in correspondence with a low pedestrian flow, a low level of emissions is estimated. Similarly, when priority is given to pedestrians, there is an increase in emissions. With the same demand flows, the increase in emissions appears to be more significant in the scenario with the narrowing crossing and a single private vehicular lane.

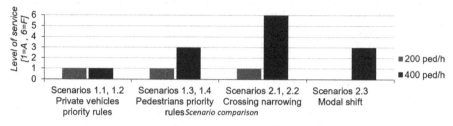

Fig. 5. Scenario comparison results - Level of service

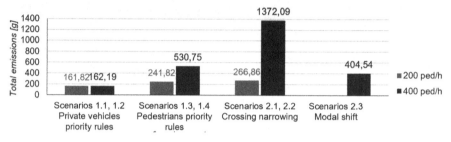

Fig. 6. Scenario comparison results - Total emissions [g]

From the analysis of the pedestrian density (Fig. 7) graph, it emerges that with moderate pedestrian flows, the consequent density is at low values and vice versa. With a pedestrian flow of 200 pedestrians per hour, it is observed a linear decrease in density deriving from the fact that by giving priority to pedestrians they move faster, thus creating less crowding; furthermore, by widening the sidewalk, the surface on which pedestrians can walk becomes more extended. A similar trend has been also found in the scenarios characterized by 400 pedestrians per hour.

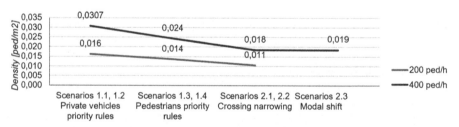

Fig. 7. Scenario comparison results - Pedestrian density [ped/m^2]

The trend of the speed graph represented in Fig. 8 is similar in both pedestrian demand configurations. Specifically, there are slightly higher speed values in scenarios with 200 pedestrians per hour. It is observed that in the case in which priority is given to vehicles, a low-speed value is found. Then, by making the improvements in terms of road geometry, it is noted that the pedestrian speed values during the crossing slightly decrease. This is due to the reduction to only one lane and therefore to a worsening of the conditions of private traffic which consequently also affect pedestrian transit.

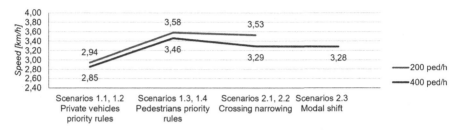

Fig. 8. Scenario comparison results - Pedestrian speed [km/h]

5   Conclusions and Future Research

The impact of COVID-19 on mobility has been and will continue to be particularly significant, both due to the severe measures adopted to reduce the risk of spreading the virus and the changing in mobility needs. In accordance with this, users are seeking solutions that can ensure social distancing, and this often leads to a preference for the use of private vehicles and the increase in walking and cycling for short distances.

This paper has proposed a methodology for evaluating the interaction between pedestrians and vehicular traffic through the implementation of a microsimulation model. Using the simulation software, it has been possible to create an accurate modelling of the road intersection within the neighbourhood of San Benedetto. By inserting detailed input data (i.e. number and width of lanes, flows and pedestrian and vehicular itineraries), it has been possible to simulate the behaviour of road users (i.e. pedestrians and drivers) in different alternative design scenarios, varying both the transport supply and the mobility demand. Moreover, quantitative assessments have been performed through the calculation and analysis of indicators (i.e. level of service, emissions, pedestrian density and speed, crossing time).

The research approach has significant implications both from a methodological and practical points of view. First, with the microsimulation it is possible to carry out controlled experiments varying different parameters to perform sensitivity analysis. In addition, the possibility of performing both qualitative (i.e. 2D and 3D visualizations) and quantitative (i.e. computation of performance indicators) scenario assessment, represent a valid decision support tool for administrations and planners in evaluating different strategies and actions for the redevelopment of urban spaces and the promotion of soft mobility.

The limitation of this simulation approach is the need of in-field measurements related to the transport demand to obtained results for operational scenario assessments. Moreover, through the calibration of the parameters related to the pedestrian simulation it would be possible to reproduce their real behavior which can be influenced by the context area. In-depth analysis of the research work moves in this direction, which will foresee the extension of the study area and the modelling of the behaviour of different categories of pedestrians (i.e. men, women, elderly people and children). Furthermore, the possibility of carrying out field surveys will allow to characterize the mobility demand that is more in keeping with reality, thus achieving simulation results that can be used in the context of operational plans and programs.

Acknowledgements. This work started and developed as a result of a project proposal within the doctoral course "Smart and Sustainable Cities (2nd edition)" held at the University of Cagliari (https://dottorati.unica.it/dotticar/smart-and-sustainablecities-2-Edizione/). This study was also supported by the MIUR (Ministry of Education, Universities and Research [Italy]) through a project entitled WEAKI TRANSIT: WEAK-demand areas Innovative TRANsport Shared services for Italian Towns (Project code: 20174ARRHT), financed with the PRIN 2017 (Research Projects of National Relevance) programme. We authorize the MIUR to reproduce and distribute reprints for Governmental purposes, notwithstanding any copyright notations thereon. Any opinions, findings and conclusions or recommendations expressed in this material are those of the authors, and do not necessarily reflect the views of the MIUR.

Authors Contribution. This paper is the result of the joint work of the authors. 'Abstract' and 'Conclusions and future research' were written jointly by the authors. VT wrote the "Introduction", VT and PL wrote 'Methodological Approach', CG wrote 'Case study', VT and AB wrote 'Results and discussion'. VT, CG and MI coordinated and supervised the paper.

References

1. Stoll, B., Müller, J., Giaconi, M., Azdad, Z.: CLEAN CITIES. Benchmarking European cities on creating the right conditions for zero-emission mobility (2022). https://cleancitiescamp aign.org/wp-content/uploads/2022/02/Clean-Cities_-City-Ranking-Rating-briefing-2.pdf
2. Statista Research Department. Number of registered passenger cars in Italy from 1990 to 2019 (2022). https://www.statista.com/statistics/452345/italy-number-of-registered-passen ger-cars/
3. Campisi, T., et al.: A new vision on smart and resilient urban mobility in the aftermath of the pandemic: key factors on European transport policies. In: Gervasi, O., et al. (eds.) ICCSA 2021. LNCS, vol. 12958, pp. 603–618. Springer, Cham (2021). https://doi.org/10.1007/978-3-030-87016-4_43
4. Kutralam-Muniasamy, G., Pérez-Guevara, F., Roy, P.D., Elizalde-Martínez, I., Shruti, V.C.: Impacts of the COVID-19 lockdown on air quality and its association with human mortality trends in megapolis Mexico City. Air Qual. Atmos. Health **14**(4), 553–562 (2020)
5. Barbarossa, L.: The post pandemic city: Challenges and opportunities for a non-motorized urban environment. An overview of Italian cases. Sustainability **12**(17), 7172 (2020)
6. OCTO Connected Forum. Connected Mobility 2025. La via italiana alla mobilità connessa (2021). https://www.octotelematics.com/it/blog/la-mobilita-del-futuro-prende-forma-allocto-connected-forum/
7. Borkowski, P., Jażdżewska-Gutta, M., Szmelter-Jarosz, A.: Lockdowned: everyday mobility changes in response to COVID-19. J. Transp. Geogr. **90**, 102906 (2021)
8. Torrisi, V., Campisi, T., Inturri, G., Ignaccolo, M., Tesoriere, G.: Continue to share? An overview on Italian travel behavior before and after the COVID-19 lockdown. In: International Conference of Computational Methods in Sciences and Engineering ICCMSE 2020 (2021). https://doi.org/10.1063/5.0048512

9. Campisi, T., Tesoriere, G., Trouva, M., Papas, T., Basbas, S.: Impact of teleworking on travel behaviour during the COVID-19 era: the case of sicily, Italy. Transp. Res. Proc. **60**, 251–258 (2022)
10. ICOS. Supplementary data: temporary reduction in daily global CO2 emissions during the COVID-19 forced confinement (2021). https://www.icos-cp.eu/gcp-covid19
11. European Environment Agency. Trends and Projections in Europe 2021 (2021). https://www.efficienzaenergetica.enea.it/vi-segnaliamo/l-agenzia-europea-dell-ambiente-aea-pubblica-il-rapporto-trends-and-projections-in-europe-2021-clima-ed-energia-2020-raggiunti-gli-obiett ivi-europei.html
12. Matemilola, S., Salami, H.A.: Net zero emission. Encyclopedia of sustainable management, pp. 1–6. Springer, Switzerland (2020)
13. Tiboni, M., Rossetti, S., Vetturi, D., Torrisi, V., Botticini, F., Schaefer, M.D.: Urban policies and planning approaches for a safer and climate friendlier mobility in cities: strategies, initiatives and some analysis. Sustainability **13**(4), 1778 (2021). https://doi.org/10.3390/su1304 1778
14. Langè, V., Gastaldi, L.: Coping Italian emergency COVID-19 through smart working: from necessity to opportunity. J. Mediterran. Knowl. **5**(1), 163–171 (2020)
15. Namiot, D., Sneps-Sneppe, M.: On content models for proximity services. In: 2019 24th Conference of Open Innovations Association (FRUCT), pp. 277–284. IEEE (2019)
16. Agba, A.O., Ocheni, S.I., Agba, M.S.: COVID-19 and the world of work dynamics: a critical review. J. Educ. Soc. Res. **10**(5), 119 (2020)
17. Daniel, S.J.: Education and the COVID-19 pandemic. Prospects **49**(1–2), 91–96 (2020)
18. Campisi, T., Ignaccolo, M., Inturri, G., Tesoriere, G., Torrisi, V.: The growing urban accessibility: a model to measure the car sharing effectiveness based on parking distances. In: Gervasi, O., et al. (eds.) ICCSA 2020. LNCS, vol. 12255, pp. 629–644. Springer, Cham (2020). https://doi.org/10.1007/978-3-030-58820-5_46
19. Canale, A., Tesoriere, G., Campisi, T.: The MAAS development as a mobility solution based on the individual needs of transport users. In: AIP Conference Proceedings, vol. 2186, no. 1, p. 160005. AIP Publishing LLC (2019)
20. Savithramma, R.M., Ashwini, B.P., Sumathi, R.: Smart mobility implementation in smart cities: a comprehensive review on state-of-art technologies. In: 2022 4th International Conference on Smart Systems and Inventive Technology (ICSSIT), pp. 10–17. IEEE (2022)
21. Garau, C., Nesi, P., Paoli, I., Paolucci, M., Zamperlin, P.: A big data platform for smart and sustainable cities: environmental monitoring case studies in Europe. In: Gervasi, O., et al. (eds.) ICCSA 2020. LNCS, vol. 12255, pp. 393–406. Springer, Cham (2020). https://doi.org/10.1007/978-3-030-58820-5_30
22. Torrisi, V., Ignaccolo, M., Inturri, G.: Innovative transport systems to promote sustainable mobility: developing the model architecture of a traffic control and supervisor system. In: Gervasi, O., et al. (eds.) ICCSA 2018. LNCS, vol. 10962, pp. 622–638. Springer, Cham (2018). https://doi.org/10.1007/978-3-319-95168-3_42
23. Torrisi, V., Inturri, G., Ignaccolo, M.: Introducing a mobility on demand system beyond COVID-19: evidences from users' perspective. In: International Conference of Computational Methods in Sciences and Engineering ICCMSE 2020 (2021). https://doi.org/10.1063/5.004 7889
24. Camporeale, R., Caggiani, L., Ottomanelli, M.: Modeling horizontal and vertical equity in the public transport design problem: a case study. Transp. Res. Part A: Policy Pract. **125**, 184–206 (2019)
25. Papa, R., Fistola, R., Gargiulo, C. (eds.): Smart Planning: Sustainability and Mobility in the Age of Change. GET, Springer, Cham (2018). https://doi.org/10.1007/978-3-319-77682-8
26. Ignaccolo, M., et al.: How to redesign urbanized arterial roads? The case of Italian small cities. Transp. Res. Proc. **60**, 196–203 (2022). https://doi.org/10.1016/j.trpro.2021.12.026

27. Distefano, N., Leonardi, S.: Evaluation of the benefits of traffic calming on vehicle speed reduction. Civil Eng. Architect. **7**(4), 200–214 (2019)

28. Ignaccolo, M., Inturri, G., Calabrò, G., Torrisi, V., Giuffrida, N., Le Pira, M.: Auditing streets' pedestrian compatibility: a study of school sites' requalification. Pedestrians, Urban Spaces Health 30–34 (2020). https://doi.org/10.1201/9781003027379-6

29. Caselli, B., Rossetti, S., Ignaccolo, M., Zazzi, M., Torrisi, V.: Towards the definition of a comprehensive walkability index for historical centres. In: Gervasi, O., et al. (eds.) ICCSA 2021. LNCS, vol. 12958, pp. 493–508. Springer, Cham (2021). https://doi.org/10.1007/978-3-030-87016-4_36

30. Rossetti, S., Tiboni, M., Vetturi, D., Zazzi, M., Caselli, B.: Measuring pedestrian accessibility to public transport in urban areas: a GIS-based discretisation approach, European transport, **76**, 2 (2020). ISSN:1825-3997

31. Torrisi, V., Garau, C., Ignaccolo, M., Inturri, G.: "Sustainable urban mobility plans": key concepts and a critical revision on SUMPs guidelines. In: Gervasi, O., et al. (eds.) ICCSA 2020. LNCS, vol. 12255, pp. 613–628. Springer, Cham (2020). https://doi.org/10.1007/978-3-030-58820-5_45

32. Torrisi, V., Garau, C., Inturri, G., Ignaccolo, M.: Strategies and actions towards sustainability: encouraging good ITS practices in the SUMP vision. In: Torrisi, V., Garau, C., Inturri, G., Ignaccolo, M. (eds.) AIP Conference Proceedings, vol. 2343, no. 1, p. 090008. AIP Publishing LLC (2021). https://doi.org/10.1063/5.0047897

33. Tilocca, P., et al.: Managing data and rethinking applications in an innovative mid-sized bus fleet. Transp. Res. Proc. **25**, 1899–1919 (2017)

34. Pellicelli, G., Rossetti, S., Caselli, B., Zazzi, M.: Urban regeneration to enhance sustainable mobility. The 2018 Call for proposals of the Emilia-Romagna Region, Tema. J. Land Use Mobil. Environ. 57–70 (2022)

35. Fellendorf, M., Vortisch, P.: Microscopic traffic flow simulator VISSIM. In: Barceló, J. (ed.) Fundamentals of Traffic Simulation, pp. 63–93. Springer, New York (2010). https://doi.org/10.1007/978-1-4419-6142-6_2

36. Lownes, N.E., Machemehl, R B.: VISSIM: a multi-parameter sensitivity analysis. In: Proceedings of the 2006 Winter Simulation Conference, pp. 1406–1413. IEEE (2006)

37. Bönisch, C., Kretz, T.: Simulation of pedestrians crossing a street. arXiv preprint arXiv:0911.2902 (2009)

38. Chauhan, B.P., Joshi, G.J., Parida, P.: Car following model for urban signalised intersection to estimate speed based vehicle exhaust emissions. Urban Climate **29**, 100480 (2019)

The Rise of E-scooters in Palermo: A SWOT Analysis and Travel Time Study

Tiziana Campisi[1]([✉]) [iD], Alexandros Nikitas[2] [iD], Muhammad Ahmad Al-Rashid[3] [iD], Andreas Nikiforiadis[4] [iD], Giovanni Tesoriere[1] [iD], and Socrates Basbas[4] [iD]

[1] Faculty of Engineering and Architecture, University of Enna Kore, 94100 Enna, Italy
tiziana.campisi@unikore.it
[2] Huddersfield Business School, University of Huddersfield, Queensgate, UK
[3] King Salman Centre for Local Governance, Prince Sultan University, Riyadh 11586, Kingdom of Saudi Arabia
[4] Department of Transportation and Hydraulic Engineering, School of Rural and Surveying Engineering, Faculty of Engineering, Aristotle University of Thessaloniki, 54124 Thessaloniki, Greece

Abstract. In recent years, e-scooters became a popular transport mode, mainly covering the "first/last mile" in the trip-chain. The recent pandemic increased the use of these vehicles because it allows social distancing. While e-scooters are already part of the daily landscape in other countries, in Italy, and especially in Sicily, their diffusion has only recently started. Operators have seen demand growth, that created several critical issues referring to vehicle maintenance and vandalism. Although e-scooters tend to be a transport solution with enormous potential, especially in overcrowded cities with increasing private car traffic, several legislative issues need also to be resolved before these can be genuinely successful. This paper shows how to improve strategic planning for e-scooter micro-mobility utilising a SWOT analysis. The paper also identifies four urban poles of attraction and analyses e-scooter suitability in terms of travel time by employing isochrones for 5, 10 and 15 min.

Keywords: E-scooter · Accessibility · Micro-mobility · Sustainable mobility · Smart city · SWOT · Travel time

1 Introduction

Recently, several strategies have been deployed to make urban mobility more sustainable (Madapur et al. 2020). Cities are undergoing continuous transformation, and the latest city models tend to encourage proximity and the use of smart technology (Green 2002).

On the one hand, local governments invest on implementing conventional cycling and walking infrastructure, both temporary and permanent (Campisi et al. 2020a; Hagen and Rynning 2021). On the other hand, national governments encourage the purchase of electric and micro-mobility vehicles (Eccarius and Lu 2020). These actions have been intensified during and in the aftermath of the pandemic (Nikitas et al. 2021b) for raising

O. Gervasi et al. (Eds.): ICCSA 2022 Workshops, LNCS 13380, pp. 469–483, 2022.
https://doi.org/10.1007/978-3-031-10542-5_32

public awareness regarding environmental sustainability and reducing the use of private vehicles, which increased after the pandemic due to the fear of contagion, especially when taking public transport (Arribas-Ibar et al. 2021; Griffiths et al. 2021). However, most big cities are not friendly to their inhabitants, especially vulnerable road users, e.g., children, pedestrians, the disabled, cyclists, the elderly (Broome et al. 2010; Hess 2009; Sundling et al. 2015).

The current infrastructure in most Italian cities is not yet adequate to guarantee safety for pedestrians, cyclists and also micro-mobility users. Several studies are trying to define whether today's cities can keep up with the pace of this new phenomenon and whether there is room for more means of transport (Campisi et al. 2020a; Campisi et al. 2021a). Other studies also highlight the need to analyse better the safety of e-scooters for the users themselves and other road users (Campisi et al. 2021a; Campisi et al. 2021b).

The main reason for this is the lack of a legal framework and rules for important questions about who, where and how can use this new mobility option.

The aim of this work is to demonstrate a dual strategic tool improving the micro-mobility service in the examined area. A first step of evaluation was conducted on the factors that characterise the operation of the existing shared mobility system in the city. Starting from the plausible assumption that e-scooters are mainly used for short-distances and they are considered really competitive for the firtst/last mile of the trip-chain, we estimate which areas can potentially be reached within 10 min from certain focal city areas.

The results lay down the foundations for the relocation and improvement of the service and evaluating some criticalities that have emerged since the start of the shared e-scooter service.

2 Literature Review

The evolution of cities is characterised by a growing urban population and a progressive tendency to pursue smart city models promoting, among others, digital evolution. Several actions have been implemented thanks to planning tools such as a sustainable urban mobility plans (SUMP), taking into account the strategic objectives of Agenda 2030 to improve the quality of life of citizens in urban areas (Campisi et al. 2020c). Studies also show that the 15-min city and smart city models are gaining popularity, especially in European cities (de Valderrama et al. 2020).

While planning focuses on strategies for improving urban spaces, it also promotes new technologies for "smart" transport including electric vehicles (Kougias et al. 2020), autonomous driving (Nikitas et al. 2021a) and e-scooters (Nikiforiadis et al. 2021; Ignaccolo et al. 2022).

Moreover, it helps in promoting multimodality in urban transport leading to efficient use of resources (Campisi et al. 2021d). SUMP evolution, i.e. the planning tools promoted by the EU and used by cities in their policy planning are often related to a fourfold SWOT analysis where the strengths of certain modal choices are defined, taking into account technological developments and vehicle characteristics and business models that may lead to threats to a city's overall mobility and liveability. Some studies in the literature focus on SWOT evaluations related to scooters, often highlighting some criticalities such as unregulated parking or careless use. Improving micro-mobility services should consider active strategic cooperation between local public authorities, public transport agencies and operators of shared e-scooter services (König et al. 2022; Sundqvist-Andberg et al. 2021). Micro-mobility has become a trend initially in China and the USA and during the last two years also in Europe. It has proved extremely attractive to inhabitants of large cities. Research has shown that more than half of all users see micro-mobility as an acceptable and suitable mode to avoid traffic congestion and stress. Shared e-scooter systems were first introduced in 2017, and in some European countries, the direct purchase and ownership of scooters through discounts and subsidies has also proved successful (Gebhardt et al. 2021; Glavić et al. 2021).

Some studies show that e-scooters can help cities with environmental issues, such as reducing air pollution (Campisi et al. 2021b). At the same time, other works highlight the need to reduce inequalities in access to transport, promote money-saving and improve mobility resilience (Campisi et al. 2021e; Nikiforiadis et al. 2021). Several studies have investigated public opinion regarding e-scooters based on who does not use them, highlighting critical issues in the lack of infrastructure and the absence of a legislative framework (Kostareli et al. 2021; Tsami et al. 2022). A small number of studies focus on the propensity to rent, share or buy scooters (Bieliński and Ważna 2020; Campisi et al. 2021a; Campisi et al. 2020b; Campisi et al. 2020c). A series of surveys have been disseminated in different European contexts to analyse the characteristics of the e-scooter sharing service and the profile of its users (Kostareli et al. 2021; Nikiforiadis et al. 2021; Raptopoulou et al. 2021).

Although the topic of e-scooters in a national context has recently been evaluated, some aspects remain unstudied. For example, the dynamic behaviour of e-scooters is not as systematically studied as that of e-bikes. This could help public administrations to plan the circulation of e-scooters in cities and advise manufacturers to improve their design by including shock absorbers to increase comfort (Boglietti, Ghirardi, Zanoni, Ventura, Barabino, Maternini, and Vetturi, 2022; Ventura, Ghirardi, Vetturi, Maternini and Barabino, 2022).

A report published by The Forum of European Road Safety Research Institutes (2020) compared the situation in 18 European countries regarding e-scooters, aiming to highlight differences in terms of the legal status of the bike, its widespread use, and safety. The majority of the members stated that e-scooters are equated with bicycles. In the Czech Republic, scooters belong to the same category as e-bikes. In some countries, the category depends on speed or maximum power (Haworth 2021). In Finland, for example, a scooter is treated as a pedestrian if it is not travelling at a speed exceeding 15 km/h; otherwise, it is classified as a bicycle. In about half the countries analysed, there is an age limit (in several European countries, scooters can only be ridden by people over the age of 14 and helmets are compulsory for people under 18) for using an e-scooter (Rahimuddin 2020). E-scooters must be ridden on cycle paths in almost all countries, if available. If they are not available, they are expected to be used on the road in Austria, France (if the speed limit for that stretch is not higher than 50 km/h), Germany, Portugal, Sweden and Switzerland (Peci and Ali 2022; Reck and Axhausen 2021). In Italy, users can use both the cycle lane and the road as long as they are in an area with a 30 km/h speed limit, as described below (Fig. 1).

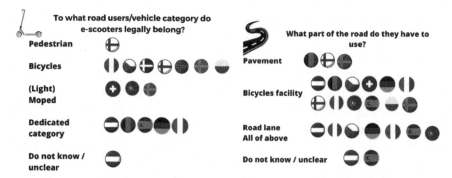

Fig. 1. E-scooter usage characteristics across European countries (data **source**: The Forum of European Road Safety Research Institutes (2020). Figure: authors elaboration)

Only in Germany, e-scooters must have a licence plate. In almost all countries, the irregular parking of e-scooters in public spaces is seen as a safety issue for pedestrians, the elderly, the blind and people with disabilities. In the Netherlands, the parking of e-scooters is not seen as a problem, thanks to the responsibility users showcase in an environment that has a well-established micro-mobility culture. Although e-scooters tend to be a transport solution with enormous potential, especially in overcrowded cities with increasing private car traffic, several legislative issues need to be resolved. In this way it would be ensured that e-scooters are not only fast and cheap, but also safe (Braniš et al. 2020). During the COVID-19 pandemic, e-scooters became more attractive. They promote social distancing and help cities not rely solely on private cars, especially short-distance travel (Campisi et al., 2021a; Li et al. 2022). Special fares have been promoted in some cities for people who start using the service, such as in Braga, Portugal (Dias et al. 2021) and Paris, France (Latinopoulos et al. 2021). The uptake of e-scooters has been also facilitated by the technological advancements (Alevras et al. 2021; Chicco and Diana 2022; Fistola et al. 2022).

2.1 E-scooters in the Italian Context

Urban areas worldwide are experiencing a rapid growth in shared micro-mobility services, mainly due to the introduction of shared bicycles and, more recently, e-scooters. Several studies have been conducted in Europe and, in particular, in Italy. For example, in Turin, research has been carried out by disseminating a questionnaire. The results indicate that both e-bikes and e-scooters are used for short trips, mainly on weekdays in the afternoon (https://www.bird.co/blog/turin-italy-micromobility-helping-red-cross-deliver-food-aid/). The peaks in use suggest that both services mostly meet the demand for non-commuting trips, in line with previous studies in other countries (Nikitas et al. 2016). Furthermore, e-scooter trips are primarily concentrated in the city centre and the vicinity of railway and metro stations, suggesting that, among other purposes, the service is used as a first and last-mile link to public transport (Baek et al. 2021).

A study carried out in the south region of Campany shows how e-scooter sharing can be a particularly effective way for university students to get to their study centres quickly, avoiding or supplementing the use of local public transport (Fistola et al. 2022). It also stresses the need to create dedicated lanes for urban micro-mobility, which would allow a considerable increase in safety during journeys and help avoid inappropriate behaviour linked to speed, the use of pavements and the inappropriate abandonment of vehicles in the middle of the road (Liu et al. 2019).

In Italy, the spread of micro-mobility can be compared to other European countries. The Italian success was strongly linked to the distribution of economic incentives; demonstrating the promotion of sustainability is still closely linked to economic development principles. Arriving in Italy at the end of 2019, scooter-sharing services achieved unprecedented numbers in the year of the pandemic.

Shared scooters increased from December 2019 to September 2020 from 4,900 to 27,150. It is just one of the numbers indicating the great change in the mobility of Italian cities, between the desire for experimentation and stricter rules. In September 2021, 65,000 light shared vehicles (excluding private ones) were registered, offered by 86 services of micro-mobility. These include 20,000 e-scooters and 45,000 bicycles. The strong growth of e-scooters in Italy was accelerated by the new rules issued in July 2019, which gave Italian municipalities a year to regulate the circulation of e-scooters, segways, hoverboards and monowheels. Milan, Turin, Rimini, Cattolica, Pesaro and Verona were the first cities to join.

The recent Italian legislation in 2021 introduced several changes to the Highway Code, including those concerning the use of e-scooters. Among the innovations introduced by the legislation is the reduction of the maximum speed from 25 to 20 km/h and the obligation to wear a reflective jacket half an hour after sunset or in poor visibility conditions, be equipped with direction indicators and brakes on both wheels. These actions were necessary considering the growing number of accidents caused or suffered by users of e-scooters. If the market for e-scooters continues growing in Italy, this is mainly due to a considerable increase of sharing services in cities.

Ease of use, and quick travel are two main characteristics of e-scooters. A substantial increase in the purchase of e-scooters was recorded in July 2020, thanks to government incentives (i.e. Bonus Mobilità 2020). The most widespread operational model in Italy is that of free-floating. For scooter sharing, the only existing business model is the B2C, with private ownership and private asset management (Foissaud et al. 2022). Campisi et al. (2021a) found that Italians chose to use e-scooters to get around the city quickly in an environmentally friendly way. As shown in Fig. 2, half of the Italians stated that getting around the city quickly and reducing emissions were main motivators to rent an e-scooter. However, only eight per cent of respondents believe that e-scooters are a safe means of transport.

The main benefits of using e-scooters can be summarised as follows:

- Ease and cost-effectiveness
- Reduction of vehicular traffic in the city
- Reduction of emissions and pollution
- Flexibility and potential to fill some gaps in public transport services

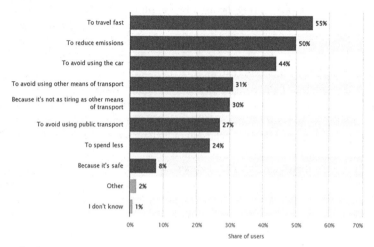

Fig. 2. Main motivators for using e-scooters in Italy. **Source:** Statista (2019)

Instead, there are several critical issues, which include: poor integration of shared micro-mobility within city transport planning; lack of guidelines on parking and dedicated areas, absence of insurance, license plate and vehicle homologation; high accident rate; and dependence on weather conditions.

Starting from these considerations, this work focuses on improving urban planning and mobility strategies in the metropolitan city of Palermo through two steps: a SWOT analysis connected to the spread of micro-mobility and an evaluation based on travel times considering four nodes in the examined city.

3 Methodology

3.1 Case Study Analysis

In recent years, the city of Palermo has been the subject of a study about the development of micro-mobility, as it was the first Sicilian city to have scooter-sharing services. By 2022, more than 20,000 rides had been recorded, and 7,000 new users had been registered. The objective of the local administration, which has been implementing strategies for more sustainable mobility for years, is to bring an integrated and multimodal service to the city, enhancing urban mobility with innovative and ecological means. Several scooter rental companies have entered into agreements with the local administration, and growing demand for transport has emerged, especially after the pandemic.

Although there has been a good take-up of the service, there are unfortunately still some problems related to the planning of the service.

Citizens have repeatedly pointed out to the responsible authorities the inappropriate use of micro-mobility vehicles, which is not limited to their circulation, but also to the release that follows the termination of the rental.

This is often done inappropriately and without respecting the law. The abandonment of these vehicles is becoming an increasingly widespread problem. From the outermost areas to the city centre, many e-scooters are abandoned on pavements, pedestrian crossings, and parking bays, even in front of essential city monuments. Unfortunately, there was a lot of vandalism in the early days of the sharing services, which initially reduced the number of operating e-scooters.

These phenomena hinder the movement of pedestrians, and cause problems in terms of safety and accessibility.

3.2 SWOT Analysis

The SWOT analysis is a simple and effective strategic planning tool that serves to highlight the characteristics of a project, and the consequent relations with the operational environment in which it is located. It also offers a reference framework for the definition of strategic orientations aimed at achieving a goal.

The SWOT analysis makes possible to think about the objective to be achieved while simultaneously taking internal and external variables into account.

The internal variables are part of the system, where it is possible to intervene, while the external ones do not depend on the organisation. They can be only kept under control to exploit the positive factors and limit the factors that obstruct the achievement of the established objectives. The SWOT analysis is implemented using a matrix divided into four fields in which we have:

- Strengths,
- Weaknesses,
- Opportunities
- Threats

As far as the context of the city of Palermo is concerned, the authors, taking into account the strategies related to the SUMP of the city but also the data of accidents and vandalism recorded by the municipal police in 2021–2022 as well as data from a series of surveys and questionnaires in the literature and related to the case study have developed the SWOT analysis as described in Table 1 below.

Table 1. Main points of SWOT analysis

Strengths	Weakness	Opportunities	Threats
Convenience and compatibility with the 'smart' cities model	Not addressing all age groups	"Smart cities" that will involve all road users	Lack of regulatory framework
Easy to ride	Not easy for family rides (adults and babies)	Sustainable goals	The transition period for cities'

(*continued*)

Table 1. (*continued*)

Strengths	Weakness	Opportunities	Threats
Easy to park	Speed range exceeds pedestrians by 4–5 times	Life quality	Infrastructure to adopt a new transportation model
Eco friendly and silent	Rapid expansion does not allow users time to adapt and comply with safety on the road	Human-friendly cities	Increased risk of non-trained e-scooter users
Enhancing multimodality	Dangerous co-existence with vulnerable road users	No congestion charge	
Suitable for first/last-mile trips	The short life cycle leads to its battery disposal and environmental burden		Lack of use of safety equipment for the users
Low cost for ownership	Operational internal and external costs	Increasing fossil fuel costs	Rise in cost of electricity
		Government subsidy for purchase	Competition in the form of electric hybrids, alternative fuels and hydrogen power cars
Energy saving-achievable in case of a regenerative braking system	Batteries changing is expensive		Presence of non-standard vehicles
			Vandalisms
			Negligence when parking scooters

The SWOT analysis approach is justified on the one hand by the simplicity of implementation and at the same time because it allows one to make an external and internal diagnosis of a phenomenon (mobility of e-scooters) in the area under investigation. The objective is to identify the strengths by highlighting the positive and negative points of the mobility service. By analysing the environment and internal factors, the shared mobility strategy can then be redefined and refined. The SWOT matrix brings together important strategic components, market analyses and evaluation opportunities that are easily readable even by non-experts. The factors defined in the table above make clear that the use of scooters still needs to be studied in terms of both regulations and safety. Although e-scooters are considerdd a useful and environmental-friendly transport mode, attention must be paid to regulating its use and its parking needs. This could ensure less negative implications on pedestrians, who often find scooters as an obstacle. Lastly, the city of Palermo, like many Italian cities, has suffered from phenomena of vandalism, so greater surveillance and control in urban areas could reduce these phenomena. Businesses, as well as local governments, are subject to many external factors over which they have limited control: relentless technological progress, demographic and social changes through to recent pandemics and wars. Moreover, the external factors to be considered in the analysis change rapidly. SWOT analysis is by nature a static snapshot and is a predictive tool that is limited on its own. Indeed, while the Strengths and Weaknesses presented in the manuscript are correlated with factors that are to some extent certain factors that local decision-makers can control, Opportunities and Threats are neither certain nor under the potential control of local decision-makers. They are by definition beyond their control and increasingly uncertain in a rapidly changing world.

3.3 Travel Time Analysis

E-scooters are one of the fastest ways to travel if you have to travel a mile or less. Generally speaking, walking on flat stretches of the road of 0.5 miles is usually done in 10 min. The same distance is covered in a third of the time if you use an e-scooter (see Table 2). If the journey is repeated over time, the e-scooter saves several hours of travel time each week.

Table 2. Distances and travel time considering walking and e-scoter use

Distance	Walking time (min)	E-scooter travel time (min)
0,5 mile (about 800 m)	10	3
1 mile (about 1600 m)	20	6
3 mile (about 2400 m)	60	18
5 mile (about 4000 m)	100	30
10 mile (about 8000 m)	200	60

Source: ScootMyCommute (2022)

Investigating further the travel times, isochrones and isolines are being drawn. Specifically, isochrones are polygons that enclose areas of the city that can be travelled at the same time with the same transport system. Isolines represent stretches of road and, therefore, the road network that is travelled at specific time-period. Three points (central nodes) in the city of Palermo have been identified and used as a basis for drawing these isochrones and isolines. These points are the following:

- Giulio Cesare main square in front of the railway station and the urban and suburban bus station
- Quattro Canti, the road intersection titled/named Quattro Canti that connected the city's two main arterial roads
- Intersection adjacent to the Teatro Massimo (main city theatre)

These nodes are located along Via Maqueda, one of the oldest streets in the city, full of offices and cultural attractions, defined as a shared space where pedestrians, cyclists and e-scooter users can easily pass. The walking route along Via Maqueda from the junction near Piazza Giulio Cesare to the junction near the Teatro Massimo is about 1.7 km. Under standard conditions, it can be covered on foot in about 19 min and with an e-scooter in about 6 min. This route has a a slight slope, about 3 m total height difference. The e-scooter almost triples the distance that can be covered in a specific time-period. Thus, guaranteeing a movement from Piazza Giulio Cesare to the intersection with Via Notarbartolo, as described in Fig. 3.

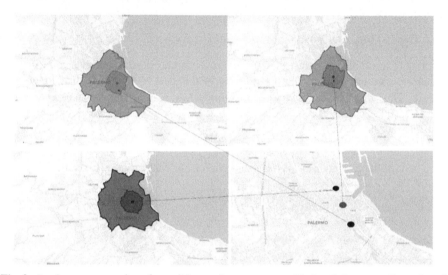

Fig. 3. Isochrones comparison for walking and e-scooter considering 3 three specific nodes of Palermo. **Source**: ISO4APP (2022)

The comparison between walking and e-scooters travel times becomes even clearer through Figs. 4 and 5, where the road network coverage for walking and e-scooters is presented respectively. It is demonstrated that e-scooters can cover a much greater distance comparing with walking in the same time-period.

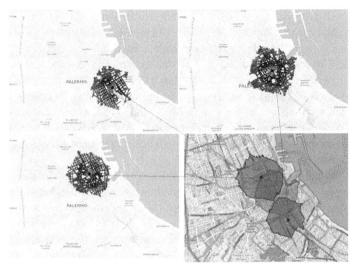

Fig. 4. Isoline street network for walking for three nodes (titled Piazza Giulio Cesare,Quattro canti and the intersection closed to Teatro Massimo) of Palermo. **Source**: ISO4APP (2022)

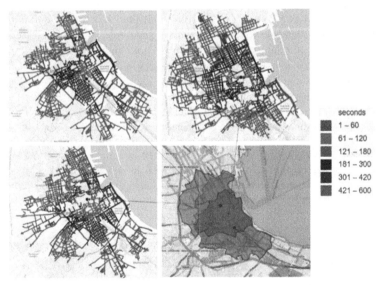

Fig. 5. Isoline street network for e-scooter considering three specific nodes of Palermo. **Source**: ISO4APP (2022)

4   Discussion and Conclusions

According to data processed by the National Observatory on Sharing Mobility, Palermo is the city (among the six analysed: Turin, Milan, Bologna, Rome, Cagliari and Palermo) that has exceeded the average values of "sharing" in 2019 in all services: scooter sharing, bike-sharing and car-sharing (http://osservatoriosharingmobility.it/).

The data confirms ann evident cultural change in mobility strongly desired by the municipal administration and shared by Palermo's citizens and many tourists who internationally recognise the efficiency and importance of sustainable mobility that in Palermo reaps actual results. Sharing mobility is one of the sustainability strategies foreseen by the Sustainable Urban Mobility Plan of the Municipality of Palermo. The local administration will continue to invest in reducing the use of private vehicles. The next step will be to expand the bike-sharing service, also with private partners, to increase the use of bicycles in urban mobility.

The SWOT analysis revealed the strengths and weaknesses of the current service, and the analysis of the travel time demonstrated the great potential that e-scooters have for attracting a large percentage of daily trips. More specifically, it was shown that e-scooters are capable of serving trips with distances up to 3–4 km from the centre using scooters; thus, potentially reducing the use of private vehicles. Yet, many barriers have to be overcome, as it is identified by the SWOT analysis. A holistic plan is therefore needed for eliminating issues related with safety and irregular use, and finally for providing the appropriate ground for a sustainable transport mode that can greatly contribute in cities' strategic objectives. The present work's key limitation is the lack of attitudinal primary data analysis; an e-survey and/or semi-structured interviews will be administrated shortly as a continuation research task. This paper provides the basis for the definition of an "impact/uncertainty" matrix in which opportunities and threats are assigned according to two parameters: an importance score (this score provides an indication of their potential impact on local economies) and a reasonable score relating to their degree of uncertainty.

Acknowledgments. The authors acknowledge the financial support from the MIUR (Ministry of Education, Universities and Research [Italy]) through a project entitled WEAKI TRANSIT: WEAK-demand areas Innovative TRANsport Shared services for Italian Towns (Project code: 20174ARRHT/CUP Code: J74I19000320008), financed with the PRIN 2017 (Research Projects of National Relevance) program. We authorize the MIUR to reproduce and distribute reprints for Governmental purposes, not-withstanding any copyright notations thereon. Any opinions, findings, and conclusions or recommendations expressed in this material are those of the authors and do not necessarily reflect the views of the MIUR.

Funding. This research work was partially funded by the MIUR (Ministry of Edu-cation, Universities and Research [Italy]) through a project entitled WEAKI TRANSIT.

References

Alevras, D., Zinas, D., Palantzas, G., Genitsaris, E., Nalmpantis, D.: Micromobility in Thessaloniki, Greece, and Madrid, Spain: a comparative study. IOP Conf. Ser.: Earth Environ. Sci. **899**(1), 012061 (2021). https://doi.org/10.1088/1755-1315/899/1/012061

Arribas-Ibar, M., Nylund, P., Brem, A.: The risk of dissolution of sustainable innovation ecosystems in times of crisis: the electric vehicle during the COVID-19 pandemic. Sustainability **13**(3), 1319 (2021). https://doi.org/10.3390/su13031319

Baek, K., Lee, H., Chung, J.-H., Kim, J.: Electric scooter sharing: How do people value it as a last-mile transportation mode? Transp. Res. Part d: Transp. Environ. **90**, 102642 (2021). https://doi.org/10.1016/j.trd.2020.102642

Bieliński, T., Ważna, A.: Electric scooter sharing and bike sharing user behaviour and characteristics. Sustainability **12**(22), 9640 (2020). https://doi.org/10.3390/su12229640

Boglietti, S., et al.: First experimental comparison between e-kick scooters and e-bike's vibrational dynamics. Trans. Res. Procedia **62**, 743–751 (2022)

Braniš, M., Balint, G., Takacs, J., Šulík, M., Galkin, A.: Shared electric scooters like a tool of a micro-mobility in cities. International Multidisciplinary Scientific GeoConference: SGEM **20**(6.1), 631–638 (2020)

Broome, K., Nalder, E., Worrall, L., Boldy, D.: Age-friendly buses? A comparison of reported barriers and facilitators to bus use for younger and older adults. Australas. J. Ageing **29**(1), 33–38 (2010)

Campisi, T., Acampa, G., Marino, G., Tesoriere, G.: Cycling master plans in italy: the I-BIM feasibility tool for cost and safety assessments. Sustainability **12**(11), 4723 (2020). https://doi.org/10.3390/su12114723

Campisi, T., Akgün-Tanbay, N., Md Nahiduzzaman, K., Dissanayake, D.: Uptake of e-Scooters in Palermo, Italy: Do the Road Users Tend to Rent, Buy or Share?. Cham (2021a)

Campisi, T., Akgün, N., Tesoriere, G.: An ordered logit model for predicting the willingness of renting micro mobility in urban shared streets: a case study in Palermo, Italy, Cham (2020b)

Campisi, T., Akgün, N., Ticali, D., Tesoriere, G.: Exploring public opinion on personal mobility vehicle use: a case study in palermo, italy. Sustainability **12**(13), 5460 (2020). https://doi.org/10.3390/su12135460

Campisi, T., Basbas, S., Skoufas, A., Tesoriere, G., Ticali, D.: Socio-eco-friendly performance of e-scooters in palermo: preliminary statistical results. Innovation in Urban and Regional Planning, 643 (2021b)

Campisi, T., Basbas, S., Skoufas, A., Tesoriere, G., Ticali, D.: Socio-Eco-Friendly Performance of E-Scooters in Palermo: Preliminary Statistical Results. Cham (2021c)

Campisi, T., Severino, A., Al-Rashid, M.A., Pau, G.: The development of the smart cities in the connected and autonomous vehicles (CAVs) era: from mobility patterns to scaling in cities. Infrastructures **6**(7), 100 (2021). https://doi.org/10.3390/infrastructures6070100

Campisi, T., Skoufas, A., Kaltsidis, A., Basbas, S.: Gender equality and e-scooters: mind the gap! a statistical analysis of the sicily region, Italy. Social Sciences **10**(10), 403 (2021). https://doi.org/10.3390/socsci10100403

Chicco, A., Diana, M.: Understanding micro-mobility usage patterns: a preliminary comparison between dockless bike sharing and e-scooters in the city of Turin (Italy). Transp. Res. Procedia **62**, 459–466 (2022). https://doi.org/10.1016/j.trpro.2022.02.057

de Valderrama, N.M.-F., Luque-Valdivia, J., Aseguinolaza-Braga, I.: The 15 minutes-city, a sustainable solution for postCOVID19 cities? Ciudad y Territorio Estudios Territoriales, 653–664 (2020)

Dias, G., Arsenio, E., Ribeiro, P.: The role of shared e-scooter systems in urban sustainability and resilience during the Covid-19 mobility restrictions. Sustainability **13**(13), 7084 (2021). https://doi.org/10.3390/su13137084

Eccarius, T., Lu, C.-C.: Powered two-wheelers for sustainable mobility: a review of consumer adoption of electric motorcycles. Int. J. Sustain. Transp. **14**(3), 215–231 (2020). https://doi.org/10.1080/15568318.2018.1540735

Fistola, R., Gallo, M., La Rocca, R.A.: Micro-mobility in the "Virucity". the effectiveness of e-scooter sharing. Transp. Res. Procedia **60**, 464–471 (2022). https://doi.org/10.1016/j.trpro.2021.12.060

Foissaud, N., Gioldasis, C., Tamura, S., Christoforou, Z., Farhi, N.: Free-floating e-scooter usage in urban areas: a spatiotemporal analysis. J. Transp. Geogr. **100**, 103335 (2022). https://doi.org/10.1016/j.jtrangeo.2022.103335

Gebhardt, L., Wolf, C., Seiffert, R.: "I'll take the e-scooter instead of my car"-the potential of e-scooters as a substitute for car trips in Germany. Sustainability **13**(13), 7361 (2021)

Glavić, D., Trpković, A., Milenković, M., Jevremović, S.: The e-scooter potential to change urban mobility-belgrade case study. Sustainability **13**(11), 5948 (2021)

Green, N.: On the move: technology, mobility, and the mediation of social time and space. Inf. Soc. **18**(4), 281–292 (2002). https://doi.org/10.1080/01972240290075129

Griffiths, S., Furszyfer Del Rio, D., Sovacool, B.: Policy mixes to achieve sustainable mobility after the COVID-19 crisis. Renew. Sustain. Energy Rev. **143**, 110919 (2021). https://doi.org/10.1016/j.rser.2021.110919

Hagen, O.H., Rynning, M.K.: Promoting cycling through urban planning and development: a qualitative assessment of bikeability. Urban, Planning and Transport Research **9**(1), 276–305 (2021). https://doi.org/10.1080/21650020.2021.1938195

Haworth, N.: E-scooters in brisbane: an overview of CARRS-Q research findings. Brisbane CBD Bicycle Users Group (2021)

Hess, D.B.: Access to public transit and its influence on ridership for older adults in two US cities. J. Trans. Land Use **2**(1), 3–27 (2009)

Ignaccolo, M., Inturri, G., Cocuzza, E., Giuffrida, N., Le Pira, M., Torrisi, V.: Developing micro-mobility in urban areas: network planning criteria for e-scooters and electric micromobility devices. Transp. Res. Procedia **60**, 448–455 (2022)

ISO4APP: Isolines for geographic network analysis. https://www.iso4app.net/ (2022)

König, A., Gebhardt, L., Stark, K., Schuppan, J.: A multi-perspective assessment of the introduction of e-scooter sharing in germany. Sustainability **14**(5), 2639 (2022). https://doi.org/10.3390/su14052639

Kostareli, A., Basbas, S., Stamatiadis, N., Nikiforiadis, A.: Attitudes of e-scooter non-users towards users. In: Nathanail, E.G., Adamos, G., Karakikes, I. (eds.) CSUM 2020. AISC, vol. 1278, pp. 87–96. Springer, Cham (2020). https://doi.org/10.1007/978-3-030-61075-3_9

Kougias, I., Nikitas, A., Thiel, C., Szabó, S.: Clean energy and transport pathways for islands: a stakeholder analysis using Q method. Transp. Res. Part d: Transp. Environ. **78**, 102180 (2020). https://doi.org/10.1016/j.trd.2019.11.009

Latinopoulos, C., Patrier, A., Sivakumar, A.: Planning for e-scooter use in metropolitan cities: a case study for Paris. Transp. Res. Part d: Transp. Environ. **100**, 103037 (2021). https://doi.org/10.1016/j.trd.2021.103037

Li, A., Zhao, P., Liu, X., Mansourian, A., Axhausen, K.W., Qu, X.: Comprehensive comparison of e-scooter sharing mobility: evidence from 30 European cities. Transp. Res. Part d: Transp. Environ. **105**, 103229 (2022). https://doi.org/10.1016/j.trd.2022.103229

Liu, M., Seeder, S., Li, H.: Analysis of e-scooter trips and their temporal usage patterns. Inst. Transp. Eng. ITE J. **89**(6), 44–49 (2019)

Madapur, B., Madangopal, S., Chandrashekar, M.N.: Micro-mobility infrastructure for redefining urban mobility. Eur. J. Eng. Sci. Technol. **3**(1), 71–85 (2020). https://doi.org/10.33422/ejest.v3i1.163

Nikiforiadis, A., Paschalidis, E., Stamatiadis, N., Raptopoulou, A., Kostareli, A., Basbas, S.: Analysis of attitudes and engagement of shared e-scooter users. Transp. Res. Part D: Transp. Environ. **94**, 102790 (2021). https://doi.org/10.1016/j.trd.2021.102790

Nikitas, A., Thomopoulos, N., Milakis, D.: The environmental and resource dimensions of automated transport: a nexus for enabling vehicle automation to support sustainable urban mobility. Annu. Rev. Environ. Resour. **46**, 167–192 (2021). https://doi.org/10.1146/annurev-environ-012220-024657

Nikitas, A., Tsigdinos, S., Karolemeas, C., Kourmpa, E., Bakogiannis, E.: Cycling in the era of COVID-19: lessons learnt and best practice policy recommendations for a more bike-centric future. Sustainability **13**(9), 4620 (2021). https://doi.org/10.3390/su13094620

Nikitas, A., Wallgren, P., Rexfelt, O.: The paradox of public acceptance of bike sharing in Gothenburg. Proc. Inst. Civil Eng.: Eng. Sustain. **169**(3), 101–113 (2016). https://doi.org/10.1680/jensu.14.00070

Peci, G., Ali, S., Fan, J., Zhu, J.: Usage pattern analysis of e-scooter sharing system: a case study in Gothenburg, Sweden. In: Bie, Y., Qu, B.X., Howlett, R.J., Jain, L.C. (eds.) Smart Transportation Systems 2022: Proceedings of 5th KES-STS International Symposium, pp. 123–132. Springer Nature Singapore, Singapore (2022). https://doi.org/10.1007/978-981-19-2813-0_13

Rahimuddin, M.: Innovation adoption of new e-scooters service in finland on consumer perspective (2020)

Raptopoulou, A., Basbas, S., Stamatiadis, N., Nikiforiadis, A.: A First Look at E-Scooter Users. In: Nathanail, E.G., Adamos, G., Karakikes, I. (eds.) CSUM 2020. AISC, vol. 1278, pp. 882–891. Springer, Cham (2020). https://doi.org/10.1007/978-3-030-61075-3_85

Reck, D.J., Axhausen, K.W.: Who uses shared micro-mobility services? empirical evidence from Zurich, Switzerland. Transp. Res. Part d: Transp. Environ. **94**, 102803 (2021). https://doi.org/10.1016/j.trd.2021.102803

ScootMyCommute: How long does it take to go a mile on a scooter. https://scootmycommute.com/scooter-distance-time (2022)

Statista: Reasons for using e-scooters in Italy. https://www.statista.com/statistics/450053/reasons-for-using-e-scooters-italy/ (2019)

Sundling, C., Emardson, R., Pendrill, L., Nilsson, M.E., Berglund, B.: Two models of accessibility to railway traveling for vulnerable, elderly persons. Measurement **72**, 96–101 (2015)

Sundqvist-Andberg, H., Tuominen, A., Auvinen, H., Tapio, P.: Sustainability and the contribution of electric scooter sharing business models to urban mobility. Built Environ. **47**(4), 541–558 (2021). https://doi.org/10.2148/benv.47.4.541

The Forum of European Road Safety Research Institutes, F.: E-scooters in Europe: legal status varies, safety effects unclear. https://fersi.org/2020/09/03/e-scooters-in-europe-legal-status-varies-safety-effects-unclear/ (2020)

Tsami, M., Giannakari, O., Panou, M., Papandreou, M.: Development of advanced, safe and sustainable micro-mobility solutions. Cham (2022)

Ventura, R., Ghirardi, A., Vetturi, D., Maternini, G., Barabino, B.: A framework for comparing the vibrational behaviour of e-kick scooters and e-bikes. Evidence from Italy. https://doi.org/10.2139/ssrn.4072708

Estimation of Pedestrian Flows in Urban Context: A Comparison Between the Pre and Post Pandemic Period

Mauro D'Apuzzo[1]([✉]) [iD], Daniela Santilli[1], Azzurra Evangelisti[1] [iD],
Vittorio Nicolosi[2] [iD], and Giuseppe Cappelli[1,3]

[1] University of Cassino and Southern Lazio, Via G. Di Biasio 43, 03043 Cassino, Italy
{dapuzzo,daniela.santilli,giuseppe.cappelli1}@unicas.it,
giuseppe.cappelli@iusspavia.it
[2] University of Rome "Tor Vergata", Via del Politecnico 1, 00133 Rome, Italy
nicolosi@uniroma2.it
[3] University School for Advanced Studies, IUSS, Piazza della Vittoria n.15, 27100 Pavia, Italy

Abstract. The Covid-19 pandemic, within a few months, radically changed the organization of daily life on a global scale; this has affected all aspects related to everyday life such as home-to-work or not home-to the work trips, accessibility of destination, recreational activities and so on.

The need to reduce coronavirus transmission, especially indoors, has imposed the "social or physical distancing" that has required administrations to reorganize roads and sidewalks for public use both to tackle this crisis and to prepare for the future pandemic challenges. Following a previous extensive study devoted to the analysis and prediction of pedestrian flows in urban area in the city of Cassino, a new experimental campaign has been recently designed and carried out in order to validate the previous methodology and/or to highlight new trends in urban pedestrian activities.

Comparison between pre-pandemic and post-pandemic data and calibrated models provided an interesting insight on the pedestrian behavioral impacts of emergency measures undertaken during pandemic. It is believed that obtained results may provide a useful knowledge for urban planners and designers to retrofit urban spaces taking into account the new pedestrian attitudes to mobility induced by the pandemic.

Keywords: Pedestrian flows prediction · Space Syntax · Hybrid model · Pre- and post-pandemic scenarios

1 Introduction

The Covid-19 pandemic can be regarded as the result of an *environmental imbalance*, generated by a disproportionate anthropogenic pressure on natural ecosystems, which has produced a virus that uses humans as a vector to spread. The strong interconnectedness of individuals, who travel from one part of the planet to another by plane, in a few hours has allowed the virus to spread rapidly on a global scale.

© The Author(s), under exclusive license to Springer Nature Switzerland AG 2022
O. Gervasi et al. (Eds.): ICCSA 2022 Workshops, LNCS 13380, pp. 484–495, 2022.
https://doi.org/10.1007/978-3-031-10542-5_33

This has generated an upheaval in people's lives by interrupting and changing their habits and passions [1].

In fact, to contain the spread of the virus, governments have been forced to impose restrictions with the consequent reduction of people's mobility (such as the blocking of flights, the temporary prohibition of intercity travel, up to total isolation in homes) and corresponding traffic volumes and public transport services. After the lockdown phase, a gradual restart has begun which required adapting the work environments and public spaces to the safety conditions required by this new risk.

Very recent observations about the impacts of the pandemic phase on habits and behaviors (conscious and unconscious) regarding the mobility, both private and public, are restituting a complex scenario: purpose, time, distance of trips and social distancing are the main affecting aspects [2, 3].

This has given rise to the problem of also modifying transport systems to ensure safe mobility for people, without losing their efficiency, since the traditional definition of such parameter for a transport system (i.e. the ability to use few vehicles to transport many people, increasing the load factor) seems to clash with the imperatives of physical distancing. In fact, it is well known that a significant amount of all trips is made during peak hours, when public transport operates near or sometimes beyond its capacity whereas it often reaches a half-empty condition during off-peak hours.

Therefore, the spatial-temporal concentration of mobility must be reduced (also exploiting technologies to mitigate queues, congestion and gatherings [4]) to avoid a sudden return to the use of the individual car (with all the consequences of congestion, climate change, degradation of urban quality of life, occupation of public spaces, road accidents, etc.).

Basing on these premises, in order to reduce the risks of contagion from Covid-19, as suggested by the World Health Organization [5], many cities are aiming at redesigning their urban spaces by promoting first and foremost pedestrian and cycling mobility (thus also yielding noticeable results in terms of mortality reduction, health, economy and society).

To this purpose the revision of mobility paradigm falls within the major issues of climate change and sustainable development, leading to a clear compliance with the Sustainability Development Goals (SDGs) defined by Agenda 2030 [6, 7], focusing above all on issues such as de-carbonization, energy independence, air quality as a measure of health resilience, promotion of local production and urban electricity logistics, integration of sustainable mobility development with the redevelopment of social spaces of urban life.

Following the urban policies undergoing in most of European countries, also in Italy, greater attention was paid to sustainable mobility in the post lockdown, leading to an increase in citizens' travel on foot and by bike (thanks also to the eco-bonus incentive policies).

The increase of dedicated spaces for pedestrians and bicycles has also led to the spread of micro-mobility. This term refers to individual transport devices (scooters, segways, monowheels and hoverboards), of small dimensions, usually with electric traction, the most representative example of which is the electric scooter.

In this particular historical period, citizens have had the opportunity to experience the benefits of walking or cycling, such as reducing the risk of many diseases and increasing psychophysical well-being.

Given the increase of vulnerable users, in order to design or to retrofit public areas such as squares or roads to accommodate the new mobility, ad hoc engineered tools are needed that allow obtaining cycle networks and sidewalks capable of guaranteeing the required physical spacing and that should be safe, usable and accessible to all [8–10].

However, since there are few and poor guidelines in Italy that can help technicians in the careful planning of these interventions, there is the need to develop engineering-based models to evaluate the impact on pedestrian or cyclist activities of new re-designed urban areas.

According to several studies pedestrian activity is indeed linked to network connectivity but at the same time is influenced by other variables such as population, land use, purpose of travel, transport supply [11–13]. Therefore, a new hybrid approach to pedestrian modelling has been proposed and experimentally calibrated in order to predict pedestrian activity on road network that is based on a combination of land use data and configurational analysis [14, 15].

However, because of the radical change in road users' behavior following the pandemic period, it has been recognized that the proposed approach needs to be compared against the new pedestrian scenarios, and therefore an additional experimental campaign has been carried out to verify the reliability of the proposed approach in capturing pedestrian flows in the post-pandemic age.

Then the obtained data have been analyzed by using the same modelling approach and a comparison between evaluation provided in the pre-Covid and post-Covid conditions has been derived in order to highlight how the propensity of vulnerable users to pedestrian mobility has changed.

The novelties of this study are first of all the comparison of pedestrian flows in pre- and post-pandemic phase, observing a reduction of pedestrians, which can be due to the general reduction of performed trips. Secondly, the proposed hybrid approach for the estimation of the pedestrian flows has been calibrated and validated also for post-pandemic scenarios, obtaining satisfactory results. Results of this study is detailed in the followings.

2   Method

In recent years numerous network analysis models have been developed to evaluate the number of users and their propensity to walk [16–18] which showed how the shape of a city affects them. In order to estimate the distribution of users on the road network, if the counting data is not available, models have been developed. These have different complexities as well as varying input requirements, making some more usable than others. Among these are the configurational models [19, 20] that show how the road and the built environment can influence the dynamics of movement of pedestrians.

This category includes the Space Syntax based approach which, through a graphic "proximity" algorithm, allows to estimate the pedestrian crowding. It is worth to be noticed that this approach is not linked to the emission, matrix or modal choice (it does not reflect a structure based on supply and demand) but addresses only to the network configuration that, in turn, may be regarded as the result of the history of urban evolution in which city centers are made up of densely meshed road networks and therefore are very connected.

Among the various indicators that allow to describe the configurational consistency of the elements, the one that according to the literature [21–27] is better related to the pedestrian activity is integration (Int). This parameter represents the minimum number of sections of a network graph necessary to reach one point from another.

Starting the simulations with the Space Syntax it was noticed that the configurational approach provided a poor estimate of the pedestrian activity since the data on population and land use that characterize an urban network are not considered. Therefore, a hybrid approach was developed and presented that considered both the population combined with specific land use parameter related to commercial activities present in the examined area.

A preliminary reconstruction of the entire road and pedestrian network within a GIS approach was undertaken and the spatial relationship of contiguity between the census sections (taken from ISTAT [28]) and the road sections composing the road network was obtained.

To each census section, represented by a centroid, the average value of the resident population was evaluated with the proximity approach by making use of a sequence of buffers with increasing radius (J^{th}), varying between 100 and 1600 m, chosen on the basis of an impedance function (blue line in Fig. 1 [29]) in order to represents the propensity to walk as a function of the distance to be traveled. This function has been developed on the regional household travel survey in the US context.

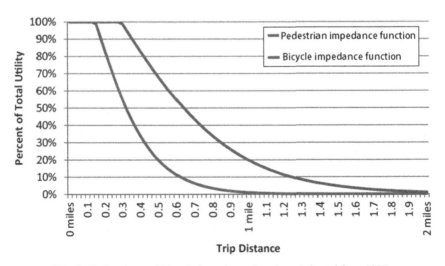

Fig. 1. Pedestrian and bicycle impedance functions (adapted from [29]).

To obtain a single Pprox weight (proximity weight) (Eq. 1) for each centroid, it is necessary to add the products of the mean population M of each annulus for the impedance function.

$$P_{prox,i} = \sum_{j=100m}^{1600m} k_{Mj}M_{ij} \tag{1}$$

By inserting these weights prior to the Space Syntax simulation, it has been highlighted that not even the population alone is able to represent the pedestrian activity of the area which indeed appears to be much more affected by purposes related to commuting. Then a correct hybrid approach was developed with an additional factor K that also took into account the impact of retail activities and other structures and attractors [15].

Once the results from the hybrid configurational analysis performed by means of Space Syntax has been obtained, it is necessary to compare these data with the on-site pedestrian counts to evaluate effectiveness of the model. Therefore, surveys were carried out on the network to estimate pedestrian crowding. The literature shows that numerous techniques have been developed over the years for the direct measurement of vulnerable users.

These are sometimes different from those consolidated for the survey of motorized traffic; this because it must be taken into account that non-motorized traffic is characterized by a greater sensitivity to environmental conditions (precipitation, temperature, darkness, etc.) and does not follow regular patterns that are not being confined to fixed lanes (vulnerable users can travel off designated footbridges and cycle paths, take unsigned shortcuts or stop unexpectedly).

According to the Federal Highway Administration [18] the most used techniques for identifying pedestrian flows can be grouped into two macro-types: manual and automatic detection. The first consists of the acquisition of data based on the direct survey of an operator for a short period of time; for this reason, the automatic survey has been developed which allows to collect data with continuity, high precision and for long periods of time. However, when there is a significant time constraint together with reduced economic resources, one can think of adopting the technique of the *mobile observer*.

According to this technique, the survey is carried out by a monitoring vehicle, equipped with video recording devices, which moves along the route to be examined. This technique has the advantage of being able to acquire data over an entire network, albeit for a shorter period of time. This makes the data unstable at a statistical level therefore it is necessary to repeat the survey several times in order to stabilize it.

Fig. 2. Location of Cassino in Italy.

3   Case Study

The experimental calibration of the model was carried out in the city of Cassino (Fig. 2). An average Italian city falling within Southern Lazio characterized by easy accessibility, by the presence of transport infrastructures (railway station, bus services, bike sharing service, etc.) and by the pedestrian-friendly peculiar features (mainly flat territory, etc.) other than by the presence of several relevant attractors such as schools, universities, restaurants, shops and public activities.

To obtain the pedestrian counts, video recordings were made after defining the position of the devices on the car and the routes to be follow, considering both the weekday and pre-holiday scenarios (Fig. 3 and Fig. 4).

Fig. 3. Post-covid weekday path. (Source plugin base-map: Open Street Map, [30]).

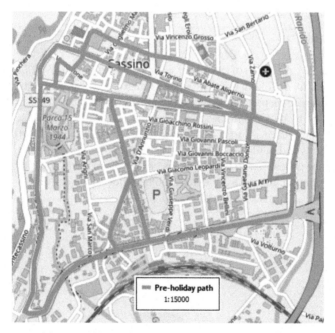

Fig. 4. Post-covid pre-holiday path. (Source plugin base-map: Open Street Map, [30]).

Following the post-processing of the acquired video footages (Fig. 5), the geo-referenced pedestrian counting data useful for the final comparison were obtained.

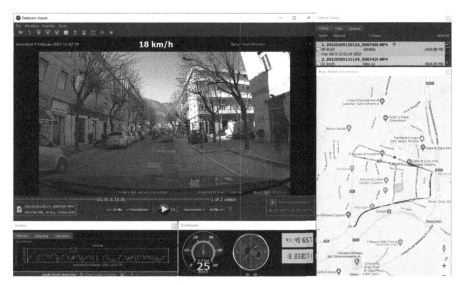

Fig. 5. Screen of the software for the analysis of the routes.

Comparing only the data of the pedestrian counts of the pre-pandemic phase (collected within 2018 and 2019 years) with post-Covid ones (collected in the end of 2021 and in early 2022) a significant reduction in walking was highlighted for most of the investigated road sections (see Fig. 6).

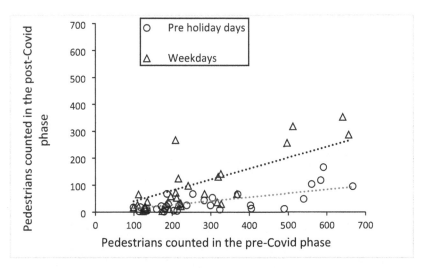

Fig. 6. Comparison of pre and post Covid pedestrian counts.

To apply the correct hybrid model, calibrated in the pre-pandemic conditions Fig. 7, the appropriate revisions were made to take into account the variations due to the restrictions that characterized the period following the lockdown or the possible closure or movement of commercial activities in the study area Fig. 8.

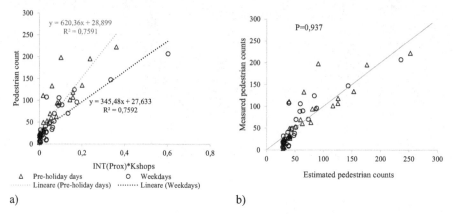

a)   b)

Fig. 7. *Pre Covid* a) calibration of pedestrian count predictive model and b) corresponding Pearson statistics between measured and predicted pedestrian flows.

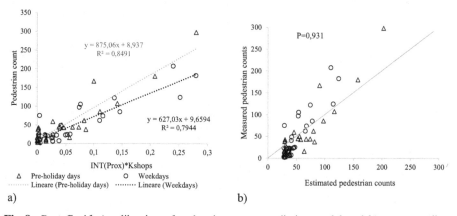

a)   b)

Fig. 8. *Post Covid* a) calibration of pedestrian count predictive model and b) corresponding Pearson statistics between measured and predicted pedestrian flows.

It can be easily observed that the hybrid approach, both in the pre- and post-pandemic scenario, presents fairly good correlations; in fact, a Pearson correlation coefficient (P) of 0.93 (see Fig. 7 and Fig. 8) can be derived for both scenarios.

This shows that pedestrian flows are affected not only by the configuration of the network but also by the presence of particular attractors (mainly retail activities), among the several land use parameters other than population distribution (embedded in the aforementioned proximity weight). Therefore, the quantitative variables used are well correlated and the model is statistically significant.

By comparing the pre- and post-Covid conditions, both in the holiday and weekday scenarios, it can be easily seen that the approach based on a linear regression model shows similar significant agreement (correlation) with the measured data thus provided the evidence for the reliability of the proposed modelling approach.

Furthermore, as far as the linear model is concerned, it is worth to be highlighted that:

- the constant term seems to have decreased, both for the weekdays and pre-holidays days, demonstrating the reduction of "basic level" movements of pedestrian activity in the post-pandemic scenario;
- the slope of the model seems to be higher for data collected in the post-pandemic period compared with those pertaining the pre-Covid period, perhaps due to the increased preference of pedestrian to choose commercial activities located closer to their residential areas.

4   Conclusion

The pandemic emergency and the need to reduce pollution levels to improve the life of the population has seen the problem of sustainability increasingly affirm itself. Among the objectives to be achieved in order to have greener cities, one is that of promoting sustainable mobility such as the *active* or *soft* one (namely walking and cycling), thus favoring traditional transport modes with zero emissions.

With this in mind, it is necessary to design or retrofit urban infrastructures to make them safe, inclusive and comfortable for new active users. Given the ever-increasing need to design routes dedicated to vulnerable users in an urban environment, an innovative method to assess pedestrian activity has been proposed.

An exposure forecasting methodology was developed that would allow planners to take a more proactive role in pedestrian area design and in risk assessment with vehicular traffic. Although pedestrian activity and trips are characterized by high levels of uncertainty compared to those pertaining the vehicular traffic, in the past, a configurational analysis was effectively used to estimate these flows, provided that pedestrian counts were made available on a daily basis.

However, data collection using these traditional approaches can be complex and time-consuming and therefore an innovative moving observer-based survey technique was suggested. In order to gain stable pedestrian crowding data and to improve calibration of the prediction model it has been necessary to replicate pedestrian counts by moving observer approach for several working and pre-holiday days. Pedestrian counts collected in such way on several road sections has been compared with those obtained from results provided by simulations via a configurational analysis enriched with the impedance function and the presence of commercial activities that characterize the area.

A recent additional survey on pedestrian flow has provided the evidence that the proposed modelling approach is indeed still effective in capturing pedestrian activities and that a dramatic drop in walking has occurred together with a higher propensity to reach closer retail activities compared with pre-Covid scenarios.

It is believed that this methodology that requires the combined use of CENSUS data, GIS tools and of Space Syntax software, can be a valid support for administrators to assess the risks deriving from the pandemic as well as the exposure to the road safety risk of pedestrian flows. In fact, once that the levels of pedestrian crowding are assessed, mitigation actions can be chosen such as accessibility limitations or restrictions for specific road user categories, in case of critical crowd-generating events or simply to limit collisions probability between pedestrians and vehicular traffic in urban areas. Following analysis are needed to evaluate the results of the methodology on other Italian or foreign context.

Acknowledgments. The help of Eng. Biagio Mancino in collecting pedestrian data within the post-pandemic period is gratefully acknowledged.

References

1. UNICEF: Generation COVID: Respond. Recover. Reimagine (2019). https://unicef.decima lstudios.com/stories/italy. Accessed Dec 2021
2. Borkowski, P., Jażdżewska-Gutta, M., Szmelter-Jarosz, A.: Lockdowned: everyday mobility changes in response to COVID-19. J. Transp. Geogr. **90**, 102906 (2021)
3. Campisi, T., Basbas, S., Tanbay, N.A., Georgiadis, G.: Some considerations on the key factors determining the reduction of public transport demand in Sicily during COVID-19 pandemic. Int. J. Transp. Dev. Integr. **6**(1), 81–94 (2022)
4. D'Apuzzo, M., Santilli, D., Evangelisti, A., Nicolosi, V.: Some remarks on soft mobility: a new engineered approach to the cycling infrastructure design. In: Gervasi, O., et al. (eds.) ICCSA 2021, Part X. LNCS, vol. 12958, pp. 441–456. Springer, Cham (2021). https://doi. org/10.1007/978-3-030-87016-4_33. ISBN 978-3-030-87015-7
5. WHO: Moving around during the COVID-19 outbreak (2019). https://www.euro.who.int/ en/health-topics/health-emergencies/coronavirus-covid-19/publications-and-technical-gui dance/environment-and-food-safety. Accessed Mar 2022
6. United Nations: The 17 Goals (2015). https://sdgs.un.org/goals. Accessed Mar 2022
7. Alleanza Italiana per lo Sviluppo Sostenibile (ASviS): L'Agenda 2030 dell'Onu per lo sviluppo sostenibile (2015). https://asvis.it/l-agenda-2030-dell-onu-per-lo-sviluppo-sosten ibile/. Accessed Mar 2022
8. Ewing, R., Cervero, R.: Travel and the built environment. J. Am. Plan. Assoc. **76**, 265–294 (2010)
9. Lee, C., Moudon, A.V.: The 3Ds + R: quantifying land use and urban form correlates of walking. Transp. Res. Part D Transp. Environ. **11**, 204–215 (2006)
10. Song, Y., Knaap, G.J.: Measuring urban form: is Portland winning the war on sprawl? J. Am. Plan. Assoc. **70**, 210–225 (2004)
11. Cervero, R., Radisch, C.: Travel choices in pedestrian versus automobile oriented neighbor-hoods. Working Paper 644, University of California at Berkeley, Berkeley, CA (1995)
12. Landis, B., Ottenberg, R., Vattikuti, V.: The roadside pedestrian environment: toward a com-prehensive level of service. Paper 990570, TRB, National Research Council, Washington, D.C. (1999)
13. Kitamura, R., Mokhtarian, P.A., Laidet, L.: A micro-analysis of land use and travel in five neighborhoods in the San Francisco Bay Area. Transportation **24**, 125–158 (1997)
14. D'Apuzzo, M., Santilli, D., Evangelisti, A., Pelagalli, V., Montanaro, O., Nicolosi, V.: An exploratory step to evaluate the pedestrian flow in urban environment. In: Gervasi, O., et al. (eds.) ICCSA 2020, Part VII. LNCS, vol. 12255, pp. 645–657. Springer, Cham (2020). https://doi.org/10.1007/978-3-030-58820-5_47. ISBN 978-3-030-58819-9. https:// link.springer.com/chap-ter/10.1007/978-3-030-58820-5_47

15. Santilli, D., D'Apuzzo, M., Evangelisti, A., Nicolosi, V.: Towards sustainability: new tools for planning urban pedestrian mobility. Sustainability **13**, 9371 (2021). https://doi.org/10.3390/su13169371
16. Raford, N., Ragland, D.: Pedestrian volume modeling for traffic safety and exposure analysis. University of California Traffic Safety Center White Paper, Berkeley, CA, USA (2005)
17. Desyllas, J., Duxbury, E., Ward, J., Smith, A.: Pedestrian demand modeling of large cities: an applied example from London. The Center for Advanced Spatial Analysis, Sendai, Japan (2003)
18. Federal Highway Administration: Guidebook on methods to estimate non-motorized travel: overview of methods. Publication No. FHWA-RD-98-165, United States Department of Transportation: McLean, VI, USA (1999)
19. McNally, M.: The four-step model. In: Hensher, D.A., Button, K.J. (eds.) Handbook of Transport Modeling. Pergamon, New York (2000)
20. Olson, J., Spring, D.: Sketch-plan method for estimating pedestrian traffic for central business districts and suburban growth corridors. Transp. Res. Rec. **1578**, 38–47 (1997)
21. Hillier, B., Penn, A., Hanson, J., Grajewski, T., Xu, J.: Natural movement: or, configuration and attraction in urban pedestrian movement. Environ. Plan. B Plan. Des. **20**(1), 29–66 (1993)
22. Dai, X., Yu, W.: Configurational exploration of pedestrian and cyclist movements: a case study of Hangzhou, China. ITU A|Z, pp. 119–129 (2014)
23. Jiang, B., Claramunt, C.: Integration of space syntax into GIS: new perspectives for urban morphology. Trans. GIS **6**(3), 295–309 (2002)
24. Ostwald Michael, J.: The mathematics of spatial configuration: revisiting, revising and critiquing justified plan graph theory. Nexus Netw. J. **13**(2), 445–470 (2011)
25. Xu, Y., Rollo, J., Jones, D.S., Esteban, Y., Tong, H., Mu, Q.: Towards sustainable heritage tourism: a space syntax-based analysis method to improve tourists' spatial cognition in chinese historic districts. Buildings **10**(2), 29 (2020)
26. Volchenkov, D., Blanchard, P.: Scaling and universality in city space syntax: between Zipf and Matthew. Phys. A Stat. Mech. Appl. **387**(10), 2353–2364 (2008)
27. Al_Sayed, K.: Space syntax methodology. Bartlett School of Architecture, UCL, London, UK (2018). Proceedings of the Ninth International Space Syntax Symposium, Seoul, Korea, 31 October–3 November 2013
28. ISTAT: Territorial Bases and Census Variables. https://www.istat.it/it/archivio/104317. Accessed Mar 2022
29. Kuzmyak, J.R., Walters, J., Bradley, M., Kockelman, K.M.: Estimating bicycling and walking for planning and project development: a guidebook (No. Project 08-78) (2014)
30. QGIS.org: QGIS Geographic Information System. QGIS Association (2022). http://www.qgis.org

An Analysis of the Integration of DRT Services with Local Public Transport in Post-pandemic Period: Some of the Preliminary Insights in the Italian Context

Tiziana Campisi[1]($\boxtimes$) , Antonino Canale[1] , Giovanni Tesoriere[1] , Nazam Ali[2] ,
Matteo Ignaccolo[3] , and Elena Cocuzza[3]($\boxtimes$)

[1] Faculty of Engineering and Architecture, University of Enna Kore, 94100 Enna, Italy
tiziana.campisi@unikore.it
[2] University of Management and Technology, C-II, Johar Town, Lahore, Pakistan
[3] Department of Civil Engineering and Architecture, University of Catania, Cittadella
Universitaria, 95125 Catania, Italy
ecocuzza@dica.unict.it

Abstract. Italy was one of the first country in Europe which was severely affected by COVID-19 pandemic. Several critical issues emerged during the different pandemic phases, especially in the health and mobility sector. Restrictions on public transport reduced the supply of transport, highlighting the need to rethink complementary transport systems. Since May 2020, in the post-lockdown phase, the provision of local public transport has been based on ordinary services, such as bus services, which are mainly intended to meet the needs of systematic travel between the places of residence and work on main development routes of the territory. These services have undergone reductions both in the on-board capacity and in some cases the complete elimination of transit routes. The rebalancing in favour of sustainable modes of transport and the reduction of the share of road mobility is pursued through the encouragement of ad-hoc measures aimed at balancing-off the supply-demand mechanism and improving the quality of services. The application of an on-demand responsive transit system has the ability to improve the transit needs in order to reach the places where personal or family services are provided or to enjoy the resources distributed within desired territory. In Italy since March 2020, new areas of weak demand for transport have been created, i.e. areas with a certain number of users that need to be transferred to and from places that have generally never had access to public transport or have had it restricted. The Demand Responsive Transport (DRT) system is, therefore, used in both urban and suburban areas, allowing even those who do not have their own means of transport (for example, disadvantaged social categories or users with a short stay in the area) or who are suitably equipped (people with reduced or no motor skills), to move around in areas easily. The present work focuses on an analysis of the current state of affairs, starting from the literature and regulations concerning the diffusion of the DRT systems in Italy, and offers some ideas for the optimisation of an integrated public transport service.

Keywords: DRT · Post pandemic mobility · Local public transport integration · Italy

© The Author(s), under exclusive license to Springer Nature Switzerland AG 2022
O. Gervasi et al. (Eds.): ICCSA 2022 Workshops, LNCS 13380, pp. 496–508, 2022.
https://doi.org/10.1007/978-3-031-10542-5_34

1   Introduction

The passenger transport and mobility sector has undergone a major transformation in the last decade. This has been caused not only by technological developments that have improved or created new services and enhanced infrastructures, but also by different trends in transport demand, i.e. different modal choices (e.g. due to changes in travel frequencies) [1, 2].

The recent pandemic and even more so the recent energy crisis has highlighted a change in travel choices. Among the mobility services that could be included as complementary to collective public transport are DRT systems [3, 4]. They can be applied through fleets of minibuses with combustion engines but recently some studies are linked to the introduction of hybrid or electric vehicles [5].

Many peri-urban areas are sparsely populated and it is widespread in Italy and in different European contexts. They often have no public transport service. People living in such areas are therefore obliged to use their own cars in order to get around [6]. Demand-responsive transport is an optimal transport service in these areas, allowing people to connect more easily to existing transport nodes, thus promoting multimodality.

Vitality and urbanity are some of the key objectives of the strategies for urban development and sustainable mobility.

These characteristics emerge from the diversity of activities in urban public spaces and have an impact on people's sense of place. They influence the propensity and frequency of travel [7, 8].

DRT complements traditional public transport services in smaller cities with low population density or in areas characterized by population dispersion (mountainous areas, rural locations, etc.) or areas not served by traditional public transport services.

It aims to offer an high quality service, closer to the needs of users, thanks to customization, comfort and a journey time of no more than 30 min.

This service can also be carried out with small vehicles, offering dedicated services and equipment for the transport of disabled people [9–11].

Several case studies indicate the willingness of both car users and those who regularly use the bus mode to use DRT services at a higher rate than current bus fares [12, 13].

Among the countries where this service has become more widespread is the UK, especially in rural areas. Drawing on the experience of a number of UK schemes, research conducted by [14] assessed the reasons for the renewed success of DRT linked to the spread of telematics systems and exemplified a number of factors including service characteristics (particularly route flexibility, flexibility of booking method and advance booking scheme), emerging markets and the overall contribution of DRT to increasing social inclusion and intermodality.

It should be considered that in recent years there has been a new potential market for DRT in workplaces outside urban areas.

Innovative solutions could be linked to the combination of freight and passenger transport systems in rural areas. In some countries the postal service operator is also a major bus operator (UK for example). Minibuses driven by volunteers are also emerging as a solution for rural areas but are not necessarily comprehensive in their coverage (popular in Japan). Although several DRT services have failed, it is not easy to identify bad practices in the development and planning of DRT services.

The main failure factors found in the literature are related to the fact that many DRT pilot projects developed and tested in past years throughout Europe were closely linked to and dependent on national, regional or EU funds. Therefore, the main reason for the discontinuation of activities is linked to the lack of public funds.

Furthermore, the service management schemes were unbalanced between private and public DRT operators.

The role of the public authority is to find the right balance between these two transport operators in order to avoid conflicts and integrate all the different mobility offers in the best possible way. Instead, the success of DRT is based on the coexistence of technological and service evolution [15, 16].

Therefore, it is possible to define three main pillars related to technological development as defined in Fig. 1

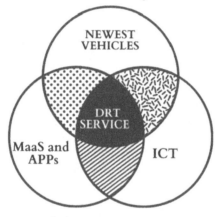

On-board vehicle units capable of accurately and precisely monitoring the position of each individual vehicle involved in the DRT solution development

End-user information tools that can reliably and easily provide relevant information to end-users and enable an easy-to-book service

Fleet management through the use of ICT technologies for more efficient planning and better routing of the different vehicles involved in DRT

Fig. 1. Technology and DRT correlations

Several research have investigated the evolution of the main technologies that can be used in DRT, including those with fixed routes (Flexible-Route Segments, Request Stops) and those without fixed routes (Demand-Responsive Connector, Feeder Service, Zone Route, Point Deviation) [17–19]. The literature review shows that despite extensive international experience in implementing DRT in practice, there are no clear criteria for determining the conditions under which it is reasonable to introduce a particular flexible passenger service technology [20]. In the following paragraphs, the literature related to DRT diffusion is presented, followed by an introduction to the European projects that have promoted DRT diffusion since 2010, and finally, attention is drawn to the Italian context, highlighting the benefits and criticalities of the current services diffused in the Italian context.

In particular the objective of this research work is related to the evaluation of the current state of the DRT service in Italy and the possibility of integrating this service as a complement to local public transport.

The research evaluated the European projects relating to the development of DRT services, subsequently focusing attention on the Italian national case.

The research is a first cognitive step of the state of affairs and of the project in Europe that provides ideas for the implementation and strengthening of these services for areas with low demand, i.e. peripheral or rural areas or even those areas in which, due to the pandemic, public transport services have been reduced or limited.

The first results of this research lay the foundations for the improvement of an integrated public transport service.

2 Literature Review

The idea of demand responsive transport (DRT) has developed since the 1970s [21]. Initially it was a call transport dedicated to specific user groups or specific areas. Among the first experiences there are replacement of regular services by shared taxis, application of "dial-a-ride systems based on telephone calls to report demand to local public transport providers" [22].

Other experiences have focused on on-call services for people with reduced mobility, "often community-based and provided by volunteers" [23]. However, the concept of demand responsive transport was formulated in the USA at the beginning of the 90s of the last century, as a solution to the rising disaffection of potential users, in particular during the night [24]. In fact, starting from the 1990s, the gradual introduction of increasingly efficient information and telecommunication technologies began, thanks to which services take on a greater level of automation and efficiency, which allows the optimization of routes and offer solutions that displaces between bus stops. The "stop-to-stop" modality spreads in opposition "of the "door-to-door": instead of picking-up and dropping users at the "doors of their houses" [25]. The DRT becomes an opportunity to offer public transport in areas with low demand and for special purpose services [26].

Thus, the implementation of innovative solutions has definitely changed the traditional concept of public transport. Several EU projects on DRT services in rural and peripheral areas and EU projects pilots have been carried out. Numerous and different solutions have been tested in Europe between 2012 and 2018, some of which, however, have already been completed as short-term pilot projects. Between these, the Kutsuplus, a service launched in 2012 in Helsinki and made operative from 2013 to 2015: a real-time demand responsive public service that uses shared 9-seater minibus, which uses a website and an app that can be used with normal smartphones. Various stops have been identified in the area identified and covered by the service, it is an on-demand micro-transit pilot [27]. Another pilot project was tested as part of the European project System for Advanced Management of Public transport Operations, SAMPO, financed within the 4th EC Program.

The objective is to improve the mobility of citizens, especially disabled and elderly people, in different rural and urban areas through integrated transport services responsive to demand. Pilot projects have been launched in several sites: urban, Florence and Campi Bisenzio (Italy) and Goteborg (Sweden); rural and peripherical area of Seinajoki and TuusulaKerva-Jarvenpaa (Finland) and the Kilkenny region (Ireland); rural, Hasselt (Belgium).

Several innovative systems are now well established in Europe. In several cities are launched bus DRT lines, that provides services for the urban and surrounding areas, both during the day and at night. The ViaVan, an on-demand transit system that takes multiple passengers heading in the same direction and books them into a shared vehicle, initially experienced in London, then in Amsterdam and Berlin, today spread around the world in more than 20 countries.

The on demand collective transport services have also spread to Italy. In 1991 a call system service was activated in Venice on a night-time line for the "Vignole" stop. The first experiments are "dial-a-ride" services booked by telephone dedicated to general users or specific user groups, like elderly or with reduced mobility people, tourists. Numerous services were launched in cities of various sizes and in different context, urban and peripheral areas and in areas with low demand, both as complementary and connection services with traditional transport services. Some services operate in extra-urban areas and offer interurban movements and connections between different cities in the same provincial region.

Other services allow to reach the interchange stops with public and rail transport. The most common are flexible transport service that use bus and mini-buses, with a schedule and a predefined route. Subsequently, thanks to technological innovations, DRT services were developed which include systems and software products for the planning and management of the service and GPS satellite systems for the location of vehicles or GIS information systems for the management of territorial information.

3 The Diffusion and Development of the European DRT Service

This paragraph illustrates the development of European projects related to the implementation and/or enhancement of DRT services in Europe in the last twenty years. After a brief analysis of the recently concluded or still active projects, attention was paid to the development of DRT services in Italy, paying particular attention to the post-pandemic period.

3.1 The Evolution of European and National Projects for DRT Deployment

Several European projects have been financed in recent years concerning the analysis of last-mile and collective and DRT mobility. Figure 2 shows the main projects and their aims.

Among the EU projects that have promoted the dissemination of DRT through the creation or promotion of certain services and the definition of test pilots, it is possible to mention the Regio-Mob project (https://projects2014-2020.interregeurope.eu/regio-mob/), which ran from 1 April 2016 to 31 March 2020.

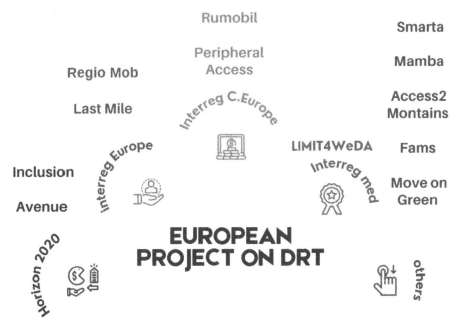

Fig. 2. European project of last 2 decades on sustainable mobility and DRT services

This project envisaged the promotion of an on-demand transport service for people with disabilities in the Ljubljana Urban Region, as well as the implementation of a Tele-bus service in the city of Krakow. The project also promoted the deployment of real-time bus passenger information systems in Edinburgh, Scotland and the application of test pilots for the analysis of light mobility for areas of weak demand (Lazio Region, Italy). In the same time frame and in particular from April 1, 2016 to September 30, 2020, the Interreg Europe project entitled LASTMILE (https://projects2014-2020.interr egeurope.eu/lastmile/) on last mile mobility took place. It focused on the implementation and study of a train service with on-demand stops from Lleida to la Pobla (High Pyrenees) (Regional Government of Catalonia) and a Nightrider, a door-to-door night bus service on demand (Luxembourg). In September 2020, the Horizon 2020 project entitled INCLUSION (http://h2020-inclusion.eu/news-and-events/final-conference/) was completed, and participatory processes were disseminated for the definition of a new DRT service in rural areas of Florence, Italy, while DRT services were tested supporting public events in Barcelona and DRT services for families with young children in the Rhein-Sieg region of Germany.

During the period May 2011–April 2014 for 36 months the Access2Montain project defined in South East Europe (http://www.access2mountain.eu/en/project/default.html) focused on the integration of different flexible transport services in Alpine areas, Alpen region Gesäuse National Park in Austria. Previously, the MOVE on GRENN-Interreg IVC project (https://keep.eu/projects/5429/MOVE-ON-GREEN-EN/) which ran from 2012 to 2014 enabled the implementation of the DRT Virtual Transport Centre in Burgos Province (Spain) and the integration of RC and taxi services. This project allowed to test a dedicated service for school children in Southern Burgenland, Austria and a DRT service in low density areas in the Regional Unit of Ioannina, Greece. On 1 May 2018, a 4-year project entitled AVENUE- H2020 (https://h2020-avenue.eu/summery/) started, which allowed to define a real-time monitoring system for DRT buses, Lyon; test an autonomous shuttle system, Luxembourg; extend an existing DRT service in Geneva and analyse DRT in Copenhagen. Even earlier, the MAMBA- Interreg Baltic Sea project (https://www.mambaproject.eu/), which ran from 2014 to 2020, allowed the study of rural route sharing and on-demand transport in the Bielsko-Biała area in Poland as well as the analysis of on-demand transport in Plön County, Germany, and also in Lithuania and Latvia. From March 2002 to 29 February 2004, the FAMS project (FP5-IST) was carried out, in which the Flexible Agency for Collective Demand Responsive Mobility Services in the Florence Metropolitan Area, Italy, and the Flexible Agency for Collective Demand Responsive Mobility Services in the Angus Region, UK, collaborated.

Particular attention was given to the project entitled DRT bad practice which focuses on the Innisfil city experiment where public transport was replaced by Uber [25]. From 2004 to 2007 the TWIST (Transport WIth a Social Target) project was carried out on a national and transnational scale (http://www.twistproject.org/EN/aspbite/categories/index.asp?tim=18:17:09). Through the partnership of the areas involved, the project envisaged the creation of an on-call transport system aimed at reducing the social and economic gap between mountain and rural areas and urban areas.

The regions that participated in the TWIST transnational project were respectively.

- Germany (city of Berlin and Brandenburg)
- Greece (Province of Ioannina)
- Italy (some cities in the regions of Abruzzo, Marche, Molise and Puglia)
- Czech Republic (the Ceske Budejovice region)
- Hungary (the PECS region)

The aforementioned areas were/are all characterized by a lack of services and infrastructures in mountain and rural areas. Starting from the analysis of the demand and supply of local public transport in the territories identified for the pilot projects, the TWIST project conducted local experiments of on-demand transport in order to develop a model for the organization and evaluation of transport to call transferable to all regions with similar characteristics of internal area and presence of weak demand. Finally, the PRIN2017 project entitled WEAKI TRANSIT is underway.

This project sees the creation of test pilots in some cities of Sicily and Sardinia and focuses on innovative shared mobility systems for areas with low demand. The goal is to study the feasibility, planning and design of demand responsive shared transport services (DRSTS), capable of providing "on demand" mobility in real time through fleets of vehicles shared by different passengers.

The project will adopt a holistic approach, studying the demand (i.e., passengers), supply (i.e., infrastructures, vehicles and technologies) and all external factors that can hinder or favour the diffusion of DRSTS, such as the regulatory framework and related constraints, and using advanced simulation tools to support the design of the service (https://sites.unica.it/weaki-transit/home/).

3.2 The Evolution of DRT in Italy

Launched in Italy in the late 1990s, on-call public transport services (in English: Demand Responsive Transport, DRT) consist of using a fleet of small public transport to allow for personalized transfers based on to the requests of the users with origin and destination chosen each time, managing the concatenation of the paths with a certain level of flexibility to be able to satisfy all requests.

The system has undoubted advantages, first of all the flexibility of timetables according to the movements, among which a not secondary aspect is represented by the rationalization of the transport lines, with the consequent reduction of trips. The benefits and criticalities of the services active in the Italian territory are briefly described below with reference to the characteristics of the services analysed up to December 2021.

The distribution of the service in the analysed context is described in Fig. 3

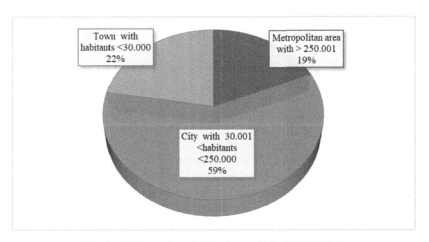

Fig. 3. DRT services distribution on Italy (2019–2021)

The regions that have benefited from pilot projects linked to national and international research projects are mainly: Abruzzo, Marche, Molise and Puglia through the TWIST project (https://www.interregeurope.eu/good-practices/the-drt-system-of-twist-transport-with-a-social-target) and Sicily and Sardinia through the WEAKI-TRANSIT project (https://www.unict.it/it/ricerca/progetti/weaki-transit). In Tuscany, on the other hand, it took place through the cooperation of the local administration with the transport service operators through the international project SAMPO (System for Advanced Monitoring of Public Transport Operations) (https://algowatt.com/en/portfolio-items/sampo/). As regards the services promoted by local administrations in synergy with the service managers, it is possible to compare three different situations corresponding respectively to a small city, a medium-large city and a metropolis, the benefits and criticalities produced are described below. To date from the DRT service. As regards the small city, the centre of Vimercate was analysed, which is located in Lombardy and is characterized by a population of about 26.200 inhabitants. Considering this context, the implementation of a DRT service took place in an experimental way from 9 to 17 from

February 2020 to July 2020 with a minivan and activation of a permanent service from September 2020 with two minivans. On 2021 a frequency of about 260 was reached/300 passengers a week, but the important fact is that they are all new users of the public service who previously had no alternative to the private vehicle. Service defined by users as fast, useful and efficient. The main benefits were:

- reduction in the use of private vehicles
- complementary service to public transport
- optimal function of the service
- simple control of stops and waiting
- simple travel reservation via the free app

Among the critical issues instead

- service not accessible to a woman with wheelchair/disabled
- bus forbidden to children (children up to 4 years in the lap of an adult instead of from 4 to 12 not access)
- it cannot be booked outside Vimercate area
- means easily recognizable by logo

As far as the medium-sized city is concerned, the city of Spoleto in Umbria has been selected, which has about 37 thousand inhabitants and is located in the center of Italy and the Call Bus service guarantees, from Monday to Saturday, for eight hours a day, possibility for the elderly over 65, for civil invalids, for the disabled with a companion and for people with reduced autonomy, an additional transport service (cemetery, pharmacy, relatives, visits, etc.). Each user has only one trip per week (round trip) to the municipalities of Spoleto, Giano, Castel Ritaldi and Campello. Among the benefits that emerged and noted by users it is possible to include:

- reduction in the use of private vehicles
- service for weak users
- booking through SUIC (citizen counter)
- partially free service

Among the critical issues instead

- service limited to certain segments of the population
- limited to 1 trip per week

Milan was selected as the metropolitan city in Northern Europe with over 1 million and 390 thousand inhabitants. The service called "Neighborhood Radiobus" has been active in the metropolis for some years, the public transport on call active every day from 10 pm to 2 am and which accompanies the user to the door of his home, at the cost of an urban ticket. (or subscription).

Starting from 4 March 2020, the "Neighborhood Radiobus" can also be booked through the ATM Milano app, which already has an average of 50,000 users per day in addition to the toll-free number. To use the service, all you need to do is have the ticket or pass that is regularly used on all ATM vehicles, or you can purchase the ticket from the app or on board at no extra charge. Two lines (Q55 and Q76) will also be activated in the coming months. In total, 15 districts of the city will be able to take advantage of this on-call service.

Among the benefits found among users, it is necessary to point out:

- reduction in the use of private vehicles
- public transport service increasingly easy to use, widespread and interconnected. In addition, the routes of some already existing Radiobus lines in the Neighborhood change with more stops and more rides.
- 15 evening and night lines for 15 different areas of Milan, increasing the offer of public transport and better connecting the individual districts within them and with the public transport network, in line with the expansion plan of the Municipality of Milan.
- booking via phone and/or Booking with customizable App ("Favorites" function will allow users to save their favourite stops, view them directly on the home page and then quickly start a booking). Using the App will allow you to reserve the Neighborhood Radiobus up to two days before the chosen date, or in real time.

Southern Italy is lacking in services with experiences limited to the test pilots of some research projects spread from 2018 to today.

4 Discussion and Conclusions

The analysis of national case studies and transnational projects allows us to highlight that in recent years there has been a growing sensation according to which conventional public transport is inflexible and unreliable as well as a vehicle for contagion. Furthermore, the growing urban expansion has meant that in some cases conventional public transport has become impracticable.

Public authorities show a growing interest in on-demand transport as a means to address the inclusion of some specific target groups, but also to achieve modal shift.

Furthermore, DRT services contribute significantly to decongest the roads, allowing travellers to easily and simply reach the main fixed lines of public transport.

Through the multimodal approach to transport, on-call transport also affects the quality of the road network and all that derives from it (accidents, parking problems, delays due to traffic jams, etc. Furthermore, from the analysis of literature and of European and national projects it is possible to underline that:

- the DRT service is an excellent complementary solution to the public transport service even in the post-pandemic phase;
- the creation of digital platforms can contribute to the improvement of modal choices and the use of the DRT;

Among the critical issues that emerged the most it should be emphasized that:
- shared transport services with highly variable travel times may become unsuitable for serving as a connecting service to public transport centres in urban areas
- There is also a certain difficulty in modelling and optimizing the routing processes of these services.

Some of these complexities arise from the difficulty of predicting behavioural responses to delayed services or customer no-shows.

The on-call services in some cases behave like a taxi service at public transport prices. As a result, they can be perceived as unfair competitors from traditional taxi services. Despite the gradual extension of the scope of services in some countries, the idea has spread that it is only for the mobility of disabled people.

This hampers the inclusion of on-demand transport in the standard public transport offer. Very few EU projects and pilot projects concern the use of on-demand services for tourism. The dial-up system is usually not included in transportation planning applications. When on-call service is provided by public transport companies that are used to serving captive markets, there is usually not enough marketing experience to attract new customers. Online bookings could make on-call transport more convenient for the general public, but not for the "socially motivated" on-call service target audience (such as elderly people or people with mobility problems);

Some niches (such as airport shuttles) have already proven to be commercially viable. In Europe, there is the potential to use on-call transport in orbital journeys in suburban and peri-urban areas, while "traditional" public transport is used for radial journeys. The on-call system could expand into the delivery of goods (e.g., library books, prescriptions and postal/parcel) as an additional source of income.

The data obtained from the analysis of the national context show a greater diffusion of the service in the city compared to the contexts of small rural centres or villages or even subways.

This layout will probably be changed in the coming months following the recent pandemic and the need to reduce pivotal transport in areas that are not characterized by adequate public transport.

The literature review also suggests paying greater attention not only to passenger transport but to combined passenger / freight transport in order to integrate the two systems and at the same time enhance the trade of small local companies.

There may also be untapped potential untapped potential for transportation in the "night economy". Finally, the most important component of variable costs is the driver's wage costs (at least in programs that are not volunteer based). Probably with autonomous mobility, this problem could vanish and this will increase the potential of on-demand transport as a mode for high-capacity public transport.

The implementation of the public transport service is considered both by the service managers and by the local Authorities, as connected to a high strategic value for the changing contexts that are subjected to relevant socio-economic pressures, such as the aging of the population or the change in the quality of life in rural areas.

Finally DRT systems must be seen not only as a more environmentally friendly means of transport, but rather as a strategy for social inclusion and socio-economic development of local communities.

Acknowledgments. This work was partially supported by the MIUR (Ministry of Education, Universities, and Research [Italy]) through a project entitled WEAKI TRANSIT: WEAK-demand areas Innovative TRANsport Shared services for Italian Towns (Project code: 20174ARRHT/CUP Code: E44I17000050001), financed under the PRIN 2017 (Research Projects of National Relevance) program. We authorize the MIUR to reproduce and distribute reprints for governmental purposes, notwithstanding any copyright notations thereon. Any opinions, findings, and conclusions, or recommendations expressed in this material are those of the authors and do not necessarily reflect the views of the MIUR.

References

1. Abdullah, M., Ali, N., Dias, C., Campisi, T., Javid, M.A.: Exploring the traveler's intentions to use public transport during the COVID-19 pandemic while complying with precautionary measures. Appl. Sci. **11**(8), 3630 (2021)
2. Campisi, T., Basbas, S., Al-Rashid, M.A., Tesoriere, G., Georgiadis, G.: A region-wide survey on emotional and psychological impacts of COVID-19 on public transport choices in Sicily, Italy. Trans. Transp. Sci. **2**, 1–10 (2021)
3. Campisi, T., Garau, C., Acampa, G., Maltinti, F., Canale, A., Coni, M.: Developing flexible mobility on-demand in the era of mobility as a service: an overview of the italian context before and after pandemic. In: Gervasi, O., et al. (eds.) ICCSA 2021. LNCS, vol. 12954, pp. 323–338. Springer, Cham (2021). https://doi.org/10.1007/978-3-030-86979-3_24
4. Abdullah, M., Ali, N., Javid, M.A., Dias, C., Campisi, T.: Public transport versus solo travel mode choices during the COVID-19 pandemic: self-reported evidence from a developing country. Transp. Eng. **5**, 100078 (2021)
5. Campisi, T., Cocuzza, E., Ignaccolo, M., Inturri, G., Torrisi, V.: Exploring the factors that encourage the spread of EV-DRT into the sustainable urban mobility plans. In: Gervasi, O., et al. (eds.) ICCSA 2021. LNCS, vol. 12953, pp. 699–714. Springer, Cham (2021). https://doi.org/10.1007/978-3-030-86976-2_48
6. Errington, A.: The Peri-urban fringe: Europe's forgotten rural areas. J. Rural. Stud. **10**(4), 367–375 (1994)
7. Garau, C., Annunziata, A.: A method for assessing the vitality potential of urban areas. The case study of the Metropolitan City of Cagliari, Italy. City Territory Archit. **9**, 7 (2022). https://doi.org/10.1186/s40410-022-00153-6, ISSN 2195-2701
8. Annunziata, A., Garau, C.: A literature review on the assessment of vitality and its theoretical framework. emerging perspectives for geodesign in the urban context. In: Gervasi, O., et al. (eds.) ICCSA 2021. LNCS, vol. 12958, pp. 305–322. Springer, Cham (2021). https://doi.org/10.1007/978-3-030-87016-4_23
9. Logan, P.: Best practice demand-responsive transport (DRT) policy. Road Transp. Res. J. Aust. N. Z. Res. Pract. **16**(2), 50–59 (2007)
10. Sörensen, L., Bossert, A., Jokinen, J.P., Schlüter, J.: How much flexibility does rural public transport need?–Implications from a fully flexible DRT system. Transp. Policy **100**, 5–20 (2021)
11. Poltimäe, H., Rehema, M., Raun, J., Poom, A.: In search of sustainable and inclusive mobility solutions for rural areas. Eur. Transp. Res. Rev. **14**(1), 1–17 (2022)
12. Ryley, T.J., Stanley, P.A., Enoch, M.P., Zanni, A.M., Quddus, M.A.: Investigating the contribution of Demand Responsive Transport to a sustainable local public transport system. Res. Transp. Econ. **48**, 364–372 (2014)

13. Coutinho, F.M., van Oort, N., Christoforou, Z., Alonso-González, M.J., Cats, O., Hoogen-doorn, S.: Impacts of replacing a fixed public transport line by a demand responsive transport system: case study of a rural area in Amsterdam. Res. Transp. Econ. **83**, 100910 (2020)
14. Brake, J., Nelson, J.D., Wright, S.: Demand responsive transport: towards the emergence of a new market segment. J. Transp. Geogr. **12**(4), 323–337 (2004)
15. Abdullah, M., Ali, N., Shah, S.A.H., Javid, M.A., Campisi, T.: Service quality assessment of app-based demand-responsive public transit services in Lahore, Pakistan. Appl. Sci. **11**(4), 1911 (2021)
16. Campisi, T., Canale, A., Ticali, D., Tesoriere, G.: Innovative solutions for sustainable mobility in areas of weak demand. Some factors influencing the implementation of the DRT system in Enna (Italy). In: AIP Conference Proceedings, vol. 2343(1), p. 090005. AIP Publishing LLC, March 2021
17. Huang, A., Dou, Z., Qi, L., Wang, L.: Flexible route optimization for demand-responsive public transit service. J. Transp. Eng. Part A Syst. **146**(12), 04020132 (2020)
18. Calabrò, G., Le Pira, M., Giuffrida, N., Inturri, G., Ignaccolo, M., Correia, G.H.D.A.: Fixed-route vs. demand-responsive transport feeder services: an exploratory study using an agent-based model. J. Adv. Transp. **2022**, 8382754 (2022)
19. Huang, D., Tong, W., Wang, L., Yang, X.: An analytical model for the many-to-one demand responsive transit systems. Sustainability **12**(1), 298 (2019)
20. Gorev, A., Popova, O., Solodkij, A.: Demand-responsive transit systems in areas with low transport demand of "smart city." Transp. Res. Procedia **50**, 160–166 (2020)
21. Pettersson, F.: An international review of experiences from on-demand public transport services. Working Paper (2019)
22. Sörensen, L., Bossert, A., Jokinen, J., Schlüter, J.: How much lexibility does rural public transport need? Implications from a fully flexible DRT system. Transp. Policy **100**, 5–20 (2021). ISSN 0967-070X, https://doi.org/10.1016/j.tranpol.2020.09.005
23. Bellini, C., Dellepiane, G., Quaglierini, C.: The demand responsive transport services: Italian approach. In: Transactions on the Built Environment, vol. 64. WIT Press (2003). ISSN 1743-3509
24. Mariz Coutinho F., van Oort, N., Christoforou, Z., Alonso-Gonz´alez, M., Cats, O., Hoogen-doorn, S.: Impacts of replacing a fixed public transport line by a demand responsive transport system: case study of a rural area in Amsterdam. Res. Transp. Econ. **83**, 100910 (2020)
25. Mulley, C., Nelson, J., Teal, R., Wright, S., Daniels, R.: Barriers to implementing flexible transport services: an international comparison of the experiences in Australia, Europe and USA. Res. Trans. Bus. Manag. **3**, 3–11 (2012)
26. Haglund, N., Mladenović, M., Kujala, R., Weckström, C., Saramäki, J.: Where did Kutsuplus drive us? Ex post evaluation of on-demand micro-transit pilot in the Helsinki capital region. Res. Transp. Bus. Manag. **32**, 100390 (2019). ISSN 2210–5395, https://doi.org/10.1016/j.rtbm.2019.100390
27. Weigl, D., Sperling, J., Henao, A., Duvall, A., Young, S.: Sustainability, Scalability and Resiliency of the Town of Innisfil Mobility-on-Demand Experiment: Preliminary Results, Analyses, and Lessons Learned (No. NREL/CP-5400–80754). National Renewable Energy Lab. (NREL), Golden, CO (United States) (2022)

International Workshop on Processes, Methods and Tools Towards Resilient Cities and Cultural Heritage Prone to SOD and ROD Disasters (RES 2022)

Resilience of Cultural Heritage in Extreme Weather Conditions: The Case of the UNESCO Villa Romana del Casale Archaeological Site's Response to the Apollo Medicane in October 2021

Fernanda Prestileo[1] , Alessandra Mascitelli[1,2(⊠)] , Guido Meli[3],
Marco Petracca[1], Claudio Giorgi[4], Davide Melfi[5], Silvia Puca[2],
and Stefano Dietrich[1]

[1] CNR-ISAC, Institute of Atmospheric Sciences and Climate, Rome, Italy
[2] National Civil Protection Department (DPC), Rome, Italy
alessandra.mascitelli@artov.isac.cnr.it
[3] Director of Works Project for the Recovery and Conservation
of the Villa Romana del Casale of Piazza Armerina, Former Director of C.R.P.R.,
Regione Siciliana, Palermo, Italy
[4] Geo-k s.r.l., Rome, Italy
[5] Italian Air Force Met Service - COMet, Rome, Italy

Abstract. The conservation strategies of cultural heritage (whether it is movable or immovable), in response to damage resulting from the natural phenomena of aging and decay but also from the occurrence of disasters (earthquakes, floods, fires, etc.), inevitably require a methodological approach aimed at planned conservation and preparedness for the risk event of the cultural site. In this perspective, between 2007 and 2012, the intervention of recovery and conservation of the archaeological site of Villa Romana del Casale in Piazza Armerina (Sicily, Italy), since 1997 inscribed in the list of UNESCO World Heritage Site, was planned and realized. The project, directed by the Centro Regionale per la Progettazione e il Restauro, Regione Siciliana, was aimed not only at carrying out the conservative intervention of the monumental site and its decorative apparatus, but also at drawing up a protocol for preventive maintenance. This protocol concerned the new covering system of the archaeological site, its protection and fruition, as well as the hydrogeological asset of the territory on which it rises. Concerning this last aspect, in fact, since the early Middle Ages the fonts document serious floods that interested the area on which the Villa del Casale is located. These floods inevitably interacted with its conservation history, even influencing its existence. The damages caused by the flood of October 1991 are documented, when the archaeological area was already excavated thanks to the archaeological campaign directed by the archaeologist Gino Vinicio Gentili. These excavations were themselves influenced by the flood of 1951 that covered the area still partially explored. This study, considering the previous impact on the UNESCO site of the weather event of October 1991, analyses the occurrence of October 2021

and the construction's positive response to the stress caused by the meteorological phenomenon. The investigation was performed using ground-
based and satellite-based measurements, to provide a detailed overview
of the extreme event that occurred, to identify the pressures that insisted
on the studied site. The analysis highlights the effectiveness of recovery
and conservation project carried out on the monumental complex and completed in 2012.

Keywords: Meteorology · Cultural Heritage · Archaeological Site ·
Flooding · Resilience

1   Introduction

At about 5 km south-west from the city of Piazza Armerina, in the province
of Enna in the heart of Sicily, Italy (coordinates: latitude 37°21'53", longitude
14°20'04.39"), at the western slopes of Mount Mangone, near the exit of a side
vallecula in the valley of the Torrent Nocciara, is located the archaeological area
of the Villa Romana del Casale (Fig. 1). Since 1997 the site is included in the
list of UNESCO World Heritage Sites as a "sublime example of a luxurious
Roman Villa" for the exceptional nature of its mosaics. Residential building of
late antiquity (IV sec. AD), built on a previous rustic Villa of the I–III sec. AD,
the site was, with alternating events and transformations, inhabited continuously
until around the 12th century AD, due to a powerful flood a thick layer of mud
has covered and delivered to oblivion [1–3].

Fig. 1. View of the Villa Romana del Casale after 2012 intervention (photo by Guido
Meli ©)

In the 15th century there is evidence of a Village called "Casale", risen above
the Roman ruins and the early medieval Arab settlement then inhabited by the
Normans. Also this rustic Village is destroyed by successive floods. The repeated

burials that occurred over time have meant that the late antique structure was preserved below the superstructures of the Byzantine and Arab-Norman periods. It is only at the end of the 18th century that the emerging ruins of the "Contrada Casale" begin to attract the interest of scholars and foreign travellers as well as antiquities dealers and clandestine diggers. Another flood in the first years of the 19th century does not allow to evaluate the entity of the damages due to the robberies perpetrated at the end of the 18th century. The first official archaeological excavations, which brought to light most of the ruins and mosaic floors, began in the first decade of the 19th century and then again in the first decades of the 20th century. However, after the Second World War, from 1949 to 1956, the archaeologist Gino Vinicio Gentili led the most complete work of discovery of the Villa del Casale site (Fig. 2) [4].

After the announcement of the competition for the design of a covering system of the monumental complex, the choice fell on the project signed by the architect Franco Minissi who carried out the work between 1957 and 1967, giving rise to an innovative architectural solution for that time that closes the perimeter wall returning the ancient volumes to the Roman Villa (Fig. 3) [5].

This solution, although valid in its design idea, will reveal itself soon disastrous from the point of view of conservation for the mosaic floors and wall paintings because of the materials used, their progressive deterioration over the years and microclimatic conditions absolutely unsuitable not only for the preservation of artefacts but also for the well-being of visitors [6]. The site, unearthed, suffers considerable damage in the 90s of the last century, in particular a flood in 1991 (Fig. 4) that again covers the rooms of the Villa with mud; in that period are

Fig. 2. Villa Romana del Casale: detail of Peristilium, during the G.V. Gentili's excavations in 50s of last century (source: Archive of Soprintendenza dei Beni Culturali ed Ambientali di Enna [7])

Fig. 3. View of the Villa Romana del Casale with F. Minissi's covering system before 2012 intervention [7]

also documented repeated acts of vandalism on the mosaics, occurred between 1995 and '98.

The progressive decay of the covering system, highlighted with more attention, activates the Centro Regionale per la Progettazione e il Restauro (C.R.P.R.), Assessorato dei Beni Culturali ed Ambientali e della Pubblica Istruzione of Regione Siciliana to start an articulated activity of study and research on the conservative issues, which characterize the archaeological site and its decorative apparatus. After a first project phase stopped in 2004, in 2005 the "Project for the recovery and conservation of the Villa Romana del Casale of Piazza Armerina" is presented by the C.R.P.R., under the direction of architect Guido Meli, then director of the C.R.P.R., and in accordance with the guidelines dictated by the newly appointed High Commissioner for the Villa Romana del Casale, Vittorio Sgarbi, whose work finally started in 2007 by the Consortium O.B.C. of Florence [7].

The complex recovery project, concluded after five years with the inauguration on July 4th, 2012 of the new musealization of the site (during this long period the archaeological area has never been closed to the public), involved not only the restoration of over 3,500 m^2 of mosaic floors and opus sectile but also the restoration of wall paintings that decorate about 50% of the walls of the rooms. The intervention included the replacement of the obsolete covering system, the design of new suspended walkways, less invasive for the visit path, as well as a new lighting system, also provided for the evening openings, and the reorganization, from the hydrogeological and naturalistic point of view, of the area on which stands the entire archaeological site. The intervention of recovery, in fact, started with the restoration of the mosaic floors, has also involved the work of drainage and regulation of the waters that cross the Villa, by means

Fig. 4. Villa Romana del Casale after flooding of 1991, details: inside on the left; outside on the right (source: Archive of Soprintendenza dei Beni Culturali ed Ambientali di Enna [7])

of canals, and those that soak the perimeter walls. The existing original system of small canals inside the Villa has been recovered and re-functionalized as well as an excavation has been made along the perimeter of the walls of the Villa, in order to create a barrier to water infiltration with a draining and breathing system for the masonry. Water has always played a major role in the existence of the site, not only as water brought into it with a sophisticated hydraulic system of canals to meet the needs of daily life, but also for the conservation history of the archaeological area, related to decay phenomena due to the presence of groundwater, surface water and rainwater. Above all, the part of the Villa exposed to the north-east was the one most at risk for the runoff of the latter because of a marked variation in the altitude of the ground that in its direction made them convey. For this reason, interventions were also made on the structure of the surrounding areas, mitigating the risk of hydrogeological instability and flooding.

A fruitful occasion for the assessment of the resilience of the Villa downstream of the safety works, was certainly the event occurred in October 2021, during which a medicane called Apollo hit central-eastern Sicily. The event was monitored and followed in its different phases, using both conventional meteorological analysis tools (i.e. rain gauges, radar, NWP models) and more recent techniques (i.e. satellite products).

In recent years, the frequent occurrence of intense meteorological events has driven the scientific community to employ more and more data sources (e.g. rain gauges [8], radar [9], radiometers [10], NWP models [11,12], satellite products [13–16], GNSS [17], lightning [18]) that, properly integrated and analysed, provide effective support in the description of these phenomena [19].

In this paper, after an overview on site features and performed structures, a focus on the Apollo event is provided employing both ground-based and satellite-based techniques. A spotlight on the area's resilience precedes the final conclusions.

2 Site and Performed Structures Overview

The entire site of Villa Romana del Casale of Piazza Armerina is located, as previously described, in an area with hydrogeological problems related to frequent flooding events, thus giving rise to numerous issues of physical-chemical and biological nature. In fact, over time, several geological movements have been registered that have created instabilities in the structures, with the formation of cracks, lesions, detachments and especially significant deformations of the mosaic surface, consisting of depressions and lifts. These consequences were more evident in the rooms where the mosaic was still lying on the original laying surface. The water coming from the foundations and from the layers of alluvial soil leaning against the external walls caused the capillary transmission of humidity on the surface and the loss of the chemical-physical characteristics of the mortars and therefore the disaggregation of the different layers of the substrate. It also contributed, in a predominant way, to the process of alteration of the different constituent materials [7]. The issue regarding the hydrogeological situation of the sites was known since a long time [4]. From the information acquired during archaeological excavations, we know that the archaeological site of the Villa del Casale has shown, since its discovery, a sensitive vulnerability to natural events such as landslides and floods. In particular, despite the absence of maps of the survey points, the investigation conducted by engineer Luigi Pappalardo in 1881 is of significance [20].

Gentili, at the conclusion of the 1956 excavations, based his thesis of a hydrogeological disaster on the objects found and on stratigraphic examination: "The Platia then moves, giving life to the current Piazza Armerina, while in the site of the Roman monument, will arise a few decades later still a rural Village of poor hovels, destined to succumb under the earthy burden of a flood that, for the changed conditions of the environment now devoid of ancient forests, came down by landslide from the hills above" [4].

The most recent and significant flooding events which have affected Sicily and which have had relevant impacts on the territory of Enna are, in particular, the one recorded on October 15th, 1951, the one of December 31st, 1972 and the most recent one of October 1991. On the October 12th, 1991 in fact, the province of Enna was affected by strong perturbations that caused the covering of vast areas of the Villa Romana del Casale (from a few centimetres up to a meter thick). The alluvial lime came from the overflow of one of the tributary channels of the Torrent Nocciara (Fig. 4), tributary of the River Gela at the highest altitudes of Mount Mangone. The formulation of a geological model of the subsoil of the Villa appeared as necessary as ever in consideration of the particular location of the same in a conoid of alluvial origin, with lithological horizons characterized by a complex lay, seat moreover of phreatic water table close to the ground level.

It was possible to delineate the geomorphologic and hydrogeological conditions of the area, to characterize the present soils from a geotechnical and geoseismic point of view. The issues addressed concerned, first of all, the effects of damming of surface waters caused by the presence of backfill materials accu-

Fig. 5. Geomorphological and hydrogeological interventions in the Villa Romana del Casale area (2007–2012): a) north western thermae area contact earths and b) related earthworks; c) and d) works for the realization of the drainage canal downstream of the Villa for the convoying of water to the river; e) works for the cleaning of the original drainage canal, realized upstream the Villa; f), g), h) execution of works to safeguard the masonry: perimeter excavation under foundation and placement of sheets and drainage pipes (photo by Guido Meli ©)

mulated downstream of the Villa (dam effect), for which it was necessary to remove a large section of these materials, in order to allow the rapid flow of water. Another issue was related to the presence of the phreatic water table close to the topographic surface. For this one, rather than assuming an artificial depression of the piezometric through forced drainage, probably harmful to the statics of the archaeological complex, it was thought to a rational exploitation in terms of balance between the quantities taken and those of natural water recharge. Finally, the conditions of morphological balance of the area close to the riverbed of the Torrent Nocciara have been improved, through the creation of a green area in the tract between the new access road to the Villa and the torrent itself, with consequent water regulation. The intervention has also planned the recovery of existing sections of the original water system of the Villa, related to networks of adduction, latrines, fountains, sheet of water, baths, aqueduct, and network of capture and disposal of water. The work carried out has allowed, in this way, to recover a correct reading of the original system of canalization of rainwater and water adduction, used inside the building of the Villa and for the operation of the thermal building, while avoiding the dispersion of water, due to clogging of the pipes, never before inspected and cleaned. The works of improvement of the water canals regulation system concerned the whole perimeter of the Villa, excavated on the back of the walls, until reaching a level lower than the sea floor. In this section of the ground, in the bottom and in contact with the masonry, a double membrane sheet was placed, breathable to the outside but, at the same time, preventing the entry of water from the outside. On the bottom of the main canal, thus created drainage pipes were placed in order to convey all the water canals to the lower part of the Villa, outside its perimeter, and then flow into the vast area (residual of the Gentili excavation) downstream of the baths (Praefurnia). In this area a drainage pipe was placed of adequate size that has allowed removing the water from the area and conveying the flow downstream to the torrent below (Fig. 5) [7].

3   Case Study: Apollo Medicane, October 2021

During the last ten days of October 2021 a Mediterranean cyclone, named Apollo, develops over the sea south of Sicily. Throughout the event analysis, the study of the atmospheric high layers clearly revealed that a split of the polar jet stream forced the development of Apollo over North Africa and Sicily; this resulted in a direct exposure of the mentioned territories and consequently of the UNESCO archaeological site discussed in this paper.

3.1   Weather Event Description

The event of interest was monitored continuously through both ground and satellite data; this allowed a detailed description of the occurrence of which here, for the sake of brevity, we provide the main outputs.

Ground Data Analysis. In Fig. 6 the product of merging between DPC radar and rain gauges , which shows the accumulated rainfall over the whole period from October 22nd, 2021 at 00:00 UTC to October 29th, 2021 at 23:55 UTC, points out the large amount of precipitation occurred on Sicily, southern Italy, during the pinpointed event.

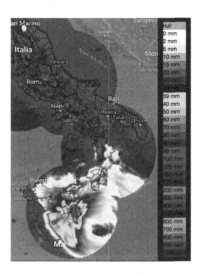

Fig. 6. Merging DPC radar and rain gauges - accumulated rainfall over the whole period from October 22nd, 2021 at 00:00 UTC to October 29th, 2021 at 23:55 UTC [21]

It is interesting to remark that throughout the analysed period the rain gauge of the Municipality of Piazza Armerina (Fig. 7) registered a total precipitation of almost 180 mm (94.2 mm only on October 22nd, 2021) [22].

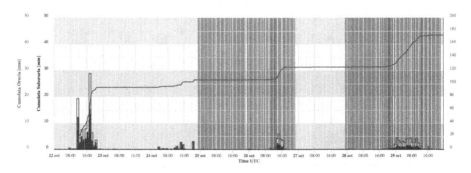

Fig. 7. Piazza Armerina rain gauge output [21] - Time period from October 22nd, 2021 at 00:00 UTC to October 29th, 2021 at 23:55 UTC

In Fig. 7 sub-hourly (blue), hourly (red) and total (green) cumulative rainfall are given; the grey areas represent the real-time data lack. Although the intense rainfall caused flooded areas and landslides in the surroundings [22], the archaeological site investigated in this study made it through the event without significant damage.

Satellite Data Analysis. A continuous monitoring of the Apollo event was carried out by satellite acquisitions, using different kind of products and data (i.e. precipitation, cloud properties, soil moisture, flooded area). In this frame, Meteosat satellite is particularly useful for observing and monitoring weather events. Using the IR channels, it is possible to follow the evolution and trajectory of the structure every 15 min. Figure 8 shows for each of the 9 days ranging from 22nd to October 30th an acquisition of the IR channel at 10.8 microns. In the afternoon of October 22nd (a), about 94 mm of rainfall were registered by the Piazza Armerina rain gauge. The phenomenon evolution is given in panels (b) and (c). In the early hours of October 25th (d), the cyclone formed close to the coasts of North Africa and continued its trajectory (e) towards the east/southeast until October 27th (f). On October 28th (g) it strengthened and moved closer to Sicily, reaching its closest point to Italy on October 29th (h). Finally, from October 30th (i) it has definitively moved south-east towards the coasts of Libya.

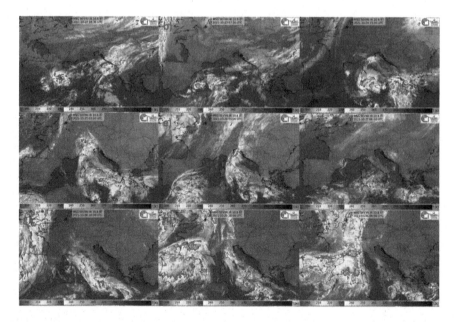

Fig. 8. MSG IR 10.8 micron acquisitions from 25th to October 30th, 2021. Red circle highlights the centre of the Cyclone for each day.

In this context, data from H SAF consortium (supported by EUMETSAT), which provides satellite-based products for hydrology purposes, are particularly useful to better analyse the phenomenon. In particular, the estimation of surface precipitation is one of the objectives pursued by this project and for sure it includes interesting products for our study.

Instantaneous precipitation rate as well as temporally accumulated (hourly up to 24-hourly) precipitation is estimated both from passive microwave (PMW) measurements from Low Earth Orbit (LEO) satellites and from IR data from geostationary (GEO) satellites [13]. So, the products that more than others allowed us to follow the evolution of the event are those based on the SEVIRI sensor on board the MSG, named respectively P-IN-SEVIRI-PMW (H60) (instantaneous) and P-AC-SEVIRI-PMW (accumulated) (H61).

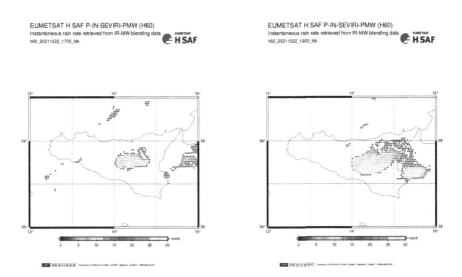

Fig. 9. Instantaneous precipitation rate (H60) - October 22nd, 2021, 17:00 UTC

Fig. 10. Instantaneous precipitation rate (H60) - October 22nd, 2021, 19:00 UTC

Both exploit the precipitation rate estimates derived from PMW sensors and the MW/IR blended rapid-update technique, and provide the instantaneous precipitation rate every 15 min (H60) and the hourly and daily accumulated precipitation (H61). Figures 9 and 10 are two images of Instantaneous precipitation rate (H60 product), whereas Figs. 11 and 12 are two pictures of Hourly accumulated precipitation (H61 product). Both products are given for October 22nd, 2021, at 5:00 p.m. and 7:00 p.m., respectively, and clearly show the magnitude of the event that hit the area. Considering the exceptional nature of the event, highlighted by the above observations, the response of the UNESCO Villa Romana del Casale site to these stresses is of particular importance and interest.

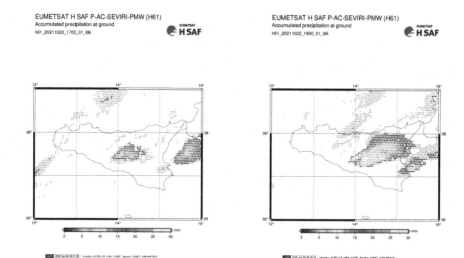

Fig. 11. Hourly accumulated precipitation (H61) - October 22nd, 2021, 17:00 UTC

Fig. 12. Hourly accumulated precipitation (H61) - October 22nd, 2021, 19:00 UTC

3.2   Archaeological Site Resilience

It can be affirmed, today, that the Villa Romana del Casale has been well protected from the recent meteoric events, of medium intensity but, also, from the exceptional meteoric event occurred at the end of October 2021, exactly three decades after the last episode (October 12th, 1991). In fact, the eaves canals built in concrete, after the flood of 1991, to collect water from the slope of Mount Mangone upstream of the site, as well as the functional recovery of the system of canals that convey water, inside the monumental building, realized under the Project of recovery and conservation of the Villa Romana del Casale managed by the C.R.P.R. and concluded in 2012, have fulfilled their task. The project, directed by architect Guido Meli, also included a plan for the preventive maintenance of the site over time. In fact, it is now well known that the policy of prevention is at the basis of planned conservation in order to avoid the recurring to restoration, considered as an exceptional event, traumatic and therefore expensive. The definition of specific protocols for planned conservation must be preceded by a careful evaluation of the phenomena and dynamics that characterize the hazards present in the area and the vulnerabilities of the cultural site in its entirety [7].

The phase of study and research preliminary to the planning of the restoration, as mentioned above, has allowed to analyse in depth all the aspects related to the geological and structural characterization of the archaeological site, as well as the knowledge from the chemical, physical and biological point of view of its decorative apparatus, being able to verify the causes of the damages detected. The overall state of conservation, after the interventions of the last thirty years, can be defined as satisfactory, but the characteristics of the site require a continuity of maintenance and care of all its constituent elements, almost continuous, able to effectively counteract the causes of the processes of decay and alteration. With regard to the risk arising from increasingly frequent extreme weather events, at the international level in general, the measures and strategies that are included in the plans for risk reduction and management are still sporadic. UNESCO, for example, is only requiring since 2019 for the inclusion of a site in the World Heritage List, the definition of the plan of risk management of the site, highlighting how important it is to develop strategies that are in line with the United Nations Sendai Framework for Disasters Risks Reduction 2015–2030 [23]. Mainly, attention was paid to "Priority 4 -Enhancing disaster preparedness for effective response", in which the European Commission is committed, also through a specific study [24], concerning the safeguarding of cultural heritage against natural and anthropogenic disasters. In the recommendations provided, for the safeguard, it is indicated the promotion of the use and application of earth observation data (satellite data), the development of dedicated alert systems and the realization of local risk maps with a high spatial resolution.

The frequency and magnitude of extreme climate events such as heavy precipitation, flooding and drought, due to climate change, produces disasters and significant damage to cultural heritage increasingly. These phenomena, defined Rapid Onset Disasters (ROD) are in addition to the natural aging processes of cultural heritage and decay due to the Slow Onset Disasters (SOD), increasing its exposure over long term risks. For this reason, there is an urgent need for analytical methodologies and technological tools for multi-risk assessment that truly enables cultural heritage managers, policy and decision makers to be able to cope with emergencies promptly and appropriately basing decisions and actions on the principles of knowledge and preparedness [23,24]. In fact, research in this area is developing new methodologies and applications [25–27].

The "Parco Archeologico della Villa Romana del Casale e delle aree archeologiche di Piazza Armerina e dei Comuni limitrofi" has drawn up its first Management Plan in 2012 [28] and since 2020 it is being updated, also comparing the current situation with the one of 2012, corresponding to the restoration work, carried out by the C.R.P.R. For this aspect, therefore, the management of this UNESCO site is at avant-garde both in the national and international context.

4 Conclusion

The definition of the Protocol for the planned conservation of the archaeological site and its decorative apparatus allowed to mitigate and, in part, to eliminate the intrinsic vulnerabilities and prevent further restoration interventions. The writing of the Villa Romana del Casale Management Plan, which is being updated since 2020 compared to the post-restoration edition of 2012, turns out to be a fundamental tool for the response of the archaeological site to possible damage from environmental and anthropogenic causes. This action is perfectly in line with what is established in Priority 4 of the United Nations Sendai Framework for Disasters Risks Reduction 2015–2030. Specifically, a proof of the effectiveness of such a management policy was provided by the occurrence of the late October 2021 flood. The exceptional meteorological event, whose evolution was presented in this work, affected, with its exceptional power, the central-eastern Sicily involving, therefore, also the area on which is located the Villa Romana del Casale. For the first time, in the history of its existence, the archaeological site did not suffer any damage because of this umpteenth flood that, instead, proved disastrous for the city of Piazza Armerina and the surrounding areas, as documented by local testimonies and reported by the main sources of information [29–31].

Acknowledgements. Agreement between CNR-ISAC and Parco Archeologico di Morgantina e della Villa Romana del Casale di Piazza Armerina (Protocol number 289, signed on 3 February 2020). Part of this work belongs to the H SAF Project. The authors would like to thank Antonio Oriente (National Civil Protection Department) for his expertise and helpfulness.

References

1. Carandini, A., Ricci, A., De Vos, M.: Filosofiana. La Villa del Casale di Piazza Armerina, Immagine di un aristocratico romano al tempo di Costantino, Flaccovio, Palermo (1982)
2. Sfameni, C.: Residential Villas in Late Antique Italy: continuity and change. In: Bowden, W., Lavan, L., Machado, C. (Eds.) Recent Research on Late Antique Countryside. Brill Leiden, Boston (2004)
3. Pensabene, P.: Piazza Armerina. Villa del Casale e la Sicilia tra tardoantico e medioevo, L'Erma di Bretschneider, Roma (2010)
4. Gentili, G.V.: Piazza Armerina. Grandiosa Villa romana in contrada Casale. In Notizie di Scavi, Serie VIII, vol. IV (1950)
5. Gentili, G.V.: La Villa Romana di Piazza Armerina. Fondazione Don Carlo, Osimo (1999)
6. Cacciatore, E., Prestileo, F.: Indagini fisiche. In: Meli G. (ed.) Progetto di recupero e conservazione della Villa Romana del Casale di Piazza Armerina, Collana I Quaderni di Palazzo Montalbo. I Grandi Restauri, n. 12/1, C.R.P.R., Palermo, pp. 97–104 (2007)
7. Meli, G. (Ed.): Progetto di recupero e conservazione della Villa Romana del Casale di Piazza Armerina, Palermo, Collana I Quaderni di Palazzo Montalbo. I Grandi Restauri, 12/1, C.R.P.R., Palermo (2007)
8. Bruno, G., et al.: Performing hydrological monitoring at a national scale by exploiting rain-gauge and radar networks: the Italian case. Atmosphere **12**(6), 771 (2021)
9. Vulpiani, G., Montopoli, M., Passeri, L.D., Gioia, A.G., Giordano, P., Marzano, F.S.: On the use of dual-polarized C-band radar for operational rainfall retrieval in mountainous areas. J. Appl. Meteorol. Climatol. **51**(2), 405–425 (2012)
10. Campanelli, M., et al.: Precipitable water vapour content from ESR/SKYNET sun-sky radiometers: validation against GNSS/GPS and AERONET over three different sites in Europe. Atmos. Measur. Techniq. **11**(1), 81–94 (2018)

11. Federico, S., et al.: The impact of lightning and radar data assimilation on the performance of very short term rainfall forecast for two case studies in Italy. Nat. Hazards Earth Syst. Sci. Discuss.(2018). https://doi.org/10.5194/nhess-2018-319. In review
12. Mascitelli, A., Federico, S., Torcasio, R.C., Dietrich, S.: Assimilation of GPS Zenith Total Delay estimates in RAMS NWP model: impact studies over central Italy. Adv. Space Res. **68**(12), 4783–4793 (2021)
13. Mugnai, A., et al.: Precipitation products from the hydrology SAF. Nat. Hazards Earth Syst. Sci. **13**, 1959–1981 (2013)
14. Massari, C., et al.: The use of H-SAF soil moisture products for operational hydrology: flood modelling over Italy. Hydrology **2**(1), 2–22 (2015)
15. Meroni, A.N., et al.: On the definition of the strategy to obtain absolute InSAR Zenith Total Delay maps for meteorological applications. Front. Earth Sci. **359** (2020)
16. Molinari, M.E., et al.: A novel procedure for generation of sar-derived Ztd maps for weather prediction: application to South Africa use case. In: 2021 ISPRS Congress, vol. 43, pp. 405–410 (2021)
17. Mascitelli, A.: New Applications and Opportunities of GNSS Meteorology. Sapienza Università di Roma (2020)
18. D'Adderio, L.P., Pazienza, L., Mascitelli, A., Tiberia, A., Dietrich, S.: A combined IR-GPS satellite analysis for potential applications in detecting and predicting lightning activity. Remote Sens. **12**(6), 1031 (2020)
19. Coletta, V., et al.: Multi-instrumental analysis of the extreme meteorological event occurred in matera (Italy) on November 2019. In: Gervasi, O., et al. (eds.) ICCSA 2021. LNCS, vol. 12956, pp. 140–154. Springer, Cham (2021). https://doi.org/10. 1007/978-3-030-87010-2_10
20. Pappalardo, L.: Caltanissetta. Aidone. Antichità, 1880–1881: relazione dell'Ing. Luigi Pappalardo sulle antichità della zona. In: Antichità e Scavi, Archivio della Direzione Generale delle Antichità e Belle Arti, busta 13, no. 23 "Caltanissetta 1861–1881" (1881)
21. Italian Civil Protection Department DPC and Research Foundation CIMA. The Dewetra platform: a multi-perspective architecture for risk management during emergencies. In: Proceedings of the Information Systems for Crisis Response and Management in Mediterranean Countries: First International Conference, ISCRAM-med 2014, Toulouse, 15–17 October 2014, pp. 165–177. Springer (2014)
22. Report d'evento Regione Sicilia. October 26*th* (2021). https://www2.regione.sicilia. it/deliberegiunta/file/giunta/allegati/N.444_27.10.2021.pdf
23. UNDRR. Sendai Framework for Disaster Risk Reduction 2015–2030, Sendai (2015).   https://www.undrr.org/publication/sendai-framework-disaster-risk-reduction-2015-2030
24. Bonazza, A., Maxwell, I., Drdácký, M., Vintzileou, E., Hanus, C.: Safeguarding Cultural Heritage from Natural and Man-Made Disasters: A Comparative Analysis of Risk Management in the EU (2018)
25. Sardella, A., et al.: Risk mapping for the sustainable protection of cultural heritage in extreme changing environments. Atmosphere **11**, 700 (2020). https://doi.org/ 10.3390/atmos11070700
26. Bonazza, A., Sardella, A., Kaiser, A., Cacciotti, R., De Nuntiis, P., Hanus, C., Maxwell, I., Drd'acký, T., Drd'acký, M.: Safeguarding cultural heritage from climate change related hydrometeorological hazards in Central Europe. Int. J. Disast. Risk Reduct. **63**, 102455 (2021)

27. Esposito, D., Cantatore, E., Sonnessa, A.: A multi risk analysis for the planning, management and retrofit of cultural heritage in historic urban districts. In: Lecture Notes in Civil Engineering, La Rosa, D., Privitera R. (Eds.) Innovation in Urban and Regional Planning, Proceedings of the 11th INPUT Conference, vol. 1 (2021)
28. Villa Romana del Casale, Piano di Gestione, Regione Siciliana - Assessorato Regionale Beni Culturali e Identità Siciliana, Parco Archeologico della Villa Romana del Casale e delle aree archeologiche di Piazza Armerina e dei Comuni limitrofi, Caltanissetta (2012)
29. MeteoWeb. October 22nd. Nubifragio a Piazza Armerina: la Sicilia è nella morsa del maltempo (2021). https://www.meteoweb.eu/video-gallery/nubifragio-a-piazza-armerina-la-sicilia-e-nella-morsa-del-maltempo/id/638004406/
30. Allagamenti a Piazza Armerina. 22 Ottobre 2021. YouTube, uploaded by Weather Italy - WS Cam, October 22nd (2021). https://www.youtube.com/watch?v=9TucoMYmiIk
31. PiazzaInDiretta. October 22nd 2021. Piazza Armerina - Emergenza Alluvioni: Assegnati i contributi per lo stato di calamità. 90.000 euro a Piazza. Serviranno per le spese di emergenza effettuate durante gli interventi di primo soccorso. https://www.piazzaindiretta.it/2021/12/10/piazza-armerina-emergenza-alluvioni-assegnati-i-contributi-per-lo-stato-di-calamita-90-000-euro-a-piazza-serviranno-per-le-spese-di-emergenza-effettuate-durante-gli-interventi-di-primo-soccorso/

Preliminary Results of the AEROMET Project on the Assimilation of the Rain-Rate from Satellite Observations

Stefano Federico[1]([✉]), Rosa Claudia Torcasio[1], Alessandra Mascitelli[1,2], Fabio Del Frate[3], and Stefano Dietrich[1]

[1] National Research Council of Italy, Institute of Atmospheric Sciences and Climate (CNR-ISAC), via del Fosso del Cavaliere 100, 00133 Rome, Italy
s.federico@isac.cnr.it
[2] Civil Protection Department, Via Vitorchiano 2, 00189 Rome, Italy
[3] Department of Civil Engineering and Computer Science Engineering DICII, University of Rome "Tor Vergata", via del Politecnico 1, 00133 Rome, Italy

Abstract. The regions close to the sea are often hit by meteorological systems that generate over the sea and then are advected towards the land. These systems impact the activities over the sea and is it important to predict their occurrence for the safety of the people as well as for the best prediction of ship-routes. The lower number of meteorological observations over the sea compared to the land and the absence of the orographic triggering mechanism, makes prediction of these storms difficult. Satellite observations are very important in this framework because they provide data over both land and sea that can help the prediction of convective storms.

The AEROMET project (AEROspatial data assimilation for METeorological weather prediction) aims to assimilate the rain-rate estimated from satellite observations into the Numerical Weather Prediction (NWP) Weather Research and Forecasting (WRF) model to improve the prediction of convective meteorological systems, especially those originating over the sea. The method to assimilate the rain-rate is straightforward: given the best estimate of the rain-rate, it is assimilated in the model through 3D-Var with a simple cloud model. Two examples, occurred on 10 December 2021 and on 15 February 2022, show the feasibility of the method, nevertheless many cases must be studied to quantify the impact of the assimilation of satellite observed rain-rate on the precipitation forecast.

Keywords: Satellite derived rain-rate · Data assimilation · WRF model

1 Introduction

The Mediterranean is a hot spot for climate change [1] and it is often struck by severe meteorological events that cause flood and flash flood in the area. The

O. Gervasi et al. (Eds.): ICCSA 2022 Workshops, LNCS 13380, pp. 527–539, 2022.
https://doi.org/10.1007/978-3-031-10542-5_36

impact of these events is amplified by the presence of a warm sea, which feeds the storm with huge amounts of water vapor, and the complex orography of the Basin which triggers, amplifies, and focuses the rainfall over specific areas [2–4]. These events are difficult to predict because of the many spatial and temporal scales involved [5]. Numerical weather prediction (NWP) models using convection permitting horizontal resolutions ($<= 3$ km) can represent the occurrence of heavy precipitation, nevertheless their precision in the representation of the convective rainfall in space, time, and amount is still challenging [6]. One of the reasons for the difficulty of precisely representing the convection in NWP is the lack of information at the local scale in the initial conditions.

Data assimilation is a powerful tool to improve the initial conditions of NWP models at the local scale as reported in many studies [7,8]. The data assimilation in the Mediterranean area is challenging when convective meteorological systems develop in the open sea, where radar observations aren't available. Lightning data assimilation has proven to be a powerful tool to predict convective storms over the land and the sea [9,10], nevertheless lightning is very few in winter and spring and are not always available, even if the launch of the new MTG (Meteosat Third Generation) satellites, with the MTG-LI (Lightning Imager) onboard will ensure the availability of lightning data.

Satellites are an important source of data over the sea and can be successfully exploited to improve the convection prediction by NWP models. The AEROMET project, funded by the regional government of Lazio, aims to explore the assimilation of the rain-rate estimated by meteorological satellites in convective environments. Specifically, the assimilation of the rain-rate is made through a simple cloud model, which is activated when rain-rate estimated by satellites is over a threshold (here 3 mm/h). It is very important to select a threshold representative of convective rainfall, to avoid an over addition of water vapor in the model. Preliminary results of the AEROMET project are shown in this paper. We show the methodology followed to assimilate the rain-rate, and the results for two case studies.

The paper is divided as follows: the WRF model settings and the 3D-Var method are introduced in Sect. 2; in this section we also introduce the dataset used in this work. Section 3 shows the results for the 10 December 2021 and 15 February 2022 case studies, while conclusions are given in Sect. 4.

2 Data and Methods

2.1 WRF Model Configuration and Experiment Description

The meteorological model used in this study is the Weather Research and Forecast (WRF) model with advanced WRF dynamic (WRF-ARW), version 4.1.3 [11]. We considered one grid with a horizontal grid spacing of 3 km and 635×635 grid points in both NS and OE directions. The vertical grid has 50 unevenly spaced levels, extending from the surface to 50 hPa. Model grid parameters are reported in Table 1. The domain (Fig. 1) covers the Italian territory, the Central Mediterranean and Central Europe.

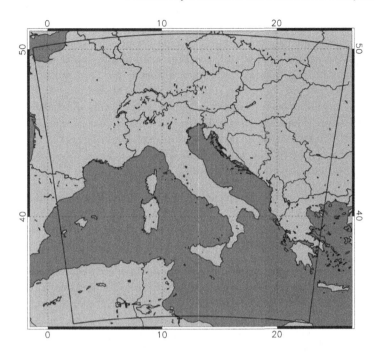

Fig. 1. The WRF domain.

Table 1. WRF model grid parameters. NNXP and NNYP are model grid points in WE and SN directions, respectively. NNZP is the number of vertical levels considered. DX and DY are the grid spatial dimensions in the WE and SN directions, respectively. Lx and Ly represent the domain extension in WE and SN directions, while Lz represents the vertical model extension. CENTLON and CENTLAT are the coordinates of the grid center.

NNXP	635
NNYP	635
NNZP	50
Lx(km)	1905
Ly(km)	1905
Lz(hPa)	50
DX(km)	3
DY(km)	3
CENTLAT	43N
CENTLON	12.5E

The main physical characteristics of the model include the new Thompson microphysics scheme [12], the Mellor-Yamada-Janjic turbulence kinetic energy scheme for the boundary layer [13], the Monin-Obukhov-Janjic scheme for surface layer physics, the five-layer thermal diffusion for land surface processes, the Dudhia scheme [14], and the rapid radiative transfer model (RRTM) [15] for shortwave and longwave radiative schemes, respectively. Radiative scheme is used every 10 min. The time step is 12 s.

Using WRF model with the configuration described above, we analyzed several case studies occurred in winter 2021–2022. For these days, we ran WRF model simulations in two different modes:

- BCKG, a background configuration, which does not assimilate satellite derived rain-rate;

- 3DV, a simulation which assimilate rain-rate data by 3DVar

WRF model was initialized using initial and boundary conditions from European Centre for Medium range Weather Forecast (ECMWF) analysis/forecast available at a horizontal grid spacing of 0.25°. The analysis/forecast cycle issued at 12 UTC on the day before the actual day to forecast were used for initialization.

The forecasts were performed using a Very Short-term Forecast (VSF) approach. More in detail, we ran 4 simulations in order to cover the whole day. Each run lasted 12 h. The first 6 h of the run are used for spin-up the model and for data assimilation in the configuration assimilating the rain-rate, while the last 6 h were used as forecast period. The assimilation scheme is shown in Fig. 2.

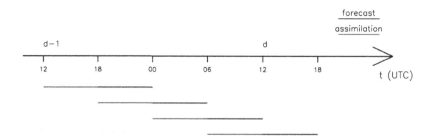

Fig. 2. Assimilation scheme. The red lines represent the assimilation phase, while the blue lines represent the forecast phase. (Color figure online)

In this paper, we focus on two case studies, in order to show the impact of rain-rate assimilation on the precipitation forecast at the short time. In particular, we will describe the period between 00 and 03 UTC on 10 December 2021 and the period between 00 and 03 UTC on 15 February 2022.

2.2   Satellite and MCM Dataset

We assimilated rain-rate estimated by satellites. More specifically we used the dataset H03B distributed by HSAF (EUMETSAT Satellite Application Facility on Support to Operational Hydrology and Water Management). The H03B product is based on a blended MicroWave - InfraRed (MW-IR) technique. The IR images come from the SEVIRI instrument on board the Meteosat satellites, while MW data come mainly from SSMIS, AMSU-A and MHS [16].

It is a near real-time product providing precipitation rate at regular time intervals of 15 min with a spatial coverage from 60° S to 67.5° N and from 80° W to 80° E [16]. The resolution varies from 3 km to 8 km over the full disk and it is consistent with the SEVIRI pixel. On the area considered in this study a spatial resolution of about 5 km is available. At each 15-min interval a calibration procedure is applied to provide one precipitation rate estimate in each grid-box. For assimilation we used the instantaneous rain-rate estimate at the 3DVar time (see next subsection for details).

The model precipitation outputs, both with and without assimilation, were compared with MCM dataset. The Modified Conditional Merging (MCM) technique permits to integrate precipitation measures coming from different instruments, in order to define a better precipitation field both in terms of positioning and amount. This method is based on the methodology, named Conditional Merging, described in [17]. Two kind of data are used as input: raingauges measurements, which give a direct indication of precipitation amount in different points of the domain, and radar estimates, which give information on the spatial structure of the precipitation field. MCM data are available every half an hour, providing the precipitation accumulated in the last hour. For comparison, we used model and MCM precipitation data, accumulated over a 3 h period.

2.3   Assimilation Method

For rain-rate assimilation we used a 3DVar technique. In particular, we used a 3DVar package developed at CNR-ISAC [18], which was employed for many assimilation experiments with RAMS@ISAC model, assimilating data from different sources, going from radar reflectivity and lightning data [2,7,19] to GPS-ZTD data [20]) and which is now applied to the WRF model.

In the AEROMET project a simple cloud model to assimilate the rain-rate is proposed in the 3D-Var framework: for grid points where the rain-rate is larger than a given threshold (3 mm/h was selected as a first threshold through trial and errors), the atmospheric column is saturated from the LCL (Lifting Condensation Level) to the −25 °C isotherm. The LCL is estimated from the model output and because the cloud top is at −25 °C. With this setting, we are assuming a convective cloud developing, with high vertical extension. For this reason, a minimum threshold of rain-rate must be considered to avoid an excessive addition of water vapor to the model that could result in too many false alarms of the predicted rainfall. After inspection of the rain-rate of the dataset

H03B for several cases and few simulations for tuning the method, a minimum threshold of 3 mm/h was adopted.

To further explore this point, we consider the results of the rain-rate data assimilation on the 10 December 2021 at 18 UTC (Fig. 3), one of the two cases considered in this paper. Figure 3a shows the rain-rate of the H03B dataset; the whole southern Italy is interested by a storm with rain-rates up to 10 mm/h. Convection occurs both over the land and over the sea. Figure 3b and Fig. 3c show the innovations at 1270 a.s.l. for the rain-rate thresholds of 3 mm/h and 5 mm/h. The innovations are represented for the mixing ratio of the water vapor, instead of relative humidity. As stated above, the model dependent variable is the water vapor mixing ratio and innovations must be converted from relative humidity to mixing ratio before being used by WRF. Interestingly, the innovations on the west side of the Italian peninsula are larger than those on the eastern side. This is caused by the fact that the background is comparatively more humid on the east side of Italy for this specific case.

Comparing Fig. 3b and Fig. 3c it is apparent that the amount of water vapor assimilated into WRF using the 3 mm/h threshold, is much more extended and representative of the observed rainfall occurring over the area compared to the 5 mm/h threshold. The subjective inspection of other cases led to the same result, and it was decided to adopt the 3 mm/h thresholds for the winter season.

It is finally noticed that, as the cloud model assumes a saturated profile from LCL to $-25\,°C$ isotherm, the innovations are always positive.

The above method was applied only when the rain-rate estimated by the H03B dataset is larger than 3 mm/h. In a future development of the AEROMET project, a neural network approach will be adopted to discriminate a threshold for the data assimilation of the rain-rate.

Rain-rate assimilation is done by generating a relative humidity pseudo-profile where the estimated rain-rate is higher than 3 mm/h, both over sea and over land. As said, this pseudo-profile is saturated between LCL and the $-25\,°C$ layer, with no data elsewhere (i.e. for heights lower than LCL and higher than $-25\,°C$). The parameter assimilated by the model is the water vapor mixing ratio and, therefore, the relative humidity profile is converted to water vapor mixing ratio before being assimilated by the model. The 3DVar method consists in the minimization of a cost function, given by:

$$J(x) = \frac{1}{2}(x - x_b)^T B^{-1}(x - x_b) + \frac{1}{2}(H(x) - y_o)^T R^{-1}(H(x) - y_o) \quad (1)$$

where x represents the state vector, $\mathbf{B}$ and $\mathbf{R}$ are the background error matrix and the observation error matrix, respectively, y_o are the water vapor mixing ratio pseudo-profiles and H is the observation operator, which is used to obtain the water vapor mixing ratio profiles in correspondence of the pseudo-observations.

The cost function is calculated by means of the conjugate gradient method. The background error matrix used for the experiment is calculated by NMC method [21] on a period representative of the season in which the case study

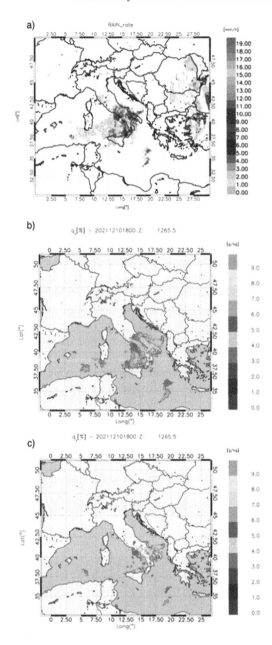

Fig. 3. (a) rain-rate from H03B at 18 UTC on 10 December 2021, (b) innovations of water vapour mixing ratio at 1270 m a.s.l. for 3 mm/h threshold, (c) as in (b) for 5 mm/h.

occurred. As said, we performed an assimilation phase of 6 h. For this phase, we ran the 3DVar every one hour.

3   Results

In this section we consider the results of the application of the method for the 10 December 2021 in the period 00-03 UTC and for the 15 February 2022 between 00 and 03 UTC.

The first period refers to the simulation started at 18 UTC on 09 December 2021 and the 00-03 UTC forecast is at the end of the assimilation period (between 18 UTC on 09 December 2021 and 00 UTC on 10 December 2021). The observations and the innovations (i.e. the difference between the analysis and background field) of the last analysis assimilated in the WRF model is shown in Fig. 4. For the innovations we consider the relative humidity field at 2830 m a.s.l., nevertheless innovations are found at all vertical levels of the WRF model, through the application of the 3D-Var method. Figure 4a shows the rain-rate derived from METEOSAT observations, which are the input of the 3D-Var in AEROMET. As stated, we consider only the grid-points with the rain-rate above 3 mm/h. There are few precipitating cells over the southern Tyrrhenian Sea and over Calabria. Other areas of precipitation are over the France, the Balkans and the Adriatic Sea. Figure 4b shows the innovations of relative humidity at about 2830 m a.s.l. The relative humidity increases by more than 20% over the southern Tyrrhenian Sea, showing several convective cells developing over the area.

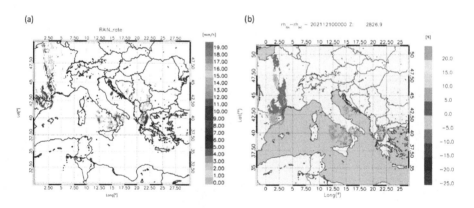

Fig. 4. (a) Rain rate estimated by H03B "copyright (2022) EUMETSAT", (b) Relative humidity field innovation at 2830 m a.s.l.

The impact of the rain-rate assimilation on the precipitation forecast between 00 and 03 UTC on 10 December 2021 is shown in Fig. 5. Comparing the precipitation forecast of the background (Fig. 5a) and of the analysis (Fig. 5b) few differences arise: the precipitation over Calabria (the southernmost tip of Italy)

(a)

(b)

(c)

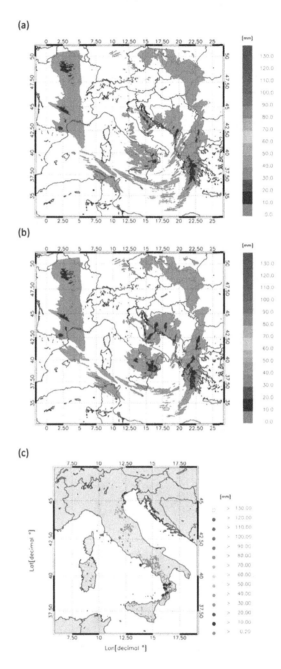

Fig. 5. Precipitation between 00 and 03 UTC on 10 December 2021 for (a) Background model (BCKG), (b) model with rain-rate assimilation (3DV), (c) MCM dataset observations.

536   S. Federico et al.

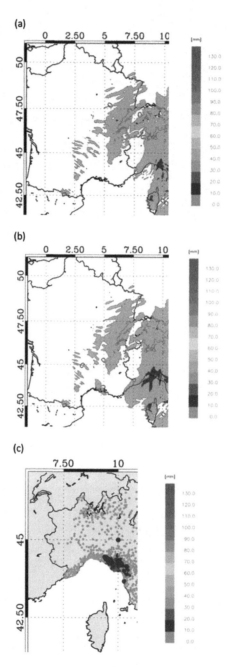

Fig. 6. Precipitation between 00 and 03 UTC on 15 February 2022 for (a) Background model (BCKG), (b) model with rain-rate assimilation (3DV), (c) MCM dataset observations. Only the northwest area of the domain is shown for clearness

is larger in the forecast with rain-rate data assimilation compared to the background, in better agreement with observations (Fig. 5c); the rainfall over Campania, underestimated by the background is correctly simulated by the forecast assimilating the rain rate.

Interestingly, the impact of data assimilation over France is reduced because the innovations are smaller (most of times <5%, Fig. 4b). There are some aspects of the forecast that are less satisfactory as the decrease of the precipitation in some parts of the Central Italy, which are better predicted by the background. It is finally noticed that rainfall increases over the sea for the simulation with data assimilation, for example over the southern Tyrrhenian Sea or north of the Balearic Islands. The impact of the rain-rate data assimilation on the precipitation forecast over the sea will be also considered in AEROMET.

A second case study refers to the 15 February 2022, between 00 and 03 UTC and affected the eastern part of the Liguria region, in the northwest of Italy. The analysis at 00UTC (not shown), which is the last analysis assimilated by the simulation, shows high water vapour innovations (>20%) in the eastern part of Liguria, west Piedmont region and southern France. Figure 6 shows the impact of data assimilation on the precipitation between 00 and 03 UTC. The domain is zoomed over the NW of Italy for clearness. Rainfall observations (Fig. 6c) show moderate precipitation over Liguria with a maxima in the range 20–30 mm/3 h. The background forecast (Fig. 6a) shows an amount between 10 and 20 mm/3 h and the precipitation area is smaller than observed. The forecast with the assimilation of the rain-rate has a better performance compared to the background: first, the observed precipitation area above 10 mm/3 h is better represented; second, the precipitation amount predicted is between 20 and 30 mm/3 h, in good agreement with observations, and the positioning of the largest precipitation amount is very satisfactory.

4   Conclusions

This paper shows the methodology and the result for two cases of the AEROMET project. The project aims at assimilating the rain-rate estimated by meteorological satellites using a simple cloud model and a 3DVar data assimilation scheme. We showed the results for two winter case studies, occurred in winter 2021–2022. In the first case a storm, acting over the southern Tyrrhenian Sea, was advected towards southern Italy affecting Calabria and Campania regions. In the second case, the storm acted over Liguria with precipitation mainly in the eastern part of the region.

Results show some improvements of the precipitation forecast at the short-range over southern Italy for the first case, and better representation of the precipitation field for the second case. While the case studies considered in this work are well representative of what AEROMET aims to investigate, because it considers meteorological system over the sea that are advected over the land, a much larger number of cases needs to be investigated in different seasons to quantify the impact of the method. Moreover, the verification of the rainfall over the sea it is another problem that AEROMET will assess.

Acknowledgments. This work was realized in the project AEROMET (AERO spatial data assimilation for METeorological weather prediction) funded by the Lazio region - FESR Fondo Europeo di Sviluppo Regionale Programma Operativo regionale del Lazio. ECMWF is acknowledged for providing part of the computational resources for the project AEROMET.

References

1. Gaume, E., Borga, M., Llasat, M.C., Maouche, S., Lang, M., et al.: Mediterranean extreme floods and flash floods. The Mediterranean Region under Climate Change. A Scientific Update, IRD Editions, pp. 133–144, Coll. Synthèses, 978-2-7099-2219-7 (2016)
2. Federico, S., et al.: The impact of lightning and radar reflectivity factor data assimilation on the very short-term rainfall forecasts of RAMS@ISAC: application to two case studies in Italy. Nat. Hazards Earth Syst. Sci. **19**, 1839–1864 (2019)
3. Federico, S., Avolio, E., Bellecci, C., Lavagnini, A., Colacino, M., Walko, R.L.: Numerical analysis of an intense rainstorm occurred in Southern Italy. Nat. Hazards Earth Syst. Sci. **8**, 19–35 (2008)
4. Lagasio, M., Parodi, A., Pulvirenti, L., et al.: A synergistic use of a high-resolution numerical weather prediction model and high-resolution earth observation products to improve precipitation forecast. Remote Sens. **11**, 2387 (2019)
5. Stensrud, D.J., et al.: Convective-scale warn-on-forecast system: a vision for 2020. Bull. Am. Meteor. Soc. **90**, 1487–1499 (2009)
6. Sun, J., et al.: Use of NWP for nowcasting convective precipitation: recent progress and challenges. Bull. Am. Meteorol. Soc. **95**, 409–426 (2014)
7. Federico, S., et al.: Impact of radar reflectivity and lightning data assimilation on the rainfall forecast and predictability of a summer convective thunderstorm in Southern Italy. Atmosphere **12**, 958 (2021)
8. Lagasio, M., Silvestro, F., Campo, L., Parodi, A.: Predictive capability of a high-resolution hydrometeorological forecasting framework coupling WRF Cycling 3DVAR and continuum. J. Hydrometeor. **20**, 1307–1337 (2019)
9. Torcasio, R.C., Federico, S., Puca, S., Vulpiani, G., Prat, A.C., Dietrich, S.: Application of lightning data assimilation for the 10 October 2018 case study over Sardinia. Atmosphere **11**, 541 (2020)
10. Fierro, A.O., Mansell, E., Ziegler, C., MacGorman, D.: Application of a lightning data assimilation technique in the WRFARW model at cloud-resolving scales for the tornado outbreak of 24 May 2011. Mon. Weather Rev. **140**, 2609–2627 (2012)
11. Skamarock, W.C., et al.: A Description of the advanced research WRF Version 4; No. NCAR/TN-556+STR, NCAR Technical Note; National Center for Atmospheric Research: Boulder, CO, USA, p. 145 (2019)
12. Thompson, G., Field, P.R., Rasmussen, R.M., Hall, W.D.: Explicit forecasts of winter precipitation using an improved bulk microphysics scheme. Part II: implementation of a new snow parameterization. Mon. Weather Rev. **136**, 5095–5115 (2008)
13. Janjić, Z.I.: 1994: The step-mountain eta coordinate model: further developments of the convection, viscous sublayer, and turbulence closure schemes. Mon. Weather Rev. **122**, 927–945 (1994)
14. Dudhia, J.: Numerical study of convection observed during the Winter Monsoon Experiment using a mesoscale two-dimensional model. J. Atmos. Sci. **46**, 3077–3107 (1989)

15. Mlawer, E.J., Taubman, S.J., Brown, P.D., Iacono, M.J., Clough, S.A.: Radiative transfer for inhomogeneous atmospheres: RRTM, a validated correlated-k model for the longwave. J. Geophys. Res. Space Phys. **102**, 16663–16682 (1997)
16. H03B Product Details, HSAF official website. https://hsaf.meteoam.it/Products/Detail?prod=h03B. Accessed 9 Apr 2022
17. Sinclair, S., Pegram, G.: Combining radar and rain gauge rainfall estimates using conditional merging. Atmosph. Sci. Lett. **6**, 19–22 (2005)
18. Federico, S.: Implementation of a 3D-Var system for atmospheric profiling data assimilation into the RAMS model: initial results. Atmos. Meas. Tech. **6**, 3563–3576 (2013)
19. Federico, S., Torcasio, R.C., Dietrich, S.: Improvement of quantitative precipitation forecast at the short range through lightning data assimilation. In: Michaelides, S. (ed.) Precipitation Science: Measurements, Remote Sensing, Microphysics, and Modeling, pp. 661–668. Elsevier (2022). ISBN: 978-0-12-822973-6
20. Mascitelli, A., et al.: Data assimilation of GPS-ZTD into the RAMS model through 3D-Var: preliminary results at the regional scale. Meas. Sci. Technol. **20**, 055801 (2019)
21. Parrish, D.F., Derber, J.C.: The National Meteorological Center's spectral statistical interpolation analysis system. Mon. Weather Rev. **120**, 1747–1763 (1992)

Finite Element Model for Wind Comfort Around a Tall Building: A Case Study of Tower of Qazaqstan

Bakdauren Narbayev[1] and Yerlan Amanbek[2(✉)]

[1] Department of Computer Science, School of Engineering and Digital Sciences,
Nazarbayev University, Kabanbay batyr 53, Nur-Sultan, Kazakhstan
`bakdauren.narbayev@nu.edu.kz`
[2] Department of Mathematics, School of Sciences and Humanities,
Nazarbayev University, Kabanbay batyr 53, Nur-Sultan, Kazakhstan
`yerlan.amanbek@nu.edu.kz`

Abstract. Pedestrian wind comfort plays an essential role in the urban environment. In our work, we consider a model obtained using Computational Fluid Dynamics (CFD) around a tall building. Our focus is the Tower of Qazaqstan or Abu Dhabi Plaza in Nur-Sultan city (Kazakhstan), which will be the tallest building in Central Asia with a height of 310.8 m. We investigated the effect of the wind velocity on pedestrians by solving the incompressible time-dependent Navier-Stokes equations in the deal.II library by the Finite Element Method (FEM) using the projection method. We present numerical simulation results for various scenarios. It has been found that the velocity profile can vary in the domain that creates different pedestrian comfort conditions including the exceeded category at places dedicated to pedestrian walking.

Keywords: Tall building · Wind comfort · Wind simulation · Navier-Stokes equations · Finite element model

1 Introduction

Understanding of wind profile around a tall building is important in modern cities for engineers because this can be useful to ensure the comfort of pedestrians. Architectural designs of buildings are becoming more complex in modern cities due to the expansion of urbanization. The wind behavior around modern buildings has an impact on humans' lives. The modeling of the wind effects allows decision-makers to take into account human activities at an early stage of the city plan.

In the literature, several studies have used Computational Fluid Dynamics (CFD) to assess wind conditions in urban areas. Most of results were obtained by various (commercial) software tools in the study of the impacts of climate conditions including wind on buildings [6–8,18]. Many places were taken into account with local weather conditions including Amsterdam [19], Hong Kong [10], Dublin [15], Dubai [16], Jeddah [11], Bursa [9] and others.

O. Gervasi et al. (Eds.): ICCSA 2022 Workshops, LNCS 13380, pp. 540–553, 2022.
https://doi.org/10.1007/978-3-031-10542-5_37

To investigate the impact of the local weather conditions, such as wind, on people, we consider a model of the Tower of Qazaqstan or Abu Dhabi Plaza in Nur-Sultan city, Kazakhstan, as shown in Fig. 1(a). According to [20] the tower is expected to be the tallest building in Central Asia with a height of 310.8 m. The tower is surrounded by four small buildings. There is a Linear Park for pedestrians behind the buildings as shown in Fig. 1(b). The location of the Nur-Sultan city is in the steppe and it is common to have windy weather near the tower. The green forest was planted around the city from 1997 to 2016, a so-called green belt zone that can help to mitigate the negative effects of winds on the city infrastructure.

In [12], the wind effect was studied for "Transport Tower" or building of the Ministry of Industry and Infrastructure Development of the Republic of Kazakhstan with 34 floors from Nur-Sultan city. As a result, the experimental measurements of the sensors at the different floors (27th and 31st floors) showed a high acceleration, $9.23 \, cm/s^2$ on a relatively calm day. However, the comfort of building under wind-induced load was the focus of their study.

Another application of CFD for some buildings from the Dostar micro district (Nur-Sultan city) was discussed in [17]. The specific configuration and orientations of buildings with the pressure profile at the height of 20 m were explored using the commercial software in the wind model.

In this paper, we study the behavior of the wind velocity around a tall building using the time-dependent Navier-Stokes flow model. To the authors' knowledge, such a model using computational fluid dynamics (CFD) has been scarcely investigated for the Tower of Qazaqstan in Nur-Sultan, Kazakhstan. To examine our model, we used the Finite Element Method (FEM) in the open-source deal.II library [3]. The deal.II library allows us to control nearly all parameters crucial to the simulation. By utilizing the library, our model solves the incompressible time-dependent Navier-Stokes equations by the finite element projection method. The numerical model is verified by the experimental data of the velocity profile near the building.

It is principal to analyze our model from the point of the pedestrians since they are the main clients of the urban environment. Hence, in this paper, we associated every obtained result with the wind comfort categories, which give information about the comfort of the pedestrians for wind conditions. These wind comfort categories can be found in Fig. 2.

2   Methodology

2.1   Computational and Mathematical Tools

To identify wind comfort categories, we compute wind velocity values in the problem domain. For that, we utilize the deal.II [5] – an open-source library specialized in solving partial differential equations numerically by FEM. The library uses the C++ programming language. Along with the classes and methods, the library maintainers created a set of programs that solve particular problems. Step-35 is one of such programs that allowed us to solve the incompressible time-dependent Navier-Stokes equations using the projection method [13].

(a) The Tower of Qazaqstan.

(b) The Linear Park and the Tower of Qazaqstan. Adapted from [1].

Fig. 1. Different views of the Tower of Qazaqstan.

The incompressible time-dependent Navier-Stokes equations themselves are as follows:

$$\mathbf{u}_t + \mathbf{u} \cdot \nabla \mathbf{u} - \nu \Delta \mathbf{u} + \nabla p = f,$$
$$\nabla \cdot \mathbf{u} = 0,$$

where $\mathbf{u}$ is the velocity of the wind, ν is the diffusion, f is the force and p is the pressure. We assume the laminar flow behavior.

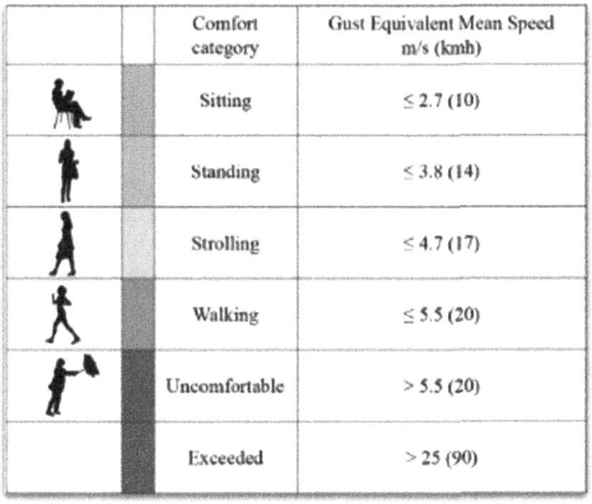

		Comfort category	Gust Equivalent Mean Speed m/s (kmh)
		Sitting	≤ 2.7 (10)
		Standing	≤ 3.8 (14)
		Strolling	≤ 4.7 (17)
		Walking	≤ 5.5 (20)
		Uncomfortable	> 5.5 (20)
		Exceeded	> 25 (90)

Fig. 2. Wind Comfort Criteria. Adapted from [2].

To solve the equations, we need specific initial and boundary conditions. First of all, we imposed no-slip boundary conditions on the top $\Gamma 1$ wall, the bottom $\Gamma 2$ wall, and the building $\Gamma 5$. Next, on the left vertical part $\Gamma 3$ of the domain we set the initial velocity values of the incoming flow. Its x-component has a parabolic structure, meaning that this component at height y has the form of $y(y_{max} - y)$, where y_{max} is the height of the considered domain. The y-component of the incoming flow velocity equals 0. So this means the incoming flow velocity achieves its highest value towards the middle of $\Gamma 3$. Finally, we set boundary conditions on the right vertical boundary $\Gamma 4$, where the values of the pressure and the y-component of the velocity equal 0 (Fig. 3).

2.2 Domain and Mesh Generation

We describe the computational flow model with its settings. The domain of our problem is the Tower of Qazaqstan and its surrounding. Since we conducted numerical simulations for various scenarios in 2D, we needed to conduct simulations in different views to solve the 3D problem. At a high level, there are 2 main scenarios. The first scenario is the view from the side of the building, and the second is from its top. The domain differs depending on the scenario.

For the side view, the domain consists of the building, a smaller area in front of it, and a larger area behind, which contains the Linear Park dedicated to pedestrians. The domain is bounded by the ground from the bottom and a smaller area for the sky from above. Since the building was under construction at the time of simulations, we assumed that it would be rectangular.

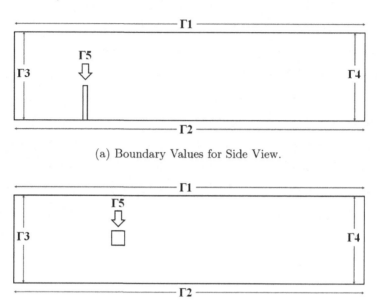

(a) Boundary Values for Side View.

(b) Boundary Values for Top View.

Fig. 3. Boundary values.

For the top view, the domain is similar except for the bottom and top boundaries. These boundaries correspond to the borders of buildings on the other side of parallel streets – Akmeshit and Turkestan, respectively. In addition, we considered two different corner structures for the building – sharp and round.

It is noteworthy that the simulations are done under the assumption that there is no other building nearby except those on the borders. In reality, the Tower of Qazaqstan is surrounded by shorter buildings. Despite that, the simulations are viable in approximating the results at greater heights. Consequently, at rooftop levels, the top view scenario does not suffer because of this assumption. However, for the side view, the results are approximated well for greater height values only.

We generated the mesh for the provided setting, and the code refined it 3 times and then discretized it for the Navier-Stokes problem. During mesh generation, we constructed finer mesh around computationally-heavy parts of the domain, that is, around the building and, especially, around its corners. This will allow us to acquire more detailed information about the wind flow around the building. The results are shown in Fig. 4 by the ParaView, which is open-source software. The exact values used for the domain and subsequent mesh generations are presented in Table 1.

Table 1. The Domain's Parameters.

The Domain'sparameters	Numerical value	Corresponding value for side view (ratio equal 3/382)	Corresponding value for top view (ratio equal 7/317)
Building's length	41 m	0.32198953	0.90536278
Building's width	41 m	0.32198953	0.90536278
Building's height	311.24 m	2.44427	6.87280757
Domain's length	1132.14286 m	25	25
Domain's height/width	317 m	6.1	7
Wind's velocity (1)	4.63 m/s	0.03636126	0.10223975
Wind's velocity (2)	23 m/s	0.18062827	0.50788643
Wind's velocity (3)	28 m/s	0.21989529	0.61829653
The mesh generation parameters		Value for side view	Value for top view
Number of active cells		8320	8448
$dim(X_h)$		67520	68608
$dim(M_h)$		8560	8704

3   Numerical Results

Different simulations were conducted in different views to investigate the wind velocity profile in the domain. Although the total number of the simulations is far more, here, we present an only important portion of it. The main emphasis was put on the parametrization of the different views on the domain, Reynolds numbers, and the highest magnitude of the incoming flow velocity (x-component). This is done to investigate the effect of different parameters on simulation results.

The most plausible values for the Reynolds number are 50, 100, and 200. For the incoming flow velocity, the chosen values are as follows. 4.63 m/s is the average velocity of the wind in Nur-Sultan. 23 m/s is slightly below the threshold value of 25 m/s, which indicates exceeded (the worst) category for pedestrian comfort [2]. Finally, 28 m/s is a higher value that represents wind velocity that occurs in Nur-Sultan regularly. Finally, we compared the velocity profile in the domain for different corner structures (round corners and sharp corners) in the top view case. Tables 2 and 3 show particular parameters for the simulation results.

3.1   Verification

Before conducting the numerical experiments, we need to verify our computational model with the similar models of other researchers. The verification of the simulation results across different meshes and different input values is necessary to understand the scope of acceptable input values for our research simulations. We compared qualitatively our top view result with results from other work, see

(a) The final mesh of the side view setting.

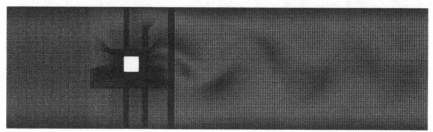

(b) The final mesh of the top view setting with sharp corners.

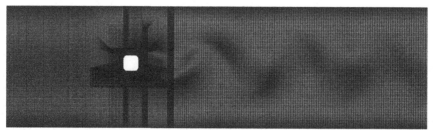

(c) The final mesh of the top view setting with round corners.

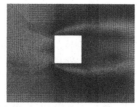

(d) The zoomed part of the final mesh of the side view setting.

(e) The zoomed part of the final mesh of the top view setting with sharp corners.

(f) The zoomed part of the final mesh of the top view setting with round corners.

Fig. 4. Generated Mesh Structures.

for more details Fig. 5. The result of one of the conducted simulations, which has a Reynolds number of 200, and a velocity value of 28 m/s, is shown below with the comparison with the result of the SimScale CFD simulation. One can see similarities in terms of the behavior of wind trails and areas of appearance of the vortexes.

Table 2. The chosen constant parameters' values for simulations in the results.

Parameter	Value
Duration	100
Time Step	5e−3
Iterations (Max)	1000
Stopping Criterion	1e−8

Table 3. The chosen variable parameters' values for simulations in the results.

Parameter	Value 1	Value 2	Value 3
View	Side	Top (Sharp)	Top (Round)
Reynolds number	50	100	200
Incoming velocity	4.63 m/s	23 m/s	28 m/s

Another approach to verify our model is to compare it with the laboratory experimental result. Now, we consider simulations for the side view case similar to the experimental setting. We used the experiment results described in [14] as a reference model. Figure 6(a) shows the experiment's setting.

In this model, the incoming velocity profile has a parabolic structure as shown in Fig. 6(b). The velocity value raises quadratically as the point of interest raises in height. Moreover, the incoming velocity profile has only x-component as non-zero, which makes it identical to that of our simulations. It is also noteworthy that the height of the building is exactly 2 times longer than its width. This allows comparing the results of different simulations with that simulation if the proportions are concerned.

Following the experiment was not an easy task since some of the computation-related parameters can only be induced. However, knowing the inflow velocity profile, adjusting mesh for different boundary conditions (here, we set a slip boundary condition with zero pressure on the top $\Gamma 1$ wall, while other boundary conditions remained the same), and optimizing the comparison across time steps we obtained the results shown in Fig. 6(c). Note that a comparison was made for the final wind velocity values along a particular vertical line connecting 61–66 points in the mesh.

3.2   Simulation of Side View

In our first run, we tried a structure that depicts the side view of The Tower of Qazaqstan. For the side view, we did only a sharp corners case. In Fig. 7 we present some of our results. Figure 7(a) illustrates the resulted magnitude and direction of the velocity of wind across thousands of points on the model. We can see that the placement of such a tall building resulted in a vortex just behind it.

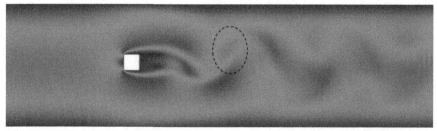

(a) The top view run with sharp corners with the maximal value of initial velocity being equal to 28 m/s. Reynolds number is equal to 200.

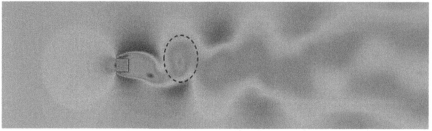

(b) The top view setting of SimScale simulation with sharp corners. Adapted from [4].

Fig. 5. Qualitative verification for top view.

Figure 7(b) shows the highest velocity areas that can be uncomfortable for pedestrians. Note that dark red depicts such places. For example, one of such places is near the bottom boundary. Here, approaching the building in reverse x-direction against the wind becomes hard. The velocity value is around 25 m/s, which is the upper threshold level for uncomfortable wind velocity for pedestrians [2]. Note that this value occurred due to comparably similar initial wind velocity at top points in the domain. It implies that the shape of the building made high levels of wind get to lower levels, meaning the building's structure resulted in an artificial increase of wind velocity near the bottom of the domain, which is the pedestrians' walking place.

3.3   Comparison of Different Corners for Top View

In the top view case, we tried a structure that depicts the rooftop view of the Tower of Qazaqstan. We studied a lot of simulations, one of which has a Reynolds number of 100 and a velocity value of 28 m/s.

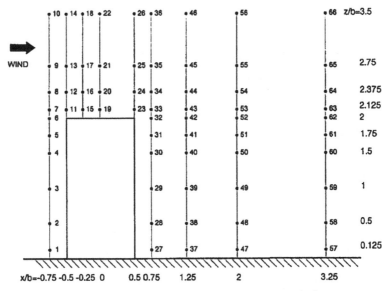

(a) The experiment's setup. Adapted from [14].

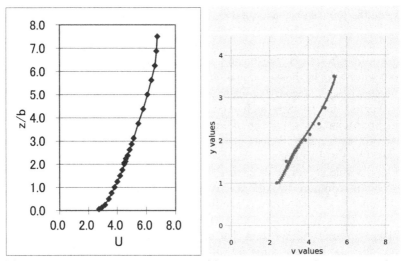

(b) The input velocity profile of the experiment. Adapted from [14].

(c) The comparison between our last experimental model results (with a final time of 1) and the experiment results.

Fig. 6. Numerical verification for side view.

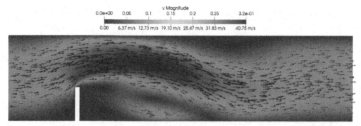

(a) The side view setting with final wind velocity values and directions.

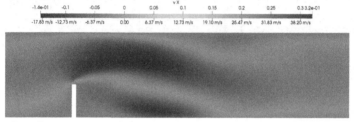

(b) The side view setting with x-components of final wind velocity values.

Fig. 7. Simulation results for the side view with the maximal initial wind velocity of 23 m/s and the Reynolds number of 200.

Figure 8(a) illustrates the results for a case with sharp corners. Here, the maximal wind velocity has a value of around 32.61 m/s, which is a wind velocity that belongs to the exceeded category of pedestrian comfort [2]. Note that this value occurred due to very high initial wind velocity at central points of the domain. So this suggests that the building's shape is affecting pedestrian comfort.

Now, we investigate the case with round corners. Other parameters remain the same. The results of one of these simulations, which has a Reynolds number of 200, and a velocity value of 28 m/s, is shown in Fig. 8(b).

Now, let us compare two different corner structures for the top view with the same parameters chosen above. Visually the difference can be seen in Figs. 8(a)–8(b). Numerically, it turns out that the maximal velocity of wind in the case with sharp corners is higher than that of the case with round corners by approximately 1.36 m/s. So this value for sharp corners is around 32.61 m/s and for round corners is nearly 31.25 m/s. This implies that round corners best serve for purpose of holding the velocity of the wind from increasing its value.

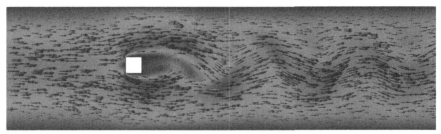

(a) The top view (sharp corners) with final wind velocity values and directions shown as magnitudes and directions of arrays, respectively.

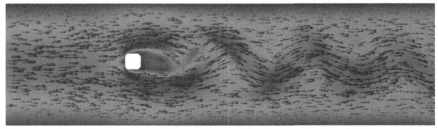

(b) The top view (round corners) with final wind velocity values and directions shown as magnitudes and directions of arrays, respectively.

Fig. 8. Simulation results for the top view with the maximal initial wind velocity of 28 m/s and the Reynolds number of 200.

4   Discussion

During the investigation of this problem, several assumptions were made due to the complexity of the research topic. Results of simulations were converted under the assumption that the conversion rate is constant as can be seen in Table 3.

The numerical results suggest that the building's structure is the reason for the wind velocity of the exceeded category in some areas. For the side view case, the height of the building is the main factor of the increase in the wind velocity. For the top view case, the corner structures affected the results more. The round corners are better than the sharp corners for pedestrian comfort.

Some of the areas with the wind velocity of the exceeded category are located in the park behind the building. It is evident to plant trees and add more obstacles in such places, where we can minimize the wind velocity so that pedestrians can walk even if outside of this structure the wind velocity is very high. Finding such places, adding more parameters such that temperature, and decreasing the error in verification for the side view case are our focus for future studies.

5   Conclusion

Using CFD with FEM, and open-source software, we investigated the problem of wind effects on a tall building. Specifically, we conducted simulations around the modeled Tower of Qazaqstan. The Navier-Stokes model was solved by the projection finite element method in the deal.II library. The verification of the model was conducted by comparing the velocity profile of the experiment with the FEM model. The different velocity profiles are presented in a domain that is one of the important parameters of the wind flow model.

We found that the shape of this tall building might cause an increase in the wind velocity around areas dedicated to pedestrians. The numerical result of the side view shows that the increase resulted in a wind velocity of 25 m/s which implies the exceeded category of wind comfort. In other words, it makes it hard for pedestrians to commute. Planting trees and adding more obstacles in such areas might reduce the wind velocity.

In addition, we found that round corners best serve for purpose of holding the velocity of the wind from increasing its value. This might give interested people new ideas on the construction of buildings.

Acknowledgements. YA wishes to acknowledge the research grant, No AP08052762, from the Ministry of Education and Science of the Republic of Kazakhstan and NUFD-CRG, Grant No 110119FD4502.

References

1. 2gis.kz: Map of Nur-Sultan: streets, houses and organizations of the city – 2GIS. https://2gis.kz/nur_sultan?m=71.427509%2C51.11999%2F17.11%2Fr%2F-103.68 (2022). Accessed 19 May 2022
2. Adamek, K., Vasan, N., Elshaer, A., English, E., Bitsuamlak, G.: Pedestrian level wind assessment through city development: a study of the financial district in Toronto. Sustain. Urban Areas **35**, 178–190 (2017)
3. Alzetta, G., et al.: The deal. ii library, version 9.0. J. Numer. Math. **26**(4), 173–183 (2018)
4. Arafat, A.: Building vortex shedding and wind load analysis, December 2016. https://www.simscale.com/projects/Ali_Arafat/demo-vortex_shedding_around_a_building/
5. Arndt, D., et al.: The deal.II finite element library: design, features, and insights. Comput. Math. Appl. **81**, 407–422 (2021). https://doi.org/10.1016/j.camwa.2020.02.022, https://arxiv.org/abs/1910.13247
6. Blocken, B.: 50 years of computational wind engineering: past, present and future. J. Wind Eng. Ind. Aerodyn. **129**, 69–102 (2014)
7. Blocken, B., Stathopoulos, T., Van Beeck, J.: Pedestrian-level wind conditions around buildings: review of wind-tunnel and CFD techniques and their accuracy for wind comfort assessment. Build. Environ. **100**, 50–81 (2016)
8. Bottema, M.: A method for optimisation of wind discomfort criteria. Build. Environ. **35**(1), 1–18 (2000)
9. Cetin, M.: The effect of urban planning on urban formations determining bioclimatic comfort area's effect using satellitia imagines on air quality: a case study of Bursa city. Air Qual. Atmosph. Health **12**(10), 1237–1249 (2019)
10. Du, Y., et al.: New criteria for assessing low wind environment at pedestrian level in Hong Kong. Build. Environ. **123**, 23–36 (2017)

11. Hegazy, I.R., Qurnfulah, E.M.: Thermal comfort of urban spaces using simulation tools exploring street orientation influence of on the outdoor thermal comfort: a case study of Jeddah, Saudi Arabia. Int. J. Low-Carbon Technol. **15**(4), 594–606 (2020)
12. Lapin, V., Yerzhanov, S., Makish, N.: Monitoring the behavior of a high-rise building under wind loads. In: IOP Conference Series: Materials Science and Engineering, vol. 953, p. 012087. IOP Publishing (2020)
13. Lee, S., Salgado, A.J.: Stability analysis of pressure correction schemes for the Navier-Stokes equations with traction boundary conditions. Comput. Methods Appl. Mech. Eng. **309**, 307–324 (2016)
14. Meng, Y., Hibi, K.: Turbulent measurements of the flow field around a high-rise building. Wind Eng. JAWE **1998**(76), 55–64 (1998)
15. Szűcs, Á.: Wind comfort in a public urban space-case study within Dublin docklands. Front. Archit. Res. **2**(1), 50–66 (2013)
16. Taleb, H., Taleb, D.: Enhancing the thermal comfort on urban level in a desert area: case study of Dubai, United Arab Emirates. Urban Forestry Urban Greening **13**(2), 253–260 (2014)
17. Tokbolat, S., Tokpatayeva, R., Al-Zubaidy, S.: CFD investigation of the effect of building passive design strategy on energy efficiency and wind comfort in extreme weather conditions in Astana, Kazakhstan. In: Applied Mechanics and Materials, vol. 253, pp. 658–669. Trans Tech Publ (2013)
18. Tokbolat, S., Tokpatayeva, R., Al-Zubaidy, S.N.: The effects of orientation on energy consumption in buildings in Kazakhstan. J. Solar Energy Eng. **135**(4), 040902 (2013)
19. Van Hooff, T., Blocken, B.: Coupled urban wind flow and indoor natural ventilation modelling on a high-resolution grid: a case study for the Amsterdam arena stadium. Environ. Model. Softw. **25**(1), 51–65 (2010)
20. Wikipedia: Abu Dhabi Plaza – Wikipedia, the free encyclopedia. http://en.wikipedia.org/w/index.php?title=Abu%20Dhabi%20Plaza&oldid=1071272342 (2022). Accessed 14 Feb 2022

International Workshop on Scientic Computing Infrastructure (SCI 2022)

Parametric Identification of a Dynamical System with Switching

Anna Golovkina[✉] and Vladimir Kozynchenko

Saint Petersburg State University, Saint Petersburg, Russia
`a.golovkina@spbu.ru`

Abstract. Many systems both in nature and created by humans give rise to time series data with complex, nonlinear dynamics. Moreover, such time series can cover different dynamical regimes which identification is of pivotal importance in system modeling. Ordinary differential equations with switching provide a tool for modeling physical phenomena whose time series data exhibit different dynamical modes. Usually, these modes are determined by changing unmeasured parameters of the system that should be learned from the available data. The paper proposes a novel learning structure in polynomial neural network (PNN) basis suitable for parametric identification of dynamical systems and doesn't require usage of numerical integration methods. The PNN weight matrices incorporate the information about the parameters of ODEs and vice versa the unknown parameters of ODEs can be recovered from the PNN weights. Transferring the knowledge about the particular states dependencies in ODEs to PNN can be carried out by finding the initial weight matrices of PNN. The paper proposes a method for PNN initialization based an iterative procedure for step by step non stationary ODE flow computing in the polynomial form. However, even when the ODEs are unknown, PNN can be learned from scratch and provide parameter identification for ODEs. We evaluate the proposed approach on synthetic dataset generated with the system of ODEs for an electrostatical deflector. As a result, PNN successfully uncovers different dynamical regimes and predict the switching dynamics for different initial conditions outside the training data range.

Keywords: Polynomial neural networks · Taylor mapping · System identification · Lie transformation · Dynamic systems

1 Introduction

A lot of dynamical processes in biology, physics, chemistry and so on can be modeled by ordinary differential equations (ODEs) usually derived from the first principles and knowledge of intrinsic nature of the considered process. So that the constructed equations adequately describe the observable process, they

Supported by Saint Petersburg State University, project ID: 90317740.

are combined with the available measurements recorded as input-output signals to find the unknown/uncertain model parameters: *system identification.* This field has been a large active research area for many years and even with several specialized sub-domains.

The interest is explained by the fact that the identified ordinary differential equations can describe responses of a dynamical process to all possible inputs and initial conditions. Thus, they provide the basis for simulation of processes dynamics, short-term and mid-term prediction along with the core for the design of control systems. That is why recently we see a growing interest in discovering the governing equations from the experimental data rather then black-box modeling, regression or curve fitting.

In should be noted that many complex dynamical signals naturally has a compositional form, in the sense that their data generating process can be decomposed into different dynamical modes [1]. Discovering of these modes in the framework of ordinary differential equations usually means identification of the unobserved parameters in the system corresponding to the different regimes.

However, parametric identification of a model in the form of ODE and its usage for making prediction requires numerical integration to get particular solution for certain parameters and initial condition. Thus, the computations start over again if the initial condition or parameters change. What is more, in general, a model is a simplified representation of the real system. In practice, due to presence of multiple sources of uncertainties and assumptions made at the model construction stage, inevitably, ODEs can mimic only essential features of the real process.

These challenges motivated the development and usage of so called physics inspired neural networks (PINN), appealed to integrate modern NN architectures and domain knowledge represented in the form of ordinary (partial) differential equations [2]. The proposed benefits behind this structure are concluded in leveraging modern NN learning algorithms to fit a model to the data in the same time preserving physical consistency of the predictions.

Usually, the governing physics equations are embedded into PINN architectures either by constraining NN output with mathematical operators (loss function) forcing to follow the prescribed dynamics or by incorporating a network to traditional numerical methods for solving differential equation. For instance, instead of classical L_2 regularization during model learning, [3,4] require the NN output to satisfy Euler-Lagrange equation, [5,6] use Hamilton's equations for this purpose, while [3] proposes energy conservation law as additional regularization. Adepts of the second approach adopts Runge-Kutta or finite-difference methods to construct neural networks [7,8]. It also should be noted that many modern learning models (e.x. general purpose recurrent neural networks (RNN), residual neural networks etc.) can be viewed by observing obvious correspondence to many of these classical algorithms. For example, it has been pointed out that the Euler scheme has similarities with NN containing residual connections [9,10].

Summing up the aforementioned points, PINN can be perceived as an analogue to the model in form of ODE (PDE) but enabling convenient interface for learning from new coming data. However, it should be noted that PINN is capable to identify only system parameters that are constant in time. In this work we overcome these limitations by exploiting the advantages of polynomial neural networks for nonstationary dynamical systems and as a particular case dynamical systems with switching.

The approach is based on Taylor mapping technique for solving ODEs first time introduced in [11,12] and developed in [13]. This paper aims to present the algorithm for non stationary PNN weights initialization in the form admitting analysis of PNN convergence to general solution of non-autonomous ODE. The algorithm is illustrated for identification of a particular non-autonomous ODEs with parametric switching. The results are compared to identification with on recurrent neural network of LSTM type.

The rest of the paper is organized as follows: Sect. 2 introduces the problem setup, Sect. 3 contains the algorithm description for transferring non-autonomous ODEs to PNN architecture, while Sect. 4 demonstrates the results of numerical experiment on parametric identification and learning carried out for non-autonomous ODEs describing deflector dynamics.

2   Problem Setup

Let us consider a dynamical system described by a system of ordinary differential equations as follows:

$$\frac{d\mathbf{X}}{dt} = F(t, \mathbf{X}) \tag{1}$$

where t is an independent variable (time), $\mathbf{X} \in \mathbb{R}^n$ is a n-dimensional state of the system, F is a known vector field mapping $F : \mathbb{R} \times \mathbb{R}^n \rightarrow \mathbb{R}^n$ and representing the prior knowledge of the system.

A curve $\mathbf{X}(t)$ solving (1) with initial condition $\mathbf{X}(t_0) = \mathbf{X}_0$ is an integral curve of a vector field F. For the fixed t,

$$\mathbf{X}(t, \mathbf{X}_0) = \mathcal{M}_F^t(\mathbf{X}_0) = \mathbf{X}_0 + \int_{t_0}^{t} F(\tau, \mathbf{X}(\tau))d\tau$$

is a flow generated by vector field F.

Solving system (1) means finding mapping $\mathcal{M}_F^t$. Traditional numerical solvers divide the interval $[t_0, t]$ into several steps and iteratively compute $\mathbf{X}(t_k)$ starting from $\mathbf{X}_0$ until reaching $\mathbf{X}_t$.

The simplest method using this general framework is explicit Euler method, in which a single step takes the following form:

$$\mathbf{X}(t_{k+1}) = \mathbf{X}(t_k) + hF(t_k, \mathbf{X}(t_k)). \tag{2}$$

More complicated numerical integration techniques preserves the same iterative structure (2) where the state vector values at the previous time step generally are not separable from the nonlinear function F. This fact means that another initial condition $\mathbf{X}_0$ generates a new sequence of points in the phase space. Its computing each time requires repetition of procedure (2).

The papers aims to find an approximate representation of the flow $\mathcal{M}_F^t(\mathbf{X}_0)$ in the form

$$\mathbf{X}(t) = \sum_{i=1}^{m} R^{1i}(t,t_0)\mathbf{X}_0^{[i]} \tag{3}$$

and derive a procedure to construct unknown $R^{1i}(t,t_0)$, $i = \overline{1..m}$ matrices. Here $\mathbf{X}^{[k]}$ means k-th Kronecker power of vector X. For example, for $\mathbf{X} = (x_1, x_2)$ we have $\mathbf{X}^{[2]} = (x_1^2, x_1 x_2, x_2^2)$, $\mathbf{X}^{[3]} = (x_1^3, x_1^2 x_2, x_1 x_2^2, x_2^3)$ after reduction of the same terms.

3   PNN Construction

3.1   PNN General Architecture

The accuracy of approximation (3) depends of the length of time interval $T = [t_0, t]$ and number of nonlinear terms m. Dividing the T in a smaller steps and increasing m, obviously, results into more precise numerical ODE solving. Flow $\mathcal{M}_F^t(\mathbf{X}_0)$ can be associated with a network consisting of a sequence of polynomial neurons shown in Fig. 1. When (1) is non autonomous, PNN's weight matrices $R^{1i}(t_j, t_{j-1})$ depend not only on the length of a time step $t_j - t_{j-1}$ but also on time itself. It means that, generally speaking, PNN's weights are not shared between the layers.

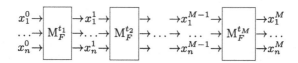

Fig. 1. Architecture of non stationary PNN with M layers

Thus, PNN architecture can represent a general solution of ordinary differential equation with the required degree of accuracy. To incorporate the knowledge about the system expressed in the ODE form into PNN, one should find weight matrices $R^{1i}(t_j, t_{j-1})$, $i = \overline{1..m}$, $j = \overline{1..M}$ directly from (1).

3.2   PNN Initialization

Let us described the proposed algorithm for the case, when $F(t, \mathbf{X}) \in C^{\infty}(\mathbb{R} \times \mathbb{R}^n)$, so it can be expanded in Taylor series in the neighborhood of $(t_0, \mathbf{X}_0)$. We consider the finite number of terms in the expansion and for the following inferences treat a non-stationary nonlinear system of ODEs with a polynomial right-hand side

$$\frac{d\mathbf{X}}{dt} = \sum_{k=0}^{N} \mathbf{P}^{1k}(t) \mathbf{X}^{[k]} \tag{4}$$

An iterative algorithm for constructing an approximate solution to nonlinear Eq. (4) in form (3) is based on the method of immersion in the space of phase moments. Let us introduce the notation for the vector of phase moment of m-th order $\mathbf{X}^{[m]}$ — Kroneker's degree of vector $\mathbf{X}$. Accepting this notation we can show that $\mathbf{X}^{[m]}$ satisfies the equation of form (5).

Theorem 1. *If $\mathbf{X}$ satisfies Eq. (4), then vector $\mathbf{X}^{[m]}$ satisfies (5) for any $m = \overline{1..N}$*

$$\frac{d\mathbf{X}^{[m]}}{dt} = \sum_{k=m}^{N} \mathbf{P}^{mk}(t) \mathbf{X}^{[k]}, \tag{5}$$

where matrices $\mathbf{P}^{mk}(t)$ $k \geq m$ can be found by the formula

$$\mathbf{P}^{mk}(t) = \left\langle \mathbf{P}^{1k-m+1}(t) \otimes \mathbf{E}^{[m]} + \mathbf{E} \otimes \mathbf{P}^{m-1k-1}(t) \right\rangle. \tag{6}$$

A proof is carried out by induction within the order of the phase moment. Obviously, the basis ($m = 1$) is hold resulting in the matrices P^{1k} from the Eq. (4). Taking the induction step, we assume that the statement holds for any given case $m = l$ and prove that it must also hold for the next case $m = l + 1$. For sake of further computing convenience, let us illustrate the procedure for $m = 2$ and introduce the necessary matrix operations.

Here and further in the transformations, we use the property of derivative of tensor product. Thus, the derivative of the vector of second phase moments can be transformed in the following way:

$$\frac{d\mathbf{X}^{[2]}}{dt} = \frac{d\mathbf{X}}{dt} \otimes \mathbf{X} + \mathbf{X} \otimes \frac{d\mathbf{X}}{dt}$$

$$= \left(\sum_{k=1}^{N} \mathbf{P}^{1k}(t) \mathbf{X}^{[k]} \right) \otimes \mathbf{X} + \mathbf{X} \otimes \left(\sum_{k=0}^{N} \mathbf{P}^{1k}(t) \mathbf{X}^{[k]} \right)$$

$$= \sum_{k=1}^{N} \left(\left(\mathbf{P}^{1k}(t) \mathbf{X}^{[k]} \right) \otimes (\mathbf{EX}) + (\mathbf{EX}) \otimes \left(\mathbf{P}^{1k}(t) \mathbf{X}^{[k]} \right) \right) \tag{7}$$

$$= \sum_{k=1}^{N} \left\langle \mathbf{P}^{1k} \otimes \mathbf{E} + \mathbf{E} \otimes \mathbf{P}^{1k} \right\rangle \mathbf{X}^{[k+1]} = \sum_{k=2}^{N} \mathbf{P}^{2k}(t) \mathbf{X}^{[k]}$$

where

$$\mathbf{P}^{2k}(t) = \left\langle \mathbf{P}^{1k}(t) \otimes \mathbf{E} + \mathbf{E} \otimes \mathbf{P}^{1k}(t) \right\rangle, k \geq 2 \tag{8}$$

While calculating matrix $P^{2k}(t)$, we use the operation of tensor multiplication and the operation of matrix addition. Taking into account the Kronecker degree definition for a vector, during tensor multiplication of matrices, we sum the columns corresponding to the same monomials $x_1^{k_1}...x_n^{k_n}$. Then, after adding the matrices, we remove the duplicate rows. The result of joint use of tensor multiplication and matrix addition according to that rule, we enclose in brackets $\langle\rangle$ (see Eq. (6))

where

$$P^{3k}(t) = \left\langle P^{1k-2}(t) \otimes E^{[2]} + E \otimes P^{2k-1}(t) \right\rangle, k \geq 3. \tag{9}$$

Let us take an induction step and assume (7) holds for $m = l$, then the derivative of the vector of $l+1$ phase moments can be transformed in the similar way

$$\frac{d\mathbf{X}^{[l+1]}}{dt} = \frac{d}{dt}\left(\mathbf{X} \otimes \mathbf{X}^{[l]}\right) = \frac{d\mathbf{X}}{dt} \otimes \mathbf{X}^{[l]} + \mathbf{X} \otimes \frac{d\mathbf{X}^{[2]}}{dt}$$

$$= \left(\sum_{k=1}^{N} P^{1k}(t) \mathbf{X}^{[k]}\right) \otimes \mathbf{X}^{[l]} + \mathbf{X} \otimes \left(\sum_{k=l}^{N} P^{lk}(t) \mathbf{X}^{[k]}\right)$$

$$= \sum_{k=1}^{N} \left(\left(P^{1l}(t) \mathbf{X}^{[k]}\right) \otimes (E\mathbf{X})^{[l]} + (E\mathbf{X}) \otimes \left(P^{lk}(t) \mathbf{X}^{[k]}\right)\right)$$

$$= \sum_{k=1}^{N} \left\langle P^{1k-l+1} \otimes E^{[l]} + E \otimes P^{lk} \right\rangle \mathbf{X}^{[k+1]} \tag{10}$$

$$= \sum_{k=l}^{N} \left\langle P^{1k-l} \otimes E^{[l]} + E \otimes P^{lk-1} \right\rangle \mathbf{X}^{[k]} = \sum_{k=l+1}^{N} P^{lk}(t) \mathbf{X}^{[k]}$$

where

$$P^{l+1k}(t) = \left\langle P^{1k-l}(t) \otimes E^{[2]} + E \otimes P^{lk-1}(t) \right\rangle, k \geq l+1. \tag{11}$$

Equation (10) together with (11) prove the theorem.

Finally, let us introduce an iterative routine for matrices R^{1i} computing, based on utilization of auxiliary matrices P^{mk} constructed with the Theorem 1. At first, we consider a linear equation ($N = 1$)

$$\frac{d\mathbf{X}}{dt} = P^{11}(t) \mathbf{X}. \tag{12}$$

The solution of this equation can be found analytically or numerically (for example $R^{11}(t, t_0) = \exp\left((t - t_0) P^{11}\right)$ if $P^{11}(t) = P^{11}$) in the form

$$\mathbf{X}(t) = R^{11}(t, t_0) \mathbf{X_0}, \qquad \mathbf{X_0} = \mathbf{X}(t_0) \tag{13}$$

Further, we consider an Eq. (4) with quadratic nonlinearity ($N = 2$) and introduce a procedure to find the solution

$$\frac{d\mathbf{X}}{dt} = P^{11}(t) \mathbf{X} + P^{12}(t) \mathbf{X}^{[2]} \tag{14}$$

Substitute solution (13) to linear Eq. (12) into the second term on the right-hand side of nonlinear Eq. (14)

$$\frac{d\mathbf{X}}{dt} = \mathrm{P}^{11}(t)\mathbf{X} + \mathrm{P}^{12}(t)\mathrm{R}^{22}(t, t_0)\mathbf{X_0}^{[2]},$$

(15)

$$\mathrm{R}^{22}(t, t_0) = \left(\mathrm{R}^{11}(t, t_0)\right)^{[2]}$$

Equation (15) becomes linear with respect to $\mathbf{X}$ and inhomogeneous, thus its solution can be written in the form

$$\mathbf{X}(t) = \mathrm{R}^{11}(t, t_0)\mathbf{X_0} + \mathrm{R}^{12}(t, t_0)\mathbf{X_0}^{[2]},$$

(16)

where

$$\mathrm{R}^{12}(t, t_0) = \int_{t_0}^{t} \mathrm{R}^{11}(t, \tau)\mathrm{P}^{12}(t)\mathrm{R}^{22}(\tau, t_0)\,d\tau$$

(17)

Then, we need to find expression for $\mathbf{X}^{[2]}$ to iteratively increase an order of non-linearity for the solution. For this, we use corresponding to (14) auxiliary system of equations with respect to vector of phase moments introduced in the Theorem 1. Substitute linear solution (13) into the second term on the right-hand side of nonlinear Eq. (5):

$$\frac{d\mathbf{X}^{[2]}}{dt} = \mathrm{P}^{22}(t)\mathbf{X}^{[2]} + \mathrm{P}^{23}(t)\mathrm{R}^{33}(t, t_0)\mathbf{X_0}^{[3]},$$

(18)

$$\mathrm{R}^{33}(t, t_0) = \left(\mathrm{R}^{11}(t, t_0)\right)^{[3]}$$

Again, the Eq. (18) is linear with respect to $\mathbf{X}$ and inhomogeneous, this its solution can be written in the form:

$$\mathbf{X}^{[2]}(t) = \mathrm{R}^{22}(t, t_0)\mathbf{X_0}^{[2]} + \mathrm{R}^{23}(t, t_0)\mathbf{X_0}^{[3]},$$

(19)

where

$$\mathrm{R}^{23}(t, t_0) = \int_{t_0}^{t} \mathrm{R}^{22}(t, \tau)\mathrm{P}^{23}(t)\mathrm{R}^{33}(\tau, t_0)\,d\tau.$$

(20)

To see the iterative pattern, let us show the introduced procedure for one step forward. We consider an Eq. (4) with cubic nonlinearity ($N = 3$)

$$\frac{d\mathbf{X}}{dt} = \mathrm{P}^{11}(t)\mathbf{X} + \mathrm{P}^{12}(t)\mathbf{X}^{[2]} + \mathrm{P}^{13}(t)\mathbf{X}^{[3]}$$

(21)

and repeat the steps to find its solution.

Substitute solution (13) into the third term on the right-hand side of nonlinear Eq. (21) and solution (19) into the second term of (21)

$$\frac{d\mathbf{X}}{dt} = P^{11}(t)\,\mathbf{X} + P^{12}(t)\,R^{22}(t,t_0)\,\mathbf{X_0}^{[2]} + P^{23}(t)\,R^{33}(t,t_0)\,\mathbf{X_0}^{[3]}. \qquad (22)$$

Again, these substitutions made (22) linear with respect to $\mathbf{X}$ and its solution can be written in the form:

$$\mathbf{X}(t) = R^{11}(t,t_0)\,\mathbf{X_0} + R^{12}(t,t_0)\,\mathbf{X_0}^{[2]} + R^{13}(t,t_0)\,\mathbf{X_0}^{[3]}, \qquad (23)$$

where

$$R^{13}(t,t_0) = \int_{t_0}^{t} R^{11}(t,\tau)\,P^{12}(t)\,R^{23}(\tau,t_0)\,d\tau$$

$$+ \int_{t_0}^{t} R^{11}(t,\tau)\,P^{13}(t)\,R^{33}(\tau,t_0)\,d\tau. \qquad (24)$$

Thus, now we can see a general pattern to find successively unknown matrices R^{1i}, $i = \overline{1..m}$. Increasing at each step the order $l \leq N$ of non-linearity in the right side of the Eq. (4) and auxiliary Eq. (5), we try to get rid of the terms higher than linear (for $k = \overline{2..l}$) by substituting

– instead of $k = \overline{2..l-1}$: the expressions for $\mathbf{X}^{[k]}$ found at the previous steps solving (5);
– instead of $k = l$: a linear solution (13).

By these means, at each successive step, we get a linear inhomogeneous equation with respect to $\mathbf{X}$ that can be solved analytically. Finally, for $l = N$ we get

$$\mathbf{X}(t) = \sum_{k=1}^{N} R^{1k}(t,t_0)\,\mathbf{X_0}^{[k]}, \qquad (25)$$

where

$$R^{ik}(t,t_0) = \sum_{j=i+1}^{k} \int_{t_0}^{t} R^{ii}(t,\tau)\,P^{ij}(t)\,R^{jk}(\tau,t_0)\,d\tau, \qquad (26)$$

$$R^{ii}(t,t_0) = \left(R^{11}(t,t_0)\right)^{[i]}.$$

Thus, this section introduces an iterative procedure to find the solution to (4) in polynomial form (3) and initialize the weights of the corresponding PNN.

4   Numerical Example

To illustrate the proposed method for identification of non-autonomous ODEs, let us consider an electrostatic deflector equations. This system is described by the following ODEs:

$$\dot{x} = y \tag{27}$$

$$\dot{y} = -2x + \frac{x^2}{p(t)}$$

where x and y are the state variables and p is a positive unknown parameter that can have different values over the time. The initial values of (27) are $x(0) = x_0$, $y(0) = y_0$. For the sake of simplicity, assume that $p(t)$ is a step function:

$$p(t) = \begin{cases} p_1, \text{ if } t \in [0, t_1] \\ p_2, \text{ if } t \in [t_1, t_2] \\ p_3, \text{ if } t \in [t_2, t_3] \end{cases}$$

The solution of the system (27) is continuous, meaning that at each switching point the following condition is hold $(x_i(t_i), y_i(t_i)) = (x_{i+1}(t_i), y_{i+1}(t_i))$, $i = 1..2$.

Let us select a set of p_i values and initial condition and generate training data using system (27) and any traditional numerical solver for ODE. We consider the time interval $T = [0; 3]$, $t_i = [1; 2; 3]$ $p_i = [10; 50; 100]$ and $(x_0; y_0) = (-2; 4)$. It should be noted, that this information is used only for generating training data, from which unknown parameters are identified.

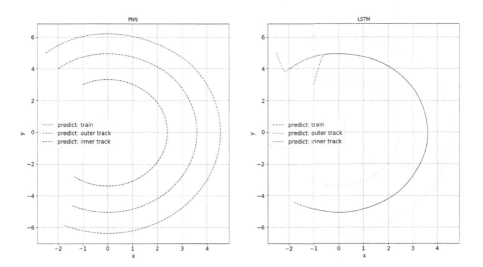

Fig. 2. Phase portrait of the reconstructed system using PNN (with weights initialization) and LSTM

Following the procedure for ODEs right hand side identification described in [14,15], we approximately find the unknown matrices P^{1i} for each of the switch intervals:

$$P_1^{11} = \begin{pmatrix} 4.07 \cdot 10^{-6} & 0.99 \\ -1.99 & 4.38 \cdot 10^{-6} \end{pmatrix} P_1^{12} = \begin{pmatrix} 1.24 \cdot 10^{-7} & 3.28 \cdot 10^{-6} & 2.00 \cdot 10^{-9} \\ 0.09 & -9.71 \cdot 10^{-8} & 3.34 \cdot 10^{-6} \end{pmatrix}$$

$$P_2^{11} = \begin{pmatrix} 2.4 \cdot 10^{-5} & 0.99 \\ -1.99 & 1.35 \cdot 10^{-5} \end{pmatrix} P_2^{12} = \begin{pmatrix} 1.68 \cdot 10^{-7} & 6.70 \cdot 10^{-7} & -4.07 \cdot 10^{-9} \\ 0.02 & -3.56 \cdot 10^{-8} & 6.95 \cdot 10^{-7} \end{pmatrix} \quad (28)$$

$$P_3^{11} = \begin{pmatrix} -4.32 \cdot 10^{-5} & 0.99 \\ -2.00 & 1.45 \cdot 10^{-5} \end{pmatrix} P_3^{12} = \begin{pmatrix} -1.44 \cdot 10^{-7} & 3.91 \cdot 10^{-7} & 6.08 \cdot 10^{-9} \\ 9.99 \cdot 10^{-3} & 1.03 \cdot 10^{-7} & 3.40 \cdot 10^{-7} \end{pmatrix}$$

The maximal order of non-linearity in the right hand side of (27) is two, so we should build PNN of the second order nonlinearity having at least two weight matrices $R^{1i}(t)$, $i = \overline{1..2}$ at each layer. The Eq. (27) is step autonomous, so the matrices R^{1i} are shared through the time steps within each of the switching interval.

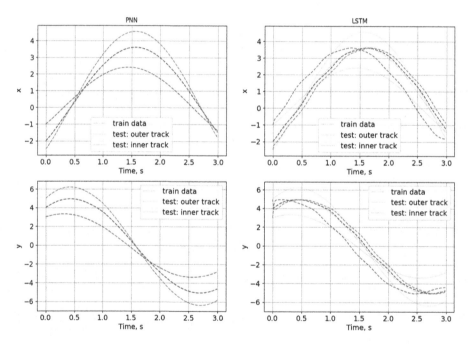

Fig. 3. System trajectories of the reconstructed system using PNN (with weights initialization) and LSTM

At first let us use the weights initialization procedure described in Sect. 3.2. We start from the system matrices obtained through the reconstruction procedure (28). To test the generalization ability of PNN, two test initial values are considered: $[-2.5; 5]$ and $[-1; 3]$. The PNN is required to reconstruct the system trajectories started form these values. The results are compared with LSTM neural network because of its internal connection with a discrete time dynamical system.

Figures 2 and 3 depict the comparison of the phase portrait and system trajectories correspondingly for the identified system predicted for the train and test initial values.

It is clearly seen from the Figs. 2 and 3 that LSTM is unable to recover the dynamics of the system just memorizing the trajectory used for training. Even for different initial conditions it can predict only seen system behaviour, while PNN correctly reconstruct the dynamics and shows great generalization ability for the initial valued laying beyond the range used for training.

Now let us compare identification abilities of PNN and LSTM for another set of switching parameters that don't provide smoothness of the trajectories: $p_i = [2; 50; 5]$ and learn PNN from scratch without reconstruction of ODEs matrices and applying weights initialization procedure described above. The results are presented in the Fig. 4.

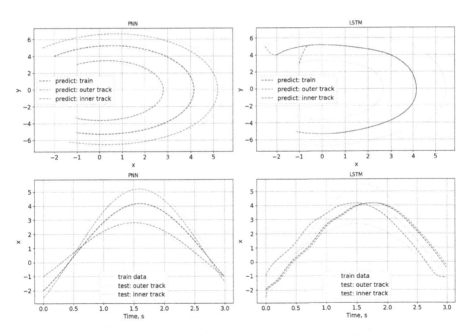

Fig. 4. Phase portrait and $x(t)$ trajectories for the reconstructed system using PNN (without weights initialization) and LSTM

Figure 4 shows that even starting from zero initial weights, PNN is able to recover the dynamics correctly. Of course, there are discrepancies between predicted and true trajectory for test initial values around the switching points, but nevertheless in general the system behaviour is captured correctly. Unfortunately, in the same time LSTM again just memorize the training data.

5   Conclusion

This paper presents an approach for system identification based on PNN that doesn't require multiple solving of ODEs with different parameters. By the design PNN can incorporate prior knowledge of dynamical system by direct transferring ODE to neural polynomial architecture (PNN). The approach is based on Taylor mapping technique for solving ODEs. It provides transformation of the dynamic system represented in the form of ODEs to the initial weights of the polynomial neural network. This paper aims to present the algorithm for non stationary PNN weights initialization in the form admitting analysis of PNN convergence to general solution of non-autonomous ODE. However, even when we don't have information about the dynamical system generated the system trajectory, PNN can be learned from scratch and still provide physically consistent results. The identification ability of PNN is illustrated in the example of ODEs with switches describing the dynamics of electrostatics deflector. Prediction results using PNN (with and without weights initialization) are compared with LSTM. They show PNN ability to recover hidden system dynamics and generalize prediction for the initial values beyond the range of the training data.

References

1. Ojeda, C., Georgiev, B., Cvejoski, K., Schucker, J., Bauckhage, C., Sánchez, R.J.: Switching dynamical systems with deep neural networks. In: 2020 25th International Conference on Pattern Recognition (ICPR), 2021, pp. 6305–6312 (2021)
2. Karniadakis, G.E., Kevrekidis, I.G., Lu, L., Perdikaris, P., Wang, S., Yang, L.: Physics-informed machine learning. Nat. Rev. Phys. **3**(6), 422–440 (2021)
3. Lutter, M., Ritter, C., Peters, J.: Deep Lagrangian networks: using physics as model prior for deep learning (2019)
4. Roehrl, M.A., Runkler, T.A., Brandtstetter, V., Tokic, M., Obermayer, S.: Modeling system dynamics with physics-informed neural networks based on Lagrangian mechanics, vol. 53 (2020)
5. Greydanus, S., Dzamba, M., Yosinski, J.: Hamiltonian neural networks, vol. 32 (2019)
6. Han, C.-D., Glaz, B., Haile, M., Lai, Y.-C.: Adaptable Hamiltonian neural networks, vol. 3 (2021)
7. Wang, Y.-J., Lin, C.-T.: Runge-Kutta neural network for identification of dynamical systems in high accuracy. IEEE Trans. Neural Netw. **9**(2), 294–307 (1998)
8. Dufera, T.T.: Deep neural network for system of ordinary differential equations: vectorized algorithm and simulation. Mach. Learn. Appl. **5**, 100058 (2021)
9. Chen, R.T.Q., Rubanova, Y., Bettencourt, J., Duvenaud, D.K.: Neural ordinary differential equations, vol. 31 (2018)
10. Rubanova, Y., Chen, R.T.Q., Duvenaud, D.K.: Latent ordinary differential equations for irregularly-sampled time series, vol. 32 (2019)
11. Andrianov, S.: Dynamical Modeling of Control Systems for Particle Beams. SPb: Saint Petersburg State University (2004)
12. Andrianov, S.: Symbolic computation of approximate symmetries for ordinary differential equations. Math. Comput. Simul. **57**(3–5), 147–154 (2001)

13. Ivanov, A., Golovkina, A., Iben, U.: Polynomial neural networks and Taylor maps for dynamical systems simulation and learning. Front. Artif. Intell. Appl. **325**, 1230–1237 (2019)
14. Golovkina, A., Kozynchenko, V., Kulabukhova, N.: Reconstruction and identification of dynamical systems based on Taylor maps. In: Gervasi, O., et al. (eds.) ICCSA 2021. LNCS, vol. 12956, pp. 360–369. Springer, Cham (2021). https://doi.org/10.1007/978-3-030-87010-2_26
15. Golovkina, A., Kozynchenko, V., Kulabukhova, N.: Reconstruction of ordinary differential equations from irregularly distributed time-series data. In: 9th International Conference "Distributed Computing and Grid Technologies in Science and Education". Crossref, December 2021

Impact of Reduced and Mixed-Precision on the Efficiency of a Multi-GPU Platform on CFD Applications

Gabriel Freytag[1]([✉]), João V. F. Lima[2], Paolo Rech[1], and Philippe O. A. Navaux[1]

[1] Informatics Institute, UFRGS, Porto Alegre, Brazil
gfreytag@inf.ufrgs.br
[2] Informatics Institute, UFSM, Santa Maria, Brazil

Abstract. The heterogeneity of modern computing architectures allows software engineers to refine their algorithms and assign the procedures with peculiar characteristics to the device with the most suitable architecture. In particular, the latest computing architectures, such as Nvidia's Graphics Processing Units (GPUs), feature mixed-precision Floating-Point Units (FPUs) that natively support double, single, and half-precision arithmetic operations. By using mixed precisions in a specific portion of the code can significantly improve both performances and computing efficiency. The challenge is to identify which procedure to run in lower precision without jeopardizing the accuracy loss.

This work explores the use of mixed-precision FPUs in Nvidia's P100 GPU for improving the performance and efficiency of High-Performance Computing (HPC) applications. We investigate the performance and power efficiency of a Computational Fluid Dynamic (CFD) application. We first use the same precision for both arithmetic operations and storage and then use single or half-precision for arithmetic operations and double, single, or half for storage. We also explore the CUDA platform's intrinsic mathematical functions, and the results show a speedup of $1.44\times$ with only 0.02% of accuracy loss in comparison to regular functions. By using half-precision for storage and single-precision for arithmetic operations, we were able to improve the performance up to more than $11\times$ and power consumption of the application up to more than $3.4\times$, with only 0.02% of accuracy loss compared to double-precision.

1 Introduction

On the path to the exascale, both hardware and software has become increasingly heterogeneous. Naturally, the plethora of existing computational problems has several distinct intrinsic characteristics that, to be quickly and efficiently computed, require a high level of affinity with the hardware's architecture. While some characteristics have a limited level of parallelism, others can be highly parallelized, require special operations, require a large amount of memory, or

O. Gervasi et al. (Eds.): ICCSA 2022 Workshops, LNCS 13380, pp. 570–587, 2022.
https://doi.org/10.1007/978-3-031-10542-5_39

need high-speed interconnections. Therefore, to match all distinct characteristics of the problems with the most suitable hardware maximizing performance, the software itself becomes heterogeneous.

Today's High-Performance Computing (HPC) systems connect a large number of devices with distinct hardware architectures that are themselves becoming heterogeneous. The most common devices are Central Processing Units (CPUs), Graphics Processing Units (GPUs), Field-Programmable Gate Array (FPGAs), and others. While some CPU devices deliver a portion of robust cores and others of reduced computational power but more energy-efficient, latest GPUs deliver a set of heterogeneous Floating-Point Units (FPUs), which have discrete floating-point precision and consequently distinct performance and power consumption.

At the same time that the heterogeneity of systems increases to support different computational characteristics, the demand for computational and storage resources exceeds current availability. Although there are a large number of optimization strategies and highly parallel systems, they do not account for the computational demand of modern large-scale applications such as scientific computing, artificial intelligence, data mining, social media, and many others. However, while some problems require exact results, others admit approximate results reducing the resource requirements and consequently improve the performance.

One of the most prevalent strategies in the approximate computing paradigm is precision scaling, which takes advantage of discrete FPUs [33]. Mixed-precision architectures usually support two or more floating-point precision arithmetic operations and allow the reduction of both storage, energy, and computational requirements. By reducing the precision of some data and arithmetic operations of the problems, it is possible to trade-off the quality of the result by the performance and energy efficiency of the execution.

Several studies explored reduced and mixed-precision in neural network training in deep learning and machine learning algorithms, increasing the performance significantly with little to no degradation in the networks' accuracy [12, 22, 31] as well as energy consumption reduction [16, 37]. However, reduced and mixed-precision also improve both performance and energy consumption of scientific applications as in iterative refinement methods [17, 18], molecular dynamics [24], and computational fluid dynamics [9]. Although the last one accelerated a CFD using mixed-precision, no half-precision arithmetic operations were available in the hardware used by the authors. Moreover, they do not exploit the CUDA platform's intrinsic mathematical functions that have improved performance in comparison to the regular ones.

In this paper, we evaluate the impact of reduced and mixed-precision on the performance, energy efficiency, and accuracy of stencil computing on a multi-GPU platform that natively supports mixed-precision floating-point operations. As a case study, we use the well-known Computational Fluid Dynamics (CFD) application called Lattice-Boltzmann Method (LBM) with a three-dimensional model, namely, D3Q19.

2   Reduced and Mixed-Precision Algorithms

In this section, we present the three multi-GPU implementations of the 3D CFD application LBM based on [27]. One version has fixed precision for data storage and computations defined at compile time. The other two versions have mixed precision for arithmetic operations, single or half, and data storage defined at compile time in any of the three precision types.

The three versions are:

multigpu The floating-point arithmetic operations and storage are in the same floating-point precision selected at compile time. This version performs all arithmetic operations with regular mathematical functions from CUDA.

multigpu_float This implementation performs all floating-point arithmetic operations in single-precision using intrinsic mathematical functions from CUDA. Data storage is defined at runtime in double, single or half.

multigpu_half2 This version does the arithmetic operations in half-precision with intrinsic mathematical functions from CUDA. In addition, it uses vectorized data types and NVIDIA's 2-way half-precision functions that perform two half arithmetic operations in parallel on a single-precision FPU.

2.1   Reduced-Precision Implementation

Our multi-GPU algorithm decomposes the data domain into subdomains where each subdomain is assigned to a device. Figure 1 shows the pseudocode of the multi-GPU implementation of our CFD application. It has five kernels, and the first (line 3) initializes the density of each particle. This first kernel runs at the pre-processing stage since this kernel runs only once. Afterwards, the simulation of the fluid flow starts by redistributing the propagation forces of each particle, as can be seen at line 8.

The next step of the simulation is the propagation of the particles (line 19) in which particles can leave one subdomain and move to another one. The fluid particles have nineteen propagation directions. After decomposing the data domain into one subdomain per device, the propagation becomes restricted to the particles of each subdomain. Consequently, each GPU device will perform disjoint simulations just with its fragment of the domain and do not contribute to the global simulation. In order to perform the simulation in parallel and synchronize each time step, we used ghost zones to synchronize the local subdomains of each GPU device with its neighbors. Each time step copies the boundaries of each subdomain to temporary buffers owned by the neighbors (line 12), and then it copies the neighbor's boundaries from the buffers into the subdomains (line 15).

As the platform that we are exploring has only four GPU devices, the decomposition of the domain in more than just one dimension is not necessary. Splitting just one of the dimensions of a domain in half results in two subdomains, and each one requires a copy to each of its neighboring subdomains of two faces and four diagonals, which in this case the faces already have they included. As we divide more dimensions in half, the number of subdomains and copies of faces doubles and diagonals triples. Thus, using only four GPUs, splitting just one of the dimensions in the number of devices involved in the computation is enough and minimizes the ghost zones' synchronization overhead in our case.

Finally, as we use up to four GPU devices in a collaborative way, manage these devices using only one CPU thread substantially harms the performance of the implementation. To manage each GPU independently, we use one CPU thread per GPU device by parallelizing the for loops We use `#pragma omp parallel for num_threads(deviceCount)` on the for loops of lines 6, 11, 14, and 17 of pseudocode from Fig. 1 to manage multiple devices in parallel.

2.2 Single-Precision Implementation

This implementation performs all arithmetics in single-precision instead of performing on the same precision used to store the domain's data in memory. Moreover, it uses intrinsic mathematical functions from CUDA platform rather than regular mathematical operations. This mixed-precision implementation uses the same multi-GPU algorithm previously described in Sect. 2.1 and only changes the kernels' arithmetic operations precision and mathematical functions.

Figure 2 shows an example of the use of the CUDA platform's intrinsic mathematical functions. To add up two single-precision (or float) numbers, instead of using the regular addition function $+$, we use the intrinsic addition function $\_\_fadd()$. We do the same for the other mathematical functions and, instead of using the regular subtraction function $-$, the regular multiplication function $*$, and the regular division function $/$, we use the respective intrinsic functions $\_\_fsub()$, $\_\_fmul()$, and $\_\_fdiv()$. For each of the single-precision intrinsic mathematical functions, we use the round to nearest even rounding mode by suffixing each function with $\_rn$. This intrinsic functions map to fewer native instructions and, therefore, are faster than the regular functions but less accurate.

2.3 2-Way Half-Precision Implementation

This version makes use of arithmetic operations in half-precision and two parallel operations in a single FPU. The implementation packs data into a *half2* vector data type in order to issue two operations per FPU. As we only use double, single, or half-precision to store the domain's data in memory, we need to convert these data to a *half2* data type before the call of computation kernels. Moreover, we need to rearrange the operands in order to avoid two computations on the same data.

Figure 3 shows an example of the 2-way half-precision arithmetic operations. At lines 1, 2, 3, and 4 of the pseudocode, we create local registers with type *half2* placing in the first position of the intrinsic function $\_\_floats2half2()$ the data of one operation, and in the second position of the function the data of the second operation. Therefore, to add up the data of *a1* and *a2* and *b1* and *b2*, first, we need to create a register *a1b1* containing the data of *a1* and *b1* (line 1) and other *a2b2* containing the data of *a2* and *b2* (line 2). Then we can add up

```
 1: Initialize parameters
 2: for Each Nx × Ny × Nz do
 3:    INITIALIZE conditions
 4: end for
 5: for Each time step do
 6:    for Each device do
 7:       for Each Nx × Ny × Nz do
 8:          REDISTRIBUTE
 9:       end for
10:    end for
11:    for Each device do
12:       COPYBOUNDARIESTONEIGHBORBUFFERS
13:    end for
14:    for Each device do
15:       COPYNEIGHBORBOUNDARIESFROMBUFFERS
16:    end for
17:    for Each device do
18:       for Each Nx × Ny × Nz do
19:          PROPAGATE
20:          BOUNCEBACK
21:          RELAXATION
22:       end for
23:    end for
24: end for
```

Fig. 1. CFD Multi-GPU algorithm.

```
 1: __half2 a1b1 = __floats2half2_rn(a1, b1)
 2: __half2 a2b2 = __floats2half2_rn(a2, b2)
 3: __half2 c1d1 = __floats2half2_rn(c1, d1)
 4: __half2 c2d2 = __floats2half2_rn(c2, d2)
 5:
 6: __half2 ab = __hadd2(a1b1, a2b2)
 7: __half2 cd = __hmul2(c1d1, c2d2)
 8:
 9: __half a = ab.x
10: __half b = ab.y
11: __half c = cd.x
12: __half d = cd.y
```

```
1: float a = __fadd_rn(a1, a2)
2: float b = __fsub_rn(b1, b2)
3: float c = __fmul_rn(c1, c2)
4: float d = __fdiv_rn(d1, d2)
```

Fig. 2. CUDA single-precision intrinsic math functions.

Fig. 3. CUDA Half2 intrinsic math functions.

these four data by calling the intrinsic addition function __hadd2(a1b1, a2b2) (line 6) and saving the result to the ab register. Finally, to get the answer to the addition of a1 and a2, and b1 and b2, we call ab.x (line 9) and ab.y (line 10), respectively.

3   Tools and Methods

This section details the hardware configuration and methodology used in our reduced and mixed-precision experiments.

3.1   Evaluation Platform

We target a experimental platform, called BLAISE, enhanced with GPUs capable of native mixed-precision floating-point arithmetics. It consists of two NUMA (Non-Uniform Memory Access) nodes, each with one Intel Xeon E5-2699 v4 (Broadwell) processor with 22 cores running at 2.2 GHz or 3.6 GHz with Turbo Boost (44 cores total), and 256 GB of main memory. The machine has 4 NVIDIA Tesla P100 (Pascal architecture) GPUs interconnected with NVIDIA's NVLink, each having 3,584 CUDA cores running at 1.48 GHz and 16 GB HBM2 global memory (a total of 14,336 CUDA cores and 64 GB of GPU global memory).

We used as software environment the C/C++ compiler GCC version 8.3 and NVIDIA's CUDA toolkit release 10.1, version 10.1.168. The flags used to compile all the three implementations were *-O3*, *-m64*, *-arch=sm_ 60*, and *-Xcompiler -fopenmp -lgomp*. All this was running over a Debian GNU/Linux 10 (buster) operational system.

3.2   Methodology

We only report the execution time of the processing stage, which is the time taken to run all the iterations of the time step for loop (lines 5 to 24 of the pseudocode in Fig. 1), that we fixed to 200 iterations in all our experiments. Since we investigate the performance of the three implementations using from 1 up to 4 GPU devices, we split the domain in the same number of subdomains as devices involved in the computation. The split step occurs in the pre-processing stage and does not appear in the execution time measurements.

The results reported are a mean of 10 samples using domains of size up to the largest one that fits in single GPU memory using double-precision. Although splitting the domain across multiple GPUs allows the use of larger domains, to investigate the impact of incrementing the number of GPUs from one to four, we run experiments using five 3D domains with size 128, 192, 256, 320, and 352. All these domains have a rectangular obstacle placed in the middle of the flow. Moreover, for each implementation, we evaluate the performance of storing the domain in memory using double, single, and half-precision floating-point.

The accuracy of the implementations was measured by the absolute floating-point error. To determine the absolute error of an experiment, we subtract its final fluid density from the exact fluid density computed using double-precision. We show the difference between the exact density and the density returned by the experiment (absolute error) as a percentage of the exact density.

To collect the GPU's resource utilization metrics, we used the NVIDIA's System Management Interface (*nvidia-smi*) command-line utility. This utility allows to query the GPU device state and retrieve information about its configuration and its instant resource utilization. During each experiment, we collect the instantaneous state of all GPUs at every teen milliseconds. In the end, we sum up all the records related to each execution and divide it by the respective number of records. Moreover, we only collect the informations of the devices involved in the respective experiment, does not including data from idle devices. Therefore, we report the mean of teen executions of each experiment for the metrics: power consumption, GPU utilization, memory usage, and GPU memory read/write utilization.

4   Experimental Results

In this section, we present the experimental results of our reduced and mixed-precision implementations by using double, single, and half-precision floating-point (FP) data types to store the CFD's domain in memory and from one up to four GPU devices.

4.1   Performance and Accuracy Evaluation

Table 1 shows the execution time, speedup with *multigpu* and single GPU on each FP as baseline, floating-point absolute error, total power consumption, GPU capacity utilization, memory usage and memory read or write overtime utilization for each of our three implementations using double, single and half-precision floating-point data types from one up to 4 GPU devices.

Looking at the execution times of the *multigpu* implementation on a single GPU, we observe that the reduction of the floating-point precision substantially improves its performance. Compared to the execution time using double-precision to store the data in memory, single-precision improves the performance of the implementation by up to 1.72× with no accuracy loss. With half-precision, performance improves by up to 2.57× with an accuracy loss of 0.53%.

Using more GPUs to perform the computation in parallel made it possible to improve the implementation's performance further. Compared to double-precision and single GPU, single-precision improved the performance of the *multigpu* implementation by up to 3.24, 4.67×, and 5.9× using two, three, and all four GPUs, respectively, and no accuracy loss. With half-precision, improvements were up to 4.86×, 7.10×, and 8.59× with an accuracy loss of 0.84%, 1.05%, and 0.22% with two, three, and four GPUs, respectively.

If we look at the performance of the *multigpu_float* and *multigpu_half2* implementations over *multigpu* with double-precision and single GPU, it is possible to see that both implementations improve the performance significantly. More precisely, *multigpu_float* improved by up to 1.21x with no accuracy loss, and *multigpu_half2* improved by 1.17x with an accuracy loss of 0.09%.

Table 1. Execution time, speedup, floating-point absolute error, power consumption, GPU utilization, amount of GPU memory used, and GPU memory utilization (read or write). It corresponds to the use of double, single, and half-precision floating-point, one up to 4 GPU devices, and a 3D domain of size $352 \times 352 \times 352$. The speedup is calculated over *multigpu*'s double-precision performance on a single GPU.

Implementation	FP	GPUs	Execution (s)	Speedup	FP Error (%)	Power (W)	GPU (%)	Memory (MiB)	Memory R/W (%)
multigpu	double	1	65.82	1.00	0.00	1985.93	99.39	12995.00	48.78
		2	35.02	1.88	0.00	1939.48	96.25	6743.00	45.53
		3	24.40	2.70	0.00	1952.66	92.44	4623.00	43.08
		4	19.47	3.38	0.00	1986.84	90.44	3583.00	40.87
	single	1	38.17	1.72	0.00	1266.33	99.35	6671.00	76.80
		2	20.34	3.24	0.00	1234.23	96.01	3547.00	72.09
		3	14.10	4.67	0.00	1240.12	93.27	2487.00	69.27
		4	11.16	5.90	0.00	1255.06	90.62	1967.00	65.60
	half	1	25.57	2.57	0.53	817.95	99.12	3511.00	86.62
		2	13.56	4.86	0.84	810.77	95.39	1947.00	81.60
		3	9.27	7.10	1.05	812.82	93.58	1419.00	79.30
		4	7.67	8.59	0.22	836.52	87.34	1159.00	72.85
multigpu_float	double	1	54.49	1.21	0.00	1492.80	99.44	12995.00	48.47
		2	29.44	2.24	0.00	1480.95	95.33	6743.00	44.42
		3	20.71	3.18	0.00	1514.98	91.28	4623.00	41.63
		4	16.81	3.92	0.00	1557.10	88.05	3583.00	39.00
	single	1	26.42	2.49	0.00	802.79	99.00	6671.00	64.99
		2	14.60	4.51	0.00	812.39	93.87	3547.00	58.64
		3	10.35	6.36	0.00	830.05	89.31	2487.00	55.13
		4	8.52	7.73	0.00	849.41	84.29	1967.00	50.44
	half	1	17.19	3.83	0.02	521.63	98.58	3511.00	73.62
		2	9.34	7.05	0.02	520.19	94.15	1947.00	68.15
		3	6.67	9.86	0.02	534.70	89.62	1419.00	64.14
		4	5.66	11.64	0.02	566.10	82.28	1159.00	57.29
multigpu_half2	double	1	56.49	1.17	0.09	1507.69	99.47	12995.00	45.40
		2	30.58	2.15	0.12	1503.53	95.55	6743.00	41.91
		3	21.53	3.06	0.15	1542.11	92.31	4623.00	39.80
		4	17.37	3.79	0.06	1587.30	88.73	3583.00	36.89
	single	1	27.40	2.40	0.09	816.62	99.06	6671.00	69.55
		2	15.12	4.35	0.12	820.43	93.92	3547.00	63.28
		3	10.66	6.18	0.15	837.15	89.90	2487.00	59.68
		4	8.72	7.55	0.06	863.72	85.72	1967.00	54.81
	half	1	18.33	3.59	0.09	560.20	98.74	3511.00	73.98
		2	10.03	6.56	0.12	562.62	93.35	1947.00	67.97
		3	6.91	9.53	0.15	570.02	91.38	1419.00	65.93
		4	5.85	11.26	0.06	595.69	84.03	1159.00	59.16

By using all four GPUs, the performance increases more than $11\times$. While *multigpu* improves by up to $3.38\times$, $5.9\times$, and $8.59\times$ with double, single, and half-precision, respectively, *multigpu_float* improves by up to $3.92\times$, $7.73\times$, and $11.64\times$, respectively. Already *multigpu_half2* improves by up to $3.79\times$, $7.55\times$, and $11.26\times$, respectively. *multigpu* and *multigpu_float* had an accuracy loss of 0.22% and 0.02%, respectively, only with half-precision, while *multigpu_half2* had an accuracy loss of 0.06% for all three precisions.

In Fig. 4, it is possible to see that difference in performance between both *multigpu_float* and *multigpu_half2* and *multigpu* becomes more prominent as the size of the domain increases. Furthermore, it is also possible to observe that the execution times of both *multigpu_float* and *multigpu_half2* are very similar on all domain sizes. Moreover, as the domain size increases, the accuracy loss of all three implementations reduces.

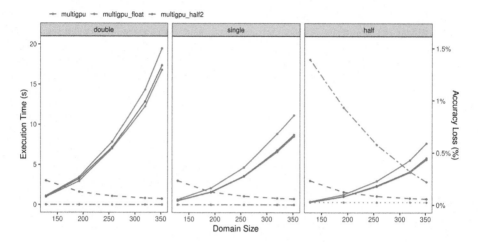

Fig. 4. Execution times of the three implementations (solid lines) using double, single, and half-precision floating-point to store the data in memory and their accuracies (dashed lines) on three-dimensional domains of size 128, 192, 256, 320, and 352 using four GPU devices.

4.2   Power Consumption Evaluation

In column seven of Table 1, we present the power consumption for each of the three implementations using from 1 up to 4 GPUs and double, single, and half-precision data types to store data. Looking only at the consumption while using a different number of GPUs within the same implementation and storage data type, it is possible to see that the power consumption remains almost the same when using one or more GPUs in parallel. The difference between the lowest and highest values for power consumption on the *multigpu* implementation is 2.38%, 2.53%, and 3.07%, for double, single, and half-precision as storage data types, respectively. Already for the *multigpu_ float* implementation, the differences are 4.89%, 5.48%, and 8.10%, and for the *multigpu_ half2* implementation, 5.27%, 5.45%, and 5.95% for double, single, and half-precision storage data types, respectively.

Let us compare the power consumption of the different storage data types on the same implementation. It is possible to observe that in all three implementations, the consumption was reduced by more than 50%, going from double to half-precision. Using half instead of double-precision on the *multigpu* implementation reduces approximately 57% of the power consumption with all four GPUs. Already on the *multigpu_ float* implementation, it reduces more than 63% and more than 62% on the *multigpu_ half2* implementation.

Now, let us analyze the power consumption between different implementations using the same data type for storage. We can see that using CUDA's intrinsic mathematical functions instead of the regular mathematical functions results in a significant reduction in power consumption. While the *multigpu* implementation consumes 1986.84, 1255.06, and 836.52 W with all for GPUs

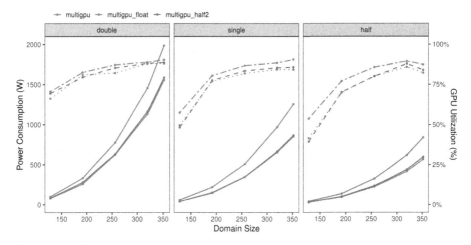

Fig. 5. Power consumption (solid lines) and the GPU utilization (dashed lines) of the three implementations using double, single, and half-precision to store the data. It corresponds to the use of four GPUs and domain size 128, 192, 256, 320, and 352.

in double, single, and half-precision, respectively, *multigpu_float* consumes only 1557.10, 849.41, and 566.10 W, and *multigpu_half2* consumes 1587.30, 863.72, and 595.69 W. This corresponds to a reduction of approximately 21%, 32%, and 32% for double, single, and half-precision on the *multigpu_float* implementation, and 20%, 31%, and 28% on *multigpu_half2*, respectively.

Figure 5 shows the power consumption of each implementation on five different domain sizes using all four GPU devices. As can be observed, the power consumption of all three implementations increases with larger domain sizes. However, let us look at the consumption of the *multigpu* implementation, which uses regular mathematical functions from CUDA, and compare it to the consumption of the *multigpu_float* and *multigpu_half2* implementations, which in turn use CUDA's intrinsic mathematical functions. It is clear that the difference in power consumption increases as the domains' size increases.

4.3 Memory Utilization Evaluation

In Table 1, we present the amount of GPUs' memory used (column *Memory*) by the three implementations to store the data in double, single, and half-precision. As can be seen, each of the three implementations used exactly the same amount of memory for each of the storage data types. With four GPUs, a total of 3583 MB, 1967 MB, and 1159 MB of global memory was used to store the data in double, single, and half-precision. However, while with a single GPU in double-precision the total amount of memory used was 12995 MB, with all four GPUs the total amount of memory used was 14332 MB, since 3583 MB of memory was used on each of the four GPUs. This is an increase of approximately 10%.

In the column *Memory R/W* of the Table 1, we also show the percentage of time in which read or write operations were performed in memory during the runtime. First, if wee look at the percentage of operations performed when using a different number of GPUs with the same data type to store the data, it is possible to see that the percentage reduces significantly as the number of GPUs increases. Second, if we compare the percentage of operations for the different storage data types, it is possible to see that it increases as the precision decreases. Third, if we look at the percentage of operations performed by the *multigpu_ float* and *multigpu_ half2* implementations in comparison to *multigpu*, we can see that the two implementations performing arithmetic operations sing CUDA's intrinsic mathematical functions have a higher percentage of memory read or write operations than the one using regular mathematical functions from CUDA.

As well as with the amount of memory, the percentage of read or write operations performed during runtime is given per GPU. Therefore, while using *multigpu*, double-precision, and a single GPU, the percentage of the time were memory operations were performed was about 48%. With all four GPUs, each GPU performed memory operations about 40% of the time.

Figure 6 shows the amount of memory and memory utilization (percentage of read or write operations performed during time) of each of the three implementations on five different domain sizes using all four GPU devices. As expected, the amount of memory used increases with larger domain sizes. Moreover, while the domain size increases, the memory read or write operations performed during the runtime increases at an even-slowing pace after domain size 256.

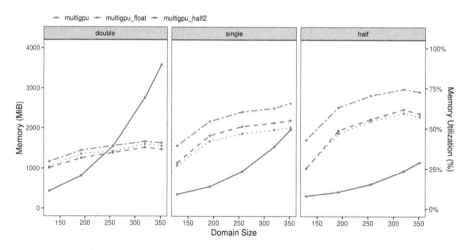

Fig. 6. Amount of memory (solid lines) and memory read/write utilization (dashed lines) of the three implementations using double, single, and half-precision to store the data. It corresponds to the use of four GPUs and domain size 128, 192, 256, 320, and 352. As the amount of memory used by the three implementations is the same on each precision, the solid lines overlap.

5 Discussion

In Sect. 4.1, it was possible to see that fastening the arithmetic operations to higher precision and storing the data in memory using a lower precision substantially improves the performance while minimizes the accuracy loss. As higher precision arithmetic operations are less likely to accumulate errors, at the moment of casting the final results to a lower precision, the loss of data is smaller and reduces the accuracy loss. Comparing the performance of the *multigpu_float* implementation using half-precision and all four GPUs against the *multigpu* implementation using double-precision and a single GPU, it is possible to see that the performance is improved by more than $11\times$ with only an accuracy loss of 0.02%.

As seen in Sect. 4.2, by reducing the precision of floating-point arithmetic operations, the total power consumption reduces substantially compared to more accurate operations. Since reduced-precision floating-point units require a lower number of hardware instructions to perform the arithmetic operations, the hardware area needed to implement the instructions is much smaller than that of higher precision FPUs. Consequently, the total amount of power consumed nearly drops by half compared to FPUs with twice the floating-point precision.

Despite reducing the floating-point precision improves the power consumption, it harms the accuracy of the arithmetic operations. As can be observed in Table 1, while using half-precision for the arithmetic operations and storage of data (*multigpu* implementation) reduces the total power consumed by nearly 58% compared to double-precision, the accuracy drops by up to 1.05% using three GPU devices. By using all four GPUs, the accuracy loss reduces to just 0.22%.

However, by mixing different floating-point precisions, it is possible to mitigate the accuracy loss maintaining the improved performance and reduced power consumption of lower precision floating-point arithmetics. By storing the data using half-precision and performing all the arithmetic operations in single-precision, it is possible to improve the performance with nearly the same power consumption than using just half-precision for both arithmetics and storage with minimal accuracy loss. As can be seen in Table 1, the performance of the *multigpu_float* implementation using half-precision and all four GPUs is approximately 35% higher than *multigpu*, consuming about 32% less power and with an accuracy loss of only 0.02%, compared to 0.22% on the *multigpu* implementation. Comparing the power consumption of half-precision in the *multigpu_float* implementation against the power consumption of double-precision in *multigpu* implementation using all four GPUs, the *multigpu_float* consumes approximately $3.5\times$ less power.

These substantial improvements, however, are not only due to the use of mixed precision, but also due to the use of faster mathematical functions. As previously mentioned in Sect. 2.2, the *multigpu_float* implementation uses the single-precision intrinsic mathematical functions of the CUDA platform, which map to a lower number of hardware instructions and, hence, are faster than the regular functions. Therefore, by storing the data using a lower precision but performing the arithmetic operations in a higher floating-point precision using faster mathematical functions, it was possible to improve the performance and power consumption while minimizing the absolute floating-point error. Comparing the performance of the *multigpu_float* implementation against the *multigpu* implementation using single-precision and a single GPU, it is possible to see that the intrinsic mathematical functions improve the performance of the *multigpu_float* implementation by up to 1.44× with an accuracy loss of only 0.02%.

Moreover, if we look at the power consumption between the *multigpu_float* and the *multigpu* implementations, it is possible to see that the use os intrinsic mathematical functions also reduce the power consumption significantly. While using single-precision and a single GPU the *multigpu* consumes 1266.33 W, the *multigpu_float* consumes only 802.79 W, a reduction of approximately 1.58× without accuracy losses. This corresponds to a reduction of about 36% only by using faster (and therefore, less precise) CUDA mathematical functions.

Furthermore, by storing the data using lower precision while performing all the arithmetic operations using a higher one, the amount of memory required to store the data reduces and contributes to the improvement of the performance and power consumption. As can be seen in Table 1, the use of half-precision instead of single-precision to store the data in the *multigpu_float* implementation reduces the amount of memory required up to 47% and the power consumption and execution time by up to 35% on a single GPU.

Not only that, but the use of intrinsic mathematical functions instead of regular functions helps to reduce the pressure on the memory. As shown in Table 1, with a single GPU and half-precision, in *multigpu* implementation, read or write operations were performed 86.62% of the time. In contrast, in *multigpu_float* implementation, operations were performed 73.62% of the time. With all four GPUs, in *multigpu* implementation, each GPU performed read or write operations 72.85% of the time and *multigpu_float* 57.29%, a reduction of about 21%.

6   Related Work

Most research on reduced and mixed precision has been devoted to neural network training in deep learning and machine learning for performance [7, 12, 22, 23, 26, 31, 36] and energy efficiency [16, 37, 40]. In [14] the authors evaluate the reliability of reduced precision on DNNs through fault injection.

In addition, many linear algebra algorithms are subject of study on reduced precision. The authors in [17, 18] evaluate the impact on in Linear solvers using NVIDIA Tensor cores, while [2] evaluated performance and energy efficiency of a GMRES solver. The works with BLAS algorithms include GPU and FPGA usage [32], batched matrix multiplication [1], and mixed precision [25]. Mixed precision in sparse linear algebra algorithms was evaluated over multiple platforms [6] and a Cell BE processor [5].

Libraries and tools have been proposed to program reduced or mixed precision algorithms in NVIDIA GPUs. In [28] the authors survey programming interfaces for half precision, and [11] proposes optimized reduction and scan operations. A library for mixed precision computations is described in [30], while [20] designed a tool to convert CUDA code into half precision for NVIDIA Pascal GPUs. An architectural model was designed in [35] in order to simulate half precision and tensor cores on NVIDIA GPUs.

Studies on scientific applications have showed an acceptable tradeoff between performance and precision error. Scientific benchmarks were evaluated on GPU [15] and Intel KNL/KNM [13]. Other applications are radio astronomy [38], earthquake city simulations [21], weather forecast [19], robotics [29], and IoT devices [34]. In CFD several works related evaluation of molecular dynamics [24] and Lattice Quantum Chromodynamics [3,4,8–10,39] on GPUs.

Compared to previous works, our paper explores a new approach with a multi-GPU algorithm based on [27] and optimized mixed-precision methods. Besides, we evaluate performance and energy in the context of multiple GPUs.

7   Conclusion and Future Work

In this paper, we presented a reduced and two mixed-precision floating-point multi-GPU implementations using as a case study, a well-known CFD application. In the first one, all arithmetic operations were performed using the same precision of the stored data and regular mathematical functions from the CUDA platform. The second and third implementations performed all arithmetics using single and half-precision, respectively, and the faster but slightly less accurate intrinsic mathematical functions. We provide results and analysis using double, single, or half-precision to store the CFD domains' data in GPU's memory on each implementation.

We show that by fastening the precision of the arithmetic operations to single and storing the CFD domains' data in half-precision improves the performance by more than $11\times$ and power consumption by more than $3.4\times$ with just an accuracy loss of up to 0.02%. These findings show that storage precision plays an essential role in the performance of reduced and mixed-precision implementations, once the reduction in storage precision minimizes pressure in memory while fixed higher precision arithmetics minimizes accuracy loss in lower storage precision. Furthermore, we point out that part of this improvement is due to the use of intrinsic mathematical functions instead of the regular ones, which improves the performance of single-precision arithmetic operations by up to $1.44\times$ with only 0.02% of accuracy loss.

As future works, we aim to extend our work on mixed-precision towards a broader set of applications, especially for computing-intensive ones. Since the performance of the implementation in which we explored the 2-way half-precision arithmetics in parallel on a single-precision FPU was nearly the same as the single-precision one, we aim to explore optimizations on these procedures. Moreover, we also intend to explore the use of intrinsic mathematical functions over the regular functions more deeply.

Acknowledgment. This research received funding from the Petrobras project, grant n. 2016/00133-9, by CAPES (Brazil) - Finance Code 001, by the project "GREEN-CLOUD" (#16/2551-0000 488-9), from FAPERGS and CNPq Brazil, program PRONEX 12/2014, and the project 406182/2021-3 from CNPq.

References

1. Abdelfattah, A., Tomov, S., Dongarra, J.: Fast batched matrix multiplication for small sizes using half-precision arithmetic on GPUs. In: 2019 IEEE International Parallel and Distributed Processing Symposium (IPDPS), pp. 111–122, May 2019. https://doi.org/10.1109/IPDPS.2019.00022

2. Anzt, H., Rocker, B., Heuveline, V.: Energy efficiency of mixed precision iterative refinement methods using hybrid hardware platforms. Comput. Sci. Res. Dev. **25**(3), 141–148 (2010). https://doi.org/10.1007/s00450-010-0124-2

3. Babich, R., Clark, M.A., Joó, B., Shi, G., Brower, R.C., Gottlieb, S.: Scaling lattice QCD beyond 100 GPUs. In: Proceedings of 2011 International Conference for High Performance Computing, Networking, Storage and Analysis, SC 2011, pp. 70:1–70:11. ACM, New York, NY, USA (2011). https://doi.org/10.1145/2063384. 2063478, http://doi.acm.org/10.1145/2063384.2063478

4. Babich, R., Clark, M.A., Joó, B.: Parallelizing the QUDA library for multi-GPU calculations in lattice quantum chromodynamics. In: Proceedings of the 2010 ACM/IEEE International Conference for High Performance Computing, Networking, Storage and Analysis, SC 2010, pp. 1–11. IEEE Computer Society, Washington, DC, USA (2010). https://doi.org/10.1109/SC.2010.40

5. Baboulin, M., et al.: Accelerating scientific computations with mixed precision algorithms. Comput. Phys. Commun. **180**(12), 2526–2533 (2009). https://doi.org/10.1016/j.cpc.2008.11.005, http://www.sciencedirect.com/science/article/pii/S0010465508003846

6. Buttari, A., Dongarra, J., Kurzak, J., Luszczek, P., Tomov, S.: Using mixed precision for sparse matrix computations to enhance the performance while achieving 64-bit accuracy. ACM Trans. Math. Softw. **34**(4), 17:1–17:22 (2008). https://doi.org/10.1145/1377596.1377597, http://doi.acm.org/10.1145/1377596.1377597

7. Chu, T., Luo, Q., Yang, J., Huang, X.: Mixed-precision quantized neural networks with progressively decreasing Bitwidth. Pattern Recogn. **111**, 107647 (2021)

8. Clark, M.A., Joó, B., Strelchenko, A., Cheng, M., Gambhir, A., Brower, R.C.: Accelerating lattice QCD multigrid on GPUs using fine-grained parallelization. In: Proceedings of the International Conference for High Performance Computing, Networking, Storage and Analysis, SC 2016, pp. 68:1–68:12. IEEE Press, Piscataway, NJ, USA (2016). http://dl.acm.org/citation.cfm?id=3014904.3014995

9. Clark, M., Babich, R., Barros, K., Brower, R., Rebbi, C.: Solving lattice QCD systems of equations using mixed precision solvers on GPUs. Comput. Phys. Commun. **181**(9), 1517–1528 (2010). https://doi.org/10.1016/j.cpc.2010.05.002, http://www.sciencedirect.com/science/article/pii/S0010465510001426

10. Clark, M., Strelchenko, A., Vaquero, A., Wagner, M., Weinberg, E.: Pushing memory bandwidth limitations through efficient implementations of Block-Krylov space solvers on GPUs. Comput. Phys. Commun. **233**, 29–40 (2018). https://doi.org/10.1016/j.cpc.2018.06.019, http://www.sciencedirect.com/science/article/pii/S0010465518302273

11. Dakkak, A., Li, C., Xiong, J., Gelado, I., Hwu, W.M.: Accelerating reduction and scan using tensor core units. In: Proceedings of the ACM International Conference on Supercomputing, ICS 2019, pp. 46–57. ACM, New York, NY, USA (2019). https://doi.org/10.1145/3330345.3331057, http://doi.acm.org/10.1145/3330345.3331057

12. Das, D., et al.: Mixed precision training of convolutional neural networks using integer operations, pp. 1–11 (2018). http://arxiv.org/abs/1802.00930

13. Domke, J., et al.: Double-precision FPUs in high-performance computing: an embarrassment of riches? In: 2019 IEEE International Parallel and Distributed Processing Symposium (IPDPS), pp. 78–88, May 2019. https://doi.org/10.1109/IPDPS.2019.00019

14. dos Santos, F.F., Navaux, P., Carro, L., Rech, P.: Impact of reduced precision in the reliability of deep neural networks for object detection. In: 2019 IEEE European Test Symposium (ETS), pp. 1–6, May 2019. https://doi.org/10.1109/ETS.2019.8791554

15. Fernandes Dos Santos, F., Lunardi, C., Oliveira, D., Libano, F., Rech, P.: Reliability evaluation of mixed-precision architectures. In: Proceedings - 25th IEEE International Symposium on High Performance Computer Architecture, HPCA 2019, pp. 238–249 (2019). https://doi.org/10.1109/HPCA.2019.00041

16. Gupta, S., Agrawal, A., Gopalakrishnan, K., Narayanan, P.: Deep learning with limited numerical precision. In: 32nd International Conference on Machine Learning, ICML 2015, vol. 3, pp. 1737–1746 (2015). http://www.jmlr.org/proceedings/papers/v37/gupta15.pdf

17. Haidar, A., Tomov, S., Dongarra, J., Higham, N.J.: Harnessing GPU tensor cores for fast FP16 arithmetic to speed up mixed-precision iterative refinement solvers. In: Proceedings of the International Conference for High Performance Computing, Networking, Storage, and Analysis, SC 2018, pp. 47:1–47:11. IEEE Press, Piscataway, NJ, USA (2018). https://doi.org/10.1109/SC.2018.00050

18. Haidar, A., Wu, P., Tomov, S., Dongarra, J.: Investigating half precision arithmetic to accelerate dense linear system solvers. In: Proceedings of the 8th Workshop on Latest Advances in Scalable Algorithms for Large-Scale Systems, ScalA 2017, pp. 10:1–10:8. ACM, New York, NY, USA (2017). https://doi.org/10.1145/3148226.3148237, http://doi.acm.org/10.1145/3148226.3148237

19. Hatfield, S., Chantry, M., Düben, P., Palmer, T.: Accelerating high-resolution weather models with deep-learning hardware. In: Proceedings of the Platform for Advanced Scientific Computing Conference, PASC 2019, pp. 1:1–1:11. ACM, New York, NY, USA (2019). https://doi.org/10.1145/3324989.3325711, http://doi.acm.org/10.1145/3324989.3325711

20. Ho, N., Wong, W.: Exploiting half precision arithmetic in Nvidia GPUs. In: 2017 IEEE High Performance Extreme Computing Conference (HPEC), pp. 1–7, September 2017. https://doi.org/10.1109/HPEC.2017.8091072

21. Ichimura, T., et al.: A fast scalable implicit solver for nonlinear time-evolution earthquake city problem on low-ordered unstructured finite elements with artificial intelligence and transprecision computing. In: Proceedings of the International Conference for High Performance Computing, Networking, Storage, and Analysis, SC 2018, pp. 49:1–49:11. IEEE Press, Piscataway, NJ, USA (2018). https://doi.org/10.1109/SC.2018.00052

22. Jia, X., et al.: Highly scalable deep learning training system with mixed-precision: training ImageNet in four minutes (2018). http://arxiv.org/abs/1807.11205

23. Jordà, M., Valero-Lara, P., Peña, A.J.: Performance evaluation of cuDNN convolution algorithms on NVIDIA Volta GPUs. IEEE Access **7**, 70461–70473 (2019). https://doi.org/10.1109/ACCESS.2019.2918851

24. Le Grand, S., Götz, A.W., Walker, R.C.: SPFP: speed without compromise - a mixed precision model for GPU accelerated molecular dynamics simulations. Comput. Phys. Commun. **184**(2), 374–380 (2013). https://doi.org/10.1016/j.cpc.2012.09.022

25. Li, X.S., et al.: Design, implementation and testing of extended and mixed precision BLAS. ACM Trans. Math. Softw. **28**(2), 152–205 (2002). https://doi.org/10.1145/567806.567808, http://doi.acm.org/10.1145/567806.567808

26. Li, Y., Wang, W., Bai, H., Gong, R., Dong, X., Yu, F.: Efficient bitwidth search for practical mixed precision neural network. arXiv preprint arXiv:2003.07577 (2020)

27. Lima, J.V.F., Freytag, G., Pinto, V.G., Schepke, C., Navaux, P.O.A.: A dynamic task-based D3Q19 lattice-Boltzmann method for heterogeneous architectures. In: 2019 27th Euromicro International Conference on Parallel, Distributed and Network-Based Processing (PDP), pp. 108–115, February 2019. https://doi.org/10.1109/EMPDP.2019.8671583

28. Markidis, S., Chien, S.W.D., Laure, E., Peng, I.B., Vetter, J.S.: NVIDIA tensor core programmability, performance precision. In: 2018 IEEE International Parallel and Distributed Processing Symposium Workshops (IPDPSW), pp. 522–531, May 2018. https://doi.org/10.1109/IPDPSW.2018.00091

29. Medhat, R., Lam, M.O., Rountree, B.L., Bonakdarpour, B., Fischmeister, S.: Managing the performance/error tradeoff of floating-point intensive applications. ACM Trans. Embed. Comput. Syst. **16**(5s), 184:1–184:19, October 2017. https://doi.org/10.1145/3126519, http://doi.acm.org/10.1145/3126519

30. Menon, H., et al.: Adapt: algorithmic differentiation applied to floating-point precision tuning. In: Proceedings of the International Conference for High Performance Computing, Networking, Storage, and Analysis, SC 2018, pp. 48:1–48:13. IEEE Press, Piscataway, NJ, USA (2018). https://doi.org/10.1109/SC.2018.00051

31. Micikevicius, P., et al.: Mixed precision training, pp. 1–12 (2017). http://arxiv.org/abs/1710.03740

32. Minhas, U.I., Bayliss, S., Constantinides, G.A.: GPU vs FPGA: a comparative analysis for non-standard precision. In: Goehringer, D., Santambrogio, M.D., Cardoso, J.M.P., Bertels, K. (eds.) Reconfigurable Computing: Architectures, Tools, and Applications, pp. 298–305. Springer, Cham (2014)

33. Mittal, S.: A survey of techniques for approximate computing. ACM Comput. Surv. **48**(4), 1–33 (2016). https://doi.org/10.1145/2893356

34. Qi, X., Liu, C., Schuckers, S.: IoT edge device based key frame extraction for face in video recognition. In: 2018 18th IEEE/ACM International Symposium on Cluster, Cloud and Grid Computing (CCGRID), pp. 641–644, May 2018. https://doi.org/10.1109/CCGRID.2018.00087

35. Raihan, M.A., Goli, N., Aamodt, T.M.: Modeling deep learning accelerator enabled GPUs. In: 2019 IEEE International Symposium on Performance Analysis of Systems and Software (ISPASS), pp. 79–92, March 2019. https://doi.org/10.1109/ISPASS.2019.00016

36. Ramirez-Gargallo, G., Garcia-Gasulla, M., Mantovani, F.: TensorFlow on state-of-the-art HPC clusters: a machine learning use case. In: 2019 19th IEEE/ACM International Symposium on Cluster, Cloud and Grid Computing (CCGRID), pp. 526–533, May 2019. https://doi.org/10.1109/CCGRID.2019.00067

37. Rojek, K.: Machine learning method for energy reduction by utilizing dynamic mixed precision on GPU-based supercomputers. Concurr. Comput. Pract. Experience **31**(6), e4644 (2019). https://doi.org/10.1002/cpe.4644, https://onlinelibrary.wiley.com/doi/abs/10.1002/cpe.4644, e4644 cpe.4644
38. Seznec, M., Gac, N., Ferrari, A., Orieux, F.: A study on convolution using half-precision floating-point numbers on GPU for radio astronomy deconvolution. In: 2018 IEEE International Workshop on Signal Processing Systems (SiPS), pp. 170–175, October 2018. https://doi.org/10.1109/SiPS.2018.8598342
39. Shi, G., Gottlieb, S., Torok, A., Kindratenko, V.: Design of MILC lattice QCD application for GPU clusters. In: 2011 IEEE International Parallel Distributed Processing Symposium, pp. 363–371, May 2011. https://doi.org/10.1109/IPDPS.2011.43
40. Vasquez, K., Venkatesha, Y., Bhattacharjee, A., Moitra, A., Panda, P.: Activation density based mixed-precision quantization for energy efficient neural networks. arXiv preprint arXiv:2101.04354 (2021)

NoSql Database Optimization Based on Metadata About Queries and Relationships Between Objects

Muon Ha⬛, Yulia Shichkina(✉) ⬛, and Roza Fatkieva⬛

St. Petersburg State Electrotechnical University, St. Petersburg, Russia
Strange.y@mail.ru

Abstract. Most experts in the field of big data agree that the volume of data generated by various devices will increase exponentially in the future. Therefore, there is no doubt the relevance of solving the problem of data storage in such a way that access to the necessary information would be as quick as possible. In this article, we propose an approach based on set theory, which is suitable for databases that store information about objects with many relationships. Such databases can include both relational and NoSQL databases. This approach takes into account the relationships between objects and the structure of the most frequently executed database queries when designing the database architecture. This allows to remove operations "join" from queries and, at the same time, to minimize the data redundancy anomaly in a separate database structural unit. We demonstrated the application of this approach on three types of databases: relational, document, and columns family.

Keywords: NoSQL · Database query · Collection · Document · Data conversion · Data format · Database structure optimization · MongoDB · Cassandra

1 Introduction

Among the databases, despite the intensive development of NoSQL and NewSQL databases, relational databases still hold the lead (Fig. 1). It is known that relational DBMSs allow to create complex data systems, and NoSQL databases and DBMSs do not support internal relationships between objects. NoSQL databases are not based on one model, and each database uses different models de- pending on the purpose of creation.

All NoSQL databases today can be divided into 4 large classes:

- key-value (Redis, MemcacheDB, etc.);
- column family - Cassandra, HBase, etc.;
- document - MongoDB, Couchbase, etc.;
- graph - OrientDB, Neo4J, etc.

© The Author(s), under exclusive license to Springer Nature Switzerland AG 2022
O. Gervasi et al. (Eds.): ICCSA 2022 Workshops, LNCS 13380, pp. 588–602, 2022.
https://doi.org/10.1007/978-3-031-10542-5_40

A lot of educational books, articles have been written about all these systems, and many different professional websites and forums on the Internet have been devoted [3, 10, 13].

In fact, a review of systems that are based on NoSQL databases allows to conclude that, for one reason or another, many developers today choose not only relational databases to create complex data systems. It is also worth noting that if the theory of designing relational databases based on functional dependencies and theorems for normalizing relational schemes has existed since the 70s [5], then for NoSQL databases there is no such theory yet, but there is a lot of research in this area. Some of the work we consider in the next section.

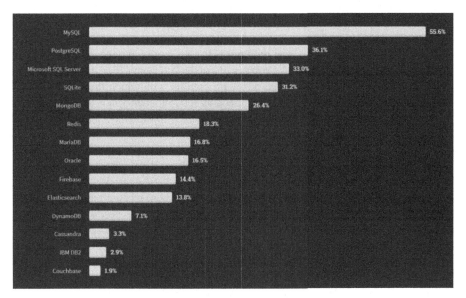

Fig. 1. Database rating [6]

And it's worth noting that many developers choose another way instead of using NoSQL to speed up access to data: denormalizing a relational database. Unfortunately, there is also no theory of optimizing data access by denormalizing a relational database, but there are many works on the Internet in which the authors describe their results of database denormalization.

The approach that we propose in this article is an attempt to create a universal apparatus based on set theory, which, in accordance with the latest proven trends in orienting databases to specific queries, allows to choose a database architecture based on formalization. We tested this approach on the three most popular in its class data type, included in the top fifteen databases [6]: MySQL, MongoDB and Cassandra. As a result, we confirmed the efficiency of the approach in queries of various complexity and showed that the approach provides the best local solution for optimizing the database in terms of query execution time. This also allowed us to compare the obtained solutions for these three databases with each other. The results of these studies are presented in this article.

The article is structured as follows. The Sect. 2 provides an overview of related work in recent years; the Sect. 3 describes an approach to creating a database architecture. The Sect. 4 presents the experimental results. In conclusion, the results of the research are summarized.

2   Related Works

Among the studies devoted to optimizing data access in various databases, the following directions can be identified:

1. Research on relational databases
    In [12], there are proposed new requirements for functional dependencies that can improve the design results of a relational database schema. For this purpose, the authors assign to tuples the value of the probability with which these tuples are in a relation, assign to functional dependencies a confidence value that indicates to which tuples these dependencies correspond. This allows, within reasonable limits, to carry out the decomposition of relations in relational databases.

    In [17], there is an algorithm for searching for possible functional dependencies between non-key attributes. As a result, the database developer can use the found functional dependencies to improve the structure of the database.

    We think that these approaches are very good when, when creating a database, queries to the database are unknown and the administrator needs to provide any options for queries. This will speed up many queries, but it will also create a redundancy anomaly where it might not have. In our case, the approach to denormalization is query-oriented and this allows us to reduce the redundancy anomaly.
2. Research on data migration between databases.
    The article [2] proposes rules for transforming an RDB schema to various NoSQL database schema, namely document-based, column-based and graph-based databases. The rules are applied based on the type of relationships that can appear in data within a database. All the rules are demonstrated by the authors on the three most popular NoSQL databases: MongoDB, Cassandra and Neo4j. We believe that the authors of [2] offer a good, but rather universal method. This method without taking into account the properties of queries will lead to the fact that on the basis of the M-1 relationship, for example, in a document database, very large documents will be created, which will slow down the work with the database. If the most frequent queries to the database are not applied to all the attributes of relations with the M-1 relationship type, then it is better to create several collections with smaller documents instead of one collection. Our approach allows to do this.

It should be noted that the topic of data migration from a relational database format to NoSQL is quite popular today, and most publications in well-known citation databases are devoted to this topic. Among such publications over the past year are [1, 8, 15] for MongoDB, an approach to transforming a model from an object-relational database to a database based on the NoSQL column family (Cassandra) [9] and many others. But, in all these studies, the structure of database queries is not taken into account.

3. Research that focuses on data indexing and query optimization. These works, for example [4, 14], are aimed at speeding up data access, but they do not directly relate to the database architecture and therefore the results of their analysis are not presented in this article.

4. Applied research on the construction of databases of various types in a given subject area. These studies are interesting and useful because the authors share their experience in creating databases, the problems of their construction, and found particular solutions to these problems. Such articles include the use of NoSQL in the Internet of Things (IoT), where a large number of sensors are used in everyday life [7]; collection and processing of data on various weather parameters for a smart home [11]; food supply chain traceability [16] and others.

The analysis of world research in the field of formalization of the approach to finding the optimal database architecture in terms of the search query execution time showed that there are currently no methods that take into account the metadata about queries and relationships between objects and are applicable to relational, documentary and column-family databases.

In this article, we present the results of a generalized approach to optimizing database architecture based on set theory that we developed and tested on three types of databases: relational, documentary, and column family.

3   Generalized Approach to Defining Database Architecture

By analogy with a relational database, we mean by a relation a finite set of values of object properties; schema of relation is a set of object attributes, object properties, data about which should be stored in the database. Functional dependence is dependence in the classic definition from the relational model [5]. Suppose there is a set of attributes X and for the attributes of a set X there is a set of declared functional dependencies.

Initially, it is assumed that the database schema consists of one relation $T = X$. Further, this scheme should be, taking into account the declared functional dependencies, reduced to the third normal form or the Boyce-Codd form. As a result, there are will be obtained the first group of sets - these are the sets of attributes belonging to a separate relation T_r, where r is number of relation, $r = 1...k$, k is quantity of relations, $T_{(r,j)}$ is an attribute in relation T_r, j is number of attribute, $j = 1...r_n$, r_n is quantity of attributes in the r-th relation Eq. 1:

$$T_r = \{T_{r,j}, j = 1, 2, ..., r_n\} \tag{1}$$

Then the set of all database attributes will be determined by the formula Eq. 2:

$$X = \{T_{r,j}, r = 1, 2, ...k | T_{r,j} \neq T_{q,i}, \forall r, q \leq k, j \leq r_n, i \leq q_n\} \tag{2}$$

where: r is the number of relation, $r = 1...k$, k is quantity of relations, j is number of attribute in the relation, $j = 1...r_n$, r_n is quantity of attributes in the r-th relation.

The length of a set is the quantity of its elements. Designation: $|X|$ - the length of the set X.

In order not to do "join" operations in the future to perform queries, it is necessary to understand what attributes are accessed by queries in the database. This requires the creation of a second group of sets - these are the sets of attributes included in the queries Eq. 3:

$$S_i = \{T_{r,j}, r \leq k, j \leq r_n\} \tag{3}$$

where: i is the number of queries $i = 1, 2, ...m$, m is the quantity of queries to the database.

Obviously, those attributes that are not referenced in the most frequent queries can be collected into a separate relation. This will be the first step towards denormalizing the resulting relation. This is because the data will enter the new relation from different relations, including those between which there was a relationship of type "$M - 1$" (Many to one), and this will lead to the creation of duplicates.

There are two ways to find such attributes:

(1) First, for each attribute, create a set of queries in which this attribute participates in any part of the construction:

$$T'_{r,j} = \{S_i, i = 1...p, p \leq m | T_{r,j} \in S_i\} \tag{4}$$

where m– quantity of queries, r – number of relations, $r = 1...k$, k – quantity of relations, j – number of the attribute in relation, $j = 1...r_n$, r_n– quantity of attributes in r-th relation. Then, among the sets that we have obtained, choose those for which the length of the set is equal to zero: $|T'_{r,j}|$. The attributes corresponding to these sets are those attributes that do not participate in queries.

(2) These same attributes can be defined as the difference between the original set of X attributes and the set of attributes included in the queries Eq. 5:

$$V_1 = X - \bigcup_{i=1}^{p} S_i \tag{5}$$

It should be noted that the first method is preferable, since in the future, we will also need to find attributes that are involved in only one database query, and formula 4 will make it easy to do this.

So, these attributes can be included in a new relationship (6):

$$V_1 = \{T_{r,j}, r \le k, j \le r_n || T'_{r,j}| = 0\} \tag{6}$$

where: m - the quantity of queries, r - the ordinal number of relations, $r = 1...k$ the quantity of relation, j - the ordinal number of the attribute in relation, $j = 1...r_n$, r_n the quantity of attributes in r-th relation.

It is possible not to follow the path of denormalization and create new relations based on these attributes (7):

$$V_i = T_i - \bigcup_{j=1}^{p} S_j \tag{7}$$

In this case, it should be noted that, firstly, a relationship cannot consist of one attribute, and secondly, if the attribute is not key, then the new relationship must include key attributes from the previous relationship. The latter is necessary in order to reduce the anomaly of lost information, which can be in any type of database.

The choice of a way to represent attributes that are not involved in queries is shown in the scheme in Fig. 2.

Note 1. The new relations should be formed taking into account the relationships between the original relations.

Example: In terms of relational algebra, composing a relation V_1 from four relations T1–T4 might look like this:

$$V_1 = \pi(T1 \rhd \lhd T2 \rhd \lhd T3 \rhd \lhd T4)_{T1_4, T2_2, T2_5, T3_5, T3_6, T4_2, T4_5, T4_6}$$

where, the operations $\rhd\lhd$ on are the natural join of the relations, $\pi(X)_{y,z}$ is the projection or vertical selection in the relation X of the attributes y, z.

With attributes that are involved in only one database query, i.e. $|T'_{r,j}| = 1$, it is possible to act in the same way as with attributes that are not involved in database queries. All the attributes $T_{r,j} \in S_i$ for which the condition $|T'_{r,j}| = 1$, is satisfied, must be separated into a new relation 8 or they can be composed of separate relations:

$$V_p = \{T_{r,j}, r \le k, j \le r_n | T_{r,j} \in S_i \& |\{T_{r,j}\}| = 1\}, p > 1 \tag{8}$$

After all attributes are removed from consideration that did not participate in database queries or participated in queries once, i.e. included in the new relations V1 and V_p, it remains to distribute those attributes that are involved in several database queries over the new relations.

This can be done iteratively by finding a new relation at each iteration as the difference of sets (9), (10):

$$V_p = I - P \tag{9}$$

$$I = P \tag{10}$$

where:

- m - the number of queries;
- $I = \bigcup_{i=1}^{m} S_i$ - the set of attributes included in database queries;
  $S_k^{'} = S_i \cap S_j, \forall i \neq j; i,j = 1, 2, ..., |I|; k = 1, 2, ..., C_{|I|}^2$ - the pairwise intersections of sets $S_i \in I$;
- $C_{|I|}^2 = \frac{|I|!}{|(|I|-2)|!2!} = \frac{|I|(|I|-1)}{2}$ - the number of pairwise intersections of sets $S_i \in I$;

The iterative process continues as long as $|I| > 1$.

When the length of the set I becomes equal to 1, the iterative process will be stopped and it is necessary to include in the new relation all the attributes from the last single intersection that are not present in other intersections (11):

$$V_{(p+1)} = X - \bigcup_{i=1}^{p} V_i \tag{11}$$

As a result of this approach, a set of new relations with attributes will be obtained (regardless of the type of database) (12):

$$V_i = \{T_{r,j}, r \leq k, j \leq r_n\} \tag{12}$$

satisfying conditions (13), (14):

$$\bigcup_{i=1}^{p} V_i = X = \bigcup_{r=1}^{k} T_r, \tag{13}$$

$$(\forall S_i)(\exists V_j)(S_i \in V_j, S_i \notin V_i, i \neq j) \tag{14}$$

where i is the ordinal number of relation ($i = 1, 2, ..., l$), l is the quantity of relations.

Note 2. The new relation could be a column family for a Cassandra database, or a collection for a MongoDB document database, or a denormalized relation for a relational database.

Note 3. In [18] we considered the second method, which is a continuation of this method for MongoDB databases and which allows you to create document collections with embedded documents of any depth.

The scheme of the described approach is shown in Fig. 2.

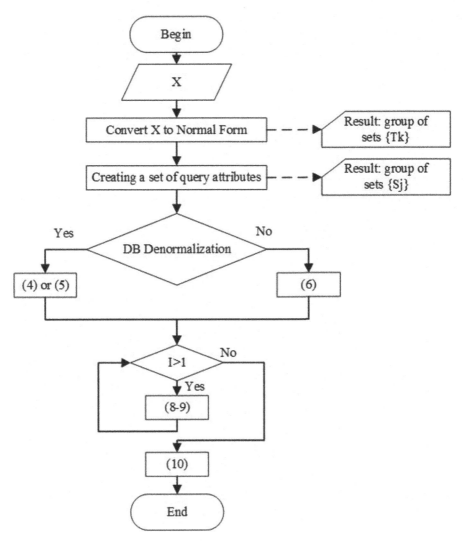

Fig. 2. Scheme of creating relations taking into account database queries

4 Testing the Approach on MySQL, MongoDB and Cassandra Databases

To test this approach, we chose a database, which in the relational model consisted of the following five relations:

- *T1(Output_phone_number,   Start_time_of_the_call,   Input_phone_number, End_time_of_the_call, Date) (or T1(f1, f2, f3, f4, f5))*
- *T2 (Output_phone_number, SMS, Input_phone_number, Time_sending, Volume, Date) (or T2(f1, f2, f3, f4, f5, f6))*

- *T3 (Phone_number, Tariff, Id_User, Contract_number, Start_date_of_the_contract, Start_date_of_the_contract) (or T3(f1, f2, f3, f4, f5, f6))*
- *T4 (id_User, Birthday, Passport, Registration, Email, Fullname) (or T4(f1, f2, f3, f4, f5, f6))*
- *T5 (Contract_number, Payment, Date_of_payment) (or T5(f1, f2, f3))*

Relationships between relations are shown in Fig. 3. To assess the effectiveness of this approach, testing was carried out on various volumes of the database:

- Volume 1: User(10.000), Number_phone(10.000), Payment(25.000), SMS(43.000), Call(32.000)
- Volume 2: User(50.000), Number_phone(50.000), Payment(65.000), SMS(81.000), Call(32.000)
- Volume 3: User(100.000), Number_phone(100.000), Payment(123.000), SMS(230.000), Call(320.000)

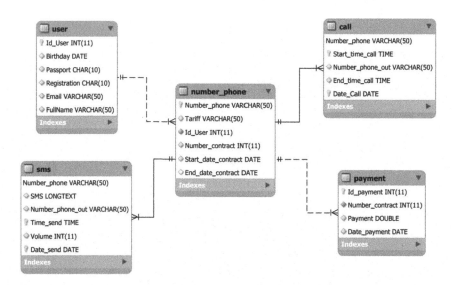

Fig. 3. Relationships between relations

Testing was carried out for 9 search queries, which were prepared in such a way that among them there were simple queries to select data from only one relation, queries to select data from several relations, queries with aggregation functions:

5. Select sum(f4 − f2); f1 From T1 Where f5 > a and f5 < b Group by f1;
6. Select count(∗); f1 From T2 Where f6 > a and f6 < b Group by f1;
7. Select T3.f1; T3.f2 From T3; T4 Where T3.f3 = T4.f1 and T4.f3 = a and T3.f6 = null;

8. Select T1.f2; T1.f3 From T1 Where T1.f1 = a and f5 > a and f5 < b Union Select T2.f3; T2.f4 From T2 Where T2.f1 = a and f6 > a and f6 < b;

9. Select T1.f2; T1.f1 From T1 Where T1.f3 = a and f5 > a and f5 < b Union Select T2.f1; T2.f4 From T2 Where T2.f3 = a and f6 > a and f6 < b;

10. Select T3.f1; T3.f2 From T3; T4 Where T3.f3 = T4.f1 and T4.f3 = a and T3.f4 $\geq$ a and T3.f4 $\leq$ b Order by T3.f4;

11. Select distinct T3.f1; T4.f6 From T3; T4 Where T3.f1 = a and T3.f3 = T4.f1;

12. Select T 5.f2; T5.f3 From T 3; T 5 Where T3.f1 = a and T 5.f3 > a and T5.f3 < b and T3.f4 = T5.f1;

13. Select T5.f2; T5.f3 From T5 Where T5.f3 in Select max(T5.f3) From T3; T5 Where T3.f1 = a and T3.f4 = T5.f1;

For the objectivity of the results, each query was tested 25 times. The table, chart, and graphs below show the average query execution time for 25 times. As a result of applying the approach described in Sect. 3, three relations were obtained:

$$V_1 = \{T2_2; \ T2_5; \ T3_5; \ T4_2; \ T4_4; \ T4_5\}$$

$$V_2 = \{T1_1; \ T1_2; \ T1_4; \ T1_5; \ T2_1; \ T2_6; \ T1_3; \ T2_3; \ T2_4\}$$

$$V_3 = \{T3_1; \ T3_2; \ T3_3; \ T3_6; \ T4_1; \ T4_3; \ T3_4; \ T4_6; \ T5_1; \ T5_2; \ T5_3\}$$

These three relations are three collections in MongoDB (Figs. 4 and 5) and three column families in Cassandra (Fig. 6).

Fig. 4. MongoDB database structure without embedded documents

Table 1 shows the results of testing databases of various architectures and types. Times are in milliseconds. These results are presented for volume 3. Columns I–VI contain the time to execute queries in the following databases: I -MySQL, the initial relational model of 5 relations, II - MongoDB database obtained from the relational model by direct data translation and therefore consisting of 5 collections, III - MongoDB database obtained using the above approach and consisting of three collections without embedded documents, IV - MongoDB database obtained using the above and additional methods [18] and consisting of three collections with embedded documents, V - Cassandra database obtained from a relational model with direct data translation and therefore consisting of 5 column families, VI - Cassandra database obtained using the above approach and consisting of three column families.

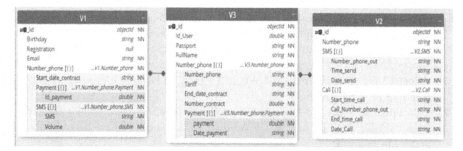

Fig. 5. MongoDB database structure with embedded documents

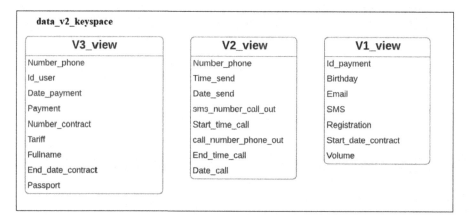

Fig. 6. Cassandra database structure

Table 1. Test results

Queries	Database type					
	I	II	III	IV	V	VI
Q1	184	114	121	104	132	106
Q2	172	84	158	125	144	127.3
Q3	465	363	117	97	121.2	103
Q4	389	282	188	110	137	119
Q5	245	219	174	127.1	125	121
Q6	718	620	179	156	148.4	94.3
Q7	652	407	172	133	166	142.8
Q8	712	457	223	145	172	157
Q9	846	550	327	221	367	181.7

Based on the test results, we created a diagram (Fig. 7), which reflects the difference in the execution time of queries for the database, depending on the type of database, query, database architecture. The diagram is built for data volume 3. In Fig. 8 there are some of the most interesting graphs illustrating the effectiveness of this approach depending on the amount of data. From the diagrams in Fig. 7 it can be seen that the approach presented in this article is the best for all cases.

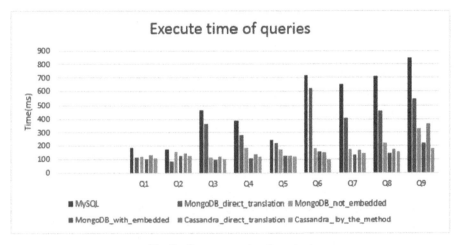

Fig. 7. Query execution time chart

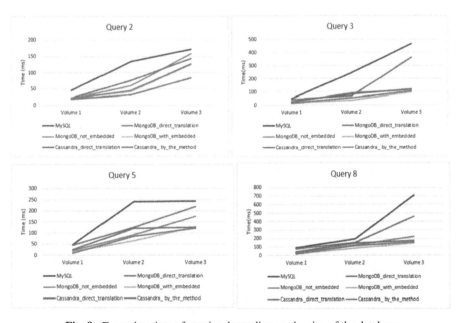

Fig. 8. Execution time of queries depending on the size of the database

It is possible to see from the graphs in Fig. 8 that the approach works differently for different queries. And in general, for a very large amount of data, the results obtained for a MongoDB database with embedded documents are much better than for a database without embedded documents, and even more so a direct correspondence of collections of a relational database in normal Boyce-Codd form. But, unfortunately, it can also be seen that with an increase in the amount of data, the approach to denormalization and adaptation of the database for queries in the Cassandra DBMS approaches in its performance a database similar in terms of the relational database scheme in the Boyce-Codd normal form.

5 Conclusion

As a result of our research, we obtained an approach that allows, based on information about the relationships between the attributes of objects in the database and the queries that will be performed most often, to build an optimal database architecture in terms of execution time for models: relational, document type, and column families. The presented approach is based on set theory and allows to automate the process of creating a database of these types. Taking into account the structure of queries to the database allows to determine the number and composition of collections for the MongoDB DBMS, tables for relational databases or column families for Cassandra, so that it is possible not to do "joins" of database structural units in the future. This method can be used when translating a database from SQL to MongoDB or Cassandra, to define collections or column families in a new MongoDB or Cassandra database, and when consolidating databases of different structures.

This method can also be applied to distributed databases. In the latter case, the distributed system architecture is taken into account besides the database schema. This approach developed by us is described in [20].

There are other possibilities for using this method, such as creating temporary collections, etc. The scientific group, which includes the authors of this article, also developed methods for automatic translation of queries from the format of one database to the format of another database (including conversion of database types), as well as methods for parallelizing queries and indexing data based on the CW-tree [19].

Further research. At the moment, research continues in the direction of supplementing the developed methods with information about a distributed database, in particular about the sharding and replication system. In the near future, we will also consider the problem of reindexing databases obtained using this approach. And finally, it is planned to take into account information about the possible parallelization of queries using methods developed by the authors based on graph theory.

Acknowledgment. The work was done within the research "Methods of constructing co-evolving intelligent systems and their prototyping in applied fields" in order to implement the ETU "LETI" Strategic Academic Leadership Program "Priority-2030", Agreement N 075-15-2021-1318.

References

1. Aggoune, A., Namoune, S.: A method for transforming object-relational to document-oriented databases. In: 2020 2nd International Conference on Mathematics and Information Technology (ICMIT), pp. 154–158 (2020). https://doi.org/10.1109/ICMIT47780.2020.9047011

2. Alotaibi, O., Pardede, E.: Transformation of schema from relational database (RDB) to NoSQL databases. Data **4**, 148 (2019). https://doi.org/10.3390/data4040148

3. Ceresnak, R., Kvet, M.: Comparison of query performance in relational a non-relation databases. Transp. Res. Procedia **40**, 170–177 (2019). https://doi.org/10.1016/j.trpro.2019.07.027

4. Chopade, R., Pachghare, V.: MongoDB indexing for performance improvement. In: Tuba, M., Akashe, S., Joshi, A. (eds.) ICT Systems and Sustainability. Advances in Intelligent Systems and Computing, vol. 1077. Springer, Singapore (2020). https://doi.org/10.1007/978-981-15-0936-056

5. Codd, E.F.: A relational model of data for large shared data banks. Assoc. Comput. Mach. **13**, 377–387 (1970). https://doi.org/10.1145/362384.362685

6. Most popular databases. https://insights.stackoverflow.com/survey/2020#technology-databases-all-respondents4. Accessed 18 Mar 2022

7. Eyada, M.M., Saber, W., El Genidy, M.M., Amer, F.: Performance evaluation of IoT data management using MongoDB versus MySQL databases in different cloud environments. IEEE Access **8**, 110656–110668 (2020). https://doi.org/10.1109/ACCESS.2020.3002164

8. Fouad, T., Mohamed, B.: Model transformation from object relational database to NoSQL document database. In: Proceedings of the 2nd International Conference on Networking, Information Systems & Security, p. 5. Association for Computing Machinery, New York (2019). https://doi.org/10.1145/3320326.3320381

9. Fouad, T., Mohamed, B.: Model transformation from object relational database to NoSQL column based database. In: Proceedings of the 3rd International Conference on Networking, Information Systems & Security, p. 5. Association for Computing Machinery, New York (2020). https://doi.org/10.1145/3386723.3387881

10. Jose, B., Abraham, S.: Performance analysis of NoSQL and relational databases with MongoDB and MySQL. Mater. Today Proc. **24**, 2036–2043 (2020). https://doi.org/10.1016/j.matpr.2020.03.634

11. Khine, S.N., Tun, Z.: MongoDB on cloud for weather data (Temperature and Humidity) in Sittway. In: 2020 IEEE Conference on Computer Applications (ICCA), pp. 1–6, Yangon, Myanmar (2020). https://doi.org/10.1109/ICCA49400.2020.9022825

12. Sebastian, L., Henri, P.: Relational database schema design for uncertain data. Inf. Syst. **84**, 88–110 (2019). https://doi.org/10.1016/j.is.2019.04.003

13. Diogo, M., Cabral, B., Bernardino, J.: Consistency models of NoSQL databases. Future Internet **11**, 43 (2019)

14. Ramya, M., Thirumahal, R.: Hybrid query system. Int. J. Comput. Sci. Eng. **7**, 8–11 (2020). https://doi.org/10.14445/23488387/IJCSE-V7I5P103

15. Leonardo, R., Fernando, V., Elder, C., D´arlinton, B., Fernando, M.: A framework for migrating relational datasets to NoSQL1. Procedia Comput. Sci. **51**, 2593–2602 (2015). https://doi.org/10.1016/j.procs.2015.05.367

16. Singh, S., Jenamani, M.: Cassandra-based data repository design for food supply chain traceability. VINE J. Inf. Knowl. Manag. Syst. (2020). (ahead-of-print), https://doi.org/10.1108/VJIKMS-08-2019-0119

17. Sug, H.: Efficient checking of functional dependencies for relations. J. Phys. Conf. Ser. **1564**, 012011 (2020). https://doi.org/10.1088/1742-6596/1564/1/012011

18. Yulia, S., Muon, H.: Creating collections with embedded documents for document databases taking into account the queries. Computation **8**, 45 (2020). https://doi.org/10.3390/computati on8020045
19. Shevskiy, V.S., Shichkina, Y.A.: Investigation of CW-tree for parallel execution of queries to database. In: Gervasi, O., et al. (eds.) ICCSA 2021. LNCS, vol. 12956, pp. 324–335. Springer, Cham (2021). https://doi.org/10.1007/978-3-030-87010-2_23
20. Ha, M., Shichkina, Y.: Translating a distributed relational database to a document database. Data Sci. Eng. **7**, 136–155 (2022). https://doi.org/10.1007/s41019-022-00181-9

Differential Privacy for Statistical Data of Educational Institutions

Ivan Podsevalov$^{(\boxtimes)}$, Alexei Podsevalov, and Vladimir Korkhov

Saint-Petersburg State University, St. Petersburg, Russia
i.podsevalov@spbu.ru

Abstract. Electronic methods of managing the educational process are gaining popularity. Recently, a large number of user programs have appeared for such accounting. Based on this, the issue of personal data protection requires increased attention. The coronavirus pandemic has led to a significant increase in the amount of data distributed remotely, which requires information security for a wider range of workers on a continuous basis.

In this article, we will consider such a relatively new mechanism designed to help protect personal data as differential privacy. Differential privacy is a way of strictly mathematical definition of possible risks in public access to sensitive data. Based on estimating the probabilities of possible data losses, you can build the right policy to "noise" publicly available statistics. This approach will make it possible to find a compromise between the preservation of general patterns in the data and the security of the personal data of the participants in the educational process.

Keywords: Differential privacy · Security · Statistics · Education

1 Theoretical Foundations Review

1.1 Introduction

The term "differential privacy" (hereinafter referred to as DP) appeared and formulated into an industrial standard in the works of several authors: Dwork, Nissim, Blum, McSherry, and Smith [1–4]. At the same time, in the classic presentation, definitions were given for entities that can be operated on during the process of working with the DP: databases, data sets, metrics for determining the "proximity" of data sets and distributions. Currently, many practical implementations have their own rules for determining the distance between the database or data sets, the sensitivity of functions, DP mechanisms, however, all implementations undergo a complete "test" for compliance with academic definitions. This indicates the complete success of the developed theory, which has been tested by practice for almost 20 years.

© The Author(s), under exclusive license to Springer Nature Switzerland AG 2022
O. Gervasi et al. (Eds.): ICCSA 2022 Workshops, LNCS 13380, pp. 603–615, 2022.
https://doi.org/10.1007/978-3-031-10542-5_41

1.2   The Concept of Differential Privacy

Differential privacy is a collection of methods based on "noise" of output data through randomization or randomness. The general idea behind this mechanism is that the information should be distributed regardless of whether the user of the information is an adversary or not. It is worth noting immediately that this is not some specific process, but, rather, a property that the process can have. The differential privacy property ensures that the result of statistical analysis of two sets of output data from one algorithm will be almost indistinguishable regardless of whether there is data of an individual in the set or not. Visually (Fig. 1), this property can be represented as follows (D_1 and D_2 differ by one line):

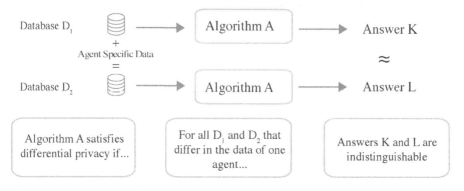

Fig. 1. Differential privacy

The meaning of the DP is the idea that any similar data sets should produce similar results based on the chosen distribution of a random variable. Reasoning more strictly and generally, the Lipschitz condition must be met for mapping "close" data sets in a random variable distribution.

The most important is the concept of the distance between two sets of data, which is necessary to determine a certain measure of "proximity" or "contiguity." We say that two sets are adjacent if the distance between them is equal to one. How close the two resulting distributions are to each other can be "measured" or determined by means of a positive parameter, called the privacy loss coefficient. In a certain, broader sense, we can refer to as a budget of the privacy loss, that is, a certain amount that can be allocated to a differential-private series of requests to the DB [14].

1.3   Local and Central Differential Privacy Models

The architecture of systems for differential privacy needs to provide both privacy and security. Privacy mechanisms control what can be excluded from data we release. Security refers to controlling who is allowed to access the database, but makes no guarantees about what can be extracted from that database.

To date there are two main architectural solutions for differential privacy, central and local models. The central privacy model is the most popular system, where data is stored centrally and each result computed on the database is differentially private by adding noise to query results. Each user of the system can send any data without any additional noise. Main industrial differential privacy solutions include Microsoft's PINQ [5], Uber's FLEX (exploring its internal analytics) [6], LinkedIn's PriPeARL (for its ad analytics) [7], Google's differential privacy open source project [8,9], and the 2020 U.S. Census disclosure avoidance system[10]. Figure 2 depicts the central model of differential privacy.

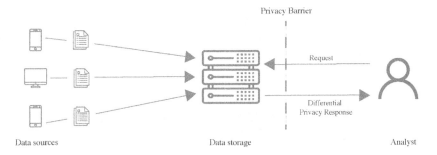

Fig. 2. The central model of differential privacy

An alternative approach is the local model, where the data curator never operates the sensitive data, so does not need to be trusted. With currently implemented systems based on local mode data is individually "noised" before being stored on a central "untrusted" server. The main implementations of local differentially private systems include Google's RAPPOR on Chrome browser [11], Apple's iOS and MacOS diagnostics [12], and Microsoft's telemetry data system in Windows 10 [13]. The Fig. 3 below demonstrates the local model.

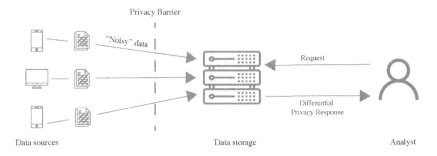

Fig. 3. Local model of differential privacy

The privacy model we are interested in for this article is the central privacy, where data is stored centrally, but we want to ensure each result requested on the data is privatized properly.

1.4   Classic Case of Differential Privacy

Let's consider an analysis on databases containing personal information about students. The analysis may be as simple as determining the average age of the students in the data, or it may be more sophisticated and involves performing some computation on data and outputting the result.

For example, consider counting queries to compute the number of objects that have some property, say how many students live in a dormitory in the first 99 records. Doing the same with the first one hundred records and determining the increase in result by one adversary can definitely find out that one hundredth record contains information about the dorm's resident. If the adversary has access to information on the hundredth record that the student came from the Kemerovo region, then in a certain case identification will happen almost instantly, because there may be a single student from the Kemerovo region in the database. That is, the organization of the process of issuing statistical data requires careful planning and determining and limiting the set of data that should be issued in response to requests.

Let's now make some notation and definitions that will be used to describe a prospective differential privacy system. To begin with, let's determine that the interaction between the analyst and the DP mechanism occurs through some kind of transformation or transcript. First of all, it is quite enough to consider the transcript as a single request to the database and the response to this request (we will consider a series of requests later).

Roughly speaking, a non-interactive mechanism M is differentially private if for any transcript and for any two sets of databases y and y' differing by one entry, the probabilities of obtaining results differ by $1+\epsilon$ (for sufficiently small ϵ) times [4]. It is technically more convenient to use exp^ϵ instead of $(1+\epsilon)$, because the former behaves more nicely under multiplication ($exp^{\epsilon_1} \cdot exp^{\epsilon_2} = exp^{\epsilon_1+\epsilon_2}$).

$$Pr(M(y) \in S) \leq exp^\epsilon Pr(M(y') \in S)$$

For greater clarity, it is necessary that the ratio of the probability distribution lies in the interval $[exp^{-\epsilon}, exp^\epsilon]$. The parameter ϵ is selected based on privacy policy considerations [21].

The mechanism is most often chosen based on the probability density distribution, such as Laplace or Gauss. We will consider the Laplace distribution, although this is not mandatory. Moreover, in general terms, differential privacy can be considered as a certain family of definitions parameterized by data sets and metrics used [5], which implies significant research opportunities.

So, the basic method for achieving differential privacy is to choose a Laplace mechanism that uses the exact calculation of the function f with the subsequent addition of noise. The noise is calculated according to the selected distribution and scaled according to the sensitivity of the function f. In this case we use sensitivity equal to 1, $\Delta = 1$.

$$M(x) = f(y) + Y, \text{ where } Y \sim Lap(1/\epsilon)$$

Note an important definition: the Laplace distribution $Lap(\lambda)$ has a probability density function $h(y) = \frac{1}{2\lambda}exp(-\frac{|y|}{\lambda})$, mean equal 0, and standard deviation $\sqrt{2}\lambda$.

Suppose we are dealing with a set D, whose elements can take the values $\{0,1\}$, and we want to count the number of units in the subset X. It is clear that if we get a set X' from a set X by adding or removing one entry, then the number of units will change by a maximum of one, $||X - X'||_1 = 1$. In this case, we can talk about calculating the difference between two data sets using the L1 norm. It is worth noting that no one restricts us in using other metrics for a database of a larger dimension.

We can define that a deterministic function of a set of real data $f : D \rightarrow R$ has a sensitivity of at least Δ if for all adjacent D and D' the condition $|f(D) - f(D')| \leq \Delta$ is satisfied.

Then the distribution mechanism takes the following form $\widetilde{f_\epsilon}(D) = f(D) + Y$, where $Y \sim Lap(\Delta/\epsilon)$. The Fig. 4 below demonstrates the distribution mechanism.

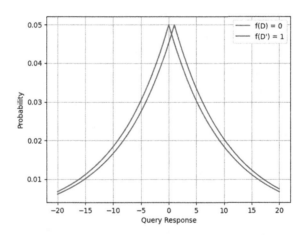

Fig. 4. Distribution of $\widetilde{f_\epsilon}(D) = f(D)+Lap(\Delta/\epsilon)$ over two inputs: $f(D) = 0$, $f(D') = 1$, sensitivity $\Delta = 1$, privacy parameter $\epsilon = 0.1$

It is clear that using continuous distribution as a mechanism can significantly reduce the performance of the program, so we should use a sample of discrete distribution. The most suitable method of generating Y is based on the generic procedure, called the inverse sampling method.

In our case, we know the probability distribution function for the Laplace distribution and this is $F(y) = Pr(Y \leq y) = 1 - exp^{-y/\lambda}$.

Thus, having random variables U in the range from 0 to 1 and an inverse function $F^{-1}(\cdot)$ at the input, one can obtain a discrete distribution: $Y \sim F^{-1}(U)$. This computing results in the procedure for sampling from the exponential distribution with parameter lambda: $\lambda Ln(U)$. Such similar transformations have already been implemented in the form of library functions for many popular programming languages.

Getting back to our example with students, we can get the following discrete distributions (Fig. 5).

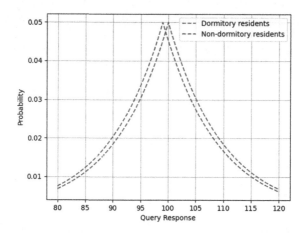

Fig. 5. Distribution of dormitory residents

1.5   Spending of the Differential Privacy Budget

In the previous section, we considered the option of non-interactive use of differential privacy, which is quite understandable and applicable for single use. However, in practice it is necessary to deal with multiple user requests to the system, moreover, with different requests. In this case, the mechanism of differential privacy should be defined as a sequence of randomized functions. In this sense, it may be interesting to apply useful consequences of the theoretical foundations of DP.

Differential privacy does not indicate the nature of the distribution used and has no relations with the auxiliary data that the adversary can get in the process from different sources. Also, the result of the DP mechanism itself is differentially private and it will not lose this property during subsequent post-processing [20]. However, when interacting with the system, it is necessary to set the total amount of allowed privacy leakage or the "privacy budget".

In fact, the privacy budget determines how many statistical queries can be made to the entire system and how accurate the results will be. In this case, it is necessary to maintain a balance: by setting the value too high, confidential data will leak, by setting it too low, the accuracy of the data will quickly tend to zero. Based on this, in many cases, the privacy budget is obtained empirically.

The quantification of privacy loss budget permits the analysis and control of cumulative privacy loss over multiple computations. Understanding the behavior of differentially private mechanisms under composition enables the design and analysis of complex differentially private algorithms from simpler differentially private building blocks [20].

A simple composition of independent differential private algorithms is differentially private and the final value of ϵ is the sum of the coefficients of ϵ for each individual algorithm [21].

It is possible to define and prove the concept of differential-private "cumulative" composition as an extension of a simple composition when the maximum value of ϵ is set, at which the database manager (or curator) stops issuing data [14]. In practice, this is expressed in the fact that we can apply the differentially private mechanism to separate parts of the database and get a simple way to account for the total loss of privacy.

Suppose we are considering class registers for two different classes and the mechanisms M_1 and M_2 are used to work with them, with coefficients ϵ_1 and ϵ_2, respectively. Both of these logs (or tables) can be combined into one large log (or table), which is a common practice in working with a database. The concept of cumulative composition DP allows us to assert that the combined mechanism $M(M_1, M_2)$ is $(\epsilon_1 + \epsilon_2)$-differentially private. This process is depicted below (Fig. 6).

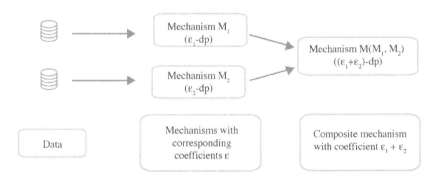

Fig. 6. Composite mechanism of differential privacy

However, such an approach is not without drawbacks related to the very nature of such a strict approach to differential privacy, when probabilities in the range $[-\epsilon, \epsilon]$ are considered, that is, tails are "lost".

To weaken such a condition, the concept of (ϵ, δ)-differential privacy is introduced, when the added coefficient δ makes sense to correct the situation in an emergency situation when the strict condition of differential privacy is violated.

That is, with a probability of $1 - \delta$, the mechanism works as a "pure" differential privacy.

Note an important definition: an algorithm M is called (ϵ, δ)-differentially private if, for any adjacent sets D, D' and any measurable S, the following is true: $Pr(M(D) \in S) \leq exp^\epsilon Pr(M(D') \in S) + \delta$.

However, with probability δ, as they say in the community, "all bets burn out", which is very inconvenient. In addition, the possibility of composing sequential mechanisms is seriously complicated [14, 16].

Ilya Mironov proposed a different mechanism - Renyi-differential privacy [15], based on the concept of Renyi divergence. Suppose we have two sets X and Y, each of which consists of n random variables. Accordingly, the probability of occurrence of each value is denoted as $p_i \in X$ and $q_i \in Y$, respectively. Then the Renyi divergence can be defined as

$$D_\alpha(X||Y) = \frac{1}{\alpha - 1} log(\sum_{i=1}^{n} \frac{p_i^\alpha}{q_i^{\alpha-1}}), \text{ where } \alpha > 0 \text{ and } \alpha \neq 1.$$

Thus, we determine the measure of similarity (or difference) of two distributions. Using this definition, we can say that $D_\alpha(A(D)||A(D')) \leq \epsilon$, i.e. the divergence of the two generated distributions should be less than the privacy loss parameter for large values of α (almost infinity). In this case, we can talk about (α, ϵ)-differential privacy when the coefficient α is finite. A remarkable feature of this mechanism is a simple way of composition, when the privacy coefficients ϵ_1 and ϵ_2 are simply summed up without any unpleasant consequences. All this makes it possible to manage the privacy budget quite simply in systems where you need to monitor a lot of requests.

2   Educational Institutions Case Study

Access to student data in Russia is regulated by the Federal Legislation of the Russian Federation, which defines basic concepts, for example, the concept of personal data. "Personal data - any information relating directly or indirectly to a certain or identifiable individual (subject of personal data)" (Federal Law No. 152-FZ of 27.07.2006 "On Personal Data").

For example, a student's personal data includes: information contained in a birth certificate, passport or other identity document; information contained in the student's personal file; information contained in the personal file of a student deprived of parental care; information contained in the class journal; information contained in the Student's Health Card; information about the state of health; a document about the place of residence; photographs; other information necessary to determine the relationship of education and upbringing. The right of access to the student's personal data may have:

– Director of an educational institution;
– Teaching staff;
– Social staff;

– Doctors/health staff;
– Other.

The section discusses 2 options - service requests for employees of educational institutions, and requests for external users. Requests for official purposes are broader in nature, requests from third-party users may be limited to a small range of functionality.

2.1 Data Structure

Let's describe our data as relational database tables in a normalized form, somewhat simplify the data schema without loss of generality. At the same time, it should be taken into account that the process of bringing to a normalized form leads to "fragmentation" of information. On the one hand, such presentation of information is convenient and familiar for developers of information systems, on the other hand, it complicates our work. However, for the sake of simplicity of understanding the principles, we will leave everything as it is.

The Fig. 7 shows the key independent data models, namely: students, teachers, subjects, classes and grades.

Student Model

Account Number	Full name	Date of Birth	Gender	Region code	Other data
10001	Ivanov Ivan Ivanovich	11.11.2007	M	47	...
10002	Sidorova Anastasia Nikolaevna	02.02.2007	Ж	10	...
10003	Yangubaeva Svetlana Salavatovna	03.03.2007	Ж	2	...
10004	Goryalov Dmitry Sergeevich	04.04.2008	M	16	...
...	...	...	...	...	...

Teacher model

Account Number	Full name	Date of Birth	Gender	Subject	Other data
20001	Sergeev Sergey Ivanovich	01.01.1981	M	1	...
20002	Docentova Irina Nikolaevna	02.02.1985	Ж	2	...
20003	Assistant Yana Lvovna	03.03.1995	Ж	3	...
20004	Petrov Petr Petrovich	04.04.1987	M	4	...
...	...	...	...	...	...

Subject Model

Account Number	Subject
1	Mathematics
2	Biology
3	Literature
4	Informatics
5	...

Class Model

Number class	Subject	Teacher	Period of study	Other data
30001	1	20001	10.01.2022 - 15.05.2022	...
30002	2	20002	10.01.2022 - 15.05.2022	...
30003	3	20003	10.01.2022 - 15.05.2022	...
30004	4	20004	10.01.2022 - 15.05.2022	...
...	...	...	...	...

Grading Model

Number class	Student	Grade	Date received	Other data
30001	10001	5	10.02.2022	...
30001	10002	3	11.02.2022	...
30001	10003	4	10.02.2022	...
30001	10004	4	11.02.2022	...
...	...	...	...	...

Fig. 7. Data models

Thus, such a structure allows to keep a very simplified accounting of the data of the educational process and organize the issuance of statistics according to user requests. We will consider the first and last tables, the rest models are explanatory.

2.2   Basic Requests

The main requests include all kinds of calculations of statistics on personal affairs of students, for example, by age, by region, by benefits. Such requests are classic from the point of view of the DP, since the personal data table contains one record per student and individual sets.

Requests for academic achievement can be considered as one of the main ones, let us focus on them. Users may be interested in statistical queries regarding academic performance in terms of subjects, class periods, etc.

If an adversary has access to accurate statistics, such as average, number, variance, then his work on identifying a particular student is significantly simplified. Having only limited access to personal data (for example: last name, first name, account number) and sufficient to the mentioned statistical data on the "classbook," it is quite realistic to restore its contents.

2.3   Histograms

Usually we talk about the database as a collection of records, each containing information about a particular person. Sometimes it is very useful to present the DB as histograms for different keys. For example, if a record of each student contains d attributes, the histogram will contain all possible combinations of these d attributes and the number of students having records with the corresponding combination.

However, a histogram with grouping by all attributes is not always informative. The most common may be histograms for a single attribute or a shorter combination of attributes, or fragments thereof. In fact, we are talking about a GROUP BY operation, often not clearly limited, and subsequent aggregation by the resulting unions. As we mentioned at the beginning about the only student from the Kemerovo region, even with the proper noise of the histogram, this will not be enough and the set of unions itself should be made differential-private [17].

If you consider the table with students' grades, you can note that each student in most cases appears in the classbook many times, these can be records of different grades for different times in different subjects. Traditional differential privacy is based on the recognition of two datasets as adjacent in the case of a difference of sets with only one record. In the case of our classbook, this has a very limited effect and potentially does not properly protect the privacy of the student. Instead, it is logical to consider adjacent datasets that either contain data about an individual or not. Naturally, such a definition of adjacency (or neighborhood) will lead to changes in calculations and performance. Suppose that we compute a histogram from a certain key combination k and previously get a list of length r. At the same time, the rules for calculating the privacy coefficient over the entire composition should also be preserved, and it is possible to evaluate ϵ_k and δ_k for each individual cluster set as the ϵ/r and δ/r, respectively, and obtain a (ϵ, δ)-differentially private mechanism as a result.

In the development of such systems, as a rule, several common problems arise:

- Restriction on the number of occurrences of an individual in a cluster;
- Predefined data grouping keys;
- Scale the solution to larger databases.

There are theoretical and practical solutions, such as Google's Plume system [18]. Another approach can be illustrated by the LinkedIn's Audience Engagement API [19], which does not impose any restrictions on entries into the cluster and significantly changes the approach to calculating the privacy loss budget, when deviations in histogram values are taken into account and the accumulation of the used budget is non-linear [6].

2.4   Architectural Solution

The strategy of spending the privacy budget can be implemented by adding an intermediate service with the calculation, accumulation and accounting of the current budget. Final implementations are no longer so obvious and require a lot of effort from developers.

The implementation of the DP can be described in the form of an independent module, which will be an addition to the software product that distributes statistics. Architecturally, the differentially private module can be divided into two services: privacy service and budget spending service. The privacy service acts as a coordinator or instructor who receives the request, processes and returns the response. The most important in this module is the budget spending service, which stores the current state of the budget, calculates the new value and regulates access to data based on the established privacy restrictions. In fact, the implementation of such a service is the main and most labor-intensive part of building a general architecture of differential privacy.

It is worth noting that budget spending implies the use of a certain starting budget value, which can be calculated from the bottom up, starting from the simplest components of the system.

Schematically, the module can be represented as follows (see Fig. 8). The privacy service does not have an internal state, it coordinates, makes the necessary calculations and gives the final result. Thus, the final pipeline will look like this:

1. Get the current value of the privacy budget and private data if the budget has not yet been spent. Otherwise, the data is not distributed, it is necessary to notify the agent;
2. Based on the data obtained, the result of the deterministic function from the set of real data is calculated $f : D \rightarrow R$;
3. Based on the obtained value of the privacy budget and the initial data, noise is calculated (use, for example, Laplace distribution), which is added to the result from paragraph (2);
4. The result of paragraph (3) is distributed with the agent.

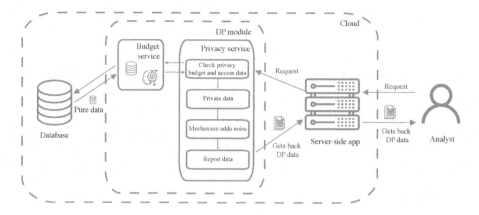

Fig. 8. Architecture for differential privacy module

Such an architectural solution is not a standard, but clearly demonstrates the direction of further work in the study of differential privacy by the community.

3   Conclusion

As part of this study, we considered a relatively new mechanism - differential privacy. We tried to demonstrate that by evaluating the probabilities of possible data losses, we can build the right policy to "noise" publicly available data. This approach makes it possible to find a compromise between maintaining the accuracy and privacy of the distributed data. We demonstrated the possibilities of practical application of this mechanism, and also described the possible architectural solution of the differentially private module. It should be noted that the community still has a lot of work to do in standardizing the principles of differential privacy; on our part, we hope that we have been able to demonstrate directions for further development.

References

1. Dinur, I., Nissim, K.: Revealing information while preserving privacy. In: Proceedings of the Twenty-second ACM SIGMOD-SIGACT-SIGART Symposium on Principles of Database Systems, PODS 2003, pp. 202–210 (2003)
2. Dwork, C., Nissim, K.: Privacy-preserving datamining on vertically partitioned databases. In: Franklin, M. (ed.) CRYPTO 2004. LNCS, vol. 3152, pp. 528–544. Springer, Heidelberg (2004). https://doi.org/10.1007/978-3-540-28628-8_32
3. Blum, A., Dwork, C., McSherry, F., Nissim, K.: Practical privacy: the SuLQ framework. In: Proceedings of the Twenty-Fourth ACM SIGMOD-SIGACT-SIGART Symposium on Principles of Database Systems, pp. 128–138. ACM (2005)
4. Dwork, C., McSherry, F., Nissim, K., Smith, A.: Calibrating noise to sensitivity in private data analysis. In: Halevi, S., Rabin, T. (eds.) TCC 2006. LNCS, vol. 3876, pp. 265–284. Springer, Heidelberg (2006). https://doi.org/10.1007/11681878_14

5. McSherry, F.D.: Privacy integrated queries: an extensible platform for privacy-preserving data analysis. In: Proceedings of the 2009 ACM SIGMOD International Conference on Management of Data, ser., SIGMOD 2009, pp. 19–30. Association for Computing Machinery, New York (2009). https://doi.org/10.1145/1559845.1559850
6. Johnson, N., Near, J.P., Song, D.: Towards practical differential privacy for SQL queries. Proc. VLDBEndow. **11**(5), 526–539 (2018). http://arxiv.org/abs/1706.09479
7. Kenthapadi, K., Tran, T.T.L.: PriPeARL: a framework for privacy-preserving analytics and reporting at LinkedIn. In: Proceedings of the 27th ACM International Conference on Information and Knowledge Management, ser., CIKM 2018, pp. 2183–2191. Association for Computing Machinery, New York (2018). https://doi.org/10.1145/3269206.3272031
8. Guevara, M.: Google developers, September 2019. https://developers.googleblog.com/2019/09/enabling-developers-and-organizations.html
9. Wilson, R.J., Zhang, C.Y., Lam, W., Desfontaines, D., Simmons-Marengo, D., Gipson, B.: Differentially private SQL with bounded user contribution. In: Proceedings on Privacy Enhancing Technologies, vol. 2020, no. 2, pp. 230–250 (2020). https://content.sciendo.com/view/journals/popets/2020/2/article-p230.xml
10. Dajani, A.N., et al.: The modernization of statistical disclosure limitation at the U.S. Census Bureau (2017). https://www2.census.gov/cac/sac/meetings/2017-09/statistical-disclosure-limitation.pdf
11. Erlingsson, U., Pihur, V., Korolova, A.: RAPPOR: randomized aggregatable privacy-preserving ordinal response. In: Proceedings of the 2014 ACM SIGSAC Conference on Computer and Communications Security, ser., CCS 2014, pp. 1054–1067 (2014). https://doi.org/10.1145/2660267.2660348
12. Apple Differential Privacy Team: Learning with privacy at scale (2017). https://machinelearning.apple.com/2017/12/06/learning-with-privacy-at-scale.html
13. Ding, B., Kulkarni, J., Yekhanin, S.: Collecting telemetry data privately, December 2017. https://www.microsoft.com/en-us/research/publication/collecting-telemetry-data-privately/
14. Dwork, C., McSherry, F., Nissim, K., Smith, A.: Calibrating noise to sensitivity in private data analysis. J. Priv. Confid. **7**(3), 17–51 (2017). https://doi.org/10.29012/jpc.v7i3.405
15. Mironov, I.: Renyi Differential Privacy (2017). https://arxiv.org/pdf/1702.07476.pdf
16. Bun, M., Steinke, T.: Concentrated differential privacy: simplifications, extensions, and lower bounds (2016). https://arxiv.org/abs/1605.02065
17. Gopi, S., Gulhane, P., Kulkarni, J., Hanwen Shen, J., Shokouhi, M., Yekhanin, S.: Differentially private set union. arXiv preprint arXiv:2002.09745 (2020)
18. Amin, K., Gillenwater, J., Joseph, M., Kulesza, A., Vassilvitskii, S.: Plume: differential privacy at scale. arXiv:2201.11603 (2022)
19. Rogers, R., et al.: LinkedIn's audience engagements API: a privacy preserving data analytics system at scale. J. Priv. Confid. **11**(3) (2021). https://doi.org/10.29012/jpc.782
20. Dwork, C., Roth, A.: The algorithmic foundations of differential privacy. Found. Trends Theor. Comput. Sci. **9**(34), 211407 (2013). https://doi.org/10.1561/0400000042. ISSN 1551-305X
21. Vadhan, S.: The complexity of differential privacy. In: Tutorials on the Foundations of Cryptography. ISC, pp. 347–450. Springer, Cham (2017). https://doi.org/10.1007/978-3-319-57048-8_7

A Systematic Literature Review on Numerical Weather Prediction Models and Provenance Data

Alper Tufek[(✉)] and Mehmet S. Aktas

Computer Engineering Department, Yildiz Technical University, Istanbul, Turkey
alper.tufek@std.yildiz.edu.tr, aktas@yildiz.edu.tr

Abstract. The weather has been an important issue for mankind since the earliest times. The need to predict the weather accurately increases every day when considering the effects of natural disasters such as floods, hails, extreme winds, landslides, etc. on many sectors from transportation to agriculture, which all depend on weather conditions. Numerical weather prediction (NWP) models, today's the de-facto tools used for weather forecasting, are scientific software that models atmospheric dynamics in accordance with the laws of physics. These models perform complex mathematical calculations on very large data (gridded) and require high computational power. For this reason, NWP models are scientific software that is usually run on distributed infrastructures and often takes hours to finish. On the other hand, provenance is another key concept as important as weather prediction. Provenance can be briefly defined as metadata that provides information about any kind of data, process, or workflow. In this SLR study, a comprehensive screening of literature was performed to discover primary studies that directly suggest systematic provenance structures for NWP models, or primary studies in which at least a case study was implemented on an NWP model even if considered in a broader perspective. Afterward, these primary studies were thoroughly examined in line with specific research questions, and the findings were presented in a systematic manner. An SLR study on primary studies which combines the two domains of NWP models and provenance research has never been done before. So we think that this work will fill an important gap in literature regarding studies combining the two domains and increase the interest in the subject.

Keywords: Numerical weather prediction (NWP) · Systematic Literature Review (SLR) · Provenance

1 Introduction

The weather has been an important phenomenon for mankind since the earliest times. It is almost impossible to find an area where the weather conditions are not effective. The magnitude of the need to predict the weather will be

O. Gervasi et al. (Eds.): ICCSA 2022 Workshops, LNCS 13380, pp. 616–627, 2022.
https://doi.org/10.1007/978-3-031-10542-5_42

better understood when considering the effects of natural disasters such as floods, hails, extreme winds, landslides, etc. on many sectors from transportation to agriculture, which all depend on weather conditions. It is for this reason that since ancient times, people have tried to predict the weather by observing various patterns in clouds or different natural events.

Today, the de-facto tools used for weather forecasting are numerical weather prediction (NWP) models. These models are scientific software that models atmospheric dynamics in accordance with the laws of physics. Their working logic is based on simulating the movement of air according to the laws of fluid dynamics and physics, and calculating the possible states of the atmosphere in future time periods, taking the current (actual) state of the atmosphere as the starting point. This is a process that performs complex mathematical calculations on very large data (gridded) and therefore requires high computational power. For this reason, NWP models are scientific software that is usually run on distributed infrastructures and often takes a long time to terminate.

On the other hand, provenance is another key concept as important as weather prediction. Provenance can be briefly defined as metadata that provides information about any kind of data, process, or workflow. For example, if it is a data product, data provenance can provide very detailed information about what processes are employed with which parameters during the production of that data from its source. Or, in situations where various simulations are run through scientific workflow applications, runtime provenance can provide useful information about all workflow stages (call traces, input parameters, artifacts, etc.).

Although there are survey or review studies on provenance systems in the literature [2,12,15] we did not find any SLR or mapping study specific to numerical weather forecasting models from the perspective of provenance. In this SLR study, a comprehensive screening study was aimed at primary studies that directly suggest systematic provenance structures for NWP models, or at the primary studies in which at least a case study was implemented on an NWP model even if considered in a broader perspective.

2   Research Methodology

In this SLR study, we followed the guidelines proposed in [13] and [6]. In this direction, primary studies on the subject were scanned in the literature. A primary study is an experimental-based study that investigates a specific research question in any field, whereas a secondary study is one in which all primary studies related to a specific research question are reviewed and the findings are compiled and synthesized.

2.1   Research Questions

In this study, we focus on primary studies that directly suggest systematic provenance structures for NWP models, or primary studies in which at least a case study was implemented on an NWP model even if considered in a broader perspective. We asked various questions to direct the knowledge synthesis. Our research questions and the main motivations behind them are shown in Table 1.

Table 1. Research questions

Research question	Main motivation
RQ1: What provenance standards/specifications are proposed/used?	PROV, OPM, or a specific representation/format
RQ2: What are the provenance sources proposed?	From where provenance is obtained: Log files, workflow app, etc.?
RQ3: What provenance storage mechanisms are proposed?	Special provenance storage system, file, or database, etc.
RQ4: What is the distribution of publications by years?	To show the trend analysis
RQ5: In which journals or conferences have related papers been published?	To identify journals and conferences where researchers publish their studies on the topic

2.2   Search Strategy

In this SLR, we specifically focus on provenance data within NWP models. We performed specific searches on all best known digital libraries to gather the primary studies [13]. These libraries are ACM Digital Library, IEEE Xplore, Scopus, SpringerLink, Elsevier's Science Direct and Web of Science. Each library has its own search engine with its own characteristics. We tried to be as much inclusive as possible when constructing query string. Numerical weather prediction models may be referred to as "atmospheric modeling", "numerical weather forecasting", etc. If supported by the search engine of the digital source, wildcards are used to include every different form of keywords, otherwise most possible variations of keywords are exclusively included in query string. The query strings used for each library and quick notes about each search engine are provided in Table 2.

Since the first Working Draft of the PROV Family of Documents [14] was published in December 2012 by W3C, papers with a publication date prior to 2012 were discarded. Also, the inclusion and exclusion criteria were defined to identify relevant works focused on in this SLR.

Inclusion Criteria (IC):

- **IC1:** Research articles or short papers that focus on provenance data in NWP workflows.

Exclusion Criteria (EC):

- **EC1:** Duplicated papers;
- **EC2:** Papers not in English;
- **EC3:** Surveys, Review Articles, Book Chapters, Posters, Tutorials, Technical Reports and Standards;

During the SLR study, StArt [16] and JabRef [5] tools were used. StArt is a free tool that aids performing SLR studies in accordance with the systematic review procedure suggested by Kitchenham [6]. JabRef (another free tool) is a reference management software that can import more than 15 reference formats, and it supports many operations such as merge, convert, export, etc. Search results obtained from digital libraries are first exported to files in bibtex, RIS or CSV formats depending on the support provided by the search engine. Next,

Table 2. Data sources and query strings used

Source	Query string	Notes
ACM	(NWP OR (numerical AND (weather OR atmospher*) AND (prediction OR forecast* OR model*))) AND provenance	Supports wildcards and boolean operators such as AND, OR, and NOT
IEEE	(NWP OR (numerical AND (weather OR atmospher*) AND (prediction OR forecast* OR model*))) AND provenance	Wildcards and boolean operators are supported. Search in Full Text & Metadata was selected
Scopus	(NWP OR (numerical AND (weather OR atmospher*) AND (prediction OR forecast* OR model*))) AND provenance	Wildcards and boolean connectors are supported
SpringerLink	(NWP OR (numerical AND (weather OR atmospher*) AND (prediction OR forecast* OR model*))) AND provenance	Wildcards and boolean connectors are supported
Science Direct	(NWP OR (numerical (weather OR atmosphere OR atmospheric) (prediction OR forecast OR forecasting OR model OR modeling))) AND provenance	Wildcards are not supported. Maximum of 8 boolean connectors are allowed. Spaces between keywords or keyword groups are implicitly interpreted as AND connector. Plurals and spelling variants are included (colour vs color, attack vs attacks)
Web of Science	(NWP OR (numerical AND (weather OR atmospher*) AND (prediction OR forecast* OR model*))) AND provenance	It supports wildcards and boolean operators. Stemming and lemmatization are applied by default to expand the search

these files were imported into the JabRef tool, grouped as a single file for each data source. Then each file per data source is imported into the corresponding search session defined for each data source in the StArt tool. With the StArt tool, it is possible to list all primary sources together, and to easily classify them as Accepted or Rejected by quickly evaluating titles, keywords, and abstracts if available.

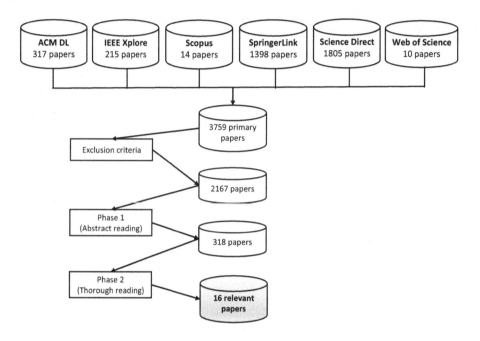

Fig. 1. Paper selection flow and summary statistics

3   Results and Analysis

We performed the extraction in January 2022. A total of 3759 results were obtained when a search was made on all search engines with the constraint of the publication years between 2012 and 2021 inclusive. After applying the exclusion criteria, there were 2176 results left (duplicate results, surveys, review articles, book chapters, posters, tutorials, etc. were removed). Then, in the next step (Phase 1), titles, keywords and abstracts were read and irrelevant articles were eliminated. At the end of this phase, there were 318 studies left. At the last stage, all the remaining articles were examined in depth and relevant papers within the scope of this SLR were identified and the findings obtained in line with the research questions were synthesized. The workflow for paper selection and the number of primary studies obtained at each stage are summarized in Fig. 1.

The findings obtained from the relevant studies and the evaluation of the synthesis results for each research question are as follows.

3.1 RQ1: What Provenance Standards/specifications Are Proposed/Used?

In most of the selected studies, OPM [9] and its improved version, PROV specification [8], were used. However, apart from these, some studies use a provenance format of their own, while some other studies use various known but less commonly used provenance formats. The provenance standards used/supported in the selected primary studies, and their explanations are summarized in the Table 3.

Table 3. Provenance standards/specifications that are proposed/used in primary studies

Study ID	Provenance standards/specifications used
S01	EML - Ecological Metadata Language
S02, S03, S04	Open Provenance Model (OPM) [9]
S05, S06, S07, S08, S14	No known provenance format specified
S09, S10, S11, S12	PROV
S13	OWL and RDF
S15	Provenance-Aware Storage System, PASS [10,11] and OPM
S16	Two extension schemas of PROV-O; CWLProv (for file-oriented provenance) and S-Prov (for streaming data provenance)

3.2 RQ2: What Are the Provenance Sources Proposed?

The provenance sources used/proposed in the selected primary studies are summarized in the Table 4. It is possible to use a variety of sources to obtain structured provenance. Scientific software is often run in a certain order according to a defined workflow through a workflow manager. Therefore, the most common source of provenance is the tracks that workflow management software keeps while running tasks within the workflow. However, in this method, there may be provenance losses for the intermediate processes of an atomic program in the workflow. Another important source of provenance is the log files created directly by the scientific software itself. In this method, it is possible to capture the details of intermediate transactions, but on the other hand, the fact that there is not a common standard for log file formats brings additional difficulties. Yet another method is the instrumentation of the source codes of the software so that the application itself generates structured provenance directly at runtime.

Each method has its own advantages and disadvantages. For example, in the source code instrumentation method, no intermediate extractor will be needed, but it is not always possible to find the source code of the software. Even if the source code is available, making additional changes to the code may cause the program to exhibit ambiguous behavior or introduce bugs.

Table 4. Provenance sources that are proposed/used in primary studies

Study ID	Provenance sources used
S01, S05, S06, S08, S13, S14	Workflow runtime provenance
S02, S03, S04	Provenance dataset consisting of provenance from different types of workflows (approximately 48,000 workflow execution instances) [9]
S07	Their private steering engine called Co^2Steer
S09	Their framework named CityPulse
S10, S11, S12	Log files
S15	Workflow traces from PASS, Karma, Tupelo [3], Taverna [7], PASOA [4]
S16	Provenance traces produced by scientific workflows of two major types: file-oriented and data-streaming. They are obtained from SPARQL endpoints [19]

3.3   RQ3: What Provenance Storage Mechanisms are Proposed?

The provenance storage mechanisms used/proposed in the selected primary studies, and their explanations are summarized in the Table 5. The most well-known system developed specifically for structured provenance storage is Karma [17]. While Karma supports the OPM standard, Komadu [18], another provenance system, which is an advanced version of Karma, fully supports PROV specification. Apart from these two systems, there are also studies that directly use a relational database (MySQL, BerkeleyDB, etc.). While some studies do not give details about the provenance storage environment, in one study, the Kepler [1] workflow manager was extended and provenance support was added.

3.4   RQ4: What is the Distribution of Publications by Years?

Looking at the final extraction results, we can say that there is not much relevant studies on the topic. This fact can be clearly seen in Fig. 2. Although there are many primary studies in the NWP domain, there are not many studies combining the NWP domain and the concept of systematic provenance, which is mostly

Table 5. Provenance storage mechanisms that are used in primary studies

Study ID	Provenance storage mechanism(s) used
S01	A provenance storage system which extends the Kepler [1] scientific workflow system
S02, S03, S04	Karma [17] provenance system
S05	A provenance module named ProvEn developed specifically for The Earth System Grid Federation (ESGF)
S06, S07, S08, S09, S14, S16	Uses their own internal databases whose details are not given in the paper
S10, S11, S12	Komadu [18] (advanced version of the Karma)
S13	Relational database (i.e. MySQL) or XML files
S15	A BerkeleyDB database storing key/value data

researched in the field of software engineering. On the other hand, although there is no general pattern in the distribution across years, we can say that there has been a relative increase in the number of studies on the subject as of 2021. With this SLR study, we think that we will fill an important gap in the literature regarding studies combining the two domains and increase the interest in the subject.

3.5 RQ5: In Which Journals or Conferences Have Related Papers Been Published?

The list of journals or conferences in which relevant studies are published can be shown in Table 6.

Since the total number of relevant studies was small, we did not expect a clustering in on single journal or conference. Indeed, only one paper per journal or conference has been published in across all journals/conferences except for the Future Generation Computer Systems journal. Three different studies have been published in the Future Generation Computer Systems journal.

4   Threats to Validity of Research

The possible threats that may affect the validity of the results obtained in this SLR study and the precautions we tried to take in response to these threats are as follows:

Selection Bias: This threat refers to the incorrect inclusion/exclusion of some primary studies in/from the SLR. In order to eliminate this possibility as much as possible, a very rigorous selection procedure has been followed and the StArt tool has been used for this end. The StArt tool facilitates the evaluation of primary studies obtained from all data sources by importing all bibliographic records into a single place. In addition, its ability to detect duplicate studies and

Table 6. Journals/conferences where related papers published

Journal/Conference name	Type	Notes
ACM Transactions on Storage (TOS)	Journal	ACM journal
Concurrency and Computation: Practice and Experience	Journal	Wiley journal
Environmental Modelling and Software	Journal	Hosted on ScienceDirect
European Conference on Parallel Processing (Euro-Par)	Conference	Covers all aspects of parallel and distributed processing
Future Generation Computer Systems (FGCS)	Journal	Hosted on ScienceDirect
IEEE Access	Journal	Open access (OA)
IEEE International Conference on Big Data and Cloud Computing (BdCloud)	Conference	Annual conference
IEEE Transactions on Cloud Computing	Journal	Dedicated to cloud computing
International Conference on Computational Science (ICCS)	Conference	Annual conference
International Conference on E-Science	Conference	Annual conference
International Conference on Semantics, Knowledge and Grid (SKG)	Conference	Annual conference
Journal of Data and Information Quality	Journal	ACM journal
Proceedings of the ACM on Human-Computer Interaction	Journal	ACM journal
Proceedings of the VLDB Endowment	Journal	ACM journal

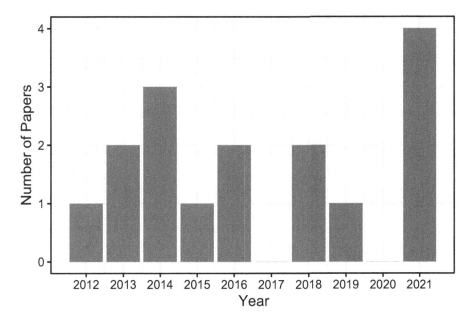

Fig. 2. The distribution of publications across years

the support for performing the selection and extraction phases separately and sequentially reduces the risk of error in the execution of the SLR process.

Publication Selection: We performed searches in all major academic data sources to avoid overlooking any studies that might fall within the scope of this SLR. While performing these searches, we preferred to query all fields (title, keywords, abstract, etc.) and full text whenever supported by the search engine. Besides, we used wildcards to include every different form of keywords if supported, otherwise we exclusively included most possible variations of keywords in query strings.

5   Conclusions

We conducted a systematic literature review to frame the studies that somehow combines the two domains of NWP models and provenance research. We identified 16 relevant papers published between 2012 and 2021. To our knowledge, this kind of an SLR study has never been done before. So we think that this work will fill an important gap in literature regarding studies combining the two domains and increase the interest in the subject.

A   Appendix: Relevant Primary Studies

S01	Behrens, H. W., Candan, K. S., Chen, X., Gadkari, A., Garg, Y., Li, M. L., ..., Sapino, M. L. Datastorm-FE: A data-and decision-flow and coordination engine for coupled simulation ensembles. Proceedings of the VLDB Endowment, 11(12), 1906–1909 (2018)
S02	Cheah, Y. W., Plale, B. Provenance quality assessment methodology and framework. Journal of Data and Information Quality (JDIQ), 5(3), 1–20 (2014)
S03	Chen, P., Plale, B., Aktas, M. S. Temporal representation for scientific data provenance. In 2012 IEEE 8th International Conference on E-Science, IEEE, 1–8 (2012)
S04	Chen, P., Plale, B., Aktas, M. S. Temporal representation for mining scientific data provenance. Future generation computer systems, 36, 363–378 (2014)
S05	Cinquini, L., Crichton, D., Mattmann, C., Harney, J., Shipman, G., Wang, F., ..., Schweitzer, R. The Earth System Grid Federation: An open infrastructure for access to distributed geospatial data. Future Generation Computer Systems, 36, 400–417 (2014)
S06	Galizia, A., Roverelli, L., Zereik, G., Danovaro, E., Clematis, A., D'Agostino, D. Using Apache Airavata and EasyGateway for the creation of complex science gateway front-end. Future Generation Computer Systems, 94, 910–919 (2019)
S07	Liu, W., Ye, Q., Wu, C. Q., Liu, Y., Zhou, X., Shan, Y. Machine Learning-assisted Computational Steering of Large-scale Scientific Simulations. In 2021 IEEE Intl Conf on Parallel & Distributed Processing with Applications, Big Data & Cloud Computing, Sustainable Computing & Communications, Social Computing & Networking (ISPA/BDCloud/SocialCom/SustainCom), 984–992 (2021)
S08	Lopez, J. L. A., Kalyuzhnaya, A. V., Kosukhin, S. S., Ivanov, S. V. Data quality control for St. Petersburg flood warning system. Procedia Computer Science, 80, 2128–2140 (2016)
S09	Puiu, D., Barnaghi, P., Tönjes, R., Kümper, D., Ali, M. I., Mileo, A., ..., Fernandes, J. Citypulse: Large scale data analytics framework for smart cities. IEEE Access, 4, 1086–1108 (2016)
S10	Tufek, A., Gurbuz, A., Ekuklu, O. F., Aktas, M. S. Provenance collection platform for the weather research and forecasting model. In 2018 14th International Conference on Semantics, Knowledge and Grids (SKG), IEEE, 17–24 (2018)
S11	Tufek, A., Aktas, M. S. On the provenance extraction techniques from large scale log files: a case study for the numerical weather prediction models. In European Conference on Parallel Processing, Springer, 249–260 (2020)
S12	Tufek, A, Aktas, MS. On the provenance extraction techniques from large scale log files. Concurrency and Computation: Practice and Experience (2021). https://doi.org/10.1002/cpe.6559
S13	Turuncoglu, U. U., Dalfes, N., Murphy, S., DeLuca, C. Toward self-describing and workflow integrated Earth system models: A coupled atmosphere-ocean modeling system application. Environmental modelling & software, 39, 247–262 (2013)
S14	Wu, C. Q., Lin, X., Yu, D., Xu, W., Li, L. End-to-end delay minimization for scientific workflows in clouds under budget constraint. IEEE Transactions on Cloud Computing, 3(2), 169–181 (2014)
S15	Xie, Y., Muniswamy-Reddy, K. K., Feng, D., Li, Y., Long, D. D. Evaluation of a hybrid approach for efficient provenance storage. ACM Transactions on Storage (TOS), 9(4), 1–29 (2013)
S16	Zhao, R., Atkinson, M., Papapanagiotou, P., Magnoni, F., Fleuriot, J. Dr. Aid: Supporting Data-governance Rule Compliance for Decentralized Collaboration in an Automated Way. Proceedings of the ACM on Human-Computer Interaction, 5(CSCW2), 1–43 (2021)

References

1. Altintas, I., Berkley, C., Jaeger, E., Jones, M., Ludascher, B., Mock, S.: Kepler: an extensible system for design and execution of scientific workflows. In: Proceedings. 16th International Conference on Scientific and Statistical Database Management, pp. 423–424. IEEE (2004)
2. Freire, J., Koop, D., Santos, E., Silva, C.T.: Provenance for computational tasks: a survey. Comput. Sci. Eng. **10**(3), 11–21 (2008)
3. Futrelle, J., et al.: Semantic middleware for e-science knowledge spaces. In: Proceedings of the 7th International Workshop on Middleware for Grids, Clouds and e-Science (2009)
4. Groth, P., et al.: An architecture for provenance system. Technical report (2006)
5. JabRef - Free JabRef Reference Management Tool. https://www.jabref.org. Accessed January 2022
6. Kitchenham, B., Charters, S.: Guidelines for performing systematic literature reviews in software engineering (2007)
7. Missier, P., et al.: Taverna, reloaded. In: Proceedings of the 22nd International Conference on Scientific and Statistical Database Nanagement (SSDBM 2010) (2010)
8. Missier, P., Belhajjame, K., Cheney, J.: The W3C PROV family of specifications for modeling provenance metadata. In: Proceedings of the 16th International Conference on Extending Database Technology, pp. 773–776 (2013). https://doi.org/10.1145/2452376.2452478
9. Moreau, L., et al.: The open provenance model core specification (v1.1). Futur. Gener. Comput. Syst. **27**(6), 743–756 (2011)
10. Muniswamy-Reddy, K.K., Holland, D.A., Braun, U., Seltzer, M.I.: Provenance-aware storage systems. In: USENIX Annual Technical Conference, General Track, pp. 43–56 (2006)
11. Muniswamy-Reddy, K.K., et al.: Layering in provenance systems. In: Proceedings of the 2009 USENIX Annual Technical Conference (USENIX 2009). USENIX Association (2009)
12. Pérez, B., Rubio, J., Sáenz-Adán, C.: A systematic review of provenance systems. Knowl. Inf. Syst. **57**(3), 495–543 (2018)
13. Petersen, K., Feldt, R., Mujtaba, S., Mattsson, M.: Systematic mapping studies in software engineering. In: Proceedings of the 12th International Conference on Evaluation and Assessment in Software Engineering (EASE 2008) (2008)
14. PROV-Overview. https://www.w3.org/TR/2012/WD-prov-overview-20121211/. Accessed 20 Dec 2021
15. Simmhan, Y.L., Plale, B., Gannon, D.: A survey of data provenance in e-science. ACM SIGMOD Rec. **34**(3), 31–36 (2005)
16. StArt - State of the Art through Systematic Review. LAPES Laboratory of Research on Software Engineering (LAPES). http://lapes.dc.ufscar.br/tools/start_tool. Accessed 10 Jan 2022
17. Simmhan, Y.L., Plale, B., Gannon, D.: Karma2: provenance management for datadriven workflows. Int. J. Web Serv. Res. (IJWSR) **5**(2), 1–22 (2008)
18. Suriarachchi, I., Zhou, Q., Plale, B.: Komadu: a capture and visualization system for scientific data provenance. J. Open Res. Softw. **3**(1) (2015)
19. W3C: SPARQL 1.1 Query Language (2013). https://www.w3.org/TR/sparql11-query/

"Smart Habitat": Features of Building It Infrastructure, Main Problems of Building Data Networks Using 5G (6G) Technologies

Alexander Bogdanov[1,2], Nadezhda Shchegoleva[1,2], Gennady Dik[3(✉)], Valery Khvatov[4], and Aleksandr Dik[1]

[1] Saint Petersburg State University, St. Petersburg, Russia
{a.v.bogdanov,n.shchegoleva}@spbu.ru, st087383@student.spbu.ru
[2] St. Petersburg State Marine Technical University, St. Petersburg, Russia
[3] LLC "System Technologies", St. Petersburg, Russia
g.dick@systechnologies.ru
[4] DGT Technologies AG, Toronto, Canada

Abstract. The main issues of digitalization of settlements in Russia based on the "Smart Habitat" (SH) technology are considered, an analysis of security problems and possible risks of 5G and 6G networks used for receiving and transmitting information is carried out, ways of organizing the protection of the used cellular networks are proposed.

Keywords: Network protection · Smart habitat · 6G networks · IoT · Data transmission systems

1 Introduction

One of the significant factors in improving the quality of life of the population in modern conditions is the use of the so-called "Smart Home"' technology, which, for the purpose of further development, develops into a whole strategic direction of building the infrastructure of the habitat called "Smart Habitat" (Fig. 1). The well-known technology "Smart Home", and then "Smart City" (SC) (hereinafter referred to as technology) has long been used in the modern world, but at the same time, the aspect of introducing these technologies in small summer cottages and villages is of increasing interest. In these settlements (habitat fragments - HFbit) there is also a need to automate life processes and ensure the personal and technical safety of residents (Fig. 1). This raises the question of SHF as a more universal and scalable option for using an interconnected system of information and communication technologies with IoT (Internet of things), which simplifies the management of the internal processes of the environment and makes the life of residents more comfortable and safer.

Within the framework of this article, SHF is considered as an environment in which engineering infrastructure, IT infrastructure, social infrastructure and business infrastructure are combined in order to improve the quality of life of the population through the digitalization of various spheres of life HFbit [1].

O. Gervasi et al. (Eds.): ICCSA 2022 Workshops, LNCS 13380, pp. 628–638, 2022.
https://doi.org/10.1007/978-3-031-10542-5_43

Fig. 1. SHF - integrated technology of a new standard of living

As for the goals and priorities of the development of the SHF, it is advisable to take as a basis six basic principles for constructing the SC, expanding and applying them to the considered HFbit according to [2]:

1. The principle of creating a comfortable environment for all SC residents;
2. The principle of coordination and interaction of all participants in the development of SC;
3. The principle of additional designation of the SHF infrastructure (priority of endowing the existing elements of the infrastructure with new functions and obtaining new results due to this);
4. The principle of sustainable development based on monitoring, analysis and forecasting;
5. The principle of sustainable development based on monitoring, analysis and forecasting;
6. The principle of forming a digital environment for self-organization of residents and businesses;
7. The principle that implies a priority orientation towards the creation of positive emotions of residents from interaction with the SC environment.

In accordance with the above principles, the SHF technology is generalized by the concept that declares different approaches to the development of a settlement of any scale.

Despite the absence of a generally accepted definition of SHF, it should be noted that the technology under consideration is a concept declaring various approaches to the development of a settlement of any size and the expected effects from the introduction of those technologies. This approach includes solving the following tasks:

– obtaining significant an economic effect;
– improving the quality of life of the population through effective management the life cycle of the settlement;
– ensuring the safety of living, life, work processes.

All these tasks should be solved by open interaction of all stakeholders (the population, government and authorities, business structures, etc.) and the use of high-tech IT infrastructure, which includes specialized equipment for retrieving and transmitting data using high-speed communication channels, as well as software and hardware systems for processing circulating information. At the same time, in the modern world there is no sufficient awareness of the principles of creating an SHF and, as a result, a unified approach for constructing both the architecture itself and the issue of organizing data transmission networks, control signals, etc. (hereinafter referred to as - information transmission networks (ITN) [2].

Within the framework of this article, it is proposed to dwell on the problems of choosing a ITN for the formation of the most effective variant of the IT infrastructure of the SHF, while paying special attention to the analysis of the architecture of building networks of the 5G standard (in the future - 6G standard) and the landscape of security threats directly related to it.

Hereby we propose the variant of an IT infrastructure for SHF technology, while paying special attention to the analysis of the architecture of building 5G networks (in the future - 6G) and the directly related landscape of security threats.

2   A Modern Approach to Organizing of Information Transmission Networks for the Concept of "Smart Habitat"

It should be noted that in practice quite often there are cases when already implemented solutions did not bring the expected effect in terms of changing the quality of life of the population. In a number of situations, the introduction of new technologies has complicated the management processes and even created an additional burden in terms of maintaining and operating the IT infrastructure itself. An example is the already well-known and widely discussed Korean city of Songdo, where the support of "smart" infrastructure has become a barrier to the development of the city. This is due to the complexity of the environmental processes, when, as a result, the introduction of individual technical solutions may affect other areas of life, and the effects of fragmented informatization are quite difficult to predict. Thus, first of all, it is necessary to identify the main shortcomings of the implemented solutions, which must be taken into account during the selection and further evaluation of the effectiveness of the proposed solutions.

In addition, if within the city there is a fairly developed switching infrastructure, then in settlements outside the city it is practically absent. Thus, there is a need for faster and broadband communication channels with wireless properties, because when introducing the SHF technology, it is not always and not everywhere possible to organize a wire cable economy.

In order to resolve this issue, 5G and 6G wireless networks are expected to provide global coverage of the surface of the entire Earth, so that users and connected IoT can access the Internet anywhere and at any time. In this case, wireless terrestrial networks must be combined with air and water (not located

on the surface of the Earth) access nodes (satellites, drones, high-altitude platforms (HAP), surface signal broadcast stations, etc.). The seamless 3-D (land,
sea and sky) coverage constructed in this way will form a global integrated communication network (Fig. 2). Thus, all terrestrial and non-terrestrial networks
will be comprehensively integrated at the system level, providing convergence
of services, wireless interfaces, various types of networks and connected user
devices.

It should be noted that such a network construction will allow users and
connected IoT to be in a single information space, regardless of their mode of
movement or location. In addition, the failure of a network fragment will not have
a significant impact on the performance of the entire SHF IT infrastructure as
a whole.

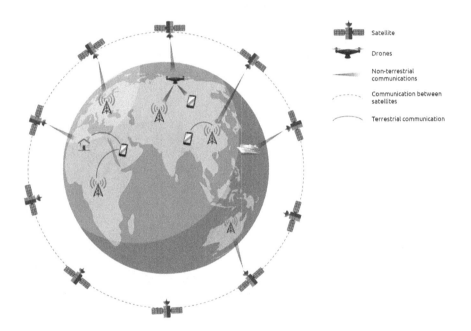

Fig. 2. Converged multilayer heterogeneous network

The presented network construction will allow not only a broadband wireless
connection anywhere and on the move, but also to organize the connection of
the following vital SHF processes:

1. Communications and disaster relief. This option is essential in response scenarios as it provides not only disaster forecasting, but also warning and emergency response and emergency communications. In some cases, duplication of
   terrestrial networks through the operation of non-terrestrial networks will provide continuity of service and support for emergency management, including

transmission of voice, data and using a video system for operational communication with the command post;

2. High-precision positioning and navigation, which will provide high-quality V2X services for vehicles, both in the urban environment, and accurate positioning and navigation services for vehicles in remote and hard-to-reach areas;

3. Monitoring of the earth's surface in real time. In this case, optical filming using visible light and partial infrared cameras, as well as radio frequency scanning, will avoid the limitations of transmitting and receiving communication channels;

In accordance with the "Smart Habitat" concept [1], one of the main tasks for creating a complex socio-technical system is to build an IT infrastructure with distributed communication support (DICS). This DICS should include a complex of information systems, consisting of local automation equipment using artificial intelligence technology (sensors, sensors, video cameras, thermal imagers, etc., the so-called "Internet of things" or "IoT") and metacognitive control technologies complex socio-cyber-physical systems based on a neural network, as well as high-performance wireless data networks, etc. (Fig. 3).

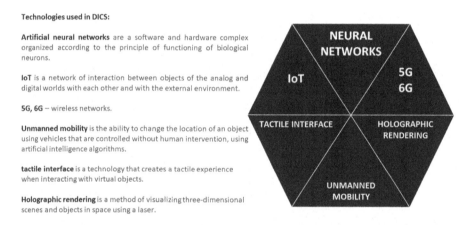

Technologies used in DICS:

Artificial neural networks are a software and hardware complex organized according to the principle of functioning of biological neurons.

IoT is a network of interaction between objects of the analog and digital worlds with each other and with the external environment.

5G, 6G — wireless networks.

Unmanned mobility is the ability to change the location of an object using vehicles that are controlled without human intervention, using artificial intelligence algorithms.

tactile interface is a technology that creates a tactile experience when interacting with virtual objects.

Holographic rendering is a method of visualizing three-dimensional scenes and objects in space using a laser.

Fig. 3. The use of modern technologies in the construction of DICS

IoT is a set of different devices and sensors united by wired and wireless communication channels and largely connected to the Internet to better integrate the real and virtual worlds, when, in fact, communication is carried out between people and devices. It is assumed that with the development of IoT technology, "things" will become active participants in business, information, and social processes, where they will be able to interact and communicate with each other, exchanging information about the environment, reacting and influencing processes occurring in the world around them, without human intervention. Thus, it can be assumed that this IoT construction is a self-organizing network of many sensors and actuators, interconnected via a radio channel. Moreover, the coverage area of such a distributed wireless sensor network can range from several meters to several kilometers due to the ability to relay messages from one element to another. The interaction under consideration is impossible without the active and comprehensive use of ITN, which ultimately leads to considering IoT as a "network of networks", where compact, loosely connected networks form larger, and then global networks (Fig. 4). At the same time, it should be noted not only the variety of primary data collection devices (gas, water, heat, electricity meters, security and fire sensors, etc.), but also the need for centralized transmission to the server through base stations and processing of incoming information. In the future, the information received is displayed in your personal account on a computer or smartphone, but it should be possible at any time to receive data from devices or send control commands to them (such as turning off the device, switching the operating mode, time synchronization, etc.) via a wireless network [3].

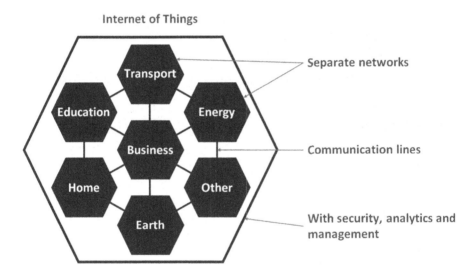

Fig. 4. IoT networks

The main advantages and disadvantages of building of an ITN based on Bluetooth, ZigBee, Z-Wave, NFC, RFID, Wi-Fi, LTE were widely illuminated in various sources [4–8]. As for the networks of remote range, i.e. cellular, then the introduction of networks of the fifth (5G), and then the promising sixth generation (6G), in contrast to the LTE network (Fig. 5), will significantly expand the ITN, taking into account three main scenarios for its use, namely:

1. Enhanced mobile broadband-eMBB: up to 25 Gbps peak data rate. Application: 4K, 8K, 3D live streaming, AR (Augmented Reality)/VR (Virtual Reality) services, cloud gaming and other high-traffic services.

2. Ultra-Reliable and Low-Latency Communication-URLLC: Reducing data transfer delays up to 1 ms and always having a connection. Application: unmanned vehicles (Vehical to Everything, V2X), remote technologies (automation of production lines, robotic surgery).
3. Mass machine-to-machine communication (enhanced Mobile BroadBand-MBB): support up to 1 million connections to the base station per 1 square kilometer with data transfer rates up to tens of gigabits per second. Application: development of consumer and industrial IoT (power supply, manufacturing, smart city, Smart living environment, etc.).

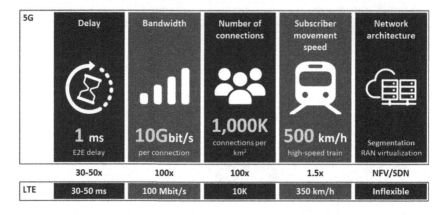

Fig. 5. Main differences between LTE and 5G networks

The 5G communication network is based on the new 5G NR (New Radio) standard and consists of the following main components:

- subscriber equipment with USIM cards;
- radio access networks (RAN), including backhaul and fronthaul networks;
- network core (5GC).

The promising 6G network is based on a similar structural one, but at the same time there are several significant differences.

3   Security Issues and Possible Risks of 5G and 6G Networks

Despite the positioning of the fifth and sixth generation ITNs as secure, the analysis below shows several security problems. [9]:

1. Significantly increased attack surface. This circumstance is primarily due to the ever-increasing number of IoT, which in turn leads to a proportional

increase in entry points for organizing targeted attacks. In addition, according to the concept of converged architecture, WiFi radio access networks, 4G-LTE, etc. must also connect to a single core 5G or 6G network, making connected devices less resistant to outside hacking. This will allow more IoT devices to be harvested and used for DDoS attacks by hackers, causing an increase in the frequency of such attacks. As a result, many connections and high bandwidth increase the attack surface, while the number of IoT devices that are less resistant to hacking is growing.

2. he architecture of the core network (network core or 5G Core) is based on cloud technologies and virtualization of network functions - software-defined network, Network Functions Virtualization (NFV), allowing you to create many independent segments and thus support services with a different set of characteristics. In addition, sharding will allow operators to provide network infrastructure as separate services. At the same time, the network infrastructures used will depend on 5G, and then on 6G, much more than on their predecessors, and a security breach in any area can become critical, and the consequences can be catastrophic. Thus, the risks should include the fact that such a construction of a network infrastructure leads to more serious consequences in case of failures and cyber-attacks, considering the scale of use.

3. Ample opportunities are opening for more aggressive conduct of various types of so-called "espionage". As you know, any IoT device with the ability to capture video or audio information (the presence of cameras and microphones) can be used by cybercriminals or software and hardware manufacturers to view and listen to uninformed users. In this case, the risks are obvious.

4. An analysis conducted by an international team of security researchers from Purdue University and Iowa State University (USA) found almost a dozen vulnerabilities in the fifth generation (5G) mobile communication standard [12]. The exploitation of the vulnerabilities allowed for several attacks, such as location tracking, the transmission of false alarms, and the complete disconnection of the phone's 5G connection from the network. A group of researchers was able to track and fix the location of the device in real time. Moreover, experts were able to intercept the phone's paging channel to broadcast fake emergency alerts, which, according to the research team, could cause "artificial chaos." It should also be taken into account that a new kind of security threat can exploit vulnerabilities in all AKE protocols, including 5G protocols, and invade the privacy of mobile device users, causing more serious damage than before. These "spyware" attacks use fake base station attacks that attackers have used to target vulnerable AKE protocols and security leaks in 3G and 4G networks, as well as an encryption vulnerability for SQNs (sequence numbers). Although the AKE protocols used in 5G and 6G networks have improved protection against base station spoof attacks, researchers have shown that relay attacks can break the SQN security of cellular networks, making it useless. These attacks are much more dangerous than the previous attacks. have an important feature: previously a user could avoid an intrusion by leaving the attack zone, but now hackers can continue

to monitor the user's activity even if he left the range of a fake base station using a new fake attack. In this case, the risks include attacks such as "monitoring the activity of subscribers", which, in addition to physical tracking of the subscriber or certain devices, create prerequisites for the security of encryption protocols.

5. 5G networks, and then 6G, involve the active use of edge computing technology (MEC - Mobile Edge Computing or Mobile Edge Computing). These can be corporate applications running on the network of operators: intelligent services, financial services, multimedia. It should be added that in this case, the operator's 5G and 6G networks are being integrated into the corporate infrastructure. At the same time, one of the advantages of 5G and 6G networks is a significantly low latency, which can be "successfully" used in the same DDoS attacks, because hackers will be able to strike faster - in seconds, not minutes. To confirm the theory, the researchers created a malicious base radio and, using the 5G Reasoner tool, successfully carried out several attacks on a smartphone connected to 5G. In one of the scenarios, a DoS attack on a phone resulted in a complete disconnection of the connection from the cellular network [10]. Thus, the risks include new opportunities to penetrate corporate networks, the placement of MEC equipment outside the protected perimeter of the organization, as well as the fact that the speed of a malicious attack becomes significantly higher.

6. The centralized network management infrastructure (O&M - Operations & Maintenance or Operation and Maintenance) used in 5G and then 6G networks is complicated by the need to simultaneously support a large number of service segments. In this case, risks can be attributed to the more serious consequences of misuse of resources and O&M configuration errors.

4   Measures for Protecting 5G and 6G Networks

Based on the analysis of possible security problems of 5G and 6G networks, it is proposed to define several levels of protection.

The first level is protection at the level of implementation of technical solutions, building the network infrastructure and equipment distribution options:

1. The use of a powerful firewall between users and the outside world, multi-level isolation and protection of the integrity of the SDN and VNF components - the hypervisor, virtual machines, OS, controllers and containers;
2. Authentication of MEC applications, use of an additional authentication factor when accessing the corporate network, whitelisting of devices and services, authorization of API requests;
3. Ensuring high availability of virtual machines for fast recovery after attacks;
4. Trusted hardware environment - secure boot devices, application of technology TEE (Trusted Execution Environment);
5. Real-time attack detection on network nodes and virtual infrastructure elements using artificial intelligence algorithms.

The second level is protection at the level of network infrastructure management:

1. Secure management of not only user data, but service, technical, analytical and other types of information involved in ensuring the solution of SHF tasks (the so-called attack on the subscriber and attack on the mobile operator), using encryption, anonymization, depersonalization and etc.;
2. Centralized management of identified vulnerabilities, as well as policies and levels of information security, the use of information during the ongoing analysis of big data to detect anomalies and quickly respond to attacks;
3. Comprehensive use of counterfeit base station detection tools based on real-time monitoring of operation and maintenance events;
4. Application of multi-factor authentication algorithms and organization of access control to segments by O&M.

The third level is protection at the level of the standard:

1. SSeparation of the layers of the protocol for receiving and transmitting data into three planes: User Plane, Control Plane, Management Plane. with complete isolation, encryption and integrity control of these planes;
2. use of encryption methods for subscriber and technological traffic with an increase in the length of the encryption key from 128 bits to 256 bits;
3. The use of a single mechanism for subscriber authentication for various types of wireless communications;
4. Support for flexible security policies for segments;
5. Use of unified standards.

At the same time, it should be noted that in addition to ensuring information security at all levels, a comprehensive approach is needed to protect networks of 5G and 6G standards, which includes an administrative and technical approach from ongoing network audit to continuous improvement of security systems. The rapidly developing technologies of new generation networks will significantly improve the interaction of consumers of ITN services through communication. And here the security issues of all types of network traffic used are most acute, which, having great potential, opens wide opportunities for cyber-attacks, invasion of privacy, serious disruption of not only IoT, but the entire SHF as a whole.

By organically combining these two access environments into one converged multi-layer heterogeneous network spanning the entire globe, 6G will provide users with a consistent experience. Providing global delivery of mobile services will be an important aspect of 6G network development.

The integrated 6G network will expand the range of services provided. For example, by integrating terrestrial and non-terrestrial networks, 6G will provide broadband and IoT services in regions and areas where there is no terrestrial network coverage, including remote farms, and even aboard ships and aircraft. In addition, 6G will help emergence of new applications such as high-precision positioning the development of objects by combined means of satellite and earth systems and high-precision survey of the earth's surface in real time for agriculture.

From a strategic point of view, this transformation is aimed at ensuring sustainable economic development, effective municipal government, providing high-quality public services to the population of the SHF, etc. But at the same time, the transition to 6G requires comprehensive compliance with more stringent requirements for mobile communication systems, especially for their security. And thus, we can speak about emerging of ecosystem based on new communication technologies, that will change both quality of life and level of control of environment.

5   Conclusions

Thus, the transition to 5G and 6G networks significantly increases the opportunities for cyberattacks and invasion of privacy. The paper discusses a list of measures that should be taken to ensure the secure connection of home devices at high speeds. It is very important that only the creation of multi-layered protection can guarantee the safe and convenient use of the Internet of Things technology for use in private homes and settlements.

The research is partially funded by the Ministry of Science and Higher Education of the Russian Federation as part of World-class Research Center program: Advanced Digital Technologies (contract No. 075-15-2020-903 dated 16.11.2020).

References

1. Argunova, M.V.: The "smart city" model as a manifestation of the new technological mode. Science and School, no. 3 (2016)
2. Mityagin, S.A., Karsakov, A.S., Bukhanovskiy, A.V., Vasil'yev, V.N.: "Smart St. Petersburg": an integrated approach to the implementation of information technologies for managing a metropolis. Control Engineering Russia 1(79) (2019)
3. Virkunin, A.O., Derevyashkin, V.M., Maksimov, A.S., Rozhentsev, V.L.: Analysis of radio access technologies for the implementation of the "smart home" system. Siberian State University of Telecommunications and Informatics (2018)
4. Wireless networks ZigBee and Thread. http://www.wless.ru/technology/?tech=1. Accessed 06 Nov 2021
5. Tkachenko, V.: WiFi technology. sib.com.ua/arhiv_2014/2014_3/statia_1_4/wifi.pdf. Accessed 06 Nov 2021
6. Bluetooth UR: https://ru.wikipedia.org/wiki/Bluetooth. Accessed 05 Nov 2021
7. LoWPAN: https://ru.wikipedia.org/wiki/6LoWPAN. Accessed 05 Nov 2021
8. Oltorak, S.: Overview of the Z-Wave protocol. https://rus.zwave.me/z-wave-knowledge-base/about-z-wave/z-wave-technical-overview. Accessed 06 Nov 2021
9. www.nttdocomo.co.jp/english/binary/pdf/corporate/technology/whitepaper_6g/DOCOMO_6G_White_PaperEN_20200124.pdf. Accessed 06 Nov 2021
10. www.securitylab.ru/news/502542.php. Accessed 06 Nov 2021

L3NS: Large Scale Network Simulation for Testing Distributed Applications

Daniil Malevanniy, Oleg Iakushkin, and Vladimir Korkhov$^{(\boxtimes)}$

Saint-Petersburg State University, 7/9 Universitetskaya nab.,
St. Petersburg 199034, Russia
st048818@student.spbu.ru, {o.yakushkin,v.korkhov}@spbu.ru

Abstract. Complex distributed applications are highly depended on the quality of service of the underlying networks connecting their components. Common approaches for testing these applications may not be sufficient to ensure stability of a distributed system during networking issues. In this paper we try to explore the possibility of using lightweight virtualization for distributed application testing. Our approach is to use a set of tools provided by the Docker containerization platform to build a virtual network model of arbitrary topology with the tested application running inside. We explore scalability of this approach both when using one or more computers for modelling and try to show how the use of the developed simulation system named L3NS can allow developers to test and benchmark large-scale distributed systems e.g. blockchain networks.

Keywords: Network simulator · Containerization · Distributed applications

1 Introduction

As the rate of microprocessor performance growth slows, distributed computing technologies are growing in popularity. Distributed computation is in essence multiple computers working together to produce a single result. In most cases network connections between the computers are used to coordinate the work.

It's obvious that the development of distributed applications requires testing. Since they are highly dependent on the underlying network, its behavior must be taken into account during testing. Otherwise, successful testing can only ensure that the application will work correctly only under ideal conditions and it won't allow any assessment of the impact of network issues on the application.

The primary objective of this paper is to demonstrate the use of a virtualization for modeling dynamic network behavior and analyzing its impact on the operation of distributed applications. To ensure the operation of the virtual network, the built-in mechanisms of the OS Linux and the Docker containerization platform are used. We also evaluate the scaling potential of this solution and explore the possibility of using distributed computing to test distributed applications.

© The Author(s), under exclusive license to Springer Nature Switzerland AG 2022
O. Gervasi et al. (Eds.): ICCSA 2022 Workshops, LNCS 13380, pp. 639–649, 2022.
https://doi.org/10.1007/978-3-031-10542-5_44

The first part of the paper describes technologies used, general architecture and principles of the developed library. The second part describes possible scenarios for using the developed library for testing distributed applications and demonstrates its use on the example of DHT Kademlia and Ethereum blockchain using one or more machines. The third part analyzes performance of the proposed solution.

2 Related Work

There are a lot of methods for emulating the impact of network behavior on the applications using it.

Discrete event-based simulators such as NS-3 [1] and Omnet++ [2] run their own network model with an arbitrary topology and provide the user with a complete set of data about all network events occurring in the model. They are intended primarily for in-depth analysis of network resource usage and network behavior. Adapting an application for testing using discrete event modeling can be extremely labor-intensive, and the computational resources required for the model to work are unacceptable for testing large-scale applications.

There are also a number of network simulators based on the use of virtualization to simulate the operation of a computer network. Some of them, such as Eve-NG [3] and GNS-3 [4], are designed primarily for emulation and debugging of network devices and topologies and aren't suitable for application testing.

Others are aimed more to simulate the overall behavior of the network and allow application testing. Examples of such simulators include CORE [5], Mininet [6], and Kathara [7]. All of them emulate the operation of the network at the link level, provide the user with a high-level API for describing the topology for the emulated network, and allow you to run arbitrary applications in it. The main difference is the toolset used to emulate network nodes: CORE uses the Linux network namespace mechanism, Mininet uses virtual machines, and Kathara uses Docker containers. Besides that, both Mininet and CORE implement distributed simulation using multiple machines using GRE protocol.

3 Methodology

3.1 Technology Stack Description

Methods used to simulate individual computers in the network and the network interactions between them are two key aspects of the implementation of the computer network model.

We decided to use containerization technology for modeling network nodes, since it is often used as a lightweight analogue of full virtualization of computing devices. It allows you to create an independent isolated environment for individual processes using the Linux kernel toolkit, which will represent separate nodes of the network.

We used Docker [8] as a containerization platform. It provides a high-level interface for managing containers, a library of images for creating predefined environments, and a set of tools for managing containers' network environment, allowing creation of network interfaces inside that can be connected via virtual bridge link, forming virtual networks. Thus, Docker is used to manage the emulation of both network nodes and their network interactions, with the actual emulation being done via Linux OS toolset.

Another important aspect of a computer network model is the level of detail of network interactions emulation. In terms of the OSI and TCP/IP models, we can choose between emulating network events at different levels.

The purpose of the developed solution is application testing. Most applications use the application layer protocols of the TCP/IP model, utilizing transport layer resources, such as TCP and UDP ports. Because of this, we decided to model the network topology only at the transport level. This will simplify virtual networks and reduce the computational overhead. The transport layer of the TCP/IP model corresponds to the third layer of the OSI model [19], which is often denoted as L3. The focus on modeling this layer is reflected in the name of the library: "Layer 3 Network Simulator", or "L3NS" for short.

To use the resources of several machines for modeling, the Docker Swarm tool was used, which comes with Docker and allows you to centrally manage containers on different machines and create virtual networks from containers running on different machines of the cluster.

These networks are based on the use of the VXLAN protocol to transfer packets between cluster nodes and an internal routing information store that allows Docker to set up ARP tables when new containers are connected to the network. Although Docker Swarm is centrally managed, virtual networks do not use the resources of a central host after initial setup, making it easy to scale the system.

To use several machines for emulation, the Docker Swarm toolset was used. It allows one to connect several computers into a cluster with a central node, and later use the central node to manage containers on different machines and create virtual networks from containers running on different machines of the cluster.

These virtual networks use the VXLAN protocol to transfer packets between cluster nodes directly, while an internal routing information is stored on the central node and used only to set up ARP tables when new containers are connected to the network. Thus, although Docker Swarm is centrally managed, virtual networks do not use the resources of a central host after initial setup, making it easy to scale the system.

It's easy to see that when the virtual subnet combines containers running on different cluster nodes, the message delay in it will be increased relative to the subnets located within the same node. In order to limit the impact of delays on the tested application, it is necessary to minimize the number of such networks. Since a computer network structure can be viewed as a hypergraph, we can use the results of hypergraph theory. This problem is known as the problem of constructing a balanced k-way cut of a hypergraph. It is shown that this problem is NP-complete [18]. To build a heuristic solution to this problem we use the KaHyPar algorithm [16].

To manage the quality of the virtual network, L3NS uses the tcconfig [10] utility, implemented in Python. The principle of its operation is based on the use of the tc (traffic control) [11] Linux system utility to create traffic control rules that allow you to limit bandwidth, add delay, add noise, duplicate, drop or change the order of IP packets processed by the network interface.

3.2   Implementation Details

The proposed solution for testing distributed applications is implemented as a Python library. Its main functionality is to deploy a computer network model with a distributed application running on top of it, as well as providing network state management and access to application nodes to test its functions.

The library is split into two main parts:

1. Partially abstract base classes that declare a generic interface, but only implement the functionality required to describe the structure of a virtual network, and are not tied to the choice of specific simulation technologies.
2. Classes that provide an interface implementation based on a particular virtualization technology or resources used to run the model.

At the selected transport layer of the TCP/IP model, the network topology has two main types of objects: hosts and IP subnets. These types are represented in the library by the abstract classes BaseNode and BaseSubnet, respectively. At the moment, there are two implementations for them: for running local Docker containers and networks, and for running on a Docker Swarm cluster.

In addition, there are two auxiliary base classes: Network, for managing the distribution of subnets IP addresses, which also acts as a single point of control for the operation of the model, and BaseOverlay, for the configuration of dynamic routing protocols, with implementations for RIP and OSPF provided based on the FRRouting [9] utility. The Network class does not have abstract methods and can be used directly. There is also an alternative implementation for it that uses the KaHyPar algorithm to optimize the distribution of computer network nodes among the nodes of the cluster used for modeling.

L3NS is implemented as a library in Python, so we can take advantage of the tools provided by the language ecosystem for distribution, such as the PIP package manager and the PyPI [14] package index. L3NS is published on github [12] or as a PIP package, available to be installed using one command on most Linux distributions:

```
pip3 install l3ns
```

4   Results

4.1   Evaluation Criteria

The main use case for the proposed solution is to model the operation of distributed applications in large virtual networks. Based on this, the most important characteristics for evaluation are the efficiency of computing resources usage and the possibility of horizontal scaling when using a cluster for simulation.

To evaluate these characteristics, we will use the following metrics collected for local and distributed simulation cases for a different number of nodes in the model:

- Host CPU load
- Host RAM usage
- Container CPU load
- Container RAP usage
- Cluster leader CPU load
- Cluster leader RAM usage

For testing we used easily reproducible virtual machines running on Amazon EC2. We used one template for all of them - r5.large, which provides a dual-core processor built on the x86_64 architecture and 16 GB of RAM. We used Ubuntu 20.04 and Docker 20.10.6 across all machines.

The distributed simulation cluster consists of three machines, two of which are used for simulation, and the third one is used to coordinate the work.

DHT Kademlia [13] was used as a distributed application for testing. It does not require intensive calculations to work, but at the same time it is extremely easy to scale. Thanks to this, it is possible to launch large-scale models necessary to evaluate the capabilities of the built testing system.

4.2   Local Testing

To test the capabilities of the L3NS library on a single machine, the simplest network structure is used with all nodes in a single subnet. The selected metrics were collected for networks of different sizes consequently.

The results are presented in Fig. 1 and Fig. 2.

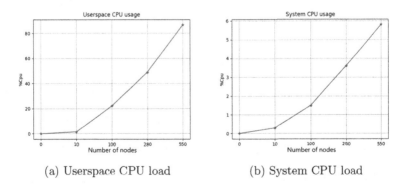

(a) Userspace CPU load   (b) System CPU load

Fig. 1. CPU load during local testing.

Some preliminary findings can be drawn from those results:

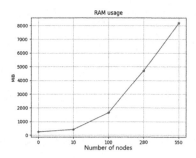 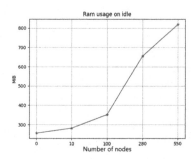

(a) RAM usage while virtual network is running.

(b) RAM usage after virtual network stopped.

Fig. 2. RAM usage during local testing.

- The occupied RAM size after the simulation is shutdown grows along with the number of nodes in the model. This may indicate a possible memory leak during start or stop of containers. After restarting the Docker server, occupied RAM size returned to the initial values, indicating a possible memory leak in the Docker itself.
- The CPU load and occupied RAM size grows linearly with respect to the number of nodes. This allows us to estimate the maximum possible size of the model for local testing with a sufficiently high accuracy based on the statistics of the small-scale model.

To get a rough estimate of the computing resources consumed by network simulation, the same metrics were collected for an identical virtual network, without an application deployed inside.

The results obtained are presented in Fig. 3.

It's easy to see that even though the CPU is practically not used to maintain the network simulation, RAM usage remains high when no application is running in the model. These results are consistent with existing Docker performance analysis [17].

4.3   Cluster Testing

For testing on a cluster, a slightly more complex network topology was used, visualized in Fig. 4. To reduce the amount of traffic between two cluster nodes, the virtual network was divided into two subnets, with each one located completely on one cluster node, and two routers connecting those subnets. The routers are connected by a distributed subnet and operate using the OSPF protocol.

As before, the same metrics were gathered for models of different sizes: 100, 400 and 700 nodes. The results are presented in Fig. 5.

Following conclusions can be drawn from these results:

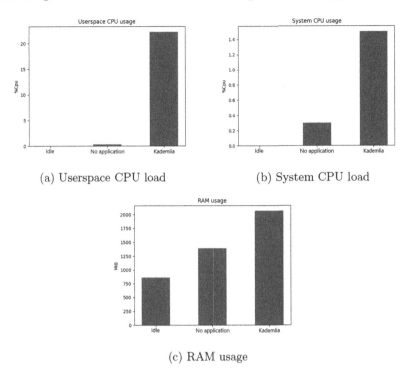

(a) Userspace CPU load   (b) System CPU load

(c) RAM usage

Fig. 3. Comparison of resource usage on idle, while emulating just network and network with DHT Kademlia running inside

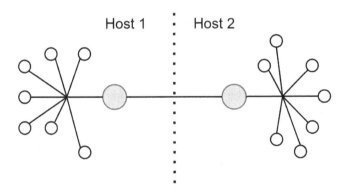

Fig. 4. Virtual network topology used in testing on cluster.

- The load on the cluster coordination node is significantly lower than the load on the modeling nodes and does not depend on the size of the model. This is due to the fact that the cluster nodes exchange traffic directly via the VXLAN protocol, and the coordination node is used only to manage the model.

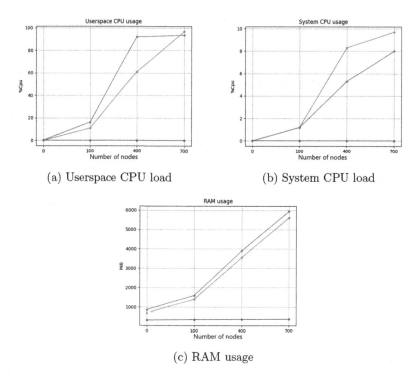

(a) Userspace CPU load   (b) System CPU load

(c) RAM usage

Fig. 5. CPU and RAM usage during testing on cluster

– The CPU load of simulation nodes is higher than during local simulation even with the same number of nodes.

Despite the increased CPU load, distributed simulation allows you to run models of larger sizes than the local one.

It is worth noting that the main obstacle to further increasing the number of nodes in the model is the need to synchronously send requests to the Docker server, which takes a significant amount of time. During testing, attempting to send parallel requests permanently corrupted the state of the Docker daemon and required a restart of the Docker daemon.

4.4 Interactive Testing

To demonstrate how L3NS can be used to interactively test or demonstrate the work of distributed applications, the Ethereum [20] blockchain was chosen. When developing smart contracts or client applications for Ethereum, access to a private blockchain may simplify development and testing workflows [21].

Developers can use L3NS to deploy a private blockchain with blockchain nodes on a single computer for testing or demonstration. Since L3NS network nodes are represented by Docker containers, they work for a long time without excessive consumption of computing power. Besides that, any container environment can be easily accessed at any time by developers.

In this example we used a network with two nodes connected by a single subnet. We used a Python script [22] to manage the virtual network, starting or stopping it depending on provided parameters.

We're using Docker built-in features to adapt virtual network model for running a blockchain: the `cpu_qouta` was used to limit the computing power available to processes running in a container. A value of 25000 corresponds to 25% of the processing power of one CPU core. Another parameter, `port`, creates a traffic forwarding rule from the host port to the container port, allowing developers external access to blockchain nodes interfaces.

Both of these options make it easier to work with the Ethereum blockchain: limiting access to the processor allows you to control the computing resources spent on mining new blocks, and external access to the container TCP port can be used to access the HTTP interface of the blockchain node to upload smart contracts to a private network or access to wallets from an external client.

4.5 Analysis

In the course of testing the functionality of the library, both its strengths and weaknesses were found. First of all, it is worth mentioning the unexpectedly high use of RAM during the operation of models and the possible memory leak that occurs at the time of starting or stopping the model.

The main positive result of testing is the demonstrated ability to scale models when running both on a cluster and on a single machine. The linear dependence of the used computing resources on the number of nodes in the model makes it possible to predict with acceptable accuracy the maximum number of nodes that can be run on one computer. In addition, it was shown that the resources of the coordinating node of the cluster are not used during the operation of the model, since all traffic exchange is decentralized. The combination of these two properties of the developed library will allow its users to calculate the cluster size required to simulate a distributed application of a given size. The main obstacle to modeling large networks is the low speed of launching models, due to the need to synchronously send to the Docker server. This problem has several possible solutions:

- Additional configuration of the Docker server for multi-threaded communication.
- Replacing containers with manual work with network namespaces.

Both solutions require a large amount of work on the library, which makes it worthwhile to conduct additional analysis of the problem to select a solution.

5   Conclusions

It's hard to overestimate the importance of testing for development or support of any application. Modern testing approaches [15] allow developers to ensure correct behavior even in cases when application workflow involves interaction between a large number of independent components. For distributed applications, however, there is an additional layer of complexity for testing, since the interaction between its components can become unpredictable depending on the quality of service of the underlying network. We investigated the possible use of lightweight virtualization techniques for testing distributed applications in varying network conditions.

Implemented testing framework allows developers to deploy distributed applications in the virtual network of arbitrary topology and quality of service. It can be later used to benchmark the stability of the application in case of networking difficulties or for general testing and demonstrations.

Two main priorities for the framework were high scalability of virtual networks and general ease of use. While it's hard to measure the usability of the library, we discussed different aspects that make it easier for developers to use, like automation of dynamic routing configuration or distribution of network nodes across cluster nodes in case of distributed modeling.

Since L3NS mostly manages Docker and system objects, like containers and virtual bridges and doesn't participate in the work of virtual network, it can play the role of an interactive environment manager, as it was demonstrated in the last example. Using L3NS in this way can simplify the process of developing and manually testing distributed applications.

In this paper we were mostly focused on analyzing the scalability of our approach. Results show that both in case of local and distributed modeling the size of the virtual network can be increased linearly along with the amount of the computational power available. In our preliminary testing we managed to launch virtual networks with up to 10 000 nodes in them.

Main limiting factor for scaling of networks is the amount of computational resources required for the tested application. If it can be roughly approximated, it's possible to predict required resources, acquire them with any cloud service provider and launch a virtual network of an arbitrary size.

References

1. Riley, G.F., Henderson, T.R.: The ns-3 network simulator. In: Modeling and Tools for Network Simulation, pp. 15–34. Springer, Heidelberg (2010). https://doi.org/10.1007/978-3-642-12331-3_2
2. Varga, A.: OMNeT++. In: Modeling and Tools for Network Simulation, pp. 35–59. Springer, Heidelberg (2010). https://doi.org/10.1007/978-3-642-12331-3_3
3. EVE-NG: https://www.eve-ng.net/
4. Al-Ani, D.R., Al-Ani, A.R.: The performance of IPv4 and IPv6 in terms of routing protocols using GNS 3 simulator. Procedia Comput. Sci. **130**, 1051–1056 (2018)
5. Ahrenholz, J.: Comparison of CORE network emulation platforms. In: 2010-Milcom 2010 Military Communications Conference. IEEE (2010)
6. De Oliveira, R.L.S., et al.: Using Mininet for emulation and prototyping software-defined networks. In: 2014 IEEE Colombian Conference on Communications and Computing (COLCOM). IEEE (2014)

7. Bonofiglio, G., et al.: Kathará: a container-based framework for implementing network function virtualization and software defined networks. In: NOMS 2018–2018 IEEE/IFIP Network Operations and Management Symposium. IEEE (2018)
8. Docker: Enterprise Application Container Platform. https://docker.org
9. FRRouting Project. https://frrouting.org/
10. Hombashi, T.: tcconfig: A tc command wrapper. https://tcconfig.readthedocs.io/en/latest/
11. Stanic, M.P.: Tc-traffic control. Linux QOS Control Tool (2001)
12. L3NS GitHub repository. https://github.com/rukmarr/l3ns
13. Maymounkov, P., Mazières, D.: Kademlia: a peer-to-peer information system based on the XOR metric. In: Druschel, P., Kaashoek, F., Rowstron, A. (eds.) IPTPS 2002. LNCS, vol. 2429, pp. 53–65. Springer, Heidelberg (2002). https://doi.org/10.1007/3-540-45748-8_5
14. L3 Network Simulator. https://pypi.org/project/l3ns/
15. Leung, H.K., White, L.: A study of integration testing and software regression at the integration level. In: Proceedings. Conference on Software Maintenance 1990, pp. 290–301. IEEE, November 1990
16. Schlag, S.: High-quality hypergraph partitioning. Doctoral dissertation, Karlsruhe Institute of Technology, Germany (2020)
17. Felter, W., et al.: An updated performance comparison of virtual machines and Linux containers. In: 2015 IEEE International Symposium on Performance Analysis of Systems and Software (ISPASS). IEEE (2015)
18. Lyaudet, L.: NP-hard and linear variants of hypergraph partitioning. Theor. Comput. Sci. **411**(1), 10–21 (2010)
19. Alani, M.M.: Guide to OSI and TCP/IP models (2014)
20. Dannen, C.: Introducing Ethereum and solidity, vol. 1, pp. 159–160. Apress, Berkeley (2017)
21. Hu, B., et al.: A comprehensive survey on smart contract construction and execution: paradigms, tools, and systems. Patterns **2**(2), 100179 (2021)
22. L3NS GitHub repository, Etherum examples. https://github.com/rukmarr/l3ns/blob/master/examples/eth/netmanager.py

Investigating Oil and Gas CSEM Application on Vector Architectures

Félix D. P. Michels[✉], Lucas Mello Schnorr, and Philippe O. A. Navaux

Institute of Informatics (INF), Federal University of Rio Grande do Sul (UFRGS), Caixa Postal 15.064 – 91.501-970, Porto Alegre, RS, Brazil
{felix.junior,schnorr,navaux}@inf.ufrgs.br

Abstract. The importance of Controlled Source Electromagnetics (CSEM) has increased in the past decade. Along with this interest, its efficiency increased, data acquisition became easier and costs went down. For the Oil and Gas industry, modeling this data is necessary for exploration. The Modeling with Adaptively Refined Elements for 2D Electromagnetics (MARE2DEM), developed at Columbia University, is one of the tools used to model CSEM data. This paper will evaluate the performance observed during the investigation and implementation of the MARE2DEM's software using the vector architecture NEC SX-Aurora. MARE2DEM is a model for 2D electromagnetic geophysics, making it possible to model the presence of natural gas and petroleum on the depths of the ocean floor. Notably, we will show how the vector machine affects MARE2DEM's performance. It will be explained how the instrumentation of MARE2DEM works and the elaboration of the experiments to perform the investigation. Furthermore, it was necessary to elucidate the modifications done to the code source. The expected result is the runtime in seconds using different parallel decomposition settings. Lastly, we show results of this novel implementation with two workloads, a synthetic input and an input provided by Petrobras (oil & gas company), for which SX-Aurora provides performance improvements up to 27%.

Keywords: MARE2DEM · SX-Aurora · Vector architecture · Geophysics · Performance

1 Introduction

Simulations are necessary and powerful tools used in various fields, from research to commercial and industrial enterprises. The investments of the petrochemical industry in controlled-source electromagnetic (CSEM) has only increased in the

This work has been partially supported by Petrobras (2016/00133-9, 2018/00263-5), CNPq under the project (406182/2021-3) and Green Cloud project (2016/2551-0000 488-9), from FAPERGS and CNPq Brazil, program PRONEX 12/2014. Experiments presented in this paper were carried out using the PCAD infrastructure, http://gppd-hpc.inf.ufrgs.br, at INF/UFRGS.

O. Gervasi et al. (Eds.): ICCSA 2022 Workshops, LNCS 13380, pp. 650–667, 2022.
https://doi.org/10.1007/978-3-031-10542-5_45

last 15 years, and the academic interest goes along with it [2,3,5]. The main reason for these investments is to reduce risk. CSEM provides more data and, therefore, more information to give new insights on the seafloor bed, consequently reducing risk. The CSEM method works as follows: A electrical-field transmitter is rested close to the seafloor but not at the bottom. Then, electromagnetic receivers are spaced at specific ranges on the seafloor, resulting in the CSEM data in these range intervals. Figure 1 represents the process mentioned above.

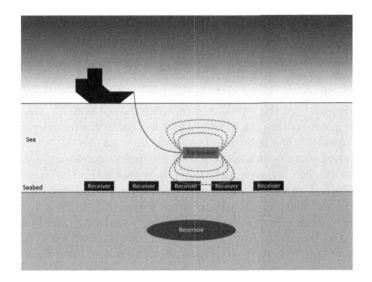

Fig. 1. Schematic view representing the CSEM method.

CSEM data acquisition produces a large quantity of data, leading to a tremendous computational problem for solving inverse modeling. Some regions with complicated geometry may require additional data, mainly to produce full 3D inversion. However, 2D inversion is much quicker and provides a more straightforward interpretation of actual data in a shorter runtime, making it a more robust, sensible, and feasible approach [21].

One necessary implementation to manage this kind of CSEM data is the application "Modeling with Adaptively Refined Elements for 2D Electromagnetics", referred to in this project as MARE2DEM [10]. MARE2DEM is an open-source code for 2D inversion of CSEM data, magnetotelluric (MT) data, and surface-borehole EM data, by parallel adaptive finite elements for onshore, offshore, and downhole environments. Due to the large quantity of data provided by CSEM, high computational power is necessary to execute such data set with efficiency. Therefore, efficient code and a powerful computer are preferred.

High-performance computing plays an essential role in various research fields, commercial sectors, and industries, especially Oil and Gas. It presents many advantages, such as facilitating evaluation to enabling new simulations and modeling [4]. Although the common strategy of increasing the density of chips is reaching its physical limits, new ways to improve performance arise [1]. One way is by Heterogeneous computing, which mainly consists in using different architectures in unison, like CPUs and GPUs. Inside this particular path, vector engines, or vector architectures, emerge once again.

Vector architectures are Single Instruction Multiple Data (SIMD), which has great potential for highly parallelizable scientific applications. Among these are numerical applications, time prediction, multimedia processing [15], collision simulation [9], data compression, and others. One prominent feature of these vector processors is the possibility of using an instruction to reproduce hundreds of operations. Moreover, all the results of the elements of a vector are independent, and therefore, checking the resulting data is not necessary. Memory access is done only once for each vector, inferring a small memory access latency.

The massive variety of architectures, while desirable and flexible, poses new challenges for the programmer [17]. Increasing the complexity of the structure will additionally extend the problem of imposing the application. Also, there are numerous frequent bottlenecks, such as these located in the memory subsystem, which encompasses cache pollution, *thrashing*, amongst others.

Vectorization can be an excellent tool for inverse modeling, especially for CSEM, in which the enormous quantity of data produces a challenging computational project. Therefore a vector architecture is a promising way to tackle this challenge and improve the performance of MARE2DEM's code, especially architectures with high memory and high memory bandwidth. NEC Corporation launched a new architecture in 2018, a vector processor known as SX-Aurora. This processor has eight processing cores at 1.6 GHz and three stages of cache memory. One of the novelties of this structure over the present ones is the dimension of its vector units, with 256 elements, eight bytes each. In addition, the NEC compiler makes choices automatically, identifying vectorizable areas and generating code for it. Nevertheless, the compiler needs the programmer's assistance to interpret the code and enhance automated vectorization, following specific guidelines. The main object of study is SX-Aurora, an excellent architecture for investigating the parallelization and vectorization of the MARE2DEM's code.

This work will investigate and analyze MARE2DEM's execution utilizing a vector architecture, the SX-Aurora, and the traditional x86 architecture. Two data sets will be used, a synthetic one and a real-world case provided by Petrobras (Brazilian Petroleum Corporation), Brazil's oil & gas corporation. Therefore, the main goals of this paper are:

- Describe the implementation of MARE2DEM on NEC's SX-Aurora. The standard Intel math library was substituted for the MARED2DEM in the SX-Aurora because NEC's architecture does not support it. All entries that required Intel's math library were rewritten, supporting NEC's mathematical libraries.
- To investigate the performance analysis of this implementation by comparing it with x86 architecture CPUs.

The article was organized as follows. Section 2 presents and discusses related works regarding the instrumentation, NEC's architecture, and MARE2DEM.

Section 3 is the methodology, workflow, and execution environment. Section 4 depicts the experimental results of three experiments. Finally, Sect. 5 presents the conclusion and possible future work.

2   Related Work

This section elucidates different scientific articles and manuals from the areas explored in this project. Thus, some studies related to the areas of performance analysis involving the SX-Aurora architecture, in which optimization techniques and vector machines or GPUs, High-Performance Computing (HPC), Score-P [13], and primarily MARE2DEM and CSEM related scientific papers and manual.

Myer, through the use of MARE2DEM, explores 2D inversion of marine CSEM and MT data [18]. The primary purpose is to make the inversion aware that the subsurface comprises similar geologic domains. The presented workflow is subjected to CSEM limitations, making fine-scale structural details hard to be resolved. However, in confounding settings, it is still possible to be used to map the rough qualities and general extent.

It is presented by Grayver a new 3-D parallel inversion scheme for CSEM data in the frequency domain based on a direct forward solver [8]. Gauss-Newton minimization provides data of model inversion, proving the approach's applicability to real-world problems, showing real-world data sets being possible to manage with only medium-sized clusters.

The application MARE2DEM [10] implements 2D forward and inversion modeling algorithms for MT and CSEM data. The inversion modeling uses CSEM information provided by a grid of electromagnetic receivers resting on the seafloor bed and its response to a transmitter below the sea's surface while being towed by a ship. This response happens in known intervals and later is converted into electrical resistivity, making it possible to study the components below the seabed.

Furthermore, MARE2DEM employs a finite element method (FEM) [11] to find the resistivity model. To accurately calculate CSEM and MT models' solutions, Kerry Key presents a parallel goal-oriented adaptive finite element method in his work. He also introduces a reliable goal-oriented error to guide the iterative mesh refinement. The overall performance is assessed utilizing clusters of 800 processors with real-world data sets, achieving execution times of only a few seconds.

Yavich and Zhdanov published their work on improving the finite element modeling through finite difference [23]. This novel implementation used a finite difference solver based on implicit factorization of the matrix. A comparison is made between their implementation and three other public available programs. One of them is MARE2DEM, and it was possible to achieve improved performance with similar accuracy.

Score-P is a unified performance-measurement infrastructure used for profiling, event tracing, and evaluating HPC applications [13]. It provides a variety of different performance evaluation tools, such as Tau [22], Periscope [7],

Scalasca [6], and Vampir [12]. Each one addresses Score-P behavior, utilizing certain factors. Score-P is a complete tool that focuses on bringing the afore-mentioned tools and being the central piece that binds them together, accom-modating all components.

Similar to this work, the publication by Komatsu et al. shows the potential of the SX-Aurora architecture. A comparison with other architectures, NVIDIA Tesla V100 and SX-Ace, among others, shows results where the SX-Aurora can run efficiently, with up to 3.5× performance, in addition to getting a higher speedup of up to 2, 8 × [14].

Yokokawa et al. demonstrate the capability of the SX-Aurora architecture for I/O applications, comparing the I/O system of the new architecture with stan-dard I/O systems. The distinct accelerated I/O function present in the architec-ture, for some instances, triples the performance in MB per second [24].

Previous work utilizes the same vector architecture, SX-Aurora [16]. Félix discusses in his work the performance analysis of the SX-Aurora architecture utilizing an artificial benchmark and a natural wave propagation application, essential to the oil and prospecting industry. Through simple optimization tech-niques, such as loop unrolling and inlining, it was possible to achieve performance improvements with the SX-Aurora up to 7, 8× with the NAS benchmark and up to 1, 9× with the actual application.

3   Methodology

The experimentation workflow follows four significant steps: preparing the envi-ronment, running the experiments, collecting data, analyzing. Figure 2 shows the steps, with additional information. The blue-green rectangles in the middle represent the significant steps. The shapes with red color are the three exper-iments performed. Moreover, the green circles show additional work related to that step.

The execution environment preparation means creating the routines for com-pilation/execution and data visualization. In this work, three experiments are presented, two of them utilizing an artificial demonstration data set and another one using a real-world data set, provided by Petrobras. The artificial demon-stration data set is relatively small compared to the real-world data set, with only 1028 and 17054 data points, respectively. It serves to test the application, providing validation to any modification implemented. Petrobras provided the second data set. The second data set is real-world data collected on the ocean floor utilizing the proper set of equipment. Since it has large amounts of data, it is perfect for testing the SX-Aurora memory bandwidth advantage.

The compiler flags for MPI Fortran (mpif90 v.7.5.0), MPI C (mpicc v.7.5.0), NEC MPI Fortran (mpincc v.2.13) and NEC MPI C (mpinfort v.2.13) utilized were -O2, -fPIC, -fpp and -cxxlib. These last two are exclusive to MPI Fortran.

Secondly, the experiments selected in the previous step are carried out in the work environment. As mentioned, there are three experiments.

Workflow

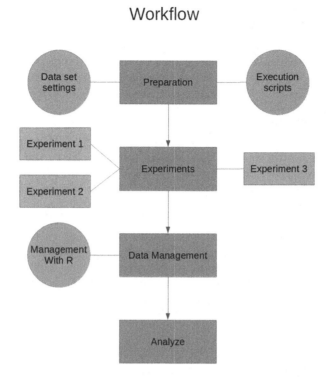

Fig. 2. Workflow of this project major steps. (Color figure online)

The first one uses the artificial demonstration data set. Several workers and data groups need to be chosen to run the application. For the x86 architecture, it was utilized 23 workers and one master corresponding to the 24 cores of the CPU and the default group distribution. NEC's architecture utilized seven workers plus one master and the same default distribution. The second experiment also utilizes the artificial demonstration data set. However, instead of 23 workers for x86 architecture and seven workers for SX-Aurora, only two will be used, which will be better explained in Sect. 4.3. Last, the third experiment uses Petrobra's data set. It utilizes 23 and 7 workers for the x86 architecture and the SX-Aurora architecture, respectively, plus the master for each. Ten executions were performed for all experiments to improve statistical rigor, achieving the mean execution time and error.

The third workflow step is data collection and management, using Score-P and R. The instrumentation of the MARE2DEM application uses Score-P. Our first step was to identify which sections of the source code implement the forward response computation, which contains the Finite Element Modeling (FEM), by the worker processes, considering a refinement group. Since we knew that the forward response parallel computation is implemented using the MPI interface, we started by searching for MPI calls inside MARE2DEM's source code, mainly implemented in FORTRAN.

Inside the source code, a subroutine is implemented, which contains the worker's logic of which task to perform, according to the message received by the manager process. Inside is the call path that leads to the forward response computation. With this in mind, it was utilized the manual region instrumentation [13] functionality of Score-P to track the timestamps of the call sequence of all workers. This sequence was grouped into a single manual Score-P region and labeled as *compute*. *Compute* is the main MARE2DEM computing phase that will be analyzed since it encapsulates the majority of the parallel MPI computation performed by the workers.

The experiments utilized the resources of the *Parque Computacional de Alto Desempenho* (PCAD) infrastructure, http://gppd-hpc.inf.ufrgs.br, at INF/UFRGS. Figure 3 shows a detailed schematic of the SX-Aurora architecture. The environment has eight-core, global memory, and cache L3, each core with memory cache L1 and L2, one unit of scalar processing (SPU), and a vector processing unit (VPU), with each VPU containing load buffer, store buffer, and 32 vector parallel pipeline (VPP) [19]. The Table 1 shows the detailed specs of the architecture, containing the specs of the processors, cache, and global memories.

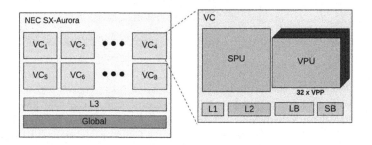

Fig. 3. Detailed scheme of each SX-Aurora core.

The Intel Cascade Lake microarchitecture represents the x86 architecture. In Table 2 you have the specifications of the Intel Xeon Gold 6226 processor, which has 12 cores operating at a frequency between 2.7 GHz and 3.7 GHz. Each core has 32 KB of the L1 cache of data and instructions and a private 1 MB L2 cache. The L3 shared across all cores has a capacity of 16.5 MB, and the machine also features 192 GB of DRAM memory [20].

Table 1. SX-Aurora Architecture.

Vector Engine	Type 10BE
Processor	8 cores @ 1408 MHz
Microarchitecture	SX-Aurora
Cache	8 × 32 KB L1I 8 × 32 KB L1D; 8 × 256 KB L2; 8 × 2 MB L3
Memory	HBM2 48 GB, 900 MHz

Table 2. Microarchitecture Cascade Lake (x86).

Processor	2 × 12 cores @ 2700–3700 MHz
Microarchitecture	Cascade Lake
Cache	12 × 32 KB L1I; 12 × 32 KB L1D; 12 × 1 MB L2; 16,5 MB L3
Memory	DDR4 192 GB, 2933 MHz

MARE2DEM implements a math library exclusive to Intel's processors. To execute MARE2DEM in the vector architecture SX-Aurora, this math library needs to be substituted by a general math library or implement NEC's math library, which works specifically to the needs of its vector engine. It was concluded that the latter is more desirable for the present work. It provides better support for parallelization and vectorization, and the nature of the library origin, being the same manufacturer of the vector engine, facilitated the porting process. Besides the math library, there were several other bugs and code rearrangements that needed to be performed.

Curiously, there were some minor discrepancies in the porting process due to different FORTRAN versions. Some syntaxes that are utilized in FORTRAN nowadays are not supported. Also, some code structures are very unreliable to work with. One of them is the bind(C) interface, which makes FORTRAN's subroutines and functions compatible with C code. This section did not work at all, luckly it was possible to rearrange the code to not need it.

One example of a substituted function is for sparse linear algebra equations. The original implementation relied heavily on intel's libraries, which were changed to use mostly NEC's functions. Using NEC's math library, it was possible to use its Sparse Basic Linear Algebra Subprograms (SBLAS) and Hetero-Solver routines. The basic structure of this function follows: matrix storage, handle initialization, solution, finalization. The following paragraphs explain these stages.

In this implementation, we utilized Compressed Sparse Row (CSR) format. It consists of representing a matrix through three vectors. So the first step consists in storing the matrix in these three arrays. Nonzero entries are stored in the first vector. The column indices of these nonzero elements are kept in the second array. The third array stores the cumulative sum of the row counts.

Secondly, we set up the handles, which are all provided by the library. We need to call for the function that creates the handles while passing all the necessary parameters, for example, the CSR arrays and column and row counts.

Next, the math library provides the solution through the sblas_execute_mv_rd function. We need to provide the input we already created in the previous steps. Lastly, we need to finalize our code by returning our solution vector and destroying the handle.

In terms of mathematical functions, six needed to be replaced or recreated. There are two functions for factoring a sparse matrix, one for complex numbers and another for real numbers. Both needed to be recreated entirely, as the workflow of both libraries is very different. The same goes for the sparse linear algebra solver, one function each for complex and real numbers. Both were recreated, as described above. Lastly, two functions to free memory for both were replaced.

4   Investigation and Results

The results section will present the main findings obtained by this work. The following result to be shown is regarding the first experiment. It uses the artificial demonstrative data set provided along with MARE2DEM's application. The following result also utilizes the same data set but different worker and refinement group configurations. The last result comes from the third experiment utilizing the real-world data set provided by Petrobras.

4.1   Outcome Validation

After the modifications were done to the math libraries exclusive to Intel, a first experiment was performed. We needed first to be sure that all the modifications had no repercussions on the final result regarding the output of MARE2DEM's execution, which is shown by Fig. 4.

Figure 4 shows the visualization of MARE2DEM final iteration. The graph on the top shows the execution of an x86 architecture. On the bottom graph, the SX-Aurora execution is shown. These graphs provide the resistivity regarding the depth of the ocean floor.

Figure 5 also shows the MARE2DEM's outcome, now related to the final iteration of the real-world data set. The top graph shows the x86 and the bottom one the SX-Aurora implementation.

We can visualize that all executions are visually identical. Therefore we can assume that the modifications implemented, the NEC's math library and all minor changes had no impact on the final result.

4.2   Initial Artificial Demonstration Runtime

After assessing the impact on the final results, we can move forward with the execution's investigation. Next, Fig. 6 shows the execution of the artificial dataset on the x86 architecture.

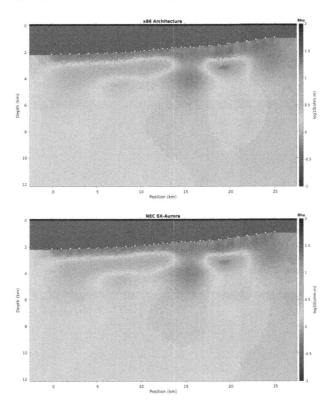

Fig. 4. Demonstration data set comparison for outcome validation between x86 and SX-Aurora.

The x86 architecture execution represented in Fig. 6 shows the runtime, in seconds, for every 23 workers. We can see that the final runtime was 206 s. The image shows the expected behavior of one iteration of MARE2DEM's execution. There is a clear division between left and right on these runtime graphs. They denote two different stages of one iteration, as the manager needs all workers to end their load to start the second stage.

Following the next result, we have Fig. 7. Here we execute the first data set, the artificial one, on NEC's SX-Aurora.

Identical to the previous graph, Fig. 7 gives the runtime for each of the seven workers. The final runtime was 237 s. So, the SX-Aurora performed slower than the x86 architecture, around 15% slower.

Both Fig. 7 and Fig. 6 show the traces collected via Score-P, which can be hard to understand at a glance. To facilitate the comparison between both runtimes, Fig. 8 is presented.

Figure 8 shows on the x-axis the experiment being run, while the y axis represents the runtime of the application in seconds. The light blue refers to the SX-Aurora architecture and the darker blue to the x86 architecture. It is easier now to see the difference in runtimes of both platforms.

Initially, it was expected for the SX-Aurora to improve the performance of MARE2DEM already. However, upon further investigation, especially if the data set was proper, it was attested that the amount of data being transferred was

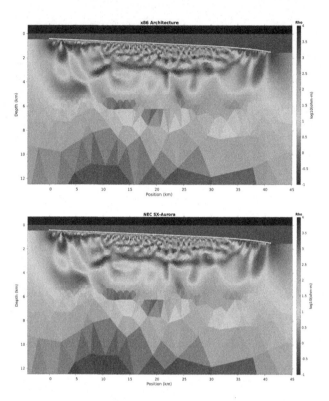

Fig. 5. Comparison for outcome validation between x86 and SX-Aurora, related to the real world data set.

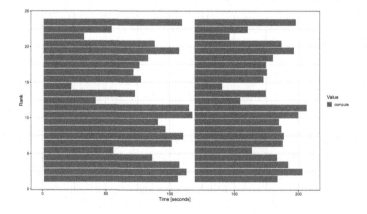

Fig. 6. Results in seconds of experiment 1 utilizing x86 architecture

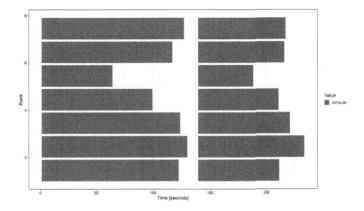

Fig. 7. Results in seconds of experiment 1 utilizing the SX-Aurora

small for each worker, which goes against the advertised advantages of this architecture. SX-Aurora has a very high memory transfer rate, and this power was not being harvested in this data set, resulting in a negative result.

4.3 Effects of One Worker on the First Data Set

After the enlightenment of the last result's investigation, a second experiment was proposed, utilizing the same dataset. A new worker and refinement group configuration was chosen in this second one, so it is possible to appropriate the advantages of the SX-Aurora architecture.

Hence, the configuration to best take advantage of SX-Aurora high memory transfer was to use only one worker, besides the manager, and one refinement group. Theoretically, it would allow for a larger-sized data set and higher data transfers during the MARE2DEM execution. Figure 9 shows these results.

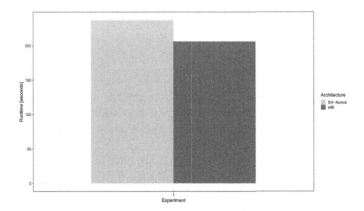

Fig. 8. Experiment 1 comparison between x86 and SX-Aurora runtimes (Color figure online)

In Fig. 9 we have a comparison of MARE2DEM's execution on the x86 and SX-Aurora architectures. The top blue line refers to the x86 execution, and the red bottom line refers to the SX-Aurora. Again, similar to the previous two graphs, on the x-axis is displayed the execution runtime. On the y axis are the two different architectures.

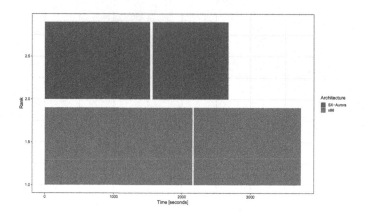

Fig. 9. Experiment 2 comparison of the runtimes between x86 and SX-Aurora. (Color figure online)

It is easier to compare both architectures' runtimes now. We can see that SX-Aurora can improve the runtime without supporting multiples cores and more significant data transfers. The x86 architecture execution runtime was of 3728 s approximately. SX-Aurora runtime reached around 2677 s. An increase in performance of approximately 39%.

This experiment shows that the SX-Aurora architecture has potential regarding performance gains. However, the experiment does not reflect any real-world use case, as both platforms are underutilized, which is evident in the total runtime of both experiments, boasting an increase in execution runtime of around 17 times more significant in the worst case.

4.4   Real World Data Set

As the last experiment was a test to investigate the potential of SX-Aurora architecture, the last experiment will put this potential to test in a real-world scenario. This data set, provided by Petrobras, is larger than the previous one, by roughly 50 times the amount of data.

Figure 10 shows a similar graph as before. We have on the x-axis the runtime in seconds. The y axis shows the workers. Particularly on this graph, we have the presence of the manager, illustrated by the first worker. This graph regards the execution of the real-world data set on the x86 architecture, achieving, for one iteration, an execution runtime of 2964 s approximately.

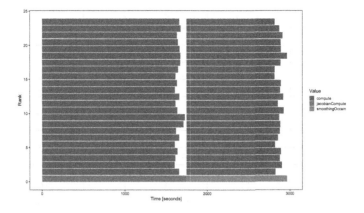

Fig. 10. Runtime for real world dataset - 1 Iteration - x86 architecture.

Next, Fig. 11 has the execution of the MARE2DEM application on the SX-Aurora architecture. As the last graph, the x-axis and y-axis are the runtime in seconds and the workers. The final runtime is around 2341 s for one iteration.

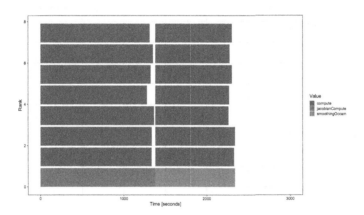

Fig. 11. Runtime for real world dataset - 1 Iteration - SX-Aurora.

To better represent the comparison between runtimes, Fig. 12 is shown. The x-axis represents the experiment, while the y axis shows the application runtime in seconds. The light blue refers to the SX-Aurora architecture and the darker blue to the x86 architecture. Here it is possible to visualize the last statistic, the SX-Aurora has an impact on performance, of around 27% increase.

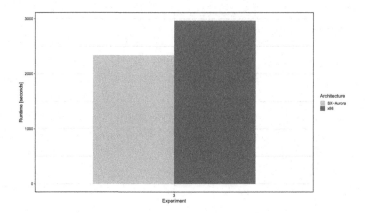

Fig. 12. Comparison of experiment 3 for x86 and SX-Aurora runtimes

Now, the last illustration, Fig. 13, elucidates and realizes some of the potentials that NEC's SX-Aurora has under the right circumstances, especially when we can take advantage of its inherent positive traits, like its vector architecture, which can perform multiple of the same calculation with only one instruction and, in this case specifically, the high memory bandwidth available.

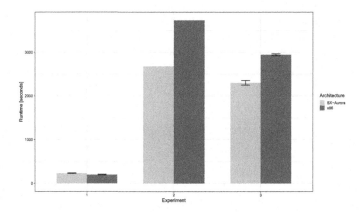

Fig. 13. Runtime comparison between x86 and SX-Aurora for all three experiments.

Figure 13 shows in the y axis the runtime of each experiment. The x-axis displays the number of all experiments that achieved the runtimes exhibited on the y axis. The light blue color gives the SX-Aurora architecture, and the darker blue represents the x86 architecture. To improve the statistical rigor, we employed ten executions to the first and last experiment to have the mean execution time and error. It is visible that the mean execution time is similar to the three experiments performed, approximately maintaining the differences in runtime between platforms.

This graph, Fig. 13 illustrates the path taken by this project. We began the runtime evaluation with worse performance for SX-Aurora. However, after analyzing and evaluating the advantages of the architecture, the two subsequent experiments utilized and realized this potential that SX-Aurora has when harvesting its potential.

5 Conclusion and Future Work

Modeling CSEM data is an arduous process. Large amounts of complex data need to be read, transferred, modified and iterated. It poses a significant challenge for developers and users. Therefore it is crucial to have the right tool for the right job. There are significant efforts in the development of vector processors to act also as performance accelerator devices. In addition to having a high SIMD processing capacity, vector accelerators stand out for allowing applications to benefit from performance gains, with little or no intervention in the application's source code, which is less frequent when accelerating with other heterogeneous architectures.

This work utilizes a SIMD architecture to try and harvest its potential on a CSEM modeling software called MARE2DEM. The chosen architecture is a vector engine titled SX-Aurora. We show that it is possible to utilize its strengths, improving general performance. However, it is necessary to consider the advantages of this kind of architecture and the specific positives the SX-Aurora has.

An extensive experimental load was carried out, which showed evidence of the strengths of vector architectures mentioned. Although there was a need to change the source code, it was mainly due to Intel-specific libraries and some FORTRAN version discrepancies. Intending to investigate the impacts that a vector engine might have, we improved performance, the runtime in seconds, of a real-world CSEM data set from around 2964 s to 2341 s, approximately 27%.

As future work, we will extend this analysis to more real-world data sets, if possible. Implementation of performance optimization techniques such as loop unrolling and inlining, similar to Félix's [16] implementation and expand it further with loop tiling and loop interchange optimizations. These techniques are advantageous in obtaining performance gains in the SX-Aurora TSUBASA vector accelerator [16]. Finally, a more in-depth study of the correlation between group refinement configurations and overall performance is desired.

References

1. Brodtkorb, A.R., Dyken, C., Hagen, T.R., Hjelmervik, J.M., Storaasli, O.O.: State-of-the-art in heterogeneous computing. Sci. Program. **18**(1), 1–33 (2010). https://doi.org/10.1155/2010/540159
2. Constable, S., Srnka, L.J.: An introduction to marine controlled-source electromagnetic methods for hydrocarbon exploration. Geophysics **72**(2), WA3–WA12 (2007). https://doi.org/10.1190/1.2432483
3. Cooper, R., MacGrego, L.: Renewed interest in CSEM in oil and gas exploration. GEOExPro **17**(5) (2020)

4. Ezell, S.J., Atkinson, R.D.: The vital importance of high-performance computing to us competitiveness. Inf. Technol. Innov. Found., 28 April 2016
5. Fanavoll, S., Gabrielsen, P.T., Ellingsrud, S.: CSEM as a tool for better exploration decisions: case studies from the Barents Sea, Norwegian Continental Shelf. Interpretation **2**(3), SH55–SH66 (2014). https://doi.org/10.1190/INT-2013-0171.1
6. Geimer, M., Wolf, F., Wylie, B.J.N., Ábrahám, E., Becker, D., Mohr, B.: The Scalasca performance toolset architecture. Concurr. Comput. Pract. Exper. **22**(6), 702–719 (2010)
7. Gerndt, M., Fürlinger, K., Kereku, E.: Periscope: advanced techniques for performance analysis. In: PARCO (2005)
8. Grayver, A.V., Streich, R., Ritter, O.: Three-dimensional parallel distributed inversion of CSEM data using a direct forward solver. Geophys. J. Int. **193**(3), 1432–1446 (2013). https://doi.org/10.1093/gji/ggt055
9. Hennessy, J.L., Patterson, D.A.: Computer Architecture. Horgan Kaufmann Publishers, Cambridge (2019)
10. Key, K.: Mare2dem: a 2-d inversion code for controlled-source electromagnetic and magnetotelluric data. Geophys. J. Int. **207**(1), 571–588 (2016)
11. Key, K., Ovall, J.: A parallel goal-oriented adaptive finite element method for 2.5-D electromagnetic modelling. Geophys. J. Int. **186**(1), 137–154 (2011). https://doi.org/10.1111/j.1365-246X.2011.05025.x
12. Knüpfer, A., et al.: The Vampir performance analysis tool-set. In: Parallel Tools Workshop (2008)
13. Knüpfer, A., et al.: Score-P: a joint performance measurement run-time infrastructure for Periscope, Scalasca, TAU, and Vampir. In: Brunst, H., Müller, M.S., Nagel, W.E., Resch, M.M. (eds.) Tools for High Performance Computing 2011, pp. 79–91. Springer, Berlin (2012). https://doi.org/10.1007/978-3-642-31476-6_7
14. Komatsu, K., et al.: Performance evaluation of a vector supercomputer SX-aurora TSUBASA. In: International Conference for High Performance Computing, Networking, Storage and Analysis, SC 2018, pp. 685–696. IEEE (2018)
15. Kshemkalyani, P.A.: Vector processors (2012). https://www.cs.uic.edu/~ajayk/c566/VectorProcessors.pdf
16. Michels, F., Serpa, M., Carastan-Santos, D., Schnorr, L., Navaux, P.: Otimização de aplicações paralelas em aceleradores vetoriais nec sx-aurora. In: Anais do XXI Simpósio em Sistemas Computacionais de Alto Desempenho, pp. 311–322. SBC, Porto Alegre, RS, Brasil (2020). https://doi.org/10.5753/wscad.2020.14079. https://sol.sbc.org.br/index.php/wscad/article/view/14079
17. Mittal, S., Vetter, J.S.: A survey of CPU-GPU heterogeneous computing techniques. ACM Comput. Surv. (CSUR) **47**(4), 1–35 (2015)
18. Myer, D., Key, K., Constable, S.: Marine CSEM of the Scarborough gas field, part 2: 2D inversion. Geophysics **80**(3), E187–E196 (2015). https://doi.org/10.1190/geo2014-0438.1
19. NEC: SX-Aurora TSUBASA A100-1 series user's guide (2020). https://www.hpc.nec/documents/guide/pdfs/A100-1_series_users_guide.pdf. Accessed Sept 2021
20. Perez, A.F., Ziv, B., Fomenko, E., Meiri, E., Shen, H.: Lower numerical precision deep learning inference and training (2018). https://software.intel.com/content/www/us/en/develop/articles/lower-numerical-precision-deep-learning-inference-and-training.html. Accessed September 2021
21. Price, A., Turpin, P., Erbetta, M., Watts, D., Cairns, G.: 1D, 2D and 3D modeling and inversion of 3D CSEM data offshore West Africa, pp. 639–643 (2008). https://doi.org/10.1190/1.3063732. https://library.seg.org/doi/abs/10.1190/1.3063732

22. Shende, S.S., Malony, A.D.: The TAU parallel performance system. Int. J. High Perform. Comput. Appl. **20**(2), 287–311 (2006). https://doi.org/10.1177/1094342006064482
23. Yavich, N., Zhdanov, M.S.: Finite-element EM modelling on hexahedral grids with an FD solver as a pre-conditioner. Geophys. J. Int. **223**(2), 840–850 (2020)
24. Yokokawa, M., et al.: I/O performance of the SX-Aurora TSUBASA. In: 2020 IEEE International Parallel and Distributed Processing Symposium Workshops (IPDPSW), pp. 27–35. IEEE (2020)

Virtual Testbed: Computational Component of Wind Waves – Ship Interaction

Alexander Degtyarev[1,3]([envelope]) [iD] and Vasily Khramushin[1,2] [iD]

[1] St. Petersburg State University, St. Petersburg, Russia
a.degtyarev@spbu.ru
[2] Krylov Scientific and Technical Society of Shipbuilders, St. Petersburg, Russia
[3] State Marine Technical University, St. Petersburg, Russia

Abstract. Marine virtual testbed is a problematic solving environment for virtual experiments conducting to study the behavior of marine objects in various conditions. These conditions may cover cases that are either very difficult or dangerous for model or natural experiments. In addition, the numerical experiment is always cheaper. To ensure the necessary accuracy at the reproduction of maritime object behavior under the action of external excitations it is necessary to have appropriate mathematical models. For effective apply of these models, numerical implementation using the advantages and features of the hardware is needed.

This article discusses the interaction of wind trochoidal waves with the maritime object in a complete formulation, taking into account the forces of Frouda-Krylov, and the diffraction component. Mathematical description of wind waves and subsurface currents is given. Modeling of vertical fluid particle oscillations is considered using finite differences. Full-fledged trocoidal waves are considered taking into account the dispersion of visible and group velocities of waves.

As a result, both the hydrostatic formulation of ship moving by arbitrary course on a stormotable waves, and complete hydrodynamic modeling, taking into account the local flow rates near the ship hull and reflection of waves are modeled in the numerical experiment.

Keywords: Virtual testbed · Hydrodynamics · Direct computational experiment · Trohoidal waves · Efficiency of ship sailing in stormy conditions

1 Introduction

The problems of the virtual testbed presented earlier in a number of articles [1–4]. Noted that the main computational task of the virtual testbed is the implementation of a complex mathematical model of an object, environment and their interaction. With a modern level of hardware development, this task is solvable at the well-known physics of the phenomenon under consideration. The second task of implementing the virtual testbed is the effective numerical implementation of mathematical models, taking into account the architecture of computing systems. The latter is possible in case of effective implementation of basic computing operations and transformation of mathematical models

© The Author(s), under exclusive license to Springer Nature Switzerland AG 2022
O. Gervasi et al. (Eds.): ICCSA 2022 Workshops, LNCS 13380, pp. 668–679, 2022.
https://doi.org/10.1007/978-3-031-10542-5_46

for these purposes. This level of operations can be attributed, for example, multiplication of the matrix to the vector, the transition from one coordinate system to another, interpolation, etc. In earlier works, we paid special attention to this topic [5–7].

In this paper, it presents and discusses tools for construction of direct computing experiments for visually demonstrative computer experiments of ship stormy seaworthiness within the marine virtual testbed. In the development of mathematical models and algorithmic solutions, special attention is paid to the efficiency of computing operations.

At the basis of stormy sea computing models, theoretical results and mathematical solutions for trochoidal big waves were used [8]. In these solutions, the parametric determination of the kinematics of the fluid particles is comparable to a corpuscular approach to the waveforming model. The conditionally free movement of cyclic displaceable cells of calculated mesh is dynamically reinterpolated to the coordinates associated with the vehicle body. This is required for the unambiguous permission of the problem of the ship's hydromechanics in stormy conditions.

The computational experiment was originally designed in the concepts of separation of solutions on physical processes [9–12]. This simultaneously allows you to use an interactive selection of both the actual models of sea waves and the nature of the power interaction of ship hull with intensive excitation.

1.1 Basic Notations

r_w [m] – local radius on the path of wave movements of fluid particles;

$\tau = 2\pi/\omega$ [s] – wave period, $\lambda = 2\pi/k$ [m] – wave length;

$C_w = \lambda/\tau = \omega/k$ [m/s] – phase speed;

$C_w = \sqrt{g/k} = \sqrt{g\lambda/2\pi}$ – phase/visible speed of trochoidal waves on deep water;

$\varphi_w = 2\pi(s + tC_w)/\lambda_w$ – phase angle for determination of displacement of trochoidal waves basis, where: s [m] – space distance, t [s] – time countdown at speed C_w [m/s];

$\omega = 2\pi \cdot C_w/\lambda = 2\pi/\tau$ [1/s] – circular frequency of wave pulsations;

$\rho = 1025$ [kg/m^3] – fluid density; g – gravity acceleration [m/s^2];

$\vec{\zeta}$ [m] – vector of fluid particle displacement in vertical plane;

$\vec{v}$ [m/s] – vector of fluid particle velocity in movement along trochoidal path.

$Volume$ – ship displacement; vW – underwater ship hull volume; $\overrightarrow{vB}$ – current coordinates of center of buoyancy, $\overrightarrow{Gravity}$ – current coordinates of center of gravity; $\overrightarrow{B}$ – vector of Archimedes force; $\overrightarrow{iV}$ – normal to wave slope; $\overset{\times}{V}$ – vector of linear velocity, $\overset{\times}{\Omega}$ – vector of angular velocity; $inMass$ – mass (volume) tensor; $\overset{\times}{r}$ – ship coordinate basis; $\overrightarrow{R}$ – distance between centers of buoyancy and gravity.

General notations using at algorithms description are shown in [7, 9].

2 Analytical Description of Computational Experiment

Sea waves in open water quakes can be modeled in various ways. One of the effective computing models reflecting all the physical characteristics of real waves is ARMA [13, 14]. For this reason, this model is implemented in the structure of the marine virtual testbed [1, 3]. Conducting serial calculations using real oceanological data on the structure of sea waves, as well as numerous data from the open sea, shows that the sea surface is most often observed wave fronts. This makes possible mathematical description of waves using simplified two-dimensional profiles of trochoid waves, which also allow you to take into account the nonlinear nature of sea waves. In this case, the distribution of current speeds can only be considered relative to the gravitational vertical.

Numerical schemes for the free propagation of surface perturbations of an arbitrary shape with a strictly specified speed C_w. are used in a computational experiment on sea waves modeling. The inclusion of high-amplitude trochoidal waves in the boundary conditions leads to the reproduction of group structures of storm waves and subsurface currents throughout the water area of the computational experiment.

The fixed phase velocity of waves C_w means the use of analogues of long-wavelength or gas-dynamic finite difference schemes, in which the dynamics of the calculated cells is strictly determined by the local rheology of an inseparable continuous medium. A similar difference solution for trochoidal and strongly swirling marine gravity waves is still unknown.

It is assumed that the waves reflected from the moving ship retain free propagation speed. This is formally acceptable for an elongated ship if the longitudinal components of the Doppler frequency shifts are neglected. The reflection of storm waves from a ship moving under its own power will, on average, be compensated by relatively small transverse displacements of the ship's hull.

In any case, the algorithms for generating shipwalking with Doppler effects are required for the existence of a numerical solution. A fixed phase speed of waves will not prevent with adequate changes in the amplitude-frequency characteristics of the reflected waves. We can consider incorrect distortion as insignificant if we exclude second action on the ship's hull.

The storm observation of waves in open sea shows the existence of several stable group structures: steep waves under the action of wind and two-three swell systems. Group structures are determined in the form of a surface rhombic network from packets, on average, of nine wave fronts. They are running in the group with a double phase rate. At the borders of the wave packets, the phase references are cyclically changed. The relative length of the fronts or the relative width of the rhombic packets increases with a decreasing of wave slops, and the line of crests of particularly steep waves are partly bending in the direction of phase velocity.

In the computational model defined in this way, sea waves are given by a superposition of three (or more) independent wave systems. These are group structures with fixed phase velocities. They are separately affect the ship. A fundamental feature of this model is the accounting of reflected waves from the oscillated ship hull. All of these independently existing wave processes are summed up to recreate the resulting surface of the storm seas and subsurface flows. Ship dynamics modeling (ship performance and motion) is carried out on the basis of this surface similarly [1, 3].

3 Mathematical and Computational Models of Trochoidal Waves

Mathematical model of trochoidal waves $\vec{\zeta}$ (t, s, z) [m] is presented in vector form on profile plate $w \in \{s, z\}$ in direction of wave front propagation s [m] with gravity vertical z [m]. Phase start of wave front in computational experiment comes from zero initial time t [s] and half-length of diagonal of model water area Lb [m].

$$\varphi_w = 2\pi(t \cdot C_w - s - Lb/2)/\lambda \text{ [rad]} \tag{1}$$

where: λ [m] is wave length moving with velocity C_w [m/s] in profile plane $w \in \{s, z\}$ at time moment t [s], from initial position s [m], taking into account the centering of initial position relatively half-length of basin diagonal Lb [m].

In the initial data, half-height of the wave is set using the trochoid radius r_w [m] at the level of the undisturbed surface of the sea $z = 0$ [m], from which the radius with depth is performed r_z [m]:

$$r_z = r_w\exp(2\pi z/\lambda)[m] \tag{2}$$

Believing the movement of particles of fluid on its own trocoidal trajectories, on which water pressure is leveled in depth under the slopes of wave ridges, a work is made for the first amendment on a local breaking:

$$r_z\times = \exp(2\pi r_z(\sin\varphi_w - 1)/\lambda)[m] \tag{3}$$

If it necessary we introduce asymmetric correction to wave profile for taking into account wind stresses Wd $[0 \div 1]$ and alignment of the middle sea level Cr $[0 \div 1]$:

$$r_z\times = \exp(2\pi r_z(Cr(\sin\varphi_w - 1) + Wd\cos\varphi_w)/\lambda)[m] \tag{4}$$

It is important to note that in the case of modeling of group wave structures with a speed dispersion, difference schemes incorrectly recreate subsurface flows of water.

The trochoidal wave profile in the mathematical model is written in vector form for a simple harmonic displacement of water particles from their initial neutral position:

$$\vec{\zeta} + = r_z\overrightarrow{\{-\cos\varphi_w, \sin\varphi_w\}}[m] \tag{5}$$

By definition, in a purely trochoid wave, fluid particles move through circular orbits with strictly equal angular velocities: $V_r = \omega \cdot r_z$ [m/s] defining phase velocity of wave crest free motion: $C_w = \lambda/\tau = \omega/k$ [m/s]. Taking the above-water space (air) conditionally weightless, the immersion of the liquid particle is counting on the level of active wave slopes, while the trochoid radii and the curvatures of the particle trajectories are scalable in the geometric proportions of the trochoidal wave as a whole (2) and (3): $V_r = \omega \cdot r_z = \omega \cdot r_w \cdot e^{kz}$, or for sea surface:

$$V_w = \omega \cdot r_w \cdot \exp(2\pi/\lambda \cdot (z + r_w \cdot (\sin\varphi - 1))), \text{ [m/s]} \tag{6}$$

where z is appliqued in the global Cartesian reference system.

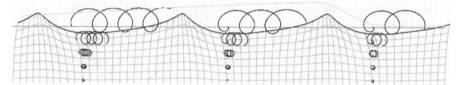

Fig. 1. Modeling of regular tropoidal waves under the action of near-water wind with correction of sea level.

Maximum amplitude in wave crest $\approx 1{,}134{\cdot}r_w$ is noticeably more than in wave trough $\approx 0{,}614{\cdot}r_w$. Ratio wave length to wave height $h = \lambda/\pi$ or $r_w = \lambda/2\pi$ corresponds to simple cycloid and approximately equal to $h{\cdot}k \approx 0{,}75$ or $\lambda/h \approx \pi \cdot 8/3 \approx 8{,}38$, where h is visible height of progressive wave from trough to crest.

Trochoidal trajectories of fluid particles illustrated dependence of drift flows from the relative height of the wave crest are show on Fig. 1. Maximum velocity of surface flows is achieved in the crest of braking progressive wave, which is approaching the value of the single wave phase velocity.

Coefficient $H_w = 8/3{\cdot}\pi \cdot h/\lambda$ normalized relative to the maximum permissible height of trichoidal waves ($h = 2{\cdot}r_w$ [m] is conditional wave height as doubled surface trochoid radius) is used for description of wave processes. Rhombic cell of the group structure has a length in the direction of movement: $L_g = \lambda{\cdot}8.89$ [m]. Largest front length (width of the rhombic water area fragment is $F_g = \cdot2\pi{\cdot}\lambda/H_w$ [m]) is inversely proportional to the relative height of the maximum wave in the center of the group structure.

3.1 Features of Algorithmic Representation of Storm Wave Models

Analysis of the stability of computational processes in time and preliminary coordination of the approximation smoothness of the simulated hydrodynamic fields precedes the construction of a computational model in finite differences.

Stability of wave equation is controlled by Courant criterion. The essence of the criterion is to prevent the intersection of the simulated perturbations of the calculation cell as a whole in one calculated cycle in time.

$$C_w < \delta s/\delta t \tag{7}$$

where C_w [m/s] is the set phase velocity of the simulated wave; δs [m] is the mesh step (common for all computational area); δt [s] is the time step for one cycle of computational experiment.

To achieve equal efficiency in modeling of three wave fields with different wavelengths, it is possible to establish as an initial condition for calculated time step δt [s]. This will naturally correlate with the ideas about the approximation smoothness of wave processes, which natural period of oscillations should be at least an order of magnitude longer. Then the spatial grid step will be assigned dynamically, as $\delta s = C_w{\cdot}\delta t$. This will create equally optimal simulation conditions for independent wave fields with predetermined phase velocities.

In practice, for a stable solution, it is necessary to slightly reduce the calculated time step δt. Usually it is enough to bring the crossing of one cell diagonally by the wavefront in two time steps ($tKrat \approx \sqrt{2}$ is the multiplicity of the time step splitting) for a rectangular grid. In a computational experiment, a change in the calculated time step does not lead to visible changes in the results of the simulation, except for a slight negative effect on the radiation conditions of the waves at the free boundaries. These are the Sommerfeld radiation conditions [15], in which for the normal component of the emitted wave it is necessary to make an adjustment to the step time form $tK = tKrat/(tKrat + 1)$.

To simplify the algorithmic writing, a dimensionless parameter-characteristic of the wave $kW = C_w \cdot \delta t / \delta s / tKrat$ (the ratio of the wave velocity to the grid speed) is introduced.

Extrapolation radiation conditions at free boundaries in accordance with Sommerfeld are determined only from sea level with respect to the normal component of the progressive wave running away from the calculated region:

$$\overset{+}{_0}\vec{\zeta} \mathrel{+}= kW \cdot (\overset{\rightarrow}{_1\zeta} - \overset{\rightarrow}{_0\zeta}) \cdot tK \;=\; C_w \cdot \frac{\delta t \cdot (\overset{\rightarrow}{_1\zeta} - \overset{\rightarrow}{_0\zeta})}{\delta s \cdot (tKrat + 1)} \quad [m] \tag{8}$$

$$\overset{+}{_n}\vec{\zeta} \mathrel{+}= kW \cdot (\overset{\rightarrow}{_{n-1}\zeta} - \overset{\rightarrow}{_n\zeta}) \cdot tK \;=\; C_w \cdot \frac{\delta t \cdot (\overset{\rightarrow}{_{n-1}\zeta} - \overset{\rightarrow}{_n\zeta})}{\delta s \cdot (tKrat + 1)}$$

where low left indexes n are used for grid knots marking; symbol (+) as left upper index shows the next time indicator.

Dynamics of liquid particles is constructed in the vertical plane of the wave profile, where grid differences divided by half of spatial step provide synchronous interaction of the displacement vectors of the liquid particles $\vec{\zeta}$ [m] (local velocities $\vec{v}$ [m/s], phase velocity of wave propagation C_w [m/s] and angle rotation ω [1/s]).

$$\overset{+}{}\vec{\zeta} \mathrel{-}= kW \cdot (\vec{v} - \underset{-}{\vec{v}}) / \omega \;=\; C_w \cdot \frac{\delta t \cdot (\vec{v} - \underset{-}{\vec{v}})}{\delta s \cdot tKrat} / \omega \quad [m] \tag{9}$$

$$\overset{+}{}\vec{v} \mathrel{-}= kW \cdot (\overset{\rightarrow}{_+\zeta} - \vec{\zeta}) \cdot \omega \;=\; C_w \cdot \frac{\delta t \cdot (\overset{\rightarrow}{_+\zeta} - \vec{\zeta})}{\delta s \cdot tKrat} \cdot \omega \quad [m/s]$$

All particles of the liquid are synchronously rotated along trochoidal radii in the direction of wave crest movement. This doubles the phase velocity relative to the group velocity. Thus, the wave packet propagates twice slowly as the apparent phase velocity. At the same time, the phase is constantly changing at the point of its first entry into the unperturbed water area:

$$\overset{+}{}\vec{\zeta} \mathrel{-}= \delta t \cdot \omega \cdot \{ -\overset{\rightarrow}{\zeta_z}, \zeta_x \} = \delta t \cdot \omega \cdot \{ -\zeta_z + \zeta_x \cdot \delta t \cdot \omega / 2, \; \zeta_x + \zeta_z \cdot \delta t \cdot \omega / 2 \} \quad [m]$$

$$\overset{+}{}\vec{v} \mathrel{-}= \delta t \cdot \omega \cdot \{ -\overset{\rightarrow}{v_z}, v_x \} = \delta t \cdot \omega \cdot \{ -v_z + v_x \cdot \delta t \cdot \omega / 2, \; v_x + v_z \cdot \delta t \cdot \omega / 2 \} \quad [m/s]$$
$$\tag{10}$$

3.2 Possible Variants of Virtual Testbed Functioning with Sea Waves Models

The undoubted advantage of computational experiments in hydromechanics is the possibility of preliminary or interactive selection of various mathematical models. This approach is in demand in many practical tasks. A variety of built-in methods for modeling sea waves is certainly useful when debugging the software that ensures the operation of the virtual testbed.

The following computational experiments with storm waves are implemented in the software package "Vessel":

1. The version of the calm sea without waves. It is necessary for experiments with the ship differentiation when gaining momentum and active braking; when simulating the heel and motion of the ship on circulation; to visualize the free or residual vibrations of the hull when sea waves excitation extracts from the calculations; as well as for observations of the ship motion under the influence of external impulse heeling moments.
2. A purely mathematical wave field of full-fledged trochoidal waves (2,3,4) and subsurface velocities of currents at uneven regularized design nodes. Such model of an unchanged storm sea allows you to work out in detail the dynamics of storm propulsion and motion of the ship without the complicated influence of high-altitude waves reflected from the ship hull.
3. The same space-temporary wave field on strictly uniform nodes with identical calculation cells. In this variant, the resulting wave field is immediately simulated without involving extra layers with fixed wavelengths. In optimized modeling of sea waves, a single vector array is used in which the z component includes sea level, and along the horizontal axes $\{x,y\}$ averaged velocities of subsurface currents. Thus, a simulation option with minimal use of computer computing resources is implemented.
4. A direct computational experiment with trochoidal wave on uneven regularized nodes, with the possibility of turning on dispersion for phase and group velocities, with showing of ship wave formation and a full reflection of external storm waves from the hull of the ship.
5. The same computational experiment, taking into account the subsurface velocities of currents, which partially reduce the force effects of storm waves on the hull of the ship by reducing water pressure while taking into account the caused currents near the hull of the ship. In this case, the computing resources of the computer are maximized.
6. Computational experiment using wave mode in full streams on uniform regular grids, with guaranteed compliance of stability criteria and approximation smoothness of differential approximations. Thus, the requests for computing resources of the computer are optimized and significantly reduced, but at the same time, the determining part of the hydrodynamic processes in the experiment is implemented quite correctly (Fig. 2).

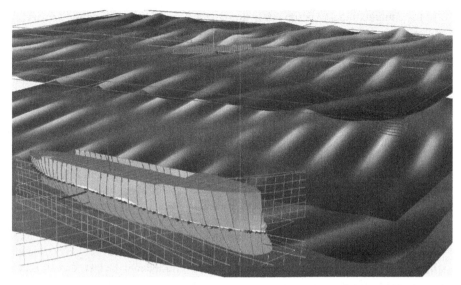

Fig. 2. Example of computational experiment with visualization of wave fields and ship dynamics.

4   Variants for Experiments in the Field of Stormy Seaworthiness

A virtual model of the ship is built in full-scale digital theoretical drawings. The surface of the general ship architecture, with mass and dynamic characteristics of the hull, propulsion and rudder control are considered. It is also possible to interactively change the application of the center of gravity directly during the experiment. This is necessary to assess the nature and intensity of the ship motion in various stormy navigation scenarios, and it can be used to return the vessel to its operating position in the event of emergency capsizing.

The virtual numerical model of the ship is digitized by full-scale theoretical drawings. This allows you to conduct simulations in real time in compliance with inertial characteristics, speed pulsations and motion periods of a real ship. During the experiment, an interactive change in the metacentric height *GM* is allowed.

Ship maneuvers in computational experiment are performed along smooth circulation trajectories. Gain and loss of speed also occur smoothly. This generally corresponds to real sailing with six degrees of freedom, occurrence of heel on the circulation and running trim during acceleration and braking of the ship, that is, with a variable speed depending on the nature of the interaction of the hull with specific crests of storm waves.

The course of the ship is held by the automatic pilot system with a limit on speed of circulation according to two conditional options for transferring the rudder to the "half-side" and "to the side" (*the angular velocity on the circulation does not depend on the travel speed*). The speed of travel is regulated by propulsion tools and the resistance in case "still water", which allows both the loss of the storm motion on intense waves, and acceleration on crests of the following waves (*when engines are stopped the damping is applied to the full drift speed*).

In the computational experiment, hydrodynamic models of ship motion of varying complexity are involved, as well as in the simulation of sea waves.

1. The simplest or test version is based on the kinematic sliding of the ship hull relative to two pairs of points along and across the hull. In the simplest case, no hydrodynamic calculations are performed at all. Graphical visualization of wave structures and ship hull sliding along the chords of the resulting wave field is performed.
2. In the simplest version of ship dynamics modeling only the vertical components of external storm forces are considered. Formally, from such vertical external forces, pitching, rolling and heaving are formed. Regardless of wave nature, the calculations involve the entire complex of finite-difference operations. They include simulations of both ship wave formation and the reflection of storm waves from the ship hull.
3. Involvement of all external forces and heeling moments. This means simulating all six components of the ship's degrees of freedom on the way of stormy conditions.
4. In variants 2 and 3, the calculations are supplemented by subsurface current velocities, which formally reduces the external force effect of storm waves by reducing the hydrostatic pressure on the ship hull while taking into account the fast currents under the crests of the waves near and along the ship hull. In this version of the simulation, additional memory resources are requested to build three-dimensional current fields near the ship hull, and, accordingly, requests for computational resources increase significantly.

4.1 Hydrodynamic Model of Ship Propulsion and Motion in Intensive Waves

The moving model of the ship interacts separately with each of the wave fields with predetermined phase velocities. This hydrodynamically correctly determines the geometric transformations and kinematic processes of waves reflection from ship hull. The resulting wave field (Fig. 3) is obtained by simply summing the sea levels and vector velocities of subsurface currents, and serves to recalculate the instantaneous force effects on all hull, including the freeboard, decks and superstructures.

At each step of the computational experiment, the geometric characteristics and hydrodynamic parameters of the hull are recalculated, taking into account the kinematics on the waves. Wave field is not created at the first cycle of calculations. The results of calculations are re-assigned to the original numerical objects to fix mass, inertial and hydrostatic parameters of the ship on still water without motion.

A computational experiment is formed by a sequence of algorithms with vector and tensor quantities: $\vec{B} = vW \cdot i\vec{V}$ is vector Archimedes forces; $\vec{W} = \{0, 0, Volume\}$ is vertical vector of mass (volume) of ship hull; $\vec{V}+ = g\left(\vec{B} + \vec{W}\right)\delta t / Volumer$ is speed of forward ship hull movements in the ship's coordinate system. After applying the damping coefficients that affect viscosity, such caused velocity is simply summed up with the current speed of the vessel. $\vec{R} = r \cdot \left(\vec{vB} - \overrightarrow{Gravity}\right)$ is moment arm of Archimedes; $\vec{\Omega}+ = \left\{\left[g\left(\vec{R} \times \vec{B}\right)\delta t\right]/r\right\}/inMass$ is renewed vector of angle velocity of ship motion. Here, damping coefficients are also used, and Archimedean force vector is supplemented by an inertial component from the current accelerations on the trajectory of the ship's mass center.

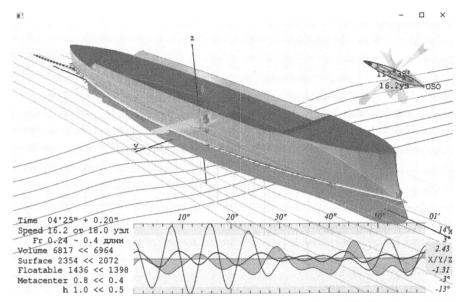

Fig. 3. Screen shot of graphical window with the characteristics of the ship hull. At the top right is a cartouche with the course of the ship and arrows of characteristic lengths, heights and directions of group wave structures movement. At the bottom of the screen are graphics of rolling, pitching and heaving are showed.

An important element of the computational experiment is the limitation of acceleration when ship becomes a given speed and two circulation modes are installed ("rudder on board" and "half-board"). This allows you to simulate the occurrence of heel on circulation and motion loss on a storm wave, the capture of the hull by a following wave and other effects of motion and propulsion on all six degrees of freedom.

To speed up the calculations, numerical structures ordered by frame-space are used that describe the hull surface. This makes it possible to enable reenterable procedures to parallelize the calculation process. At each step of the experiment, the current waterline is re-interpolated and beams are placed to dynamically separate the underwater and overwater volumes of the hull. Modified submerged hull volumes, shifted centers, and new moments of inertia are calculated. The metacentric characteristics of the hull are used only to formally control the dynamics of the ship within the framework of traditional representations of ship theory. To do this, the area, position of the center and moments of inertia of the current waterline area are additionally calculated.

5   Conclusion

Direct computational experiments within the framework of the marine virtual testbed are widely used in practice. The obtained results can serve as an experimental justification for technical proposals in the design of promising ships and vessels of increased storm seaworthiness. The described approach can also be useful as part of on-board navigator counting and solving devices or expert information systems in the maritime services of captains-mentors, for the synthesis of operational recommendations to navigators in strong and stormy seafaring conditions.

The experimental computing environment has a full three-dimensional visualization of all structures of the sea wave. It shows the trajectory of movement and instant positioning of the virtual model of the ship with visualization of hydrodynamic characteristics and parameters. OpenGL's standard graphics tools make it possible to adjust the transparency of sea waves with a choice of options for continuous or contour drawings of ship contours and surface architecture of the ship. This gives the user of the virtual testbed the opportunity to visually analyze and predict in advance the conditions and effectiveness of the storm seagoing, including to prevent potentially dangerous or emergency situations on the high seas.

The new toolkit opens up a popular area of research in the field of ship fluid mechanics, the significant advantages of which are a completely optimal requirement for RAM and performance of computers, which makes it possible to recommend new software complexes for widespread use in production, research and academic purposes.

Acknowledgment. The research is partially funded by the Ministry of Science and Higher Education of the Russian Federation as part of World-class Research Center program: Advanced Digital Technologies (contract No. 075-15-2020-903 dated 16.11.2020).

References

1. Bogdanov, A., Degtyarev, A., Gankevich, I., Khramushin, V., Korkhov, V.: Virtual testbed: concept and applications. In: Gervasi, O., et al. (eds.) ICCSA 2020. LNCS, vol. 12254, pp. 3–17. Springer, Cham (2020). https://doi.org/10.1007/978-3-030-58817-5_1
2. Gavrikov, A., et al.: Virtual testbed: simulation of air flow around ship hull and its effect on ship motions. In: Gervasi, O., et al. (eds.) ICCSA 2020. LNCS, vol. 12254, pp. 18–28. Springer, Cham (2020). https://doi.org/10.1007/978-3-030-58817-5_2
3. Gavrikov, A., et al.: Virtual testbed: simulation of ocean wave reflection from the ship hull. In: Gervasi, O., et al. (eds.) ICCSA 2020. LNCS, vol. 12254, pp. 29–39. Springer, Cham (2020). https://doi.org/10.1007/978-3-030-58817-5_3
4. Degtyarev, A., Bogdanov, A., Korkhov, V., Gankevich, I., Pylnev, Y., Eibozhenko, A.: Virtual testbed as a case for big data. CEUR Worksh. Proc. **2267**, 58–64 (2018)
5. Bogdanov, A., Degtyarev, A., Korkhov, V.: New approach to the simulation of complex systems. EPJ Web Conf. **108**, 01002 (2016). https://doi.org/10.1051/epjconf/201610801002
6. Bogdanov, A., Khramushin, V.: Tensor arithmetic, geometric and mathematic principles of fluid mechanics in implementation of direct computational experiments. EPJ Web Conf. **108**, 02013 (2016). https://doi.org/10.1051/epjconf/201610802013
7. Degtyarev, A., Khramushin, V.: Coordinate systems, numerical objects and algorithmic operations of computational experiment in fluid mechanics. EPJ Web Conf. **108**, 02018 (2016). https://doi.org/10.1051/epjconf/201610802018
8. Gerstner, F.J.: Theorie der Wellen samt einer daraus abgeleiteten Theorie der Deichprofile. (Prag, 1804)
9. Degtyarev, A., Khramushin, V.: Design and construction of computer experiment in hydrodynamics using explicit numerical schemes and tensor mathematics algorithms. Mat. Model. **26**(11), 4–17 (2014)

10. Bogdanov, A., Degtyarev, A., Gankevich, I., Khramushin, V.: On agreement of computational experiment in interactive simulation of the ship hydromechanics on a stormy sea. CEUR Worksh. Proc. **2267**, 493–498 (2018)
11. Degtyarev, A., Khramushin, V., Shichkina, Y.: Tensor methodology and computational geometry in direct computational experiments in fluid mechanics. AIP Conf. Proc. **1863**, 110006 (2017). https://doi.org/10.1063/1.4992291
12. Bogdanov, A., Degtyarev, A., Khramushin, V.: Features of physical distribution processes modeling in continuum-corpuscular computational experiments. CEUR Worksh. Proc. **1787**, 124–129 (2016)
13. Degtyarev, A., Reed, A.: Synoptic and short-term modeling of ocean waves. Int. Shipbuild. Prog. **60**(1–4), 523–553 (2013)
14. Degtyarev, A.: New approach to wave weather scenarios modeling. Fluid Mech. Appl. **97**, 599–617 (2011)
15. Sommerfeld, A.: Vorlesungen über theoretische Physik. 2. Mechanik der deformierbaren Medien, Akad. Verlag Ges. Geest & Portig, 371p. (1949)
16. Degtyarev, A., Gankevich, I., Kulabukhova, N., Khramushin, V.: Computational model of unsteady hydromechanics of large amplitude gerstner waves. EPJ Web Conf. **226**, 02009 (2020). https://doi.org/10.1051/epjconf/202022602009

New Technologies for Storing and Transferring Personal Data

Nadezhda Shchegoleva[1,3]([✉]), Natalia Zalutskaya[2], Alina Dambaeva[1], Jasur Kiyamov[1], and Aleksandr Dik[1]

[1] Saint Petersburg State University, St. Petersburg, Russia
n.shchegoleva@spbu.ru, {st069509,st080634,
st087383}@student.spbu.ru
[2] Federal State Budgetary Institution «Bekhterev National Medical Research Psychiatry and Neurology Center», St. Petersburg, Russia
[3] State Marine Technical University, St. Petersburg, Russia

Abstract. Medical information about a person's state of health, data on the diagnostic evaluation of his symptoms and complaints, especially those related to the field of mental health, require a special reliability of the information storage system, since their disclosure often leads to stigmatization of the patient. The article proposes a new technology for storing and transmitting personal data based on "zeroing the LSB layers" (least significant bit (LSB) component of the Red, Green and Blue color image) and filling these layers with QR-codes containing AES-encrypted personal medical data of the patient. Specified the approach allows you to remove personal data from open access, since the presence of a barcode in the LSB layer practically does not change the image, therefore, without knowing about its presence, an attacker will not pay attention to it, moreover, using existing applications or scanners, it is impossible to read information, and decryption of information is hindered by the lack of an encryption key.

Keywords: Medical data · Barcoding · Color barcodes · Encryption · Data protection · Personal data

1 Introduction

Over the past few years, information technology has been developing at a dizzying pace, and every year the connection between the real and virtual worlds is becoming stronger. The format of communication and information exchange between people and groups of people united by the same interests, government organizations, companies, corporations, etc. has changed significantly. However, unlike the real world, any information that appears in the virtual space is distributed almost instantly, and it is extremely difficult, and sometimes almost impossible, to remove it from the network.

The number of data leaks is growing exponentially every year. News of another company system hack, customer information theft, or demand for payment or ransom is becoming commonplace. The governments of almost all countries are making tremendous efforts to increase the level of information security - a number of new laws are being developed that provide data protection and provide for liability for violation of the requirements for their processing and illegal distribution [1–5]. Those facts draw increased attention to the methods of storage, processing and distribution of personal information, and also force organizations to strengthen data protection measures in order to prevent their leakage.

According to the Data Leakage & Breach Intelligence (DLBI) intelligence service, medical institutions are among the organizations in which data breaches are most often recorded [6]. Varonis, an information security company, believes that the losses of medical institutions in 2020 from data leaks amounted to $7.13 million, an increase of 10.5% compared to the previous year, and judging by the dynamics of 2021, these losses will increase. This is evidenced, for example, by the appearance in the public domain of data of 300,000 people who recovered from COVID-19, the publication of stolen Pfizer data on the COVID-19 vaccine on the network, etc.

It should be noted that the detection of cyber-attacks on financial institutions is quite fast, but theft and misuse of electronic health records is an almost invisible crime. Since it is usually discovered in an emergency for the owner, when the consequences can be very life-threatening.

An article published on the zdravexpert portal notes that "the life cycle of a leak in the healthcare sector - from the commission of an attack to its detection and remediation - reached a record 329 days in 2020." Obviously, this is due to the catastrophic lack of time to analyze incidents in the health sector, all efforts of which were aimed at combating the pandemic. And in this situation, health care institutions were unable to adequately protect the main thing - the personal data of citizens, including information protected by law on the state of health, examination results and medical recommendations.

Cybersecurity experts note new trends in the black market: information and medical products - various kinds of filing cabinets - are gaining more and more popularity. In January 2022, news broke that the data of 48 million coronavirus vaccination certificates for $100,000 were put up for sale on the darknet. The data of medical policies, medical records, personal data of patients in private and public clinics are put up for sale. Offers are in high demand, from criminal associations for financial gain to pharmaceutical companies, tour operators and funeral service agencies.

It is worth noting a special category of medical personal data related to the field of mental health. Labeling a person as mentally ill often entails serious social consequences, starting with attributing certain negative characteristics to a person, and as a result falling into social isolation and distancing others, and ending with the infringement of rights. Especially when this information falls into the hands of incompetent people who do not have a psychological or psychiatric education, knowledge and experience, but who want to protect other people from a non-existent danger, thus harming an innocent person.

2 Data Encryption

To protect data in practice, several groups of methods are used, including:

– creation of obstacles in the way of the alleged kidnapper, physical and software means.
– data masking or transformation by cryptography and steganography methods.

– development of legal acts and a set of measures aimed at shaping the correct behavior of users.
– creation of such conditions under which the user will be forced to comply with the rules for handling data.

Recently, one of the most effective approaches is data protection in depth, that is, the use of several successive measures to prevent third parties from accessing information. This approach uses multiple levels of data protection, which increases the security of the system and reduces the risk of unauthorized access to information.

In this paper, it is proposed to use two levels of protection. The first is implemented using a cryptographic encryption algorithm that provides data protection by converting it into a form that is incomprehensible and useless for an attacker. The second level of protection is provided with the help of steganography, that is, an algorithm that hides not only the content of the stored information, but also the very fact of storing or transmitting some data embedded in the image. Since a person "at a glance" is not able to accurately estimate the difference between the size of an image without data embedded in it and with data, the main task is to make the embedded data invisible. This approach will be discussed in the next section.

An analysis of the proposed encryption technologies showed that the most promising is the use of symmetric encryption technology. In this case, the block cipher is used to encrypt the identifier using a secret key, which is both a pseudo anonymization secret and a recovery secret.

The advantage of symmetric encryption algorithms is their simplicity, since one key is used for both encryption and decryption, so such algorithms are much faster than their asymmetric encryption counterparts, require less computing power, do not reduce Internet speed, and allow you to quickly encrypt a large the amount of data.

The most promising and one of the most common symmetric encryption algorithms is AES (advanced encryption system) [7], also known as Rijndael. It was developed as an alternative to DES and became the new encryption standard after being approved by NIST in 2001.

AES uses substitution and permutation methods. In the first step, the unencrypted data is converted into blocks, and then encryption is applied using the key. The encryption process consists of various processes such as row shifts, column mixing, and adding keys. Depending on the key length, 10, 12 or 14 such transformations (rounds) are performed. It is worth noting that the last round is different from the previous ones and does not include a mixing sub-process. Thus, AES is faster, more flexible, and more secure because it allows keys of various lengths, and the longer the key, the more difficult it is to crack.

Today, AES is the most popular encryption algorithm - it is used in many applications, including security:

– wireless applications,
– processors and files,
– websites - in SSL/TLS protocol,
– Wi-Fi,
– mobile applications,
– VPN (virtual private network), etc.

3   New Technology for Storing and Transferring Personal Data

To store and analyze the results of various tests and medical examinations of patients at the Research Institute named after V. M. Bekhterev an information system was developed should ensure the protection of personal data, as well as research results containing information that allows you to identify the patient directly or indirectly. This is an extremely difficult task, since in future this system should be integrated with other brain research systems within the framework of international collaborations.

Currently, bar codes are widely used in most medical institutions for fast and accurate management of patient flows. In information systems, barcodes are used to register and record patients, generate medical records and referrals for procedures, extracts and prescriptions, while there is no explicit information about patients on the documents.

An analysis of the characteristics of existing barcodes shows that QR-codes (Quick Response) are of the greatest interest [8, 9], having the highest capacity for recording information from ASCII, Cyrillic characters and, moreover, allow recovering up to 30% of lost information. The generation and reading of this kind of barcodes is quite simple, there are many different kinds of sensors and applications on the market that allow reading using mobile devices. Of particular note the recently appeared color QR-codes, which actually consist of 3 QR-codes, so their capacity for recording information is three times higher. An additional advantage is the description of QR-code as ISO standards, which does not require any royalties.

However, when realizing access to information, financial and material resources within the framework of a corporate network through barcodes in a significant number of medical institutions, there is an almost open transmission of patient information through communication channels. In this case, there are many opportunities for intercepting confidential and personal data, their substitution or replacement of these data by modifying them, since the barcode decryption algorithms are open and the programs implementing this process are also in the public domain.

Therefore, in order to protect the personal data of patients in accordance with the adopted laws, an additional step of hiding data from being read by illegal users should be implemented.

In [10] presents a method and algorithms for embedding QR-codes with embedded biometric and documentary information in color images to form BIO QR-codes.

The idea of the algorithm proposed by the authors is based on "zeroing the LSB layers" (least significant bit (LSB) of the Red, Green and Blue components of the original color image and filling these layers with the corresponding QR-codes. This is what makes it possible to remove personal data from public access, since using existing applications or scanners is impossible on the one hand, and on the other hand, the presence of a barcode in the LSB layer practically does not change the image, therefore, without knowing about its presence, an attacker will not pay attention to it.

4 Algorithm for Embedding Personal Information in a Color Image

Considering the recommendations [11], the process of embedding personal information in a color image will consist of the following steps.

1. Preparation of messages for QR-codes with documentary information.

   To form a message that will be used to generate a QR-code, it is necessary to group the initial personal textual and digital information (for example, full name, year and place of birth, profession, etc.), biometric data information (weight, height, etc.), examination results, established diagnoses, etc. by arranging them into semantic groups to record them in three barcodes. At the same time, separator characters (for example, #) can be used to structure information.

   Such an organization of the message makes it possible to preserve the semantic structure of biometric and documentary information. This makes it possible to simplify the process of generating QR-codes from them and decoding them to read information to the recipient. Depending on the purpose of using the information, it is possible to generate QR-codes containing different sets of personal data and documentary information, while embedding one, two or three codes in the corresponding LSB layers of the Red, Green and Blue components.

   In the original algorithm, the next step is to write the generated messages into QR-codes, but in this case, the information will be stored in its original form and can be easily read. Therefore, as shown above, in order to protect information, it must be encrypted. Therefore, a modification of the algorithm is required.

2. Encryption of messages for QR-codes with documentary information

   The results of the study showed that the most efficient, secure, fast and flexible encryption algorithm is AES, the advantage of which is the ability to use keys with different lengths, which can be selected based on user needs and system limitations.

   Therefore, the next step is to encrypt prepared messages for QR-codes with documentary information using the AES algorithm and generate a key, the length of which is selected by the user in accordance with security requirements, and contains the parameters of the QR-code in the image.

3. Writing encrypted messages to QR-codes

   Graphically, QR-codes are halftone images in ".png" format. In [10] it was shown that this image format provides a representation without compression noise, full preservation of information in memory exchange operations, which means that the QR-code will not be distorted by the noise of restoring the recorded information.

4. Preparing the container image

   The container can be any color image, the size of which exceeds the size of the barcode. To do this, the input color image is decomposed into three components R, G and B, which are three matrices of size $M \times N$ (where M and N are the size of the image in pixels). In graphical representation, we get three halftone images - components R, G and B, which are shown in Fig. 1.

Fig. 1. Original color image and the result of its decomposition into components R, G, B.

From halftone images, the R, G and B components are removed in the LSB (least significant) layer, the part whose size corresponds to the size of the embedded QR-code.

5. Formation of the container image.

In place of the removed part of the LSB layer of halftone images, the R, G, B components and the contents of the QR-codes are embedded. Next, the reverse operation is performed - combining all the layers of grayscale images and the R, G and B components into one color image that contains personal information in the form of QR-codes. The result of the process of embedding QR-codes in a color image is shown in Fig. 2.

Figure 3 shows a diagram of the process of embedding information in color images and the stages of information transformation: defining a set of personal data, preparing messages for each component R, G, B, AES encryption, generating QR-codes, embedding the corresponding bar codes in the components.

Reading information from a filled container image is carried out in reverse order (from right to left) by extracting embedded QR-codes from the LSB layers of components, decoding QR-code messages, decrypting messages, reading message information in accordance with the accepted record structure.

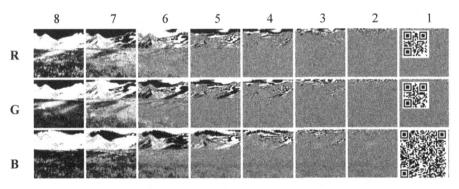

Fig. 2. R, G, B components of the "filled container image".

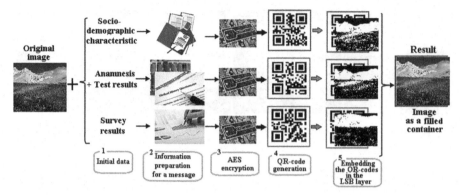

Fig. 3. Scheme of the process of embedding information in color images.

5   Selecting a Container Image for Storing and Transferring Data

The purpose of forming a container image is to hide information during the transfer and storage of personal data. However, as experiments show, not every image can be used for these purposes. This is due to the fact that all barcodes recorded in one area of the LSB layers can lead to a slight distortion of the original image. At the same time, this distortion may not be noticeable to an ordinary user, and at the same time, a specialist will notice a difference, which can be explained by errors in data transmission, but re-sending will not correct the situation, which will lead to increased attention to this image, and this contradicts the task. Example of such image is shown in Fig. 4a. This problem can be solved in different ways, which will be discussed in this section.

Image Selection Based on Color Histogram. The first and easiest way is to choose an image that will change slightly when barcodes are added to the LSB layers. To do this, we calculate the color histograms of the image obtained from the original color image. In this case, the larger the range of values, the more suitable the image will be for using it as a container. Figure 4 shows sample images and their color histograms. At the same time, Fig. 4a shows an example of an image in which the appearance of a barcode will be noticeable, Fig. 4b shows an image in which distortions will be hardly noticeable, and Fig. 4c shows an image that should be chosen as a container.

Selection of the Content of the Barcode. Let's consider the content of the barcode in more detail. A QR-code consists of six components: indentation, search pattern, alignment pattern, sync bars, version, data cells. The first two components - the indent and the search pattern (see Fig. 6, highlighted in color), which correspond to the largest areas that have one color, which can distort the original image, have the greatest importance for the formation of the barcode image.

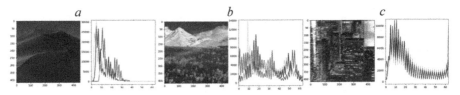

Fig. 4. Color histograms of images.

The padding is the white border around the outer edge of the QR-code. Without this frame, the scanner will not be able to determine what needs to be read - the surrounding elements will interfere with it.

The search pattern is three black squares: in the lower left, upper left and upper right corners, they show where the outer borders of the QR-code are and how it is oriented.

These components have a size strictly limited by the standard, so they can be removed before being placed in the container and added when reading the barcode. The content part, namely the data itself, will then have the form shown in Fig. 5 right. Obviously, such a barcode image is already becoming less noticeable in the original image.

Fig. 5. Separation of barcodes and options for their recording in the image-container.

It should be noted that in this case, the information can also be read using the modification of the content of the barcode described above. Therefore, the next step, which will make the code invisible, will be dividing it into several parts and writing it to different parts of the image, and the positions for writing in each layer may be different. An exampleы of possible ways to separate barcodes (see Fig. 2) and options for writing them to the container image is shown in Fig. 6.

Barcode Image Conversion. Another approach that allows you to hide the information contained in a barcode is the use of geometric transformations of image matrices: rotation by an angle that is a multiple of 90°, matrix transposition, rotation around an axis that coincides with one of the rows or columns, etc. Several examples of such transformations are shown in Fig. 7.

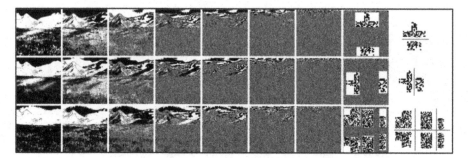

Fig. 6. Examples of barcode image transformations.

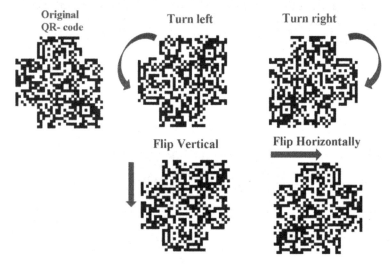

Fig. 7. Examples of barcode image transformations.

Similarly to the transformation of the barcode image, it is possible to perform transformations of its parts shown in Fig. 6. In this case, for each part, its own method of change can be used.

Note that the image shown in the pictures is small (446 * 417 pixels), so you may notice a slight distortion of the picture that looks like "broken" pixels. However, if the image has a significantly larger size, then the human eye will hardly see the changes made. And in this case, such a change will serve to hide, and therefore protect the data placed in the container image.

At the same time, the proposed methods for changing the barcode image do not require complex mathematical transformations, graphic libraries and have low computational complexity, which allows them to be used for a wide range of data transmission and storage systems.

Until now, the question has remained aside, how does the recipient of such an image-container with the patient's personal data find out about the performed barcode conversions?

The solution to this problem can be implemented either by generating an encryption key in such a way that it contains values corresponding to certain transformations in certain places, and then the recipient of the message can perform all the necessary actions. Other way around is on the basis of a preliminary agreement between the sender and recipient of the order and list of transformations to be performed. The combination of the above approaches is also possible.

In view of the foregoing, the proposed new technology for storing and transferring personal data will consist of the following steps (see Fig. 8):

1) Preparation of messages for QR-codes with documentary information.
2) Encryption of messages for QR-codes with documentary information
3) Selection of the content of the barcode image
4) Dividing the selected content part of the barcode image into several parts
5) Application of geometric transformations of image matrices of barcode parts (rotation by an angle multiple of 90°, matrix transposition, rotation around an axis that coincides with one of the rows or columns, etc.)
6) Writing the converted parts of the barcode to different areas of the container image.

Accordingly, the extraction of information is carried out in the reverse order.

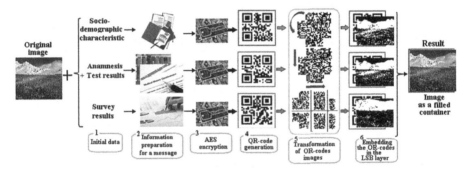

Fig. 8. New technology for storing and transferring personal data.

6 Practical Implementation

The new data storage and transmission technology proposed in this article was implemented as an application consisting of two modules - for the sender and the recipient. An example of the application is shown in Fig. 9 - data input for forming a container image and Fig. 10 - the process of extracting data from a container image.

At the same time, as can be seen from the presented figures, it is enough for the sender of personal data to simply select the necessary information from the Excel table, specify the encryption key and select an image to form the container. Knowing the key, the recipient can easily extract information from the container image. It is worth noting that the original image has not changed much and without knowing about the presence of any information in it, the attacker will not pay attention to it, and therefore we will be able to safely store and transfer personal medical data.

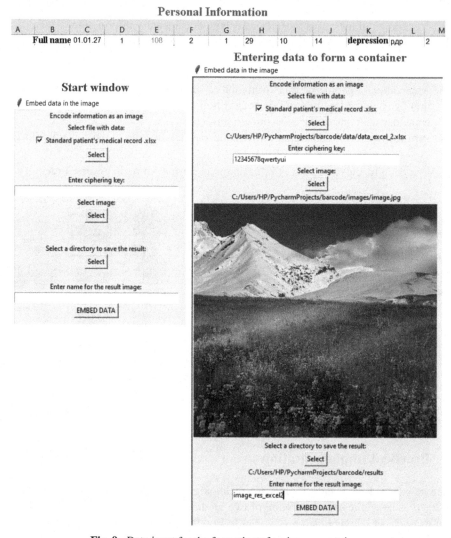

Fig. 9. Data input for the formation of an image-container.

Selecting a image-container

The result of extracting data from the image-container

A	B	C	D	E	F	G	H	I	J	K		L	M
	Full name	01.01.27	1	108	2	1	29	10	14	depression	рдр	2	

Fig. 10. The process of extracting data from a image-container.

7   Conclusion

It should be noted that container images obtained in this way do not make it possible to detect the existence of documentary information in them. The use of color images with QR-codes embedded in them containing encrypted information as a storage and carrier of personal data will ensure the protection of this information, as well as restrict open access to it, since the embedded information can be read and decrypted only if the encryption key is present and knowledge of the structure of information is known.

The proposed new technology will make it possible to apply a universal standard when transferring personal data over a network, exchanging information, including through international channels, without losing any part of it and/or replacing it, as well as significantly reduce the losses of medical institutions from data leaks and significantly increase security of personal data processing.

Acknowledgments. The research is partially funded by the Ministry of Science and Higher Education of the Russian Federation as part of World-class Research Center program: Advanced Digital Technologies (contract No. 075-15-2020-903 dated 16.11.2020).

References

1. General Data Protection Regulation – GDPR
2. NIST.SP.800-122. Guide to Protecting the Confidentiality of Personally Identifiable Information (PII)
3. NIST.SP.800-53. Security and Privacy Controls for Federal Information Systems and Organizations
4. NIST.SP.800-37. Risk Management Framework for Information Systems and Organizations A System Life Cycle Approach for Security and PrivacyNIST.IR.8053. De-Identification of Personal Information
5. NIST PRIVACY FRAMEWORK 1.0 (PRAM): A tool for improving privacy through enterprise risk management
6. Data Leakage & Breach Intelligence. https://dlbi.ru/data-base-leaks-risks/
7. Advanced Encryption Standard (AES)
8. Kukharev, G.A., Kaziyeva, N., Tsymbal, D.A.: Barcoding technologies for facial biometrics: current status and new solutions. Sci. Tech. J. Inf. Technol. Mech. Opt. 18(1), 72–86 (2018). https://doi.org/10.17586/2226-1494-2018-18-1-72-86. (in Russian)
9. Kaziyeva, N., Kukharev, G., Matveev, Y.: Barcoding in biometrics and its development. In: Chmielewski, L.J., Kozera, R., Orłowski, A., Wojciechowski, K., Bruckstein, A.M., Petkov, N. (eds.) ICCVG 2018. LNCS, vol. 11114, pp. 464–471. Springer, Cham (2018). https://doi.org/10.1007/978-3-030-00692-1_40
10. Nazym, K.: Methods and algorithms of barcoding for facial biometrics. Academic Dissertation Candidate of Engineering (2020)
11. Patent of the Russian Federation No. 2714741. Method for generating a color QR-code according to images of faces and a device for its implementation. In: Kukharev, G.A., Kazieva, N., Shchegoleva, N.L.

Use of Digital Twins and Digital Threads for Subway Infrastructure Monitoring

Alexander Vodyaho[1] (ID), Elena Stankova[2] (ID), Nataly Zhukova[3] (ID),
Alexey Subbotin[1](✉) (ID), and Michael Chervontsev[1] (ID)

[1] Saint-Petersburg State Electrotechnical University, Professor Popov Street 5,
197376 St. Petersburg, Russia
alesu1543@gmail.com

[2] St. Petersburg State University, 7-9, Universitetskaya nab., 199034 St. Petersburg, Russia

[3] St. Petersburg Institute of Informatics and Automation of the Federal Research Center at the
Russian Academy of Sciences (FRC RAS), 14th Line V.O. 39, 199178 St. Petersburg, Russia

Abstract. The article deals with the problem of using digital twins and digital threads in complex distributed cyber-physical systems with a high level of structural and functional dynamics. A three-level model of the life cycle of a complex cyber-physical system is proposed. At the upper level, the observed system is described in terms of a continuous architecture. At the middle level, the observed system is described in terms of an agile architecture. At the lower level, the observed system is described in terms of a multigraph, which allows describe both the observed system structure and behavior. In the case study the solution of the problem of monitoring the state of the subway infrastructure is considered. The proposed approach has shown its effectiveness and can be applied in other domains such as smart cities.

Keywords: Digital twin · Digital thread · Event monitoring and visualization · Smart city · Machine learning · Neural network algorithms

1 Introduction

One of the distinguishing features of the modern stage of society's development is very rapid changes in people's lives and production methods. Modern companies and organizations are transforming their strategies, business models, products and services, as well as business processes and information systems by increasing the level of their digitalization [1] with the help of intelligent services and products usage. The potential of the Internet and related digital technologies, such as the Internet of Things, artificial intelligence, data analysis, computing services, cloud computing, mobile systems, collaboration networks and cyber-physical systems (CPS), are strategic factors that allow the development of digital platforms and ecosystems [2] based on intelligent services.

O. Gervasi et al. (Eds.): ICCSA 2022 Workshops, LNCS 13380, pp. 693–707, 2022.
https://doi.org/10.1007/978-3-031-10542-5_48

Currently, digital transformation is the main trend of the modern business development. Digital technologies are the main driving forces of digitalization, as they are a way of doing business. Digital technologies provide three main opportunities for a changing business [1]: i) ubiquitous data distribution; ii) unlimited connectivity; iii) huge computing power.

Using the term "digitalization" [6], we mean something more than just digital technologies. Digitalization [3] is the result of digital transformation [4, 5], which is a transition from analog-digital to fully digital technology. Thanks to this replacement, analog media are replaced by digital media with the same commercial value, while the digital addition functionally enriches the corresponding converted analog media.

Thus, digitalization [6] is more associated with the transition of processes to highly automated digital business processes, and not only with communication via the Internet.

It is obvious that digital transformations [4, 6] are closely related to digital technologies.

Digitalization [3] promotes the development of large-scale IT systems with distributed structures, such as the Internet of Things or mobile systems. Data, Information and Knowledge (DIK) are fundamental concepts of our daily activities and are the driving force of digital transformation [4] of modern global society [3].

The implementation of the digital transformation of society and industry requires reaching a new level of complexity of the created man-made systems. As a measure of the complexity of the created man-made systems can serve not only the number of elements, the number of hierarchy levels, the number of connections between the elements of the system, but also the complexity of the behavior of systems, which can be expressed in the expansion of the set of implemented functions, in the complexity of the functions themselves and the ability of systems to adaptation. New classes of systems are constantly appearing, in addition, the concept of a complex system is expanding. It includes such concepts as a complex phenomenon, a complex process, while the elements of a complex system are not only software components, but also elements of a very different nature (technological equipment, transport systems, natural phenomena, biological systems), as well as people responsible for the extraction, accumulation and use of knowledge. This approach is used in the construction of cyber-physical systems (CPS), the functioning of which can be described using models that are not directly tied to a specific implementation [1–11].

It can be argued that modern anthropogenic systems are mostly large-scale distributed heterogeneous systems that can be classified as System of Systems (SoS) with an agile architecture [12].

The emergence of fundamentally new classes of complex systems and large scale technical complexes requires the use of new architectural solutions and design approaches. When building modern information-oriented systems, such new architectural paradigms as flexible architectures, continuous architectures, CPS, and ambient intelligence systems are increasingly used. Platforms such as cloud and fog computing, the Internet of Things, and the Industrial Internet of Things are actively used as platforms.

Model-based approaches, which are widely used in system design, can be considered as such approaches. In particular, in recent years the Digital Twins (DT) and Digital Threads (DTh) paradigms have been widely used for SoS building.

DT and DTh paradigms can be considered both as implementations of a model-based approach and as virtualization mechanisms. DT can be used at different stages of the system Life Cycle (LC), in particular at the stages of production and operation. The idea of DTh can be viewed as a generalization of the idea of DT, according to which digital models (twins) accompany the system throughout its LC.

The use of DT can be seen as a means of integrating heterogeneous elements into a system, and the use of DTh can be conceded as an approach to the efficient organization of the production process.

The key problem that limits the widespread use of both DT and DTh is the rather high cost of developing and maintaining models up to date. In this context, the task of automating the process of building models comes to the fore, especially when it comes to systems with variable structure and behavior, when building common models is impossible.

2 Digital Twins and Digital Threads

There are a number of definitions of the concept of DT [13]. The most general definition of DT according to ISO/IEC is the following "*a digital twin is a virtual representation of real-world entities and processes, synchronized at a specified frequency and fidelity*".

One can define the following typical approaches to the use of DT: i) DT is a controller of a physical entity; ii) DT is an intelligent controller of a physical entity; iii) DT is a simplified model of the Observed System (ObS); iv) DT is a full functional analog of the ObS; v) DT is the access port to other systems, in particular, physical systems.

In the first case, DT is conceded as a passive adapter which can track the status and synchronize with a physical entity. In the second case, the DT can support ObS agility mechanisms. In the third case, DT is a simplified ObS models which are built for the needs of the concrete stakeholder. In the fourth case, DT is considered as a full functional ObS analog. In this case ObS can be replaced by the DT. In the fifth case, DT is considered as an instrument of SoS building. Each system that is a part of a SoS can have an arbitrary number of DTs that describe the system in the vocabularies that are understandable by other SoS elements. In this case, DT can be considered as a service available to other SoS elements.

A DTh can be defined as a set of models belonging to different stages of the LC and a set of mechanisms for the transformation of these models. It should be noted that the models at different stages of the LC differ significantly, and the task of transforming the models is quite complex [13].

It can be argued that nowadays the concept of DT is a multidimensional concept and is most closely related and based on paradigms such as evolutionary, continuous and agile architecture [9].

When using approaches based on DTh, the task of transforming models related to different stages of the system LC becomes important.

This article discusses the possibility of using the DT paradigm in relation to large and complex systems with a high level of structural and functional dynamics. Special attention is paid to the stage of functioning where the data collection (acquisition) task about the current state of ObS is of high importance.

3   Three-Level Model of a Continuous Agile Architecture

The large-scale CPS can be described with the help of a three-level model. The proposed model describes the LC in terms of a continuous agile architecture in five life cycle stages and three levels.

The structure of the model is shown in Fig. 1.

Top level: Continuous architecture
Intermediate: Agile architecture
Lower level: Structural-functional run-time model

Fig. 1. Continuous agile architecture model.

At the top level, the ObS is described in terms of a continuous architecture LC.

At the middle level, the system architecture as an agile architecture is described.

At the lower level, structural and functional models are used that describe the functioning of the ObS in terms of current states.

Upper Level. At this level, the process of transforming the architectural representations of the system during the transition between different stages of the LC is described (Fig. 2).

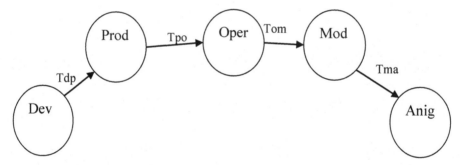

Fig. 2. Artifact transformation.

In general, 5 phases of the LC cycle can be distinguished: Development (Dev), Production (Prod), Operation (Oper), Modernization (Mod), Anigilation (Anig). The chain of transformations in terms of artifacts (Art) can be represented as follows: Art Dev → Tdp → Art Prod → Tpo → Art Oper → Tom → Art Mod → Tma → Art Anig where Tdp, Tpo, Tom, Tma are the operations of artifacts transformations between LC phases.

At each phase of the LC, a certain set of artifacts is formed. Artifacts belong to the classes defined as Art::=<Model|Code|Physical entity>. Each phase uses its own set of artifacts.

There are 4 basic types of transformations that can be defined:

$M_i \rightarrow M_{i-1}$, $M \rightarrow$ Code, $M \rightarrow$ PhE where $M_i \rightarrow M_{i-1}$ is a transformation of a model of the i-th level to the models of the i−1 level, PhE is a physical entity.

In addition, more complex transformations can be distinguished (Fig. 3), such as operation of adding extra models, e.g. additional views (Fig. 3,a) and operation of DT creation (Fig. 3,b). Other types of transformations are also possible.

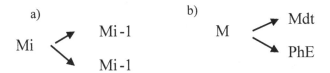

Fig. 3. Compound transformations.

In the general case, at each LC stage its own set of entities is used.

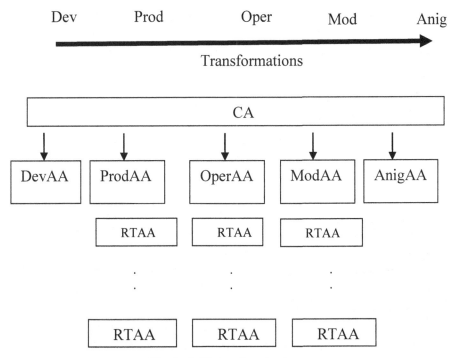

Fig. 4. Artifact system structures.

The structure of the artifact system is shown in Fig. 4. At the top level, one can talk about the single model. At the middle level, each phase uses its own artifacts. Each phase has its own Agile Architecture (AA). To each AA architecture a set of Run-Time Agile Architectures (RTAA) is assigned.

Each phase uses its own artifact systems.

Models can be divided into two groups: models that describe classes and models that describe entity instances.

A model and a model entity can be in the following relationship: i) implementation of the M → E model; ii) building the model E → M; iii) synchronization of a model and an entity instance M ↔ E.

In Fig. 5 an automaton model is presented that describes the behavior of the ObS in terms of the change of architectural states (ASt) under the action of external or internal events (Ev) and control actions (RecScr), which transfer the ObS to a new architectural state. Using this model, it is possible to describe the agile architecture [12–16, 21] in terms of changes in architectural states.

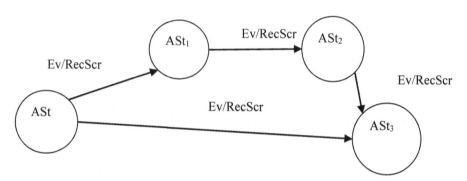

Fig. 5. High level automaton model.

The architectural state ASt can be defined as ASt = <AL, R2LLM>, where AL is an attribute list and R2LLM is the reference to LLM. The automaton presented in Fig. 4 is a distributed Relatively Finite State Operating Automaton (MLRFSOA) operating in discrete space and discrete time, which describes the level-by-level behavior of the ObS.

MLRFSOA is an automaton, in which the functions of transitions and outputs explicitly depend on time, $Ai + 1 = F (Ai, t)$ or $A = (X(t), Y(t), S(t), T (t), s0)$, where Xt are input signals, Yt are outputs, St are internal states, Tt is a transition function, s0 is an initial state. Since the automaton operates in discrete time and with discrete states, it can be assumed that at each moment of time the automaton is in the state which can be defined as $A = (X(si), Y(si), S(si), T(si), s0)$. It is known that automata with a variable structure can generally be reduced to an ordinary automaton, but the number of the states becomes very large, which makes it difficult to define them. This can be dealt with in 2 ways: by generating a new automaton "on the fly" or by considering special cases when the number of new states is a countable set. It seems appropriate to consider special cases, in particular, when an automaton switches to a new state, only separate elements of its description are changed. In this case, an automaton with a variable structure can be defined as a set of automata, $Ai \in A$, $Ai = Ai - 1$, $\Delta i - 1$, i, where Δ is a set of actions to restructure the automaton, the execution of which leads to the construction of the required automaton.

It should be noted that only in the simplest cases, the structure of the considered automaton can be determined at the design stage. Most often, especially when ObS belongs to the SoS class, knowledge about the structure of the automaton is incomplete. In this case, it is necessary to solve the problem of constructing (synthesizing) an automaton. These issues are considered in sufficient detail in the works of the authors [17–20].

LLM describes a specific ASt in terms of structure and behavior and is considered as a Structural and Functional Model (SFM), which can be defined as LLM = <MS, MB>, where MS is a structural model, and MB is a behavior model. It is often necessary to obtain information only about the structure or behavior, or even about certain aspects of the structure and/or behavior, for example, about the relationships between elements.

4   Structural-Functional Run-Time Model

Suggested SFM describes the run time structure and behavior of the ObS.

The following basic requirements for the structural-functional runtime models can be formulated.

The main requirements for structural models are the following: i) the ability to describe a constantly changing multi-level structure of arbitrary complexity; ii) the ability to automatically build a structural model based on limited information received in the form of logs.

The main requirements for behavioral models are the following: i) the ability to track the progress and correctness of Business Processes (BP) execution by incoming logs, ii) the ability to adjust the structure of BP when their structure changes.

An additional requirement for both models is the relative ease of implementation.

Because of it the most preferable is to use graph models, e. g. work flow graph-based models, there are a number of effective algorithms and tools for work flow graph processing such as process mining algorithms.

The SFM can be presented as a bipartite multigraph constructed on the basis of the workflow graph: SFM = <OPV, OPA, RV, RA, ORA>, where OPV are operator vertices, OPA (OP arcs) are arcs connecting operator vertices, RV are resource vertices, RA (R arcs) are connections between resource vertices, ORA (OR arcs) are connections between operator vertices and resource vertices.

OPV are operators of any level of complexity, operators are connected by OP arcs, which can be colored in one of 4 colors: arcs through which data is transmitted, arcs through which control signals are transmitted that allow OPV execution, arcs through which requests for operator execution are transmitted, arcs through which signals about the availability of resources are distributed. There are 16 different ways to check the readiness of operators for execution, which determine the strategies for managing the Business Process (BP). BP can be described with the help of a modified workflow graphs. Modified process mining algorithms can be used to construct data flow, control flow, and demand flow graphs [21]. To build a resource graph, which is essentially a structural graph, different mechanisms can be used at different levels.

The dynamics of the execution of the SFM can be described in terms of calculating the readiness of the operator to execute. The following conditions act as conditions for the operator's readiness: the availability of initial data, the availability of the necessary resources, and the availability of a request and the presence of a control signal to launch the operator.

The decision on the readiness of the operator is made in dynamics. However, some of the readiness conditions can be checked statically at the level of input language schemas or even at the algorithm level. In other words, a limited number of conditions are checked in dynamics, the rest are considered to be fulfilled by default.

5 Data Collection Virtual Machine

The conceptual structure of the virtual machine for supporting data collection is shown in Fig. 6.

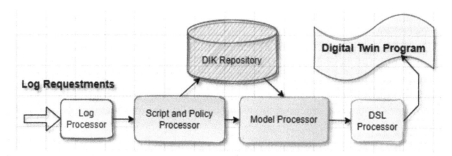

Fig. 6. Virtual machine structure.

The virtual machine consists of 4 asynchronously functioning virtual machines (processors): a log processor (Log P), a model processor (MP), a script and policy processor (SPP), a Domain Specific Language (DSL) processor (DSLP) and a DIK repository (DIKR). All listed elements are distributed.

Log P is responsible for logs processing through the implementation of scripts. MP implements two main functions: maintaining the adequacy of models and generating responses to user requests. The Script and policy processor is responsible for generating policy-based scripts. DSL Pr is an interpreter of a set of DSLs with which different categories of users work.

Algorithm for keeping the model up to date.

1. Launching the monitoring procedure.
2. Reception of logs.
3. Cleaning and sorting logs.
4. If correction of the model is required, then continue, otherwise go to step 2.
5. Correction of the model and transition to step 2.

Algorithm for processing user requests.

1. Waiting for a request from the user.
2. Receiving a request and transforming DSL → MQL (Model Query Language).
3. Request to the model in MQL.
4. If the answer is not received then continue, otherwise MQL → DSL and go to step 1.
5. Policy definition.
6. Synthesis of the script.
7. Execution of the script.
8. Construction of the required ObS model.
9. Request for a new model.
10. MQL → DSL and transition to item 1.

6 Case Study

The usage of the suggested approach can be illustrated on the example of a subway station, which can be conceded as an element of smart city ecosystem [1, 4, 5].

The functional model for the DT of a subway station is shown in Fig. 7. The operators are presented in ovals, the arcs that connect the vertices, define the conditions for their execution. The model assumes that first the data is received, then its type is determined. Depending on the type of data (video, audio, sensors), further information processing takes place. The video is divided into frames, then a series of frames is processed in a fog computing environment or cloud using machine learning algorithms for identifying objects on the images. The audio is also divided into frames and processed by machine learning algorithms.

Sensors are initially defined as either analog or discrete. If the sensors are discrete, then the events that occur on the subway stations are determined immediately, and if the signal from the sensors is analog, then the event is determined using machine learning. Processing the signal from an analog sensor resembles audio processing, which differs only in amplitude and certain sine wave characteristics. In any case, regardless of the type of information (video, audio, sensors), data and results of its processing are transferred to the database and used to build digital twins of the metro stations.

The algorithm for building DT of the metro stations contains the following steps:

1. Determining the type of the received data (video, audio, sensors).
2. If this is a video stream, then division into frames (with a frequency of 10 frames per second, but not more than 24 and a resolution from 720 × 1280 to 1920 × 1080 using a Panasonic Full HD 1080p HC-V730 camcorder, zoom 20×/60×).
3. If this is data from a sensor, then determine the type of the sensor (discrete or analog).
4. If this is audio stream, then the division into frames (based on the Meridian Lossless Packing (MLP) codec with a bit rate of 18 Mbit/s, divided into fragments from 2 to 5 s).
5. Determination of objects based on series of video frames using machine learning (using the methods of convolutional neural networks, deep learning, recurrent neural networks using the library TensorFlow 2.0 on Python 3.8).

6. Determination of events based on audio frames using machine learning (using deep learning neural network methods from frameworks PyTorch, CNTK and MXNet).
7. Determination of events based on data from sensors (using internal sensor algorithms that are based on the analysis of an analog signal, where the sinusoid crosses a certain set threshold with a certain intensity, which indicates a certain event).
8. Creation of logs.
9. Saving data and results of its processing to the database to build a DT.

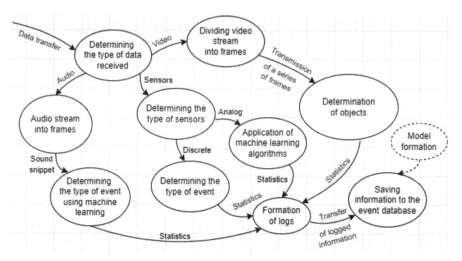

Fig. 7. Functional model of the DT of the subway station.

The functional model of the of the subway station monitoring is shown in Fig. 8. It starts from receiving data from the database, including the data about the objects of the subway station (structures, stairs, tracks, police offices, cash desks, etc.). Next, information is obtained from the event database. The type of event is determined and, depending on the degree of its danger and specificity, it is forwarded to the appropriate service. After contacting the service, logs are generated and information about the measures taken is stored. If a hardware error occurs, the information is stored in the database and the digital twin model of the station is re-built, taking into account the faulty hardware (cameras, sounds, sensors). If no dangerous events are identified, then the process is waiting for new information about events.

The steps of the algorithm of the subway station monitoring are the following:

1. Receiving data from the database.
2. Building the initial digital twin, that contains data about all objects of the station (call to algorithm 1).
3. Getting information about events.
4. Determining of the degree of danger of the event (the level of danger is determined on the basis of three sources of information: sensors, images and sounds).

5. If no dangerous events are identified, then the process is in the pending state, return to step 4.
6. If the event is identified as dangerous, then information about the event is transmitted to the appropriate service.
7. Formation of logs and reporting.
8. Saving to the database the information about the event for further analysis and the information about the hardware failures.

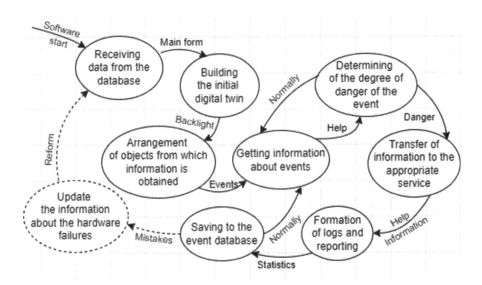

Fig. 8. Functional model of the of the subway station monitoring.

For dynamical building of the DTs of the subway stations a program was implemented. Due to using DT it provides for the employees of the subway the possibilities to determine the dangerous events quickly and thus prevent the incidents or take timely measures to help passengers. Usage of DT also allowed increase the accuracy of the event identification as for building the DT three data sources (cameras, sounds, sensors) are used and data is processed using machine learning algorithms [23, 26, 27]. Decision-making speed is enhanced because the employee works with an exact digital copy of the station that allows determine the place where the dangerous event has occurred accurately. The usage of DT also allowed increase the speed of reaction for the employees of the subway. The passengers can use the program to define location of subway employees when they need help.

The main frame of the developed program displays the objects of the station (stairs, exits, railway tracks, office premises, help kiosks, police departments, etc.), their status and the location of subway employees (Fig. 9). Also, the following information is available: processing time for a series of frames, connections, settings for encrypted channel, framing, finding images, rebuilding DTs and other. Also, it is possible to gather application performance metrics (accuracy, speed). At the bottom there are control buttons for collecting data (Stop, Restart, Start) to control the process of events identification. At the bottom there are two more buttons (Timer and Logs) to open additional frames for viewing logs and set timer settings to stop measuring the speed and accuracy of events identification. In Fig. 9 both forms are shown on the top of the main frame. At the far right of the main frame of the program there are buttons (with arrows) for moving around the entire platform, since the platform occupies a considerable area and is much larger than the size of the screen. At the bottom right are settings for collecting data (sources of three types: Cameras, Audio, Sensors) and settings for managing history files (viewing in an external editor by clicking the Open button and completely clearing the logs by clicking the Clear button). Additional settings are opened by clicking the Advanced button. By default, the program logs are stored in text files in the "/opt/mnt/tw/logs/" directory, which can be changed.

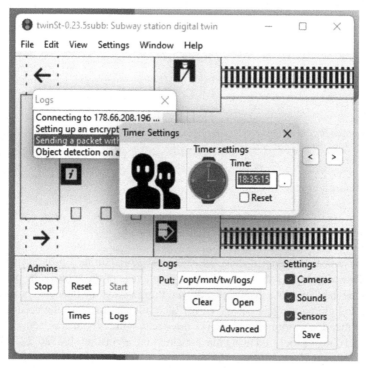

Fig. 9. The main frame of the program that implements a digital twin of a subway station.

The process of building and rebuilding the DT takes place in the cloud or fog computing environment. Python scripts that use TensorFlow for identifying events using machine learning are executed in the cloud. The log preprocessing is also located on the servers in the cloud.

After measuring the accuracy of the events identification, the following results were obtained (Table 1). The accuracy of event detection using the digital twin has increased by 10.56%.

Table 1. Event identification accuracy.

Event	Only logs are processed (visualization and monitoring program is not used)	Logs are processed and visualization and monitoring program is used	DT is used	Increase of the accuracy when using digital twin
Hanging on the edge of the platform	0.71	0.83	0.94	11.7%
Falling things and objects on the railroad tracks	0.78	0.86	0.97	11.3%
Running or fast moving on a platform	0.75	0.84	0.95	11.58%
Smoky or hazy environment	0.73	0.85	0.92	7.6%
Average				10.56%

To reproduce the experiments, it is necessary to develop a program for collecting data, a visualization program, and a "Digital Twin" program. Develop a program to summarize data or open logs in Microsoft Excel, apply filtration, summation, mathematical rounding and average. After that, fill in the resulting tables. The experiments were carried out on an HP Laptop 17-cp0092ur with technical specifications: 17.3″, 1600 × 900, SVA (TN + film), AMD 3020e, cores: 2 × 1.2 GHz, RAM 4 GB, SSD 256 GB, AMD Radeon Graphics, Windows 11. For cloud computing, an HP server was used at Immers (https://immers.cloud/) with the name "nvme.4.16.120" and technical characteristics: 16384 RAM, 4-core Intel Xeon Gold processor 6th Scalable series (Cascade Lake) using the OpenStack virtualization API with the "ninja_vm" command and pre-installed Debian 11.3 (https://www.debian.org/).

7 Conclusions

In the course of the study, a three-level model of a continuous agile architecture was developed. The use of this model allows describe all system LC stages.

The suggested approach was used for solving the problem of monitoring the state of the subway stations using three information sources (cameras, sounds and sensors). The research materials are recordings of video, sound and signals from sensors obtained at the subway station.

The program for DT building has been developed and measurements of its efficiency were carried out, which showed an increase in the accuracy of determining events by an average of 10.56%. The usage of DT approach has shown to be effective for solving the problems of the subway, but it can be applied in more complex cases, in particular, at plants, factories, bridges and other complex structures.

References

1. Calinescu, R.C., Camara Moreno, J., Paterson, C.: Socio-cyber-physical systems: models, opportunities. In: Proceedings of the Open Challenges 5th International Workshop on Software Engineering for Smart Cyber-Physical Systems, Montreal, QC, Canada, 28 May 2019
2. Sanfelice, R.G.: Analysis and design of cyber-physical systems. A hybrid control systems approach. In: Rawat, D., Rodrigues, J., Stojmenovic, I. (eds.) Cyber-Physical Systems: From Theory to Practice. CRC Press, Boca Raton (2016). ISBN 978-1-4822-6333-6
3. Mahmood, Z.: Guide to Ambient Intelligence in the IoT Environment Principles, Technologies and Application, 289p. Springer, Cham (2019). https://doi.org/10.1007/978-3-030-04173-1
4. Marques, G., Pitarma, R., MGarcia, N., Pombo, N.: Internet of Things architectures, technologies, applications, challenges, and future directions for enhanced living environments and healthcare systems: a review. Electronics 8, 1081 (2019). https://doi.org/10.3390/electronics8101081
5. Korzun, D., Balandina, E., Kashevnik, A., Balandin, S., Viola, F.: Ambient Intelligence Services in IoT Environments: Emerging Research and Opportunities, 199p. IGI-Global, Hershey (2019). https://doi.org/10.4018/978-1-52258973-0
6. Wu, Y., Hu, F., Min, G., Zomaya, A.Y.: Big Data and Computational Intelligence in Networking, 530p. Taylor & Francis Group, LLC, Boca Raton (2018)
7. Weilkiens, T., Lamm, J., Roth, S., Walker, M.: Model-Based System Architecture, 375p. Wiley, Hoboken (2016)
8. Babar, M.A., Brown, A.W., Mistrik, I.: Agile Software Architecture Aligning Agile Processes and Software Architectures, 292p. Morgan Kaufmann, Burlington (2014)
9. Ford, N., Parsons, R., Kua, P.: Building Evolutionary Architectures, 272p. O'Reilly Media, Sebastopol (2017)
10. Gasevic, D., Djuric, D., Devedzi, V. (eds.): Model Driven Architecture and Ontology Development. Springer, Heidelberg (2006). https://doi.org/10.1007/3-540-32182-9
11. Bass, L., Weber, I., Zhu, L.: DevOps: A Software Architect's Perspective, 463p. Pearson Education, Inc., London (2015)
12. Bloomberg, J.: The Agile Architecture Revolution: How Cloud Computing, REST-based SOA, and Mobile Computing are Changing Enterprise IT, 278p. Wiley, Hoboken (2013)
13. van der Valk, H., Hunker, J., Rabe, M., Otto, B.: Digital twins in simulative applications: a taxonomy. In: Proceedings of the 2020 Winter Simulation Conference. https://www.researchgate.net/publication/341235159_A_Taxonomy_of_Digital_Twins. Accessed 5 May 2022
14. Digital Thread. https://searcherp.techtarget.com/definition/digital-thread. Accessed 5 May 2022
15. What is the Digital Thread? Digital Thread Definition. https://nxrev.com/2018/05/digitalthread/. Accessed 5 May 2022
16. Rozanski, N., Woods, E. (eds.): Software Systems Architecture: Working with Stakeholders Using Viewpoints and Perspectives, 576p. Viewpoints, Poland (2005)
17. Erder, M., Pureur, P., Woods, E.: Continuous Architecture in Practice Software Architecture in the Age of Agility and DevOps, Upper Saddle River, NJ, USA, 321p. (2021)
18. Shaw, M., Garlan, D. (eds.): Software Architecture: Perspectives on an Emerging Discipline, 242p. Prentice-Hall Inc., Hoboken (1996)

19. Vodyaho, A.I., Zhukova, N.A., Shichkina, Y.A., Anaam, F., Abbas, S.: About one approach to using dynamic models to build digital twins. Designs **6**, 25 (2022)

20. Osipov, V., Stankova, E., Vodyaho, A., Lushnov, M., Shichkina, Y., Zhukova, N.: Automatic synthesis of multilevel automata models of biological objects. In: Misra, S., et al. (eds.) ICCSA 2019. LNCS, vol. 11620, pp. 441–456. Springer, Cham (2019). https://doi.org/10.1007/978-3-030-24296-1_35

21. Osipov, V., Zhukova, N., Vodyaho, A.: About one approach to multilevel behavioral program synthesis for television devices. Int. J. Comput. Commun. **11**, 17–25 (2017)

22. Vodyaho, A., Osipov, V., Zhukova, N., Chernokulsky, V.: Data collection technology for ambient intelligence systems in Internet of Things. https://doi.org/10.3390/electronics9111846. Accessed 5 May 2022

23. Osipov, V., Lushnov, M., Stankova, E., Vodyaho, A., Zukova, N.: Inductive synthesis of the models of biological systems according to clinical trials. In: Gervasi, O., et al. (eds.) ICCSA 2017. LNCS, vol. 10404, pp. 103–115. Springer, Cham (2017). https://doi.org/10.1007/978-3-319-62392-4_8

24. Capilla, R., Bosch, J., Kang, K.C. (eds.): Systems and Software Variability Management, 317p. Springer, Heidelberg (2013). https://doi.org/10.1007/978-3-642-36583-6

25. Xing, L.: Cascading failures in Internet of Things: review and perspectives on reliability and resilience. IEEE Internet Things J. **8**, 44–64 (2020). https://doi.org/10.1109/JIOT.2020.3018687

26. Vodyaho, A., Zhukova, N., Subbotin, A., Anaam, F.: Towards dynamic model-based agile architecting of cyber-physical systems. Sensors **22**(8), 3078 (2022). https://doi.org/10.3390/s22083078

27. Subbotin, A., Zhukova, N., Man, T.: Architecture of the intelligent video surveillance systems for fog environments based on embedded computers. In: Proceedings of the 2021 10th Mediterranean Conference on Embedded Computing (MECO), Budva, Montenegro, 7–10 June 2022, pp. 1–8 (2022). https://doi.org/10.1109/MECO52532.2021.9460270

Author Index

Printed in the United States
by Baker & Taylor Publisher Services